Collins

PSYCHOLOGY AS
FOR AQA A

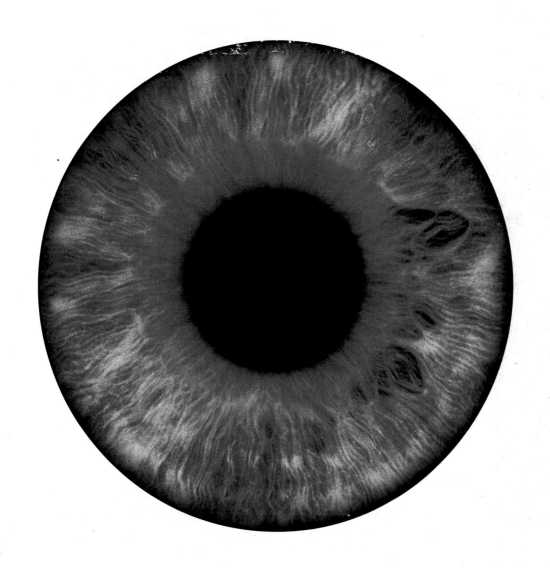

CARDWELL CLARK MELDRUM

FOURTH EDITION

William Collins' dream of knowledge for all began with the publication of his first book in 1819. A self-educated mill worker, he not only enriched millions of lives, but also founded a flourishing publishing house. Today, staying true to this spirit, Collins books are packed with inspiration, innovation and practical expertise. They place you at the centre of a world of possibility and give you exactly what you need to explore it.

Collins. Do more.

Published by HarperCollinsPublishers Limited
77–85 Fulham Palace Road
Hammersmith
London W6 8JB

Browse the complete Collins catalogue
at **www.collinseducation.com**

© HarperCollinsPublishers Limited 2008

Psychology for A Level first published 1996
First AS edition published 2000
Second edition first published 2003
Third edition first published 2008

Reprint 10 9 8 7 6 5 4 3 2 1

ISBN 978-0-00-725503-0

Commissioned by Marie Insall
Project managed by Hugh Hillyard-Parker
Edited by Rosamund Connelly
Cover design by Oculus
Internal design template by Jordan Publishing Design
Typesetting by Hugh Hillyard-Parker
Cartoons by Mike Parsons, Barking Dog Art, Gloucestershire
Illustrations on pp. 150, 153 and 171 by Oxford Designers and Illustrators Ltd
Index compiled by Christine Boylan
Production by Simon Moore
Printed and bound by L.E.G.O. S.p.A. - Lavis (TN) ITALY

Acknowledgements

Mike Cardwell acknowledges his enormous debt to his ever-patient wife Denise. She provides the secure emotional base that allows him the luxury of long hours spent staring at a computer screen and 'doing' psychology.

Liz Clark would like to thank her husband, Charley, for his continued support and patience through both the planned and unplanned periods of disruption to home life during this latest major editing project. Also, to family and friends near and far for always being there to provide those all-important words of support and encouragement when deadlines loom and threaten to take over one's entire life. Finally, for children of friends and colleagues who are studying AS psychology, using our book – there's nothing like some robust and focused feedback from a lively group of psychology students to trigger significant improvements to this latest edition!

Claire Meldrum once again would like to thank Stuart upon whose encouragement and steadfast support she can always depend. Thanks also go to her past students and colleagues for their insights and constructive comments over many years.

The editors would also like to thank the staff at HarperCollins, particularly Marie Insall whose lively, hands-on approach has cheered us on our way and kept us on our toes! Marie's attention to detail, commitment and enthusiasm for this book has been an inspiration throughout. We also wish to thank Hugh Hillyard-Parker, who once again is responsible for the book's editorial production.

Mike Cardwell, Liz Clark and Claire Meldrum
April 2008

Contents

Using the book

This book provides detailed coverage of all aspects of Specification A of the AS psychology course offered by the Assessment and Qualifications Alliance (AQA).

What's new in A-level psychology?

The most important change is that the Qualifications Curriculum Authority (QCA) has classified psychology as a science and this is reflected in the new AQA specification.

How has this affected the new specification?

Since psychology is a science, students will now study psychological research and scientific methodology. This has been incorporated into the specification as *How Science Works*, which is a set of core concepts that enable the student to understand and contextualize science for themselves, and also to appreciate how scientists investigate scientific phenomena in order to explain the world about us. These concepts are shown in detail in the subject specification published by AQA (**www.aqa.org.uk**).

We like to think of *How Science Works* as a thread of principles that run throughout your entire AS psychology course and that hold all the key elements together. Thus, *How Science Works* isn't something that can be studied in isolation, but rather is intrinsic to all aspects of the study of psychology.

The other significant change in the new specification is that research methods are now studied in the context of specific areas of psychology rather than in isolation.

How are these changes reflected in this book?

How Science Works

We have woven *How Science Works* into the main text – from Chapter 1 to Chapter 8 – and into the key features of the book and we flag up its presence by using an icon (shown above), so that you can see exactly when you are practising these skills.

Research Methods

To enable you to understand psychological research fully, we first take a look at the role it plays in the context of psychology and the work undertaken by psychologists (Chapter 1). We then develop this further in Chapter 2, where we provide an in-depth look at specific types of research method. Finally, we incorporate the study of research methods into the specific areas of psychology of the AS course: Cognitive, Developmental, Biological, Social and Individual Differences. In each chapter, you'll find research methods flagged up by an icon (shown above) whenever it occurs in the main text and in individual features.

What are the benefits of using this book?

- **A full coverage of the new AQA specification at exactly the right depth** – delivering all the content and up-to-date research to ensure complete coverage
- **Bringing psychology to life** with our 'Psychology in context' feature that looks at psychology in your everyday world
- **Even more student support and exam preparation** with exam-style practice and in-depth guidance from experienced examiners
- **A strong focus on *How Science Works* and Research Methods** to develop essential evaluation and analysis skills
- **A student-friendly approach** with topic maps, engaging activities and visual features – written by teachers and examiners who understand the needs of psychology students.

AQA (A) AS specification and examination

The specification

The AS-level specification is designed to be midway between the skills required for GCSE and the full A-level (A2), and to take account of the target age (17+) of the majority of students who will be taking this exam.

The AQA (A) AS-level course is organized into two assessment units:

- **Unit 1**: Cognitive Psychology, Developmental Psychology and Research Methods
- **Unit 2**: Biological Psychology, Social Psychology and Individual Differences

You will learn about the five core areas of psychology and also about research methods within the context of each of them. Each of these core areas is represented by a topic that will give you a good introduction to that area of psychology. The five core areas and their related topics are as follows:

Core area	Topic
Cognitive Psychology	Memory
Developmental Psychology	Early social development
Biological Psychology	Stress
Social Psychology	Social influence
Individual Differences	Psychopathology (Abnormality)

The exam

All areas of this specification are compulsory – this means that you must cover everything in this book. The specification entries are very carefully worded and questions will tend to reflect that wording. We have endeavoured to use the same wording as the specification, wherever possible, to make it easier for you to track your route through each topic. When questions are set, the question-setter will attempt to sample (eventually) all areas of the specification. Therefore, it is unwise to leave out any areas, even small ones, simply because they do not appeal to you.

There is no choice of questions in the examination; every question is compulsory. There will not necessarily be a question on everything that appears in the AQA specification. However, there will be a set of questions on every area (i.e. Cognitive, Developmental, Biological, and so on), so a good proportion of the specification will be covered in every examination.

The examination will test:

- your knowledge and understanding (known as 'Assessment Objective 1' or AO1)
- your analysis and evaluation skills (known as AO2)
- the degree of knowledge, understanding and appreciation that you show of *How Science Works* (across both units, and known as AO3).

You will find more information on these skills and how they are assessed in Chapter 8.

Several entries on the AQA specification are preceded by the words 'including' or 'e.g.'. The word 'including' indicates prescribed material on which questions may be asked, whereas the use of 'e.g.' is merely illustrative of appropriate subject material. We have covered all prescribed material in this book, and have endeavoured, wherever appropriate, to cover all the examples mentioned in the specification as well.

Do, please, let us know, care of the Publisher, what you think of the book. Feedback from readers is enormously helpful and we always pay close attention to it when we come to write the next edition of the book. We do hope you enjoy the course!

Mike Cardwell, Liz Clark, Claire Meldrum

Overview of the book

Key features

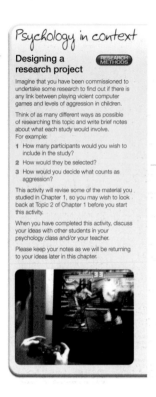

Psychology in context

Designing a research project

RESEARCH METHODS

Imagine that you have been commissioned to undertake some research to find out if there is any link between playing violent computer games and levels of aggression in children.

Think of as many different ways as possible of researching this topic and write brief notes about what each study would involve.
For example:

1 How many participants would you wish to include in the study?

2 How would they be selected?

3 How would you decide what counts as aggression?

This activity will revise some of the material you studied in Chapter 1, so you may wish to look back at Topic 2 of Chapter 1 before you start this activity.

When you have completed this activity, discuss your ideas with other students in your psychology class and/or your teacher.

Please keep your notes as we will be returning to your ideas later in this chapter.

See at a glance how this book delivers the specification content by the **Explaining the specification** table at the start of each chapter.

Immediately engage with new ideas through **Psychology in context** at the start of each topic.

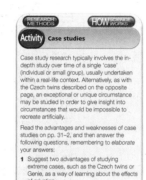

RESEARCH METHODS · HOW SCIENCE WORKS

Activity Case studies

Case study research typically involves the in-depth study over time of a single 'case' (individual or small group), usually undertaken within a real-life context. Alternatively, as with the Czech twins described on the opposite page, an exceptional or unique circumstance may be studied in order to give insight into circumstances that would be impossible to recreate artificially.

Read the advantages and weaknesses of case studies on pp. 31–2, and then answer the following questions, remembering to *elaborate* your answers:

1 Suggest two advantages of studying extreme cases, such as the Czech twins or Genie, as a way of learning about the effects of privation.

2 Suggest two weaknesses associated with studying extreme cases, such as the Czech twins or Genie, as a way of learning about the effects of privation.

3 Suggest two ethical issues that might apply to such studies, and suggest how the researchers might have dealt with each of these.

Answers are given on p. 275 ▶

Practise as you learn, using the **Activities** throughout the book.

EXPLAINING THE SPECIFICATION

Specification content	The specification explained
Attachment	In this part of the specification you are required to explain the nature and origins of the emotional bond between parent and child, and what happens when this bond is broken. To do this you need to be able to:
Explanations of attachment, including learning theory, and evolutionary perspective, including Bowlby	■ Describe and evaluate at least two explanations of attachment – these should include learning theory and Bowlby's explanation of attachment. ■ Offer outline descriptions of these explanations, which means being able to précis each explanation in about 50 words.
Types of attachment, including insecure and secure attachment and studies by Ainsworth	■ Outline the characteristics of secure and insecure attachment, including the difference between them. ■ Describe and evaluate Ainsworth's research using the Strange Situation, and link this to different types of attachment.
Cultural variations in attachment	■ Describe and evaluate research into cultural differences in attachment. The most obvious study that does this is by van IJzendoorn and Kroonenberg (1988). Studies of cultural differences in childrearing methods tend to explain why there are differences in attachment.
Disruption of attachment, failure to form attachment (privation) and the effects of institutionalization	■ Describe and evaluate research showing what happens when the attachment bond is disrupted (e.g. separation or deprivation). ■ Describe and evaluate research showing what happens when the attachment fails to form (privation). ■ Describe and evaluate research showing the effects of institutionalization (e.g. growing up in an orphanage) on development of the attachment bond. ■ Be aware of the difference between bond disruption and privation.
Attachment in everyday life	In this part of the specification you are required to explain how being cared for outside the home affects the development of the child, and how research in this area has informed childcare practices. To do this you need to be able to:
The impact of different forms of day care on children's social development, including the effects on aggression and peer relations	■ Describe and evaluate research into the impact of at least two different types of day care (e.g. childminding and day nurseries) on children's social development. Because *aggression* and *peer relations* are named here (note the use of the term 'including'), these should be the areas of social development covered.
Implications of research into attachment and day care for childcare practices	■ Comment on how psychological research into attachment and day care might shape our approach to the care of children. This should not be speculative or subjective, but based on research (which you should be able to describe and evaluate) that you have studied.

Get to grips with **key research studies**, which are clearly broken down into aims, procedures, findings, conclusions and evaluations of the research. Many of the key studies feature a further analysis section, which enables you to further develop important analytical skills.

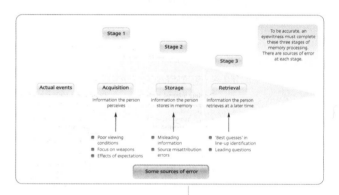

Psychological material is made even more accessible through the frequent use of **diagrams**, **tables** and **pictures**.

Working memory in chess
A study by Robbins *et al.* (1996)

Aim	To study the role of the central executive in remembering chess positions by investigating the effect of generating random letter strings.
Procedure	Twenty chess players were asked to memorize in 10 seconds the positions of 16 chess pieces from a real game. The procedure was repeated 20 times using a different game each time. While memorizing the positions, participants either: ■ simultaneously engaged the central executive by generating random letter sequences, concentrating to avoid any meaningful combinations (such as H, G, V), or ■ simultaneously, carried out an articulatory suppression task (saying 'the, the, the' in time with a metronome) After 10 seconds, the participants' memory was tested by asking them to arrange chess pieces on another board to match those they had just seen.
Findings	■ Participants in the articulatory suppression condition performed well in recalling the positions of the chess pieces. ■ Participants in the letter generation condition performed poorly.
Conclusion	■ The impaired performance of those generating the letter sequences demonstrated that the central executive played a role in remembering chess positions. ■ The good performance of participants in the articulatory suppression condition indicated that the phonological loop was not involved in remembering the chess positions.
Evaluation	■ This well-designed study enables us to conclude that the different tasks (articulatory suppression and letter sequence generation) did cause the difference in performance. ■ Generating meaningless letter sequences has been claimed by many cognitive psychologists as a valid way of engaging the central executive as it requires considerable attention.
FURTHER ANALYSIS	In another condition of this experiment, participants' visuo-spatial scratchpad was suppressed by requiring them to press keys systematically on a calculator while they were memorizing the chess positions. This resulted in the participants performing as poorly in the memory test as those who had experienced a suppressed central executive. Therefore, Robbins and colleagues concluded that both the central executive and the visuo-spatial scratchpad are involved in recalling chess positions.

Each stage represents the focus for pleasure (libido) from different parts of the body.

1	**Oral stage** (0–18 months)	Pleasure gained, for example, from eating and sucking. Weaning is the most important developmental achievement.
2	**Anal stage** (18–36 months)	Pleasure gained from expelling or retaining faeces. Bowel and bladder control are important achievements.
3	**Phallic stage** (3–6 years)	At this most vital stage, the child becomes aware of its gender and the focus is on the genitals. At this stage, the Oedipus complex occurs for boys and the Electra complex for girls, when an unconscious rivalry develops between the child and its same-sex parent for the affection of its opposite-sex parent. At this time, boys experience castration anxiety and girls experience penis envy. According to Freud, this complex is resolved when the boy, repressing his desire for his mother, identifies strongly with his father and when the girl sublimates her penis envy into a desire to have a baby. Successful (normal) development through this stage requires the development of a firm gender identity. One of Freud's most famous case studies concerns a young boy who is in this stage of development (see case study 'Little Hans' below).
4	**Latency stage** (6 years to puberty)	The focus is on social rather than psychosexual development. This is sometimes seen as the calm before the storm of adolescence.
5	**Genital stage** (puberty to maturity)	If the conflicts experienced during the earlier stages have been satisfactorily resolved, the greatest pleasure comes from mature heterosexual relationships.

For each topic in Chapters 3 to 7, the **Eye on the exam** provides an examiner's commentary on key issues when answering questions in this area.

Eye on the exam

'Outline two explanations of how people sometimes resist pressures to conform' *(3 marks + 3 marks)*

When faced with a question like this which requires *two* explanations, each with its own mark allocation, provide *two separate* accounts. The two explanations do not have to be exactly the same length but each must earn its own 3 marks. In other words, you cannot compensate for one weak explanation by providing a better, more detailed second one.

Material from the chapter that you might use to answer this question includes: desire for deindividuation or control, being confident or having made a prior commitment that differs from the majority opinion, finding someone who thinks the same as you do (see pp. 203–4).

For more exam advice, visit **www.collinseducation.com/psychologyweb**

Understand key concepts and terms by using the **Glossary** of key terms at the back of the book.

Glossary

Abnormality: see psychological abnormality or psychopathology.

Aim: the intended purpose of an investigation, i.e. what the research investigation in question is actually trying to discover.

Alternative hypothesis (may be referred to as the **experimental hypothesis** in an experiment): predicts that something other than chance alone has produced the results obtained; in a well-designed experiment this should be the effects of the independent variable.

Anxiety: a state of apprehension, worry or fear.

Attachment: a strong emotional and reciprocal bond between two people, especially between an infant and its caregiver(s). Attachments serve to maintain proximity between infant and caregiver because each experiences distress when separated.

Aversion therapy: a behavioural treatment that aims to rid the individual of an undesirable habit (e.g. smoking) by pairing the habit with unpleasant (aversive) consequences.

Bar chart: a series of vertical bars of equal width used to illustrate the frequencies of a non-continuous variable displayed on the x-axis. It is superficially similar to a histogram.

Behaviour categories (or **behavioural categories**): categorizing behaviour is a process carried out in observational research where the investigator(s) classify examples of the behaviour to be observed. For example, behaviours in a discussion group might include categories of 'giving advice', 'asking for advice', 'seeming friendly' and 'seeming unfriendly'.

Behavioural approach to psychopathology: a view that abnormal behaviours are maladaptive, learned responses which can be replaced by more adaptive responses

Benzodiazepines (BZs): anti-anxiety drugs often used for the short-term relief of severe anxiety.

Beta-blockers: used in the treatment of high blood pressure (hypertension), beta blockers reduce activity in the sympathetic nervous system.

Biological (somatic) therapies: an approach to the treatment of mental disorders that relies on the use of physical or chemical methods. Biological therapies include drug treatment, electroconvulsive therapy and psychosurgery.

Biological approach to (or biomedical model of) psychopathology: a view of abnormality that sees mental disorders as being caused by abnormal physiological processes such as genetic and biochemical factors. Abnormality according to this model is seen as an illness or disease

Capacity: the amount of information that can be stored in memory at any particular time.

Case study: case study research typically involves the in-depth study over time of a single individual or small group and is usually undertaken within a real-life context.

Catharsis: in psychoanalysis, catharsis is the process whereby the expression of an emotion removes its pathological effect - the release of pent-up emotion that happens when a client recalls and relives a repressed earlier emotional catastrophe and re-experiences the tension and unhappiness.

Central executive: the most important component of Baddeley's working memory model, it controls attention.

Chemotherapy: treatment by using drugs.

Classical conditioning: a form of learning where a neutral stimulus is paired with a stimulus that already produces a response, such that over time, the neutral stimulus also produces that response.

Cognitive approach to psychopathology: a view that stresses the role of cognitive problems (such as illogical or irrational thought processes) in abnormal functioning

Cognitive behavioural therapy (CBT): a technique that involves helping clients to identify their negative, irrational thoughts and to replace these with more positive, rational ways of thinking.

Cognitive development: the changes that take place throughout one's life with respect to mental abilities, including memory, perception, language and intelligence.

Cognitive Interview/Cognitive Interview Schedule (CI): a method for questioning witnesses which requires them to recreate the context, recall all details, recall events in different orders, and use different perspectives to aid memory recall.

Conditioning: a learning process in which an organism's behaviour becomes dependent on a learned association with an existing stimulus (classical conditioning) or on the consequences of that behaviour (operant conditioning).

Conformity: a result of social influence where people adopt the behaviours, attitudes and values of the majority members of a reference group.

Confounding variable: an uncontrolled variable that produces an unwanted effect on the dependent variable and so distorts the findings by obscuring any effect of the independent variable.

Content analysis: a systematic research technique for analyzing transcripts of interviews and other documents that involves formally categorizing and counting how often things in the text (such as words or ideas) occur.

Correlation: a term that refers to the extent to which values on (usually two) different variables co-vary.

Correlation coefficient: a descriptive statistic with a numerical value on a scale between –1 and +1. It demonstrates the strength and direction of any relationship that exists between two sets of data. The sign of the coefficient tells us if the relationship is positive or negative. The numerical part describes the magnitude of the relationship.

Correlational analysis: a technique used to test a hypothesis using an association that is measured between two variables that are thought likely to co-vary (e.g. height and weight).

Counterbalancing: a technique used in a repeated measures design to overcome the impact of order effects, practice, boredom and fatigue on performance in an experiment. It involves ensuring that each condition is equally likely to occur in a particular order within the study. If there are only two conditions, then each is equally likely to be carried out first or second by participants.

Counterconditioning: a therapeutic technique for treating phobias. A phobic patient is helped to relax while imagining the feared situation (going from the least feared to the most feared situation). The relaxation response is incompatible with the fear previously associated with the situation. This leads to the fear being extinguished.

Critical period: a period of time during development when the brain is open to a particular type of experience, resulting in the development of a particular characteristic. Outside this 'window of opportunity', such development is no longer possible.

Cross-cultural variation: variations between people of different cultures. A culture is a set of beliefs and customs, e.g. about child-rearing practices, that bind a group of people together.

Cultural relativism: the idea that judgements about definitions of human behaviour (e.g. abnormal behaviour) cannot be made in absolute terms but only within the context of a given culture

Daily hassles: relatively minor events arising out of day-to-day living, such as the everyday concerns of work, caring for others and commuting.

Day care: a form of care for infants and children, offered by someone other than close family, taking place outside the home. Day

278

A **Check your understanding** feature at the end of each topic will help you review what you have just read and help you pinpoint any areas you need to revisit.

CHECK YOUR UNDERSTANDING

Check your understanding of social influence in everyday life by answering these questions. Try to do this from memory first. You can check your answers by looking back through Topic 2.

1. What do you understand by the term 'independent behaviour'?
2. How many participants in Asch's line-length study of conformity acted independently throughout the procedure (see Topic 1)?
3. Outline three explanations that have been proposed for people resisting pressures to conform.
4. Outline three explanations that have been proposed for people resisting pressures to obey authority.
5. In what way have levels of moral reasoning been linked to the likelihood that a person will obey?
6. Explain the terms: 'internal locus of control' and 'external locus of control'.
7. According to Blass, under what circumstances were participants with an internal locus of control most likely to resist obedience pressures?
8. What gender differences (if any) did Milgram find in his research on obedience?
9. Outline the procedures and findings of the study by Sistrunk and McDavid (1971) that investigated gender differences in conformity.
10. What conclusion did Sistrunk and McDavid draw from their research?
11. What cultural differences have been found in people's responses to pressures to conform?
12. In what way did research into social influence (e.g. by Milgram and Zimbardo) affect how psychologists have addressed ethical issues when they have carried out research subsequently? (See also Chapter 2, p. 63, to help you answer the question.)
13. How should minorities behave if they are to be influential and bring about social change?
14. What is meant by the foot-in-the-door technique as a means of changing behaviour and whose research on social influence demonstrated its effectiveness?
15. What implications does Zimbardo's research on conformity to social roles have for the training of those in positions of power?

A visual overview of the key points in the chapter content is provided by the **Chapter summary** – ideal for revision.

Chapter 5: Summary

Stress – A lack of fit between the perceived demands of a situation and a person's perceived ability to cope

Stress as a bodily response

Stress in everyday life

The body's response to stress

Pituitary adrenal system

1. Higher brain centres activate hypothalamus
2. Hypothalamus releases CRF
3. Pituitary releases ACTH
4. Adrenal cortex releases corticosteroids into bloodstream
5. Corticosteroids cause 'fight-or-flight' changes

Evaluations

- 'Fight or flight' – a male stress response
- 'Tend and befriend' – a female response

Sympathomedullary pathway

1. Activation of SNS causes bodily arousal
2. SNS also activates adrenal medulla
3. Releases adrenaline and noradrenaline
4. Both support sympathetic activation

Evaluations

- Stress response adaptation to stressors faced by ancestors
- Fight-or-flight response prepared body for energy expenditure.

Stress and the immune system

- Immune system – seek outs and destroys antigens
- Stress may affect immune system directly
- May also have an indirect effect

Research on short-term stressors

- Natural killer cell activity
- Wound healing
- Additional stressors (e.g. daily hassles)

Research on chronic stress

- Conflict in interpersonal relationships
- Death of a spouse
- Care giving

Evaluations

- Women report more stress-related problems than men
- Younger people report more stress than older people
- Older people show more adverse changes in response to stress

Life changes and daily hassles

Life changes

- Discrete stressors
- Measured by SRRS
- Higher SRRS, more illness (Rahe *et al.* 1970)
- Link between undesirable life changes and illness

Evaluations

- Individual differences – impact varies
- Correlational rather than causal
- Doesn't distinguish between negative and positive events

Daily hassles

- Relatively minor events
- Higher hassles score, lower mental health
- May accumulate for more serious stress reactions
- May arise from pre-existing chronic stressors

Evaluations

- Correlational rather than causal
- Cultural differences important in buffering effects

Workplace stressors

- Physical environment
- Work overload
- Lack of control

Evaluations

- Extraneous variables not controlled
- Job control – stressful for some people
- Individual differences – e.g. cultural differences

Personality factors

- Type A personality (Friedman and Rosenman 1974)
- Hardiness (Kobasa and Maddi 1977)

Evaluations

Type A

- Lack of consistent research support
- Role of hostility

Hardiness

- Non-representative participants
- Components of personality not well defined

Emotion-focused and problem-focused coping

Problem-focused coping

- Active to eliminate stressful situation
- Used to deal with potentially controllable events
- Associated with overall good health outcomes
- More by males

Emotion-focused coping

- Regulates emotional distress of stressful situations
- Short-term measure to reduce arousal levels
- Used first to deal with high anxiety levels
- More by females

Methods of stress management

Physiological methods

Drugs

- BZs – enhance GABA
- Beta-blockers – reduce arousal

+ve: fast action and effective

–ve: dependency, side effects, only targets symptoms

Biofeedback

- Strategies to reduce physiological measures
- Effectiveness – no more effective than muscle relaxation alone

Psychological methods

Stress inoculation

- Promotes confidence in ability to deal with stress
- Conceptualization; skills training and practice; real-life application

+ve: greater confidence to handle stressful situations

–ve: requires high levels of motivation and commitment

Hardiness training

- Increases hardiness and resilience
- Focusing; reliving stressful encounters; self-improvement
- Problems – theoretical issues and practicality

Credits

Text permissions

The following permission to reproduce material is gratefully acknowledged. Numbers refer to pages:

American Psychological Association (21/table); Allyn & Bacon (45/Fig. 2.3); Holt, Rinehart & Winston (45/Fig. 2.4); Blackwell Publishers (46/Table 2.3, 48/Table 2.4, 55–7/Table 2.5); Social Trends (62/Graph B). Academic Press (72/diary extract; Dept of Psychology, Temple University, Philadelphia (85/Fig. 3.1); Academic Press Ltd (90/graph); Child Development (127/Table 4.1); Elsevier (158/Table 5.1); Blackwell Publishers (189/Zimbardo interview); New York Times (191); The American Psychology Association (194/Table 6.2); John Wiley & Sons Ltd (230/Table 7.3); American Medical Association (235/Fig. 7.4).

Whilst every effort has been made to contact the copyright holders, this has not proved possible in every case.

Photographs

The publishers would like to thank the following for permission to reproduce photographs. The page number is followed, where necessary, by T (top), B (bottom), C (centre), L (left) or R (right).

Rex (3), Getty Images (6, 7, 8), Photos.com (9, 10), iStockphoto (12), Photos.com (13, 14), Alexandra Milgram (15, 16), Getty Images (18), Rex (21), iStockphoto (24), Rex (27), Photos.com (29), Isopress/Rex (37), Photos.com (40), Philip Zimbardo (53), Photos.com (57), iStockphoto (59, 60), Topfoto (74, 79L), Rex (79R), iStockphoto (80), Photos.com (81), iStockphoto (94, 99), Corbis (100), iStockphoto (101, 104, 106 both, 110, 112), Rex (117), Science Photo Library (119, 120), iStockphoto (121, 128), Mary Evans (129), iStockphoto (131), Photos.com (132), Rex (134), Photos.com (138), iStockphoto (141), Rex (144), Photos.com (145), Rex (149L&R), iStockphoto (149C), Rex (149), iStockphoto (150), Photos.com (152, 155, 156), Rex (157), iStockphoto (158L), Getty Images (158R), iStockphoto (160 all, 162 both, 167), Photos.com (168, 172), Rex (174), Photos.com (175), iStockphoto (176), Getty Images (181T), Photos.com (181C), iStockphoto (181B), Science Photo Library (184), Getty Images (187 both), Philip Zimbardo (188), Getty Images (190, 191T), Reuters (191B), Alexandra Milgram (193, 194, 196), Shout pictures (199), Photos.com (200), Getty Images (201), Edinburgh City Council (203), Rex (204, 217 all), iStockphoto (218), Reuters (219), Rex (219, 220 both), Photofusion (224T), Hugh Hillyard-Parker (224B), Photos.com (230), iStockphoto (232, 233), Science Photo Library (238 both), Getty Images (239), Science Photo Library (240), iStockphoto (241, 243), Rex (244, 250), Photos.com (267, 268, 269, 270, 271).

Author biographies

Mike Cardwell

Mike Cardwell is Senior Lecturer in Psychology at Bath Spa University, where he teaches courses in social psychology, and a former Chief Examiner for A-level psychology. Mike is also an Editor of the journal *Psychology Review* and a regular contributor to student conferences. Although psychology takes up most of his time, he still avidly follows the fortunes of his home-town football teams, Premier League Liverpool and Marine of the Unibond League.

Liz Clark

Although a psychologist at heart and also by training, and someone who is passionate about learning and good teaching, Liz Clark has worked in healthcare education for the past 22 years. Whilst Head of Distance Learning at the Royal College of Nursing (RCN), she was responsible for developing and delivering a range of distance learning degree programmes for qualified nurses, as well as bite-sized chunks of learning for the RCN Learning Zone to support RCN members' personal and professional development. Liz Clark currently works at The Open University (OU) and is the Deputy Director for the OU–RCN Strategic Alliance.

The experience of creating effective and highly accessible learning resources that can be studied with the minimum of teacher support contributed to the original ideas and vision behind the first edition of this book published in the mid 1990s.

The editors and the publisher believe that AS-level students deserve texts that intrigue, support and challenge, and above all that kindle their curiosity to find out more and embark on a journey of lifelong learning.

Claire Meldrum

Claire Meldrum has taught A-level psychology for many years, in both schools and colleges. She has written AS revision and examination guides, and has contributed to books on applied psychology for nurses and social workers.

CHAPTER 1

Psychology, psychologists and research methods

EXPLAINING THE SPECIFICATION

Specification content	The specification explained
Research methods and techniques Candidates will be expected to demonstrate knowledge and understanding of the following research methods, their advantages and weaknesses: ■ experimental method, including laboratory, field and natural experiments ■ studies using a correlational analysis ■ observational techniques ■ self-report techniques, including questionnaires and interviews ■ case studies.	**In this part of the specification you need to describe:** ■ the experimental method, including laboratory, field and natural experiments and the advantages and weaknesses of each of these three types of experiment ■ studies using a correlational analysis and their advantages and weaknesses ■ observational techniques and their advantages and weaknesses ■ self-report techniques, including questionnaires and interviews, and their advantages and weaknesses ■ case studies and their advantages and weaknesses. **You also need to be able to evaluate the advantages and weaknesses of research studies that you read about as part of your psychology studies. We will help you to do this by providing lots of examples and activities throughout the book that will enable you to develop your evaluation skills in relation to research. These activities are highlighted with Research Methods and/or** *How Science Works* **icons, shown here, and will help you prepare for the** *How Science Works* **(AO3) component of the two AS exams.** RESEARCH METHODS / HOW SCIENCE WORKS

Introduction

This chapter is divided into two topics. The first topic will provide a brief overview of psychology, including its goals, the main approaches in psychology and what it is that psychologists do. We will also explore the difference between psychology and common sense, and examine how psychology lives up to its claim of being a science.

The second topic focuses on the range of research methods used by psychologists: experimental research, studies using correlation analysis, observational techniques, self-report techniques, including questionnaires and interviews, and case studies. The advantages and weaknesses of each research method will be discussed.

If this is the first time you have studied psychology, you will probably be wondering what it's all about and what it is that people who call themselves psychologists actually do for a living. Some psychologists (and I have to admit to being one of these) are reluctant to tell others what they do, particularly when out with friends. This is because as soon as I say that I am a psychologist, I inevitably get the response 'Well I suppose that you can read my mind then' or 'I really don't know why anyone bothers to study psychology because it's all just common sense'. So, we begin this first chapter by asking an important question, 'What is psychology?' before we go on to ask an equally important question, 'What do psychologists do?' This sets the scene for our discussion of research methods in Topic 2.

Topic 1: What is psychology? HOW SCIENCE WORKS

Psychology in context

Big Brother

The *Big Brother* series has become a regular feature on television. During 2007, serious accusations of racism, bullying and harassment on the programme resulted in newspaper headlines and TV news features. You may have noticed that psychologists are employed as advisers to the *Big Brother* programme.

1 In what ways do you think that psychologists could contribute to the programme at the planning stage, including the selection of the participants?

2 Try to watch an episode of the programme and discuss with other students on your course how you think that psychologists can help interpret the behaviour of the residents of the Big Brother house. If you are not able to see the programme, think about this question based on your knowledge of the programme.

3 Do you think that psychologists would be able to predict reliably how each housemate would cope with life inside the house? Give your reasons.

4 Do you think that a psychologist could reliably predict the likely winner at the outset of the series, based on their knowledge of each of the participants? Give your reasons.

5 Finally, why do you think that the Big Brother series have become so popular over the years and are watched, talked about and written about so much?

Before you read any further, we would like you to carry out a short activity to find out what you and a few others think the study of psychology is all about.

Psychology is concerned with understanding the experience and behaviour of humans and what makes people 'tick'. Psychologists also study non-human behaviour. As human beings we are able to reflect on our own behaviour and its causes. We also observe other people and watch how they react to us and to others. We listen to what people say. As a result of all this activity we sometimes create our own personal theories, based on our experiences and observations. For example, I might believe that 'people who wear glasses look intelligent' or that 'politicians are self-seeking and can't be trusted'. Have you ever developed any personal theories like these, based on your own observations and experiences?

Once we have developed a theory we tend to test it out by continuing to observe others, looking out for examples that support our theory in order to confirm what we already believe. This means that many of our ideas about people are based on rather limited and biased observations, and on simplified beliefs and assumptions that are influenced by our family upbringing, our personality and sometimes our prejudices. Clearly, there is no real relationship between wearing glasses and a person's IQ; not all politicians are self-seeking and some can be trusted! This is where psychology has an important contribution to make. Psychologists carry out systematic research because they know that we cannot rely on intuition and common sense alone. Nor can we rely on our own observations and experiences (which are inevitably limited) to answer important questions about people's behaviour and experience. Questions such as: How can we improve our memory? Why are girls achieving higher average grades at GCSE than boys? Does watching violent films on TV affect levels of violence on the streets? What are the benefits of using online support groups to help victims of domestic violence? These are just a few examples of the vast number of interesting questions that psychologists are interested in. So, psychologists enhance our understanding of many aspects of human behaviour and experience

Activity Studying psychology

First, list what you think you will be studying during your AS course. How does this help you answer the question 'What is psychology?' Note down a few of your ideas.

Then, spend a few more minutes asking members of your family and/or some of your friends the same question, and make a note of their ideas.

Try to summarize all the ideas you have gathered in one sentence that reads 'I think psychology is concerned with studying ...'.

When you have completed this activity, read on to find out more about what psychology is all about and what psychologists do.

Activity Shocking treatment?

Think for a moment about what you predict would happen in the scenario described below:

Imagine you and some of your friends have agreed to take part in a learning **experiment** carried out in a psychological laboratory. In this study, you have been designated as the 'teacher' and have been paired with a learner who has agreed to take part in a study of whether punishment can help people to learn. You are also introduced to a third person (whom you have never met before), who is alongside you throughout the study and asks you to give an electric shock (as punishment) to the learner every time he or she gets an answer wrong. The electric shocks range on a scale from very mild to very severe shocks (450 volts) that are potentially lethal. The learner is hidden behind a screen, but you can hear what they say and any cries of distress when a shock is administered. Once you have delivered a particular level of shock, you can only give a stronger shock the next time the learner gives a wrong answer. Alternatively, you can opt out of the study by saying that you don't want to continue to participate in the study.

1 What percentage of people do you think would be willing to give severe, potentially lethal shocks to the learner in this context?

- less than 15 per cent
- 15 to 30 per cent
- 31 to 45 per cent
- 46 to 60 per cent
- 61 to 75 per cent
- more than 75 per cent

2 Would this differ if the 'teacher' heard more and more anguished cries from the 'learner' as the study progressed and higher voltage shocks were administered? If so, how do you think it would differ?

As you may have already guessed, this was based on a real study involving deception. Milgram (1963) was interested in studying obedience to authority, but for obvious reasons he could not tell those participating in the study that this was what he was studying because it would inevitably have affected the results. This raises some important ethical questions for you to consider:

(a) Is there any way that Milgram could have conducted a study of obedience without using deception?

(b) What are the possible physical and psychological risks to the participants in Milgram's study?

(c) How might the researcher reduce the risk to participants?

and also of non-human behaviour by carrying out carefully designed research studies that answer these research questions and test predictions systematically. As we shall see, this is a very different approach to searching selectively for evidence to support one's existing beliefs (personal theories).

Psychology is more than common sense

From the above it should be clear that psychology offers much more than a common-sense understanding of people's behaviour and experience. In fact, some of our so-called common-sense ideas are contradictory. Think for a moment about proverbs that give inconsistent messages. For example, if 'many hands make light work' then why do we say that 'too many cooks spoil the broth'? If common sense suggests that 'absence makes the heart grow fonder', how can we reconcile this with the statement 'out of sight, out of mind'? Also, 'he who hesitates is lost' and 'look before you leap' offer contradictory advice.

Of course, psychology sometimes provides evidence that supports what we often call common sense or 'gut feelings' (intuition). For example, most people believe that children who are raised in caring and loving families are well placed to be warm and loving parents in their turn. Psychologists who have carried out research in this area have confirmed this 'common-sense' view. On other occasions, psychological research has played a significant role in demolishing commonly held beliefs, such as the myth that only by using regular punishments can parents raise well-behaved children or teachers instil discipline in their pupils. Owing to the research of psychologists, such as Skinner (Chapter 7, p. 232), we now know that rewarding desirable behaviour is more important and effective for learning than punishing what is undesirable. Before reading on, try the activity 'Shocking treatment' on the left.

You may have already heard about this research, carried out by the American psychologist Stanley Milgram in 1963, as it is quite often written about and has also been featured on TV. This is mainly because it raises so many interesting questions about the ethics of carrying out such a study and whether what Milgram did was defensible. Although Milgram presented the study in the context of a learning experiment, as described in the activity, he was actually interested in studying obedience to authority. However, it is the use of deception that contributed to the controversy over this particular experiment.

Before carrying out this study, Milgram asked a number of people (including some psychologists and psychiatrists) to predict how far they thought the teachers would be prepared to go, i.e. what level of electric shock they would be prepared to give to the learner. Remarkably, in the actual study, he found that 65 per cent of the participants (the 'teachers') obeyed the stranger and gave increasingly severe electric shocks to the learner, who made lots of mistakes, and continued until they had administered the highest, potentially lethal, electric shock (450 volts). Certainly, none of the people whom Milgram had asked predicted that so many people would be willing to administer such extreme electric shocks. In fact, most predicted that the majority would either refuse to administer any shock at all or only the very mildest ones. What did you guess?

Sometimes, therefore, psychological research produces results that are not at all what you would expect. Such findings are what are called 'counter-intuitive'. Here, our common-sense understanding was definitely unreliable and Milgram had to try to explain his findings. Milgram's research is discussed in more detail in Chapter 6 on pp. 192–8, where the ethics of carrying out such a study are also considered.

The important point to remember is that psychology studies its subject matter systematically and therefore bases its claims on research evidence, not hunches, intuition, guesswork, anecdote or people's limited experience.

The importance of evaluating everything you read

Of course, the quality of the research evidence produced by psychologists varies. You cannot, therefore, trust all the conclusions that psychologists draw when they have carried out research. Some research evidence is very sound, while some is weaker. As you work through this psychology book, you will learn to evaluate (judge) how convincing the evidence is that is being presented to you. When we introduce the different research methods that psychologists use in Topic 2 of this chapter, we will consider the advantages and weaknesses of each method. Then, whenever we provide a description of a research study in later chapters of this book, we would like you to evaluate the study in terms of its strengths and also any flaws in the design. This will enable you to judge whether the findings of the study are reliable and valid, and give clear reasons why you think a particular piece of research is, or is not, sound. (See Chapter 2, p. 50, or the Glossary for the meaning of the important terms **reliability** and **validity**.)

The ability to evaluate is an important skill to develop not only for your psychology studies, but also for other aspects of your life. The activity on the right encourages you to start practising this skill.

Once you start doing this, you are likely to notice that newspaper headlines and their brief accounts of research are sometimes biased or misleading, and that the research being described in the article may be seriously flawed and, therefore, unreliable. However, they make good headlines and interesting reading! As a discerning reader you will soon be able to judge which findings you can trust and which should be dismissed because the research study was not well designed, was poorly carried out, or the results were not properly analyzed and interpreted. We hope you will notice how much your ability and confidence to evaluate research improve over the course of your AS studies.

Activity Judging the media

It is important to start challenging everything you read, including reports of research in the media.

Read about the same research in two different newspapers, including a tabloid newspaper such as *The Sun*.

- How are the accounts similar and how do they differ?
- Do you think that one account is more accurate than the other, and if so, why?

Some definitions of psychology

The word 'psychology' comes from the Greek word *psyche* (which means mind, spirit or soul) and *logos* (meaning study or knowledge of). This suggests, therefore, that psychology is the study of the mind. However, this statement does not capture the complex subject matter that psychologists actually study. In fact, it is quite difficult to come up with a straightforward definition of psychology. Below are some of the definitions in a number of psychology textbooks, starting with one of the very earliest definitions from the late 19th century:

- '... the science of mental life, both of its phenomena and of their conditions ... The phenomena are such things as we call feelings, desires, cognition, reasoning, decisions and the like.' (William James 1890)

- Eysenck (2005) defines psychology as 'The science of mind, behaviour, and experience'.

- 'Psychology is the scientific study of behaviour and mental processes (the mind), and psychologists are interested in every aspect of behaviour and every type of mental process.' (This was the definition used in the previous edition of this textbook by Cardwell *et al.* 2003.)

■ 'Psychology is commonly defined as the scientific study of behaviour and cognitive processes (or mind or experience).' (Gross 2005)

If you look carefully at each of these definitions you will notice that although they differ, they include some common themes. They all emphasize psychology's *scientific approach* to the subject matter of *behaviour*, *mental processes* and *experience*. However, as we shall see, not all psychologists approach their work in the same way. Perhaps not surprisingly, the range of topics studied by psychologists has necessitated the development of different approaches (sometimes referred to as 'schools of thought'). During the course of this book, we will provide you with a clear sense of what psychology is, and you will also get a hint of some of the very real tensions that exist within a discipline that sets out to explain human behaviour and experience. However, it could be argued that these differences are actually beneficial, because different approaches provide different kinds of insights into the subject matter.

Approaches in psychology

Wundt, introspection and the first psychology laboratory

People have always been interested in how the mind works and the causes of behaviour. The roots of modern psychology can be traced back to the ancient Greek philosophers of the 4th and 5th centuries BC. However, it was only towards the end of the 19th century that psychology became established as a branch of knowledge (discipline) in its own right, when Wilhelm Wundt (1832–1920) set up the first experimental psychology laboratory in 1879 in the University of Leipzig (Germany). In this laboratory, Wundt (who trained as a physiologist) and his colleagues studied the human mind through what is called **introspection** (**observation** used by early psychologists to study and analyze the elements of their own conscious mental processes).

The methods used by Wundt and colleagues involved measuring and recording their introspections under controlled conditions. Introspection was later rejected as a suitable method because it was considered to be too subjective – the accuracy of introspective data could never be checked because it relied on what one person told another person about their private, and therefore invisible, thought processes.

Since then, many different approaches (perspectives) have been developed in psychology. Some of the most important current approaches are outlined below.

Freud and psychoanalysis

This approach developed from the work of Sigmund Freud (1856–1939). The term 'psychoanalysis' is used to describe both the theory that much of our behaviour is motivated by unconscious thoughts, and also the therapy that Freud developed for treating neurotic conditions. In the course of treating psychiatric patients, Freud became convinced that problems in adulthood often have their origins in early experiences, particularly those that occur during the first five years of a person's life. To help people gain access to the unconscious mind, Freud developed a number of psychoanalytic techniques, including dream interpretation and free association. By these means, he sought to uncover unconscious conflicts, help people understand the causes of these, and come to terms with their problems. You will read more about Freud's work and ideas in Chapter 7 (see pp. 227–31).

The couch used during Freud's psychoanalysis sessions, overlaid by a portrait of Freud

Watson and behaviourism

Behaviourism dates from 1913 when John Watson (1878–1958) argued that psychologists should focus on studying observable behaviour rather than mental processes. Unlike mental processes, behaviour is visible and can be directly observed and measured, and other people can independently check (verify) any observations and measurements that are recorded, making the account more objective. The roots of behaviourism stretch back to the Russian physiologist, Ivan Pavlov (1849–1936), who was famous for his work on conditioning animals.

So, introspection was replaced by methods that were used by other scientists, such as biologists, chemists and physicists. By using the same methods that were used in the natural sciences, psychology could claim to be scientific (which you may recall was one of the key themes in the four definitions above). Behaviourism had a profound effect on psychology for about 50 years and some of its basic ideas are still influential in psychological thinking today. For example, one important legacy from the behaviourist approach is the scientific concept of an **operational definition**, which is a precise statement of how a concept, such as aggression, is recognized and measured. You will learn more about the importance of operational definitions when you study Chapter 2 (see p. 48) and you will find out more about behaviourism in Chapter 4.

Psychologist Dr John Broadus Watson, author of the book entitled Behaviourism

Social learning theory

In the 1960s, social learning theorists, such as Bandura, demonstrated that sometimes learning was possible without the need for reinforcement (being rewarded for a behaviour). All that was needed was the chance to observe the behaviour of others. This observational learning was called imitation or modelling.

The cognitive approach

Psychology was initially accepted as a scientific discipline by restricting its subject matter to the study of human and non-human behaviour, as reflected in the work of behaviourists such as Watson and Skinner. However, in the later 1950s/early 1960s, some psychologists returned to an interest in mental processes and the human mind (the subject matter of the very early psychologists such as Wundt). They began to study the mental (cognitive) processes that people use to acquire, store, retrieve and use the knowledge they have about the world.

This approach arose as a reaction against the narrow view taken by behaviourists, which concentrated solely on observable behaviour and neglected complex activities like perceiving, remembering, processing information, problem-solving and planning. Although these mental processes are 'private' events and cannot be studied directly, unlike behaviour, it is now accepted that they can be inferred (conclusions reached from evidence) by using specific tests of problem-solving, perception, memory, etc. How people perform on such tasks or what they report is considered to be valid data. In Chapter 3, you will read about the cognitive approach when we consider the study of human memory.

The physiological (biological) approach

Physiological psychologists believe that, in order to describe and explain human behaviour and experience, we need to look closely at human biology. For example, how do different areas of the brain contribute to behaviours? In Chapter 5, you can read about the physiological response to stress, while

Cartoon of English naturalist Charles Darwin (1809–82), propped up on two cushions and in the chair with wheels that he used to propel himself round his workroom.

Chapter 7 discusses the biological treatment of severe depression, including the controversial use of **electro-convulsive therapy** (ECT).

The evolutionary approach

The evolutionary approach also emphasizes the importance of biological factors. Its starting point is Darwin's theory of evolution: that processes of natural selection have shaped human behaviour and experience.

According to evolutionary psychology, our modern behaviours are shaped by the problems faced by our ancestors millions of years ago, and the solutions that led to some surviving and reproducing and others falling by the wayside. While this approach has become popular in recent years, there are many who criticize it, pointing out that social and cultural factors influence behaviour and shape it in a way that has nothing to do with natural selection. You will learn more about the evolutionary approach if you go on to study psychology at A2 level.

Looked at together, as in the four definitions above, these approaches demonstrate that contemporary psychology focuses on the study of behaviour (human and non-human), mental processes and experience, although in different ways.

Before we look at what psychologists do, let's consider what we mean by science and how we can judge whether a discipline is scientific.

How science works

Most chapters in this textbook include *How Science Works* features. These are designed to help you understand how scientists investigate specific phenomena as they attempt to explain particular aspects of the world around us. We will start by examining the main characteristics that characterize a science and help us to decide that one particular discipline is scientific (e.g. biology) and another discipline, such as philosophy, is not. The key characteristics of any scientific investigation are highlighted in italics in the text below.

Key characteristics of science and how they apply to psychology

- Any science has a *clearly defined subject matter* – While this has changed over the years for psychology, there is now broad agreement that it involves the study of human and non-human behaviour, mental processes and experience.

- *Scientific activity is systematic* – Recognized techniques are used to collect data (these are referred to as 'research methods' in the AS exam specification). The research methods used in psychology are discussed in the second topic of this chapter.

- *Scientific evidence must be empirical* – This is a statement about the type of evidence that is acceptable. All scientific knowledge and theory must be based on evidence derived from direct observation or experience (this is known as empirical evidence), rather than on intuition, personal opinions or beliefs. Scientific claims therefore stand or fall on the basis of empirical evidence. Science makes claims that are regarded as true according to criteria that are public and available for all to see and judge – hence the emphasis on objectivity. We shall see how psychologists strive to be objective and minimize bias when we discuss the research methods they use to study behaviour, mental processes and experience.

■ *Theories are constructed in an attempt to explain behaviours that have been repeatedly observed.* Theories are then investigated systematically by generating and testing hypotheses. A **hypothesis** is a precise prediction, based on a theory, about what will happen under particular conditions. In this book you will be reading about a number of psychological theories, including attachment theory and learning theory (both discussed in Chapter 4, which focuses on early social development).

Scientists use different methods to examine and investigate aspects of our world

Science aims to understand and explain specific aspects of the world we live in; different scientific disciplines investigate different aspects of our world. So, for example, biology investigates living organisms by examining their structure, function, growth, origin, evolution and distribution. Chemistry investigates the interactions of chemical substances with one another, and the energy changes that accompany chemical reactions. All scientific investigation involves a detailed, systematic and objective examination of the subject matter that is being studied; it has four main objectives:

■ to describe

■ to explain

■ to predict

■ and, where appropriate, to control.

The goals of psychology

Description

In psychology, the first step towards understanding behaviour is to describe it accurately. For example, if we wish to find out whether boys are more physically aggressive than girls, we must first describe exactly what we mean by 'physical aggression'. Once we have a clear definition we can begin to observe whether there is any difference in levels of physical aggression between boys and girls.

Explanation

Once something has been described, the next goal is to explain why it occurs, i.e. to understand what causes it. Psychologists often start with a hypothesis (based on scientific theory) about an observed behaviour and they then test the hypothesis to see if the evidence supports the theory. For example, our hypothesis could be 'Boys are more physically aggressive than girls because they are rewarded more often than girls for physically aggressive behaviour'. To test this prediction, we might carry out an observation study to see if boys do, indeed, receive more reinforcement than girls for their aggressive acts.

Prediction

After describing and explaining a particular aspect of behaviour, psychologists will often try to predict when that behaviour is likely to occur (i.e. the set of circumstances that trigger it). For example, we know that lacking a sense of control over aspects of our life is associated with so-called stress symptoms such as migraine and gastric ulcers. We might predict, therefore, that people whose work is monotonous, repetitive and regulated by others will be more likely to have high rates of absenteeism than people whose job allows them some freedom to organize their work. Chapter 5 looks in more detail at the causes of stress.

Control

Finally, scientists aim to control or modify a specific phenomenon by manipulating the factors that cause it. In certain circumstances it may be desirable to modify behaviour. Take, for example, the use of token economy in prisons or psychiatric hospitals in order to discourage antisocial behaviour. Tokens, used to reward any examples of desired behaviour, can be collected and then exchanged for privileges. See Chapter 7 for more information on therapies based on operant conditioning.

The goals of prediction and control are particularly important to applied psychologists who use psychological knowledge and theories to bring about improvements in many aspects of people's lives. We will now return to the second question that we raised at the beginning of this chapter: what do psychologists actually do?

What do psychologists do?

> 'Psychology, like all other sciences, can be misapplied. But, rightly used, psychology can make an immense contribution to human happiness.'
> (Rex and Margaret Knight, 1959, p. 264)

Put simply, psychologists study psychology, carry out research, apply psychological knowledge in the course of their day-to-day work, or do any combination of these activities. Some psychologists teach their discipline in schools, colleges and universities, while others practise psychology in the world at large. The latter, sometimes called 'applied psychologists', include many different occupations:

- *Clinical psychologists* focus on the treatment of psychological disorders, often carrying out psychological assessments and tests with people in hospitals, health centres, social services, community health services and mental health services; they also provide a range of therapies such as cognitive-behavioural therapy or psychotherapy.

- *Educational psychologists* work with children and young people in a range of settings, including schools, colleges, family centres, nurseries and residential children's homes. They carry out psychological assessments and administer psychometric tests (including IQ and personality tests), diagnose and treat educational, emotional and behavioural problems, and provide advice and guidance to parents and teachers on how best to support children and young people who have a physical impairment or learning difficulty.

- *Forensic (or criminal) psychologists* use psychological theories and principles in their work with the criminal justice system; they are employed in prisons, young offender units, the probation service, secure hospitals and rehabilitation centres.

- *Health psychologists* usually work in hospitals and community health centres, focusing on the causes of health and illness. They are concerned with health promotion and apply psychological principles and theories to bring about changes in people's beliefs, attitudes and behaviours that affect their health, in order to improve their overall health, wellbeing and life style (e.g. through smoking cessation programmes).

- *Occupational (or organizational) psychologists*, as their name suggests, are concerned with people at work. They provide advice and guidance on a range

Many trained psychologists work in the field of education

of work-related issues, including working conditions, matching the person to the job, recruitment and selection of staff, vocational guidance, advising on training/retraining needs, designing training programmes and the development of assessments and tests.

Since 1987, psychologists in the United Kingdom (UK) have been able to apply for chartered status through the British Psychological Society, which is the only professional body for psychologists in the UK authorized through its Royal Charter to keep a Register of Chartered Psychologists. This provides important protection for the general public because it prevents people calling themselves chartered psychologists, without having completed the required qualifications and gaining the necessary experience. Anyone who is listed on the official register (which is available for checking) is fully qualified to be working as a psychologist without supervision. The different types of applied psychologists listed above, who work with members of the general public (including quite vulnerable people), are all required to be chartered before they are permitted to practise.

In the rest of this chapter, we will be looking at how psychologists carry out research. In particular, we will consider the range of research methods they use to answer questions about aspects of human and animal behaviour and human experience, and we will examine the strengths and limitations of each method. This will help you judge the quality of particular research studies in later chapters of this book.

CHECK YOUR UNDERSTANDING

Check your understanding of the approaches in psychology, its goals, the key characteristics of science and what psychologists do by answering the following questions. Try to do this from memory. Check your answers by looking back through Topic 1.

1 Complete the following sentence:
'Psychology is concerned with studying ...'

2 Why is it important to evaluate everything you read in psychology?

3 When was the first psychology laboratory opened? What kind of research was carried out there?

4 What are the main differences between introspection as a means of collecting research data and the methods later used by behaviourists such as John Watson?

5 What would be the main criticisms that behaviourists would wish to highlight when evaluating the work of Freud and psychoanalysts?

6 What are the main subject areas studied by cognitive psychologists?

7 List the four key characteristics of science.

8 What are the four main goals of psychology?

9 Select three types of psychologist from the list below and write brief notes on the range of activities that each one does: clinical psychologist; educational psychologist; forensic psychologist; health psychologist; occupational psychologist.

RESEARCH METHODS   HOW SCIENCE WORKS

Psychology in context

How to study behaviour

As we have seen, psychologists study aspects of human and non-human behaviour. How would you go about investigating each of the areas listed below? Note down your ideas and then discuss them with other students on your course.

1 the effects of day care on children's social and cognitive development

2 the effect of learning multiplication tables by heart on children's ability to solve mathematical problems

3 a study of a 3-year-old child as she adapts to life as a singleton after separation from a conjoined twin

4 children's views about pocket money

5 a study of the relationship between intelligence and academic achievement

6 the effect of watching violent films on levels of aggression in young people

7 an investigation of the amount of time unemployed young adults spend on social networking Internet sites in a month, compared with those in full-time employment.

What problems might arise when studying these topics? How could you overcome the problems you identify?

When you have completed Topic 2, return to your answers and make notes on any changes you would want to make in the light of studying a range of research methods.

RESEARCH METHODS   HOW SCIENCE WORKS

Topic 2: Research methods and techniques

All of us have our own personal theories about why people think and behave in the ways that they do. However, psychologists differ from 'lay people' (i.e. non-psychologists) in that they develop scientific theories, which they then test by carrying out carefully designed research studies. The main methods used by psychologists to carry out their research include:

- experiments
- correlation techniques
- self-report techniques, including questionnaires and interviews.
- observational techniques
- case studies

Psychologists use research methods and techniques to gather and make sense of the data they produce. The data they collect can be either quantitative or qualitative. **Quantitative data** have a numerical basis (e.g. time in seconds, stress ratings), whereas **qualitative data** are non-numerical (e.g. verbal reports of how research participants feel about something). Each of these research methods has its own advantages and limitations. Once you understand how each of these methods is used, you will be in a better position to evaluate research findings and the scientific theories that are offered to explain behaviour and mental processes. As we shall see, the type of research method used depends on the purpose of the study and also the topic that is being investigated.

For many years the **experimental method**, and in particular the **laboratory experiment**, was the main research method used by many psychologists. However, increasing dissatisfaction with the realism of the findings from experimental research carried out in laboratories and the relevance of such studies to everyday life has led some psychologists to seek alternative methods. This has resulted in an increase in the use of research methods that produce qualitative data, as well as quantitative data. It is now recognized that both experimental and non-experimental research methods have their place in psychology, and have an important contribution to make and should therefore be considered complementary to one another.

We will consider the main advantages and weaknesses of each research method, and some of the ethical issues associated with its use, illustrating each method in the context of an actual study discussed elsewhere in the book. For example, Milgram's studies of obedience and Zimbardo's prison simulation study, in Chapter 6, are examples of experimental methods, but also highlight the importance of research ethics. These are two of the most hotly debated studies in the entire history of psychology, because people still disagree about whether they should ever have been carried out, in spite of the important insights they provided. The specific examples will also consolidate your understanding of how psychologists have used particular methods to address a range of topics.. The advantages and weaknesses of the specific study will also be outlined, to help you learn how to evaluate psychological research – an important skill that is required for the AS exam.

This section discusses all the research methods that are included on the AS specification, but may not cover all the methods you may encounter when studying psychology. Bear in mind, too, that although research methods can be divided into specific categories, these methods can merge into each other. For example, the boundary between experimental and non-experimental research is not always clear cut. What really matters is that the most *appropriate* research method is used to investigate a particular problem or research question.

Experimental method in psychology

When carrying out an experiment, a researcher always intervenes directly in the situation being investigated by manipulating at least one variable. A **variable** is quite simply anything that can be measured and that can change (or vary) such as age, weight, response times, reading scores and IQ scores. The true experiment is regarded as being the most powerful research method used by psychologists because of its potential to investigate the causes of events, and thus identify cause-and-effect relationships. A true experiment has three key features:

1 The researcher manipulates an **independent variable** (IV) in order to investigate whether there is a change in a second variable, known as the **dependent variable** (DV) (see Figure 1.1).

2 All other variables, which might influence the results, are either controlled, held constant or eliminated.

3 Participants are allocated to the experimental conditions randomly.

The researcher formulates a hypothesis (a prediction) that one variable (the IV) will affect another variable (the DV). In the simplest form of experiment, the researcher deliberately manipulates the independent variable, while all the other aspects of the study are held constant in order to see what effect the IV has on the results (i.e. how it affects the DV).

Consider for a moment a hypothetical experiment to investigate which of two methods of teaching young children to read is more successful. Method A is a new approach that seems promising, but which has not yet been systematically evaluated for its effectiveness. Method B is the standard approach to teaching reading in many schools. The teaching method is the IV and the DV would be some measure of the children's reading ability (for example, scores derived from a standardized test of reading ability). Notice the wording above includes the phrase 'is more successful'. In order to make such a comparison, some children would need to be taught to read using the standard teaching method, while others would need to be taught by the new (untested) method. We will consider how best this comparison might be achieved a bit later.

To be confident that only the IV produced any change in the DV, the researcher must ensure that all other variables are held constant. If they cannot be held constant, then the effect of these variables needs to be eliminated. These unwanted variables are known as **confounding variables**, and might include the following:

▪ *Differences in the instructions* given by an experimenter or in the stimulus materials being used – This can be overcome by standardizing the instructions and materials for all participants in the experiment.

▪ *Differences between participants* (e.g. in their age) – This can be eliminated by using a single age group, or can be held constant by ensuring that the age structure of each of the groups taking part in the experiment is similar.

The logic of the true experiment is that, if all variables other than the IV have either been successfully controlled or eliminated, then any change that is

Figure 1.1
Linking the independent and dependent variable

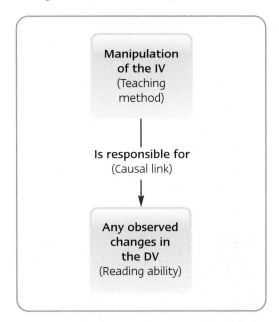

Manipulation of the IV
(Teaching method)

|

Is responsible for
(Causal link)

↓

Any observed changes in the DV
(Reading ability)

produced in the DV must be the result of manipulating the IV. When reading about an experiment, it is always important to consider carefully the design of the study to check whether any other variable (a confounding variable) could have caused the results, in which case you can have no confidence in the results or any conclusions drawn from them.

A principle of good experimental design is that the researcher must either allocate participants randomly to the groups that make up the study (i.e. give all those who have agreed to participate an equal chance of being selected for a particular group), or permit all participants to experience each condition. Returning to our earlier example, it would not be feasible to expose the children to both teaching methods (which would confuse the children and also render the study meaningless). However, if the teachers involved agreed, it would be possible to use both teaching methods in one school, and allocate the children randomly to Method A or to Method B. Alternatively, the researcher could seek out two schools – one that has adopted the new method of teaching reading and another that uses the standard method (Method B). The reading abilities of the children in these two schools could then be compared.

As we have seen, it is not always possible to meet all three of the requirements for a true experiment. The term **quasi-experiment** (the prefix 'quasi' means 'resembling but not really the same as') is used to describe an experiment where the investigator lacks complete control over the IV and/or the allocation of participants to groups. For example, if a psychologist was interested in studying the effectiveness of an antibullying strategy in schools, it probably would not be possible to introduce the strategy for some pupils but not for others. An alternative approach would be to undertake a quasi-experiment, comparing the levels of bullying in schools where a strategy has been implemented with bullying levels in similar schools where a strategy has not been introduced. This is a quasi-experiment because the researcher has no control over the allocation of participants to the two experimental conditions – exposure or no exposure to the antibullying strategy.

Returning to our hypothetical investigation of methods of teaching children to read, if the children from one school were randomly allocated to one or other of the teaching methods, this would be a true experiment. If two different schools were used, this would be a quasi-experiment. You must, therefore, look carefully at the design to determine what type of experiment it is.

Advantages of the experimental method

- By holding all variables constant between groups, except for the IV, and eliminating any confounding variables, an experimenter may be able to establish a cause-and-effect relationship between the IV and the DV. No other research method can do this directly. However, it is important to remember that cause-and-effect relationships are notoriously difficult to demonstrate in experimental research involving human participants undertaken outside a highly controlled laboratory setting.

- The use of experiments allows researchers to force the pace of the research because they do not have to wait for natural events to reproduce the appropriate scenario needed to investigate a particular issue. It allows psychologists to study behaviour that rarely occurs or that cannot easily be studied in another way, such as bystander attitudes to an emergency. Also, it allows the researcher to select *when* and possibly *where* an experiment will be carried out.

In an experiment investigating different methods of teaching children to read, how would you allocate the participants to groups?

- An experiment generates quantitative data (numerical measures of the DV) which can be analyzed using inferential statistical tests. These statistical tests (which are beyond the specification requirement for AS) allow the researcher to state how likely the results are to have occurred *by chance*, rather than as a result of manipulating the IV.

- Once the data from experimental research have been obtained and analyzed, it is possible to generalize the findings to the rest of the population from which the sample of participants has been draw, provided that a representative sample of participants was selected to take part in the original research study.

Disadvantages of the experimental method

- Participants in many experimental investigations reflect an overrepresentation of males and of specific cultures (usually the US and Europe), and have often been volunteers drawn from university campuses. It is important, therefore, to question how far it is appropriate to generalize the results of such experimental studies to groups of people beyond those who actually took part.

- Participants usually know that they are taking part in a psychological experiment and may therefore react either positively or negatively to this knowledge. This can affect the results of the study.

- It is not always possible to carry out an experiment because it would either be inappropriate or unethical to do so. For example, discipline in schools would be better studied by an observational study or **survey** research than by any form of experimental research.

Now try the activity on the right.

Laboratory experiments

Laboratory experiments provide the highest level of control over variables and are widely used in psychology. The psychology laboratory may be the only place where some sophisticated technical equipment can be used and accurate measurements made. Researchers who are interested in memory and other cognitive processes often carry out laboratory experiments. For example, Stroop (1935) carried out a well-known series of laboratory experiments. He studied how colour name words have an interfering effect on the time taken to name the ink colours of non-matching colours. For example, naming the ink colour of the word 'blue' written in green ink takes longer than it does for the same word written in blue ink. This effect has become known as the 'Stroop effect' (see the activity on the next page).

When reading an account of research that has been carried out in a laboratory, it is important to think carefully about the design of the study. Just because the study has been carried out in a laboratory does not mean that it is necessarily a laboratory experiment. Some observation studies have been carried out in laboratories, so the setting alone is not a reliable indicator of the type of research.

Advantages of the laboratory experiment

- *Replicability of procedures* – A laboratory experiment that is carefully designed, well carried out and clearly reported can easily be repeated (replicated) by other researchers to see if they obtain similar results. If this happens and the findings are similar, then confidence is increased in the results. Without this ability to replicate studies fairly easily in a laboratory setting, researchers would have to wait indefinitely for the precise set of

RESEARCH METHODS

Activity Identifying independent and dependent variables

After reading the brief descriptions below of three memory studies, identify the IV and DV in each one.

1 Baddeley (1966) investigated the effects of acoustic similarity on serial recall performance by presenting participants with a list of five short words that sound alike (e.g. man, mat, map, can, cap) and five short words that do not sound alike (e.g. pen, day, few, cow, pit).

2 Tyler *et al.* (1979) gave participants two sets of anagrams to solve: one set was easy (e.g. doctro) and the others were more difficult (cdrtoo). They were then unexpectedly asked to recall as many of the words as possible. The aim was to test the prediction that it is the amount of processing effort rather than depth of processing that affects memory retention.

3 Psychologists have been interested in the effects of the learning environment on memory recall. Smith (1979) gave participants a list of 80 words to learn while sitting in a distinctive basement room. The following day he tested some of the participants in the same basement room, others in a fifth-floor room with very different decor, and a third group in another upstairs room where participants were instructed to imagine themselves back in the basement room.

Answers are given on p. 272 ▶

A participant is briefed in Milgram's research into obedience (see Chapter 6, p.193) – a classic laboratory experiment

RESEARCH METHODS

Activity — The Stroop effect

In one experiment, Stroop (1935) selected five colour names – red, blue, green, brown and purple. For the experimental condition, each word was printed several times in a grid, but never printed in the colour it named (i.e. the word blue was never printed in blue ink). Instead, each word appeared an equal number of times in each of the other four colours. A second sheet was produced of the same words, but this time they were presented in reverse order.

The control condition experienced the same arrangement of ink colours, but this time each ink colour was represented by a coloured block. The researcher manipulated whether the stimulus sheets consisted of words in ink colours that conflicted with the colour names or were in the form of colour blocks.

The times taken to name the ink colours for each condition were compared. On average, it took participants 47 seconds longer to name the ink colours of a stimulus sheet in the experimental condition than in the control condition.

1 What is the IV in this experiment?
2 What is the DV?
3 How many conditions are there in this experiment?
4 Were the collected data quantitative or qualitative?
5 What cause-and-effect relationship do the findings suggest?

   Compare your answers with those on p. 272 ▶

You can try the Stroop test yourself online at **http://faculty.washington.edu/chudler/words.html**

Stanley Milgram with the 'shock' generator

circumstances required for a particular experiment to recur before the study could be replicated.

- *Sophisticated measuring and recording equipment* can be used more easily in a psychological laboratory compared with other settings outside the laboratory. This is particularly important with technical equipment, which may be highly sensitive to the external conditions.

- *Control over variables* – It is far easier to control potential confounding variables in the laboratory than in any other setting or with any other research method, so high levels of precision can be achieved. If all variables other than the IV are either tightly controlled or eliminated, then a cause-and-effect relationship can be established.

Weaknesses of the laboratory experiment

- *Loss of validity* – By establishing high levels of control, and narrowly defining IVs and DVs, an experimental situation is likely to become artificial and therefore recognizably different from real-life situations. Laboratory studies were originally designed for use in the natural sciences, such as biochemistry, chemistry and physics, where matter reacts in exactly the same way to external events under a given set of conditions. Human behaviour is far more complex and is affected by internal factors, such as self-awareness, emotions and motives relating to human consciousness, as well as by external variables that can be manipulated by the researcher.

  Ecological validity is concerned with the extent to which results may be generalized to settings other than the one in which the research took place, such as those outside the laboratory. For example, memory experiments have often been conducted using word lists, which are rarely learned in everyday life. However, in some research the artificiality of the laboratory situation may not really matter, such as when carrying out research on newborn infants or on auditory perception. Ecological validity is discussed more fully in Chapter 2.

- *Demand characteristics* – These occur when participants try to make sense of the research situation they find themselves in and adjust their behaviour accordingly (Orne 1962). **Demand characteristics** can seriously threaten the validity of an experiment. The demands placed on participants in a laboratory situation are not helped if the experimenter sticks rigidly to a standardized procedure and acts in an unemotional way, which is necessary if confounding variables are to be avoided. Participants may respond to subtle cues made either consciously or unconsciously by an investigator, such as differences in the tone of voice used or non-verbal signs of encouragement, and this may prompt them to try to guess what hypothesis is being tested. Some participants may also try to behave in a way they believe will be helpful to the researcher. Or, if they feel irritated by something, they may set out deliberately to confound (upset) the results.

  Other potential problems include evaluation apprehension, where participants demonstrate concern over what an experimenter might find out about them, or social desirability effects, where participants change their normal behaviour so that they may be perceived more favourably.

Ethical issues

- *Consent* – In all psychological research, the fully informed consent of all the participants must be obtained. However, once in the laboratory setting, participants might become so overawed by the environment that they feel unable to withdraw from the procedure, even if they wanted to. So, it is vital to abide by the guidelines about participants' right to withdraw from an investigation (see p. 55).

■ *Deception* – Some experiments undertaken by social psychologists involve deception. In these situations, it is important to debrief participants about the true nature of the study and to obtain their consent to use the data collected (for example, see Chapter 6, pp. 195–8, to read more about the ethical issues raised by Milgram's research on obedience).

■ *Use of animals* – Animals are sometimes used in laboratory experiments because this offers greater opportunities for experimental control in research procedures, compared to similar research with humans. For example, Harlow and Harlow's deprivation studies with rhesus monkeys, described in Chapter 4 (see p. 119), could not have been carried out on humans. Since animals are not able to consent to their involvement in research, they must not be subjected to unnecessary suffering. There are tight guidelines about what is permissible that have to be adhered to.

Field experiments

Field experiments are experimental investigations carried out in the natural environment of those being studied, e.g. in homes, schools or on the street. These experiments attempt to improve the realism of the research. As with the laboratory experiment, the researcher still deliberately manipulates an IV to produce a change in a DV. Therefore, much of what has been written in the previous section about the laboratory experiment also applies to the field experiment, so here we will focus on the key differences.

The field experiment is used in situations where it is considered particularly important for research to take account of the natural environment. For example, field experiments are widely used when studying non-human animals.

Advantages of field experiments

■ *Improved ecological validity* – By carrying out an experiment in a natural, real-life setting, the artificiality of the laboratory environment is avoided. This helps to eliminate the main criticism made of laboratory experiments that it can be difficult to generalize the findings to real-life situations.

■ *Reduction of demand characteristics* – Participants may be less conscious that they are taking part in a research study, so the likely influence of demand characteristics may be reduced.

Weaknesses of field experiments

■ *Establishing controls* – It is difficult to establish high levels of control in a field experiment, not only control over IVs and in measuring DVs, but also over any potentially confounding variables. For example, non-participants may intrude through conversation or simply by being present in the location where the experiment is taking place. Because of the increased difficulty of establishing controls, it may be more difficult to replicate precisely a field experiment than a laboratory experiment.

■ *Generalizing to other situations* – Although realism is high in a field experiment, the results cannot be generalized to other real-life situations that differ from the one in which the field experiment took place.

- *Cost* – Field experiments are often more costly to undertake than those carried out in laboratory settings and may also take longer to complete.

- *Use of technical equipment* – It can be more difficult to use sophisticated technical equipment outside a laboratory, restricting what can be measured and studied.

Ethical issues

- *Consent* – Ethical issues relating to informed consent and to participants' right to withdraw from a study at any time during the research are similar to those for laboratory experiments.

- *Confidentiality* – Since field experiments are undertaken in real-world settings, such as schools and hospitals, the identity of any organizations and participants involved in the research must be protected. Simply removing the names of organizations or people, and substituting descriptive characteristics (such as 'a large teaching hospital in Sunderland', or by referring to the age and gender of participants) may not be good enough to guarantee anonymity. Where confidentiality or anonymity cannot be guaranteed, the participants must be warned of this in advance.

- *Use of animals* – When animals are used in field experiments, their natural environment is being altered in some way because of the very nature of a field experiment. Such tampering with nature in order to understand it places great responsibilities on researchers to ensure they minimize the disruptive effects of any such manipulation.

Natural experiments

In a **natural experiment**, the researcher makes use of naturally occurring differences in the independent variable. This means that the researcher does not directly control the IV. The approach is therefore best described as a quasi-experiment (see p. 14), although some purists might even regard it as non-experimental study.

Examples of natural experiments can be found in the adoption studies discussed on p. 227 in Chapter 7.

Occasionally, an unforeseen event in the environment permits a natural experiment to be undertaken, such as the effect of widespread witnessing of violent crime on levels of violence subsequently recorded. Berkowitz (1970) hypothesized that witnessing violence makes people more violent. He recorded and examined data on violent crime before and after the assassination in 1963 of President Kennedy in the United States of America, which appeared on TV in North America and throughout the world. Berkowitz was able to demonstrate a sudden rise in violent crime after the assassination, thereby supporting his hypothesis. Some of the data gathered by Berkowitz are shown in Figure 1.2.

Advantages of natural experiments

- *Reduction of demand characteristics* – Participants may be less conscious that they are taking part in an experiment, and so demand characteristics may be avoided.

- *Lack of direct intervention* – The experimenter does not intervene directly in the research situation, although it is possible that the mere presence of the researcher may still produce an effect on the participants' behaviour.

President Kennedy, with his wife Jackie, arriving in Dallas on the morning that he was assassinated, 22 November 1963

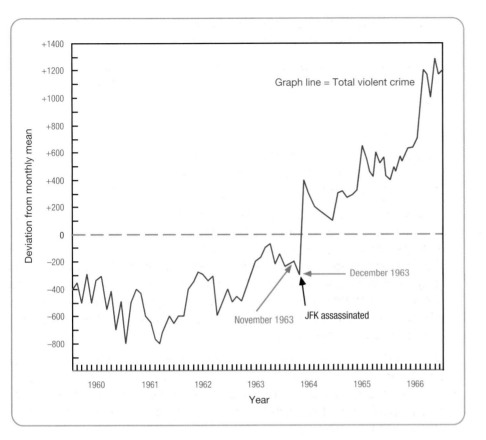

Figure 1.2 The assassination of President Kennedy and recorded levels of violence in the USA

Weaknesses of natural experiments

■ *Loss of control* – Since the investigator does not directly control the IV or assign participants to experimental conditions, the overall degree of control exercised by the researcher is significantly less than in either a laboratory experiment or a field experiment. This, in turn, greatly increases the likelihood of confounding variables affecting the results. The researcher cannot therefore be confident that the outcome is due to the IV, making it very difficult to establish a cause-and-effect relationship.

■ *Likelihood of the desired behaviour being displayed* – The naturally occurring situation that the researcher wishes to study may occur only rarely, thus reducing the available opportunities for research. This is illustrated in Berkowitz (1970) study of violent crime referred to above.

Ethical issues

■ *Consent* – Ethical issues relating to obtaining fully informed consent and safeguarding participants' right to withdraw from a natural experiment are similar to those for field experiments.

■ *Protection of participants* – This is also essential. For example, probing participants' views about the death penalty, following an increase in widely reported murders or terrorist atrocities might increase anxiety levels and lead to unwarranted distress associated with the research.

■ *Confidentiality* – Participants in natural experiments have the right to expect that the information they provide will be treated confidentially and, if published, will not be identifiable as theirs. Where confidentiality or anonymity cannot be guaranteed, participants must be warned of this in advance.

Non-experimental research methods

Having discussed the experimental method and three different types of experiment, we will now examine some types of research in which variables are not deliberately manipulated by the researcher. These research methods and techniques can be broadly categorized as 'non-experimental'. Each of the non-experimental research methods allows psychologists to study behaviour in more natural settings. However, this potential benefit also has its costs. Reduced levels of control make it far harder for the researcher to draw any conclusions concerning cause-and-effect relationships. As we saw in Topic 1, this type of relationship is important if we are to understand behaviour as fully as possible and go beyond description in order to explain, predict and, where appropriate, control it.

The non-experimental methods discussed here are:

- **correlational analysis**
- observational techniques
- **self-report techniques**, including **questionnaires** and **interviews**
- **case studies**.

The activity on the left will help you think about what claims can be made by researchers where non-experimental methods have been used and no control has been possible.

Studies using correlational analysis

The term correlation refers to a statistical technique that measures the relationship between two variables, i.e. the extent to which high values on one variable are associated with high values on another (known as a positive correlation), or the extent to which high values on one variable are associated with low values on another (a negative correlation). Many correlational techniques calculate a correlation coefficient, a statistic that has a value on a scale between +1 (which is a perfect positive correlation) and –1 (a perfect negative correlation). The strength of a correlation (i.e. the degree of the relationship) increases as a calculated correlation coefficient moves away from zero and becomes closer to +1 or –1. Correlation coefficients are discussed more fully in Chapter 2, pp. 64–5.

As it is a statistical technique, correlation is not strictly a research method, but the term is also used to refer to the design of non-experimental investigations which specifically aim to identify the relationship between variables.

Correlational research (or a study using correlational analysis, to use the phrase from the AS specification) is typically used to investigate the extent of relationship between variables that are thought likely to co-vary. For example, Murstein (1972) was interested in whether we select partners who are of similar physical attractiveness to ourselves (see the panel on the opposite page).

Correlation analysis can also be used in the early stages of research on a particular topic, especially when it is important to isolate relationships from a web of complex variables. For example, studies using Holmes and Rahe's Social Readjustment Rating Scale (1967) have found a correlation between life change units (scores derived from using the scale) and the incidence of sickness or depression (see Chapter 5, p. 158).

RESEARCH METHODS

Activity **'Dramatic increase in bullying in local schools'**

Imagine that you have just read a newspaper article with this headline. It reports that a short questionnaire was circulated to pupils of all the five secondary schools in your town. Sixty-five per cent of the respondents stated that they had been bullied at school during the past two years. The article then goes on to suggest that this dramatic increase is the result of poor discipline in the schools and holds the teachers responsible for this terrible state of affairs.

You have decided to contact the researcher and ask some questions, in order to prepare a report for your school magazine about this research.

1 Make a list of questions to ask the researcher who carried out the study. You want to find out whether you can be confident that the findings reflect the true incidence of bullying in the schools.

2 The newspaper article accuses teachers of using poor discipline. How might you go about researching whether or not this is true?

3 Imagine you discover that bullying is more common in schools with poor discipline. Can you be sure that the poor discipline causes the bullying? If not, why not and what other factors might be involved?

Physical attractiveness and marital choice
A study by Murstein (1972)

Murstein hypothesized that individuals tend to select marital partners of comparable physical attractiveness to themselves. He set out to investigate whether partners forming premarital couples were more similar in terms of their physical attractiveness than one would expect by chance.

Ninety-eight couples who were described as 'engaged' or 'going steady' participated as paid volunteers in his research. All participants were asked to rate the physical attractiveness of their partner and also to estimate their own physical attractiveness using a five-point scale. Photographs were also taken of all the participants. Independent judges were asked to rate the physical attractiveness of each couple.

The following correlation coefficients were obtained:

Relationship between:	Correlation coefficient:
Male participants' perception of their own and their partners' attractiveness	+0.50
Female participants' perception of their own and their partners' attractiveness	+0.45
Independent judges' ratings of the physical attractiveness of partners	+0.38

All the correlation coefficients were highly significant ($p < 0.01$), meaning that the likelihood of these results occurring by chance was highly unlikely (less than 1 in a 100). The data therefore supported Murstein's hypothesis about the relationship between physical attractiveness and marital choice.

David and Victoria Beckham – according to Murstein's (1972) research, it is not surprising that they selected each other as partners

Correlational techniques also play a major role in establishing the reliability and validity of psychological measuring instruments, such as psychometric tests of intelligence and personality.

The concepts of validity and reliability are discussed further in Chapter 2.

Now try the activity on the right.

Advantages of using correlational analysis

- *Measuring the strength of relationships* – Correlational techniques provide a precise quantitative measure of the strength of the relationship between specific variables.

- *Value to exploratory research* – Correlational techniques allow for the measurement of many variables and the relationships between them. They are useful, therefore, when trying to unravel complex relationships and are a powerful tool for exploratory research.

Weaknesses of correlational analysis

- *The issue of causality* – It is not possible to establish cause and effect through research investigations using correlational analysis; it can only measure the degree of interrelationship between different variables. For example, Snedecor (1956) reported a near perfect negative correlation of –0.98 between the production of pig iron in the USA and the birth rate in Britain for the years 1875 to 1920! The possibility of highlighting spurious relationships is a real

RESEARCH METHODS

Activity Bowlby's '44 thieves' study

Read the description of Bowlby's (1944) study of 44 juvenile thieves on p. 130. Then answer the questions below:

1 What type of study did Bowlby undertake?
2 What hypothesis was being tested?
3 Did the findings support the hypothesis?
4 What type of data did Bowlby collect in this study?
5 Do the results allow us to conclude that there was a link between frequent early separations and emotional maladjustment, or that frequent early separations cause emotional maladjustment?
6 Would it be possible to design an experiment to demonstrate a causal relationship between early separation and subsequent emotional maladjustment? Give reasons for your answer.

Answers are given on p. 272 ▶

Figure 1.3 Linking the independent and dependent variable

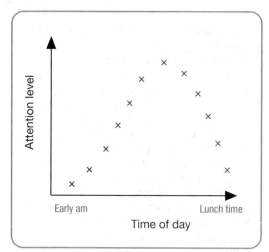

drawback of the technique and must be avoided at all costs because of the potential to be highly misleading.

To illustrate the problem, there is a well-established correlation between the presence of symptoms of schizophrenia and the high availability of the neurotransmitter dopamine. However, there is insufficient evidence to state that excess dopamine causes schizophrenia. It remains possible that it is schizophrenia which causes the increase in available dopamine or, indeed, that there may be other links in the causal relationship that have yet to be discovered. Nevertheless, the existence of this correlation has provided a useful avenue for further research.

● *Measurement of non-linear relationships* – Non-linear relationships cannot be measured by commonly used correlational techniques. For example, Figure 1.3 shows the relationship between time of day and attention level in a group of students. Initially, there is a positive correlation between the two variables, but as lunchtime approaches this changes into a negative relationship. When such data are analyzed, the positive and negative relationships tend to cancel each other out, with the result that no meaningful relationship is indicated by the calculated correlation coefficient. It is important therefore to plot non-linear relationships visually in order to understand what is happening.

Ethical issues

● *Consent* – The same issues of fully informed consent and right to withdraw (as discussed under 'Natural experiments') apply here.

● *Use of findings* – In socially sensitive research, such as an investigation of sexual offences against children and drug abuse, the question of who 'owns' the data is very complex. It raises possible concerns about research findings being used for reasons other than those for which they were originally intended. Researchers must, therefore, consider in advance how their research might be used. Participants can then give their informed consent not only to their participation in the study, but also to the ways in which the findings will be disseminated and used.

Observational techniques

In observation research, behaviour is observed and recorded and there is usually no deliberate manipulation of variables. It therefore provides an alternative to tightly controlled research methods such as the laboratory experiment. The emphasis is placed on how people or non-human animals behave in specific situations; no attempt is made to influence the behaviour being investigated in any way (unless, of course, observation is used as part of an experimental study, in which case it would be classified as an experiment). The method can, therefore, be used in situations where any other form of research intervention would be either entirely inappropriate (e.g. when studying weddings or funerals) or unethical (e.g. intervention with children).

Observational research can differ in several important ways, depending on:

● the setting in which the study is carried out

● the role of the researcher

● the amount of structure that is imposed.

We will look at each of these briefly in turn.

The study setting

Observation studies are often carried out in a natural setting such as a school canteen or a pub. Studies that focus on people's naturally occurring behaviour in everyday settings are usually referred to as naturalistic observation. The wide range of uses of naturalistic observation includes topics such as driver behaviour, the behaviour of children in school settings and studies of the workplace. It is also useful where behaviour might be difficult to recreate in a laboratory setting or as a preliminary study before a laboratory investigation is carried out. An example of naturalistic observational research is that by Rosenhan (1973) described in the panel on the right. Read the study now and then try the activity beneath it.

Naturalistic observation has always been popular in research carried out on non-human animals. Examples include the classic research by Lorenz on imprinting (see p. 120). The method is particularly useful when studying species that do not thrive in, or adapt to, laboratory conditions (e.g. red deer or marine mammals).

Observational research can also be laboratory based – a setting that is likely to make the behaviour observed seem rather artificial and structured. It is therefore tempting to assume that observation carried out in a laboratory environment cannot be naturalistic observation. However, some species (e.g. rats) appear to adapt well to laboratory conditions and the behaviour displayed in psychological laboratory settings may be considered sufficiently natural for naturalistic observational research to be carried out. Psychological laboratories can also be designed to resemble playrooms. Once children have become completely accustomed to such a room, their behaviour, which may be observed through a one-way mirror, may also be sufficiently natural for the observational research to be regarded as naturalistic.

The role of the researcher

A distinction is often made between participant observation, in which the observer actually joins the group of people being studied, and non-participant observation, in which the observer remains external to those being observed. Observers also have to decide whether to remain disclosed or undisclosed, so that the participants are either made aware of the research that is taking place or remain unaware of it. However, there are important ethical issues to consider when observation is undisclosed and when video recorders, concealed cameras and one-way mirrors are used. In the study by Rosenhan (1973), the researcher adopted the role of an undisclosed participant observer, which resulted in some very interesting findings.

The structure of observation activity

The amount of structure imposed on an observation can also differ. Participant observers may be most interested in trying to understand the meaning of the behaviours they are observing, in which case they typically produce detailed verbal descriptions of the behaviour they observe. Another form of observation research involves far more structure, with the observer using a coding system in order to count the number of times specific behaviours occur. Categories are needed so that the observer can count the number of times each **behavioural category** occurs during a given period of time. This kind of an approach produces quantitative data that can be analyzed statistically. If, for example, a researcher was observing children's aggressive behaviour, they might develop and use a coding system based on a series of relevant categories of behaviour. These might include 'angry shouting at another person', 'provoked hitting another

On being sane in insane places
An observational study by Rosenhan (1973)

Eight people who were entirely free of any psychiatric symptoms presented themselves to different psychiatric hospitals in the United States of America. All reported the same symptom – they said that they heard a voice say 'dull', 'empty' and 'thud'. Apart from this single symptom, they were all instructed to behave normally and to give honest answers to any other questions they were asked. All were believed to be genuine patients and were admitted to the psychiatric hospitals concerned, seven with a diagnosis of schizophrenia. Once admitted into a hospital, the 'patient' immediately stopped reporting that they had been hearing voices. They were later discharged seven to 52 days later, with diagnoses of 'schizophrenia in remission'.

Rosenhan attributed these diagnoses to the context in which their behaviour was observed. None of the so-called patients actually displayed symptoms of schizophrenia, but the context in which the symptoms were reported led to an expectation that these 'pseudopatients' were indeed mentally ill.

RESEARCH METHODS
Activity Rosenhan's study

1 What kind of observational study did Rosenhan (1973) conduct (see study above).

2 What conclusions can be drawn from this study?

3 What, if any, ethical issues does Rosenhan's study raise?

4 If such a study were to be replicated (repeated) today, do you think that it would produce similar results? Give reasons for your answer.

Answers are given on p. 272 ▶

person with great force', 'provoked hitting another person with lesser force', 'unprovoked hitting another person with great force' and 'unprovoked hitting another person with lesser force'.

Advantages of observational techniques

- *Value as a preliminary research tool* – Careful use of observation can lead to the identification of appropriate hypotheses for further investigation or may, on the other hand, help to prevent time being wasted in carrying out unrealistic experiments. It is also a useful technique for studying unknown or little-known behaviours. For example, Clutton-Brock and colleagues provided much of our knowledge about the behaviour of red deer through their pioneering studies carried out on the island of Rum (Rhum) in the Hebrides (e.g. Clutton-Brock and Albon 1979).

- *Validity* – Naturalistic observation can provide a useful means of checking whether experimental findings apply outside laboratory conditions. Realism and ecological validity can be good, provided that the observer remains undetected. The overall quality of the research may be improved through increased familiarity with the research setting, so that the researcher becomes a familiar figure, totally accepted as part of the environment by both human and non-human participants. Demand characteristics are minimized because behaviour is not affected either by anxiety or by inhibition associated with being in a laboratory situation. Also, with undisclosed naturalistic observation, there can be no feeling of a need to impress the researcher, as long as the observer remains undetected.

Weaknesses of observational techniques

- *Control* – The level of control over potentially confounding variables is poor in all types of observation, but particularly naturalistic observation, although some degree of control may be possible by, for example, restricting the focus of the study. This means that cause-and-effect relationships cannot be established.

- *Replication* may be difficult due to the problems that arise when trying to control variables such as differences between naturalistic settings. Problems may sometimes be minimized with the appropriate use of sound or video recordings, so that a record exists that can be used by others to check the researcher's own interpretation of observed behaviours.

- *Observer effects* – It is possible that the presence of an observer may change the behaviour of those being observed, especially when a small group is being studied. This can also be an issue when observing non-human animals. For example, breeding patterns may be disturbed by the mere presence of an observer. Additionally, the potential exists for bias on the part of observers themselves, particularly participant observers, based on their expectations or interpretations of events.

- *Ecological validity and realism* are likely to be lower in observational research carried out in laboratory settings compared with naturalistic observation.

- *Costs* can be high when undertaking naturalistic observation – for example, the cost associated with travel and the cost of transporting recording equipment.

- *Coding systems* used in structured observational research may limit or constrain how the data gathered are categorized (using behavioural categories), affecting the interpretation of behaviour; behaviours may also be

Much of our knowledge about the behaviour of red deer comes from naturalistic observation carried out on the island of Rum by Clutton-Brock and Albon (1979)

observed that do not easily fit into any of the categories. For example, identical behaviour in children might be classified as 'aggressive' by one researcher and as 'rough and tumble play' by another researcher.

- *Generalizability of the findings* – The uniqueness of each observational situation may make it difficult, or even impossible, to generalize the results of observational research to other occasions or other settings.

Ethical issues

- *Privacy* – Studies based on observation must respect the privacy and psychological wellbeing of the individuals studied. Unless those being observed give their consent to being observed, observational research is only acceptable in situations where those observed would expect to be observed by strangers (e.g. in the high street of a major town). Particular care should be taken to respect local cultural values and avoid the possibility of intruding upon the privacy of individuals who, even while in a normally public space, may believe they are unobserved. Those who are observed have the right to expect that any information they provide will be treated confidentially and, if published, will not be identifiable as theirs.

- *Confidentiality and consent* – If researchers do not disclose that they are undertaking observational research and collect data in a non-public setting, such as a hospital ward or a school playground, they should subsequently inform those who were observed about the study and obtain their consent to use the data collected. If confidentiality or anonymity cannot be guaranteed, the participant must be warned of this.

- *Use of findings* – The same issues arise as discussed under 'Studies using correlational analysis' on p. 22.

Self-report techniques: questionnaires

Self-report techniques enable those participating in a study to provide information knowingly about specific things relating to themselves (e.g. what they think, believe or do), as opposed to the researcher observing these things directly. One form of self-report technique that is widely used is the questionnaire, which is a printed series of questions used to gather information about specific areas of interest, such as views on healthy living, in the context of survey research.

A survey involves the systematic gathering of data from large numbers of people, usually by means of a postal questionnaire. If smaller numbers of people participate in a survey, the researcher may choose to use interviews instead of a questionnaire (interviews are discussed in the next subsection). Vast amounts of data are regularly collected by large-scale surveys from households across the UK and are published in tables and charts in reports such as *Social Trends*. This provides a range of fascinating social and economic data about British society today, including population statistics, data about households and families, education, the labour market, health and lifestyles. You can access *Social Trends* via the National Statistics website at: **www.statistics.gov.uk/ socialtrends**.

Most surveys are carried out on carefully selected representative groups (referred to as samples) so that the researcher can generalize the findings to the wider population from which any such group was drawn. The main exception is the national census which is carried out every ten years and which involves every adult in the UK (i.e. the total adult population) and not a sample of the population.

Figure 1.4 Examples of closed questions

- **Checklists** – respondents tick any items that apply.

  For example: Please tick the subjects in the following list that you studied at GCSE level.

  ☐ Art   ☐ English

  ☐ Geography   ☐ History

  ☐ Mathematics   ☐ Psychology

  ☐ Science   ☐ Sociology

- **Placing items in rank order**

  For example: Place a number against each of your GCSE subjects, placing them in rank order from most liked (given the number 1) to least liked.

- **Attitude scales**

  For example: Underline the response that best reflects your attitude to the statement: 'A university education is essential if you are to succeed in the employment market'.

  Do you: ☐ strongly disagree?

             ☐ disagree?

             ☐ neither disagree or agree?

             ☐ agree?

             ☐ strongly agree?

- **Likert scales** – based on a numerical rating.

  For example: How important are the following factors to the relationship between you and your partner? (Please circle the appropriate number.)

	Very important	→			Very unimportant
Sense of humour	1	2	3	4	5
Common interests	1	2	3	4	5
Mutual respect	1	2	3	4	5

- **Semantic differential scales** – where respondents are asked to rate each item on a scale, based on a series of pairs of opposite adjectives.

  For example: How would you rate your feelings about your AS-level Psychology course? (Place a tick at the appropriate point on each scale.)

  Warm |__|__|__|__|__|__|__| Cold

  Satisfied |__|__|__|__|__|__|__| Dissatisfied

Questionnaire surveys can be used in a wide range of research situations. They allow researchers to ask participants questions about, for example, their attitudes, behaviours or intentions. They can be used whenever a pen-and-paper method is appropriate, allowing the researcher to gain information from a large sample of participants relatively quickly, efficiently and cheaply. The researcher does not need to be present when the questionnaire is administered, although the researcher's presence may be helpful to answer any queries that the respondent has. Questionnaire surveys can be conducted by post, telephone, via the Internet, or left for participants to collect from some central point and complete in their own time. As we shall see both qualitative and quantitative data may be produced.

Questions can be of two broad types:

- *Closed questions* are those where the researcher determines the range of possible answers; respondents often reply by ticking boxes or circling appropriate answers. These questions are best used when straightforward factual information is required. They produce information which is easy to quantify and analyze, but which may lack realism due to the forced choices of answers available to the respondents. Examples of different forms of closed questions are shown in Figure 1.4.

- *Open-ended questions* are those in which the researcher does not restrict the range of available answers. So, for example, a researcher might start an interview by asking: 'What are your views on the use of corporal punishment by parents?' Open-ended questions produce a lot of detailed, verbal information (qualitative data) but at a cost: the answers are usually more difficult to analyze because the range of possible answers is so wide.

- *Leading questions* are questions where the choice of wording used suggests that the respondent should reply in a particular way. For example, 'You do find studying psychology interesting don't you?' Such a question is leading the respondent to say 'yes' and actually makes it quite hard for the respondent to disagree by saying 'no'. Another less obvious but important form of leading question involves the use of the word 'the' rather than 'a', as illustrated in the following example: 'Did you see the young woman who was carrying a dog under her arm?' Use of the word 'the' in this leading question implies that there was indeed a young woman carrying a dog under her arm and therefore the respondent should have seen her. Compare this with the question, 'Did you see a young woman carrying a dog under her arm?' which does not imply that there was such a woman and does not, therefore, lead the respondent to agree with the statement in quite the same way. It is important, therefore, always to examine carefully the precise wording of questions in order to identify inappropriate use of leading questions in interviews and questionnaires.

When carrying out research using a questionnaire, it is good practice to:

- keep the number of questions to a minimum
- use short questions
- phrase questions very clearly and carefully to avoid any ambiguity or possible misunderstanding
- avoid questions that are emotionally charged.

Ideally, any questionnaire should be carefully piloted before it is used in a research study. (Pilot studies are discussed in Chapter 2.)

Questionnaire surveys produce descriptive and/or explanatory information that can be tailored to fit a wide range of research situations. They can be carried out as a 'one-off' or, more powerfully, they can be conducted both before and after some event in order to examine the impact of that event. The flexibility of questionnaires means that they are valuable both as a preliminary research tool and also as a source of in-depth information on a topic of interest.

Examples of well-known questionnaires include the Social Readjustment Rating Scale (Holmes and Rahe 1967, see Chapter 5, p. 158) and the Hassles and Uplifts Scale, developed by Kanner *et al.* (1981, see Chapter 5, p. 161).

Advantages of questionnaires

- *Simplicity* – Once developed and piloted, questionnaires can be used with a minimum of training. Quantitative data obtained from closed questions are usually easy to analyze, so it is often easy to compare answers from different individuals or groups of respondents.

- *Speed and cost* – Large amounts of information can be gathered fairly quickly and cheaply from a large number of respondents within a fairly short period of time.

- *Less influence of interpersonal variables* – Researchers do not usually sit with respondents when they complete a questionnaire, so there is less opportunity for the researcher to influence the information provided.

Weaknesses of questionnaires

- *Problems with question wording*:

  - If the wording of questions is ambiguous, then respondents may interpret the question in different ways and their answers may reflect this. Meaningful analysis of the responses would therefore be difficult.

  - Leading questions may also influence the responses given. For example, it is clear what answer is being encouraged by the question: 'Don't you think that spending money on education is important?'

  - Different interpretations of language can also be problematic. For example, there may be different interpretations of the term 'rarely' when used in a question about days off work due to illness. To one person, 'rarely' may mean once or twice a month; to another, once or twice a year.

  - Finally, social desirability bias may also be an issue: respondents may not provide truthful answers, especially to personal or potentially embarrassing questions; they may wish their answers to be seen in the best possible light.

- *Poorly designed questionnaires* produce poor quality data. Many people underestimate the amount of time and effort required to develop, pilot and refine a questionnaire before it is ready to be used to collect useful data.

- *Response rates* (i.e. the proportion of people who are sent the questionnaire who choose to respond) can be quite low – Often, around 30 per cent or fewer of those who were sent the questionnaire actually complete it and return it to the researcher. This means that the sample is not representative of the wider group (the population) from which it was drawn and the results cannot therefore be generalized beyond those who actually participated in the research.

What factors might influence the respondent in this survey setting?

- *Researcher effects and biases* – If a researcher administers the questionnaire personally, respondents may be influenced by factors such as the researcher's ethnic origin, age, appearance, gender or mode of dress. Even unintentional nods, smiles or frowns may have an effect on the results.

  Researcher bias may also be a problem when interpreting the data. For example, a researcher might provide one possible answer on a questionnaire that is perceived as being more socially desirable than other possible answers. Responses in this category might be wrongly interpreted as providing genuine support for the researcher's particular (biased) viewpoint. (See Chapter 2 for further detail about the wording used in questionnaires.)

Ethical issues

- *Privacy* – Studies based on questionnaire surveys must respect the privacy and psychological wellbeing of all those who agree to complete the questionnaire. Those responding have the right to expect that any information they provide will be treated confidentially and, if published, will not be identifiable as theirs. If confidentiality or anonymity cannot be guaranteed, the participant must be warned of this in advance.

- *Consent* – Researchers need to protect respondents' right to withdraw some or all of their data from the study, and respondents should give their consent for their data to be included in the findings.

- *Risk of harm* – Investigators have a primary responsibility to protect respondents from psychological harm during an investigation. Normally, the risk of harm must be no greater than in ordinary life. Where a questionnaire probes behaviour or experiences that respondents may regard as personal and private, the respondents must be protected from stress by a range of appropriate measures, including the assurance that answers to personal questions need not be given. In research involving children, great care should be taken when discussing results with parents, teachers or those *in loco parentis*, since evaluative statements may carry unintended weight and, again, may cause distress.

- *Debriefing and support* – Questions on socially sensitive topics can cause distress to respondents, and appropriate debriefing and support mechanisms must be made available. However, survey researchers must also be vigilant regarding any questions that may appear straightforward such as asking parents about their views on disciplining children. Questions like this may trigger psychological distress in some respondents who may subsequently require debriefing and support.

Self-report techniques: interviews

'Conducting interviews is a complex, labour intensive and uncertain business, fraught with tricky issues that social science researchers, and particularly psychologists, are often ill-equipped to address.' (Banister et al. 1994)

Despite the difficulties outlined in the quotation above, the interview is a common way of carrying out research; it may form the basis of a case study or may be used as one of the ways of conducting a survey.

Some research establishes a distance between the researcher and the research participants, but that approach is challenged by the face-to-face nature of the interview, which is both personal and public. In order to encourage the flow of information from the interviewee to the interviewer, the interview needs to have an explicit purpose and specific aims.

Like questionnaires, interviews also need very careful planning and piloting (see Chapter 2). **Structured interviews** usually aim to produce quantitative data and include questions that are decided in advance in order to structure and categorize the interviewee's responses. In this sense, they are similar to experimental research because the researcher largely determines the focus of the response.

A structured approach has several advantages:

- The interviewer and interviewee are less likely to deviate from the topic that is the desired focus of the interview.
- Data analysis may be simpler.
- Results are easier to generalize.
- Less training is needed for interviewers.
- There is less risk of the results being affected by interviewer bias, since the interviewer is more likely to be objective.

However, there are limitations, as well as benefits:

- The researcher cannot follow up any new lines of enquiry that emerge during the interview.
- Validity may be threatened by participants reacting to the formality of the research situation.

In other forms of interview, the focus of the interview may involve some negotiation between the interviewer and interviewee:

- **Unstructured interviews** are far less rigid and very little, if anything, concerning their nature will be decided in advance. They often start with one or two set questions that are broad in their focus, with further questions picking up on issues that the interviewee raises. These interviews can be more difficult to analyze, but have greater validity, as interviewees will be more likely to say whatever they wish to express, and the interviewer can be flexible in the approach they use.

What are the advantages and disadvantages of different types of interview?

- The **semi-structured interview** is often the most successful approach, with the use of some prepared questions by the interviewer, supplemented by additional questions that provide opportunities for the interviewee to expand their answers.

The diversity of interviews also means that interviewing is a skill that requires careful development.

Researchers sometimes choose to interview a small group of people at the same time rather than individuals; these are known as **focus groups**. Focus groups have some advantages but also some limitations. On the plus side, they can alert a researcher to important issues and areas for further enquiry. Observation of group dynamics can also indicate something of the way in which the topic is understood and can reveal social customs relating to a subject in a way that individual interviews might not. However, an account of a focus group interview may not necessarily be representative of the views of everyone involved. More confident members of the group may dominate the discussion and influence what is discussed by steering the group towards issues of particular interest to them. The researcher needs, therefore, to be a skilled group facilitator in order to enable the group to have a representative and wide-ranging discussion of the

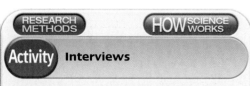

Activity Interviews

Carry out two interviews on a topic of your choice. Use a structured interview with one person (i.e. a set series of five or six questions about the chosen topic) and an unstructured interview with another person. What are the main differences in the information you gather from these different forms of interview?

topic. It can also be extremely demanding to observe the group and monitor what is being said, and the researcher can easily become overloaded with information.

Interviews (whether individual or group) can be used to supplement the information obtained by other research methods. For example, Milgram (1963) enriched his work on obedience (see Chapter 6) by interviewing the participants after the experiment was complete. Two areas where the approach has been of particular value are social psychology (see, for example, the use of interviews in the research on conformity by Asch, discussed in Chapter 6) and psycho-pathology (for example, in exploring the family histories of sufferers from anxiety disorders). A study by Kim and McKenry (1998) used interviews to investigate the social networks in a range of ethnic groups in America: African-Americans, Asian-Americans, Hispanics and Caucasian (White) Americans (see Chapter 5, p. 162).

Advantages of interviews

- *Flexibility* – The interview can enable the researcher to explore complex issues that may be difficult to investigate using other techniques. The interviewer can tailor questions to the responses of an interviewee so that issues can be explored in depth.

- *Tackling sensitive topics* – Interviews also allow researchers to identify aspects of behaviour that are private or personal to the individuals concerned (such as fear of dying or concerns about sexual health and sexually transmitted diseases). Topics such as these would be more difficult to explore using more impersonal research techniques.

   Different types of interview (structured, semi-structured and unstructured) generate different types of information and, therefore, the way information is gathered can be tailored to the requirements of a particular research study.

Weaknesses of interviews

- *Interpreting data* – Misinterpretation or partial interpretation of data can occur. Ideally, the interviewer needs to be detached from the interviewee, which can be difficult to achieve in face-to-face situations where there is the potential for bias and subjectivity. Qualitative data gathered from unstructured interviews may also be very time consuming to transcribe (it can take up to three or four hours to transcribe what was said during a 30-minute interview) and can be difficult to analyze.

- *Time and effort involved* – Some people may not be willing to invest the time or effort to meet an interviewer at a pre-arranged time and place in order to complete the interview. This may limit the number of people who are available to be interviewed.

- *Limitations in interviewees' responses* – Interviewees may be unable to articulate their thoughts clearly.

- *Effects of interpersonal variables* – A range of factors, including gender, ethnicity, personality, class and age of both interviewer and interviewee, may affect the interaction between the two, as well as the amount and quality of information provided in the course of the interview.

- *Demand characteristics* may also occur, such as social desirability bias where those being interviewed provide answers that cast them in a favourable light or are intended to impress the interviewer, rather than truthful answers.

■ *The need for training* – Some interviewers may require training before they are able to carry out effective interviews; this is particularly true for unstructured interviews, which require the use of probes to pursue an interesting line of enquiry in more depth.

■ *Cost* – The cost of carrying out interviews can be quite high in terms of the time involved to meet with each individual, particularly if extensive travel is involved. The use of telephone interviews can reduce travel costs.

Ethical issues

The ethical issues associated with interviews are similar to those associated with the use of questionnaires (see p. 28), especially with regard to:

■ respecting the privacy and psychological wellbeing of interviewees

■ obtaining informed consent and respecting participants' right to withdraw some or all of their data

■ maintaining confidentiality and anonymity

■ protection from harm

■ debriefing and support.

Case studies

Case study research typically involves the in-depth study over time of a 'case', which is usually a single individual or small group. Case study research is usually undertaken within a real-life context. This may involve a representative case – for example, the decision-making of a person who decides to undergo gender reassignment surgery after becoming increasingly unhappy with their birth gender.

Alternatively, an exceptional or unique circumstance may be studied, such as twins separated at birth and raised in very different families, before being reunited at the age of 10 when they went to live with the same foster parents. Data are mainly gathered through interviews and observation and are usually qualitative (i.e. non-numerical data). You will come across many case studies in psychology – for example, the harrowing case study of Czech twin boys who experienced severe isolation is reported on p. 134.

Case study research usually produces some measurement data and also a powerful narrative account that provides an overall picture; Sandelowski (1996) refers to this as 'understanding a particular in the all-together'. Details of the context of the research are important aspects of any case study. Sometimes, several cases are studied – referred to as multiple case studies. Freud, for example, created his theory of the unconscious on the basis of studying multiple cases of patients he labelled as 'hysterical'. However, this should not be confused with sampling. Each case study is selected on the basis of what it might contribute to a developing pool of data, so that patterns may emerge over time.

Advantages of case studies

■ *Rich and interesting data* – Case studies produce data that have a high degree of realism and can therefore provide valuable new insights into the phenomenon being studied and which might not be accessible via any other form of investigation. For example, important information about brain function has been deduced from case studies of brain-damaged individuals. The sad case of Clive Wearing, whose memory was severely impaired following brain damage after a viral infection, is one such example (see p. 79).

■ *Challenging existing theory* – If the findings of a single case contradict a well-established theory, then we have to consider modifying the theory in some way to accommodate the new evidence. For example, if a child who was deprived of social contact from birth was found to have developed some rudimentary language skills, then our theory of the effects of severe deprivation might have to be refined.

Weaknesses of case studies

■ *The low reliability of much case study research* – This is a significant weakness, as the findings are unlikely to be replicated, even when a similar case is studied with a view to generalizing the findings. However, those who conduct case studies do not usually intend to make such generalisations.

■ *The findings may be subjective* – Case studies are often based on lengthy in-depth interviews and observations, during which a relationship may be established between the researcher and the individual(s) being studied.

■ *Selecting from large amounts of data* – Masses of data are usually gathered when carrying out case study research, so the researcher may have to select which aspects of the data to include or leave out of the case study. This can also make the findings subjective.

■ *Distortions* – If an individual is required to recall historical events, the data can become distorted as a result of memory errors.

Ethical issues

■ Observation and interviews are typically used in case study research to gather data, so the ethical issues are broadly the same as those already discussed in the relevant subsections of this topic. In addition, the researcher needs to take care that the level of intrusion that may occur when carrying out detailed research on a single individual or small group does not render the study unethical.

Qualitative data comes in many forms and can be challenging to analyze

CHECK YOUR UNDERSTANDING

Check your understanding of research methods and techniques by answering the following questions. Try to do this from memory. Check your answers by looking back through Topic 2.

1 What are quantitative data?

2 What are qualitative data?

3 List the three key features of a true experiment. Give two advantages and two weaknesses of laboratory experiments.

4 What is a field experiment? Give two advantages and two weaknesses of field experiments.

5 What is a natural experiment? Give two advantages and two weaknesses of natural experiments.

6 Define what is meant by an independent variable.

7 Define what is meant by a dependent variable.

8 What is correlational analysis and when is it used in psychology? Give two advantages and two weaknesses of studies using correlational analysis.

9 What is naturalistic observation and when is it used in psychology?

10 What is meant by the term 'participant observation'?

11 Give two advantages and two weaknesses of using observational techniques to collect research data in psychology.

12 What is meant by the term 'self-report techniques'?

13 What is a questionnaire and when are questionnaires used in psychological research?

14 What is an 'open-ended' and a 'closed' question in a questionnaire or interview?

15 Give two advantages and two weaknesses of using questionnaires as a method of collecting research data.

16 Define what is meant by an interview and describe when it is used in psychological research.

17 What are the key differences between structured, unstructured and semi-structured interviews?

18 Give two advantages and two weaknesses of using interviews as a method of collecting research data in psychology.

19 When do psychologists use case study research?

20 Give two advantages and two disadvantages of case study research.

Chapter 1: Summary

Psychology and psychologists

Psychology, psychologists and research methods

What is psychology?

Definitions of psychology

- Psychology is more than common sense
  - Importance of evaluating everything you read

Approaches in psychology

- Wundt, introspection and the first psychological laboratory
- Freud and psychoanalysis
- Watson and behaviourism
- Social learning theory
- Cognitive approach
- Physiological (biological) approach
- Evolutionary approach

Goals of psychology

- Description
- Explanation
- Prediction
- Control

How science works

Key characteristics of science

- Clearly defined subject matter
- Systematic activity
- Evidence must be empirical
- Theories are created in an attempt to explain research findings

What psychologists do

- Clinical psychologists
- Educational psychologists
- Health psychologists
- Occupational psychologists (organizational psychologists)

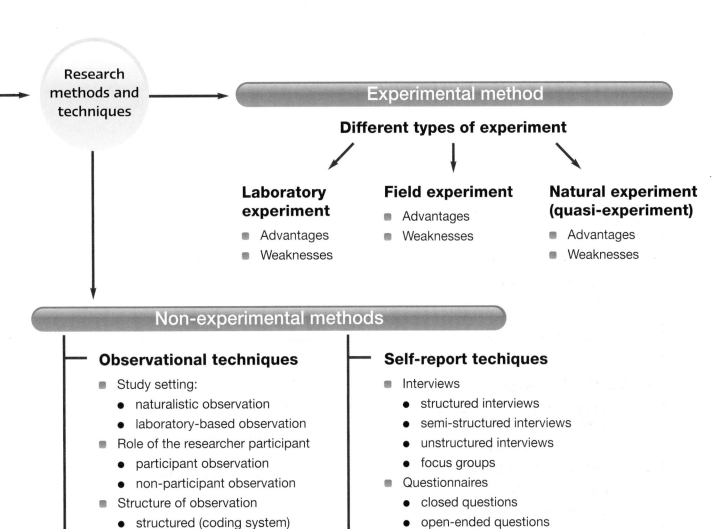

Research methods and techniques

Experimental method

Different types of experiment

Laboratory experiment
- Advantages
- Weaknesses

Field experiment
- Advantages
- Weaknesses

Natural experiment (quasi-experiment)
- Advantages
- Weaknesses

Non-experimental methods

Observational techniques
- Study setting:
  - naturalistic observation
  - laboratory-based observation
- Role of the researcher participant
  - participant observation
  - non-participant observation
- Structure of observation
  - structured (coding system)
  - unstructured

- Advantages of each technique
- Weaknesses of each technique

Studies using a correlational analysis
- Advantages
- Weaknesses

Self-report techiques
- Interviews
  - structured interviews
  - semi-structured interviews
  - unstructured interviews
  - focus groups
- Questionnaires
  - closed questions
  - open-ended questions
  - leading questions

- Advantages of each technique
- Weaknesses of each technique

Case study approach
- Advantages
- Weaknesses

Investigation design, data analysis and presentation

EXPLAINING THE SPECIFICATION

Specification content	The specification explained
Investigation design	In this part of the specification you should be familiar with the key features of investigation design. To do this, you need to be able to:
■ Aims ■ Hypotheses, including directional and non-directional ■ Experimental design (independent groups, repeated measures and matched pairs) ■ Design of naturalistic observations, including the development and use of behavioural categories ■ Design of questionnaires and interviews ■ Operationalization of variables, including independent and dependent variables ■ Pilot studies ■ Control of extraneous variables ■ Reliability and validity ■ Awareness of the BPS *Code of Ethics* ■ Ethical issues and ways in which psychologists deal with them ■ Selection of participants and sampling techniques, including random, opportunity and volunteer sampling ■ Demand characteristics and investigator effects	■ Describe how the purpose of an investigation is articulated in the aim(s) of the study and for experimental research in a hypothesis (or hypotheses), and distinguish between directional and non-directional hypotheses. ■ Describe and identify three different types of experimental design – independent groups, repeated measures and matched pairs – and evaluate the advantages and weaknesses of each design. ■ Describe and evaluate the design of naturalistic observations and the development and use of behavioural categories. ■ Describe how questionnaires and interviews are designed and distinguish between questions that are clear and unambiguous and poor questions. ■ Describe precisely (operationalize) independent and dependent variables. ■ Discuss the role of pilot studies (small-scale trial runs) in designing good research. ■ Discuss and evaluate the control of extraneous variables and the ways in which the reliability and validity can be assessed and improved. ■ Be aware of the British Psychological Society (BPS) *Code of Ethics*, discuss ethical issues and evaluate ways in which psychologists deal with them. ■ Describe the selection of participants and three sampling techqniues – random, opportunity and volunteer sampling – and evaluate the advantages and weaknesses of random and non-random sampling methods. ■ Discuss the social dimensions of research, including demand characteristics and investigator effects, and evaluate their possible impact on the outcomes of a study.
Data analysis and presentation	In this part of the specification you should be familiar with the key features of data analysis, presentation and interpretation. To do this, you need to be able to:
■ Presentation and interpretation of quantitative data, including graphs, scattergrams and tables ■ Analysis and interpretation of quantitative data. Measures of central tendency, including median, mean and mode. Measures of dispersion, including ranges and standard deviation ■ Analysis and interpretation of correlational data. Positive and negative correlations and the interpretation of correlation coefficients ■ Presentation of qualitative data ■ Processes involved in content analysis	■ Describe and evaluate the presentation and interpretation of quantitative data when presented in graphs, scattergrams and tables. ■ Discuss the analysis and interpretation of quantitative data and be able to calculate and interpret three measures of central tendency – the median, mean and mode for a set of data. Describe and interpret three measures of dispersion – the range, interquartile range and standard deviation. ■ Discuss and interpret correlational data, including positive correlations, negative correlations and correlation coefficients. ■ Describe the presentation of qualitative data and the use of content analysis to analyze qualitative data.

Introduction

Chapter 1 discussed some of the research methods used by psychologists. The first topic of this chapter builds on the first chapter and examines a range of issues associated with research design and the analysis, presentation and interpretation of data. We begin by considering how to generate appropriate research aims and hypotheses. We will then discuss the design of experiments, naturalistic observations, questionnaires and interviews. A range of factors associated with research design is examined, including the operationalization and control of variables, the role of pilot studies, how two important factors in research – reliability and validity – can be assessed and improved. Ethical issues associated with psychological research are also discussed, as are the major sampling methods that psychologists use to select participants. The topic ends by examining the social dimensions of psychological research and the effect of the relationship between researcher and participants, including demand characteristics and investigator effects.

Topic 2 examines some of the ways in which psychologists analyze and present their data. You may recall from Chapter 1 that the data from psychological investigations can be either quantitative or qualitative. The nature of the data depends on the aim(s) of the research, the topic under investigation, as well as the research method(s) used. We will consider how quantitative data can be presented and interpreted using descriptive statistical techniques and correlational analysis, and also discuss how qualitative data can be presented and analyzed using content analysis.

Topic 1: Investigation design

RESEARCH METHODS

Aims, research questions and hypotheses

The purpose of a research study can be expressed as an **aim**, research question or **hypothesis**. We will consider what is meant by each of these terms, starting with research aims.

Generating research aims

The starting point for any psychological research study is for the researcher to think carefully about what the investigation is trying to discover and generate an appropriate aim to make the focus of the study clear. In order to generate the aim (or aims), a researcher needs to be clear about the purpose of the investigation. In some observational or survey research, the research aim may be fairly broad – it may simply be to describe what is happening rather than to measure something in order to test a prediction. For example, the research aim might be 'To describe the incidence of cigarette smoking in 12 to 16 year olds in the United Kingdom'. In experimental investigations, on the other hand, the aim may be to test a hypothesis.

The aim of a research study may be further refined into a research question (or questions) and in the case of experimental research into a hypothesis (or hypotheses).

Psychology in context

Designing a research project

Imagine that you have been commissioned to undertake some research to find out if there is any link between playing violent computer games and levels of aggression in children.

Think of as many different ways as possible of researching this topic and write brief notes about what each study would involve.
For example:

1 How many participants would you wish to include in the study?

2 How would they be selected?

3 How would you decide what counts as aggression?

This activity will revise some of the material you studied in Chapter 1, so you may wish to look back at Topic 2 of Chapter 1 before you start this activity.

When you have completed this activity, discuss your ideas with other students in your psychology class and/or your teacher.

Please keep your notes as we will be returning to your ideas later in this chapter.

Generating research questions

Research questions also differ in how broad they can be. Some are very precisely worded and indicate how the research study will focus on a specific issue: 'How do children aged between five and seven come to terms with the news that a sibling has recently been diagnosed as having a life-threatening illness?' Others are deliberately worded in such a way that they allow the researcher to explore issues more widely, such as 'What meanings do young children attach to the diagnosis of a life-threatening disease?'

Formulating hypotheses

A hypothesis can be defined quite simply as a statement that is testable. It is a general prediction made at the outset of an experimental investigation about what the researcher expects to happen. However, in order to assist the analysis of data obtained from the research study, it is essential to phrase the hypothesis carefully, so that it is unambiguous and testable. This is the process of hypothesis formulation, i.e. refining the prediction so that it is stated in precise terms.

For example, consider the research hypothesis that 'The use of leading questions affects eyewitness testimony'. As stated, it raises too many questions and could not, therefore, be tested precisely. For instance, what kind of leading question are we talking about, or in what ways is the testimony of witnesses affected? If this statement is to be converted into a format suitable for the analysis of the results, then its wording must be clear and unambiguous. A more tightly worded statement would be: 'More witnesses subsequently report seeing a knife in a crime scene when a leading question suggests the existence of a knife as a murder weapon'.

The process of formulating hypotheses highlights a fundamental issue relating to experimental research. If the wording of the research hypothesis is too general, it could be difficult to test. On the other hand, when a hypothesis is more clearly defined and testable, it may lack more general application (see p. 48 for a discussion of the **operationalization** of variables).

Two different forms of hypothesis are important when analyzing and interpreting the results of experimental research – the alternative hypothesis and the null hypothesis.

Alternative hypothesis

The alternative hypothesis (in an experiment this is often referred to as the experimental hypothesis) predicts that something other than chance variation alone has played a part in producing the results obtained.

Consider an experiment investigating the effect of a mnemonic on memory recall (a mnemonic is a device for aiding memory, such as using the phrase '**R**ichard **O**f **Y**ork **G**ave **B**attle **I**n **V**ain' to remember the order of the colours in a rainbow). In such an experiment, the alternative hypothesis might predict a difference in memory recall between those in the experimental condition who use a mnemonic and those in the control group who do not. Only if the design of the investigation is completely watertight will the researcher be left with just one plausible explanation for the results (i.e. that the **independent variable** – in this case the use of a mnemonic – is responsible for any observed difference in the outcome). In practice, this can be quite difficult to achieve, as we shall see when we consider various issues that need to be addressed in a well-designed experiment.

The alternative hypothesis can either be directional or non-directional:

- As its name suggests, a **directional hypothesis** predicts the direction in which results are expected to occur. For example, 'More words are recalled from a list when using rehearsal as a mnemonic technique than when no mnemonic technique is used'. In this case, we are predicting not only that there will be a difference in the number of words recalled, but that more will be recalled by participants in the condition where a mnemonic technique is used, than in the control group where it is not.

- A **non-directional hypothesis** does not predict the expected direction of outcome. For example, 'There is a difference in the number of words recalled from word lists presented with or without the presence of background music'. In this statement a difference is predicted, but no prediction is made about the direction of the difference, i.e. about which of the two conditions will result in a greater number of words recalled.

Directional and non-directional hypotheses are sometimes referred to as one-tailed and two-tailed hypotheses respectively. In this textbook, however, we use the terminology directional and non-directional hypothesis.

Null hypothesis

The null hypothesis predicts that the results of an experiment can be explained by chance variation alone rather than by the manipulation of the independent variable. For example, in an experiment investigating the effect of a mnemonic on memory recall, the null hypothesis would predict no difference in the memory scores for the two conditions. If small differences occur, these are assumed to be due to chance, rather than the manipulation of the independent variable (in this case, use of a mnemonic). The researcher has to decide whether the null hypothesis should be retained because it is supported by the data or rejected. If the likelihood of the results occurring by chance is remote, then the null hypothesis is rejected and the researcher will argue that the alternative hypothesis provides the most plausible explanation of the findings.

The null hypothesis therefore predicts that the alternative hypothesis is not true. Although the researcher is likely to be more interested in the alternative hypothesis, the null hypothesis is actually the more important of the two hypotheses, since it is the null hypothesis that is actually tested when the quantitative data are analyzed using a statistical test. The probability value (p value) that you often see included in the results section of a report of experimental research is the probability that the null hypothesis is true. So if the probability value is high, then the null hypothesis is accepted and the alternative hypothesis is rejected as a plausible explanation of the findings. It is only when the probability value is very low that the null hypothesis is rejected and the alternative hypothesis is accepted as being the most plausible explanation of the findings.

Now try the activity on the right.

RESEARCH METHODS   **HOW SCIENCE WORKS**

Activity Writing hypotheses

For each of the following studies, write a suitable alternative hypothesis and null hypothesis and indicate whether your alternative hypothesis is directional or non-directional.

1 Loftus (1979) – a study of the role of anxiety in eyewitness testimony (Chapter 3, p. 98)

2 Godden and Baddeley (1975) – an experiment to investigate the effect of retrieval context on learning (Chapter 3, p. 111)

3 Kiecolt-Glaser et al. (2000) – a study of chronic stress (Chapter 5, p. 156)

4 Johansson et al. (1978) – a study of stress in a Swedish sawmill (Chapter 5, p. 164)

5 Moscovici et al. (1969) – a study of minority influence (Chapter 6, p. 212)

An example is given below to help you get started.

Suggested suitable answers are given on p. 273 ▶

Study	Alternative hypothesis	Directional (D) or Non-directional (ND)	Null hypothesis
Baddeley (1966) – acoustic coding in short-term memory (p. 85)	Words that sound different will be recalled better than words that sound similar.	D	Words that sound different will not be recalled better than words that sound similar.

Investigation design: some key decisions

When undertaking research, a number of important design issues need to be considered. These may include the following:

- *Choosing an appropriate research method* – What is the most appropriate research method or methods to achieve the research aim and how can each method best be used? (This is the focus of Topic 2 in Chapter 1.)

- *Deciding how many participants to study* – Researchers conducting an experiment or a survey involving a questionnaire have to decide how many participants to recruit for the study. As a general rule, the larger the sample, the less biased it is likely to be; a sample of 25 or 30 participants is often regarded as a reasonable number for any small-scale study in which quantitative data are to be collected and analyzed. However, in observation research, the researcher sometimes has little or no control over the sample size and may need to recruit whoever is available. Also, when using unstructured interviews lasting up to one hour, it may only be possible to involve a few participants (say 8 to 10) because of the time it takes to transcribe (i.e. record in writing) everything that is said during each interview in order to analyze the data. It can take up to six hours to transcribe a single one-hour interview.

- *Using an appropriate sampling method* – This is essential where a **sample** of participants is selected to represent the larger population from which the sample is drawn. The researcher also needs to decide how representative the participants are of a particular **target population**. (Sampling methods are discussed later in this chapter.)

- *Deciding how to brief participants* – An important question is whether participants should be aware or unaware of the specific nature of the investigation or even that they are taking part in research. This raises the important **ethical issue** of informed consent (discussed later in this chapter). Sometimes researchers disclose their intent to participants – this is usual in survey research using questionnaires or interviews and in many experiments. The researcher may even spend time getting to know the participants before the research is carried out in order to put them at their ease prior to the study. It is hoped that this process encourages more natural behaviour. With naturalistic observation, the researcher may choose whether to inform participants that an investigation is being carried out on them. Where informed consent is not given, the researcher needs to consider very carefully the ethical issues that arise (see p. 55).

Decisions need to be made early on about how to record data

- *Deciding how to record the data and the techniques to be used* – A written record may be made (often by the participant in the case of questionnaires and some experiments), or behaviour may be recorded for subsequent analysis, e.g. on video/audio tape or using a computer. A combination of these methods is often used. The researcher also needs to decide which behaviour to record and which to ignore. If a written record is made, the researcher may need to devise an appropriate coding system for recording behaviour (an example is provided in Figure 2.3 later in the chapter). The technique used may be highly structured (as in many experiments, research using questionnaires or structured interviews and some observational studies), or it may be unstructured (as in some interviews). The main aim is to collect data that can be appropriately analyzed.

Experimental design

Selecting an appropriate experimental design is essential for the success of any experimental investigation. It involves balancing the advantages and weaknesses of different designs. The aim of successful experimental design is to:

- provide an overall plan for the experiment
- ensure that appropriate and precise measurements can be made
- enable all the data collected to be analyzed correctly
- eliminate all potential sources of ambiguity or bias
- ensure high levels of control over the independent variables and **dependent variables**.

When deciding on an appropriate design, the researcher must consider carefully the precise nature of the experimental task, how to control the relevant variables and the availability of participants. This section considers three types of experimental design that you are likely to encounter in your reading:

- the **independent groups design** (different participants are used in each condition of the experiment)
- the **repeated measures design** (the same participants are used in each condition of the experiment)
- the **matched pairs design** (each group of participants is carefully matched on all the variables considered to be relevant to the experiment).

Independent groups design

An independent groups design involves using different participants in each condition of the experiment. (This may also be referred to as an independent measures/participants/subjects/samples design, or as a between groups/participants/subjects/samples design.)

Experiments using this design typically involve:

- a control condition and one or more experimental conditions, or
- two (or more) experimental conditions.

See Figure 2.1 for an example of how this design might operate in practice.

In the former case, the group of participants who are given the experimental treatment is referred to as the experimental group (or experimental condition), and the group that provides the comparison and receives no experimental treatment is the control group (or control condition). Ideally, participants should be allocated randomly to the conditions (i.e. allocated in such a way that each participant has an equal chance of being selected for each condition).

This procedure of random allocation to groups aims to ensure that characteristics of the participants (sometimes referred to as the participant variables) do not differ systematically between the conditions at the start of the study. Otherwise, individual differences relevant to the experiment concerned might lead to the results being confounded. (A discussion of confounding can be found on p. 49.) For example, in a study of learning ability it would be inappropriate if all the fast learners were allocated to the same condition. However, random allocation will not necessarily produce groups of participants that have identical characteristics. The researcher may still, through chance, fail to eliminate individual differences if, for instance, the fastest learners happen to be allocated to one of the groups.

Figure 2.1

Allocation of participants in three different experimental designs

1 Independent groups design:

Participants (Ps) may be allocated to the conditions randomly. For example:

Condition A	Condition B
P1	P3
P2	P5
P4	P6 ... *and so on.*

2 Repeated measures design:

Each participant undertakes all conditions of the experiment. For example:

Condition A	Condition B
P1	P1
P2	P2
P3	P3 ... *and so on.*

3 Matched pairs design:

Pairs of participants are matched on appropriate variables relevant to the experiment; the members of each pair are then allocated to each condition (sometimes randomly). For example:

Condition A	Condition B
P1a	P1b
P2a	P2b
P3b	P3a ... *and so on.*

However, the likelihood of this occurring is minimal when random allocation is used. For example, imagine the likelihood of the numbers one to six inclusive coming up in that order on the National Lottery, or the probability of dealing out all four suits of a pack of cards in both suit and number order. The chances of events such as these happening are extremely remote but, of course, any single combination, including those described above, is as likely to happen as any other single combination.

By randomly allocating participants to groups, a researcher aims to avoid any conscious or subconscious bias in the allocation of participants to groups. When an independent groups design is used and there are sufficient participants in each group, it is highly unlikely that individual differences between the groups will be a confounding factor.

The random allocation of participants to conditions can be achieved in several ways. The simplest method is to draw names from a hat. More sophisticated ways include the use of a random number table or a computer program that draws and allocates random numbers.

In natural experiments (see Chapter 1, pp. 18–19), the allocation of participants to conditions is decided by the naturally occurring event, which is treated as the independent variable. For example, if the independent variable is the different reading scheme used in two different schools, then the experimenter does not have full control over the allocation of participants to the conditions of the study.

See Table 2.1 on the next page for the advantages and weaknesses of an independent groups design.

Repeated measures design

A repeated measures design involves exposing every participant to each of the experimental conditions, so, in effect, participants are used as their own controls. (This design may also be referred to as a related measures, related samples, within participants or within subjects design.) Figure 2.1 on p. 41 provides an example of how participants might be arranged in an experiment using this design. One of the conditions in a repeated measures design may be a control condition, which serves the same purpose as the control condition in an independent groups design – that is, it provides a baseline against which the responses from an experimental condition can be compared.

Table 2.1 on the next page summarizes the advantages and weaknesses of a repeated measures design. The weakness associated with order effects can be minimized in two ways: by **counterbalancing** or by **randomization**.

Counterbalancing

Counterbalancing involves equal numbers of participants undertaking the required tasks in different orders. Figure 2.2 shows two examples of how this might take place, with participants performing the conditions alternately until all participants have been tested. Note that there needs to be an even number of participants if counterbalancing is to be implemented fully. In the first example in Figure 2.2, a multiple of two participants would be required, and in the second a multiple of six, reflecting the number of possible task orders in each case.

Occasionally, however, it is not appropriate to apply counterbalancing as a strategy to minimize order effects. Problems can occur, for example, when performing one condition helps the performance of another more than the other way round.

Figure 2.2

Examples of counterbalancing in two- and three-condition experiments

Counterbalancing in a two-condition experiment:

Participant number	First condition undertaken	Second condition undertaken
1	A	B
2	B	A
3	A	B
4	B	A
		... and so on.

Counterbalancing in a three-condition experiment:

Participant number	First condition undertaken	Second condition undertaken	Third condition undertaken
1	A	B	C
2	B	C	A
3	C	A	B
4	A	C	B
5	B	A	C
6	C	B	A
			... and so on.

1 Independent groups design

Advantages
- There is no problem with order effects which occur when participants' performance is positively or negatively affected by taking part in two or more experimental conditions. For example, performance in a second or subsequent condition may be improved through practice of a task carried out in a previous condition, whereas negative effects may result from fatigue or boredom. An independent groups design has a wide range of potential uses and can be used where problems with order effects would make a repeated measures design impractical (e.g. an investigation of the effect of background noise or no noise on the performance of a problem-solving task).

Disadvantages
- There is the potential for error resulting from individual differences between the groups of participants taking part in the different conditions. Also, if participants are in short supply, then an independent groups design may represent an uneconomic use of those available to participate, since twice as many participants are needed to collect the same amount of data as would be required in a repeated measures design with two conditions.

2 Repeated measures design

Advantages
- Individual differences between participants are removed as a potential confounding variable. Also, fewer participants are required, since data for all conditions are collected from the same group of participants.

Disadvantages
- The range of potential uses is smaller than for the independent groups design. For example, it is inappropriate to use two different reading schemes to teach young children to read within the same group of children – only an independent groups design could be employed in this case.
- Order effects may result when participants take part in more than one experimental condition. Order effects can confound the results in two ways – either negatively through the effects of fatigue or boredom, or positively through the effects of learning or practice.

3 Matched pairs design

Advantages
- A matched pairs design combines the advantages of both an independent groups and a repeated measures design.

Disadvantages
- Achieving matched pairs of participants can be difficult and time consuming. It depends on the use of reliable and valid procedures for pre-testing participants to identify the matched pairs. Complete matching of participants on all variables that might affect performance can rarely be achieved. Matched pairs designs are, therefore, relatively uncommon, with their use restricted to specific situations where a matching process is highly desirable in order that experimental success can be achieved. For example, in a study of the effect of psychological stress on recovery time following physical illness or on wound healing, the researcher would need to match the particpants carefully in terms of variables such as age, family support, family income and history of illness.

Table 2.1

Advantages and disadvantages of different experimental designs

Consider the following memory experiment:

- *Condition A*: Learning a set of words presented randomly

- *Condition B*: Learning a matched set of words using a mnemonic technique to assist memory.

There may be no problem when participants undertake Condition A first, followed by Condition B. However, when Condition A is presented after Condition B, it is likely that participants still have the mnemonic technique fresh in their minds. As a result, Condition B might help performance on Condition A more than A helps B, which is likely to confound the results. In such circumstances, counterbalancing would be inappropriate and a researcher would be advised to use an independent groups design.

Randomization

Randomization involves adopting a strategy for randomly determining the order of presentation of experimental conditions by, for example, drawing lots or tossing a coin. This procedure, however, fails to provide a guarantee that the presentation order of conditions will not influence results, because it is still possible, through chance, that differences will remain in the number of participants experiencing the conditions in particular orders.

Randomization can also be used as a technique for deciding the order of presentation of, for example, individual stimuli within a condition. It works best when there is a large number of items within each condition. For example, suppose an investigation involves each participant rating 20 photographs for their attractiveness. If all participants experience the same presentation order, then some rating biases might occur. For example, the photo presented first is likely to be given an average rating by many participants, simply because they are rating this photo in an average manner because they feel they may wish to use more extreme ratings in either direction for subsequent photos.

Finally, it is possible to combine an independent groups design and a repeated measures design. For example, children from two different age groups might be given two different cognitive tasks. The independent groups element of the design would involve a comparison of the two age groups, and the repeated measures element would be a comparison of performance on the two cognitive tasks.

Matched pairs design

A matched pairs design aims to achieve the key advantages of an independent groups design (i.e. no problems with order effects, as different people are used in each condition), and a repeated measures design (i.e. a reduced risk of problems resulting from individual differences as participants are matched). A matched pairs design is sometimes referred to as a matched participants or a matched subjects design. This design involves matching each participant in one of the experimental conditions as closely as possible with another participant in the second condition on all the variables considered to be relevant to performance in the study. For example, pairs of participants might be matched for age, gender and scores on intelligence and personality tests. Once pairs of participants have been identified, members of each pair can be randomly allocated to the conditions (see Figure 2.1 on p. 41). The assumption made is that members of each pairing are so similar on the relevant variables that they can, for research purposes at least, be treated as if they are the same person. At the same time, however, participants perform in one condition of the experiment only, thereby eliminating the problem of order effects. See Table 2.1 on the previous page for the advantages and weaknesses of a matched pairs design.

Now try the activity on the left.

Design of naturalistic observations

Naturalistic observation is introduced in Topic 2 of Chapter 1 (p. 23), so you might like to reread that section now to refresh your memory.

A key design issue with naturalistic observational studies is deciding how to sample the behaviour to be studied. The possibilities include:

- *time interval sampling* – observing and recording what happens in a series of fixed time intervals (e.g. every 10 minutes or other suitable time interval)

- *time point sampling* – observing and recording the behaviour which occurs at a series of given points in time (e.g. meal times)

- *event sampling* – observing and recording a complete event, such as a teacher encouraging a pupil.

RESEARCH METHODS   **HOW SCIENCE WORKS**

Activity   **Identifying the design used in research studies**

The following studies are described in Chapter 3 or Chapter 5:

- Bahrick *et al. (1975)* – a study of the duration of very long-term memory, described on p. 87

- Kiecolt-Glaser *et al (1984)* – a study of the effects of stress on the immune system, described on p. 155

- Glanzer and Cunitz (1966) – a study of the multi-store model of memory, described on p. 90

- Johansson *et al.* (1978) – a study of stress in a Swedish sawmill, described on p. 164.

For each of these studies, turn to the description and note down whether (a) an independent groups design, (b) a repeated measures design, or (c) a matched pairs design was used. Make a note of any potential weaknesses of the design that was used and whether you think an alternative experimental design would have been preferable, outlining the reasons why.

Answers are given on p. 273 ▶

A further issue that needs careful consideration relates to behavioural categories, that is, the way in which data are organized and recorded. Possible methods include preparing written notes, producing a checklist or tally chart, or using a rating scale. Figure 2.3 shows a simple tally chart, which was developed for an observational study on the state of a baby. Figure 2.4 is a simplified example of the tally chart devised by Bales (1970) as part of his Interaction Process Analysis (IPA) technique, which can be used to observe and record changes in the interactions within small groups.

Now try the activity on the right.

State of baby during 30-second time period	No. of observations
Deep sleep:	llll llll l
Active sleep:	llll llll llll llll l
Quiet awake:	llll llll llll llll llll ll
Active awake:	llll lll
Crying, fussing:	llll llll lll

Figure 2.3
Specimen checklist of behaviours and tally chart (the behavioural categories are taken from Bee 1999)

RESEARCH METHODS **HOW SCIENCE WORKS**

Activity Observing and recording interactions

Using the set of behavioural categories developed by Bales (1970) shown in Figure 2.4, spend up to 10 minutes observing and recording the interactions of one person participating in a small-group discussion (involving no more than five other people). If possible, ask someone else to observe the same person for the same period of time. Compare your records of the behaviours you observed and answer the following questions:

1 What difficulties, if any, did you encounter while recording the interactions?

2 Note any differences between your record of interactions and those of the other observer (if you used one).

3 Why do you think these differences occurred?

4 When might it be useful to carry out an observation like this?

A suggested answer to question 4 is given on p. 273 ▶

Figure 2.4
Simplified version of a tally sheet used by Bales (1970)

Each observer records the interactions of one participant for the period of the discussion, which lasts for 10 minutes. This 10-minute period can be divided into two 5-minute halves to allow comparison between behaviours over time. From this sheet, the total number, type and direction of a participant's interactions can be calculated and compared with those of other participants.

Name of observed person _____

Person being addressed

Categories	Person A 1st half	2nd half	Person B 1st half	2nd half	Person C 1st half	2nd half	Person D 1st half	2nd half	Person E 1st half	2nd half	The group 1st half	2nd half
Seems friendly												
Jokes												
Agrees												
Gives suggestion												
Gives opinion												
Gives guidance												
Asks for guidance												
Asks for opinion												
Asks for suggestion												
Disagrees												
Shows tension												
Seems unfriendly												

Activity Developing a questionnaire

Prepare a brief questionnaire (consisting of no more than 10 questions) that could be used to investigate a person's health over the last 12 months. When you have prepared the first draft of your questionnaire, review each of the proposed questions to check you have addressed all the issues highlighted in Table 2.2 on the opposite page. Have you asked each question in the best possible way? Think carefully about the sequence of the questions you want to ask. Finally, prepare a set of standardized instructions for respondents, telling them what you want them to do. Remember to make it clear in your questionnaire that your respondents need not answer any question they would prefer to omit.

We will return to your questionnaire later in this chapter (p. 49), when you will be asked to pilot your questionnaire to test out how well it works in practice.

Design of questionnaires and interviews

To remind yourself of the self-report techniques of questionnaires and interviews you may wish to turn back to pp. 25–31 of Chapter 1. We will now examine some important issues that need to be considered when designing questionnaires and interviews.

Questionnaires

Questionnaires can be administered face to face, by post or via the Internet.

Some of the key decisions that need to be made when designing a questionnaire are outlined in Table 2.2 on the opposite page. Once a questionnaire has been developed it should be piloted (see p. 49). Piloting allows the researcher to check that all the questions can be answered and contribute to the purpose of the research, and any ambiguity or other issue that comes to light can be rectified before it is used to gather data in an actual research study.

Interviews

Interviews may be conducted face to face or by telephone. A checklist for planning interviews is shown in Table 2.3 below. Table 2.4, on p. 48, is an example of an interview schedule that would generate qualitative data, which was prepared for a study of gender identity.

Table 2.3 A checklist for planning interviews (based on Dyer 1995)

1	**The preliminaries to the interview**	Have you:
		☐ clearly described the research problem?
		☐ stated the aim of the interview?
		☐ linked the problem to an appropriate theory?
		☐ identified the general categories of data that you will need to collect?
2	**The questions**	Have you:
		☐ generated an appropriate set of questions?
		☐ planned the order in which the questions will be presented?
		☐ planned the interview to obtain the required balance between structured and unstructured interviewing?
3	**The interview procedure**	Have you:
		☐ considered the issues of self-presentation?
		☐ identified and approached potential respondents?
		☐ planned the pre-interview meeting?
		☐ planned the post-interview debriefing?
		☐ decided how the information is to be recorded in the interview?
		☐ considered the ethical issues raised by the proposed research and sought advice if necessary?

Table 2.2 Designing effective questionnaires

Closed or open questions?	■ Closed questions are frequently used in questionnaires because they are easy to score and analyze. Closed questions invite the respondent to choose an answer from various possible answers (e.g. by answering 'yes' or 'no', ticking a category – it is important that the categories are non-overlapping – or placing a list of options in order from the most important to the least important).
	■ Open questions, on the other hand, do not constrain respondents, allowing them to answer in whatever way they like. They may, therefore, generate more informative answers, but the disadvantage is that these can be more difficult to analyze. Any question – whether open or closed – that is long or complex is liable to be misunderstood by respondents and should be avoided.
Number of questions and question order	■ Only questions that are absolutely necessary for the purpose of the research should be included. However tempting it might be, it is not appropriate to add extra questions just in case they might generate some interesting information! Questions relating to demographic characteristics (e.g. age, gender, marital status, sexual orientation) are usually included at the end of a questionnaire. An important principle is that any highly sensitive questions should not be placed at the beginning of a questionnaire if it can be avoided.
Use clear language	■ Plain English should always be used, so that the wording of every question is clear and unambiguous. Questions that are ambiguous are likely to be interpreted in different ways by respondents, making meaningful comparisons impossible at the data analysis stage.
	■ Jargon or technical language should be avoided wherever possible. For example, 'Do you support affirmative action in employment?' To answer this question respondents would need to be familiar with the concept of 'affirmative action'. If this understanding cannot be assumed, an explanation of any technical terms used should be provided before the particular question is asked.
Avoid leading, biased or value-laden questions	■ Question wording should never lead the respondent towards a particular answer. It is better to ask 'What colour was the young boy's shirt?' than 'Was the boy's shirt green or blue?'
	■ Questions should not include any value judgements. Here is an example of a biased, value-laden question: 'Do you think the British government should allow immigrants to settle in our overcrowded country now that the European Union has been enlarged to include 27 member states?'
Ask one question at a time	■ It is sometimes tempting to ask two separate questions rolled into one, but this does not allow the respondent to give a different answer to each part of the question and therefore the response to each part of the question is likely to be unclear. It is important therefore to avoid questions such as 'Do you think that life is more stressful today than it was 30 years ago, or do you find that modern technology has reduced the stresses of modern living?' Instead, two separate questions should be asked.
Avoid using emotive language when asking questions	■ Use of emotive language can bias the response. The question 'Do you think that the use of defenceless animals in psychological laboratory studies should stop?' (which is both leading and emotive) could be rephrased as: 'What do you think about the use of animals in psychological laboratory studies?'
Ask questions that are clear and unambiguous	■ It is important to avoid asking questions that are vague or ambiguous. For example, 'Do you take time off work? (please tick one): ☐ Never ☐ Rarely ☐ Sometimes ☐ Often' Using categories such as these is problematic because each category may mean something different to different people responding to this question. All participants need to treat a particular question in the same way if the data collected are to be meaningful and produce useful results. Instead, the possible responses could be presented as: ☐ Never ☐ 1–5 days a year ☐ 6–10 days a year ☐ 11–20 days a year ☐ More than 20 days a year
Avoid making inappropriate or insensitive assumptions	■ Avoid asking questions that incorporate an assumption and could therefore cause embarrassment to some respondents. For example, the question 'What is your occupation?' assumes that every respondent is employed. Instead, the question could be asked: 'Are you currently in paid employment? Yes/No If your answer is 'yes', is your employment: ☐ Full-time (30 or more hours per week) ☐ Part-time (16–29 hours per week) ☐ Part-time (15 hours or less per week)

RESEARCH METHODS

Activity   Asking suitable questions

1 What do you think are the advantages and the weaknesses of asking open questions?

2 What do you think are the advantages and the weaknesses of asking closed questions?

3 Look at the nine questions in Table 2.4 and decide whether each question is clear or whether it could be improved. Make a note of all your suggestions for possible improvements and discuss these with another student in your psychology class and/or your teacher.

Title of project: A study of the development of gender identity

Topic: Contribution of early school experiences

Date of interview:

1 Can you begin by giving me a general description of the school you attended at the age of 5, so I can begin to understand what kind of a place it was?

2 Looking back, how did your school deal with the issue of gender in general? For example, were boys and girls treated in different ways?
Could you give me some examples of that?

3 How did this compare with what you experienced at home?

4 How was children's behaviour dealt with? For example, was a clear distinction made between what was considered appropriate behaviour for boys compared to girls?

5 Did the school generally reinforce or challenge stereotyped gender definitions? Can you give me some examples of that?

6 How do you now think this affected you during your early school life? Can you give me some examples?

7 Can you give me some examples of the kind of thing that would have happened if a boy behaved in a way the teachers thought was more appropriate to a girl?

8 Can you give me any examples of the ways in which the rules about appropriate behaviour were enforced? How do you feel about them now?

9 What would have happened if you had been found breaking a rule like that?

Table 2.4
An example of an interview schedule (based on Dyer 1995)

RESEARCH METHODS

Activity   Defining terms

Think carefully about what you understand by the term 'aggressive behaviour'. Imagine that you are one of a team involved in designing an observational study of aggressive behaviour in young children in school playgrounds. You have been asked to prepare a definition of the term 'aggressive behaviour' that could be used by the research team. You may wish to look back at your notes from the 'Psychology in context' activity at the beginning of this chapter.

When you have decided on your own definition, compare your ideas with those of another student in your psychology class. How are the definitions similar and how do they differ. Try to agree a single definition that you are both happy with.

Key aspects of investigation design

This section examines some of the key factors associated with research design. It looks at:

- how variables in research can be defined and operationalized

- the use of pilot studies to improve research quality

- the control of **extraneous variables**

- techniques for assessing reliability and validity

- ethical issues associated with research

- selecting participants and sampling techniques.

Defining and operationalizing variables

A variable is a thing that may vary or change in some way and which can either be categorized or measured (IQ, memory span, personality and stress levels are some examples of variables that psychologists study). The control, manipulation and measurement of variables are central to psychological research. Psychologists need to be able to define variables clearly if their research is to be scientifically credible and worthwhile. This is by no means an easy task. Try the activity on the left for yourself.

When you thought about your definition, you probably included different forms of violent behaviour – but did you include things such as spitting, swearing, glaring or invading personal space? Even a smile can sometimes have aggressive intent! It is even harder to define variables when they are less tangible, such as 'stress' or 'concentration levels'. For example, psychologists may be able to measure the visible signs of the effects of 'stress' on a person, and also attempt to measure its effects on an aspect of behaviour. However, can they be confident that they are measuring the actual variable – stress – itself?

Operational definitions

Operational definitions of variables being investigated are precise descriptions of what a particular researcher understands by a particular term.

In experimental research, the key variables are the independent variable and the dependent variable (see Chapter 1, p. 13). Operationalizing these variables usually results in narrowing down the research focus. For example, the general statement that 'mnemonics improve memory' might be refined into an independent variable that specifies the presence or absence of imagery, and a dependent variable that specifies the number of words correctly recalled. This process can have important implications for the extent to which research findings can be generalized – the more precise the operational definition, the narrower the research focus and the more limited the extent to which results can be generalized.

Conducting pilot studies

An important step in designing a good research study is to undertake a **pilot study**. This is a small-scale trial run of a specific research investigation to test out the planned procedures and identify any flaws and areas for improvement, before time and money are invested in carrying out the main study. It is carried out on a small number of participants to find out whether there are any problems with:

- the design
- the clarity of standardized instructions for participants and the procedures
- the measuring instrument(s) employed, including the use of behavioural categories in observation research.

A questionnaire or interview should be piloted on people from the appropriate target population.

A pilot study also enables the researcher to practise carrying out the research task and provide useful information on how long its takes, which can be useful when creating a schedule for the actual study. The researcher will usually inform participants that they are taking part in a pilot study and ask them to highlight any problematic areas or ambiguities they come across during the trial run. In the light of direct experience and feedback from the pilot study, the researcher makes changes to address the issues raised before the main study is conducted. Now try the activity on the right.

Control of extraneous variables

If a variable other than the independent variable produces a change in a dependent variable, the results of the study are said to have been confounded. Unwanted variables (i.e. those which could confound results) are known as extraneous variables. They need to be controlled because they can obscure the effect of an independent variable on a dependent variable, or provide a false impression that an independent variable has produced changes when in fact it

RESEARCH METHODS

Activity Operationalizing definitions

Refine the definition of 'aggressive behaviour' you generated in the previous activity into a fully operationalized definition that could be used in an observational study of aggressive behaviour in young children.

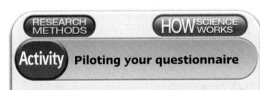

RESEARCH METHODS **HOW SCIENCE WORKS**

Activity Piloting your questionnaire

Pilot the standardized instructions and the short questionnaire that you prepared as part of the Activity, 'Developing a questionnaire', on p. 46 with two or three members of your psychology class, family or friends. Ask each person who completes your questionnaire to tell you whether the questions were clear and presented in a logical order, and to give you any other feedback about their experience of answering the questions.

Revise any questions that have been identified as confusing or difficult to respond to. What did you learn from this pilot? Why is it important to carry out a pilot before embarking on a research project?

The effects of random errors cannot be predicted ...

has not. Extraneous variables can result from either random error or constant error, and need to be either eliminated or controlled as far as possible.

- *Random errors* – the effects of random errors cannot be predicted. Possible sources of random error include:
  - a participant's state of mind
  - a participant's level of motivation
  - incidental noise
  - room temperature
  - previous experiences on the day of the study (e.g. an argument with a friend).

  It is hoped that random errors resulting from variables such as these will not systematically affect one condition of an experiment more than any another condition. By allocating participants randomly to experimental conditions, psychologists usually assume that random errors balance out across the experimental conditions. Such errors might, however, result in some loss of sensitivity of the results.

- *Constant errors* affect the dependent variable in a consistent way and therefore create a more serious problem for the researcher than random errors, since they may not affect all conditions of an experiment equally.

  Constant errors might include:
  - a failure to counterbalance or randomize the presentation order of experimental conditions
  - participant differences
  - errors of measurement which affect one condition more than another.

Wherever possible, the researcher will aim to eliminate these two sources of error by good experimental design.

Reliability and validity

Psychologists are keen to demonstrate the consistency of a measure or an effect (its **reliability**) and also the extent to which a test actually measures what is intended (its **validity**). In this section we will outline the ways in which reliability and validity can be assessed and improved.

Assessing and improving reliability

The term reliability means dependability or consistency, which is vital if a psychologist is to obtain meaningful data. The term can be applied in a general way to the findings from psychological research. If the findings are replicated consistently, then the results can be said to be reliable. The term 'reliability' is also used in specific contexts. There are several ways in which reliability can be assessed and improved, and this section will consider some of these. Assessing reliability often involves using a **correlational analysis** to assess the consistency of observer ratings or psychological measuring instruments such as psychometric tests. Before reading on, check you understand the meaning of the term **correlation**, including **positive correlation**, by turning to p. 20.

Assessing and improving observer reliability

Observer reliability can be assessed by measuring the extent to which different observers achieve similar results when observing and scoring the same participants. Observers record their own data individually and then the sets of data obtained from each observer are correlated to establish the degree of similarity in the scores. Observer reliability is achieved if there is a significant positive correlation between the scores of the different observers.

Ideally, more than one observer should be used in observational studies. Inter-rater reliability is a procedure that allows a researcher to measure the extent to which different observers agree on the behaviours they have observed. Correlational analysis is used to establish the inter-rater reliability. Independent checks for reliability can also be made by using audiotapes or videotapes.

Observer reliability can be improved in a number of ways. For example:

- All observers should be trained thoroughly in the techniques they are required to use.

- Operational definitions of the key terms involved in the research should be both clear and understood fully by all the observers involved in gathering data. Consider the example used in the activity, 'Defining terms', on p. 48, of an observational study of aggressive behaviour in children's playgrounds. If more than one observer is used, it is essential that all the observers understand exactly which behaviours can be categorized as examples of 'aggressive behaviour'. In other words, the term 'aggressive behaviour' needs to be operationalized and all the observers need to be fully familiar with all aspects of the operationalized definition.

Assessing and improving test reliability

Another important aspect of reliability concerns the reliability of tests employed by psychologists (such as intelligence or personality tests or questionnaires). Psychologists use several methods to do this, including the split-half method and the test–retest method.

- The *split-half method* can be used as a way of assessing the extent to which individual items in a particular test or questionnaire are consistent with other items in the same test. The method involves splitting the test or questionnaire into two parts after data have been obtained from the participants. This splitting might be done by, for example:
  - comparing the results obtained from odd- and even-numbered questions
  - comparing the results from the first half of the test with those from the second half
  - randomly splitting the test into two parts.

  The two sets of responses (whichever method is used to obtain them) are then correlated. A significant positive correlation between the two sets of responses would indicate that the test was reliable. If the correlation is not sufficiently high, the researcher would need to check the procedure used for constructing the test or questionnaire carefully and revise the test items. The aim of the revision would be to produce an improvement in the reliability of the particular test or questionnaire.

- The *test–retest method* is used to assess another important aspect of consistency – the stability of a test or questionnaire over time. This method involves presenting the same participants with the same test or questionnaire on two different occasions, with no feedback given after the first presentation. The time interval between presentations needs to be selected carefully. If it is too short, participants may remember their previous answers, but if it is too long, then the participants may possibly have changed in the meantime in some way relevant to the test or questionnaire. Once again, correlational techniques are used to indicate the test stability. If there is a significant positive correlation between the scores obtained from the test and retest phases, the test is deemed to be stable. Test items and/or testing procedures can be revised (e.g. by rephrasing instructions) if a sufficiently high correlation is not obtained.

Assessing and improving validity

Validity is concerned with the extent to which something measures what it actually sets out to measure. This is not quite as simple as it might first appear. For example, there is ongoing debate over issues, such as whether personality tests are valid measures of personality, or whether diagnostic classification schemes used in the mental health field really are valid indications of a person's mental health status. Different types of validity can be tested, including internal validity, external validity and test validity.

Internal validity is concerned with the extent to which we can be sure that research findings are due to the mechanisms suggested. For example, in an experiment, the key issue might be whether we can be certain that differences in the results obtained are due to manipulation of the independent variable and not to the action of some other unwanted (extraneous) variable, such as individual differences or the effects of practice. Internal validity is also compromised if no effect is found in a research study when in fact an effect actually exists.

External validity is concerned with the extent to which results can be generalized to other settings beyond those in which the study was actually carried out. A distinction can be drawn between the following:

- *population validity* – the extent to which results from research can be generalized to other groups of people
- *ecological validity* – the extent to which research findings can be generalized to situations outside the research setting.

Note that laboratory experiments do not automatically lack ecological validity by the mere fact that they are carried out in a laboratory setting. While some do lack ecological validity, many laboratory studies are ecologically valid and their results can be generalized beyond the laboratory. Similarly, the fact that research is carried out in a natural setting does not guarantee ecological validity. This may or may not be achieved – it all depends on whether or not the results can be generalized.

Test validity

Psychologists use various techniques to assess the validity of a specific test. Four of these are outlined below:

- *Face validity* is the simplest technique – independent experts assess whether a measuring instrument appears to be appropriate and may suggest improvements to the researcher. Because of its subjectivity, the assessment of face validity usually only takes place in the early phases of constructing a measuring instrument, e.g. when a draft examination paper is submitted for approval.
- *Content validity* is superficially similar to face validity. Again, independent experts are asked to assess the validity of the measuring instrument concerned. This time, however, the procedures are more rigorous, and there is a detailed and systematic examination of all the component parts of the measuring instrument that is being assessed.

- *Concurrent validity* involves obtaining two sets of scores at the same time: one from the new procedure with unknown validity, and the other from an alternative procedure or test for which validity has already been established. The scores obtained from both the new and the existing test will then be correlated with each other to assess the validity of the new procedure. A highly significant positive correlation would suggest that the new procedure is valid. For example, a new procedure for the diagnosis of a psychopathological condition might be compared with an established method of diagnosis for which the success rate is already known. If the correlation obtained is not sufficiently high, further refinement of the criteria might be necessary in order to improve concurrent validity.

- *Predictive validity* involves a similar strategy, but this time the two sets of scores are obtained at different points in time. An example from abnormal psychology might be the correlation of initial diagnoses with information gained in the light of experience with the patients concerned over a period of time. In other words, a diagnostic procedure or test with high predictive validity would allow fairly accurate forecasts to be made about future behaviour. If the test indicates that certain behaviours should occur, and they do not occur, then the test has low predictive validity.

Ethical issues and the ways in which psychologists deal with them

As we saw in Chapter 1, most psychological research is carried out on people and animals, and so there is the potential to harm participants, which raises important ethical issues. Over the years, psychologists have become increasingly aware of these issues and have recognized that some research previously undertaken by psychologists has been ethically questionable. This includes some very well-known studies. The two studies that are most frequently discussed in this context were both undertaken in the United States of America in the 1960s and 1970s: the prison simulation study by Zimbardo (1973) and Milgram's study of obedience to authority (Milgram 1963). These studies are described in Chapter 6 on pp. 187–90 and pp. 192–8 respectively. Read these descriptions now before reading any further.

Psychologists now have to defend their proposed research very carefully to an ethics committee before they are allowed to proceed. Although this provides an important safeguard, it is interesting to note that the question about whether these studies should ever have been permitted, or whether the important results justified the means, continues to be debated.

Ethics is the science of moral principles or rules of behaviour. Since there are no absolutes about what is deemed to be 'right' or 'wrong', different groups, including professional societies, determine what is considered to be acceptable or unacceptable for their members. In the United Kingdom, the British Psychological Society (BPS) is responsible for promoting ethical behaviour among psychologists and has developed clear ethical principles and standards to protect the public from harm.

The BPS acknowledges that psychologists owe a debt of gratitude to everyone who agrees to take part in their studies and requires its members to treat research participants with high standards of consideration and respect. This respect for individuals is reflected in a change in the language used to describe those who take part in research from the term 'subjects' (which can seem highly impersonal) to 'participants'.

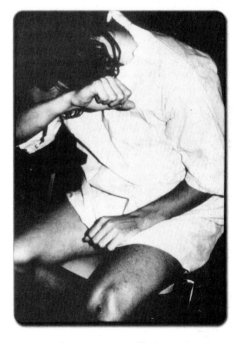

Participants in Zimbardo's prison simulation suffered considerable emotional distress and many people have questioned the ethics of the study (see Chapter 6, p. 189).

British Psychological Society *Code of Ethics and Conduct*

In March 2006, the British Psychological Society (BPS) published a *Code of Ethics and Conduct*. This code aims to promote ethical decision-making and behaviour by practising psychologists; it outlines the guiding principles or 'rules' by which all psychologists should operate, including those carrying out research. It also helps to clarify the conditions under which psychological research is acceptable. Unfortunately, the mere existence of a code does not guarantee ethical practice – it has to be implemented conscientiously for this to happen. Good psychological research is only possible if there is mutual respect and confidence between investigators and participants. It may be that some areas of human experience and behaviour cannot be investigated for sound ethical reasons.

Table 2.5 on pp. 55–7 outlines the four ethical principles on which the BPS *Code of Ethics and Conduct* is based: respect, competence, responsibility and integrity, and summarizes how these principles are operationalized in the context of research.

The BPS has also produced additional sets of guidance for researchers:

- Ethical principles for conducting research with human participants (BPS 2000 and currently being revised).
- Guidelines for minimum standards of ethical approval in psychological research (BPS 2004).

The views of what constitutes ethical conduct and ethical research are not fixed, so codes of ethics have to be updated from time to time. The latest versions of all these documents and the *Code of Ethics and Conduct* are available on the BPS website and it is worth getting your own copies for reference purposes.

Read the Guidelines on pp. 55–7 now; then do the activity on the left.

Evaluation of ethical guidance

- The *Code of Ethics and Conduct* and the ethical guidelines provide guidance and not hard-and-fast rules; they are sometimes criticized for being vague and difficult to apply.

- *Guidelines differ across cultures* – Different guidelines exist in different countries. For example, the guidelines of the American Psychological Association (APA) are more detailed than the guidelines developed by the BPS. Most codes concentrate on the protection of participants from physical and psychological harm and on the confidentiality of the data they provide. On other matters, however, there is more variation between codes. In Holland, the guidelines provide more general advice to investigators while the British guidelines are more concerned with the details of research procedures. In Canada, the guidelines advise going beyond the immediate concerns of the participants in order to analyze any long-term risks or benefits to both groups and individuals that might be affected. There is, therefore, no universal set of guidelines that applies to psychologists worldwide.

- *The limited scope of BPS guidance* – Condor (1991) criticized an earlier version of the BPS guidelines for limiting the concerns to the relationship between the investigator and the participant and for ignoring the role of psychologists in society at large. Others accuse psychologists of perpetuating negative stereotypes (e.g. of people who are elderly) in books and research papers, and believe that ethical issues in psychology should go beyond the traditional issues of confidentiality, deception or privacy (Gale 1995).

RESEARCH METHODS **HOW SCIENCE WORKS**

Activity **Your views on the BPS *Code of Ethics and Conduct***

After you have read the summary of the BPS *Code of Ethics and Conduct*, make a list of the key ethical issues that need to be considered either when reading reports of psychological research or when designing some research.

Use your summary list as a reminder when you discuss the following questions with others in your class:

1 To what extent do you think that the BPS *Code of Ethics and Conduct* adequately protects the interests of all those who participate in psychological research?

2 Should all psychologists who undertake research be compelled to follow a strict ethical code? If so, how could this be achieved? What do you think should happen to anyone who is found not to have followed the code?

3 Think back to the description of the study of obedience to authority carried out by Milgram (1963) or Zimbardo's prison simulation study (Zimbardo 1973). Is either study defensible on ethical grounds? Do you think such a study would be permitted today? Give your reasons.

Answers are given on p. 274 ▶

Table 2.5 British Psychological Society *Code of Ethics and Conduct* (BPS 2006)

1 Respect

Psychologists should respect people's dignity and their rights to privacy and to have a say in what happens to them (this is known as self-determination); they must also be sensitive to issues regarding perceived authority and influence over those with whom they work. This means that psychologists should respect individual and cultural differences, including those relating to age, disability, education, ethnicity, family status, gender, race, religion, sexual orientation and socio-economic status.

Informed consent

Psychologists should ensure that all participants are helped to understand fully all aspects of the research that are likely to influence their willingness to participate, including the nature and objectives of the investigation, so they can give their fully informed consent to take part. Special care is needed when planning to carry out research with children or other vulnerable individuals. Wherever possible, the real consent of children and of adults with impairments in understanding should be obtained. If an individual is unable to give his or her own consent, a parent/guardian (if the child is under the age of 16) or legal representative can provide additional consent, making this decision on what is in the individual's best interests.

Where the researcher is in a position of authority or influence over the participants (e.g. students or employees), care needs to be taken to ensure that this relationship does not cause individuals to feel obliged to agree to take part in, or remain in, an investigation.

If a study is carried out over an extended period of time or if there is any significant change in the focus of the study, it may be necessary to seek additional informed consent.

Proposed alternatives for when it is not possible to gain fully informed consent are shown in the panel on the right.

Confidentiality and anonymity

Except where disclosure is required by law or has been agreed at the outset, participants have the right to expect that all data collected during a research study remain confidential and will be stored securely in accordance with the UK Data Protection Act, 1998. If the findings are published, the data should remain anonymous and should be presented in such a way that specific information cannot be linked to particular individuals. Participants should be warned at the start of a study if confidentiality and anonymity cannot be guaranteed, prior to giving their consent to take part.

Right to withdraw at any time

At the outset it should be made clear to participants their right to withdraw from a research investigation at any time, without having to give a reason and to request that any data relating to them that have been collected are removed from the study and destroyed. This right applies in all situations, including when financial payments have been made. Participants should also be informed of their right to decline to answer specific questions or to participate in a particular aspect of a study.

Deception

Withholding information or misleading participants about the purpose of a study is unacceptable if the participants subsequently become uneasy when they have been debriefed about its true purpose at the end of the study. If there is any

---

Alternatives to fully informed consent

There are alternatives to informed consent that may be used in situations when revealing the purpose of the investigation to participants would invalidate the study:

Presumptive consent

For example, we may take a large random sample from the population to be studied and introduce them to the research design, including the use of deception. If they agree that they would still have given voluntary informed consent had they known the true aims of the investigation, then we may assume that they represent the views of that population group. Another sample from that population would then be selected for use in the study without being told its true purpose.

Prior general consent

In this case, people who might be used as participants in a study are told that sometimes participants are misinformed about the true purpose of a study. Only those who agree that such a practice is acceptable would be selected as participants for this type of study. Therefore, they have given general informed consent, but they do not know whether or not the actual study they participate in uses misleading information.

Table 2.5 continued
British Psychological Society *Code of Ethics and Conduct* (BPS 2006)

Alternatives to using deception

Complete information

Provide participants with complete information about the purpose of the investigation. In a study by Gallo *et al.* (1973), participants were told that the study concerned the extent to which people would conform. The results for these informed participants were no different from those for deceived participants who thought they were involved in an investigation of depth perception. However, a second study by the same researchers produced opposite findings.

Role-playing

Tell participants about the general nature of the study (although not the detailed hypothesis being tested) and ask them to role-play the experimental procedure as though they were naive participants. Mixon (1972) used this method in a set-up similar to that used in Milgram's obedience studies. He found that provided the role-playing participants were led to believe that the experimenter carried the responsibility for any distress caused to the 'learner', they behaved much as Milgram's participants did. However, if those role-playing were led to assume responsibility, their levels of obedience were significantly lower than those found by Milgram. More often than not, studies using role-play procedures result in different findings from those where investigators have concealed their true purpose from participants.

doubt about the possible impact of deception, careful consultation should take place prior to the investigation.

Intentionally deceiving participants about the purpose and nature of the investigation should be avoided wherever possible and is only ever deemed to be acceptable in very exceptional circumstances. Information should only be withheld from participants if it is crucial to do so in order to maintain the integrity of the research. If any form of deception is used, the nature of the deception should be disclosed to participants at the earliest possible opportunity and participants have the right to request that their data are excluded from the study and destroyed. Proposed alternatives to using deception are outlined in the panel on the left.

Observation research

Studies based on observation should always respect the privacy and psychological wellbeing of the individuals studied. Unless those being observed give their informed consent, observational research is only acceptable in public places where those being observed would expect to be observed by strangers. Careful account should be taken of local cultural values – researchers should avoid the possibility of invading the privacy of individuals for whom it is important that they are not being observed, even though they are in a public space (e.g. when taking part in a religious ceremony).

2 Competence

Psychologists should be committed to the *Code of Ethics and Conduct* and to maintaining their levels of competence, while at the same time acknowledging any limits of their knowledge, skills, education and experience. This means that they should recognize and resolve the ethical dilemmas that arise out of a proposed research study and be able to defend all their decisions and actions on ethical grounds.

3 Responsibility

Psychologists undertaking research should understand their responsibilities to the general public, including their research participants, which includes their protection from harm or undue risk at all times.

Protection of research participants

- *Risk of harm* – Investigators have a key responsibility to protect all participants from physical and mental harm during research – the risk of harm should normally be no greater than in their everyday life. Therefore, psychologists should always think very carefully about both the ethical implications and psychological consequences of the research for the participants. This involves considering the study from the participants' perspective to eliminate any foreseeable threats to physical health, psychological wellbeing, personal dignity or values.

- *Understanding the implications of an investigation* – The researcher may not, however, have sufficient knowledge about the implications of an investigation for all participants, particularly if they are drawn from different groups in terms of key factors such as age, cultural background, disability, gender, education, ethnicity, language, marital status, race, religion, sexual orientation and social background. In which case it may be necessary to consult others who are more knowledgeable – the best judges of whether an investigation is likely to cause offence are members of the same population from which the research participants are to be drawn.

- *Protection from stress* – Where research involves behaviour or experiences that are considered to be personal and private, the participants should be protected from undue stress, and given assurance that they need not answer personal questions.

- *Inducements* – Financial incentives or other inducements should not be used to encourage individuals to take part in research and risk harm beyond that which they would normally risk without payment in their normal, everyday life.

- *Professional advice* – A researcher has a responsibility to inform a participant of any psychological or physical problem that emerges during the course of research, and about which the participant seems to be unaware, if the problem identified is likely to affect his/her future wellbeing adversely. If any professional advice is requested in the course of research, a referral should be suggested to someone who is suitably qualified to deal with the matter raised.

- *Non-human animals* – When carrying out research with non-human animals the highest standards of animal welfare should be observed; the animals should not be subjected to any more pain, discomfort, suffering, fear, distress, frustration, boredom than is absolutely necessary. All decisions and actions must be strictly justified and should adhere to the BPS *Guidelines for Psychologists Working with Animals*.

Debriefing

At the end of an investigation where the participants were aware they had taken part in a study, the researcher should take time to discuss the study with the participants. This is known as debriefing and should involve informing the participants about the nature and outcomes of the research. During the debriefing session the researcher should also discuss the participant's experience of the study in order to identify any unforeseen discomfort, distress or other negative effect of the research, and offer professional support should this be deemed necessary. Care is required to avoid making any evaluative statements during a debriefing session since these can take on unintended significance when provided by a psychologist, especially when discussing results involving children with their parents, teachers or those in *loco parentis*.

As a result of debriefing or in the light of experience of the investigation, a participant has the right to withdraw any consent given retrospectively, and to require that all their personal data be removed from the study and destroyed.

A researcher should never use the provision of debriefing sessions as justification for any unethical aspects of an investigation.

4 Integrity

Psychologists should be honest, accurate, clear and fair in all their dealings with people, including research participants. They should also seek to promote integrity in all scientific activity. In the context of research, this should include being accurate and honest when recording and analyzing data, and when reporting research findings and acknowledging any limitations of the results and the conclusions drawn.

It is also important to emphasize that participating in research is entirely voluntary and there should never be overt or covert coercion to do so. It needs to be clear that participation in research will not affect in any way the provision of resources or services to which the individual is otherwise entitled. This is particularly important when the researcher is in a position of authority or power over the participants (e.g. a teacher and his/her students). Someone who is unwilling to participate or who withdraws during the course of a study would receive exactly the same services and resources as those who participated.

The scientific community shares the responsibility for the ethical conduct of research and ethical treatment of research participants. A psychologist who believes that another person may be carrying out research in the UK that is not in accordance with the BPS *Code of Ethics and Conduct* is expected to encourage that investigator to re-evaluate the study and make changes where appropriate.

(Adapted from *the BPS Code of Ethics and Conduct 2006*)

Table 2.5 continued
British Psychological Society *Code of Ethics and Conduct* (BPS 2006)

Debriefing is an essential part of research. What would the effect be on a participant if they took part in upsetting or challenging research and were sent home without any chance to talk through their experience?

- *Role of ethics committees* – Most universities and other institutions where research is carried out have ethics committees to scrutinize research proposals to ensure that the rights of all participants are fully respected. The effectiveness of ethical guidelines and codes of conduct depends on the rigorous evaluation of research proposals by ethics committees. It is important that such committees include non-psychologists in their membership to represent the lay person's point of view.

- *Enforcing the guidelines* – Enforcement of ethical standards depends on psychologists being willing to punish those who contravene the published guidelines. The BPS and the APA impose penalties on any of their members if they infringe their ethical code. However, there is no obligation on psychologists (unlike the medical profession) to belong to the BPS, for example, and so threats of expulsion may carry little weight. Furthermore, every year, psychology students carry out investigations and these are not always supervised by BPS members or even by qualified psychologists. Therefore, there is potential for ethical guidelines to be breached. Examination bodies and universities, however, always provide clear guidance on how psychology projects should be conducted.

- *Revision of guidelines* – Ethical codes are revised regularly to keep pace with social change. This is essential as society's views about morality change over time. The interests of psychologists also change, so that new ethical issues may arise (e.g. when to maintain confidentiality in research in the area of child abuse). The need for such revisions reminds us that ethical codes are not entirely dependent on universal, unchanging truths.

The activity on the left will enable you to check your understanding of key ethical issues.

It can be easier to identify the 'big' ethical issues when thinking about a particular research study (e.g. the use of deception in Milgram's research on obedience to authority). When you completed the activity on 'Ethical issues', did you recognize that interviews could also raise unanticipated ethical issues? For example, questions about how children should be brought up may reawaken uncomfortable thoughts or painful memories about the past. Also, memory researchers often do not tell the participants beforehand what they are expected to remember or even that they are taking part in a memory experiment. This is because to do so may cause the participants to change the way they approach the task. This type of temporary minor deception, which does not cause any harm, is usually regarded as being acceptable.

Selecting participants and sampling techniques

A target population is a group of people who share a given set of characteristics, about which a researcher wishes to draw conclusions (e.g. all students registered for AS-level psychology examinations in a given year). However, a target population is usually far too large for each individual to be investigated, so a subset of the population – a sample – is investigated instead. A representative sample is part of the target population and shares all the main characteristics of the population despite its smaller size. If, and only if, a sample is truly representative, it can be used by psychologists as a basis for generalizing the results of the study and the conclusions drawn to the remainder of the target population. It follows from this that a sample that is not truly representative may result in wasted time and effort because the results would only apply to the specific sample studied and cannot be generalized to the target population.

RESEARCH METHODS

Activity **Ethical issues**

Describe in as much detail as you can at least one ethical issue that is important in relation to each of the following research methods: (a) laboratory experiment, (b) naturalistic observation, (c) questionnaire, (d) interviews and (e) case study research.

Try to select a different ethical issue to discuss in relation to each method.

Discuss your thoughts with someone in your psychology class and combine your ideas.

Some suggestions for relevant ethical issues are given on p. 274 ▶

A general principle is that the larger the sample, the more likely it is to provide an accurate estimate about the nature of the population from which it has been drawn. Deciding sample size, therefore, reflects a delicate balancing act between the need to represent accurately the target population on the one hand, and practical considerations, such as saving time and money, on the other. In practice, some degree of sampling error is likely to result – the researcher's task is to minimize this error. Statistical tables can be used to advise on the sample size needed to achieve acceptable levels of sampling error in target populations of different sizes.

Samples can be selected in several different ways. We will discuss three methods of sampling: **random sampling**, **opportunity sampling** and **volunteer sampling**.

Random sampling

In a random sample, every person or item in a given target population has an equal chance of being selected for inclusion. This means that it is necessary to have a list (sometimes referred to as a sampling frame) that identifies every person or item in the target population in order to generate a random sample. Selection of the sample must take place in an unbiased way. However, selecting a random sample does not guarantee a sample that is totally representative of the population concerned. Nor does it mean that any two random samples drawn from the same target population will share identical characteristics. By its very nature, a random sample can only come with a guarantee that it has been selected in an entirely unbiased manner (e.g. by using one of the techniques described for randomly allocating participants to conditions earlier in this chapter on pp. 41–2). However, as long as the target population and sample size have been chosen carefully, the laws of probability predict that the chance of selecting a biased sample through random sampling techniques is minimal.

There are several other methods of sampling that psychologists use, but most of these are beyond the requirements of the AS psychology specification. Two non-random sampling methods that you need to know about are opportunity sampling and volunteer sampling.

Opportunity sampling

Opportunity sampling is a widely used non-random method of sampling because it is convenient (in fact it is sometimes referred to as a convenience sample). Its main weakness is that it is unlikely to generate a sample that is representative of the wider target population from which it was drawn. Opportunity sampling involves the researcher selecting anyone who is available to take part in a study from a given population, such as the staff or students within a particular college. This means that the data gathered from an opportunity sample are unlikely to be representative of the target population and so the findings of the study cannot be generalized.

Volunteer sampling

Volunteer sampling (also referred to as self-selected sampling) is another non-random sampling technique that involves participants selecting themselves to take part in a research study, often by replying to an advertisement. This type of sampling has been widely used in university research. A well-known example was in Milgram's research on obedience in the 1960s (see Chapter 6). Potential weaknesses of using a volunteer or self-selected sample are that the majority of a given target population are unlikely to respond to the request to participate, and that those who do respond (i.e. volunteers) may be not be typical of the target

Your classmates might provide a ready source of participants for psychological research, but what might be the drawbacks of using them?

population in some way. Therefore, the data gathered from this potentially biased sample are also unlikely to be representative of the target population and so the findings of the study cannot be generalized.

The relationship between researchers and participants

When psychologists study people, the research situation has its own social dimensions and it is therefore to be expected that a relationship may develop between the researcher and the participants. A research investigation is, therefore, liable to be influenced by those who are taking part. Research participants may be affected by **demand characteristics**, while investigators themselves may have unintended effects on the outcome of research – known as **investigator effects**.

Demand characteristics

Demand characteristics occur when participants try to make sense of the research situation they find themselves in and act accordingly. Demand characteristics have already been described in the section on laboratory experiments (Chapter 1, pp.18–19), but they may occur in any research scenario in which the participants are aware of taking part. They become a problem as soon as participants act differently from the way that they would outside the research situation. Well-designed research aims to minimize the effects of demand characteristics as much as possible.

Demand characteristics might include the following participant behaviour:

- Trying to guess the purpose of the research and acting in a way that they feel is helpful to the researcher – or, indeed, acting in a way that is unhelpful if the participant decides not to cooperate with the requirements of the research.

- Acting nervously and out of character because of being in a research situation – for instance, participants may feel they are being evaluated in some way (e.g. that their personality is being assessed) and be anxious about this.

- Displaying social desirability bias by wanting others to see them in the most favourable way possible, e.g. in the responses given to a questionnaire on moral standards.

Investigator effects

Investigator effects result from the effects of a researcher's behaviour and characteristics on an investigation. There is a wide range of possibilities here. Expectation effects can occur where a researcher is deeply committed to achieving a particular outcome. This may be a particular problem when observing events that can be interpreted in more than one way (an example might be the difficulty in distinguishing between children fighting or indulging in rough-and-tumble play). Even overt fraud is a possibility by 'massaging' the data to produce the desired results, although this is highly unlikely.

In naturalistic observational studies, the presence of the observer can cause participants to behave in ways that are different from their normal behaviour – for example, participants' behaviour may either be more restrained or more exuberant than usual. When research is carried out using questionnaire surveys or interviews, then many different aspects of the investigator may have an influence, including the investigator's age, gender, ethnic group, appearance, facial expressions and communication style.

In what ways might the relationship between researcher and participant affect the research?

CHECK YOUR UNDERSTANDING

Check your understanding of investigation design by answering the following questions. Try to do this from memory. You can check your answers by looking back through Topic 1.

1. What is an alternative hypothesis?

2. What is a null hypothesis?

3. Name the experimental design where all participants take part in all the conditions of the experiment.

4. Give one advantage and one weakness of an independent groups design.

5. Give one advantage and one weakness of a matched pairs design.

6. What does the term 'event sampling' mean in observational research?

7. Describe one way in which observer reliability can be assessed.

8. Suggest one way in which observer reliability might be improved.

9. Name two techniques for assessing test reliability.

10. Explain what the term 'external validity' means.

11. Name three of the techniques that a psychologist can use to assess test validity.

12. What are the four ethical principles that underpin the BPS *Code of Ethics and Conduct* published in 2006?

13. What is meant by the term 'informed consent' and how is it achieved? What special arrangements are needed when seeking informed consent to study children aged less than 16?

14. How is informed consent addressed in the context of observation research carried out in public places?

15. Is it ever ethically defensible to deceive participants about the purpose of a research study?

16. What does the term 'debriefing' mean? What is its main aim and when is it used?

17. The BPS *Code of Ethics and Conduct* (2006) refers to the 'avoidance of harm. What does this mean in the context of research undertaken by psychologists?

18. Why is it necessary to revise codes of ethics and ethical guidelines from time to time?

19. Define the term 'random sample'.

20. Why is an opportunity sample unlikely to be representative of the target population?

21. What is meant by the term 'demand characteristics'?

22. What is a pilot study and why is it important to carry one out?

Psychology in context

Presenting data effectively

Look at the two graphs carefully and answer the questions that follow:

1 Describe in words what Graph A tells you.

2 Describe in words what Graph B tells you.

3 Which graph do you believe to be the more accurate and informative? Give your reasons.

4 What changes would need to be made to the graph that you felt to be less informative in order to make it more informative?

Graph A: Long-lasting efficacy – The best way to eliminate dandruff and prevent it recurring

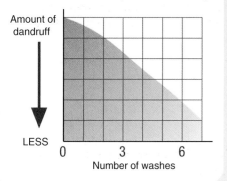

Graph B: Library books issued per person in the UK

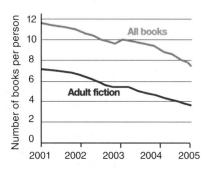

Look at some newspapers or magazines and try to find at least one good example of graphical presentation of numerical data and one poor example. Write a few notes about each one, highlighting what you feel to be the good and the less effective features of each example. Discuss these with another student in your psychology class and/or your teacher.

Topic 2: Data analysis and presentation

This topic looks at various ways of analyzing, presenting and interpreting both quantitative and qualitative data. We start by considering the presentation and interpretation of data, using line graphs, bar charts, histograms, frequency polygons, scattergrams and tables. Quantitative data can also be summarized using descriptive statistics, including the median, mean, mode, range and standard deviation. The analysis of quantitative data using inferential statistical tests is outside the scope of the AS psychology specification.

The final section focuses on the presentation of qualitative data derived from naturalistic observation studies and studies using questionnaires and interviews. The use of content analysis to analyze qualitative data is also described.

Before reading on, try the activity in 'Psychology in context' on the left.

Presentation and interpretation of quantitative data

As you will realize by now, psychologists often gather masses of quantitative (numerical) data; these are the raw data. The raw data must be presented, analyzed and interpreted in order to make sense of them. The data can be presented visually in tables, graphs, bar charts, histograms and scattergrams, and they can also be analyzed statistically. In this section we will consider a range of methods that can be used to summarize and present quantitative data visually.

First, however, we need to consider the different levels (or scales) of measurement because these affect the organization and display of data. Measurement of a variable involves either assigning it to a category or using a number to represent it. The choice of method of visual data display and the selection of statistical techniques to analyze quantitative data depends on the scale of measurement used. The four scales of measurement – nominal, ordinal, interval and ratio – are defined and illustrated in Table 2.6 on the next page.

Presenting and interpreting graphs

Graphs act as visual aids that help make sense of quantitative data obtained from psychological investigations. They provide an overall picture that helps to summarize the results; when well constructed, they can show us at a glance any patterns which occur in the data.

A line graph joins together continuous values using a single line; it is often used to indicate changes over time. For example, a line graph could be used to present data relating to the number of students enrolled every year for the AS psychology exam over a 10-year period in the United Kingdom. Alternatively, the same data could be presented for England, Northern Ireland and Wales using three different lines so that comparisons can be made between the three countries.

It is important to ensure that continuous data only are presented in a line graph to prevent inappropriate inferences being drawn. If, for example, the number of road traffic accidents, involving motorbikes, was known for January, March, May and July 2007 and these data points were joined using a line graph, there would be a danger that the data for February, April and June might be inferred from the line graph. This inference would, however, be entirely meaningless. Such data should be presented in a bar chart (see p. 64).

Table 2.6 Scales of measurement

Nominal scale of measurement	Nominal scale of measurement simply involves distinguishing between different categories of a variable. Data are allocated to categories that are mutually exclusive (e.g. male/female; smoker/non-smoker; left-handed/right-handed). The category labels are merely names (the term 'nominal' comes from the Latin word *nomen*, which means 'name'), so there is no inherent order of the categories.
Ordinal scale of measurement	Ordinal scale of measurement involves organising the measured characteristics into categories (as for nominal data above), but the main difference is that these categories can be placed in a logical order, based on their meaning. However, the differences between the values on an ordinal scale are not the same (as, for example, in the categories used to measure social class). Ordinal categories indicate the rank position in a group – for example: ■ very confident, confident, not at all confident ■ strongly agree, agree, neither agree nor disagree, disagree and strongly disagree.
Interval scale of measurement	An interval scale involves measurements that can be ordered and the intervals on the scale are equal because they are based on some standard unit of measurement. However, the point used to indicate zero is arbitrary. An example of interval data is IQ scores; it is not possible to claim that someone with an IQ of 120 is twice as intelligent as someone with an IQ of 60.
Ratio scale of measurement	As for interval measurements, ratio data are measurements on a scale that has equal intervals but also a genuine zero point – for example, height in centimetres or weight in kilograms. With a fixed zero point it is possible to make ratio statements, i.e. to claim that someone whose height is 1.9 metres is twice as tall as someone who is 95 cms.

It is also important to be aware that manipulation of the way that the axes in graphs are drawn can easily bias the interpretation. Before reading on, try the activity, 'Presenting data', on the right, which illustrates the kind of visual deception that can occur.

The two graphs will produce very different impressions, even though they are based on identical data – see Figures 2.12 and 2.13 on p. 274, which show the graphs to scale at a reduced size. Shortening or extending the axes, or manipulating their labelling, can convey a desired impression and may be highly misleading to the observer. The important lesson from this exercise is that there is no single correct way to select the scales used on the axes of graphs. However, there are certain conventions that facilitate the presentation of information in an unbiased way and reduce the risk of misunderstanding or misinterpretation:

■ Plot frequency of scores on the y-axis (as in the examples that you have just drawn); this is the conventional mode of presentation.

■ Adopt the three-quarter-high rule: this states that when frequencies are plotted, the length of the y-axis should be determined in the following way. It should be presented in such a way that the distance of the highest point on the graph (i.e. the point which represents the score with the highest frequency) from the x-axis is approximately equal to three-quarters of the total length of the x-axis.

■ It is possible to break the x-axis or y-axis of a graph if labelling of the axis from zero would give a poor visual impression, due to the large amount of empty space that would result.

■ Remember that all graphs and charts need to have each axis clearly labelled and also have a clear and informative title.

RESEARCH METHODS

Activity **Presenting data**

A psychology software publisher asks one of its sales representatives to present her sales figures for the last three years to the company's senior management. Her sales are:

2005	1000 items
2006	1050 items
2007	1100 items.

The company is dissatisfied with the sales performance, but the sales person is desperate to keep her job. Both parties decide to present the sales figures by means of a line graph, with the years 2005 to 2007 on the x-axis (horizontal) and number of items sold on the y-axis (vertical). The sales person draws a graph with 3 cm representing one year, the management opt for 4 cm = one year. The y-axis of the sales person's graph is 16 cm long and extends from 1000 items sold to 1100. However, the management draw their y-axis 10 cm long, and label it from 0 items sold to 10 000. Draw or sketch the two graphs and see the bias created.

Answers are given on p. 274 ▶

Figure 2.5

Bar chart showing the number of observations of different behaviours in a group of children

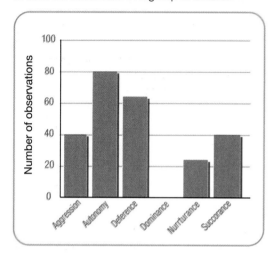

The ideal situation to aim for is that someone looking at any graph should be able to understand what it is about without the need to refer to any additional explanation from the surrounding text. It is also important when reading other people's work to look out for examples of graphs and charts that are misleading.

Presenting and interpreting bar charts, histograms and frequency polygons

Bar charts and histograms are two of the most widely used graphical techniques. Simple forms of these are discussed here, but alternative forms exist, such as compound or three-dimensional ones, which show data from more than one condition simultaneously.

Bar charts

A bar chart is usually used when the data are in categories (nominal or ordinal data) or to illustrate the average scores from different samples. It consists of a series of vertical bars of equal width on the x-axis, but varying height to indicate the frequency of each category (on the y-axis). Unlike the histogram, each bar is usually separated from each of the others on the x-axis so that a continuous variable is not implied (as shown in Figure 2.5). When data are at a nominal level, bias should be avoided in the order in which the bars are presented; these can be presented in any order because there is no inherent logic to the ordering. Consequently, they are often presented in alphabetical order or in ascending (or descending) order of frequency. However, when data are measured on an ordinal scale, the order of the categories on the x-axis would be predetermined.

Figure 2.6

Histogram showing the number of words recalled in a memory experiment

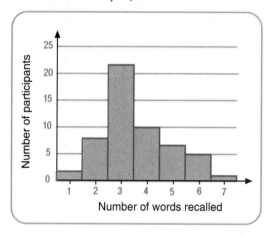

Histograms

Histograms are a useful form of graphical representation that can be used when presenting continuous data on interval or ratio scales of measurement. A histogram consists of a series of vertical bars of equal width to represent each score or group of scores (class interval) presented on the x-axis. The height of each bar on the y-axis represents the frequency of occurrence of each score or class interval. A histogram is drawn with the bars representing the frequencies actually touching each other. An optimum number of bars is between six and eight. Sometimes, single values can be used for each bar, but if the scale used on the x-axis has a large number of points, then the data can be clustered into class intervals.

Figure 2.7

Frequency polygon showing the number of words recalled in a memory experiment

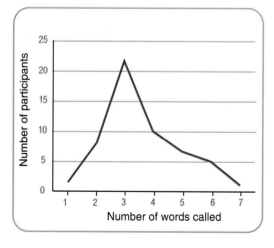

Frequency polygons

The frequency polygon is a particularly useful technique when it is necessary to compare two or more frequency distributions. It is used as an alternative to the histogram. A frequency polygon can be drawn by linking the midpoints from the top of each bar contained in a histogram, as in the example in Figure 2.7. A frequency polygon may be the preferred technique when the results from two or more conditions of an investigation need to be presented at the same time; this is because two or more lines can be drawn on the same graph to show direct comparison of results.

Presenting and interpreting scattergrams

The term 'correlation' and the concepts of correlation coefficients, and positive and negative correlations, were introduced in Chapter 1 (p. 20). Reread that section now to refresh your understanding of these terms. One way of presenting correlational data is the scattergram (also referred to as a scattergraph or

Figure 2.8

Scattergraphs illustrating different correlation coefficients

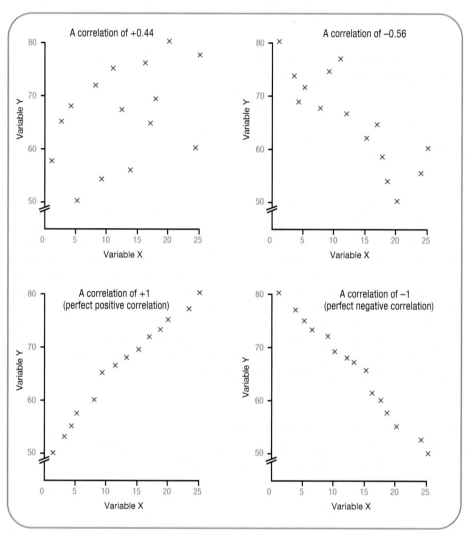

Table 2.7

Frequency table showing the number of hours spent preparing for an exam

Total number of hours spent preparing for an exam	Number of students (frequency)	Percentage (%)
18	1	1.2
17	0	0
16	3	3.5
15	5	5.9
14	5	5.9
13	4	4.7
12	10	11.7
11	6	7.1
10	10	11.7
9	8	9.4
8	7	8.2
7	5	5.9
6	5	5.9
5	1	1.2
4	4	4.7
3	7	8.2
2	2	2.4
1	2	2.4
TOTAL	N=85	100

scatterplot). Data from one of the variables is presented on the x-axis and data from the second variable on the y-axis (see Figure 2.8).

Study the four scattergrams in Figure 2.8, which illustrate what a correlation coefficient of +1, +0.44, −0.56 and −1 look like when the correlation data are presented in a scattergram.

Presenting and interpreting tables

The raw data collected in a psychological investigation are sometimes presented in a table in an appendix rather than in the body of the research report. Although all the data are captured, such a table is not particularly useful because it is difficult to make much sense of the data and identify any clear patterns within the data. Presenting these data in a **frequency table** is more useful and helps to make any patterns within the data more obvious.

Table 2.7 is an example of a frequency table showing the total number of hours that a group of 85 students on a AS psychology course spent preparing for their exam. When presenting a table, it is important that the columns and rows are always clearly labelled.

Table 2.8
Grouped frequency table showing the number of hours spent preparing for an exam

Total number of hours spent preparing for an exam	Number of students (frequency)	Percentage (%)
16–18	4	4.7
13–15	14	16.5
10–12	26	30.6
7–9	20	23.5
4–6	10	11.8
1–3	11	12.9
TOTAL	N=85	100

When a large number of different values exist for a variable, presenting the data in a frequency table can become rather cumbersome. Instead, the different values can be organized in a smaller number of grouped values and presented in a **grouped frequency table**. It is important that the intervals used are mutually exclusive, exhaustive and of equal width. Table 2.8 is an example of a grouped frequency table for the total number of hours spent preparing for an exam, using intervals of three.

Descriptive statistical techniques

Descriptive statistical techniques enable the researcher to obtain summary descriptions of sets of quantitative data. Two types of descriptive statistical techniques are:

- **measures of central tendency**, which give average values
- **measures of dispersion**, which look at the variability of scores.

Each of these techniques provides a single value that can help to summarize a set of data that might otherwise be difficult to interpret. This potential benefit has its drawbacks however. When any single value is obtained, the process of adding the scores together inevitably produces a loss of individual information.

Measures of central tendency and measures of dispersion are also valuable to the psychologist in that they form the basis for analyses using inferential statistics, although this is outside the scope of AS psychology.

Measures of central tendency

You are probably already familiar with measures of central tendency and refer to them as *averages*. A measure of central tendency provides a single value which is representative of a set of numbers by indicating the most typical value. Three measures of central tendency are discussed here:

- the median – the middle value of scores arranged in ascending or descending order
- the mean – the arithmetic average
- the mode – the most frequently occurring value.

Each of these has its own particular uses, and therefore advantages and weaknesses, for particular sets of data.

The median

The median is the middle value of a set of numbers that has been placed in numerical order (i.e. in order from the lowest to the highest score, or the highest to the lowest). Therefore, half of the scores in a given set of data will lie above the median, and half below it. When there is an even number of scores, however, there will be two middle values. In these circumstances, the median is calculated by adding the two central values together and dividing by two. The panel on the left, 'Calculating the median', provides an example of both situations.

When calculating the median, you may find it helpful to cross out the lowest and highest values alternately until you are left with the middle value(s).

The main advantage of the median is that it remains relatively unaffected by any outlying values. It is therefore a safe measure of central tendency to use when we are unsure about the reliability of extreme values. Also, it can be used with

Calculating the median

To calculate the median when there is an odd number of scores:

Place scores in numerical order

2 4 5 (6) 8 10 11

Median = 6

To calculate the median when there is an even number of scores:

Place scores in numerical order

2 4 5 (6 8) 10 11 13

Median = $\frac{6 + 8}{2}$

Median = 7

Normal and skewed distributions

A normal distribution curve is a bell-shaped curve which is symmetrical about its mean, median and mode (see Figure 2.9). It is called 'normal' because it describes the theoretical distribution of a great many naturally occurring variables. Various characteristics of individuals are considered to be normally distributed (e.g. height and body weight) and sometimes a particular measure is deliberately constructed in a way that a normal distribution of scores results (e.g. some intelligence tests). In theory, a normal distribution curve should result when a large random sample of measurements is taken from an appropriate population. In practice, however, it would be very rare for a distribution to fit a normal distribution curve precisely – there are always likely to be at least some minor irregularities.

Notice the key features of this curve:

- The curve is symmetrical about its mean value, which occurs at the central point of the distribution. (This value is also the median and mode.)
- The curve has a characteristic bell shape, curving downwards close to the mean and outwards further away.
- The outer extremities of the distribution (known as the tails) will never touch the horizontal axis.
- The properties of this distribution mean that certain statements about probability can be made – a very important feature when a researcher wishes to express clearly the relationship between sample data and data from the population that the sample represents.

However, all variables are not normally distributed; some distributions can be best described as skewed (see Figure 2.10).

Figure 2.9 Normal distribution

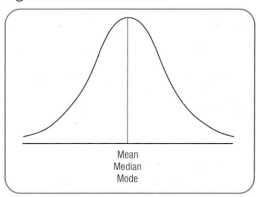

Mean
Median
Mode

Figure 2.10 Examples of skewed distributions

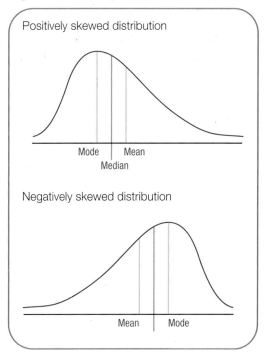

Positively skewed distribution

Mode   Mean
Median

Negatively skewed distribution

Mean   Mode

data from skewed distributions (i.e. where there is a cluster of values at one end of the range, see the panel above, 'Normal and skewed distributions'. Unlike the mean, it can be used when data are on an ordinal level of measurement (for example rating scales, where data are not measured in fixed units with an equal distance between each point on the scale concerned).

A weakness of the median, however, is that it does not work well with small data sets and is affected by any alteration of the central values in a set of values. For example, if we have two sets of data:

| 10 | 12 | 13 | 14 | 18 | 19 | 22 | 22 | and |
| 10 | 12 | 13 | 14 | 15 | 19 | 22 | 22 | |

the median would be 16 in the first case and 14.5 in the second, despite only one value being different in the two sets of data.

The mean

The mean is the arithmetic average of a set of data, and is probably the average with which you are most familiar. It is calculated by adding all the values together and dividing the total by the number of scores. An example is shown in the panel 'Calculating the mean', on the right.

The main advantage of the mean is that it makes use of all the available data. As such, it is the most powerful of the measures of central tendency available. However, it needs to be used with caution. One limitation of the mean is that when it has been calculated, decimal points may be less meaningful if all the data consist of whole numbers (as in the example in the panel on the right).

Calculating the mean

To find the mean of:

2 4 5 5 6 6 6 7 8 10

Add all the values together:

$2 + 4 + 5 + 5 + 6 + 6 + 6 + 7 + 8 + 10 = 59$

Divide this sum by the number of scores

(there are 10 scores):

$$\text{Mean} = \frac{59}{10}$$

$$\text{Mean} = 5.9$$

Also, the distribution of values needs to be taken into account. The mean can be used appropriately as the measure of central tendency with sets of data (such as normally distributed data – see the panel 'Normal and skewed distributions' on the previous page) that do not have extreme outlying values. When such extreme values are present, the median should be used instead.

For example, calculate the mean of 8, 10, 10, 12, 60. What does the mean tell us about any of these scores?

In this example, the mean is 20, which tells us very little about the four low scores and the single high score. In circumstances where such outliers occur, it would be more appropriate to use the median (10), which would at least summarize the first four values reasonably successfully (coincidentally, 10 is also the mode in this example).

The mean can be used most successfully with data on interval or ratio levels of measurement (i.e. data measured in fixed units, where each point on the scale of measurement is an equal distance apart). Caution needs to be used if the mean is used with data on ordinal levels of measurement, where data are capable of being placed in rank order, but no assumptions can be made about points on the scale being an equal distance apart.

For example, consider the situation where a teacher rates pupils using a seven-point scale which measures how hard they have worked on their psychology coursework. Students are rated from 1 ('very hard working') to 7 ('no effort'). Given the arbitrary nature of this scale, we have no way of knowing whether all those rated at 4 on this scale ('average level of work') actually invested precisely the same amount of work, or whether the points on this scale are an equal distance apart. Therefore, calculating the mean would be inappropriate. In a similar way, it would be wholly inappropriate to work out a mean GCSE grade – these grades are measured on an ordinal scale, as some grade bands cover a wider range of marks than others.

Using a measure of central tendency is insufficient on its own to describe a set of data. Take, for example, the data shown in Table 2.7 on the left. The mean for each set of data is 100, yet the distribution of scores is very different in each case. In data set A, the scores are all very close to 100, while in data set B, they are dispersed much more widely. This is where measures of dispersion have an important role to play (see p. 35).

Table 2.7 Two data sets

Data set A	Data set B
100	100
101	40
99	120
102	60
98	180
100	100

The mode

The mode is the value that occurs most frequently in any set of scores. For example, with the following series of numbers:

2   4   6   7   7   7   10   12

the most frequently occurring number is 7, and so the mode = 7.

Although the mode provides information about the most frequently occurring value and is easy to identify, it has its limitations and is not widely used in psychological research. One reason for this is that when there are only a few scores representing each value, then even very small changes in the data can radically alter the mode. For example:

3   6   8   9   10   10 Mode = 10
3   3   6   8   9   10 Mode = 3

A further possible problem is that there may not be a single modal value. For example, take the series of numbers:

3   5   8   8   8   10   12   16   16   16   20

In this situation, there are two modal values (8 and 16), known as the *bimodal values*. With cases such as this, the bimodal values may still provide a useful summary statistic. It is, of course, possible to have several modal values, in which case the distribution is referred to as multimodal and the value of the statistic becomes even more limited.

For example:

2   2   4   7   7   8   8   10   11   11   13   13

Here, five values occur twice: 2, 7, 8, 11 and 13.

The mode has an advantage in that it is a figure that actually does always occur in a given sequence, which may not be true of the other measures of central tendency. However, its weakness is that it tells us nothing about the other values in the distribution concerned.

Now try the activity on the right.

Measures of dispersion

Measures of dispersion enable us to examine the variability within our data sets, and help us to understand whether scores in a given set of data are similar to, or very different from, each other.

Range

The range is easy to calculate because it is simply the difference between the highest and lowest scores in a given set of data, with one added if the scores are all whole numbers. A sample calculation is shown in the panel on the right. Similarly, if values are recorded to one decimal place, then the range is the difference between the lowest and highest values with 0.1 added (to two decimal places, it is the difference plus 0.01, and so on). If values are recorded to the nearest half unit, then the range has 0.5 added to the difference between the lowest and highest value.

The range has the advantage of being quick to calculate, but also has some important limitations. It does not provide any idea of the distribution of values around the centre, nor does it take individual values into account (remember that the only values used when calculating the range are the two most extreme values). Following on from this point, the range is seriously affected by any outlying values in a given set of data.

Interquartile range

In an attempt to overcome the potential effect of outlying values, the **interquartile range** is often preferred. The interquartile range measures the spread of the middle 50 per cent of values when they are placed in numerical order (known as rank ordering). The top 25 per cent and the bottom 25 per cent of values are ignored, which has the effect of removing the influence of outlying values, and providing an indication of grouping around the central value. The panel on the right explains how it is calculated.

Standard deviation

The standard deviation is a measure of the variability or spread of a given set of scores from its mean. As with the mean, its calculation involves using all the scores in a given set of data; this makes the standard deviation the most powerful of the measures of dispersion available to the researcher. The actual calculation is beyond the scope of the AS psychology specification, although if you continue

RESEARCH METHODS

Activity   Measures of central tendency: advantages and weaknesses

There are three measures of central tendency: median, mean and mode. For each measure, draw a three-column table, using the format shown below for the median. In the appropriate columns, give a definition, and the advantages and weaknesses for each measure. Use the material on pp. 66–9 to help you complete the three tables. Don't look at the answers on p. 274 until after you have tried to complete the tables yourself.

The median		
Definition	Advantages	Weaknesses

Calculating the range

To calculate the range of:

3   7   8   10   11   16   18   21   22   26

Find the difference between the highest score (26) and the lowest (3), and add 1.

Range = 26 − 3 + 1 = 24

Calculating the interquartile range

To calculate the interquartile range for the following data:

2   3   7   8   10   11   16   18   21   22   26   26

We first need to calculate the median:

The median = $\dfrac{11 + 16}{2}$

Median = 13.5

There are six scores above the median, and six below it. The interquartile range will therefore include the six scores that lie closest to the median, and exclude the remaining six. So, for the scores lying above the median, this means that 16, 18 and 21 will be included within the interquartile range, and 22, 26 and 26 excluded.

The upper boundary of the interquartile range will therefore be the mean of the values immediately below it (21) and immediately above it (22), i.e. 21.5. Similarly, the lower boundary will be the mean of 7 and 8 (i.e. 7.5). The interquartile range is, therefore, the difference between 21.5 and 7.5 (i.e. 14).

Figure 2.11
The percentage of scores that lie between a given number of standard deviations either side of the mean

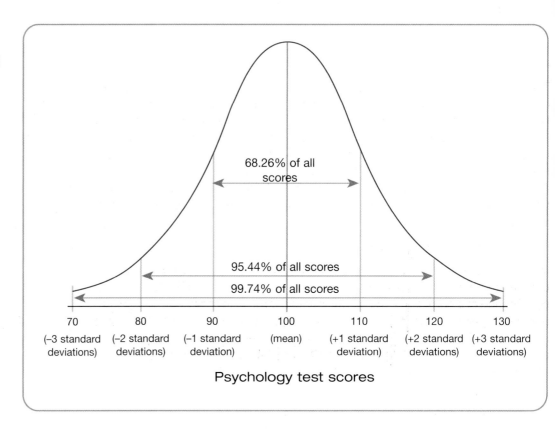

Psychology test scores

to A2 level, you may need to calculate it in order to describe the variability in data sets.

The standard deviation allows us to make statements of probability about how likely (or how unlikely) a given value is to occur. This ability to make inferences is based on the relationship between the standard deviation and a normal distribution curve (refer back to the panel on p. 67). Meaningful use of the standard deviation not only requires data which are approximately normally distributed, but also data measured on interval or ratio levels of measurement (i.e. data measured in fixed units, where each point on the scale of measurement is an equal distance apart). The standard deviation becomes a less effective measure when there are any outlying scores that skew the data distribution.

The percentages of values that lie between the mean and a given number of standard deviations above and below the mean are fixed properties, which help to make the standard deviation a particularly useful measure. These fixed properties are:

- 68.26 per cent of all values lie within one standard deviation either side of the mean

- 95.44 per cent of all values lie within two standard deviations either side of the mean

- 99.74 per cent of all values lie within three standard deviations either side of the mean.

Figure 2.11 illustrates how this works, using some data where the standard deviation is 10. As the mean value is 100, this means that 68.26 per cent of the psychology test scores in the population can be assumed to lie between 90 (minus one standard deviation from the mean) and 110 (plus one standard deviation from the mean).

Analysis and interpretation of correlational data

The term correlation was introduced in Chapter 1, where the concepts of correlation coefficients, and positive and **negative correlations** were introduced. Reread that section now to refresh your knowledge of these terms. As far as interpreting correlation coefficients is concerned, the strength of a correlation increases as the obtained coefficient becomes closer to +1 or −1. As we have seen, a useful way of depicting correlational relationships is the scattergram (sometimes referred to as a scattergraph or scatterplot). Data from one of the variables being correlated are presented on the x-axis and data from the second variable on the y-axis (see Figure 2.8 on p. 65).

Now try the activity on the right.

In order to interpret a correlation coefficient fully, it is necessary to test the correlation coefficient obtained for statistical significance. This is because the significance of a correlation coefficient is linked directly to the key variable of the number of pairs of scores being correlated. If you go on to study psychology at A2 level, you may have the opportunity to carry out a correlational study and analyze the correlational data statistically to see whether the relationship between the variables is significant.

Presentation of qualitative data

Qualitative data include data that are not in the form of numbers generated from observational research and from open questions in interviews and questionnaires. The task of the researcher, therefore, is to analyse large volumes of narrative accounts, including transcripts from interviews, detailed descriptions of what was observed or the written answers to questionnaires.

When analysing qualitative data, the researcher is usually concerned with searching for the underlying meaning in what people do or say, and this relies heavily on the researcher's interpretive skills. Researchers use a number of different techniques to analyze qualitative data, involving categorizing the data and trying to identify themes within the data. This is very different from the use of statistical tests to analyze quantitative (numerical) data.

Data from naturalistic observational studies

The use of naturalistic observational techniques is discussed in Chapter 1. These techniques differ widely both in terms of the approaches used and in the ways in which behaviour is recorded and classified, so it is hardly surprising that they also differ widely in terms of how behaviour is analyzed and presented. Data interpretation may also produce ideas for hypotheses that can be tested using other research methods.

When qualitative data are generated, these may be presented in different ways, including diary descriptions and specimen descriptions of behaviour. An example of a diary description from an observational study is shown in the panel on the next page; it illustrates the social rituals through which a child's ability to name can arise.

Although ecological validity may be a strength of observational studies, the use of behavioural categories to record behaviour may challenge their validity. Are the operational definitions used the best ways to define specific behaviours?

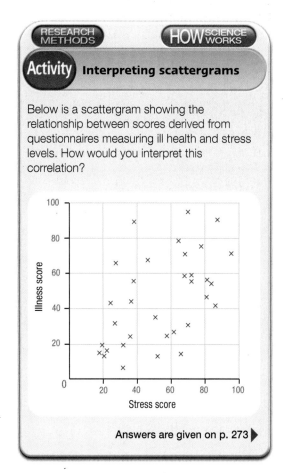

RESEARCH METHODS · HOW **SCIENCE WORKS**

Activity Interpreting scattergrams

Below is a scattergram showing the relationship between scores derived from questionnaires measuring ill health and stress levels. How would you interpret this correlation?

Answers are given on p. 273 ▶

Diary description

Mary, aged 11 months. Mother takes Mary out of her high-chair and puts her on the potty. Her toys are all in a box on the table in front of her chair.

Mother (*spontaneously*): "Do you want Teddy?"

Mary: "aah"

Mother: "Where is he?"

Mary looks around and makes to get off her potty and go to the table, but Mother restrains her. Mary looks at the table and points.

Mother (*going to table opposite and bringing down the box of toys*):

"That's right, he's there, isn't he? Here he is. What does he say? What does Teddy say?"

Mary: "aah"

Mother: "Yes, he does, doesn't he?"

Mary: "aah"

Mother pats Teddy.

Mary: "aah"

Mary's attention moves to the box containing her other toys, which Mother has placed on the floor near her.

Mother: "Oh, what can you see in there? Doggie? (*takes doggie out*) Let's see who else is in here. Who's that? Is it duckie? and what does the duck say?"

Mother squeaks the duck.

Mary: "aah"

Mother: "He doesn't! What does the duck say? What does he say?"

Mary: "argh" (*reaching towards it*)

Mother: "Yes, I know you want it. What does he say?"

Mary: "woraghagh"

Mother: "He doesn't, he says (*she squeaks it concurrently*) 'quack, quack, quack', doesn't he? 'quack, quack, quack'."

Mary: "gh, gh"

Mother: "Yes, he does."

Mary (*looking at Teddy*): "aah"

Mother: "And that's aah is it, that's aah Teddy?"

Mary: "aah"

Mother: "And who's this, what does he say? What does duck say? What does duck say?"

No response from Mary. Mother squeaks duck.

Mary: "gah"

Mother: "Quack!"

Mary: "gah"

Mother: "Ooh, aren't you clever."

Source: Lock (1980, p. 110)

For instance, are the definitions comprehensive enough, or too comprehensive? It is important, therefore, that the structure of a study is fully justifiable in terms of its theoretical basis, and also sufficiently complete, i.e. it should include all the behaviours of interest.

Other potential threats to validity are:

- inadequate sampling (e.g. too few samples, or sampling undertaken at inappropriate times)

- mishandling or inadequate handling of the system used (e.g. through pressure or lack of familiarity in a research situation).

These challenges to validity highlight the need for careful analysis and presentation of observational data if the potential benefits from the richness of the data gathered are not to be compromised.

Data from questionnaires

Much of the data gained from conducting research that uses questionnaires are analyzed using quantitative methods. However, data from open questions, which invite participants to answer in whatever way they choose, need to be analyzed qualitatively. In contrast to closed questions, the use of open questions may help to reduce researcher bias and the impact of the researcher's own views on what is important by constraining the possible answers. Open questions enable the interviewer to uncover what the respondents think is really important.

A further possibility for the analysis of data derived from questionnaires is to convert qualitative data to quantitative by, for example, counting the number of times that a particular item is mentioned (see the section on content analysis, p. 74). This is a common way of analyzing data and shows the extent to which qualitative and quantitative data may be interdependent.

Data from interviews

Interviews are often just one of the techniques used by the researcher in association with other research methods in a particular research study. As such, they may help to provide a validity check on the results obtained. Interpreting the information gathered from interviews is a complex procedure.

Qualitative data may include many elements that need to be taken into account when interpretation takes place. These include description of features of interest, such as:

- the actual behaviour observed by the interviewer

- the context(s) in which the behaviour occurs

- self-reports of behaviour by the participant(s)

- self-reports of cognitions which cannot be observed directly – for example, the feelings, thoughts and attitudes of the participants in the study

- interpretations made by the researchers

- implications of the study for any theory.

From this list, it can be seen that distinctions need to be made between the aspects of a report that:

- describe what actually happened

- are based on the interpretations and inferences made by the researcher

- are based on the interpretations and inferences of the participant(s).

If reporting is to be objective, the distinctions between these need to be made clear to the reader when a report of an investigation is published. Inevitably, the potential for bias in reporting is considerable. For example, researchers might report only those aspects of behaviour that support their own theoretical standpoint, or are particularly relevant to their beliefs and assumptions. Also, decisions about what information to include and what to leave out may be subjective. Carefully reported investigations will always make clear to the reader the criteria used to select participants, and how decisions were made about what information to present.

The close, and often prolonged, relationship between the researcher and the participant(s) in interview-based research may heighten the importance of interpersonal interaction. This interaction may be very productive or it may reduce objectivity.

Although the qualitative data generated by interviews may add to our current understanding, the data can also produce evidence that challenges theory or our existing understanding, thereby stimulating further research and, perhaps, a new theoretical perspective.

The nature of the data obtained often reflects the extent to which the interview was structured or unstructured (see Chapter 1, p. 29). Where data are qualitative, the researcher is able to present results more flexibly, but it can be challenging to organize and present a mass of descriptive data in a meaningful way. Some of the issues the researcher needs to consider are listed below:

- Examine carefully the background theory for a study involving interviews before the research is undertaken, and then decide how the data can be categorized appropriately.

- Solicit opinions from the interviewees on how they would wish their material to be presented. Has information been presented in the spirit in which it was told?

- Decide how any selection or paraphrasing of material is going to be undertaken. (Particular care needs to be taken with this if bias in reporting is to be avoided.)

- Decide whether verbatim quotations will be used to enrich the presentation of data. If so, how will they be selected and used?

Categorization of qualitative data is an important task for the person reporting an interview. It involves the grouping of like items together, e.g. statements by the interviewee concerning particular topics or themes. A good computer database can be helpful when doing this.

Perhaps inevitably, because of their nature, the interpretation of qualitative interview data is partial or incomplete. Something may be lost in terms of reliability, and something gained through the sensitivity and depth of the approach. This may have the important benefit of providing a new basis for interpretation. See the panel on the next page for an example that provides interesting insights about the Bristol riots of the early 1980s derived from interviews.

Processes involved in content analysis

Content analysis is a systematic research technique for analysing transcripts of interviews, documents or text (visual or written), including advertisements, children's books, TV programmes, cartoons, films, song lyrics, newspapers and

Riots and representations: the Bristol riots of the 1980s
Source: Foster and Parker (1995)

In-depth interviews that generate qualitative data can add a great deal to our understanding of social processes, and can illuminate events that appear, at first sight, to be incomprehensible. A series of street disturbances in Britain in the early 1980s, for example, raised the spectre of 'mob rule', and the idea that people who get together in crowds are overtaken by a 'group mind'.

Journalists tend to see people in crowds (particularly when they attack the police) as if they are animals who have been stripped of the veneer of civilization that usually holds them in check. Social psychologists who have been influenced by the theories of the French writer, Gustave LeBon, have been just as negative. LeBon (1947, but first published in 1895) argued that the behaviour of people in crowds fell several rungs down the evolutionary ladder, to the level of 'beings belonging to inferior forms of evolution, women, savages, and children, for instance' (LeBon 1947, p. 36). These ideas take on a quite nasty political flavour when they are used to describe 'riots' by black people in inner-city areas, and the task of the psychologist should be to look at how popular images work, and how people in the crowd understand their actions. In-depth interviewing can move to an 'insider' perspective on these events, and so assist in this task.

One of the first 'riots' in the 1980s, in the St Paul's area of Bristol, was studied by Reicher (1984), a social psychologist whose training had been in the experimental tradition. Reicher was carrying out research on social identity at Bristol University when the April 1980 'riot' broke out, and he was able to interview participants. Their accounts did not correspond with either standard social psychological or journalistic images of people who had lost their minds, and the 'inside' story was of a community trying to defend itself against the police. One of the striking aspects of the insider accounts was that both black and white people who were in the crowd refused to accept the outsider claims that this was a racial disturbance. Private homes and shops within the community were left untouched, whereas the banks and the unemployment office were seen as legitimate targets. The stories collected in these interviews also corresponded with the descriptions of the damage given by the authorities. An examination of the accounts of outsiders and insiders by Reicher and Potter (1985) illustrated the ways in which traditional 'scientific' explanations of crowd behaviour fail to account for the insider perspective which, in the case of St Paul's, stressed the meaningfulness of crowd action, and the feelings of solidarity and emotional warmth that came with defence of the community.

magazines, and websites. The researcher creates a coding system of predetermined categories at the outset of the study, which is then used on the selected materials in a transparent and consistent manner. A pilot study is often used to generate and test the coding system to be used. Care is needed to ensure the categories are discrete and do not overlap so that they can be applied systematically.

Coding qualitative data consists of assigning specific elements of the material to be analyzed to a specific category and then drawing inferences about the themes reflected in the content. The frequency of occurrence of specific words is sometimes analysed (e.g. the incidence of words to describe socially desirable characteristics, such as 'young', 'attractive', 'good looking' or 'fun loving', in dating adverts published in different newspapers). In this way, the researcher can count how many times each code (or word) occurs, thereby extracting quantitative data (frequency data) from qualitative data in an objective way.

In a content analysis of advertisements on British television, Cumberbatch (1990) reported that only around 25 per cent of the women appeared to be over 30 years of age, compared to about 75 per cent of the men, and that around 90 per cent of the voice-overs used authoritative male voices. The findings of this study highlighted some interesting issues relating to gender and age.

It is important that the coding categories used in content analysis are clear and that the allocation of material to specific categories is consistent. One way of achieving this is to invite a second person either to check the coding of the data or, even better, to code the data independently and compare the outcome, negotiating where necessary to reconcile any coding differences. Analyzing qualitative data in this way enables the researcher to defend the inter-rater reliability of the study findings.

Now try the activity on the right.

CHECK YOUR UNDERSTANDING

Check your understanding of data analysis and presentation by answering the following questions. Try to do this from memory. You can check your answers by looking back through Topic 2.

1. List four methods of presenting quantitative data visually. When would you use each method?

2. What is the main difference between a histogram and a bar chart?

3. When might a frequency polygon be used instead of a histogram to present frequency data?

4. What is a scattergram and when is it used?

5. Name three measures of central tendency.

6. Which measure of central tendency is the middle value of a set of numbers placed in numerical order?

7. Explain what is meant by the term 'measure of dispersion'?

8. Name three measures of dispersion.

9. Why is it necessary to provide a measure of dispersion, as well as a measure of central tendency, when describing a set of data?

10. When might the interquartile range be used rather than the range as a measure of dispersion?

11. What are the main properties (characteristics) of the normal distribution curve?

12. Does the following statement indicate a positive or a negative correlation?

    'The more people exercise, the less risk they have of a heart attack.'

13. What is content analysis and how is it used to analyze qualitative data?

14. How might a researcher, using content analysis, check that the allocation of material to coding categories is consistent?

RESEARCH METHODS — HOW SCIENCE WORKS

Activity Planning a study

Now that you have reached the end of this chapter and have learned more about designing research and analyzing data, look back to the first activity on p. 37. Choose just one research method to investigate whether there is any link between playing violent computer games and levels of aggression in children.

Use what you have learned in this chapter to prepare a plan. Issues to consider when planning a research study are:

- the aim of the study and any research hypothesis
- who the participants will be – how many and how you would select them
- what design you will use, if you plan to undertake experimental research
- whether you will need to carry out a pilot study
- what the main ethical issues are associated with the proposed study and how you would address them
- what type(s) of data you will collect and how you will analyze the data.

Chapter 2: Summary

Issues to address when designing an investigation

Research aims

Hypotheses

- Alternative hypothesis
  - directional (one-tailed) *or*
  - non-directional (two-tailed)
- Null hypothesis

Experimental design

- Independent groups
- Repeated measures
- Matched pairs

Design of naturalistic observations

- Behavioural categories
- Behaviour sampling
  - time interval
  - time point sampling
  - event sampling

Design of questionnaires and interviews

- Open or closed questions
- Question order
- Question wording

Operationalization of variables

- Independent variable
- Dependent variable

Use of pilot studies

Control of extraneous variables

- Independent groups
- Repeated measures
- Matched pairs

Reliability

- Techniques to test reliability
  - correlation
  - split half
  - test–retest
- Improving reliability
  - training observers
  - use of operational definitions

Validity

- Internal validity
- External validity
  - population validity
  - ecological validity
- Techniques to test validity
  - face validity
  - content validity
  - concurrent validity
  - predictive validity

Awareness of BPS *Code of Ethics and Conduct*

Four ethical principles

1 Respect
  - informed consent
  - confidentiality and anonymity
  - right to withdraw at any time
  - use of deception
  - observation research

2 Competence

3 Responsibility
  - protection of research participants
  - risk of harm
  - understanding the implications of an investigation
  - protection from stress
  - use of inducements
  - professional advice/support
  - studying non-human animals

4 Integrity

Selection of participants and sampling techniques

- Random sampling
- Opportunity sampling
- Volunteer sampling

Demand characteristics and investigator effects

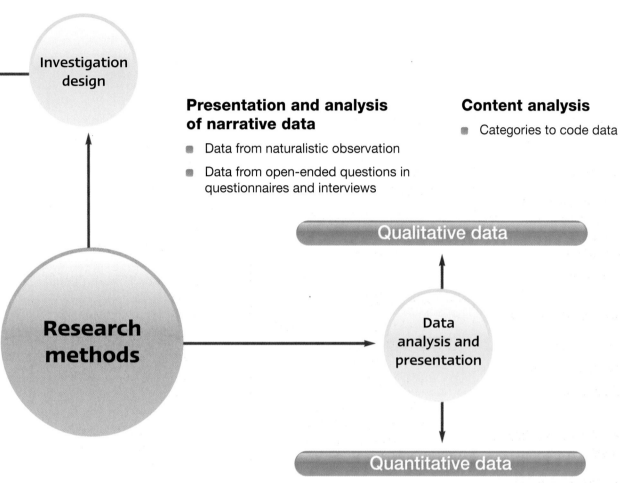

**Presentation and analysis
of narrative data**

- Data from naturalistic observation
- Data from open-ended questions in
  questionnaires and interviews

Content analysis

- Categories to code data

Qualitative data

Investigation
design

Research
methods

Data
analysis and
presentation

Quantitative data

**Presentation and interpretation
of numerical data**

- Scales of measurement
  - nominal
  - ordinal
  - interval
  - ratio
- Graphs
- Bar charts
- Histograms
- Frequency polygons
- Tables
  - frequency table
  - grouped frequency table

Use of descriptive statistics

- Measures of central tendency
  - median
  - mean
  - mode
- Measures of dispersion
  - range
  - interquartile range
  - standard deviation
- Analysis and interpretation of
  correlational data
  - correlation coefficients
  - positive correlation
  - negative correlation

EXPLAINING THE SPECIFICATION

Specification content	The specification explained
Models of memory	In this part of the specification you are required to know about two explanations (models) of how memory functions. To do this, you need to be able to:
The multi-store model, including the concepts of encoding, capacity and duration. Strengths and weaknesses of the model.	■ Describe the **multi-store model**, that is, you need to know about the sensory, short- and long-term stores that make up the model and how information is encoded in and transferred from one store to the next. You also need to know about the capacity and duration of short-term and long-term memory. ■ Discuss the research that has investigated the multi-store model. ■ Evaluate the model in terms of its strengths and weaknesses.
The working memory model, including its strengths and weaknesses.	■ Describe the **working memory model**, that is, describe the components (the central executive and the slave systems) of the model and understand the functions of each component. ■ Discuss the research that has investigated the working memory model. ■ Evaluate the model in terms of its strengths and weaknesses.
Memory in everyday life	In this part of the specification, you are asked to look at the importance of memory in everyday life. Memory is important in many aspects of life, but two areas are specified here and so you must study both of them.
Eyewitness testimony (EWT) and factors affecting the accuracy of EWT, including anxiety, age of witness.	■ Research has shown that many factors can affect the accuracy of **eyewitness testimony** (EWT) – memory for significant events such as road accidents or crimes. Only **two** factors, however, are specified in this subsection and you must study both of these: anxiety and age of witness. Other factors are also described in the chapter, but these are optional. To demonstrate an understanding of the factors affecting EWT you will need to be able to describe and evaluate research in this area.
Misleading information and the use of the Cognitive Interview.	■ **Misleading information** is an important factor that can adversely affect the accuracy of EWT. Research on its effects looks at what happens when a witness is asked a question that suggests wrongly that something has taken place. You need to be able to discuss such research. ■ The **Cognitive Interview** (CI) aims to improve the accuracy of witness recall. You need to be able to describe the CI, including its four techniques, and evaluate its effectiveness.
Strategies for memory improvement	■ Psychologists have proposed a number of **strategies for improving memory**, drawing on different theoretical perspectives, e.g. using hierarchies to organize material and the encoding specificity principle to recreate learning contexts. The specification requires you to know about **at least two** of these strategies, although no particular strategy is specified.

Introduction

Memory is studied within the branch of psychology known as cognitive psychology. This research field focuses on the mental processes that humans use to acquire, store, retrieve and use their knowledge about the world. Cognitive psychologists have investigated a wide range of topics, including perception, attention, language, problem solving and decision-making. In this chapter, we shall look at memory, which is central to all cognitive processes, because we use it whenever we need to maintain information over time.

In the first topic in the chapter, we will look at research that has investigated the processes involved in memory, including the concepts of encoding, capacity and duration. We will also discuss two important models of memory, i.e. two explanations of how memory works.

Psychologists are increasingly turning their attention to more everyday aspects of memory. In Topic 2, we will look at two such practical applications, namely research into eyewitness testimony and strategies for improving memory.

Topic 1: Models of memory

Your answers to the questions in 'Psychology in action' will have highlighted that we would all be virtually helpless without our memory. In fact, we take memory so much for granted that it can be hard to imagine the impact of its loss on our daily lives. The case of Clive Wearing, who suffers particularly profound amnesia, illustrates just how devastating memory loss can be. After contracting a viral infection called encephalitis, Clive Wearing, a highly educated and talented musician and broadcaster, was left with extensive brain damage, which has caused major memory disruption. He is still able to talk, read and write and can still sight-read music and play quite complex piano pieces. In all other respects, however, his memory is dramatically impaired. For example, he has no recollection of his wedding, pictured here (Baddeley 1997).

Psychologists have learned a great deal from the study of people who suffer from loss of memory (amnesia) after brain damage. Clive Wearing's case demonstrates that memory is crucial to our well-being and everyday functioning. It also demonstrates the enormous complexity of human memory. The fact that Clive continues to be able to talk, walk, play music, read and write, in spite of huge impairments in his memory for personal history and general knowledge suggests that memory is not a unitary system. Even more disturbing is his apparent inability to lay down new memories. Clive is convinced that he has only just woken up and keeps a diary in which he records this obsessive thought. There are pages of closely written text, in which he gives the date and time followed by the statement, 'I have just regained consciousness' or 'I'm conscious for the first time'. Whenever his wife visits, he greets her effusively as if he has not seen her for ages. If she leaves the room for a couple of minutes, the emotional greeting is repeated and this can happen time and time again. Years after the onset of the

Psychology in context

Fascinating memory

Do you recall the news item about the so-called 'piano man' who was found wandering on the beach on the Isle of Sheppey in 2005? For nearly four months he convinced many people that he was suffering from amnesia. The press gave him the name 'piano man' because of a rumour that he was a talented pianist – a rumour that seems to have had little foundation in fact. Eventually, it was revealed that he was not suffering from amnesia and he was repatriated to his home in Germany. Before this revelation, however, his apparent amnesia intrigued the public, the press and the medical profession.

We can see the fascination that exists about the effects of memory loss in some of the films that have explored this subject. You may have seen *The Bourne Trilogy*, *Mulholland Drive* or the critically acclaimed *Memento*. In this latter film, Leonard Shelby (played by Guy Pearce, shown in the photo) is suffering from short-term memory loss and is unable to recall any event or person he has met just minutes before. He is trying to find out who murdered his wife and left him brain damaged. Why does the idea of losing our memory fascinate and frighten people so much?

Imagine for a moment what would happen if you woke up one morning to find that you had completely lost your memory. To help you think about this, try to answer the following questions:

1 What do you normally do in a day that you would no longer be able to do because of your memory loss? Consider, for example, when you need to know your name, your age and where you live.

2 What would you be unable to do if you could not recognize your friends or members of your family?

3 How would you plan your day if you were not able to recall what you were thinking about just moments ago?

illness which caused Clive's memory loss, he is still trapped in an eternal present – he cannot use the past to anticipate the future. He is unable to enjoy books or television because he cannot follow the thread, and he does not read newspapers because he has no context within which to make sense of the news stories. He cannot go out alone because he immediately becomes lost and is unable to tell anyone who finds him where he is going or where he has come from. Clive himself has described his situation as 'Hell on earth. It's like being dead.'

Clive's case also raises a number of questions for cognitive psychologists. For example, why do you think that Clive cannot recall a visit from his wife just two minutes earlier? One possible explanation is that her visit never actually registered in his brain and so no memory trace was laid down. Another possibility is that the memory trace was laid down, but that it faded away very quickly. The third possibility is that the memory trace was laid down, still exists but now cannot be retrieved. The answer is not clear, but it is important to recognize that a normally functioning memory system must be capable of:

- registering/ acquiring (encoding) information
- storing (retaining) information over time
- retrieving (recovering) information when required.

Types of memory

The **multi-store model of memory** (Atkinson and Shiffrin 1968) is based on the assumption that there are three kinds of memory:

- **sensory memory**
- **short-term memory**
- **long-term memory**.

We will consider each of these in turn. It is important to note, however, that some memory researchers no longer accept this distinction. The multi-store model is outlined and evaluated later in the chapter.

Sensory memory

Sensory memory is a storage system that holds information in a relatively unprocessed form for fractions of a second after the physical stimulus is no longer available. Baddeley (1988) suggested that one function of this kind of storage is to allow information from successive eye-fixations to last for a long enough time to be integrated and so to give continuity to our visual environment. For example, if you watch a film, your conscious experience is of a continuous visual scene in which all of the action appears to be moving smoothly. In fact, the film is actually being presented as a rapid series of frozen images interspersed by fleeting moments of darkness. In order to make sense of it, your sensory store has to hold the information from one frame of film until the next is presented. Such everyday examples seem to suggest that we are capable of storing visual images for very brief periods. It is assumed that we have separate sensory stores for all the senses (including an echoic store for auditory information), but it is the visual sensory store (**iconic memory**) which has attracted most research.

Memory researchers, however, have focused their interest more on short-term and long-term memory.

When you watch a movie, which is a series of frozen images, your sensory store makes sense of it by holding the information from one frame of film until the next is presented

Short-term memory

Short-term memory (STM) is a system for storing information for brief periods of time. Some researchers (e.g. Atkinson and Shiffrin 1968) see STM simply as a temporary storage depot for incoming information, whereas others (e.g. Baddeley 1986) prefer to use the term '**working memory**' to indicate its dynamic, flexible aspects. We shall return to this difference of opinion later in this topic. For the moment, we will look at specific aspects related to the nature of STM:

- **capacity** – the amount of information that can be stored in STM at any one time
- **duration** – the length of time that information can be held in STM
- **encoding** – the way that sensory input is represented in STM (e.g. as images or sounds).

The capacity of short-term memory

Please try the activity on the right before you read any further.

You probably found problem (a) extremely easy, and that problem (b) was also possible. Problem (c), however, is likely to have posed much more of a challenge because it will have stretched the limits of your STM by requiring you to carry too much information at once. It can feel quite frustrating as you struggle to hold on to relevant bits of information while manipulating others.

This exercise indicates that STM has a limited capacity; that is, we can only hold a small number of items at any one time. One way of assessing how much your STM can hold – its capacity – is by finding out how many digits you can repeat in correct order immediately after hearing them. This is known as your **immediate digit span**. This technique, which has frequently been used in psychological studies of memory, usually involves reading out a list of random digits and requiring the participant to repeat them back in the correct order. The sequences usually begin with about three digits and steadily increase in length until it becomes impossible to recall them in serial order (i.e. the order in which they were presented). Over a number of trials, the sequence length at which the participant is correct 50 per cent of the time is defined as their digit span. Most people have a digit span of 'seven, plus or minus two' (Miller 1956). This has been called Miller's magic number seven. Miller claimed that this finding holds good for lists of digits, letters, words or larger 'chunks' of information. According to Miller, chunking occurs when we combine individual letters or numbers into a larger meaningful unit. For example, the digits 9 3 7 1 would represent four separate items to most people, but would form a single chunk for you if they happened to be your bank Personal Identification Number (PIN).

Factors affecting the capacity of STM

- *Influence of long-term memory* – There are some difficulties in using immediate digit span as a measure of STM capacity. One problem is that it is difficult to exclude the influence of long-term memory. For example, Bower and Winzenz (1969) found that digit strings that are repeated within a series of immediate memory span trials become progressively easier for participants to recall. This indicates that information stored in long-term memory (LTM) is helping to increase STM capacity temporarily.

- *Reading aloud* – If participants read the digits aloud before attempting to recall them, performance is better than when they simply read them without speaking (subvocally) to themselves.

Most people have a digit span of seven (plus or minus two), i.e. can remember a list of seven (±2) random digits

■ *Rhythmic grouping* – Performance also improves if the numbers are grouped together rhythmically. This is probably why we tend to divide up telephone numbers into rhythmic clusters rather than reciting the whole string of numbers.

■ *Pronunciation time* – Other researchers have found that pronunciation time may be a more important indicator of STM capacity than Miller's digit span. Schweikert and Boruff (1986) tested immediate span for a number of different types of stimulus, e.g. letters, colours, shapes and nonsense words. They found that people consistently remembered as many items as they were able to pronounce in approximately 1.5 to 2 seconds. Naveh-Benjamin and Ayres (1986) have tested immediate memory span for speakers of various world languages. They found, for example, that the digit span for native English speakers is considerably greater than for Arabic speakers. The only explanation for this finding is that Arabic numbers take longer to pronounce than English numbers. These results confirmed earlier findings in a classic experiment by Baddeley and colleagues (1975) – see key study below, 'Capacity of STM'.

The duration of short-term memory

However capacity is measured, it seems clear that STM is only able to hold a few items at any one time. It is also the case that, by its very nature, STM has a brief duration. STM is a temporary store and anything we need to remember for

Capacity of STM
RESEARCH METHODS

Study of word-length effect on immediate memory span by Baddeley *et al.* (1975)

Aim	To see if people could remember more short words than long words in a serial recall test and so demonstrate that pronunciation time, rather than the number of items to be recalled, determines the capacity of short-term memory.
Procedure	■ The reading speed of the participants was measured. ■ Participants were then presented with sets of five words on a screen. ■ The words were taken from one of two sets: a set of one-syllable words (e.g. harm, wit, sum) or a set of polysyllabic words (e.g. opportunity, aluminium, university). ■ Participants were asked to write down the five words in serial order immediately after presentation. They recalled several lists of both short and long words.
Findings	■ Participants could recall considerably more short words than long words. ■ They were able to recall as many words as they were able to articulate in about 2 seconds. ■ There was a strong positive correlation between reading speed and memory span.
Conclusion	Immediate memory span represents the number of items of whatever length that can be articulated in approximately 2 seconds.
Evaluation	■ It might simply be that short words are easier to recall than long words because they are more familiar to us. ■ Baddeley and colleagues responded to this criticism in later versions of the study and showed clearly the importance of pronunciation time over familiarity. ■ Miller had not been able to account for the findings of research which showed that immediate memory span depends on the nature of the stimulus, i.e. the kinds of words and the language in which they are spoken. This study can explain such findings.
FURTHER ANALYSIS	This was a laboratory experiment using lists of unconnected words and so did not reflect everyday use of STM. However, what might be lost in terms of realism is compensated for by the high levels of control that Baddeley enjoyed by using a laboratory experiment. In the laboratory he was able, for example, to present the words on a screen at exactly the same speed for each condition (i.e. short words and long words).

Duration of STM

Study of duration of STM by Peterson and Peterson (1959)

Aim	To test how long STM lasts when rehearsal is prevented.
Procedure	■ Participants (Ps) were briefly shown a consonant trigram (i.e. three letters such as CPW or NGV). ■ Participants were asked to count backwards in threes from a specified number to stop them rehearsing the letters. ■ After intervals of 3, 6, 9, 12, 15 or 18 seconds, participants were asked to recall the original trigram. ■ The procedure was repeated several times using different trigrams.
Findings	■ Participants were able to recall about 80 per cent of trigrams after a 3-second interval (see the graph on the right). ■ Progressively fewer trigrams were recalled as the time intervals lengthened. ■ After 18 seconds, fewer than 10 per cent of the trigrams were recalled correctly.
Conclusion	See the Research Methods activity below and provide your own conclusions for this study.
Evaluation	■ Trigrams are rather artificial things to remember and may not reflect everyday memory. ■ It is possible, however, that **interference** from the earlier trigrams (not merely **decay**) caused the poor recall. ■ Note that the experimental method used in this study allows us to see the (causal) effect of time passing (independent variable) on recall (dependent variable).

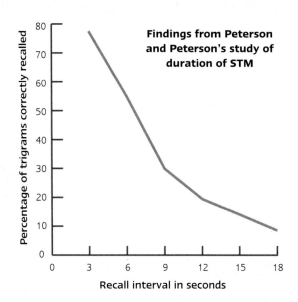

Findings from Peterson and Peterson's study of duration of STM

(Graph: y-axis "Percentage of trigrams correctly recalled" from 0 to 80; x-axis "Recall interval in seconds" at 0, 3, 6, 9, 12, 15, 18)

---

longer needs to be transferred to LTM. The first attempts to measure the duration of STM used an experimental method known as the Brown–Peterson technique. The key study, 'Duration of STM' (see above), explains how Peterson and Peterson (1959) used the technique in this experiment.

Factors affecting the duration of short-term memory

■ *Maintenance rehearsal* – The key point about findings based on the Brown–Peterson technique is that items disappear from STM only when rehearsal is prevented. New items can only take their place if existing items move on – either to LTM or because they are forgotten. If we want to remember something for a short period of time, we tend to repeat it to ourselves, as for example when we look up a number in the phone book and need to hold it in our memory for long enough to dial it accurately. This repetition serves as a method of continually reinserting the information into STM (i.e. maintaining it in STM) and thereby strengthening the memory. Without rehearsal, the duration of STM is very brief.

■ *Deliberate intention to recall* – Sebrechts and his colleagues (1989) briefly presented participants with lists of three common English nouns and then gave them an unexpected test where they had to recall the words in the correct order (this is called a 'serial recall test'). Correct recall of the items fell to 1 per cent after only 4 seconds. Studies such as these demonstrate that information can vanish from STM in a matter of a few seconds if people do not make a conscious effort to retain it.

Activity **Difference between findings and conclusions in research studies**

The findings (often called the results) of a study are what the researchers find out. In Peterson and Peterson's experiment, the finding was how the independent variable affected the dependent variable – in other words, that fewer trigrams were correctly recalled as the interval between learning and recall increased. However, to reach a conclusion about this finding you need to interpret it. Try to do this yourself before reading any further and before looking at p. 275 where some suggestions are provided.

1 What does this finding tell us about the duration of STM?

2 What does this tell you about how information is maintained in STM?

3 What does this tell you about how (the mechanism by which) information is often quickly lost from STM?

Answers are given on p. 275 ▶

A stimulus input can be encoded visually as a word or picture (top left), acoustically (top right) or semantically (left). Can you work out how you process stimuli?

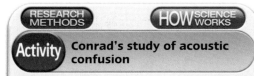

Activity Conrad's study of acoustic confusion

Reread the description of the study of acoustic confusion (Conrad 1964). When you are confident that you understand what Conrad did and what the findings were, try to answer the following questions:

1 Why do you think that Conrad used the experimental method to test the theory that people use acoustic encoding in STM?

2 Identify the independent and the dependent variables in Conrad's study.

3 At the beginning of a research study, investigators make a prediction about what they expect the findings of their study to be. What prediction do you think Conrad was testing? This prediction is called a hypothesis and is expressed as a statement, not a question (see Chapter 2 for more information about hypotheses).

4 Note down one important criticism of this study that limits the usefulness of the findings.

Answers are given on p. 275 ▶

■ *Amount of information to be retained* – Murdock (1961) presented participants with either a single three-letter word such as CAT or three unrelated words like HAT, PEN, LID. He then followed the same procedure as in the Brown–Peterson technique. **Forgetting** for the three unrelated words was the same as for the consonant trigrams in the Peterson and Peterson study. However, the single, three-letter word (which could be processed as one chunk) was remarkably resistant to forgetting, and accurate recall level was still at 90 per cent after 18 seconds. This shows that, as in Miller's digit span, the important factor is the number of chunks to be remembered rather than the number of individual items, i.e. letters.

Encoding in short-term memory

When information arrives at the sensory registration stage, it is still in its raw form or original modality. For example, information presented visually is still in the visual modality. Psychologists have been interested in the question of what happens to such information when it reaches the STM. Does it stay in its original modality or is it re-coded in some way?

There are various ways in which we can encode stimulus inputs. Imagine looking at the word 'glove'. This could be stored as a visual representation so that you form a visual image of either the printed word itself or a pictorial image of an actual glove. You could form an acoustic representation by saying the written word aloud or under your breath – this has the effect of converting the written word into a verbal or speech code. Alternatively, you could form a semantic representation, which depends on your knowledge about the meaning of the word. You might, for example, think about the circumstances in which you need to wear gloves or a specific pair of gloves that you own (as in the illustration on the left).

It is not possible simply to ask people what codes they are using because memory processes are often unconscious. Much of the evidence about coding comes from studies into so-called substitution errors. These occur when people confuse one item for another. If, for example, they confuse letters, which sound alike, it indicates that acoustic coding is being used. If, however, letters that look similar are confused, it indicates that visual coding is being used.

Conrad's (1964) study on acoustic confusion looked at whether people use acoustic coding in STM even when the information is presented visually. Participants were shown a random sequence of six consonants projected in rapid succession onto a screen. The strings of consonants were either acoustically similar (e.g. P, C, V, T, B, D) or acoustically dissimilar (e.g. L, Z, F, X, H, W). Participants wrote down the letters in the same order as they had appeared. The letters were presented too rapidly for the participants to keep up and so they had to rely on memory. Conrad noted that most of the errors made involved the substitution of a similar sounding letter (e.g. 'B' for 'D' or 'S' for 'X'). Participants found that it was more difficult to recall strings of acoustically similar letters in the correct order than acoustically dissimilar letters, even though they were presented visually. Conrad concluded that items are stored in STM in some form of acoustic code. Other studies, however, have shown that acoustic coding is not exclusively used in STM. When steps are taken to prevent acoustic coding, visual coding may be substituted (see the study by Brandimonte *et al.* (1992) on pp. 85–6).

Now try the Research Methods activity on the left.

Factors affecting encoding in short term memory

- *The sound of words* – Conrad's (1964) study suggested that STM relies heavily on acoustic coding. Other researchers thought that the type of stimulus to be remembered might affect the way it was encoded. Baddeley (1966), for example, wondered whether Conrad's results were dependent on using consonants as his stimulus material. After all, they tend to be more similar in sound than in any other characteristic, such as visual form or meaning. Baddeley set about testing this idea by presenting participants with words rather than consonants and comparing the effect of acoustic similarity with similarity of meaning (semantic similarity) – see the key study below 'Encoding in STM'.

- *Other ways of encoding* – it seems likely that acoustic coding is the preferred method of encoding in STM, but there are several studies, which show that other modes of representation are also possible.

An interesting study by Brandimonte and her colleagues (1992) demonstrates not only that visual coding can be used in STM, but that, under certain circumstances, it is a superior method. Participants were presented with six line drawings of familiar objects like the ones shown in Figure 3.1 and asked to memorize them in order.

Participants were then asked to form a mental image of each one in turn and to subtract a specified part of the drawing as shown. They were then asked to name

> **HOW** SCIENCE WORKS
>
> The experimental investigation of encoding in STM illustrates how scientific explanations can change over time. On the basis of Baddeley's evidence, which has been reproduced many times, it is tempting to conclude that acoustic encoding is always preferred in STM. However, the more recent evidence from Brandimonte's experiment shows that in different circumstances visual encoding is preferable. We are reminded that scientific knowledge is tentative in nature and may change in the light of new scientific evidence.

Figure 3.1 Sample of the line drawings used by Brandimonte and colleagues

Encoding in STM
A study by Baddeley (1966)

RESEARCH METHODS

Aim	To explore the effects of acoustic and semantic encoding in STM
Procedure	Participants were divided into four groups. Each group heard a list of five words drawn from one of the following categories: ■ acoustically similar words (e.g. man, mad, map) ■ acoustically dissimilar words (e.g. pen, day, few) ■ semantically similar words (e.g. great, big, large) ■ semantically dissimilar words (e.g. hot, old, late). Immediately after hearing the five words, they were asked to recall them in the correct order. The procedure was carried out four times.
Findings	■ Acoustically similar words were much harder to recall in the correct order (only 55 per cent accuracy) than words with dissimilar sounds (about 75 per cent accuracy). ■ Similarity of meaning had only a very slight detrimental effect ■ The effects of sound similarity disappeared when he tested participants' long-term learning (see the key study, 'Encoding in LTM' on p. 88). This suggests that a major factor affecting encoding is whether the items are being stored in STM or LTM.
Conclusion	These findings support those of Conrad: STM relies more on the sound of words than on their meaning, as shown by the difficulty participants had in recalling the correct order of words that sounded similar.
Evaluation	■ The use of the experimental method allows a causal link to be drawn between type of coding used in STM and the accuracy of recall. ■ However, the conclusion of this study might not reflect the complexity of encoding. Evidence from other studies has shown that, in certain circumstances, STM may use other forms of encoding (see the study by Brandimonte *et al.* (1992) described above).

the resulting image; for example, the left-hand image is a wrapped sweet, but it becomes a fish when the right-hand section of the image is removed. Participants were able to name on average 2.7 of the six items.

Another group of participants was given the same tasks to do except that they were prevented from articulating during the learning stage. While they were being shown the original pictures, they were asked to repeat the meaningless chant 'la-la-la-…'. This prevented them from converting the pictorial image into a verbal code, as they would have done under normal circumstances. They were actually more successful when it came to identifying the subtracted image and were able to name 3.8 items correctly. Because they were using visual coding, they found it easier to subtract a part from the visual image than the first group of participants who had coded the original stimulus in verbal form.

This study shows that the nature of the task may affect the type of coding used. If prevented from using acoustic coding, visual coding may be substituted. There is also some evidence that items in STM can be coded in terms of their meaning. So it seems reasonable to conclude that acoustic coding is generally the preferred, rather than the exclusive, method of representation.

Long-term memory

Long-term memory (LTM) holds a vast quantity of information that can be stored for long periods of time. The information kept here is diverse and wide-ranging and includes all of our personal memories, our general knowledge and our beliefs about the world. It also includes plans for the future and is where all our knowledge about skills and expertise is deposited. It seems likely that LTM is not a single store, but a number of different systems with slightly different functions. LTM is not a passive store of information, but a dynamic system that constantly revises and modifies stored knowledge in the light of new information. LTM is a much larger, more complex memory system than STM and it differs from STM in terms of its capacity, duration and encoding. The specific aspects of LTM that we will look at here are:

- **capacity** – the amount of information that can be stored in LTM at any one time
- **duration** – the length of time that information can be held in LTM
- **encoding** – the way that memories are represented in LTM (e.g. as images or sounds or meaning).

Capacity of long-term memory

It is not possible to quantify the exact capacity of LTM, but most psychologists would agree that there is no upper limit – we are always capable of more learning. The huge capacity of LTM requires a highly organized structure, otherwise items would be difficult to retrieve. Many researchers have suggested that LTM is divided into a number of different memory systems. This would explain why Clive Wearing (the case described on pp. 79–80) can remember some things from his LTM but not others.

Duration of long-term memory

The duration of the memory trace in LTM is considerably longer than in STM and can last almost a whole lifetime. Bahrick and colleagues (1975) suggested the term 'permastore' to refer to memory held for a very long time – see the key study, 'Duration of LTM' on the opposite page).

Duration of LTM
A study by Bahrick *et al.* (1975)

Aim	To establish the existence of very long-term memory (VLTM) and to see whether there was any difference between recognition and recall.
Procedure	■ Investigators tracked down the graduates from a particular high school in America over a 50-year period. ■ 392 graduates were shown photographs from their high-school yearbook. ■ Recognition group: for each photo, participants were given a group of names and asked to select the name that matched the person in the photo. ■ Recall group: participants were simply asked to name the people in the photos without being given a list of possible names.
Findings	■ In the name-matching (recognition) condition, participants were: 　– 90 per cent correct even 14 years after graduation 　– 80 per cent accurate after 25 years 　– 75 per cent accurate after 34 years 　– 60 per cent accurate after 47 years. ■ In the recall group, who had to identify the photos without any name cues, participants were not quite as successful. They were: 　– 60 per cent accurate after 7 years 　– less than 20 per cent accurate after 47 years.
Conclusion	■ People can remember certain types of information for almost a lifetime. ■ Very long-term memory appears to be better when measured by recognition tests than by recall tests.
Evaluation	■ Unlike many memory experiments, this study used meaningful stimulus material (high-school yearbooks) and tested people for memories from their own lives. ■ It is unclear whether the drop-off in accuracy after 47 years reflects the limits of duration or a more general decline in memory with age.

Factors affecting the duration of long-term memory

■ *Childhood amnesia* – Try to jot down some of your earliest memories. You will probably find that you have some quite vivid memories, but it is unlikely that you can accurately remember many events from before your third birthday. If you can, it is likely to be because you have been told about these events by your family or have seen them recorded in photos. The most likely explanation for this so-called childhood amnesia is that very young children are incapable of laying down well-organized and integrated memories and so they are not available for later recall.

■ *How duration is measured* – Another factor that seems to be important when measuring the duration of LTM is the method used to tap into memory. As you can see from the study by Bahrick and colleagues, people are much better at remembering information from long ago if they are tested by recognition rather than by free recall.

■ *Thorough learning* – It also seems that people are more likely to hold material in permastore if they learned it very well in the first place and if they continued to learn about related material in the interval. Bahrick and Hall (1991) tested long-term memory (LTM) for algebra and geometry. They found that people who had only taken maths up to high-school level showed a steady decline in the accuracy of their recall over the years, whereas students who had taken

Activity **Natural experiments**

In a natural experiment (or quasi-experiment), the researcher:

■ does not control the independent variable (IV) or assign participants to conditions

■ uses naturally occurring differences in the IV.

1 What naturally occurring difference did Bahrick *et al.* (1975) use as the IV in their natural experiment?

2 In what way does the use of a natural experiment limit the conclusions that Bahrick and colleagues can draw from their study?

Answers are given on p. 275 ▶

Encoding in LTM
A study by Baddeley (1966)

Aim	To explore the effects of acoustic and semantic coding in LTM.
Procedure	Participants were divided into four groups and shown a list of ten words drawn from one of the following categories: ■ acoustically similar words (e.g. man, mad, map) ■ acoustically dissimilar words (e.g. pen, day, few) ■ semantically similar words (e.g. great, big, large) ■ semantically dissimilar words (e.g. hot, old, late). After an interval of 20 minutes, during which they were given another task to do, participants were asked to recall, in correct order, the ten words they had heard. This procedure was carried out four times.
Findings	■ Recall was much worse for semantically similar words (55 per cent accuracy) than for semantically dissimilar words (85 per cent accuracy). ■ Recall was the same for acoustically similar and acoustically dissimilar words.
Conclusion	LTM primarily makes use of semantic coding, as shown by the difficulties participants had in recalling the correct order of words that had similar meanings. (Note that these findings and conclusions contrasted with those where STM was being investigated. STM uses acoustic encoding – see p. 84.)
Evaluation	The use of the experimental method allows a causal link to be drawn between the type of coding used in LTM and the accuracy of recall.
FURTHER ANALYSIS	In this study, only LTM for words (semantic memory) was tested. Other types of LTM, such as memory for past events (episodic memory) or how to ride a bike (procedural memory), might use different types of encoding.

a higher maths course at college showed remarkably high levels of accuracy as much as 55 years later.

Encoding in long-term memory

As far as coding is concerned, there is some evidence that the meaning of the stimulus is often the main factor here. In other words, semantic coding is important (see key study above, 'Encoding in LTM').

Factors affecting encoding in long-term memory

It is clear from our own experience that material can be represented in other ways as well. It seems that the type of stimulus material can affect the way we encode in LTM.

■ *Acoustic encoding* – our ability to recognize sounds, such as police sirens and telephones ringing, shows that we can store material in an acoustic form.

■ *Visual encoding* – we can also easily bring to mind pictorial images of people or places that suggest some visual coding in LTM.

Now, try the activity on the left, which asks you to summarize the features of STM and LTM. By doing this you will be able to see the main differences between the two memory stores.

Activity **Differences between STM and LTM**

As you will have noticed, there are differences in capacity, duration and encoding between STM and LTM. Draw a chart based on the one shown below and use it to list the characteristics that distinguish STM from LTM.

	Capacity	Duration	Encoding
STM			
LTM			

Answers are given on p. 275 ▶

Models of memory

A model of memory is a way of representing or explaining how the process of memory works.

Multi-store model (Atkinson and Shiffrin 1968)

A number of memory theorists have proposed that the memory system is divided into three stores as outlined in the previous section. Atkinson and Shiffrin (1968) proposed a multi-store model of this type.

Key features of the multi-store model

- The model arose from the information processing approach where memory is characterized as a flow of information through a system. The system is divided into a set of stages and information passes through each stage in a fixed sequence (see Figure 3.2 below).

- There are capacity and duration limitations at each stage.

- Transfer of information between stages may require re-coding.

- External stimuli from the environment first enter sensory memory, where they can be registered for very brief periods of time before **decaying** (i.e. fading away) or (if given attention) being passed on to the short-term store.

- STM contains only the small amount of information that is actually in active use at any one time. Information is usually encoded acoustically at this stage.

- Memory traces in STM are fragile and can be lost within about 30 seconds, through **displacement** or decay, unless they are repeated (rehearsed).

- Material that is rehearsed is passed on to the long-term store where it can remain for a lifetime, although loss is possible from this store through decay, **retrieval failure** or **interference**.

- Coding in LTM is assumed to be in terms of meaning, i.e. semantic.

In summary, Atkinson and Shiffrin described the structural features (memory stores) of the memory system, and various control processes (strategies) used by individuals to manipulate the information flowing through the system. The most important of the control processes is rehearsal which allows information both to be recycled within STM and also passed into LTM.

Eye on the exam

Outline the key features of the multi-store model of memory.   (6 marks)

This is a straightforward question that asks you to demonstrate your knowledge about the multi-store model. Remember ,this question requires only AO1 skills and you are expected, therefore, to demonstrate your knowledge and understanding. You are not required to provide any analysis or evaluation of the model.

You must also remember that a model is an explanation or theory. It is not a study.

Take care to provide a balanced answer. If, for example, you spend too much time describing (rather than briefly outlining) the memory stores, you will not have enough time to do justice to the other aspects of the model.

Your answer should include a short account of:

- the three separate stores (sensory, short-term and long-term) and their main characteristics in terms of encoding, capacity and duration

- the processes used to transfer information from one store to another (attention to pass information on from the sensory store, and rehearsal to pass information from STM to LTM). Recoding may also be needed between one store and the next

- why information may be lost from each store (through decay from sensory, through decay and displacement from STM and through interference and retrieval failure from LTM).

For more exam advice, visit **www.collinseducation.com/psychologyweb**

Figure 3.2 Summary of the Atkinson and Shiffrin (1968) model of memory

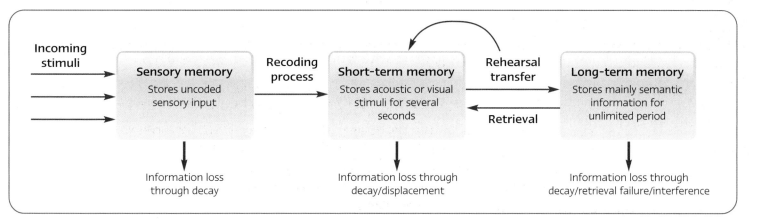

Brain damage and memory
A study by Milner (1965)

Using case study research (see Chapter 1, pp. 31–2), Milner (1966) studied a young man referred to as H.M. who was left with severe memory impairment after brain surgery. He was able to talk normally and to recall accurately events and people from his life before the surgery, and his immediate digit span was within normal limits. He was, however, unable to retain any new information and could not lay down new memories in LTM. When told of the death of his favourite uncle, he reacted with considerable distress. Later, he frequently asked about his uncle and, on each occasion, reacted again with a level of grief appropriate to hearing the news for the first time. Cases such as this and that of Clive Wearing (see p. 79) lend support to the multi-store model by pointing to a clear distinction between LTM and STM.

Strengths of the multi-store model

- A crucial aspect of the multi-store model is that it distinguishes between short-term and long-term stores in terms of capacity, duration and encoding. Evidence in support of the distinction between STM and LTM comes from case studies of people with brain damage that has given rise to memory impairment (see the Case study on the left).

- Further evidence for the existence of separate stores comes from laboratory experiments that have investigated primacy and recency effects. These are demonstrated, for example, when people are presented with a list of about 20 words, one at a time, and then immediately asked to recall the words in any order. The words at the beginning of the list are easily recalled. This is called the primacy effect. Words at the end of the list are also well remembered. This is called the recency effect. Glanzer and Cunitz (1966) conducted an experiment that investigated what would happen when they delayed recall.

Read the key study below, 'Evidence in support of the multi-store model', and then try the activity at the top of the opposite page.

Evidence in support of the multi-store model
A laboratory experiment by Glanzer and Cunitz (1966)

Aim	To see if they could find evidence for the existence of separate short-term and long-term memory stores
Procedure	Participants were presented with a list of words, one at a time, and then asked to recall the words in any order (free recall). Participants were divided into two groups: ■ Immediate recall group: participants participants recalled the words immediately after they had been presented. ■ Delayed recall group: participants counted backwards for 30 seconds before they recalled the words.
Findings	■ The immediate recall group remembered the first and last words best. ■ The delayed recall group remembered the words from the beginning of the list best. ■ Both groups had difficulty in recalling the words in the middle of the list.
Conclusion	■ Both groups easily remembered words from the beginning of the list because they were already stored in LTM. Words at the end of the list, however, were still in STM. When recall was delayed by a distraction task, such as counting backwards, participants were unable to rehearse the words in STM and consequently they were not maintained in STM or passed into LTM and so were forgotten. ■ These findings support the concept of separate memory stores by showing that delayed recall interfered with STM store and caused the recency effect to disappear but had no effect on LTM store and left the primacy effect almost unaltered.
Evaluation	Other researchers have interpreted these findings differently. Crowder (1993), for example, proposed that recency effects occur because the most recent items are the most distinctive, not because they are held in a separate STM store.

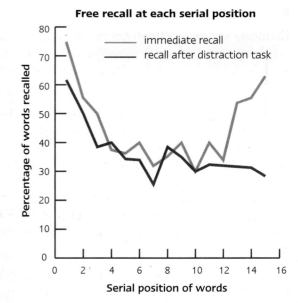

Free recall at each serial position

immediate recall
recall after distraction task

Percentage of words recalled / Serial position of words

Weaknesses of the multi-store model

- Although the multi-store model has stimulated considerable research, it is too simplistic and inflexible to explain the entire memory system. It fails to take account of factors such as the strategies people employ to remember things. It also places emphasis on the amount of information that can be processed rather than its nature. Some things are simply easier to remember than others, perhaps because they are more interesting, more distinctive, funnier, etc. The multi-store model cannot account for this.

- The multi-store model is also criticized for focusing on the structure of the memory system at the expense of adequately explaining the processes involved. For example, visual stimuli registering in sensory memory must be changed to an acoustic code for access to STM. However, in order to translate the pattern of the letter 'M' into the sound 'em', the individual needs to access knowledge about letter shapes and sounds which is stored in LTM. This means that information from LTM must flow backwards through the system to the re-coding stage prior to STM. This suggests that the flow of information through the system is interactive rather than strictly sequential as Atkinson and Shiffrin (1968) suggested. Now try the activity on the right, 'The interactive flow of information between STM and LTM'.

- The suggestion that rote rehearsal is the only means of transfer from STM into LTM has also been criticized. Rehearsal may be important for storing some information in LTM but people acquire new knowledge continually without using conscious rehearsal.

- The working memory model of memory casts doubt on the assumption of Atkinson and Shiffrin that STM is a single (unitary) store with a severely limited capacity – see the next section.

The working memory model (Baddeley and Hitch 1974)

The working memory model replaces the concept of a unitary STM. It proposes a multi-component, flexible system concerned with active processing and short-term storage of information.

Baddeley and Hitch (1974) conducted a dual-task study in which participants were given digit strings to rehearse while, at the same time, carrying out verbal reasoning tasks similar to those in the activity on the right ('Verbal reasoning task'). Try the activity now.

Imagine trying to do these reasoning tasks while simultaneously rehearsing a string of digits – you probably think that this would be very difficult if not impossible. However, the participants in the study were able to recall six-digit strings and perform accurately on the reasoning task. This finding is not compatible with Atkinson and Shiffrin's view of a short-term store with approximately seven slots. Instead, it suggests that STM, or working memory as Baddeley and Hitch prefer to call it, consists of several different components that can work independently of one another and so handle more than one task at a time.

Baddeley and Hitch concluded on the basis of this and other studies that STM is a flexible and complex system that consists of a central control mechanism assisted by a number of subsidiary (or 'slave') systems. The model has been modified slightly in the light of experimental studies and is shown in simple form in Figure 3.3.

Answers are given on p. 275

Activity — Evidence in support of the multi-store model

Read the key study on the opposite page and then answer the following questions

1 Identify the independent variable in the experiment by Glanzer and Cunitz (1966).
2 Identify the dependent variable in the same study.
3 What is the main difference between the recall performances of the two groups?

Activity — The interactive flow of information between STM and LTM

1 Why do you think it is that keen football fans can more accurately recall match scores from STM than those who are not fans (Morris et al. 1985)?
2 Note any other similar examples you can think of that can be explained in the same way.

Activity — Verbal reasoning task

Read the following list of ten short statements and decide for each one, as quickly and as accurately as you can, whether it is true or false.

1	B is followed by A	BA
2	A does not follow B	BA
3	A is not preceded by B	BA
4	A is not followed by B	BA
5	B follows A	AB
6	B is preceded by A	BA
7	A does not precede B	BA
8	B is not preceded by A	BA
9	B is followed by A	AB
10	A follows B	AB

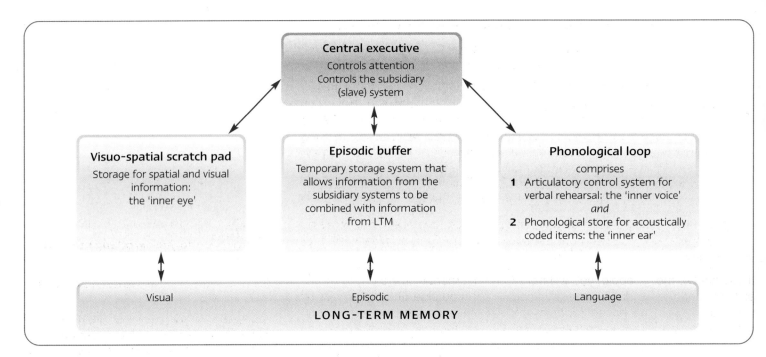

Figure 3.3 The multi-component model of working memory (from Baddeley 2000)

Key features of the working memory model

1 The **central executive** is the most important component in the model and is involved in problem solving and decision-making. Its features include:

- It controls attention and plays a major role in planning and synthesizing information, not only from the subsidiary systems but also from LTM.

- It is flexible and can process information from any modality.

- It has a limited storage capacity and so can attend to a limited number of things at one time.

2 The **phonological loop** stores a limited number of speech-based sounds for brief periods. It is thought to consist of two components:

- The *phonological store* (inner ear) allows acoustically coded items to be stored for a brief period.

- The *articulatory control process* (the inner voice) allows subvocal repetition of the items stored in the phonological store. Repetition can be prevented by a technique known as 'articulatory suppression'. This involves having a research participant repeat aloud a sound that is irrelevant to the memory task (such as 'the the the') in order to prevent the phonological loop from retaining any further information.

3 The **visuo-spatial scratch pad** stores visual and spatial information and can be thought of as an inner eye.

- It is responsible for setting up and manipulating mental images.

- Like the phonological loop, it has limited capacity but the limits of the two systems are independent. In other words, it is possible, for example, to rehearse a set of digits in the phonological loop while simultaneously making decisions about the spatial layout of a set of letters in the visuo-spatial scratchpad.

4 More recently, Baddeley (2000) proposed an additional component to the working memory model – the **episodic buffer** – that integrates and manipulates material in working memory. Its features include the following:

- It has limited capacity, depending heavily on executive processing.

- It is capable of integrating (binding together) information from different sources into chunks or episodes, hence the term 'episodic'.

- One of its important functions is to integrate material from LTM to meet the requirements of working memory. Baddeley offers a humorous example to illustrate this. Imagine an elephant playing ice hockey. Bizarre as this image may be, we can easily conjure it up by using our existing knowledge (from LTM) about elephants and about ice hockey and integrate and manipulate these to create a novel scenario. The episodic buffer, in other words, allows us to go beyond what is already in LTM and combine it in different ways when working memory requires it.

Baddeley (1997) suggested that you can get a good idea about how working memory operates by carrying out the activity on the right, so please try it for yourself now.

If you are like most people, you will have formed a mental image of your home and counted the windows either by imagining the outside of the house or by walking through the house room by room. The image will be set up and manipulated in your visuo-spatial scratch pad and the tally of windows will be held in the phonological loop as you count them subvocally. The whole operation will be supervised by the central executive, which will allocate the tasks and recognize when the final total has been reached.

Strengths of the working memory model

- The working memory model appears to have a number of advantages over the concept of STM as outlined in the multi-store model. It effectively explains our ability to carry out tasks such as mental arithmetic by storing information briefly, while at the same time actively processing it.

- *Evidence supporting the phonological loop* – There is a considerable body of empirical research that seems to support the existence of the phonological loop slave system. For example, Baddeley *et al.* (1975) conducted a series of studies that investigated the word-length effect (see the key study on p. 82). However, when participants were prevented from rehearsing the words subvocally by being asked to repeat an irrelevant sound such as 'la-la-la …' (articulatory suppression – as shown in Brandimonte's study – see p. 85), the word-length effect disappeared (i.e. short words were not recalled any better than long words). It is assumed that the articulatory suppression task fills the phonological loop and, therefore, removes the advantage of rehearsal. However, since some words could be recalled, it is likely that the central executive takes over the recall task.

- *Evidence supporting the visuo-spatial scratch pad* – The visuo-spatial store has not been investigated in the same depth as the phonological store, but there is experimental evidence that supports its existence. For example, Baddeley *et al.* (1973) gave participants a simple tracking task that involved holding a pointer in contact with a moving spot of light. At the same time, participants were asked to perform an imagery task. Participants were required to imagine the block capital letter 'F' and then, starting at the bottom, left-hand corner, were to classify each angle as a 'yes' if it included the bottom or top line of the letter and as a 'no' if it did not. Participants found it very difficult both to track the spot of light and to classify accurately the angles in the letter imagery task. However, they were perfectly capable of carrying out the tracking task in conjunction with a verbal task. This suggests that the tracking and letter imagery tasks were competing for the limited resources of the visuo-spatial scratchpad, whereas the tracking task and the verbal task

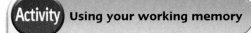

Activity Using your working memory

Try to work out how many windows there are in your home.

When you have completed this task, make a note of how you did it and then discuss your answer with someone else in your class. Did you use similar strategies?

were making use of the separate components of the visuo-spatial scratchpad and the phonological loop respectively.

- The working memory model has been influential and is still being developed and expanded (as illustrated by the recent addition of the episodic buffer).

Weaknesses of the working memory model

- The main weakness is that the component we know least about (the central executive) is the most important. It has a limited capacity, but no one has been able to quantify it experimentally.

- Richardson (1984) argues that there are problems in specifying the precise functioning of the central executive. He believes that the terminology is vague and can be used to explain any kind of results. In other words, it can give rise to a circular argument. For example, if we give participants an articulatory suppression task and this affects performance, we assume the phonological loop is normally utilized in the task, but if performance is not affected, we assume the central executive is normally utilized in the task, rather than the phonological loop. Therefore, it is difficult to falsify the model. Some recent studies, however, have provided more information on the role of the central executive. See the key study below, 'Working memory in chess'.

Working memory in chess
A study by Robbins *et al.* (1996)

 RESEARCH METHODS

Aim	To study the role of the central executive in remembering chess positions by investigating the effect of generating random letter strings.
Procedure	Twenty chess players were asked to memorize in 10 seconds the positions of 16 chess pieces from a real game. The procedure was repeated 20 times using a different game each time. While memorizing the positions, participants either: ■ simultaneously engaged the central executive by generating random letter sequences, concentrating to avoid any meaningful combinations (such as H, G, V), or ■ simultaneously, carried out an articulatory suppression task (saying 'the, the, the' in time with a metronome) After 10 seconds, the participants' memory was tested by asking them to arrange chess pieces on another board to match those they had just seen.
Findings	■ Participants in the articulatory suppression condition performed well in recalling the positions of the chess pieces. ■ Participants in the letter generation condition performed poorly.
Conclusion	■ The impaired performance of those generating the letter sequences demonstrated that the central executive played a role in remembering chess positions. ■ The good performance of participants in the articulatory suppression condition indicated that the phonological loop was not involved in remembering the chess positions.
Evaluation	■ This well-designed study enables us to conclude that the different tasks (articulatory suppression and letter sequence generation) did cause the difference in performance. ■ Generating meaningless letter sequences has been claimed by many cognitive psychologists as a valid way of engaging the central executive, as it requires considerable attention.
FURTHER ANALYSIS	In another condition of this experiment, participants' visuo-spatial scratchpad was suppressed by requiring them to press keys systematically on a calculator while they were memorizing the chess positions. This resulted in the participants performing as poorly in the memory test as those who had experienced a suppressed central executive. Therefore, Robbins and colleagues concluded that both the central executive and the visuo-spatial scratchpad are involved in recalling chess positions.

CHECK YOUR UNDERSTANDING

Check your understanding of models of memory by answering these questions. Try to do this from memory first. You can check your answers by looking back through Topic 1.

1 What is meant by the terms encoding, capacity and duration?

2 What type of encoding is preferred in STM?

3 What is the capacity of STM?

4 What is the duration of STM?

5 What type of encoding is preferred in LTM?

6 Outline the findings from one study of duration in LTM.

7 Outline two key features of the multi-store model of memory.

8 How might information be lost from LTM.

9 Outline one strength of the multi-store model.

10 Outline one weakness of the multi-store model.

11 Outline the three key components of the working memory model.

12 What is the main difference between working memory and the concept of STM as described in the multi-store model?

13 Name the 4th component of working memory that integrates material from LTM to meet the requirements of working memory.

14 Outline one strength of the working memory model.

15 Outline one weakness of the working memory model.

Topic 2: Memory in everyday life

Psychology in context

PQRST method for improving memory

One way in which research on human memory has been successfully applied in everyday life is in advising students on how to make best use of their textbooks to help them with their studies. This advice may be given as part of a 'Self-help guide to study' or be tailored for a particular textbook. By following the advice offered by psychologists, a student should avoid feeling overwhelmed and frightened by a new textbook that contains lots of new material to be learned.

One of the most popular techniques is called the PQRST method , which is based on three principles for improving memory:

● organize material
● elaborate material
● practise retrieval.

The name of the technique derives from the first letters of its five stages. We will illustrate how this would work when you want to get to grips with a new chapter in a textbook.

(Adapted from Smith *et al.* 2002)

P **Preview the chapter** – Skim read the introduction; pay particular attention to chapter headings and subheadings; look at the chapter summary. In this way you are beginning to organize the material by gaining an overview of the topics covered.

Q **Question** – Turn the first section heading into a question, e.g. 'What is meant by short-term memory?' Do the same for each subheading. This process encourages you to elaborate material as you encode it. Then work through Steps R and S before moving on to the next section.

R **Read** – Read the section carefully so that you understand its meaning. You may want to mark some of the text but be careful not to overdo this. Try to answer the questions you posed in the previous step to trigger more elaboration.

S **Self-recitation** – Now it's time to recall the main ideas from the section that you have read. Recite in your own words and aloud if possible and check with the text that you are recalling information correctly. You will be able to spot any gaps in your knowledge and organize the material better.

T **Test** – Test and review the content of the whole chapter by practising retrieval. Check that you know the main facts and understand how the different topics link together. The best time to test yourself is shortly after you have completed reading the chapter, but it is also important to test yourself again after an interval that is well before your exam!

Activity **Memory for familiar things**

Without looking anything up, try to do the following:

1 Draw a picture of a 10p coin.

2 Which person is shown on the back of a new £5 note? And what words are written at the top of the front of a note of any denomination (i.e. £5, £10, £20 and £50)?

3 Draw a picture or write a brief description of the front cover of this textbook, including the three names printed there.

You may be surprised how difficult it is to remember exactly what a 10p coin looks like without having one in front of you. If you compare your drawing with a real coin, you will probably find a number of inaccuracies. In everyday life, you do not need to remember every detail, as long as you are able to recognize coins so that you can use them appropriately. Similarly, you may not have remembered that Elizabeth Fry is shown on the back of a £5 note or that the words 'Bank of England I promise to pay the bearer on demand the sum of 5 pounds' are written on the front. And even though you use this textbook regularly you may not be able to recall the detail of the front cover. In other words, there are many areas of everyday memory where we do not need exact recall. However, in certain instances, such as taking exams or giving testimony about a crime, accuracy is vitally important.

Factors affecting eyewitness testimony (EWT)

In 1978, Neisser criticized contemporary psychologists for concentrating almost exclusively on theoretical concepts and ignoring practical issues about memory. One exception to this was the work of Bartlett (1932), but his ideas had little influence at the time. Since Neisser's challenge there has been a growing interest in practical, applied aspects of memory in everyday life. One particular area of interest is **eyewitness testimony**, that is, the evidence given by a witness to a significant event such as a crime or serious accident. The evidence usually takes the form of personal identification or a verbal account of what happened. Such evidence is based on the memory of the eyewitness and, unfortunately, witness memory is not always accurate. Problems can occur at any point in the memory process: during acquisition (encoding), during storage or during retrieval (see Figure 3.4 below).

Figure 3.4 Stages of memory in eyewitness testimony

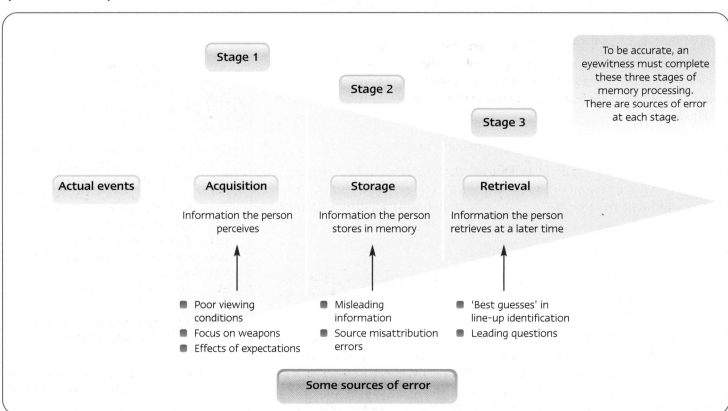

Inaccurate eyewitness testimony can have very serious consequences leading to wrongful convictions and, in some cases in the US, to the death penalty (Loftus and Ketcham 1991). For example, Rattner (1988) reviewed 205 cases of wrongful arrest and found that, in 52 per cent of cases, this was due to mistaken eyewitness testimony. It is not surprising, therefore, that psychologists have been interested in investigating some of the reasons why eyewitness testimony may be unreliable and some of the ways that accuracy might be improved. A number of different avenues of research have been pursued, including:

- the role of **anxiety**
- the role of **schemas**
- the age of the witness
- use of **leading questions**
- the consequences of the testimony
- how witnesses are tested
- the effects of **misleading information**
- use of the **Cognitive Interview**.

The role of anxiety

Jurors often place considerable importance on the evidence provided by eyewitnesses (i.e. on eyewitness memory). Baddeley (1997) has reported that 74 per cent of suspects were convicted in 300 cases where eyewitness identification was the only evidence against them. However, numerous research studies have identified several problems with eyewitness testimony, including anxiety experienced by witnesses at the time of the incident, that is, during the encoding (acquisition) stage of the memory process. One of the leading researchers in this field is Elizabeth Loftus.

When considering the reliability of eyewitness testimony, it is important to bear in mind the type of crime that is being recalled. Some crimes, such as those involving violence, are associated with high levels of **anxiety** in victims or bystanders. Whether such anxiety leads to unreliable remembering depends on a number of factors.

Research on the 'weapon focus' phenomenon

Loftus (1979) reported a laboratory study (see key study on the next page), which demonstrated the powerful role that anxiety can play in undermining the accuracy of eyewitness memory. After reading it, try the Research Methods activity on the right.

Research on witnessing real-life events

You might think that being a victim of a robbery would make you more anxious and so less reliable as a witness than someone who was merely a bystander. Evidence suggests otherwise.

Yuille and Cutshall (1986) provided evidence for the accuracy of testimony regarding real-life events. They interviewed 13 witnesses to a real-life shooting involving the owner of the store and an armed thief. The storeowner was wounded but recovered. The thief was shot dead. Some witnesses had seen the incident close to, while others were more distant. The interviews showed that:

What factors affect the quality of eyewitness testimony?

Activity Risks for participants?

Imagine that you were a participant in either the study where you saw the bloodstained paper knife or the study where you watched the violent film. Try to imagine how you might feel during and after the investigation. Now, try to answer the following questions:

1 What potential harm might participants suffer as a result of being a participant in either study?

2 How might any risks to participants be reduced?

3 Give some reasons why you think it was ethical or unethical to carry out these studies.

Look at p. 53 in Chapter 2 for a discussion of ethical issues in psychological research ▶

The role of anxiety in eyewitness testimony
A laboratory experiment by Loftus (1979)

Aim	To find out if anxiety during a witnessed incident affects the accuracy of later identification
Procedure	Participants were exposed to one of two situations: 1 They overheard a low-key discussion in a laboratory about an equipment failure. A person then emerged from the laboratory holding a pen and with grease on his hands. 2 They overheard a heated and hostile exchange between people in the laboratory. After the sound of breaking glass and crashing chairs, a man emerged from the laboratory holding a paper knife covered in blood. Participants were then given 50 photos and asked to identify the person who had come out of the laboratory.
Findings	1 Those who had witnessed the man holding the pen accurately identified the person 49 per cent of the time. 2 Those who had witnessed the man with the bloodstained paper knife were successful only 33 per cent of the time.
Conclusion	This finding has come to be known as the 'weapon focus' phenomenon, where the witness concentrates on the weapon (in this case, the bloodstained paper knife) and this distracts attention from the appearance of the perpetrator. Loftus concluded that the fear or anxiety induced by the sight of a weapon narrows the focus of attention and gives rise to very accurate recall of the central details of the scene, but less accurate recall of peripheral details.
Evaluation	Later research by Loftus and Burns (1982) has provided support for this finding. Participants watched either a violent or non-violent short film of a crime. Those who saw the violent version, in which a boy was shot in the face, were less accurate in recalling information about the crime. However, it is mainly laboratory studies that produce this result. They could be accused of lacking validity, as a rather different picture emerges if we look at field studies of real-life events (see below). This experiment raises ethical issues about the welfare of the participants who were deceived and who also may have been upset by witnessing a bloodstained paper knife.

- Witnesses gave impressively accurate accounts several months later.

- Those closest to the event provided the most detail.

- Misleading questions had no effect on accuracy.

- Those who had been most distressed at the time of the shooting proved the most accurate five months later – it appeared that the heightened arousal associated with anxiety enhanced the accuracy of EWT in this case.

Christianson and Hubinette (1993) questioned 110 witnesses who had, between them, witnessed a total of 22 genuine, as opposed to staged, bank robberies. Some of these witnesses had been onlookers who happened to be in the banks at the time, whereas others were bank employees who had been directly threatened in the robberies. The researchers found the following:

- Victims were more accurate in their recall and remembered more details about what the robbers wore, their behaviour and the weapon used than people who had been bystanders.

- This superior recall continued to be evident, even after a 15-month interval.

Christianson and Hubinette concluded that people (especially victims) are good at remembering highly stressful events if they occur in real life rather than in the artificial surroundings of the laboratory.

Now try the activity on the left which asks you to think about the Research Methods used by Christianson and Hubinette.

 Activity

RESEARCH METHODS

Christianson and Hubinette (1993)

1 What type of study did Christianson and Hubinette (1993) carry out?

2 What do you think is the main strength of their study?

3 Why is it sometimes important for researchers, such as Christianson and Hubinette, to study recall after a long period of time (e.g. after a 15-month interval), rather than just gather data over short periods of time only, as tends to be the case in much laboratory-based memory research?

Answers are given on p. 275 ▶

The role of schemas

Schemas are knowledge packages which are built up through experience of the world and which enable us to make sense of familiar situations and aid the interpretation of new information. Imagine, for example, that you are going for a meal in a restaurant. Through past experience you will already be familiar with the kinds of things you would expect to see in a restaurant (for example, tables, chairs, waiters, menus, other customers) – in other words, you will have a restaurant schema. This is sometimes called a 'script' if it includes knowledge of appropriate events or actions that should occur in a particular social setting.

In the 1970s, there was a revival of interest in the idea of schemas and their effects on memory. Cohen (1993) has suggested five ways in which schemas might lead to reconstructive memory:

1 We tend to ignore aspects of a scene that do not fit the currently activated schema.

2 We can store the central features of an event without having to store the exact details (e.g. the gist of a conversation rather than the exact words).

3 We can make sense of what we have seen by 'filling in' missing information (e.g. we see someone running and a bus pulling away from a bus stop and assume that the person was running for the bus).

4 We distort memories for events to fit in with prior expectations (e.g. we might 'remember' that a bank robber wore a stocking mask, whereas he had actually worn a cap).

5 We may use schemas to provide the basis for a correct guess (e.g. if we cannot recall exactly what we had for breakfast last Tuesday, our schema for weekday breakfast suggests 'cereal' and this has a good chance of being correct).

This means that schemas, which are usually useful to us because they help us direct our attention and make our experiences more predictable, may also lead to distortions in memory.

Research findings on the role of schemas

Brewer and Treyens (1981) investigated the effects of schemas on visual memory by asking their 30 participants, one at a time, to wait in a room for 35 seconds. The room was designed to look like an office and contained 61 objects. Some objects were compatible with an office schema, such as a desk, calendar, typewriter (this was 1981!), etc., but a few items were included which were incompatible, such as a skull, a brick, a pair of pliers, etc. In a subsequent, unexpected recall test, the findings showed the following:

- Participants were most likely to recall the typical office items, i.e. items with high schema expectancy, but were less successful at recalling the incompatible items such as the brick.

- Eight participants, however, recalled the really bizarre item – the skull (see the activity on the right).

- Most of the errors in recall were substitutions, i.e. participants tended to recall falsely the presence of objects, such as books, pens and a telephone, which would have high schema expectancy, but which were not actually present on this occasion.

A boy is running; a bus is pulling away – we use schemas to make sense of the situation: he was running for the bus

Activity **A skull in the office!**

1 Why do you think that some participants recalled seeing a skull in the office (Brewer and Treyens 1981)?

2 What implications does this finding have for schema theory?

Answers are given on p. 275 ▶

Other errors involved wrong placement of items, e.g. a note pad was 'remembered' as being on the desk (where it might be in an office schema), instead of being on the seat of a chair (as it was in reality).

These findings suggest that participants were using schemas to ensure rapid encoding of the visual information available to them during their 35-second wait. At the retrieval stage, the schema influenced recall so that typical items were recalled, even if they were not actually present. The Brewer and Treyens (1981) experiment showed that people can sometimes falsely remember objects that did not exist. To summarize, people tend to 'remember' what is consistent with their schemas and filter out what is inconsistent. List's (1986) shoplifting scenarios (see below) give another example of how schemas influence what is recalled.

Influence of schemas on recall
List's shoplifting scenarios (1986)

List asked people to rate various events in terms of their probability in a shoplifting scenario. She then compiled a video showing eight different shoplifting acts, each of which incorporated some of the events rated as high-probability and some rated as low-probability. She showed this video to a new set of people and, one week later, tested their recall. She found that they were more likely to recall high- rather than low-probability events and that, if they made inclusion errors of events that had not actually occurred in the video, they were more likely to be high-probability events.

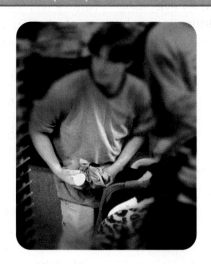

Activity: Based on a study by Bransford and Johnson (1972)

1 Read the following passage through once at your normal reading speed. Then cover it up and write down as many points from the passage as you can remember.

2 On a scale of 1 to 5, rate the passage for comprehensibility (that is, how well you understood it). Give a score of 5 if the passage is entirely understandable.

'The procedure is actually quite simple. First you arrange items into different groups. Of course one pile might be sufficient depending on how much there is to do. If you have to go somewhere else due to lack of facilities, that is the next step; otherwise you are pretty well set. It is important not to overdo things. That is, it is better to do too few things at once than too many. In the short run this may not seem important but complications can easily arise. A mistake can be expensive as well. At first the whole procedure will seem complicated. Soon, however, it will become just another facet of life. It is difficult to see any end to the necessity for this task in the immediate future, but then one never can tell. After the procedure is completed one arranges the material into different groups again. They then can be put into their appropriate places. Eventually they will be used once more and the whole cycle will then have to be repeated. However, this is part of life.'

Answers are given on p. 275 ▶

Evaluation of the role of schemas

- In addition to the studies already described, Bransford and Johnson (1972) also provided evidence to show how schemas affect our ability to store information. They constructed some prose passages that would be difficult to understand in the absence of context. They then compared recall performance between a group of participants who had been supplied with contextual information and a group who had not received this additional information. You can try one of their studies for yourself in the activity on the left.

- You probably found the task in the activity quite difficult because the passage was hard to understand – in other words, you lacked an appropriate schema and so could not relate the passage to stored information. However, if you are told that the appropriate schema for the passage is 'washing clothes' and then read the passage again, you will probably be able to recall more items. Bransford and Johnson found that recall was significantly better for the group given the schema than for the group that simply read the passage.

- There seems little doubt that we do use stored knowledge and past experience to make sense of new information and that memory for events can be reconstructed (distorted) because of this. This may well account for some instances of inaccurate eyewitness testimony. However, schema theories have been criticized on several counts (Cohen 1993). The main problems are that a schema is rather a vague concept and schema theory offers no explanation as to how the schemas are acquired in the first place.

The age of the witness

People tend to think that children are unreliable witnesses and that their testimony should be treated as suspect (Yarmey and Jones, 1983). There are times, nevertheless, when a child may be the only witness to a crime and so the only person who can provide eyewitness testimony (e.g. in many cases of sexual abuse). Therefore, the reliability of children's testimony is an important, although controversial, issue. You will have realized from reading the rest of this chapter that adults are far from being infallible when it comes to recalling events accurately or identifying people in police line-ups. How then do children perform?

When evaluating children's testimony, it is worth bearing in mind the useful distinction that Koriat *et al.* (2001) made. They looked at the amount of information given by children and also at its accuracy.

- *How much is remembered?* – Most researchers agree that children are generally inferior to adults when it comes to providing a complete account of past events, and that the amount of information that children can recall or recognize generally appears to increase with age. Inferior encoding, storage and retrieval capabilities and a lack of prior knowledge (schemas) to help them see links between elements and events have been suggested as possible explanations for this finding.

- *How accurate is the memory?* – The picture is less clear here. Some studies have found that children are less accurate than adults. For example, Geiselman and Padilla (1988) found that children aged between 7 and 12 years were less accurate than adults when it came to reporting details of a filmed robbery. However, other researchers have failed to find such differences, especially when open-ended, free recall is used (e.g. Cassel *et al.* 1996).

Factors affecting accuracy of children's eyewitness testimony

Researchers concerned with what might affect the accuracy of children's EWT have explored factors operating during each stage of the memory process:

1 *Encoding* – According to Ceci and Bruck (1993), one reason why children may be inaccurate in providing EWT is their lack of an appropriate schema or script for the event witnessed. This makes it difficult for them to encode the event accurately. However, Ceci and Bruck acknowledge that there are times when a child can be more accurate than an adult. Adults' prior knowledge and expectations may sometimes cause them to 'see' things that are not there.

2 *Storage* – As the time between encoding and retrieval increases, recall and recognition declines in both adults and children. Studies have compared the effects of storage interval on the performance of children and adults. Although research findings are contradictory, it seems as though children's EWT is likely to suffer more than adults' as the storage interval increases (Thomson 1988). The type of information being stored and then recalled is also a factor. After a delay, descriptions of people are less accurately reported than details of actions.

How would you approach the task of choosing a suspect from an identity parade if you knew your choice could make all the difference in getting someone convicted?

3 *Retrieval* – Children omit more information than adults, but relevant, non-suggestive, cues can help elicit accurate information from them (Saywitz 1987). However, when children are asked leading questions (e.g. 'He had black hair, didn't he?') they are more likely than adults to give the answer implied by the question (Goodman and Reed 1986). Leichtman and Ceci (1995) investigated the effects of misleading information when questioning children. A misleading question is one that wrongly implies that something has happened (e.g. How often did he push the girl?). They found that if 3- and 6-year-old children were given repeated misleading information in questions, they eventually incorporated it into their memory.

Ceci and Bruck (1993) have reviewed research findings on children's memory and summarized the main factors that they believe can affect children's EWT. These include:

■ *Interviewer bias* – When the interviewer has a fixed idea about what really happened, this can lead to attempts (via leading questions) to get the child to confirm the interviewer's bias.

■ *Repeated questions* – Young children are more likely to change their answers when the same question is repeated.

■ *Stereotype induction* – Children may come to assume and report negative things about someone they have previously heard described as a bad person.

■ *Encouragement to imagine and visualize* – If encouraged too much to 'think really hard' about a person or event, a child may come to 'remember' events that never actually happened.

■ *Peer pressure* – Peer pressure can influence what children report. Research has also shown that children may incorporate events into their own memories that others have told them about, even though they themselves were not witnesses.

■ *Authority figures* – Children may be susceptible to misleading information in their desire to please an authority figure who is interviewing them. Research on identification also shows children's willingness to do what someone in authority asks them to do – read the research studies in the panel on the left.

Ceci and Bruck (1993) drew a number of conclusions and made a number of recommendations:

■ While pre-school children are capable of providing relevant EWT, they are more suggestible than older children who, in turn, are more suggestible than adults.

■ If exposed to leading questions and misleading interview techniques, children may get not only peripheral details wrong, but also the central gist of events.

■ Whenever possible, interviews with children (especially where children are giving evidence about suspected sexual abuse) should be audio- or video-taped from the first interview onwards.

■ Much of the evidence concerning the suggestibility of children has come from laboratory studies, which may lack validity as they can never mirror real-life experiences or questioning. However, it is ethically impossible to make laboratory studies as intense and distressing as real life may be for some children.

Accuracy in identification
A study by Kent and Yuille (1987)

Kent and Yuille (1987) found that younger children (9-year-olds) were more likely than older children (14-year-olds) to select someone from a photo display when they were asked to identify a person seen earlier, even though the person's picture was not included in the display.

Further research in this area has shown that children as young as 5 years could reliably identify a previously unknown person (the target) with whom they had interacted briefly two days earlier when asked to pick the person out of a photo line-up. However, when the target person was absent from the photo line-up, the children performed poorly (by wrongly selecting a picture), even when they had interacted with the target person at length only two days earlier (Gross and Hayne 1996).

It seems that young children find it difficult to 'admit' to the questioner that they do not recognize anyone! See the Research Methods activity on 'Demand characteristics' on the opposite page.

■ It is the responsibility of all those involved in collecting and evaluating children's EWT to be knowledgeable about the factors that can affect the accuracy of what children report.

Now try the activity on the right.

Use of leading questions

The term **leading question** refers to a question that is worded in such a way that it might bias how a respondent answers. Research has shown how even subtle changes to the wording of a question can affect eyewitness testimony.

Loftus and Palmer (1974) showed participants a film of a car accident and then asked them: 'How fast were the cars going when they hit each other?' All participants were asked the same type of question, except that the word 'hit' was variously replaced with 'smashed', 'collided', 'bumped' or 'contacted'. It was found that the word used affected the estimation of speed. See Table 3.1 below for details of the results.

Moreover, when people were asked, one week later, if they had seen any broken glass, those in the 'smashed' group were consistently more likely to answer 'Yes' (this was the wrong answer).

In a similar study, in which film footage of a car accident was shown, participants were asked either 'Did you see *a* broken headlight?' or 'Did you see *the* broken headlight?' People who had seen a version of the film in which there really was a broken headlight were equally likely to answer 'Yes' to either of the questions. However, people who had seen a version with no broken headlight were more than twice as likely to recall having seen one when asked about 'the' broken headlight rather than when asked about 'a' broken headlight.

The consequences of the testimony

As we have already seen, findings from laboratory studies have not always been supported by evidence from real life. It is possible that participants in experiments are less accurate than genuine witnesses because they realize that inaccuracies will not lead to serious consequences.

Foster *et al.* (1994) tested this possibility in a study where participants were shown a video of a bank robbery and subsequently asked to identify the robber in an identity parade. One group of participants was led to believe that the robbery was a real event and that their responses would influence the trial, while the second group assumed that it was a simulation. Identification of the robber was more accurate for the first group, suggesting that the consequence of identifying someone is an important factor for witnesses.

How witnesses are tested

Loftus often used forced-choice tests (e.g. picking one of two slides), but this may give a false picture. Koriat and Goldsmith (1996) have shown that witness accuracy can be dramatically increased if tests do not rely on forced-choice format and if witnesses are allowed to give no answer if they feel unsure. It also seems to be the case that witnesses are able to produce far more accurate memories for events if they are given the appropriate cues. The Cognitive Interview Schedule (see the next page), for example, seems to trigger memories that are more accurate and richer in detail than other types of questioning.

Activity Demand characteristics

Demand characteristics are features of a research situation that prompt a participant to interpret the situation in a particular way and to act accordingly. Studies, such as those by Kent and Yuille (1987) and Gross and Hayne (1996), provide examples of a situation where demand characteristics could arise. The children were invited to identify a person from a photo line-up and, in their eagerness to please the researcher, they interpreted the situation as one where they 'should' identify a picture. Consequently, they chose a picture incorrectly.

Loftus and Palmer's (1974) experiment on the effect of leading questions when estimating car speeds (described on the left) is another study where demand characteristics might have existed, so that participants might have guessed what was expected.

Do you think that children might be more susceptible to demand characteristics than adults? Give reasons for your answer.

Table 3.1
Speed estimates of collision in response to different forms of question wording

Question: 'How fast were the cars going when they _____ each other?'

Different words used to complete the question	Average speed estimates in miles per hour hour
Contacted	31
Hit	34
Bumped	38
Collided	39
Smashed	41

Misleading information and the Cognitive Interview

The effects of misleading information

We have already seen how prior knowledge (schemas) can affect the way we encode and remember events. Elizabeth Loftus, however, has been particularly interested in the effects on memory of information provided *after* the event. She and her colleagues have carried out many studies, which show that memory for events can be changed or supplemented by providing misleading information later. This usually takes the form of a question or statement that wrongly implies that something happened when it did not, following an eyewitness experience.

They used the experimental method, which has the advantage of the controlled environment of the laboratory, but which uses stimulus material that mimics real-life situations. In a typical experiment, participants are first shown a film or series of slides showing an event such as a car accident. In the interval between viewing the slides and being tested for recall, participants are then provided with information which either conflicts or is consistent with the original witnessed event.

Research on misleading information after the event

For example, Loftus (1975) showed 150 participants a film of a car accident. After they had seen the film, participants were divided into two groups and each group was asked 10 questions about what they had seen.

- *Group 1* was asked 10 questions which were all entirely consistent with the original film, e.g. 'How fast was the white sports car going when it passed the 'Stop' sign?'

- *Group 2* was asked the same questions, except for one: 'How fast was the white sports car going when it passed the barn when travelling along the country road?' This question was deliberately misleading because there was no barn in the film.

After one week, the participants were all asked a further 10 questions and both groups were asked a final question: 'Did you see a barn?'

Loftus found that:

- only 2.7 per cent of the participants in Group 1 gave the incorrect answer 'Yes' to the question about the barn, whereas

- 17.3 per cent of those in Group 2 (i.e. those given the misleading question) answered 'Yes'.

Loftus concluded that for those in Group 2, the non-existent barn had been added to the original memory representation of the event at the question stage, so that it was now recalled as being part of the original event (see the key study, 'Eyewitness testimony' on the opposite page for another example.)

So far we have looked at factors that seem to increase witness fallibility, but recall seems less susceptible to error under some circumstances.

The effects of misinformation that is blatantly incorrect

People are generally not misled by information if it is blatantly incorrect. Loftus (1979) showed participants a set of slides that showed the theft of a large, red purse from a handbag. In an immediate recall test, 98 per cent of the participants

In her experiments, Elizabeth Loftus used films of car accidents to investigate the effects of misleading information on witnesses' recall

---

Eye on the exam

Within the area of EWT, what is meant by the term 'misleading information'? (2 marks)

It is not enough just to write 'information that misleads a witness'. This does little more than recycle the words of the original question. It is better to write that misleading information (often found in the form of a question) uses a form of words to imply wrongly that something has happened so that a witness is enticed to give inaccurate testimony.

It would be OK to answer this question with reference to an example.

For more exam advice, visit **www.collinseducation.com/psychologyweb**

Eyewitness testimony

A study of the effects of misleading information on accurate recall by Loftus *et al.* (1978)

Aim	To see whether participants would recall an event inaccurately if they were asked misleading questions.
Procedure	■ Participants were divided into two groups and were shown a set of slides showing the events that led up to a car accident. ■ The slides for each group were identical, except for one slide: – Group 1 saw a red car stopping at a junction with a 'Yield' (Give Way) sign. – Group 2 saw the same car stopping at a junction with a 'Stop' sign. ■ After the slide presentation, both groups were asked a set of 20 questions. ■ Half the participants in each group were asked the question: 'Did another car pass the red one while it was stopped at the 'Stop' sign?' For the other half of each group, the critical question was: 'Did another car pass the red one while it was stopped at the 'Yield' sign?' (This meant that half the participants were asked a misleading question and half were asked a question that was consistent with what they had actually seen.) ■ After 20 minutes, all the participants were given 15 pairs of slides, presented in random order, to look at. They had to pick from each pair of slides presented, the slide that had been included in the original set (this was a recognition test). The critical pair of slides consisted of one slide showing the car stopped at the 'Yield' sign and the other slide showing the car stopped at the 'Stop' sign.
Findings	■ 75 per cent of participants who had received the consistent questions picked the correct slide compared with 41 per cent who had been given the misleading question. ■ When the recognition test was delayed for a week, accuracy in the group that had been misled fell even further to 20 per cent.
Conclusion	■ Loftus and her colleagues concluded that the misleading question had served to delete the correct information from memory and replace it with false information. That is, the original memory was no longer stored. ■ The effect of misleading questions becomes more pronounced over time.
Evaluation	■ The conclusions of this study have been supported by other research. For example, Loftus and Loftus (1980) found that accuracy in the misled group did not increase, even when participants were offered money for picking the correct slide. ■ Although the results of this study were statistically significant, it is important to note that by no means everyone in the group that was misled was inaccurate in the recognition task. ■ Participants were simply shown static slides. We cannot conclude that memory would be affected by misleading questions in the same way in a real-life situation.
FURTHER ANALYSIS	This study illustrates a phenomenon known as 'source misattribution'. Misleading questions may cause a problem with source monitoring – a process that people use to identify the source of their memories. Participants, for example, who saw a 'Stop' sign but were asked the post-event misleading question about a 'Yield' sign then had two different items of information. This becomes a problem if they then mix up where they encountered each item of information. In this case, some participants wrongly located (misattributed) the source of the 'Yield' information and thought they had seen it during the slide show. 'Source misattribution' is a popular explanation for the effects of misleading information that is provided after the event.

correctly remembered the colour of the purse. They were then asked to read an account of the incident that was allegedly written by a professor of psychology (this information was designed to lend weight to the accuracy of the account). One of these accounts contained errors relating to unimportant items in the slide sequence, e.g. the wrong colour was given for items that were not important to the central action. The other account contained, in addition to these minor errors, the more glaring statement that the purse was brown. In a second recall test, all but two of the participants resisted this blatantly wrong information and still correctly recalled that the stolen purse had been red. This suggests the following:

How reliable is EWT?

With the introduction of DNA evidence, the issue of mistaken identity has assumed a newfound prominence. It has been cited as a factor in nearly 78 per cent of the first 130 convictions in the United States that were later overturned by DNA testing, according to the New York-based Innocence Project, which works to free those who have been wrongly convicted. As a result, a number of researchers are helping police departments and juries to understand better the circumstances under which eyewitnesses observe crimes and later identify a suspect (Stambor 2006).

Elizabeth Loftus, the American psychologist, is probably the best-known expert witness in psychology. Her area of expertise is accuracy of EWT and she has been called upon in many court cases to outline to juries and judges all the various factors that need to be considered when they evaluate the reliability of EWT.

Accounts from eyewitnesses are often fallible and incomplete

- Memory for information that is particularly noticeable and salient at the time is less subject to distortion than memory for peripheral details.

- People can ignore new information under certain circumstances and so their original memory representation remains intact.

Evaluation of research on misleading information

- Loftus and her colleagues have made an important contribution to our understanding of the fallibility of eyewitness testimony. It seems clear from her research that memory for events can be fundamentally altered in the light of misleading post-event information. This has important implications for the way in which the police question witnesses and also how witnesses are questioned in court.

- However, Loftus' studies have been criticized for their artificiality. In real life, events that might have to be recalled later in a court of law often take place unexpectedly and in an atmosphere of tension. It is difficult to reproduce such conditions in the laboratory for various practical and ethical reasons, and it is quite possible that eyewitnesses remember real events rather differently from staged events (e.g. see Christianson and Hubinette (1993) on p. 98).

- Loftus has also been criticized for her method of testing recall. People are much more accurate if they are asked questions in a logical order (Bekerian and Bowers 1983) and if they are not forced to answer if they are unsure. The success of the Cognitive Interview Schedule has demonstrated that the type of questioning has a significant effect on witness accuracy (see below).

What happens to the original memory?

In the light of misleading information, Elizabeth Loftus believes that the original memory is deleted and replaced by the new, false memory. Other researchers have disputed this and claim that the original memory trace is still available, even though it has been obscured by new information. Bekerian and Bowers (1983) replicated the study by Loftus *et al.* (1978) in which a car is shown stopping at either a 'Stop' or a 'Yield' sign (see the key study on the previous page). In the recognition phase of the study, the participants were presented with the pairs of slides in chronological order, i.e. the order in which they were first shown (unlike the study by Loftus and colleagues, where presentation had been random). Under these circumstances, recall of the misled participants was almost exactly as accurate as the recall of the control group. Bekerian and Bowers concluded that the original memory representation had not been lost for these participants. Looking at the slides in the correct sequence provided enough cues to reactivate the original memory in spite of the misleading information that was provided after the event. However, other researchers have failed to replicate this result, so it remains unclear whether the original memory trace is destroyed or merely obscured.

The Cognitive Interview

In view of the finding that accounts from eyewitnesses are often fallible and incomplete, psychologists have attempted to develop memory retrieval techniques aimed at eliciting more accurate information. One example is the **Cognitive Interview Schedule**, developed by Geiselman *et al.* (1985) and designed to be used by police investigators. This interview technique is based on four instructions:

- To *recreate the context of the original incident* – this does not involve revisiting the scene of the crime, but trying to recall an image of the setting including details such as the weather, the lighting, distinctive smells, any people nearby, what you were feeling at the time, etc.

- To *report every detail* – you are required to report back any information about the event you can remember, even if it does not seem to have a bearing on the crime.

- To *recall the event in different orders* – you are encouraged to describe the event in reverse order, or to start with an aspect of the scene which seems most memorable and work backwards or forwards from that point.

- To *change perspectives* – you are asked to attempt to describe the incident from the perspective of other people who were present at the time.

Research on the Cognitive Interview

Geiselman and colleagues tested the effectiveness of the Cognitive Interview Schedule by comparing it with standard police interviewing techniques. They showed police training videos of violent crimes to a group of 89 students. About 48 hours later, the students were interviewed individually by American law enforcement officers (detectives, CIA investigators and private investigators). The interviewers had either been trained in standard police interviewing techniques or in the new Cognitive Interview Schedule. Each interview was taped and analyzed for accuracy of recall. Results were recorded as:

- the number of correct items recalled

- the number of errors – this category was subdivided into:
  (a) *incorrect items* (the number of items incorrectly recalled, i.e. the assailant was wearing a brown coat instead of a black one)
  (b) *confabulated items* (the number of items described that were not actually shown in the video).

As you can see in Table 3.2, the students recalled considerably more items in the Cognitive Interview than in the standard interview, although the error rates were very similar. It is important to note that the participants in this study were undergraduate students who watched videotapes and so the study could be criticized for its artificiality. However, Fisher *et al.* (1989) later trained a group of detectives in Florida in the use of the Cognitive Interview Schedule and then assessed their performance when interviewing genuine witnesses to crimes. When their performance was compared with the pre-training levels, it was found that the information gain was as much as 47 per cent.

Evaluation of the Cognitive Interview

- There have since been a number of studies that have investigated the effectiveness of the Cognitive Interview Schedule. Bekerian and Dennett (1993) reviewed 27 such studies and found in all cases that the Cognitive Interview Schedule has provided more accurate information than other interview procedures.

- More recently, research has shown that a modified Cognitive Interview Schedule is also useful for interviewing children. Holliday (2003) showed two groups of children, aged 4 to 5 and 9 to 10 years, a five-minute video of a child's birthday party. The next day all the children were interviewed about what they had seen, using either a standard interview or Cognitive Interview. The findings showed that use of the Cognitive Interview Schedule resulted in

Eye on the exam

Research into EWT

A researcher wished to find out whether the type of interview used to question eyewitnesses to a crime affected how accurately they remembered what they had seen. To carry out the investigation, the experimenter asked 40 adult participants to watch a short video of a bank robbery. Participants were then questioned about what they had seen using either the Cognitive Interview or a standard interview technique.

Total marks: 11

(a) Which type of design was used in this investigation – independent groups or repeated measures? *(1 mark)*

(b) Identify one advantage and one disadvantage of the type of design used in this study *(2 marks)*

(c) Write a suitable non-directional hypothesis for this study *(2 marks)*

(d) It is important that those interviewing eye-witnesses avoid using leading questions. Give an example of a leading question and explain why it is a leading question. *(3 marks)*

(e) Why might this study be accused of lacking validity? *(3 marks)*

For more exam advice, visit
www.collinseducation.com/psychologyweb

Table 3.2 Average number of items recalled in the standard interview and the Cognitive Interview (based on Geiselman 1988)

	Cognitive	Standard
Correct items	41.5	29.4
Incorrect items	7.3	6.1
Confabulated items	0.7	0.4

more correct details being recalled about the video compared with the standard interview.

Strategies for memory improvement

An important application of memory theory in everyday life is memory improvement. Believe it or not, everyone can improve their memory. The trick is to develop and practise strategies that enhance recall. As you might expect, psychologists have plenty of advice to offer. Some of this advice is outlined below, including:

- paying attention
- use of elaborative rehearsal
- organization
- avoiding interference effects
- using the **encoding specificity principle**
- using **mnemonics**
- spacing your studies.

Pay attention!

If you are serious about remembering something you need to attend to it. In class, it is important to avoid distractions and focus on what you need to learn. Likewise, when studying on your own, try to choose a location that helps you concentrate on what you want to remember rather than an environment that offers more attractive distractions!

Use of elaborative rehearsal

Craik and Watkins (1973) distinguished between maintenance and elaborative rehearsal. Maintenance rehearsal is a strategy that is often used by young children – it involves simply repeating information over and over again – but it only helps maintain information for a few seconds (i.e. in STM). To encode information successfully into LTM, more elaborate forms of rehearsal are required. In other words, the information must be made meaningful – for example, perhaps by linking it to pre-existing knowledge. Elaborated memories are easier to recall because several different routes can be used to reach items in memory.

Organization

As you know, organizing items of information into meaningful chunks can increase the capacity of STM. To improve your LTM, it is helpful to create hierarchies to organize material into meaningful patterns. In 1969, Bower *et al.* asked participants to learn a list of words. The experimental group saw the words organized in conceptual hierarchies, while the control group saw the words presented randomly. (In Figure 3.5 on the opposite page, you can see an example of one of the hierarchies used by Bower and colleagues in their experiments.)

In a total of four trials, participants saw 112 words. The results were as follows:

- The experimental 'organized' group recalled on average 73 of the 112 words correctly (i.e. 65 per cent).
- The control group recalled only 21 words correctly (19 per cent).

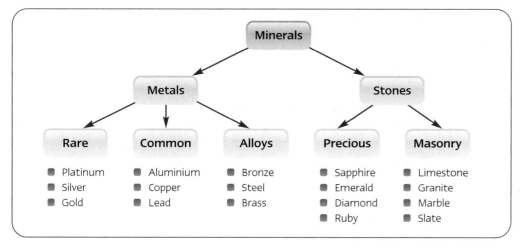

Figure 3.5 An example of a conceptual hierarchy used by Bower *et al.* (1969)

Organization clearly helped with remembering in this study. The most meaningful hierarchies, however, are the ones you create for yourself. Try organizing the contents of one of the chapters in this book into a hierarchy.

In a different study, Bower and Clark (1969) investigated another form of organization involving the use of a story. The participants were asked to memorize 12 lists of 10 unrelated words by organizing each list into a story (see example on the right). When tested later, the participants could recall more than 90 per cent of the words. By comparison, participants in the control group who did not (we must assume) use an organizational strategy recalled only 10 per cent.

Studies like these have been criticized for lacking realism. In exams, for example, you are not required to learn lists of unrelated words and the material you are expected to recall is already organized. However, the principle remains the same – by organizing aspects of a topic and seeing links between topics you will increase the meaningfulness of the material and remember it better. As you may recall, semantic (meaningfulness) encoding is preferred in LTM.

Avoid interference effects

One of the most important factors that can impair retrieval of information is interference from similar material. A distinction has been made between two types of interference:

- *Retroactive interference* – when new information interferes with old information. For example, if you change your telephone number, you soon find that the new number replaces the old in your memory.

- *Proactive interference* – when an old memory trace disrupts new information. You may, for example, suddenly find yourself giving someone your old number even though you have not used it for months.

Retroactive interference was widely studied up until the 1960s, but has attracted less attention since then. Such studies typically made use of the paired-associates technique in which a word is associated with one word on list A (e.g. apple – fish) and with a completely different word on list B (e.g. apple – shoe). Participants were required to learn list A and then to learn list B. When given the stimulus 'apple' and asked to recall its paired associate from list A, participants frequently suffered from retroactive interference – in other words, they recall the paired associate from list B.

Using your memory
Based on a study by Bower and Clark (1969)

'A VEGETABLE can be a useful INSTRUMENT for a COLLEGE student. A carrot can be a NAIL for your FENCE or BASIN. But a MERCHANT of the QUEEN would SCALE that fence and feed the carrot to a GOAT.'

An example of turning a list of 10 unrelated words into a story. Words in capitals were the words on the list (after Bower and Clark 1969).

The effects of interference
A study by McGeoch and MacDonald

McGeoch and MacDonald asked participants to learn and relearn lists of adjectives and then compared their performance on recall tests after delays during which they carried out unrelated tasks. They found the following:

- Forgetting rates were lowest when participants simply had to rest during the interval between learning and recall.

- Forgetting rates increased when participants were required to learn unrelated material, such as nonsense syllables, in the interval.

- Forgetting rates were even higher when other adjectives were learned in the interval and were highest when the adjectives to be learned were similar in meaning to the original list.

Conclusion: This study demonstrates that forgetting increases as a function of the similarity of the interfering material. Therefore, if you have to revise more than one subject during a limited period of time, select subjects that are dissimilar in order to reduce potential interference effects.

Underwood (1957) studied proactive interference. He noted that students who had learned a list of nonsense syllables showed a greater rate of forgetting when tested after 24 hours than would be expected. Given that these students had not been required to learn any more nonsense syllables in the intervening period, Underwood decided that retroactive interference was not causing the forgetting. Instead, he realized that this group of students had taken part in a number of his earlier memory experiments and so concluded that the interference responsible for their forgetting was proactive. He confirmed this suspicion by gathering data about the number of previous studies completed by the students and found that, the more lists of nonsense syllables they had previously been required to learn, the more likely they were to forget a new list over a 24-hour period.

McGeoch and MacDonald (1931) carried out one of the classic studies into the effects of interference (see study left).

There seems to be little doubt that we should avoid interference from similar material if we wish to learn and recall effectively. Trying to learn both Spanish and French vocabulary in the same evening is probably not the best strategy. Recall can be impaired both from prior learning (proactive interference) and from later learning (retroactive interference) and, in both cases, the greater the similarity of the interfering material, the greater the interference. However, much of the evidence for interference theory has come from artificial laboratory experiments that have limited relevance to everyday situations.

Use the encoding specificity principle

According to Tulving and Thompson's (1973) encoding specificity principle (ESP), when we acquire memories we encode them with links to the context which existed at the time of learning. This context becomes a potential **retrieval cue**, that is, a prompt or clue to help recall stored information from LTM. Therefore, the closer retrieval cues are to the original coding situation, the better the retrieval. This may explain why recognition memory is usually better than recall memory. In recognition tasks, there is a greater overlap with the information originally encoded. According to the ESP, forgetting occurs because the correct retrieval cues are not available. We are all familiar with the feeling that we know something but just cannot bring it to mind – the name of an actor in a film or TV series, for instance.

Tulving has conducted much of the research into retrieval cues. For example, Tulving and Osler (1968) presented participants with lists of words, each of which was paired with a weakly associated cue word, e.g. city – dirty. Participants were then tested either for free recall (i.e. required to recall the first word of the pair without any prompt) or were cued with the associated word, i.e. given the word 'dirty'. Cued recall consistently produced better performance than free recall.

To counteract the argument that any semantically associated word might have elicited the target, Tulving and Osler gave some participants weak, semantic associates that had not been the original cue words, e.g. 'busy'. Such cues did not facilitate recall, so Tulving and Osler (1968, p. 593) concluded that 'specific retrieval cues facilitate recall if, and only if, the information about them is stored at the same time as the information about the membership of the word in a given list'.

Although Tulving has continued to stress the importance of cues at the memory encoding stage, he later (1983) acknowledged that cues not present at the time of learning can be helpful under certain circumstances.

Context-dependent retrieval	RESEARCH METHODS
A study by Godden and Baddeley (1975)	

Aim	To investigate the relationship between learning and retrieval environments
Procedure	Divers acted as participants and learned a list of 40 unrelated words, *either* on land *or* 15 feet under water.
	Their recall was then tested in either the same or a different location. That is, half of the divers switched locations before they all tried to recall the 40 words.
Findings	Those who learned and recalled in the same location remembered the most words – 12.5 on average (see Table 3.3).
Conclusion	The findings support the encoding specificity principle: information (cues) about the learning environment was encoded along with the words. When participants were tested in the same location they benefited from retrieval cues that were denied to those who recalled the words in a different environment.
Evaluation HOW SCIENCE WORKS	The findings of this scientific study have useful practical applications. For example, some of the complex skills required by divers working in the oil and gas industries are now practised in the underwater situations where these skills will be used.

Table 3.3 Relationship between recall and environment in Godden and Baddeley's (1975) study

Group	Location for learning	Location for recall	Mean recall score
A	Beach	Beach	13.5
B	Beach	Under water	8.6
C	Under water	Under water	11.4
D	Under water	Beach	8.4

Context-dependent retrieval

Findings consistent with the encoding specificity principle come from research on context-dependent retrieval. For example, Smith (1979) gave participants a list of 80 words to learn while sitting in a distinctive basement room. The following day, he tested some participants in the same basement room and others in a fifth-floor room with completely different furnishings and atmosphere. Average recall for the basement group was 18 items, but for those in the fifth-floor room, recall averaged 12 items. A third group were tested in the upstairs room, but first were instructed to imagine themselves back in the basement room. These students recalled an average of 17 items.

See the key study above for another example of context-dependent retrieval.

Evaluation of research on context dependent retrieval

The findings from these studies raise the question of whether students will perform better in exams if they are tested in their original lecture rooms. In general, it has been found that environmental differences need to be substantial before any significant difference in recall performance can be demonstrated. It has also been shown that simply imagining the original setting can be helpful.

Improving memory for medical advice

Do you always follow all the advice your doctor gives? If you do, you are definitely in the minority. Why do we often fail to comply with medical advice?

There are many reasons for not complying with medical advice, but thanks to research carried out by psychologists, it is now recognized that one of the key reasons is that patients often misunderstand or forget the advice they have been given! A review of research studies in this area by Ley (1988) found that people tend to recall only 50 per cent of what their doctor tells them during a consultation. It is now part of medical training for doctors to be taught techniques for presenting medical information in ways that enhance the understanding and recall of their patients. Successful methods include:

- simplifying instructions by using clear, straightforward language and short sentences
- making use of the primacy effect by giving the most important information first and stating why it is important
- using concrete, explicit statements – e.g. 'walk one mile a day for the first week, and two miles after that' rather than advising 'daily exercise'
- categorizing information – e.g. 'Now I am going to tell you what is wrong; what tests will be needed; what the treatment will be; and what you must do to help yourself get better. First, I think you have bronchitis. You'll have to have an X-ray and a blood test to make sure. I'll give you an antibiotic to take on an empty stomach at least two hours after your last meal. Make sure that you take the full course of tablets. To help yourself you should not smoke and should stay indoors if the weather is foggy or cold. Come and see me this time next week.' (after Ley 1988)
- asking patients to repeat instructions using their own words in order to check their understanding
- giving written information that the patient can keep.

State dependent retrieval

There is also some evidence that the internal environment (i.e. physiological state or mood) can also affect retrieval. Goodwin and colleagues (1969) found that heavy drinkers who learn things in a drunken state are more likely to recall them in a similar state. Eich (1980) has shown this effect with a range of other drugs, including marijuana.

Evaluation of research on state dependent retrieval

Although there is less conclusive evidence that mood affects retrieval, a review of research studies into mood dependence (Ucros 1989) found a moderately strong relationship between mood at the learning and retrieval stage. She also found that mood dependence was more likely if the stimulus material was about real-life rather than artificially constructed material and that adults were more likely to demonstrate mood dependence than children.

Use of mnemonics

Mnemonics are memory improvement techniques based on encoding information in special ways. These techniques are useful for remembering things such as shopping lists and for some academic material. Most mnemonic devices have two key features:

- a good encoding technique, so that a strong memory trace is established
- effective retrieval cues.

You are probably already familiar with using initial letters as memory aids, e.g. '**R**ichard **o**f **Y**ork **g**ave **b**attle **i**n **v**ain' to help recall the colours of the rainbow (red, orange, yellow, green, blue, indigo and violet). Another well-known mnemonic uses rhyme to facilitate memory, e.g. 'Thirty days has September, April, June and November....'. You may be less familiar, however, with the two techniques outlined next, but these are among the oldest mnemonics known and are still widely used.

Method of loci

The *method of loci* dates back to ancient Greece and Rome. 'Loci' is the Latin word for places. To use the method of loci you need to identify a set of familiar places (e.g. 15 locations in your house) that you can imagine walking through. The number you choose depends on the number of items you need to remember. Convert each item you want to remember into an image and mentally place it in a location. For example, to recall a grocery list, you might imagine a loaf of bread on your front doorstep, eggs smashed on the hall floor, bacon rashers on the kitchen table and so on. When you are ready to recall the grocery list, you imagine walking through the various locations you used. The locations act as retrieval cues because you already know them well.

Peg-word method

The *peg-word method* is based on the same principles as the method of loci except that the retrieval cues are a set of learned 'pegs'. One example of this method involves learning a set of objects that rhyme with numbers 1 to 20, e.g. one is gun; two is shoe; three is tree, etc. After you have learned these, you convert each item you wish to remember into an image and then imagine it interacting with the 'peg' word. For example, returning to the grocery list, you could imagine shooting the loaf of bread, walking on eggs and a tree with rashers in its branches. The learned pegs act as retrieval cues. According to Bellezza

(1996), peg-word mnemonics are more flexible and effective than the method of loci.

Try using the peg-word method for yourself by carrying out the activity on the right.

Spacing your studies

We all know it is foolish to leave studying to the last minute so that we have to cram but, despite best intentions, many students use massed practice to cram information just before an exam. The student who organizes study time effectively will use spaced (distributed) practice, which permits rest periods between learning sessions. In a review of 63 studies, Donovan and Radosevich (1999) found that distributed practice produced superior learning and remembering compared to massed practice (cramming).

CHECK YOUR UNDERSTANDING

Check your understanding of memory in everyday life by answering these questions. Try to do this from memory first. You can check your answers by looking back through Topic 2.

1. Define what is meant by 'eyewitness testimony' (EWT).
2. What is a schema?
3. Outline two ways in which research has shown that schemas affect EWT.
4. What is meant by the 'weapon focus' effect?
5. In studies of real-life events, how does anxiety appear to affect EWT?
6. Name two ways in which children's EWT has been found less accurate than that of adults.
7. What is a 'leading' question?
8. Outline the procedures and findings of Loftus and Palmer's (1974) study into the effects of leading questions when estimating the speed of a car.
9. What is meant by the term 'misleading information'?
10. What conclusions did Loftus and colleagues (1978) draw from their 'Yield/Stop sign' study of misleading information on accuracy of recall?
11. Outline the four processes involved in the Cognitive Interview.
12. In a short paragraph, evaluate the effectiveness of the Cognitive Interview Schedule in improving accuracy in EWT.
13. Outline the findings from the experiments carried out by Bower and colleagues on the role of organization as an aid to memory.
14. Describe and evaluate one other strategy for improving memory.

Activity: Using 'rhyming pegs'

Try a simple version of the peg-word method for yourself. You could use the 10-word list given here or make up a list of your own.

Ask a friend to give you a list of 10 items to remember. Use the peg-word method to see how quickly you can recall the items in the correct order.

1 – gun	6 – sticks
2 – shoe	7 – oven
3 – tree	8 – plate
4 – door	9 – wine
5 – hive	10 – hen

Chapter 3: Summary

Multi-store model (Atkinson and Shiffrin 1968)

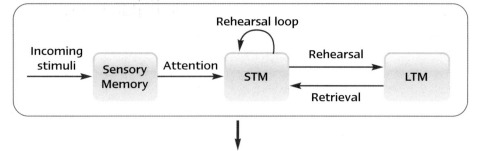

- One-way (linear) flow of information
- Unitary, separate stores

Research findings on STM and LTM stores

STM

- encoding mainly acoustic
- capacity – very limited (e.g. 7±2 chunks)
- duration – about 20 seconds

LTM

- encoding mainly semantic
- capacity – unlimited
- duration – up to a lifetime

Evaluation of multi-store model

+ve: support from clinical case studies and laboratory experiments

–ve: too simplistic – stores not unitary and information flow not linear

Eyewitness testimony

Factors associated with inaccurate testimony

- Anxiety of witness in laboratory studies
- Schemas
- Age
  - children give less complete testimony
  - children more susceptible to misleading information
- Misleading information (e.g. Loftus)
  - distorts memory for witnessed event
  - is original memory diluted or obscured?
- Leading questions – subtle effects

Factors associated with accurate testimony

- Anxiety of witness in real-life situations
- Serious consequences of testimony
- Blatantly inaccurate misinformation
- Cognitive Interviews
  - recreate context
  - report all details
  - recall events in different order
  - change perspective

Models

Memory

The process of encoding, storing and retrieving information

Memory in everyday life

Working memory model (Baddeley and Hitch 1974)

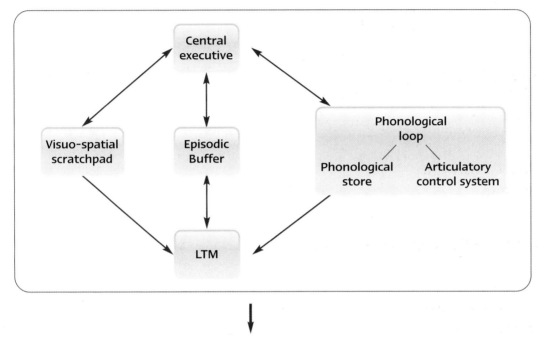

Research findings

- Evidence to support existence of visuo-spatial and phonological loop

Evaluation of working memory model

+ve: demonstrates that STM has more than one component
explains how we can carry out more than one cognitive task at a time

−ve: capacity of central executive not quantified
no clear explanation of how central executive works

Strategies for improving memory

- Pay attention
- Rehearse
- Organize
- Avoid interference
- Use cues, e.g. context
- Mnemonics, e.g. method of loci, peg word method
- PQRST method for textbook study
- Spaced (distributed) practice

CHAPTER 4 Early social development

EXPLAINING THE SPECIFICATION

Specification content	The specification explained
Attachment	In this part of the specification you are required to explain the nature and origins of the emotional bond between parent and child, and what happens when this bond is broken. To do this, you need to be able to:
Explanations of attachment, including learning theory, and evolutionary perspective, including Bowlby	■ Describe and evaluate at least two explanations of attachment – these should include learning theory and Bowlby's evolutionary explanation of attachment. ■ Offer outline descriptions of these explanations, which means being able to précis each explanation in about 50 words.
Types of attachment, including insecure and secure attachment and studies by Ainsworth	■ Outline the characteristics of secure and insecure attachment, including the difference between them. ■ Describe and evaluate Ainsworth's research using the Strange Situation, and link this to different types of attachment.
Cultural variations in attachment	■ Describe and evaluate research into cultural differences in attachment. The most obvious study that does this is by van IJzendoorn and Kroonenberg (1988). Studies of cultural differences in childrearing methods tend to explain why there are differences in attachment.
Disruption of attachment, failure to form attachment (privation) and the effects of institutionalization	■ Describe and evaluate research showing what happens when the attachment bond is disrupted (e.g. separation or deprivation). ■ Describe and evaluate research showing what happens when the attachment fails to form (privation). ■ Describe and evaluate research showing the effects of institutionalization (e.g. growing up in an orphanage) on development of the attachment bond. ■ Be aware of the difference between bond disruption and privation.
Attachment in everyday life	In this part of the specification you are required to explain how being cared for outside the home affects the development of the child, and how research in this area has informed childcare practices. To do this, you need to be able to:
The impact of different forms of day care on children's social development, including the effects on aggression and peer relations	■ Describe and evaluate research into the impact of at least two different types of day care (e.g. childminding and day nurseries) on children's social development. Because *aggression* and *peer relations* are named here (note the use of the term 'including'), these should be the areas of social development covered.
Implications of research into attachment and day care for childcare practices	■ Comment on how psychological research into attachment and day care might shape our approach to the care of children. This should not be speculative or subjective, but based on research (which you should be able to describe and evaluate) that you have studied.

Introduction

When you become 'attached to' someone, it means you have formed a special bond or relationship with that person, and they with you. Relationships and attachments are important throughout people's lives, but they have a special importance during infancy. In Topic 1, we will consider explanations of *why* an infant becomes attached, and why they become attached to one person rather than another. (Note that psychologists generally use the term 'infant' to refer to children aged less than 2 years; the term 'child' is used to refer to anyone between the age of 2 and adolescence.) We will then look at how development varies from one individual to another, including the work of the American researcher, Mary Ainsworth, and her research using the 'Strange Situation'. Ainsworth and others have made an extensive study of the childrearing methods in different cultures, and this has led to some startling discoveries about how attachment differs from culture to culture.

If attachments are so important, then this would lead you to expect that a loss of attachments would have negative consequences for an individual. Some of these consequences are relatively short-term, but others may have an enduring long-term effect on the future development of an individual. Psychologists have tended to make a distinction between the loss (or disruption) of an attachment bond, and the failure to develop a bond in the first place. The term 'deprivation' has generally been used in the literature to refer situations of loss of attachment, and 'privation' to the non-formation of attachment. In recent years, the harrowing images of children growing up in orphanages in Romania and Iraq have brought the effects of institutionalization on development to wider notice. Psychologists have been studying these effects and we will look at the results of that research here.

This type of psychological research also has implications for many people on a more daily basis; it is relevant to concerns about the effects of separation when parents go out to work and their children are placed in day care. Does this affect the social development of their children? Topic 2 considers this critical issue with respect to two important areas of social development – aggression and peer relations. We finish by looking at how research on attachment and day care might shape the way we bring up our children, particularly how such insights might shape social policies in this area.

Topic 1: Attachment

Attachment is a strong emotional tie that develops over time between an infant and their primary caregiver(s), i.e. the person or person to whom they are most strongly attached. It is a reciprocal tie because each partner is attached to the other. Maurer and Maurer (1989) suggested that attachments 'are welded in the heat of interactions'. In other words, attachments depend on *interaction* between two people rather than them simply being together. Maccoby (1980) identified four characteristics of this emotional tie:

- seeking proximity, especially at times of stress
- distress on separation
- pleasure when reunited
- general orientation of behaviour towards the primary caregiver.

Psychology in context

International adoption

In 1951, eminent attachment theorist, John Bowlby, speculated that 'in skilled hands adoption can give a child nearly as good a chance of a happy home life as that of the child brought up in his own home'. In the 1950s, very little was known about attachment, let alone the long-term effects of adoption. Since then, that position has changed dramatically, with research consistently showing that adopted children can and do enjoy the same 'happy home life as that of the child brought up in his own home'.

When celebrities are involved, the process of adoption occurs under the intense scrutiny of the media, particularly when the children concerned are from a completely different culture. Angelina Jolie and Brad Pitt have adopted children from Cambodia and Ethiopia (see photo right), while Madonna made headlines over her adoption of 13-month-old David from Malawi. Adopting a child from a different culture presents the same challenge of predicting outcome as that faced by Bowlby in 1951. International adoption involves more than 40 000 children a year, moving among more than 100 countries. In most cases, these children have experienced malnutrition, maternal separation and neglect in orphanages prior to being adopted, but how do they fare *after* adoption?

Juffer and van IJzendoorn (2005) carried out a meta-analysis involving over 15 000 international adoptees to investigate the effects of international adoption on later behavioural and mental health problems. Results showed that most of these children were well adjusted. Surprisingly, perhaps, international adoptees have fewer behaviour problems and have fewer mental health problems than children adopted from within the home culture. Rather unsurprisingly, international adoptees with higher levels of adversity prior to adoption have more problems than those without evidence of extreme deprivation. How our celebrity adoptees fare remains to be seen.

Answer the two questions below, making some brief notes about what you think and why. When you have read the first topic on attachment, come back and answer these questions again, noting whether your original answers have changed.

1 Do *you* think adopted children have the same chance to live the same 'happy home life as that of the child brought up in his own home'?

2 What particular problems do you think would be faced by international adoptees?

Activity **What is attachment?**

In psychology, the term 'attachment' is used to describe a special kind of relationship or 'affectional bond' between two people. According to Mary Ainsworth (1989), an affectional bond is a 'relatively long-enduring tie in which the partner is important as a unique individual ... [and where there] is a desire to maintain closeness to the partner'.

An attachment is a special type of affectional bond where, in addition to desiring closeness, you feel a sense of comfort and security when with the other person. The other person can also be used as a safe base from which to explore the rest of your world.

Since both the terms 'affectional bond' and 'attachment' refer to internal states, psychologists can only infer their existence by looking at specific behaviours.

Some questions for you to think about:

1 Make a list of the people with whom you have an affectional bond.

2 Now select from your list any people with whom your relationship would be better described as an attachment.

Now work in a small group to discuss the following:

3 If an attachment is designed to maintain proximity to another person, what attachment behaviours are commonly used by:

(a) infants to maintain closeness to their parents or to those who care for them?

(b) school-aged children to maintain closeness to their parents or to those who care for them?

(c) adults to maintain closeness to their parents or to those who cared for them?

4 Imagine that you have been observing how several infants react when they are separated from their mothers. One infant (Child A) cries a lot when the mother leaves the room and does not settle until the mother returns. Another infant (Child B) does not show any sign of distress when her mother walks out of the room, but is clearly very pleased when her mother comes back into the room a few minutes later. Is it reasonable to infer that Child A is more strongly attached to her mother than Child B? Is there any other possible explanation of their different behaviour when their mothers left the room for a short period of time?

Explanations of attachment

Why then, do infants become attached to one person rather than another? What is the purpose of attachment? We will focus on two explanations – learning theory and the evolutionary perspective as exemplified by Bowlby's approach. Learning theory takes the view that attachment is a learned process (nurture), whereas Bowlby argued that attachment is an inherited behaviour (nature). These are examples of the nature–nurture debate.

Learning theory

Learning theory is the view put forward by behaviourists to explain how all behaviour is acquired, using the principles of **conditioning**:

■ *Classical conditioning* – Dogs salivate when they feed. Salivation is an unconditioned response (UR) to an unconditioned stimulus (food – the US). The stimulus (US) and response (UR) are innately linked. If a bell is rung every time food appears, the animal comes to associate the sound of the bell and food, so that the bell alone will produce the UR. The bell was a neutral stimulus (NS), but is now a conditioned stimulus (CS) and the salivation is now a conditioned response (CR). Thus the animal has learned a new stimulus–response link.

■ *Operant conditioning* – An animal is placed in a cage where food will be delivered if it presses a lever. At first the animal presses the lever accidentally and is rewarded by receiving food. This reward increases the probability that the behaviour (lever pressing) will be repeated. The food or reward is then said to be reinforcing. If the lever press results in an electric shock, this will decrease the probability of the response being repeated. The shock acts as a punishment.

Classical conditioning

We can explain attachment in terms of the principles of **classical conditioning** (see Chapter 7, p. 231). An infant is born with reflex responses. The stimulus of food produces a response of pleasure – an unconditioned stimulus and an unconditioned response respectively. The person providing the food (usually the mother) becomes associated with this pleasure and therefore becomes a conditioned stimulus. The food-giver then becomes a source of pleasure, irrespective of whether or not food is supplied. According to learning theory, this is the basis of the attachment bond.

Operant conditioning

Dollard and Miller (1950) proposed a further adaptation of the learning theory account of attachment, based in part on **operant conditioning**, but with the inclusion of a mental state (mental states are usually excluded from behaviourist accounts). Dollard and Miller suggested that when hungry, the human infant feels uncomfortable and experiences a drive state. This drive motivates the baby to find some way to lessen the discomfort of being hungry. Of course, in early infancy the baby can do little more than howl and it is up to other people to feed it. Being fed satisfies the infant's hunger and makes it feel comfortable again. This results in drive reduction, which is rewarding, and the child learns that food is a reward or primary reinforcer. The person who supplies the food, the mother, is associated with the food and becomes a secondary reinforcer. From then on, the infant seeks to be with this person because she is now a source of reward. The infant has therefore become attached.

The formation of love in infant monkeys
A research study by Harlow and Harlow (1962)

Perhaps the most famous study to show that attachment is not based on the supply of food was conducted by Harlow and Harlow (1962) on infant monkeys. The infant monkeys were placed in a cage with two wire mesh cylinders, each with a face. One cylinder was bare and provided the baby monkey with milk from a teat (the 'lactating mother', while the other cylinder was covered with towelling (giving contact comfort). If food were the cause of attachment then we would expect the monkeys to cling to the bare cylinder that supplied the milk. In fact, the monkeys spent most of their time on the towelling-covered cylinder and they would jump on to this cylinder when frightened, which is a characteristic of attachment behaviour. They also used the towelling-covered cylinder as a secure base from which to explore – another characteristic of attachment behaviour. This study indicated that simply supplying food is not sufficient for the formation of attachment.

However, the towelling-covered 'mother' did not provide sufficient 'love' to enable healthy psychological development. In later life, the monkeys were either indifferent or abusive to other monkeys and had difficulty with mating and parenting. This shows that contact comfort is preferable to food comfort, but not sufficient for healthy development. Presumably, infants need a responsive carer.

In another experiment, four young monkeys were raised on their own, without any 'mother'. They spent the first few months huddled together, but gradually they developed more independence and finally appeared to have suffered no ill effects. This suggests that the infant–infant affectional bond can be just as effective as the mother–infant bond.

This work, which would now be considered unethical, was critical in demonstrating that neither feeding nor physical contact could explain attachment and healthy development.

Evaluation of learning theory as an explanation of attachment

Clearly, learning theory predicts that an infant's attachment will be to the person who gives greatest pleasure or drive reduction, probably the person who feeds the infant. Schaffer and Emerson (1964) found that this was not always true. In their study, fewer than half of the infants had a primary attachment to the person who usually fed, bathed and changed the infant. Another source of evidence that does not support the role of reinforcement came from classic research by Harlow and Harlow on the behaviour of rhesus monkeys (see the panel above, 'The formation of love in infant monkeys'). This, again, showed that feeding was not the main source of reinforcement and, therefore, not the sole basis for attachment. However, Harlow and Harlow did find that contact comfort was a key source of reinforcement, but that this was not sufficient for healthy development. We should, of course, be cautious about making any generalizations about human behaviour on the basis of research carried out with rhesus monkeys.

Learning theory is often criticized for being reductionist. The term 'reductionist' means that it 'reduces' the complexities of human behaviour to overly simple ideas such as stimulus, response and reinforcement. It then uses these concepts as building blocks to explain complex human behaviours such as attachment. It may be that these learning theory (behaviourist) concepts are too simple to explain complex behaviour, including attachment.

Activity — Learning theory

Learning theory predicts that an infant's attachment will be to the person who gives greatest pleasure or drive reduction. Look at the research undertaken by Harlow and Harlow (1962), described on the left. Does the evidence from this study: (a) confirm, or (b) contradict the predictions from learning theory? Explain the reasons for your answer.

One of the monkeys in the Harlow and Harlow research, shown with the cloth-covered 'mother'

RESEARCH METHODS — HOW SCIENCE WORKS
Activity — Harlow and Harlow's research study

The study by Harlow and Harlow (1962) described above is an experiment. Experiments explore the relationship between an independent variable and a dependent variable. Look again at this study.

1 What is the independent variable (IV) in this study?

2 What is the dependent variable (DV)?

3 Experiments are especially useful to psychologists because they enable them to establish a cause-and-effect relationship between the IV and DV. Apart from the cause-and-effect relationship, what other advantages were there for using an experiment?

4 Nowadays this experiment would be considered 'unethical'. What is meant by the term 'unethical', and why do you think this particular study would be considered unethical today?

Answers are given on p. 276 ▶

The evolutionary perspective – Bowlby's theory

John Bowlby (1969) proposed that attachment was important for survival. Infants are physically helpless and need adults to feed, care for, and protect them; they cannot survive without such assistance. Therefore, it is likely that human beings have evolved in such a way that infants are born with an **innate** tendency to form an attachment that serves to increase their chances of survival. The term 'innate' refers to any behaviour that is inherited. Since attachment is a reciprocal process, it is also likely that adults are innately 'programmed' to become attached to their infants – otherwise they would not respond to their infant, and the attachment bond would not develop.

It is also likely that attachment has a long-term benefit in addition to the short-term benefit of ensuring food and safety. In the long term, it may be of fundamental importance for emotional relationships because it provides a template for relationships, as a result of the **internal working model**. These short- and long-term effects of attachment are similar to the effects of imprinting observed in some non-human animals (see the panel below, 'Imprinting in non-human animals').

There are three important features of Bowlby's theory:

- Infants and carers are 'programmed' to become attached.

- As attachment is a biological process, it takes place during a critical period of development or not at all.

- Attachment plays a role in later development – the continuity hypothesis (see opposite page) and monotropy (see p. 128).

Innate programming

Bowlby (1969) suggested that attachment could be understood within the framework of evolutionary principles, that all psychological and physical

Konrad Lorenz being followed by the goslings that have imprinted on him rather than their natural mother

Imprinting in non-human animals
A research study by Lorenz (1952)

Our views about attachment are partly derived from research using non-human animals. Konrad Lorenz (1952) studied the behaviour of geese who are likely to imprint on the first moving object they see. This 'imprint' has important short- and long-term effects.

In the short term, the young follow their mother figure. Lorenz (1937) demonstrated this with a clutch of gosling eggs that were divided into two groups. One group was left with their natural mother and the other eggs were kept in an incubator. When the eggs in the incubator hatched, the first living (moving) thing they saw was Lorenz and they soon started to follow him around. Lorenz marked the two groups to distinguish them and then placed them together with their mother. The goslings quickly divided themselves up, one followed their natural mother and Lorenz's brood followed him.

It is easy to see the evolutionary value of this behaviour. A young animal that follows its mother is more likely to be safe from predators, more likely to be fed and to learn how to find food. In short, it is more likely to survive and reproduce, so that the genes for this behaviour are perpetuated. This is the basis of the evolutionary approach. Inherited behaviours that promote reproduction are naturally selected.

characteristics are naturally selected. A characteristic is selected because it helps those individuals who possess that characteristic to survive and reproduce. It is important to realize that this notion of selection is a passive one – no one is doing the selecting – it is selective pressure. The essential principle is that any inherited behaviour that increases an individual's chances of survival and reproduction will be passed on to the next generation and thus continues to reappear in subsequent generations. It has been selected because of its usefulness.

The result is that infants are born 'programmed' to become attached and adults are also 'programmed' to form this kind of relationship with their infants. Social releasers are necessary to ensure an interaction takes place. These are social behaviours that elicit a caregiving reaction from another, such as smiling, crying, cooing and simply looking appealing. Bowlby suggested that these behaviours are innate in infants (and other non-human animals), and that the responses are innate in caregivers. They are critical in the process of forming attachments.

A critical period

The concept of a **critical period** is a feature of biological characteristics. If development does not take place during a set developmental period, then it may not take place at all. For instance, during the development of the human embryo, the arms begin to develop between Day 24 and Day 26. Any interference with development at this critical stage will permanently affect the development of the arms. If attachment is innate and therefore biological, we would expect there to be a critical period for its development. Bowlby suggested that if a child does not form an attachment before the age of $2\frac{1}{2}$ years, then it would not be possible thereafter. We will consider the evidence for this in the section on deprivation and privation.

The continuity hypothesis

The argument behind the continuity hypothesis is that the relationship with one special attachment figure (monotropy) provides an infant with an internal working model of relationships. Secure children develop a positive working model of themselves, based on their feelings of security derived from having one sensitive, emotionally responsive and supportive primary caregiver (known as the *caregiver sensitivity hypothesis*). In contrast, avoidant children are assumed to have a primary caregiver who is rejecting, resulting in their having a working model of themselves as unacceptable and unworthy. Ambivalent children have a primary caregiver who is inconsistent and, consequently, the children tend to have a negative self-image and exaggerate their emotional responses as a way to obtain attention. This continuity hypothesis provides one possible explanation of the fact that early patterns of attachment are related to later child characteristics.

Evaluation of Bowlby's theory

The continuity hypothesis

The Minnesota longitudinal study by Sroufe *et al.* (1999) has followed a cohort of children from the age of 12 months to adolescence. The children were rated throughout their childhood by teachers, trained observers and camp counsellors at special events arranged for the children. Those children who were rated as being securely attached in infancy were also subsequently rated as being more popular, having more initiative, and being higher in social competence, self-confidence and self-esteem. In other words, social competence was associated

Activity Social releasers

A social releaser is any behaviour that encourages a caregiver reaction from another person.

- Work with one other person to draw up a list of ten social releasers used by infants, children or individuals of any age.

- For each social releaser on your list, state whether you think that the behaviour is innate (I) or learned (L) and identify what response(s) you think it might elicit from a caregiver.

- Do you think that the caregiver's responses to the social releasers are innate or learned?

- To what extent do you think caregivers differ in their responses to the same social releaser, and why?

Figure 4.1 Relationship success by attachment type

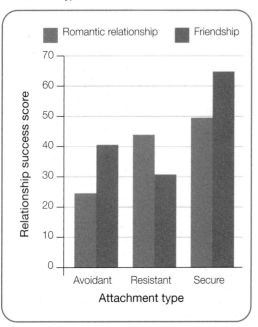

RESEARCH METHODS

Activity **Research into types of attachment**

Figure 4.1 presents data from an (imaginary) investigation into the relationship between attachment type (i.e. avoidant–insecure, resistant–insecure and securely attached) and scores on a measure of 'relationship success'. Students between the ages of 18 and 21 responded to an advertisement in a local newspaper to take part in the study. They were first assessed using the **Adult Attachment Interview**, and then asked a series of questions about their relationships in the previous year to assess things like length of romantic relationships, number of friends, popularity, etc.

1 What type of graph is this?

2 Suggest two conclusions that might be drawn from Figure 4.1?

3 Suggest two weaknesses about the way this study was carried out.

Answers are given on p. 276 ▶

with early attachment style, supporting Bowlby's views of continuity from infancy to adulthood in terms of social development.

McCarthy (1999) also used attachment data from infancy. A group of women were contacted who had been assessed in infancy as insecurely attached. The study recorded their attitudes and experiences of friendships and romantic relationships. Women previously classified as 'avoidant–insecure' were more likely to have romantic problems and those classified as 'resistant–insecure' were more likely to have problems in friendships (see key study, 'Findings', on p. 124 for an explanation of these classifications).

Even though there are positive correlations between early experiences and later social experiences, you may remember that there is an alternative explanation to that of the internal working model – namely that some infants may simply be better than others at forming relationships. This is known as the *temperament hypothesis* (see p. 125). Children who are appealing to their parents are also likely to be appealing to other people and this could explain continuities.

A second study that investigated the continuity hypothesis perhaps offers some better support for it because it involved individual's attitudes. Hazan and Shaver (1987) published a 'love quiz' in an American newspaper, collecting information from people about (a) their early attachment experiences, and (b) their current romantic attitudes and experiences. They found that individuals who were securely attached as infants tended to have happy and lasting love relationships and to believe that love was enduring and about mutual trust. By contrast, insecure types found relationships less easy, were more likely to be divorced and felt that true love was rare. This supports Bowlby's concept of an internal working model because it assesses attitudes generated from an internal working model.

Critical or sensitive period?

More recent research has led to a modification of Bowlby's notion of a critical period in the development of attachments. Studies of infants (e.g. Rutter *et al.* 1998) abandoned or orphaned and raised in institutions in Eastern Europe prior to adoption by families in the US or UK have shown that these adoptees *were* able to form attachment relationships after the first year of life and also made notable developmental progress following adoption. However, the later these children were adopted the slower their progress. This tells us that although it may take them longer, children who fail to form attachments *during* the so-called critical period are nonetheless still able to form them outside this period. This evidence, then, is consistent with the notion of a *sensitive* period (during which children find it easier to form attachments) rather than a critical period for the development of the first attachment relationship.

A summary of Bowlby's theory

- Attachment is adaptive and innate: infants are born with a drive to become attached.

- They elicit caregiving through innate social releasers; adults respond to social releasers.

- Bonds are formed with adults who respond most sensitively.

- This must occur during a critical period of development.

- Infants form one special relationship – Bowlby referred to this as *monotropy*.

- This leads to an internal working model (a schema) and the continuity hypothesis (evidence from Sroufe *et al.* 1999 and Hazan and Shaver 1987).

There are also flaws with the theory. For example, it does not explain *why* some children are able to cope with poor attachment experiences while others suffer long-term consequences, as we will see in the next section on deprivation and privation.

One final point we should note is that the evolutionary argument is a *post hoc* (after the fact) assumption rather than proven fact. In other words, we are making the judgement by looking backwards and arguing that a specific behaviour must be adaptive because it persists. We cannot *know* this is true, but are assuming it is likely. It could be that the value of the behaviour is simply neutral rather than positive.

Despite the criticisms, Bowlby's theory continues to:

- be the major theory of attachment
- generate a great deal of research (an important positive feature of any theory)
- have an enormous impact on the emotional care of young children.

Types of attachment

We will now move from *explaining* how attachments form to explaining different *types* of attachment. One way to distinguish between individual infants is in terms of the quality of the attachment bond between them and their mother figure (or primary caregiver).

Secure and insecure attachment – Ainsworth's studies

Mary Ainsworth, who worked with Bowlby in the 1950s, sought to develop a reliable method of measuring quality of attachment using a procedure called the **Strange Situation**, which is described below and in the key study on the next page. Read the key study on the next page now.

Other research into secure and insecure attachment

The main reason to need a method of classifying attachment is to be able to measure the effects of attachment on later behaviour – the long-term consequences of early attachment. Bowlby claimed that early attachment is important for healthy psychological development. In order to test this, we need some reliable and valid measure of early attachment. Any form of measurement (such as a ruler) should be reliable or consistent. It should also be valid – it should be measuring something that is real.

In general, studies have found that for a particular child the Strange Situation classification (SSC) is usually the same at different ages (i.e. it is reliable). For example, a study conducted in Germany found 78 per cent of the children were classified in the same way at ages 1 and 6 years (Wartner *et al.* 1994). When differences occur, these are often associated with changes in the form of care, such as changes in family structure (Melhuish 1993).

On the other hand, there are studies that challenge the meaning or validity of the SSC. For example, it has been found that infants behave differently depending on who they are with. For example, they may be classified as having a **secure attachment** to their mother and an avoidant relationship with their father (Lamb 1977). This suggests that what is being measured is particular attachments rather than a general attachment type. For example, if an infant is securely attached to his mother but appears **insecurely attached** to his father, then what can be concluded about the infant's attachment type? This leads us to conclude that

Eye on the exam

How good is an explanation?

When asked to evaluate an 'explanation' of attachment, you are being asked to do more than simply describe material that may be useful in this context; you are being asked to demonstrate how this enhances or detracts from the overall value of your chosen explanation. Examination questions always present you with a fairly challenging task in the final part of each question. These AO1 + AO2 questions test your ability to work with the material you have learned in order to consider a particular issue in a more critical light. In practical terms, these questions always have equal marks available for descriptive content and for analysis and evaluation, so it is important to get the balance right. When asked to 'consider' an explanation of attachment, it is tempting to spend much of the time available describing it and not enough on evaluation.

Take the learning theory explanation of attachment as an example. Answering an AO1 + AO2 question requires a brief descriptive response followed by an evaluative response of a similar length. For example:

Give a brief account of, and evaluate, one explanation of attachment.

- *Task 1* – Can you summarize this theory in such a way that it illustrates how learning theory has been used to explain attachment (rather than just describing learning theory itself). Remember that this part of your response is only worth 6 marks (or sometimes 4, if this is an 8-mark question), therefore it needs to be correspondingly brief. On the previous page, we considered the main points of Bowlby's explanation of attachment, but can you do the same for the learning theory explanation?

- *Task 2* – Is your evaluation informed (i.e. how much is there, and is it relevant?) and is it effective (i.e. have you done more than identify some critical points)? This is not always as easy as it sounds, so it is important to look carefully at the evaluation covered on the preceding pages.

The secret of effective performance then, is to choose your material carefully, make sure you are using it in an evaluative context, and elaborate each point you make sufficiently to give it impact.

For more exam advice, visit
www.collinseducation.com/psychologyweb

Individual differences in attachment

A study measuring secure and insecure attachment by Ainsworth and Bell (1970)

Aim	To produce a method for assessing quality of attachment by placing an infant in a situation of mild stress (to encourage the infant to seek comfort) and of novelty (to encourage exploration behaviours). Both comfort seeking and exploration behaviours are indicators of the quality of attachment.
Procedures	■ About 100 middle-class American infants and their mothers took part in this study. ■ A method of controlled observation was developed. This involved observing infants with their mothers during a set of predetermined activities (this is known as the Strange Situation). All the sessions, except the first one, took three minutes. 1 Mother and child are introduced to the room. 2 Mother and child are left alone and the child can investigate the toys. 3 A stranger enters the room and talks with the mother. The stranger gradually approaches the infant with a toy. 4 Mother leaves the child alone with the stranger, and the stranger interacts with the child. 5 Mother returns to greet and comfort the child. 6 The child is left on its own. 7 The stranger returns and tries to engage with the child. 8 Mother returns, greets and picks up the child. The stranger leaves inconspicuously. ■ Observers recorded the infant's and mother's behaviours, noting the following in particular: – separation anxiety: the unease the infant shows when the caregiver leaves – the infant's willingness to explore – stranger anxiety: the infant's response to the presence of a stranger with or without the caregiver present – reunion behaviour: the way the caregiver was greeted on return.
Findings	The observational records led Ainsworth and Bell to classify the infants into three broad groups: ■ One group of infants tended to explore the unfamiliar room; they were subdued when their mother left and greeted her positively when she returned. These were described as *securely attached* infants (called type B) and 66 per cent of infants were classified in this group. Their mothers were described as being sensitive. ■ A second group did not orientate to their mother while investigating the toys and room; they did not seem concerned by her absence, and they showed little interest in her when she returned. These were described as *avoidant–insecure* infants (type A) and 22 per cent of infants were classified in this group. It was observed that these mothers sometimes ignored their infants. ■ A third group showed intense distress, particularly when their mother was absent, and rejected her when she returned. These were called *resistant–insecure* infants (type C) and 12 per cent of infants were classified in this group. These mothers appeared to behave ambivalently towards their infants.
Conclusions	■ This study shows that there are significant individual differences between infants, and that these can be represented using three broad categories or types. ■ It also shows that most of the North American children who were observed were securely attached. ■ Furthermore, there appears to be an association between the mothers' behaviour and the infants' attachment type which suggests that mothers' behaviour may be important in determining attachment type.
Evaluation	■ It would be unreasonable to make generalizations about all infant behaviour on the basis of this sample. The study and its findings are restricted to middle-class American infants, i.e. the findings and conclusions are culturally biased. ■ In a later study, Main and Cassidy (1988) identified a further group of children; this classification group is referred to as disorganized (type D). These children show inconsistent behaviour, confusion and indecision. They also tend to freeze or show stereotyped behaviours such as rocking.
FURTHER ANALYSIS	Further analysis: You can add an evaluative link to research methods by commenting on the validity of this study. One of the major concerns with any study is the extent to which it is valid, i.e. that the findings of the study are legitimate or real. A study that is based on a particular group of people (in this case, North American infants) can only really tell us about how *this* particular group of people behaves. This is called population validity.

the Strange Situation only measures particular relationships and not some general characteristic of the child.

Van IJzendoorn *et al*. (1992) discussed this multiple caregiver paradox, which is the idea that infants have qualitatively different relationships with different caregivers (mother, father and perhaps a professional caregiver). They found that the best predictor of later development was an aggregate of all the child's attachments – by considering a kind of average of all the child's attachments. This suggests the Strange Situation measurement is valid but that attachment type must be derived from a consideration of more than just one attachment relationship.

One important question about attachment types is whether they are *caused* by the primary caregiver's behaviour or by something else. Why are some children securely attached whereas others are not? Ainsworth and Bell (1970) supposed that secure attachments were the result of mothers being sensitive to their children's needs. Isabella *et al*. (1989) has supported this in a study that found that mothers and infants who tended to be responsive to each other at one month were more likely to have a secure relationship at 12 months. Those who had a more one-sided pattern of interaction tended to have insecure relationships. Ainsworth *et al*. (1974) called this the *caregiver sensitivity hypothesis* – i.e. attachment depends on the warm and loving responsiveness of the caregiver.

There is an alternative explanation. Some infants may form secure attachments because they are born with a tendency to be more friendly. This is called the *temperament hypothesis* (Kagan 1982). Certain innate personality or temperamental characteristics might account for behaviour in the Strange Situation rather than it being the result of the caregiver's sensitivity. It may be that some children are innately more vulnerable to stress, so each child will respond differently according to their innate temperament. Research has found, for example, that newborns who showed signs of 'behavioural instability' (e.g. tremors or shaking) were less likely to become securely attached to their mother than were newborns who did not (Belsky and Rovine 1987). Thus, there is a possibility that infant temperament, rather than caregiver sensitivity, contributes to the form of attachment and to later behaviour.

Evaluation of the Strange Situation technique

The importance of the Strange Situation as a research tool is that it enables us to assess whether or not children are securely attached, and how this attachment type relates to later behaviours. We have already considered some evidence about the reliability and validity of the SSC, including the question of ecological validity – do these findings apply to settings beyond the laboratory? In addition, do these findings apply to societies other than middle-class North Americans – i.e. population validity? In the next section we will consider the validity of the Strange Situation in relation to research conducted in different cultural settings.

Cross-cultural variations in attachment

Most psychological research has been conducted in America, which means that most psychological theories are based on this group of people and it is assumed that all other people the world over will be similar. In the last few decades, psychologists have come to recognize that this is a narrow view of human behaviour. To redress the balance, psychologists endeavour to look at studies conducted in different cultural settings. This enables them to investigate whether their theories are universal (i.e. apply to all people because they concern innate

---

RESEARCH METHODS

Activity Validity

Validity refers to whether a test of measurement actually measures what it is intended to measure. For example, the Strange Situation is intended to measure the attachment type of a child – i.e. secure, insecure–avoidant and so on. However, some critics suggest that the Strange Situation is not a valid measure of attachment, but rather it measures the *quality* of a relationship instead. For example, Main and Weston (1981) found that children behaved differently depending on which parent they were with. Perhaps this is not such a problem for the validity of the Strange Situation, as ultimately it is only one relationship (i.e. the one with the primary attachment figure) that determines attachment type. Validity of any measure, however, is vital, as without it, we may be measuring something else completely, and any conclusions drawn might be inappropriate. In particular, psychologists are concerned with the ecological validity of measures such as the Strange Situation (i.e. the extent to which the findings might be generalized to situations outside the narrow context of the laboratory). Now consider the following four questions:

1 Why would a lack of validity be a problem for the Strange Situation?

2 Why would a lack of reliability be a problem for the Strange Situation?

3 How could you assess the ecological validity of the Strange Situation?

4 How could you assess the reliability of the Strange Situation?

Answers are given on p. 276 ▶

behaviours) or are culture-bound (apply only to the culture in which the research took place because the behaviour is related to cultural practices).

Research into cross-cultural variations in attachment

An increasing number of studies have measured attachment behaviours in cultural settings outside middle-class America, e.g. the key study described below. Strictly speaking, these are not *cross*-cultural studies as they do not

	Cross-cultural variations Study of Japanese children by Takahashi (1990)	
Aims	To consider whether it is appropriate to use the Strange Situation procedure with Japanese children. The key question is whether the Strange Situation is a valid procedure for cultures other than the original one, i.e. other than American middle-class, White, home-reared infants and their mothers. By making comparisons between the American and Japanese group, it may be possible to reveal the cultural assumptions on which the procedure is based.	
Procedures	■ The participants were 60 middle-class, Japanese infants, aged 1 year, both boys and girls, and their mothers. They were all raised at home. ■ The infants and mothers were observed in the Strange Situation (as described on p. 124).	
Findings	■ 68 per cent of the infants were classified as securely attached, almost identical to the original American sample. ■ There were no infants classified as avoidant–insecure. ■ 32 per cent were classified as resistant–insecure. ■ When the observational data were examined in more detail, differences emerged. The Japanese infants were much more disturbed after being left alone. In fact, the 'infant alone' step was stopped for 90 per cent of the participants because the infants became so distressed. If the infants had not been so distressed, many more of them (possibly more than 80 per cent) would have been classified as securely attached (the observation of distress led to an alternative classification).	
Conclusions	■ The findings suggest that there are **cross-cultural variations** in the way infants respond to separation and being left alone. This difference may be due to the fact that Japanese infants experience much less separation – for example, they generally sleep with their parents until over 2 years of age, are carried around on their mothers' backs and bathe with parents. Japanese infants are almost never left alone. This means that the Strange Situation was more than mildly stressful for Japanese infants. This also means that the behaviours observed were reactions to extreme stress, which was not the original aim of the Strange Situation. ■ The findings also highlight a second cross-cultural variation – the total lack of avoidant behaviour in this sample. This can also be explained in cultural terms. Japanese children are taught that such behaviour is impolite and they would be actively discouraged from such behaviour. ■ The final conclusion must be that the Strange Situation does not have the same meaning for the Japanese as it does for American participants and is not, therefore, a valid form of assessment for that culture.	
Evaluation	■ Research with children, especially with infants, needs to be especially careful in terms of potential psychological harm to participants, which is an important ethical issue. ■ Takahashi's study was carried out on a limited sample of only middle-class, home-reared infants (as was the original study by Ainsworth and Bell, 1970). It may, therefore, not be appropriate to generalize these findings to all Japanese people, although the results do demonstrate that there are important cultural or subcultural differences in attachment.	
FURTHER ANALYSIS	A common means of evaluating any study is to consider ethical issues and ethical guidelines, but to boost your marks you must be clear about *why* any particular study infringes ethical guidelines (which are considered in Chapter 2). One of these guidelines is that all participants should be protected as far as possible from psychological harm. Takahashi showed sensitivity by stopping those observations when infants became too distressed. However, the study itself was not stopped, even though it became obvious that extreme distress was likely.	

always explicitly make comparisons between two or more different cultures. However this comparison is implicit in many of the studies, as is demonstrated by their conclusions about cultural variation. One point to make before we look at one study in detail is to note that 'culture' is not a group of people, but is about the beliefs and customs that a group of people shares, such as child-rearing practices. A 'subculture' is a group within a society that shares many practices and so on with the dominant culture, but which also has some special, different characteristics. Now try the activity on the right.

Research on secure and insecure attachment

Researchers in many different countries have used the Strange Situation to investigate secure and insecure attachment. The results of 32 such studies undertaken in eight different countries have been summarized (this is called a 'meta-analysis') by van IJzendoorn and Kroonenberg (1988), as shown in Table 4.1.

Table 4.1 Cross-cultural differences in secure and insecure attachment

Country	Number of studies	Percentage of each attachment type (to the nearest whole number)		
		Secure	Avoidant	Resistant
West Germany	3	57	35	8
Great Britain	1	75	22	3
Netherlands	4	67	26	7
Sweden	1	74	22	4
Israel	2	64	7	29
Japan	2	68	5	27
China	1	50	25	25
United States	18	65	21	14
Overall mean (average)		**65**	**21**	**14**

Source: Van IJzendoorn and Kroonenberg (1988, pp.150–1)

Bee (1999) points out that the most striking finding of the data that Van IJzendoorn and Kroonenberg (1988) bring together is that there is considerable consistency across cultures. She concludes that it is likely that the same caregiver–infant interactions contribute to secure and insecure attachments in all cultures. However, the universal nature of caregiver–infant interactions may be cultural rather than innate. Van IJzendoorn and Kroonenberg observe that the similarity between countries may be due to the increasing effects of the mass media (i.e. nurture rather than nature).

The finding of consistency across cultures is in direct contrast to the conclusions drawn by Takahasi (1990) and others, such as Grossmann and Grossmann (1991) who studied German infants, and found that these infants were more likely to be classified as insecurely attached. This may be related to the German cultural norm of keeping some interpersonal distance between parents and children, so infants do not engage in proximity-seeking behaviours in the Strange Situation and thus *appear* to be insecurely attached. It may not be appropriate to make comparisons between different countries or cultures because it appears likely that the Strange Situation may not mean the same thing in different cultures.

RESEARCH METHODS **HOW SCIENCE WORKS**

Activity Criticizing Takahashi's study

Read the description of Takahashi's study (1990) investigating whether it is appropriate to use the Strange Situation procedure with Japanese children. As you read it, think carefully about any criticisms you can identify in relation to:

1 the ethical issues in this study

2 the sample used and whether it would be reasonable to generalize the findings to all Japanese children.

Make a note of your answers to these two questions before reading any further.

Answers are given on p. 276 ▶

HOW SCIENCE WORKS

Activity Cross-cultural differences

Look carefully at Table 4.1. Perhaps the most obvious conclusion to draw from this table is that the findings about secure attachments are remarkably consistent across the different countries. A secure attachment is the most common type of attachment found in each of the eight countries.

Questions for you to consider:

1 Why do you think that a high percentage of Japanese infants were classified as 'resistant' compared to infants from most other countries?

2 Why do think that such a high proportion of German infants were classified as 'avoidant' compared to babies from the other countries?

3 Why do you need to be cautious when interpreting the figures presented in Table 4.1? What further information would you like to know?

When you have answered these questions, compare your notes with the answers in the text below Table 4.1.

Another limitation of the data presented in Table 4.1 is that although it tells us how many studies were included from each country, it does not include the number of infants involved in each study. You need, therefore, to be cautious about interpreting these figures because in many cases the sample sizes were fairly small. For example, there were only 36 infants in the single Chinese study.

When using any kind of psychological assessment, it is important to be cautious about attributing what is measured (in this case the type of attachment) to the individual. It could be that there is something about the test situation that makes some of these infants *appear* to be insecurely attached.

Research on monotropy and multiple attachments

Bowlby (1969) claimed that infants need one special attachment relationship, which is qualitatively different from all others, in order to develop an internal working model and emotional maturity. He used the term monotropy, which literally means 'being raised by one person', to describe this special relationship which is at the top of the hierarchy of all other relationships. The **internal working model** is a mental model of the world that enables individuals to predict, control and manipulate their environment. Individuals have many such models or schema (a concept you should be familiar with from your study of cognitive psychology in Chapter 3, *Memory*). Some schema are concerned with the environment or world in general, and others are 'organismal' and tell us about ourselves and our relationship with the world. One such organismal model is concerned with the relationship between oneself and one's primary caregiver, and Bowlby suggested that this model provided a basis for all other relationships.

There is considerable debate about whether this primary bond (monotropy) is universally true. In some cultures, children have equivalent relationships with many caregivers, and still develop into psychologically healthy adults. Thomas (1998) questions whether the tendency to form a single main attachment is actually good for healthy psychological development. It might be more desirable to have a network of attachments to sustain the needs of a growing infant who has a variety of demands for social and emotional interactions. Thomas claims that in Caribbean cultures, multiple attachments are the norm. Even in Western European culture, infants do form several attachments and these are all beneficial, probably precisely because of their qualitative differences. For example, fathers' style of play is more often physically stimulating and unpredictable, whereas mothers are more likely to hold their infants, soothe them, attend to their needs and read them stories (Parke 1981).

On the other hand, Schaffer and Emerson (1964) found that even though infants do form multiple attachments, they appear usually to have one primary attachment. Ainsworth (1967) studied members of the Ganda tribe of Uganda, where the pattern of childcare involved multiple carers, and concluded that the infants nevertheless formed one primary attachment. Tronick *et al.* (1992) studied the Efe (Pygmies from Zaire, Africa) who live in extended family groups. Infants and children are looked after by whoever is closest to hand. They are breastfed by different women, but usually sleep with their own mother. Tronick and colleagues found that by the age of 12 months, the infants still show a preference for their mothers – a single primary attachment.

A study by Fox (1977) looked at life in Kibbutzim, where children spend most of their time with nurses called metapelets, but see their mothers for a few hours a day after work. When the children were placed in the Strange Situation, they protested equally when either mother or metapelet left, but were more comforted by their mothers at reunion. This would again suggest that, despite having

Studies in Africa found the existence of a single primary attachment even when childcare involved multiple carers

multiple carers, the infants still had one special relationship. However, the metapelets changed fairly frequently and also had to divide their attention among many children and had less interest in any one individual, which would explain why the children were usually less attached to their metapelet. On the other hand, the children slept communally, which might reduce their maternal attachments.

Disruption of attachment

Around the time of the Second World War, a number of psychologists became interested in the negative effects of disruption of the attachment bond, in particular **separation** from the primary caregiver. This led eventually to a formal statement of the link between separation and emotional maladjustment – Bowlby's maternal **deprivation** hypothesis.

Bowlby's maternal deprivation hypothesis

Some 20 years before the publication of his attachment theory, Bowlby proposed the maternal deprivation hypothesis (Bowlby 1953). This hypothesis was the forerunner of the attachment theory (described on pp. 120–3) and was considerably less complex (note that it was called a 'hypothesis' and not a 'theory').

The maternal deprivation hypothesis stated the belief that if an infant was unable to develop a 'warm, intimate, and continuous relationship with his mother (or permanent mother-substitute)' (Bowlby 1953, p.13), then the child would have difficulty forming relationships with other people and be at risk of behavioural disorders.

There are three important things to note:

- The hypothesis focuses on the importance of a continuous relationship between a child and mother (or mother-substitute). Relationships that are discontinuous (i.e. where there are separations) become unstable and less predictable, which disrupts the development of the relationship.

- Bowlby suggested that the development of this continuous relationship must occur during a critical period. If a child experiences repeated separations before the age of $2\frac{1}{2}$ years, they are likely to become emotionally disturbed. Bowlby felt that there was a continuing risk of disturbance up to the age of 5. After that age, children are better able to cope with separation.

- Bowlby did not suggest that the relationship had to be with the child's mother. The term 'maternal' was used to describe mothering from a mother 'or any mother-substitute'. He did believe that a child needed to form a relationship with one primary caregiver for healthy emotional development to take place (the concept of monotropy). This is most likely to be a child's mother but does not have to be.

Note that there is no mention in this hypothesis of evolutionary principles, of adaptiveness, of social releasers, of internal working models or of the continuity hypothesis. It is important to be able to distinguish between Bowlby's attachment theory and his maternal deprivation hypothesis.

The key contribution of this hypothesis was to identify the importance of emotional care in healthy emotional development. In the 1940s it was a common belief that children simply needed a good standard of physical care and that emotions would look after themselves. Bowlby famously said 'mother-love in infancy and childhood is as important for mental health as are vitamins and proteins for physical health' (Bowlby, 1953 p. 240).

HOW SCIENCE WORKS

Activity | **Your own experiences of separation**

Separation is about being physically set apart from something. In the context of attachment, it means to be physically apart from someone you love. Think back to some of your own experiences of separation from the people you love – either when you were younger and/or more recently.

1 How did you respond to each example of separation that you identified? How did the separation make you feel?

2 What things helped you feel better?

3 In a small group, consider the following four examples and identify what possible short-term and longer-term effects you think that the separation might have on the individuals concerned:

(a) a 1 year old who goes into hospital for nearly three weeks for major surgery that involves some time in intensive care during the recovery period

(b) two 8-year-old twins who go off to boarding school for the first time; their older brother is already at the same school

(c) a family of two children, aged 3 and 5, whose parents suddenly have to go away for two weeks, leaving their children to be looked after in their own home by an aunt they adore, but rarely see.

(d) two sisters, aged 12 and 15, who had always lived in Glasgow with their mother and step-father, who were evacuated during the Second World War to a farm in a very rural, English community a long way from any city.

4 Do you think that the age of the children and the context of the separation may have an effect on the short- and longer-term consequences?

During World War II, thousands of children experienced the shock of separation from loved ones

Research into the effects of deprivation

One source of evidence for Bowlby's maternal deprivation hypothesis was his own research of the effects of deprivation, described below.

Further research into the effects of deprivation

A number of studies conducted in the 1930s and 1940s strongly influenced Bowlby's views and led to the development of his maternal deprivation hypothesis. For example, Spitz and Wolf (1946) studied 100 apparently normal children who became seriously depressed after staying in hospital. The children generally recovered well if the separation lasted less than three months. Longer separations were rarely associated with complete recovery.

The effects of deprivation

A study of 44 juvenile thieves by Bowlby (1944)

RESEARCH METHODS

Aim

To test the maternal deprivation hypothesis, i.e. to see if frequent early separations were associated with a risk of behavioural disorders, in particular a disorder termed 'affectionless psychopathy'. Bowlby used this term to describe individuals who have no sense of shame or guilt and lack a social conscience. Is it possible that such individuals were more likely to have experienced a disrupted early childhood?

Procedures

- The participants in this study were 88 children, ranging in age from 5 to 16, who had been referred to the child guidance clinic where Bowlby worked.
- Forty-four of the children had been referred to the clinic because of stealing (the 'thieves'). Bowlby identified 16 of these thieves as 'affectionless psychopaths' (described above).
- The remaining 44 children in the study had not committed any crimes. They were emotionally maladjusted but did not display antisocial behaviour. None of this 'control group' was diagnosed as affectionless psychopaths.
- Bowlby interviewed the children and their families and was able to create a record of their early life experiences.

Findings

- Bowlby found that a large number (86 per cent) of those thieves diagnosed as 'affectionless psychopaths' had experienced 'early and prolonged separations from their mothers'.
- Only 17 per cent of the other thieves (the ones who weren't classed as affectionless psychopaths) had experienced such separations.
- Even fewer (4 per cent) of the control group (the 'non-thieves') had experienced frequent early separations.

Conclusions

- These findings suggest a link between early separations and later social and emotional maladjustment.
- In its most severe form, maternal deprivation appears to lead to affectionless psychopathy. In its less severe form, it leads to antisocial behaviour (theft).
- These findings support the maternal deprivation hypothesis.

Evaluation

- The evidence is correlational, which means that we can only say that deprivation/separation and affectionless psychopathy are linked, but not that one *caused* the other.
- The data on separation were collected retrospectively and may not therefore be reliable. Parents may not have recalled separations during infancy accurately. They may have overestimated or underestimated the frequency. In addition, how do we know whether these children experienced deprivation (the loss of emotional care) or whether they had good substitute emotional care during the separations?

FURTHER ANALYSIS

The issue of causation is a frequent problem in many developmental studies where it is difficult to manipulate an independent variable. Bowlby's study demonstrated a link between two variables: frequent early separations and emotional maladjustment. The maternal deprivation hypothesis proposed that the first *causes* the second, but the evidence cannot support this causal relationship. It could be, for example, that children from unhappy homes are more prone to becoming ill. This leads them to spend more time in hospital and also leads to emotional maladjustment. In this case, it would be the unhappy home that is the causal factor and not the separations. This is discussed further on p. 132, where we consider Rutter's evaluation.

Research into separation

There is often an interchangeable use of the words 'separation' and 'deprivation'. Bowlby believed that separation threatened the attachment relationship and led to emotional deprivation. However, research done by James and Joyce Robertson (Robertson and Robertson 1971) showed that separation need not lead to emotional deprivation. A mother and child may be separated, but if substitute emotional care is provided, then deprivation may be avoided.

The Robertsons filmed various children under the age of 3 during short separations. One boy, John, spent nine days in a residential nursery. The staff had little time to attend to his personal needs. The film shows John being overwhelmed by the strange environment and clinging to a teddy bear rather like Harlow's monkeys clung to the wire mother when they were frightened. John progressively became more withdrawn and despairing, and when his mother came to collect him he even tried to get away from her. He continued for months to show outbursts of anger towards his mother.

In contrast, several other children were filmed while Joyce Robertson, a foster mother, cared for them in her own home. She arranged for the children to visit their mothers in hospital and to bring things from home with them, thus maintaining emotional bonds with home during the separation. These children ate and slept well while staying in foster care, and welcomed their parents at the end of their stay.

From the Robertsons' research, it would appear that separation need not lead to deprivation, as long as separation is minimized and substitute emotional care is provided. This conclusion is supported by another early study by Skeels and Dye (1939). They compared the development of one group of orphans raised in a home for women who were mentally retarded (where the women there gave them attention) with a control group who remained in the original institution. After one and a half years, the IQs of the control group fell from an average of 87 to 61 points, whereas the average IQs rose from 64 to 92 points in the group who were transferred to the home. Skeels (1966) assessed the children 20 years later and claimed that the effects were still apparent. This was credited to the emotional care they received from the adults that reduced the emotional deprivation experienced in the institution.

Evaluation of Bowlby's maternal deprivation hypothesis

There are various issues to be considered. First, much of the evidence used to generate and support the maternal deprivation hypothesis came from studies of children in institutions where they were deprived in many ways. Therefore, it may not be *maternal* deprivation, but other forms of deprivation (e.g. physical deprivation) which affected the children's subsequent development.

Second, not all research has found that deprivation leads to maladjustment. Another study by Bowlby *et al.* (1956) found no such ill effects. A group of children with tuberculosis was studied. They were under the age of 4 when they were first hospitalized. The nursing regimes tended to be strict and the care provided was impersonal. Many of the children were visited weekly by their families, but this probably did little to prevent emotional deprivation (John in the Robertsons' study was also visited regularly by his father). Data were collected about these children when they were between 7 and 14 years old. Psychologists assessed them, and their teachers were also interviewed. When the children who had TB were compared with a control group of children who had not been in hospital, it was found that there were no differences in terms of delinquency or problems in forming social relationships. Therefore, it would appear that deprivation does not

Did you have a favourite toy or 'cuddly' as a child that gave you comfort when you were anxious?

HOW SCIENCE WORKS   **RESEARCH METHODS**

Use of film in research on separation

In 1948, John Bowlby hired James Robertson to carry out observations of young children who were hospitalized or in some other way physically separated from their parents. After two years of collecting data in hospitals, Robertson felt compelled to do something for the children he had been observing, and so bought a cine camera and, together with his wife Joyce Robertson, made the deeply moving documentary film '*A two year old goes to hospital*'.

> 'Laura, aged 2, is in hospital for 8 days to have a minor operation. She is too young to understand her mother's absence. Because her mother is not there and the nurses change frequently, she has to face the fears, frights and hurts with no familiar person to cling to.' (A quotation from the film notes)

Robertson made careful use of time sampling, documented by the clock that was always in the picture, to show that the film segments were not specially selected. This film was first shown in November 1952 and, together with his other films, subsequently played a crucial role both in the development of attachment theory and also in challenging an outdated practice that had excluded parents from visiting hospital wards for over 100 years. For example, at the time the film was made, no visiting of children was allowed at the West London Hospital, while at St Thomas's Hospital, parents were allowed to see children only when they were asleep between 7pm and 8pm. Robertson's documentary of the emotional consequences of separation improved the fate of children not only in hospitals and nurseries in the UK, but also in many other areas of the world.

Eye on the exam

Confusing correlation with causality

Examination questions often ask you to interpret correlational data or perhaps suggest a limitation of it. A problem for Bowlby's maternal deprivation hypothesis is that his data was *correlational* only and so could not demonstrate a *causal* relationship between the two variables concerned (i.e. early maternal deprivation and later emotional maladjustment). This is a limitation of all studies that produce correlational data, not just Bowlby's. The problem when interpreting such studies is that it is so easy to convince ourselves that there is a causal relationship, simply because it makes sense that there would be. This is the trap that many people fall into and one that you should guard against. If, for example, a study found that among a population of 25- to 65-year-old males, the more facial wrinkles a person had, the richer they were, we would not be tempted to conclude that facial wrinkles make you richer (both perhaps are a consequence of increasing age). We should, therefore, always guard against reading too much into correlational data. Of course, it is quite possible that there is a causal relationship between early maternal deprivation and later development, but correlational data can only suggest this possibility rather than demonstrate it. The only way to determine if there is a causal relationship between two things is by carrying out an experiment (this would clearly be inappropriate in this context).

For more exam advice, visit
www.collinseducation.com/psychologyweb

The maternal deprivation hypothesis has had an enormous impact on the treatment of children in hospitals

inevitably have harmful effects. Bowlby and colleagues suggested that individual differences might be important. For example, children who are securely attached may cope better with deprivation.

Michael Rutter (1981) identified some further problems with the maternal deprivation hypothesis in a classic book entitled *Maternal Deprivation Revisited*. Rutter supported Bowlby's hypothesis in general, but felt refinements were needed. He claimed that:

- Bowlby confused 'cause and effect' with an 'association'. The fact that early separation and later maladjustment are linked does *not* mean that one caused the other. Rutter suggested that, instead, it could be that some families are 'at risk' because of, for example, poor living conditions or unsettled interpersonal relationships. These factors might lead to both early separation and later maladjustment. Rutter (1976) interviewed over 2000 boys and their families on the Isle of Wight and found that delinquency was most common in cases where boys had experienced separations due to discord in their families. This supports Rutter's hypothesis that it is family discord, rather than separation on its own, that causes delinquency and emotional maladjustment.

- Bowlby did not distinguish between different kinds of deprivation. An infant or child can be deprived of a caregiver's presence, meaning that the child had formed attachment bonds, but these were now disrupted; or the child can suffer from **privation**, which is the lack of ever having had any attachments. It may be privation rather than deprivation that has permanent and irreversible effects.

Before moving on to consider privation as distinct from deprivation, there is one final point to make. Bowlby's maternal deprivation hypothesis was developed in the early 1950s. He later went on to formulate the more positive 'attachment theory' (described on pp. 120–3). As we have seen, this theory focuses on the benefits of attachment rather than the consequences of deprivation.

The maternal deprivation hypothesis also had an enormous impact on the way we treat children. For example, it changed the treatment of children in hospitals. In the 1950s, parents were discouraged from visiting their children because it was thought to cause too much distress to them; today, parents are encouraged to stay overnight when their children are in hospital because it is recognized that this prevents emotional deprivation and promotes quicker recovery through reduced anxiety.

Privation and the effects of institutionalization

Rutter suggested it might make better sense to look at privation (lack of attachments) rather than deprivation (loss of attachments). Bowlby's hypothesis may be refined as the maternal privation hypothesis and again tested to see if it is correct.

Research into the effects of privation

There are three main types of evidence regarding privation:

- longitudinal studies of children in institutional care

- case studies of children raised in extreme isolation

- studies of reactive attachment disorder, a category of mental disorder attributed to a lack of early attachments.

Longitudinal studies of children in institutional care

One way to study privation is to consider the effects of institutionalization, in situations where infants have never had the opportunity to form any attachments. Hodges and Tizard conducted a large-scale investigation of institutionalized infants over a period of 16 years. Their study is described below.

The effects of privation

RESEARCH METHODS

A longitudinal study of ex-institutional children by Hodges and Tizard (1989)

Aims	To investigate the effects of early privation on subsequent social and emotional development, and to test the maternal deprivation (or privation) hypothesis. The study aimed to follow the same children over a long period of time (a longitudinal study) to collect reliable information linking early experiences to later outcomes for the same individuals.
Procedures	■ This longitudinal study was a natural experiment. The independent variable (attachment experiences) varied naturally. The participants were 65 children who had been placed in an institution when they were less than 4 months old. There was an explicit policy in the institution against caregivers forming attachments with the children. This would suggest that the children experienced early privation. ■ By the age of 4 years, 24 of the institutionalized children had been adopted, 15 had returned to their natural homes, and the rest remained in the institution. ■ Assessment at age 8 and 16 involved interviewing those children who were adopted and those who had returned to their original homes. Their parents, their teachers and their peers were also interviewed. Data were also collected from a control group of 'normal' peers.
Findings	■ There were some differences between the adopted and 'restored' children. The adopted children generally had close attachments to their parents and good family relationships, whereas this was much less true for the restored children. ■ However, there were similarities in the behaviour of the adopted and restored children outside the family. For example, both groups were more likely to seek adult attention and approval than the control children, and both groups were less successful in peer relationships.
Conclusions	■ There is evidence that does *not* support the maternal deprivation hypothesis. The two ex-institution groups, adopted and restored, differed *within* their family relationships. The restored children had often returned to the same difficult circumstances that had precipitated the need for care in the first place, and to parents who may have felt ambivalent about them. In contrast, adopted children went to homes where the parents had very much wanted to have a child. This shows that recovery is possible given the right circumstances. ■ There is evidence that does support the maternal deprivation hypothesis. Outside the family environment it would appear that early privation did have an effect on subsequent social development. Clarke and Clarke (1979) put forward a transactional model to explain the findings. It may be that the adopted children in Tizard's studies got on well within their families because the families made special efforts to love them, whereas they did not experience this outside the home and thus were unable to form relationships as easily or well.
Evaluation	■ Random allocation of participants to experimental groups is used to ensure that the participant groups in an experiment are equivalent. In Hodges and Tizard's study, there may have been important differences between the two groups – the adopted and the restored group – in addition to the independent variable. It is possible, for example, that the children selected for adoption were the more attractive and socially able children. The children's temperament thus becomes a confounding variable in this study – a variable that confounds the finding because it provides an alternative explanation of the results. This means that we cannot infer a causal relationship between the effects of early privation on later social and emotional development from this study. ■ Attrition is a common problem in longitudinal research and is one that you should always bear in mind when interpreting the findings of any longitudinal study. Inevitably, some participants are no longer available or willing to take part in the study as the years pass by. It is possible that a certain kind of individual is more likely to drop out from the study – for example, those who are less highly motivated or, in the case of Hodges and Tizard's study, those who were less well adjusted. This leaves the study with a biased sample. If a study sample is biased, the researchers have to be very careful about what conclusions they can draw and it is not appropriate to generalize the findings.

After the fall of the brutal Ceaucescu regime in Romania in 1989, scores of orphanages yielded up their grim secret of thousands of children subjected to conditions of extreme deprivation. Here, in 1990, a group of orphans in their dormitory receive gifts from aid agencies.

Further research into institutional care

One of the consequences of psychological research into the effects of institutionalization has been to reduce greatly the extent to which children are placed in care. As a result, it has not been possible to replicate such studies until recently, when a natural opportunity for further study presented itself. In Romania, many children were placed in orphanages from birth (though by no means all were orphans) and experienced considerable deprivation. Rutter *et al.* (1998) studied 111 Romanian orphans adopted in the UK before the age of 2. On arrival, these children were physically undersized, but by the age of 4, they had caught up with age-related milestones. However, age at adoption was negatively correlated with attainment of developmental milestones. In other words, the later the children were adopted, the slower their progress. This suggests that the longer children experience emotional deprivation, the longer it will take for them to recover, but that recovery is possible.

An earlier study by Quinton *et al.* (1985) found the reverse. The researchers followed a group of women who had been reared in institutions (ex-institutional women). These women had extreme difficulties when they became parents – for example, their children were more frequently in care and the women were less sensitive, less supportive and less warm with their children than a control group of non-institutionalized women who were also observed. However, it may not be early privation that explained their lack of parenting abilities. It may more simply be that they had inadequate models for how to parent and this made them less able to cope as mothers.

A recent study by Rutter *et al.* (2007) followed a group of Romanian orphans, assessing them at 4, 6 and 11 years old. These children had spent their early years in conditions of extreme physical and emotional privation in Romania before being adopted. Those children adopted by British families before the age of 6 months have shown normal levels of development when compared to UK children adopted at the same time. However, children adopted *after* the age of 6 months showed disinhibited attachments (i.e. superficially accepting anyone as a caregiver) and problems with their peers. This important study suggests that the long-term consequences of privation may not be as severe as first thought if children have the opportunity to form attachments within the first six months.

Case studies of children raised in extreme isolation

Case studies of children who have been raised in isolated and deprived circumstances demonstrate two things:

- Some children never recover from their early privation.
- Other children show remarkable recovery.

Two case studies are described in the panels on the left and on the next page.

Why did Genie fail to recover while the other children seemed to be more resilient? It may be due to the length of time in isolation. Genie was 13, which may be beyond the age of recovery, whereas the others were much younger. It may be because of the actual experiences in isolation. The Czech twins had each other, although Genie's mother claimed to have had a relationship with her daughter (Rymer 1993). It may be related to some unique characteristic of the individual – Genie's father had locked her up because he thought she was retarded. It may be related to subsequent care – the Czech twins were cared for by a pair of loving sisters, whereas there is uncertainty about the quality of the foster care that Genie received because there were continuing wrangles about who should look after her. Also, she was later fostered by a family where she was abused.

Cases of isolation 1
Czech twins (Koluchová 1976)

The first case involves Czechoslovakian, male, identical twins whose mother died after giving birth. The children went to a children's home for 11 months, then spent six months with their aunt, and next went to stay with their father and stepmother. The father was of low intelligence and the stepmother was exceptionally cruel. The boys were never allowed out of the house and were kept in either a small, unheated closet or in a cellar. When discovered at 7 years, the children could hardly walk, had acute rickets, were very fearful and their spontaneous speech was very poor. After placement in a hospital and then a foster home, excellent gains were made. The children are now adults and appear well adjusted and cognitively able.

These questions highlight some of the problems with the case history approach. The evidence is also retrospective, so we cannot be sure about the actual conditions the children endured; nor is it possible to make generalizations about human behaviour on the basis of individuals who may have unique characteristics. Nevertheless, we might cautiously conclude from these case histories that recovery from privation does seem possible when good emotional care is offered at a sufficiently young age.

Studies of reactive attachment disorder

Some children who experience early disruptions in the attachment process do appear to be unable to recover. These are children who are diagnosed with *reactive attachment disorder*. The symptoms include a lack of ability to give and receive affection, cruelty to others especially pets, abnormalities in eye contact and speech patterns, lying and stealing, lack of long-term friends, and extreme control problems (Parker and Forrest 1993). It is suggested that the cause of this disorder is a lack of primary attachments due to early maternal rejection and separation. For example, one typical case history described a young boy whose mother had not wanted him and offered him for adoption. This was followed by a series of foster homes until he was finally adopted at 18 months old. However, he appeared unable to accept the affection that his adopted parents tried to give him and, as an older child, engaged in lying, stealing, sending death threats and flying into wild rages (Flanagan 1996).

Maternal rejection can occur even when the mother remains present, as in the case of primary rejectors (Jones *et al*. 1987). These tend to be middle-class women who have had an unwanted child, a difficult pregnancy and/or experienced early separation from their infant due to problems at the time of birth. The mothers may well have good relationships with other offspring and are able to offer a good standard of physical care. Rejection starts from the time of birth and the mother–infant relationship never recovers. Gradually the guilt and lack of empathy that the mother feels turns into anger and later, as the child grows up, a period of stress or naughtiness may result in excessive punishment and abuse.

However, it is possible that the reason for the initial breakdown between caregiver and child was some aspect of the child's temperament, and this has continued to affect other attempts to form relationships.

Are these effects reversible?

Some of the evidence suggests that the first two years of life are decisive for emotional and social development. For example, Hodges and Tizard's study showed that all the ex-institutional adolescents had difficulty coping with schoolmates. It may be, however, that they were simply less mature than their 'normal' peers and this made it more difficult to cope socially rather than being due to early deprivation. Studies of reactive attachment disorder suggest that the effects of early privation are irreversible, but it is not certain that privation is the *cause* of such a disorder.

The case study of Genie suggests that it is not possible to recover from early privation, even with good subsequent care, although she probably suffered a range of early privations and may have been retarded from birth. She was also quite old when she was discovered. Other studies of isolated children, such as the Czech twins, indicate that when children are offered good emotional care,

Cases of isolation 2
Genie (reported by Curtiss 1977)

Genie, the second case, was found when she was 13 years old (Curtiss 1977). Her history was one of isolation, severe neglect and physical restraint. She was kept strapped to a child's potty in a bare room. Her father punished her if she made any sound. On discovery, aged 13, her appearance was that of a 6- or 7-year-old child. Curtiss described her as 'unsocialized, primitive, and hardly human'; she made virtually no sounds and was hardly able to walk. Genie never achieved good social adjustment or language despite intervention and being placed with a foster family.

RESEARCH METHODS · HOW SCIENCE WORKS
Activity · Case studies

Case study research typically involves the in-depth study over time of a single 'case' (individual or small group), usually undertaken within a real-life context. Alternatively, as with the Czech twins described on the opposite page, an exceptional or unique circumstance may be studied in order to give insight into circumstances that would be impossible to recreate artificially.

Read the advantages and weaknesses of case studies on pp. 31–2, and then answer the following questions, remembering to *elaborate* your answers:

1 Suggest two advantages of studying extreme cases, such as the Czech twins or Genie, as a way of learning about the effects of privation.

2 Suggest two weaknesses associated with studying extreme cases, such as the Czech twins or Genie, as a way of learning about the effects of privation.

3 Suggest two ethical issues that might apply to such studies, and suggest how the researchers might have dealt with each of these.

Activity Research into attachment

From your reading of this chapter and/or from your own reading, select:

- one study of the development of attachments
- one study of the effects of privation
- one study of the effects of institutionalization.

For each study, complete a table like the ones used to present studies in this chapter, using the following headings:

(a) Topic

(b) Aim

(c) Procedure

(d) Main findings

(e) Main conclusions

(f) Evaluation.

even after the age of 5, they can recover. However, they may have formed attachments with each other through their early, critical years. You may recall that Harlow and Harlow (1962) found that monkeys isolated from their mothers but reared with peers were reasonably well adjusted.

There is other evidence that at least some individuals, in some circumstances, can and do recover. The study of Romanian orphans, undertaken by Rutter and colleagues (Rutter *et al.* 2007) showed that such children could recover, although earlier adoptions were associated with more positive outcomes than later adoptions. However, a study by Triseliotis (1984) examined about 40 adults who had been adopted late in childhood. They all appeared to have recovered well, even after late adoption.

The answer about whether early privation is irreversible appears to be uncertain, but in general it is likely that children can recover given the right set of circumstances. All of the studies mentioned so far relate to privation, not deprivation. Research on deprivation indicated reasonable recovery where substitute emotional care was provided.

However, there are many problems in interpreting the data, as we have already noted. Perhaps most importantly, many of these children experienced more than emotional deprivation/privation. It is difficult to conduct well-controlled studies in this area of psychology

CHECK YOUR UNDERSTANDING

Check your understanding of attachment by answering the following questions. Try to do this from memory. You can check your answers by looking back through Topic 1.

1. Fill in the blank space: 'Attachments depend on _____ between two people.'

2. List four characteristics seen in an 'attached' infant.

3. According to learning theory, what two processes explain the development of attachment?
Give one criticism of the learning theory explanation of attachment.

4. The explanation of attachment that sees the infant forming an attachment with the mother merely because she provides food and so becomes a secondary reinforcer is _____ conditioning.

5. What was Harlow and Harlow's main finding?

6. What does the term imprinting mean?

7. What is a 'social releaser'?

8. Why does the Minnesota longitudinal study support Bowlby's theory of attachment?

9. List the steps in the Strange Situation procedure.

10. What are the three types of attachments that Mary Ainsworth identified?

11. In which country have most Strange Situation studies been carried out?

12. Define the term 'monotropy'.

13. What did Bowlby's maternal deprivation hypothesis (1953) predict?

14. List the three most important elements of Bowlby's maternal deprivation hypothesis.

15. What are the three main conclusions from Bowlby's (1944) study of 44 juvenile thieves?

16. Give two criticisms of this study of juvenile thieves.

17. Define the term 'privation'.

18. Are the following three statements true or false?

(a) The answer about whether early privation is irreversible appears to be uncertain, although in general it is likely that children can recover given the right set of circumstances.

(b) Research on deprivation indicates that reasonable recovery is unlikely, even where substitute emotional care was provided.

(c) It is easy to conduct well-controlled studies into privation and deprivation in children.

Topic 2: Attachment in everyday life

The impact of day care on social development

Employment and **day care** are two interrelated issues that pose a dilemma for many mothers. Mothers often feel torn between the wish to care for their child and the wish for independence and income; related to this are concerns about whether day care can be an adequate substitute for the care they provide for their child. This makes answering questions about the effects of day care on social development especially important.

Our focus in this section concerns the effects of day care on **social development**. Social development involves the growth of a child's abilities to interact with others and behave in a prosocial manner, such as comforting, helping and sharing. There are several factors that might lead us to expect that the experience of day care might affect social development:

- Bowlby (1953) raised fears that the separation of children from their mother would have adverse effects on child development and could even be a cause of delinquency. These claims have been challenged by findings from subsequent studies (see pp. 131–2).

- Attachment theory predicts that children who are secure in their relationships with important figures in their lives will later on have more positive relationships with others.

- On the other hand, the opportunities for social interaction that occur in day care might promote social development. For example, children in day care are more likely to have to learn negotiation skills and how to interact with others, and could have more intellectual challenges. Research has often shown that children with older bothers and sisters achieve milestones related to social understanding earlier than firstborn or single children.

Issues to consider

Methodology

There are a number of methodological reasons why it is very difficult to get clear-cut answers to questions about the effects of day care. Perhaps the most important reason is that ethical considerations mean that researchers cannot conduct an experiment where children are randomly allocated to a condition where they remain with their mothers or are allocated to day-care provision. As a result, it is not possible to investigate the effects of day care on children experimentally.

It is always possible that mothers with certain characteristics will choose day care, and mothers with different types of characteristics will decide to look after their child. These two sets of characteristics could then influence the social development of children. Most large-scale studies make sure that the comparisons between children in and not in day care involve families with very similar characteristics, and try to make statistical adjustments if there are differences. However, the ethical considerations mean that we can never be as certain of the effects of day care as we would be if a controlled experiment were carried out.

Psychology in context

Is day care harmful?

Headline in the *Daily Telegraph* (21/10/2006):

Day nursery may harm under-3s, say child experts

A letter written by a group of eminent childcare experts, including Sir Richard Bowlby (son of John Bowlby), called for an 'urgent national debate' about whether children under 3 should be cared for by anyone other than trusted, familiar figures in their lives.

One approach, which is based on attachment research, is the 'attachment-based childcare' model. This allows a carer to provide age-appropriate childcare. Before enrolling in day care, infants must have formed a primary attachment bond to their primary caregiver (usually the mother), and this approach provides an appropriate secondary attachment figure who is sensitive to the child's emotional needs. Some key features of this approach are:

- Infants and young children between the ages of 6 and 30 months have access to a trusted secondary attachment figure whenever their primary attachment figure is not available.

- Carers look after no more than three children well spaced in age (one aged 6 to 18 months, one between 18 and 36 months, and one over 36 months), so they have the energy and resources to meet the needs of each child.

- Carers are trained and supported to meet the physical and emotional demands of the children in their care, so that their secondary attachment needs are met.

- Parents are supported in maintaining their child's primary attachment bond to them.

Even the most sensitive non-parental care is usually more stressful to children aged between 6 and 30 months, than being cared for at home by their primary attachment figure. However, age-appropriate day care with a secondary attachment figure does not appear to constitute a significant long-term risk factor for young children. Children may actually benefit from day care if their attachment needs are met.

1 Day care comes in many forms. Make a list of what you think are the most important factors which could influence the quality of day care. You'll be asked to return to this question when you have completed Topic 2.

Types of day care

Another issue is that there are many different forms of day care, and these forms can vary in the quality of the care that is provided. When we talk about 'day care', we are usually talking about some regular form of childcare that takes place during the day while parents work or engage in some other activity that prevents them looking after their own children. This tends to take place outside the child's own home, and may be group based (e.g. day nurseries) or more individual based (e.g. childminders). In addition, children may experience day care for a morning or afternoon only (e.g. playgroup or pre-school) or occasional care while the parent is doing something else for a short period (e.g. a workplace crèche).

When we add in all the other types of childcare situations, including babysitters, home child carers, out-of-school care, au pairs and nannies, we begin to see how wide the field of day care really is. In this section, we identify two quite distinct forms of day care which differ primarily on the number of children and the amount of individual attention provided by the carer:

- *Day nurseries* – In the UK, most nurseries provide for between 26 and 40 children, although some are smaller and some larger. Children are usually divided into smaller groups based on their age. There should be one member of staff for every eight children aged 3 to 5, one member of staff for every four children aged 2 to 3, and one member of staff for every three children aged under 2. Nurseries are regularly inspected to ensure that they conform to these regulations. A day nursery will employ qualified staff.

- *Childminders* – By contrast, a childminder will have a maximum of three children in their care and will usually look after children in a home environment. Childminders must be registered and inspected by the Office for Standards in Education (Ofsted) who carry out regular checks on the home and childminder. Not all childminders have childcare qualifications.

Day nurseries cater for a large number of children in groups of varying sizes

Quality of day care

A further important consideration is that the quality of day care can vary along a number of dimensions:

- the number ratio of staff to children
- the staff turnover (see Penelope Leach, below, and Melhuish, opposite)
- the physical provisions
- the training of the staff
- the dedication of the staff
- the type of children recruited, and so on.

The problems in the quality of day care were highlighted in 1998 when Penelope Leach and colleagues began a study involving 1200 children and their families from North London and Oxfordshire. Mothers were interviewed when their babies were 3 months old and again when they were 10, 18, 36 and 51 months old. When the results of this study were published in 2007, the authors concluded that young children who are looked after by their mothers do significantly better developmentally than those cared for in nurseries, or by childminders, or by relatives. Babies and toddlers fared worst when they were given day nursery care, whereas those cared for by nannies or childminders were rated second only to those cared for by mothers. Leach and colleagues also observed nurseries in both areas, raising more questions about the quality of care in day nurseries. Problems included high staff turnover (between 30 per cent and 40 per cent annually in the UK) and a relatively high staff to child ratio.

Effects of day care on social development

One aspect of social development that could be affected by day care is a young child's attachment to its parents. However, the findings do not provide a clear message. A number of early studies failed to identify marked differences in the quality of mother–infant attachment between infants who were reared at home and those that attended day care (Belsky and Steinberg 1978; Rutter 1981). For example, Clarke-Stewart *et al.* (1994) found no evidence of attachment differences between children cared for at home or by childminders, and those in group-based day care. However, some investigations suggested that extensive non-parental care was associated with increased avoidance and insecurity of attachment (Schwartz 1983). Belsky and Rovine (1988) found that children who spent more than 20 hours per week in day care were more insecurely attached (as assessed in the Strange Situation) than home-cared children.

Research has also shown that securely attached children may respond differently to day care compared to insecurely attached children. Egeland and Hiester (1995) found that day care appeared to have a negative effect for secure children, but had a positive influence for insecure children. We might be able to explain this in terms of the fact that insecurely attached children *needed* compensatory care, and therefore benefited from day care, whereas the securely attached children did not require this extra attention, and separation from good-quality care was detrimental. There are also indications that the effects of day care may be influenced by the child's temperament (DiLalla 1998).

Despite these worrying findings, research on the effectiveness of pre-school enrichment has suggested a number of benefits for social development. Between 1962 and 1967, the High/Scope Perry Pre-school Project provided high-quality pre-school education to 3- and 4-year-old African-American children living in poverty and assessed to be at high risk of school failure. Children who took part in this project subsequently had lower delinquency rates in adolescence, were less likely to have a criminal record as adults and were less likely to be receiving welfare as adults compared to a control group who did not take part in the project (Schweinhart *et al.* 1993). Now try the activity on the right.

Effects of day care on aggression

A number of investigations have reported that children who have been in day care are more likely to exhibit higher levels of aggression. The Effective Provision of Pre-school Education (EPPE) project has followed 3000 children in the UK, since the age of 3, in a variety of pre-school settings, including nurseries, childminders and play groups. Read the key study on the next page now.

The findings (Sammons *et al.* 2003) indicate that there is a slight risk of increased antisocial behaviour when children spend more than 20 hours per week in nurseries, and this risk increases noticeably when they spend more than 40 hours in care. Melhuish (2004), one of the researchers involved in the EPPE project, has also warned of increased aggression among children whose carers are constantly changing.

A large US-Government-funded study suggested that young children cared for outside the home were more likely to exhibit problem behaviour. The NICHD (National Institute of Child Health and Human Development) Study of Early Child Care studied children who were $4\frac{1}{2}$ years old and currently in kindergarten, with data being recorded on social competence and problem behaviours, including being aggressive, but also behaviour that one might classify as challenging,

The High/Scope Perry Pre-school Project (Schweinhart *et al.* 1993)

In this study, 123 African-American children living in poverty were randomly assigned at ages 3 and 4 to either a programme (pre-school education and care) or a control (no-programme) group. Programme groups received daily classes with child-planned learning activities and weekly home visits to families. Both groups were followed into adulthood, and assessed on a variety of measures including the percentage of each group who were in receipt of state welfare (e.g. social security) payments.

1 Why was it important to 'randomly assign' children to groups?

2 What is the purpose of the control (no-programme) group in this study?

3 Why did the researchers think it necessary to include weekly visits to families as part of the study?

4 Explain what conclusions you might draw from Figure 4.2 below.

Answers are given on p. 276 ▶

Figure 4.2 Comparison of no-programme and programme groups

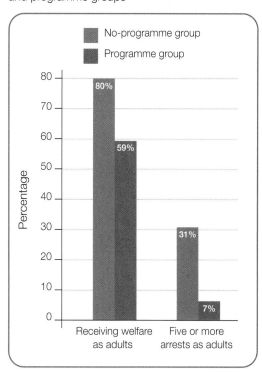

such as talking back to adults and demanding lots of attention (NICHD 2003). Compared to the one-to-one care offered by childminders, the group care offered in day nurseries tended to have more adverse effects. The more time children spent in group care, the more aggressive and disobedient they were between 2 and 6 years old. These effects remained, even when quality and type

The Effective Provision of Pre-school Education (EPPE) project
A study by Sylva *et al.* (2003)

 RESEARCH METHODS

Aims

The EPPE project studied the impact of pre-school on young children's intellectual and social/behavioural development, in particular whether it reduced social inequalities.

The project also aimed to find out whether some types of pre-school experience were more effective than others in promoting children's development, and to discover the characteristics of an effective pre-school setting.

Procedures

- EPPE studied 3000 children from 141 different pre-school centres. The sample was selected to include urban, suburban and rural areas, and a range of ethnic diversity and social disadvantages.
- Six main types of pre-school provision were included in the study. These were playgroups, local authority or voluntary day nurseries, private day nurseries, nursery schools, nursery classes, and centres combining care and education
- Researchers assessed children individually at 3/4 years old. Assessments were undertaken to create a profile of each child's intellectual and social/behavioural development using standardized assessments, observations and reports from the pre-school worker who knew the child best.
- Children were assessed again at entry to primary school and analyses were carried out to compare children's progress, taking into account a range of background factors such as parental and home background. These assessments were undertaken to assess the 'value added' by pre-school.

Findings

- When children's development during pre-school was compared to that of 'home' children, researchers found that pre-school attendance improved **cognitive development** for all children, as well as aspects of social behaviour, such as independence, cooperation, conformity and relationships with other children (peer sociability).
- Disadvantaged children are more likely to have adverse social profiles both at age 3 and at school entry. The EPPE study suggests that this increased risk of antisocial behaviour could be reduced by high-quality pre-school when children were aged 3 and 4.
- The type of pre-school a child attends was found to have an important effect on their developmental progress. Integrated centres (i.e. those that combined education with care) promoted both better intellectual *and* social development, even after taking account of children's backgrounds and prior social behaviour.
- Disadvantaged children did better in settings with a mixture of children from different social backgrounds rather than in settings containing mostly other disadvantaged children.

Conclusions

- The EPPE study has shown that pre-school can have an important positive impact on children's intellectual and social development. It can help to overcome the effects of social disadvantage and can provide children with a better start to school. Investing in good-quality pre-school provision is therefore likely to be an effective means of achieving overcoming social exclusion and breaking the cycle of disadvantage.
- The quality of the pre-school experience was seen as particularly influential, with higher-quality pre-school care offering children a significant developmental boost prior to starting school. Higher-quality pre-school appears to offer both intellectual and social advantages to children rather than being restricted to just one aspect of developmental gain.

Evaluation

- The EPPE project has become well known for its contribution to 'evidence-based policy' (i.e. making decisions about policies and programmes using the best available evidence from research) in early-years education and care. Its findings are robust because they are based on sound research methods. As a result, the conclusions from this study have been acted upon at both national and local level.
- Despite the recommendations of the EPPE study, some critics have argued that the application of its principal findings (e.g. through the Sure Start programme – see p. 144) has not been widespread enough. A Department for Education and Skills survey (Bryson *et al.* 2006) found that a quarter of all families (or 1.3 million), had reported being unable to find a childcare place when they needed it.

of childcare, maternal sensitivity and other family background factors were taken into account.

Following the introduction of universal day care in Quebec, the proportion of 0 to 4 year olds in day care rose by 14 per cent, accompanied by a sizeable increase in the number of married women returning to the workplace. Baker *et al.* (2005) analyzed data on 33 000 children of two-parent families, and found that in the post-universal day care period, aggression among 2 to 4 year olds increased by 24 per cent in Quebec, compared with one per cent in the rest of Canada. The wellbeing of parents also declined, with a greater incidence of hostile parenting and dissatisfaction with spouses.

Effects of day care on peer relations

Findings about the relation between day care and peer relations are mixed. In the EPPE project, attending a pre-school institution was associated with greater independence, cooperation, conformity and sociability with other children. These effects were greatest in institutions with higher-quality care involving staff with higher qualifications, and where there was an equal value placed on social and educational development.

Clarke-Stewart *et al.* (1994) found that children in group-based day care were actually more sociable and better able to negotiate with peers than children cared for at home or at childminders. Harvey (1999) reached a similar conclusion (see the panel below).

Researchers have found that children in group-based pre-school care achieve high levels of sociability, including negotiating skills

'Children not harmed by working moms'
Report of research by Harvey (1999)

A study by Harvey (1999) evaluated the development and health of more than 6000 youngsters and found that children of women who work outside the home suffered no permanent harm because of their mother's absence.

Harvey's study came to a different conclusion compared with some earlier studies of the same group of children. The new work examined the children at a later age – 12 years old. This suggests that problems detected in children of working mothers at age 3 and 4 may have gone away by the time the children were 12.

According to Harvey, the study suggests that in raising children, issues exist that are more important than outside employment of the mother. These include the quality of the parent–child relationship and the quality of the child's daycare arrangement. 'The message should be that being at home during the early years, or being employed during those years, are both good choices', Harvey said. 'Both can result in healthy, well-developed children.'

Adapted from the *Beloit Daily News*, 1 March 1999

Field (1991) examined the amount of time children spent in day care and the quality of the day care they received. She found that the more time children spent in day care, the more friends they had and the more extracurricular activities they engaged in. Field also found that children who had experienced high-quality day care showed more physical affection during peer interactions. Campbell *et al.* (2001) took Field's research a stage further, and showed that as well as the amount of time spent in day care and the quality of the day-care experience, the age at which a child enters day care is also vital for their social development.

Their results showed that social competence with peers begins to stabilize at around $3\frac{1}{2}$ years. Therefore, the amount of out-of-home care prior to $3\frac{1}{2}$, and the quality of that care, play an important role in shaping children's social skills.

Some investigators have failed to find evidence that group-based day care affects a child's long-term relations with other children. For example, Larner *et al.* (1989) carried out a longitudinal study of 120 Swedish children, beginning at age 12 months and following the children until the age of 10. Sixty of the infants were enrolled in high-quality, municipally operated day-care centres, and 60 were cared for at home. At age 10 years, individual differences in children's development were overtaking the effects of their early care arrangements. No evidence was found that the children who had experienced out-of-home care were any more negative or aggressive in their behaviour with peers or adults compared to children who had been cared for at home.

Conclusions

Comparing the effects of day care and home caring on social development is difficult because of methodological problems. This has resulted in some investigators, such as Belsky (1998), suggesting that a more relevant question is: what determines the quality of day care? Comparisons suggest that extensive day care might have an impact on attachment and social relationships with parents, and that children in day care at later ages might be more aggressive. However, these findings are not reported in all studies. There also seem to be positive effects of high-quality day care, including better social relationships with other children and better preparedness for school.

In conclusion, we may take heart from Schaffer (2004), who suggests that when determining whether or not a child in day care might benefit or suffer because of maternal employment, we must take into account a number of factors, including the degree to which the mother receives support from her husband or from other family members, her ability to cope with her occupational and domestic duties, and her motivation for working. Where conditions are optimal, claims Schaffer, 'children of employed mothers may actually benefit compared with those of non-employed mothers, largely as a result of extra experiences with other adults and with peers in day-care settings ...'

To end this part of Topic 2, try the activity on the left, 'Designing research into day care'.

Implications of research for childcare practices

Start this section by trying the activity on the left, 'Applying your knowledge'.

Studies of day care tend to focus on the question of whether or not it is harmful, but it may be more productive to consider the question: 'What factors contribute to *good* day care?'

Schaffer (1998) suggests that consistency and quality of care are important. According to Schaffer, the question of consistency is an organizational matter. A day-care centre needs to find some way of ensuring minimal turnover of staff and arranging that each child is assigned to one specific individual who is more or less constantly available and feels responsible for that child. It may also be important to establish consistent routines and physical environments.

It is probably more difficult to define quality, although Schaffer suggests that it can be expressed in terms of the following:

- The amount of verbal interaction between caregiver and child, which should ideally be one to one as far as possible – Tizard (1979) found evidence that, irrespective of social class, the conversations between mother and child were more complex than between nursery teacher and child.

- Having sufficient stimulation such as suitable toys, books and other play things.

- Giving sensitive emotional care – the NICHD study found that about 23 per cent of infant care providers gave 'highly' sensitive infant care, while 50 per cent of them provided only 'moderately' sensitive care, and 20 per cent were 'emotionally detached' from the infants under their care.

A study by Howes et al. (1998) considered the value of a programme designed to improve the quality of caregiver interactions. A number of caregivers were involved in in-service training to increase their sensitivity. Six months after training, Howes and colleagues found that the children (aged around 2 years old) became more secure and the caregivers were rated as more sensitive after training. There was a control group of caregivers who received no training. The attachment of the children in their care and their own sensitivity remained unchanged. The results of this study suggest that a modest intervention programme that is directed at improving caregiving practices can improve the attachment security of the children in day care.

Implications of attachment research

Hospital admissions

Research on attachment has helped improve hospital admissions involving young children. For example, research by James and Joyce Robertson (see p. 131) showed that in situations where children experience physical separation from their primary attachment figure, the negative effects of disruption could be avoided if substitute emotional care was provided, as well as links with existing attachment figures. As a direct result of the Robertsons' work, together with the impact of Bowlby's own research on maternal deprivation, government policies, hospital attitudes and parents' expectations changed. Children's wards now routinely allow parents to stay with their children and also actively involve them in planning and implementing their child's care.

Adoption

Attachment research has also been influential in the adoption of children. In the past, mothers who were going to give a baby up for adoption were encouraged to nurse the baby for as long as possible. However, by the time the baby was adopted, the sensitive period for attachment formation may have passed, making it difficult to form secure attachments. Bowlby's research led to significant changes in the timing of adoption, such that most babies are now adopted within the first week of birth. Nowadays, research shows that adoptive mothers and children are just as securely attached as non-adoptive children and their mothers (Singer et al. 1985).

Also, recent research undertaken with children adopted from Romania by British couples has shown that children who were 6 months or younger when adopted had higher IQs and experienced fewer attachment disorder behaviours than children who had spent more time in orphanages (Rutter et al. 2007).

RESEARCH METHODS

Activity   Using control groups

A control group is a group of people who do not receive the independent variable under investigation. As a result, they serve as a baseline for comparison, a measure of how the experimental group might have behaved without the independent variable. In the study by Howes et al. (1998) described on the left:

1 What was the independent variable that would be missing from the control group?

2 What would researchers have to take into consideration when putting together a control group for this study?

3 Is this study more likely to have been a 'repeated measures' design or an 'independent groups' design? Explain your answer.

4 Suggest one advantage and one weakness of using this type of experimental design.

Answers are given on p. 276 ▶

UK Prime Minister Gordon Brown, with his wife Sarah and son Fraser, born July 2006

The 'theatre of attachment'

The 'theatre of attachment' is an innovative therapeutic approach that helps bring about attachment between adoptive parents and children who have suffered abuse and neglect in their family of origin (Moore 2006). Because children of hostile parents often display fear of adults' proximity, play is used as a way of increasing empathy between the children and their adoptive parents. Through the medium of 'make-believe' fantasy play, children begin to reassess their survival of adversity as 'heroes' rather than 'victims'. They begin to explore troublesome problems through theatrical enactment and so create new perspectives and, ultimately, new ways of seeing themselves and those around them. The shared emotional experience brings parent and child closer, and parents gain more confidence to support their children.

Implications of day-care research

Sure Start

As we have seen, the opportunities for social interaction that occur in day care can, in the right circumstances, promote social development. For example, Field (1991) found that the more time children spent in day care, the more friends they had and the more extracurricular activities they engaged in. In 2001, a Government initiative entitled 'Sure Start' was implemented with the aim of breaking the cycle of poverty that plagues much of the Western world by providing high-quality day care for children and support for their families.

Sure Start Local Programmes (SSLPs) target children under the age of 4 and their families in over 500 geographic areas throughout England where there are high concentrations of families at risk. The aim of these SSLPs is to enhance the life chances of young children by enhancing existing services for children and families and, whenever necessary, developing new ones.

The National Evaluation of Sure Start (NESS) study looked at 9- and 36-month-old children and their families in 150 SSLP areas and in 50 comparison communities (Tunstill *et al.* 2005). Overall, some beneficial effects of living in SSLP areas have emerged from this study. For example, mothers of 36 month olds are less likely to use physical methods of dealing with unacceptable behaviour in their children (e.g. slapping or physical restraint) when living in SSLP areas, compared to comparison communities. Children from relatively less disadvantaged families appear to benefit more from living in SSLP areas, whereas children from relatively more disadvantaged families (e.g. teenage mothers, workless households) appear to benefit less from living in a SSLP community.

The 'Effective Provision of Pre-school Education' (EPPE) project

The EPPE project (see p. 140) has demonstrated the positive effects of high-quality, pre-school provision on children's development up to the end of Key Stage 1 in primary school (Sylva *et al.* 2003). This project has shown that high-quality day care that emphasizes early education, as well as care, gives children a valuable head start as they begin school ready to learn. This finding led the Government to commit to the promise of a pre-school place for every 3 year old from 2004. The EPPE study also found that spending time in group-based day care (e.g. day nurseries), or too much time with childminders before the age of 2, was associated with higher levels of antisocial behaviour later on. This finding led the then Chancellor, Gordon Brown, to announce in December 2004 that paid parental leave after childbirth would be extended from six to nine months, with an intended eventual increase to 12 months.

CHECK YOUR UNDERSTANDING

Check your understanding of day care by answering the following questions. Try to do this from memory. You can check your answers by looking back through Topic 2.

1 Define day care.

2 Give two possible reasons why day care involving separation from a parent might be thought to affect social development.

3 Which of the following statements are true and which are false:

(a) Opportunities for social interaction, such as negotiation skills, that occur in day-care situations may serve to promote children's social development.

(b) All research undertaken to date has found that day care has negative effects on social development.

(c) Research has shown that children who begin day care before the age of $3\frac{1}{2}$, later show better peer relations than those who start after that age.

(d) Schweinhart and colleagues (1993) found that children who took part in the High/Scope Perry Pre-school Project had similar delinquency rates in adolescence and were just as likely to have a criminal record when young adults than a control group who did not take part in the project.

4 Suggest four factors that have been shown to affect the experience of day care.

5 Why do the factors that you listed above make it hard to make any definitive statements about day care?

6 Cite (name) one study that found day care does harm to children's development, one study that found no evidence of harm, and one study that reported evidence of day care having beneficial effects.

7 How has research on attachment been used to improve hospital admissions involving children?

8 How has research on attachment influenced the adoption process?

9 List at least four ways in which research findings can be used to improve day care.

10 What are EPPE and Sure Start, and why are they important?

Having completed this topic, what is your view about the benefits and drawbacks of day care? Would you choose it for your children?

Chapter 4: Summary

Learning theory explanation

- Classical conditioning
- Operant conditioning

Evaluations

- Harlow and Harlow (1962) – importance of 'contact comfort'
- Reductionist – attachment more complex than stimulus–response

Evolutionary perspective (Bowlby)

- Infants and carers 'programmed' to become attached
- Biological process
- Continuity hypothesis

Evaluations

- Empirical support (e.g. Sroufe et al. 1999)
- Individual differences in coping

Attachment

Early social development

Types of day care

- Day nurseries – group-based care for 26 to 40 children, controlled staff–child ratio
- Childminders – individual-based care for maximum of three children, usually home–based

Quality of day care

Determined by:

- Ratio of staff to children
- Staff turnover
- Physical provisions
- Staff training and dedication
- Type of children recruited

Day care

Attachment in everyday life

Day care and aggression

- NICHD study – more time in day care, more evidence of later problem behaviours
- EPPE study – too much time in day care in first two years led to antisocial behaviours later on

Link to 'type' of day care

- Group-based day care, where caregivers are constantly changing = aggression more likely
- Canada – introduction of universal group-based day care increased aggression among 2 to 4 year olds by 24%

Day care and peer relations

- More time children spent in day care, more friends they had (Field 1991)
- Age child enters day care vital for shaping social skills (earlier = better – Campbell et al. 2001)
- Day care may inhibit the socialization of some children (DiLalla 1998)

Link to 'type' of day care

- Children in group-based day care no more negative in their behaviours than those in home-based care (Larner et al. 1989)
- Group-based day care more likely to produce sociable children than are childminders (Clarke-Stewart et al. 1994)

Disruption of attachment

Definition and types

Definition

A strong emotional tie that develops over time between an infant and their primary caregiver(s)

Types of attachment

- Secure – insecure-avoidant – insecure-resistant
- Ainsworth and Bell (1970) – Strange Situation
- Association between mothers' behaviour and infants' attachment type
- Caregiver sensitivity hypothesis
- Temperament hypothesis

Deprivation

= loss of attachment relationship

- Maternal deprivation hypothesis (Bowlby 1953)
- Research evidence – juvenile thieves (Bowlby 1944)
- Children in brief separation (Robertson and Robertson 1971)

Evaluations

- Deprivation doesn't always lead to maladjustment
- Separation due to family discord was determinant of delinquency rather than separation alone
- Privation rather than deprivation more likely to have irreversible effects (Rutter *et al.* 2007)

Privation

= attachment relationship never developed

- Earlier studies
  - Czech twins
  - Genie
- Later studies
  - e.g. Rutter *et al.* (2007) – recovery from privation possible

Evaluations

- Problems in interpreting data from early case studies
- Evidence that some individuals do recover from privation

Implications for childcare practices

Key issues

- Consistency and quality of care important (Schaffer 2004)
- Minimal turnover of staff
- Staff constantly available and responsible for each child

Quality of day care determined by

- Amount of verbal interaction between caregiver and child
- Having sufficient stimulation (e.g. toys and books)
- Giving sensitive emotional care
- Howes *et al.* (1998) – intervention programme to improve caregiving

Implications of attachment research

- Hospital admissions
- Adoption
- Theatre of attachment

Evaluations

- Hospital admissions – supported by Robertsons' research
- Adoption – Singer *et al.* (1985)
- Theatre of attachment – enables children of abusive families to reassess themselves as 'heroes' rather than 'victims'

Implications of day-care research

- Sure Start programme
- EPPE project

Evaluations

- NESS study (Tunstill *et al.* 2005) – evidence of beneficial effect of Sure Start Local Programmes
- EPPE findings – effect on government policy

EXPLAINING THE SPECIFICATION

Specification content	The specification explained
Stress as a bodily response	**In this part of the specification you need to be able to:**
The body's response to stress, including the pituitary–adrenal system and the sympatho-medullary pathway in outline	■ Outline the body's response to stress. The words 'in outline' are important here. Many students get bogged down unnecessarily in the underlying physiology of the stress response. Note that these 'responses' appear under many different headings in the literature, but you should recognize the common mechanisms.
Stress-related illness and the immune system	■ Describe research showing a link between stress and the immune system. Stress has been shown to have many negative consequences for the individual, including ill health.
	■ The specification requires you to study only the effects of stress on the immune system, although passing reference to other aspects of illness (e.g. cardiovascular disorders) will help you to understand the overall relationship between stress and illness.
	■ Evaluate research into stress and the immune system.
Stress in everyday life	**In this part of the specification you need to be able to describe:**
Life changes and daily hassles	■ Describe research into the effects of life changes on the individual. You do not have to study specific life changes, so are free to concentrate on the impact of at least two of your choice.
	■ Describe research into the effects of daily hassles on the individual. There is no requirement for you to study specific hassles, but rather the contribution of daily hassles in general.
	■ Evaluate research into life changes and daily hassles.
Workplace stress	■ Describe research into the effect of workplace stressors on the individual. It is wise to be able to identify at least two workplace stressors and to consider research that demonstrates their impact.
	■ Evaluate research into the effects of workplace stressors.
Personality factors, including Type A behaviour	■ Describe the role of personality in the experience of stress. People clearly differ in the way they are affected by stressful situations. Coverage of Type A behaviour (or Type A personality) is required, but study of a second personality factor (e.g. hardiness) is needed as more than one factor is asked for.
	■ Discuss research evidence supporting the link between personality and stress.
Distinction between emotion-focused and problem-focused approaches to coping with stress	■ Distinguish between emotion-focused and problem-focused coping. Emotion-focused and problem-focused coping are the terms used to refer to a broad range of different coping strategies. The *distinction* between them concerns whether people focus on dealing with the stressful situation itself (problem-focused) or the emotions it has created (emotion-focused).
	■ Discuss research into each type of coping approach.
	■ Evaluate each coping approach in terms of its strengths and weaknesses.
Psychological and physiological methods of stress management, including Cognitive Behavioural Therapy and drugs	■ Describe psychological methods of stress management. It is prudent to cover at least two methods, although only Cognitive Behavioural Therapy (CBT) is specified. CBT encompasses a variety of different methods, one of which, stress inoculation, is covered in this chapter.
	■ Describe physiological methods of stress management. Many different drugs are used in the management of stress; benzodiazepines and beta-blockers are considered here. These would suffice as two *different* physiological methods; however, biofeedback is included as another method.
	■ Evaluate psychological and physiological methods of stress management in terms of their strengths and weaknesses.

Introduction

Stress is a common topic of conversation nowadays. For instance, we often hear friends say 'I'm feeling really stressed at the moment'. Stress is believed to account for high levels of anxiety and depression, for increased vulnerability to colds and flu, and for heart attacks and strokes (damage to the brain's blood supply). Every week in papers and magazines there are articles on how to cope with the high levels of modern-day stress, and thousands of professional and amateur psychologists make a living out of helping people to manage stress and its consequences. You will notice that stress is generally referred to in a negative way. Yet, Selye (1956) pointed out that stress can be associated with positive as well as negative experiences. To distinguish between the two, he referred to 'eustress' and 'distress'. Eustress is the amount of stress needed for an active, healthy life. However, when levels of stress increase and exceed a person's ability to cope, it becomes potentially harmful; this is distress. The focus of this chapter will be on the negative experiences associated with stress.

People use the term stress to mean different things. The three most common ways of defining stress are:

- stress as a *response* to something in the environment
- stress as a *stimulus* (**stressor**) in the environment
- stress as a *lack of fit* between perceived demands and perceived ability to cope with those demands. In other words, the key to understanding how much stress individuals experience lies in their *perception* of themselves and their world.

An important feature of this third approach is the recognition of a central cognitive element in the experience of stress. This approach to stress is called the **transactional model** and is the most popular among psychologists. The transactional model allows us to look at the role of individual differences in explaining how people perceive and react to stressful situations. It also means that we can use cognitive strategies to help people cope with stressful experiences, as we shall see later.

In this chapter, we shall look at the background to modern stress research, and evaluate the evidence for links between stress and physical illness. We shall see that some common assumptions about the effects of stress are well founded, but that some are not supported by experimental evidence. We shall also see how successful methods of coping with stress have to take into account the causes of stress and the physiological mechanisms of the stress response.

Topic 1: Stress as a bodily response

The body's response to stress

The term stress, as we use it today, was first used by the American physiologist Walter Cannon in 1914. However, it was the experimental work of Hans Selye in the 1930s that really introduced the topic into the scientific and psychological world. After studying the reactions of rats to the stress of repeated daily injections, Selye proposed that in animals and humans, the body responds to a range of psychological and physical stressors with the same pattern of

Psychology in context

Stress and you

Being 'stressed' is a fact of life. We are all stressed from time to time; indeed, to listen to some people it is not uncommon to be stressed all the time! For our ancestors, millions of years ago, 'stress' as we know it was what kept them alive in the face of danger. The physiologist Walter Cannon identified a pattern of bodily changes that are initiated whenever we are faced with imminent danger. He called this the 'fight-or-flight' response (see p. 151). To early humans, this meant preparing the body (e.g. increasing heart rate and depth of breathing) for the rapid physical action that might be necessary when faced with a sabre-toothed tiger or a very angry Neanderthal! This response to stress persists today (although sabre-toothed tigers as stressors have been replaced by malfunctioning computers and insurmountable debt). Unfortunately, the fight-or-flight response doesn't help us much when dealing with these, so if they persist we get ill. Hitting your broken computer with a large rock or climbing a tree to escape a large telephone bill may make you feel better in the short term, but clearly this is not the best form of **stress management**.

1 Look at the three photos above. Do any of these photos show something that you typically find stressful?

2 Identify some of the other causes of stress that you experience in your life (e.g. people, situations, yourself).

3 How do you *know* that you are stressed? What are the symptoms that you associate with the experience of stress?

4 Compare your lists with those of friends. Do they have different stressors? Are their symptoms the same as yours?

5 What do you *do* when you are stressed? Does it work?

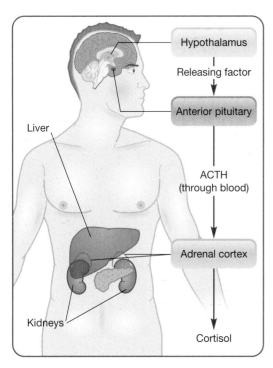

Figure 5.1 Pituitary–adrenal system

Stressful relationships

Stress, it appears, is an inevitable part of our lives. For example, you are most probably reading this because you are studying for an examination, you might lack enough money to make ends meet, and we all feel stressed by personal relationships from time to time.

Theodore Robles *et al.* (2006) were interested in finding out how couples' positive and negative behaviours contributed to changes in their ACTH and cortisol levels. They gave 90 newlywed couples a conflict task and observed their behaviour using a marital interaction coding system. Guess what? High levels of positive behaviour from husbands led to

significant *decreases* in ACTH and cortisol in their wives. This tells us that constructive discussion promotes healthier responses to interpersonal conflict, lowering the negative impact of stressful situations, such as dealing with money problems.

physiological activation. He called this pattern of physiological activation the **General Adaptation Syndrome** (Selye 1956), and suggested that it could in some circumstances lead to harmful changes in the body. This was the beginning of the modern study of stress.

There are two main ways in which our body responds to stress, and both involve the *adrenal gland.* We have two adrenal glands, lying just above the kidneys. Each adrenal gland is made up of two distinct sections – the *adrenal cortex* and the *adrenal medulla*. These two sections release different sets of hormones into the bloodstream (see Figure 5.1) and are controlled by two different pathways:

- the pituitary–adrenal system
- the sympathomedullary pathway.

The pituitary–adrenal system

The **pituitary–adrenal system**, which involves the adrenal cortex, is under the control of the *hypothalamus* and the *pituitary gland*. The hypothalamus is a small structure at the base of the brain, while the pituitary lies in the skull cavity just below the hypothalamus, to which it is connected by the *infundibulum*).

When the higher brain centres evaluate a situation as being stressful, they instruct the hypothalamus to release **corticotrophin releasing factor (CRF),** which travels to the pituitary gland. The pituitary has been called the 'master gland' of the body because it releases a number of hormones into the bloodstream, which in turn control many vital body functions. One of these hormones is *adrenocorticotrophic hormone (ACTH),* which travels to the adrenal cortex and stimulates the release of hormones called *corticosteroids* into the bloodstream. There are a large number of corticosteroids, which have a range of effects on the body and are a vital part of the stress response.

The sympathomedullary pathway

The control of the adrenal medulla is very different. The *autonomic nervous system (ANS)* is a network of nerve pathways running from centres in the lower parts of the brain (the brainstem) out to the organs of the body such as the heart, digestive system, the circulatory (blood) system, and various glands, including the adrenal medulla. The ANS centres in the brainstem are in turn controlled by higher brain structures, especially the hypothalamus. The role of the ANS is to maintain the normal functioning of bodily systems in response to demands. When we run, for example, we need more energy and oxygen supplied to the muscles, so our energy reserves (fats and carbohydrates) have to be 'mobilized' into sugars and fatty acids in the bloodstream, and our heart rate and blood pressure have to increase. All this is carried out by the ANS without our conscious control.

To help it carry out its functions, the ANS has two subdivisions – the sympathetic and the parasympathetic. Each division has nerve pathways running to the internal organs of the body:

- When the *sympathetic* subdivision is activated, we see a pattern of bodily arousal: heart rate and blood pressure increase; fats and carbohydrates are mobilized; activity in the digestive tract slows down – a pattern known as *sympathetic arousal.*

- When the *parasympathetic* subdivision is activated, we see the opposite picture: heart rate and blood pressure return to normal and digestion speeds up – a pattern of calm and bodily relaxation.

The adrenal medulla is controlled by the ANS, and activation of the sympathetic branch stimulates it to release the hormones *adrenaline* and *noradrenaline* into the bloodstream (in the USA, these are called *epinephrine* and *norepinephrine*). Adrenaline is well known as an arousal hormone, and noradrenaline has similar effects. Together they reinforce the pattern of sympathetic activation, stimulating heart rate and blood pressure, and further mobilizing energy reserves.

In stressful situations, therefore, the hypothalamus activates both the pituitary–adrenal system and the **sympathomedullary system** pathways.

Activating the body's stress response

Selye identified the activation of these two pathways as the main components of the body's response to stressors. He also began the debate about *why* they should be activated in this way.

The key to this is to understand that the two systems, when aroused, prepare the body for energy expenditure. Corticosteroids, adrenaline and noradrenaline mobilize energy reserves and sustain blood flow and heart rate to get oxygen to the muscles. They do this under normal circumstances to supply our daily energy needs, but in stressful situations we also have to consider the role of higher brain centres. Normally, the hypothalamus and the ANS function perfectly well without the involvement of higher brain centres, making sure that the body's physiological systems function within normal limits. However, we do need the higher centres when things happen in the world around us to which we have to respond quickly.

To our ancestors, the appearance of a sabre-toothed tiger on the horizon was a signal to run for their lives. Alternatively, if they were hunting, the appearance of a suitable target was a signal to chase. Either way, the reaction was due to higher brain centres in the cortex and limbic system perceiving and evaluating the situation as either threatening or attractive. But to run in any direction needed energy. So, to make sure the energy was available, the higher centres would communicate with the hypothalamus and the ANS, and thus stimulate a pattern of bodily arousal; ACTH would be released from the pituitary, leading to the secretion of corticosteroids from the adrenal cortex, and sympathetic ANS arousal would lead to the secretion of adrenaline and noradrenaline from the adrenal medulla. When the emergency was over, the systems would return to their normal level of functioning.

Cannon (1914) called this pattern of bodily arousal the 'fight or flight' response. Selye's experimental studies showed that it was also central to the stress response he observed in rats. Later, he proposed that any physical or psychological stressor activated the two pathways. Selye developed a model, the General Adaptation Syndrome (GAS), which explained the short-term effects of exposure to stressors, but also accounted for stress-related illnesses such as gastric ulcers.

The General Adaptation Syndrome

The GAS (Selye 1956) has three stages (see Figure 5.2 on the right):

- In the first *alarm* stage, the presence of a stressful event (a stressor) is registered; this could be a threat or an injury or illness affecting the body. The hypothalamic-pituitary system secretes a surge of ACTH which, in turn, releases corticosteroids from the adrenal cortex, while sympathetic ANS activation leads to increased adrenaline and noradrenaline being secreted

Eye on the exam

The skill of précis

Given the precise nature of exam questions, it pays to have different versions of the same material to address differently 'weighted' exam questions. In the first example below (a 6-mark version), five key points have been identified. In the second example (a 3-mark version), these can be reduced to just two or three main points. You could try this same technique for the sympathomedullary pathway.

The pituitary–adrenal system *(6-mark version)*:

- This pathway is activated when higher brain centres evaluate a situation as stressful.
- These higher brain centres instruct the hypothalamus to release **corticotrophin releasing factor (CRF)**, which travels to the pituitary gland.
- CRF causes the pituitary gland to release adrenocorticotrophic hormone (ACTH) into the bloodstream.
- ACTH travels to the adrenal cortex and stimulates the release of corticosteroids into the bloodstream.
- These corticosteroids have a variety of effects throughout the body and form part of the stress response.

The pituitary–adrenal system *(3-mark version)*:

- When the brain evaluates a situation as stressful, the hypothalamus sends a message to the pituitary gland to release ACTH into the bloodstream.
- ACTH in turn prompts the adrenal cortex to create corticosteroids, which have a variety of effects, as part of the body's response to a stressor.

For more exam advice, visit **www.collinseducation.com/psychologyweb**

Figure 5.2 The three stages of Selye's General Adaptation Syndrome

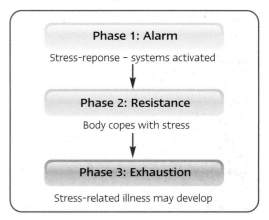

Activity How do you feel when you experience stress?

1 Think back to the last time that you felt stressed because you were in a frightening situation – perhaps you were walking home along an unlit street late at night? How did you feel? What happened to your heart rate? How did your mouth feel? How did your stomach feel? How did you deal with this situation?

2 Now think of the last time you were stressed because you were struggling to finish some homework by the deadline for handing it in, or you had to give a presentation but hadn't had enough time to prepare properly. Again, how did you feel and how did you react? What are the possible signs of stress that others might notice in you (e.g. moodiness, irritability)?

3 Were there any similarities in the way that you felt about each of these situations? Did you deal with each of these in similar or in different ways?

The transactional model emphasizes the role of individual differences in how people perceive and react to stressful situations. What is stressful to one person may not be so for another person.

Activity The transactional model and your stressors

Look back at the list of stressors you wrote in response to the questions in the activity on p. 149. For each stressor you noted, write down how the transactional model of stress (see p. 149) would help to explain why it causes you stress.

from the adrenal medulla. The body is thus prepared for energy expenditure, ready to respond to the perceived threat, poised for fight or flight.

- In the second stage of *resistance*, the body's stress response is fully activated and is apparently coping with the stressor, and so from the outside things seem to be under control.

- However, if the stressor is long lasting or chronic, the body enters the third stage – *exhaustion*. Selye thought that hormone reserves became depleted, and it is at this point that stress-related conditions, such as raised blood pressure, ulcers, depression and anxiety, may develop.

Today most people's concerns are dominated by psychological stress, yet our stress response is still geared to providing the resources we need for physical action. Therefore, it provides energy that has nowhere to go. If a psychological stressor is long lasting and the physical response to it occurs over long periods, then damaging effects of stress can occur, as we shall see in the next section.

Now try the activity on the left to explore how you feel when you experience stress.

'Fight or flight' or 'tend and befriend': Gender differences in the stress response

In 2005, of the 33 000 people in the UK who died of coronary heart disease before the age of 75, approximately 70 per cent were male and 30 per cent female. Several explanations have been proposed for this gender difference. Some psychologists who are particularly interested in the evolutionary explanations of human behaviour suggest it may be the way our *ancestors* dealt with stress that now determines the way *we* react and why there are different consequences of this for the health of men and women. Their argument is that, in the past, human beings dealt with threats using a 'fight-or-flight' response, making use of the body's resources for rapid action. However, while this fight-or-flight response may be help the individual survive, it puts defenceless offspring at a much greater risk of being harmed. Compared to males, females make a greater investment in their offspring, first in pregnancy and then in supporting them to maturity. Consequently, this greater maternal investment has resulted in the evolution of female stress responses that do not jeopardize the safety of offspring in times of threat, but rather maximize the chances that they will survive. Shelley Taylor *et al.* (2000) believe that this should favour the development of biological mechanisms which *inhibit* the fight-or-flight response in females when they are faced with a threat. Females would shift their attention to tending the young (i.e. showing attachment behaviour) and befriend other females as a defensive network against outside threats.

Taylor and colleagues claim that:

- high sympathetic nervous system activation (which is targeted primarily at the cardiovascular system, thereby optimizing physical performance) and high cortisol responses are characteristic biological components of the *male* stress response

- neurophysiological mechanisms within the female brain inhibit the fight-or-flight response, and instead promote attachment behaviour, called the 'tend-and-befriend' response to stress.

It is possible that these differences also apply to the non-life-threatening stressors of daily life, and could play a role in the fact that men are more likely than women to die of coronary heart disease.

Stress-related illness and the immune system

The last phase of Selye's GAS is the stage of exhaustion. In Selye's time, it was thought that the constant outpouring of stress hormones eventually depleted our stores, so that a literal state of 'exhaustion' occurred and it was this that led to stress-related illness. Nowadays, the view has changed – hormones themselves are believed to be responsible for the negative effects of stressful situations. The two main reasons for this change in view are that:

- hormone supplies are rarely exhausted – even under the most severe pressure
- we now know far more about the widespread effects of these hormones on the body.

As well as activating body systems that prepare us for action (e.g. increasing the blood supply to the heart and muscles and increasing glucose in the bloodstream to bolster our energy reserves), the stress response also shuts down some body systems, e.g. cutting down the blood supply to the digestive tract, which might contribute to the development of gastric ulcers if the stress is long-lasting. The stress response also inhibits the **immune system** (called **immunosuppression**).

The immune system

The immune system is our main defence against infection by foreign agents. It is an immensely complicated network of cells and chemicals throughout the body that functions to seek out and destroy invading particles. Any agent that stimulates an immune response is called an antigen. Familiar antigens are bacteria, viruses and fungi (such as moulds and yeasts). Sometimes, particles that are normally harmless, such as dust and pollen, cause an overreaction of the immune system, and this is the basis of allergies. Key players in our immune system are the white blood cells, which are manufactured in the bone marrow and circulate in the bloodstream.

The two types of white blood cell are lymphocytes and phagocytes, and these provide three different mechanisms of immunity:

- *Non-specific immunity* – Phagocytes are cells that surround and ingest foreign particles wherever they encounter them. One example is the macrophage (see Figure 5.3), which acts like a scavenger looking for invading pathogens. When it finds them, it alerts other macrophages to come and destroy the invaders. Macrophages also activate helper T cells.

- *Cell-based immunity* – Lymphocytes called T cells (because they mature in the thymus gland) seek out and destroy any cells recognized as foreign (e.g. in transplanted tissues), and cells infected with antigens such as viruses and bacteria. Helper T cells activate cytotoxic T cells (e.g. natural killer cells) which destroy infected body cells, and also activate another class of lymphocyte, the B cell.

- *Antibody-based immunity* – B cells (so-called because they mature in the bone marrow) destroy invading agents while they are still in the bloodstream and before they enter the body's tissues. They do this by forming plasma cells, which in turn produce antibodies. These attach themselves to the virus or bacteria, slowing them down, and making it easier for them to be destroyed by other immune cells such as the phagocytes and cytotoxic cells.

The immune system is complex, and stress-response hormones can affect it directly. For example, high levels of corticosteroids can shrink the thymus gland,

Figure 5.3 The immune response

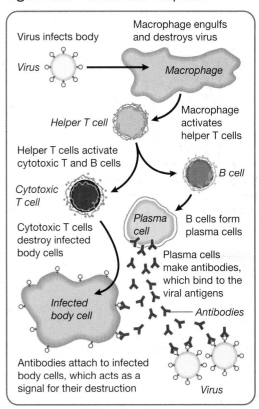

preventing the growth of T cells. The immune system is also more sensitive to stress than was originally thought. Even short-lasting life events, such as brief marital strife, can cause immunosuppression, while chronic (long-term) life stress causes parallel long-term reductions in immune function (Willis *et al.* 1987). On the other hand, exercise, diet and social support can improve immune function, and as a self-regulating system it will also recover from suppression if the stressful situation is resolved (Sapolsky 1994).

Short-term suppression of the immune system is not dangerous, but chronic suppression leaves the body vulnerable to infection and disease. A current example of this danger is AIDS, which involves long-term immunosuppression and leaves the sufferer vulnerable to a host of possible illnesses. So, we would expect chronic stress to lead to more frequent illnesses and infections. We will look at the experimental evidence in the next section.

Some effects of stress on the immune system

- *Infection and diseases* – Stress causes physiological changes that tend to weaken our immune system. As a result, our health can be negatively affected: infections and illness occur more frequently and recovery takes longer.

- *Indirect effects* – Stress causes the release of ACTH from the pituitary gland in the brain, which signals the adrenal glands to release anti-inflammatory hormones. These inhibit immune cell functioning.

- *Psoriasis and eczema* – Symptoms of inflammatory skin disorders such as psoriasis and eczema worsen with stress. Stress interferes with the immune system's ability to deal with the inflammation associated with these disorders.

Complete the activity 'Indirect effects of stress ...' on the left before reading on.

You will probably have identified a range of behaviours that might result from being in a stressful situation and could indirectly affect a person's health in the longer term. These might include smoking, drinking excess alcohol, drug abuse or neglecting oneself by eating a poor diet over a period of time, making it more likely that the person will suffer from illnesses such as colds and coughs. Later in the chapter, we will consider a range of techniques that can help to reduce the negative effects of stress.

Short-term stressors and the immune system

It has become well established in recent decades that psychological stress can adversely affect many aspects of immune function (Glaser and Kiecolt-Glaser 2005). Even fairly brief periods of stress, such as school or college examinations, can result in significant suppression of immune-system functioning. (See the study by Kiecolt-Glaser *et al.* (1984) on the opposite page and the activity 'Stress and the immune system' on the left.)

These effects include a decline in the ability of white blood cells (leucocytes) to perform their functions in fighting antigens (Kiecolt-Glaser and Glaser 1991) and a decrease in natural killer cell activity during examination periods (Kang *et al.* 1997). Natural killer cells attack cancer cells and cells infected by viruses.

Stress can also slow down wound healing. The immune system plays an important part in healing wounds by preparing tissue for repair by means of cytokines (secreted proteins which initiate inflammation in the area of a wound) that promote healing. Transient stressors such as examinations can alter the production of cytokines, and so slow down this process. The adverse effects of such stressors on immune-system functioning may be increased when

Activity Indirect effects of stress on health and wellbeing

As we have seen, the chronic experience of stress can lead directly to physical illness. For example, it can produce physiological changes in the body that contribute to diseases such as heart disease or weakening of the immune system. Sometimes, however, stress may cause physical illness *indirectly*, by altering the way people behave, which, in turn, could damage their health.

In what ways might a stressed person behave that could later increase the risk of damage to their physical health? To help you start thinking about this, consider the following three 'stressful' scenarios:

1 a student studying for an exam in a subject that they find quite difficult

2 a person who has just broken up with their girl/boyfriend after several years of being together

3 someone caring for a relative who is terminally ill.

RESEARCH METHODS

Activity Stress and the immune system

Kiecolt-Glaser and colleagues' 1984 study was a *natural* experiment. As you will have read in Chapter 1 (pp. 18–19), in a natural experiment, the researcher makes use of naturally occurring differences in the independent variable. This means that the researcher does not directly *control* the IV.

1 What do you think were the advantages of using a natural experiment in this study on the effects of stress on the immune system?

2 What might the disadvantages have been?

3 Can the researchers draw confident conclusions about the cause-and-effect relationship between stress and immune functioning?

4 Can you generalize the findings of this study to the general adult population?

Answers are given on p. 277 ▶

	The effects of stress on the immune system
	A study of the effects of important exams on the functioning of the immune system by Kiecolt-Glaser *et al.* (1984)

Aim	To investigate whether the stress of important examinations has an effect on the functioning of the immune system.
Procedures	■ This was a natural experiment using 75 medical students. ■ Blood samples were taken: (a) one month before their final examinations (relatively low stress), and (b) during the examinations (high stress). ■ Immune function was assessed by measuring T cell lymphocyte activity in the blood samples. ■ The students were also given questionnaires to assess psychological variables such as life events and loneliness.
Findings	■ T cell activity was significantly reduced in the second blood sample, taken during their final examinations, compared with the first sample (taken one month before their final examinations). ■ T cell activity was most reduced in participants who also reported high levels of life events and loneliness.
Conclusions	■ Examination stress reduces immune function, potentially leaving the individual vulnerable to illness and infections. ■ Immune function is also affected by psychological variables such as the stress of life events and feelings of loneliness. These long-term stressors may make individuals more vulnerable to the added effect of short-term stressors such as examinations.
Evaluation	■ This study used medical students, who might be considered a non-representative group. This limits the extent to which these results can be generalized to other groups in society.

| **FURTHER ANALYSIS** | Accepting criticism at face value may get you good marks, but you can boost the impact of your critical commentary by looking a bit deeper. Students may well be a special group, but these results are in line with other studies linking stress to reduced immune function. Kiecolt-Glaser's research group has shown that immune function is significantly reduced in highly stressed groups such as carers for Alzheimer patients (Kiecolt-Glaser *et al.* 1991) and women going through divorce proceedings (Kiecolt-Glaser *et al.* 1987). Even short periods of marital conflict have been known to lead to immunosuppression, with women showing a greater and longer-lasting reduction than men (Kiecolt-Glaser *et al.* 1998). |

individuals are already in an elevated level of stress. For example, students taking examinations show greater immune-system dysfunction if they additionally report stress caused by daily hassles such as arguments with parents or a broken-down car (Marshall *et al.* 1998).

Chronic stress and the immune system

Given that such short-term stressors as examinations can cause suppression of immune-system functioning, it is not surprising that chronic, long-lasting stress has also been found to have consequences for immune-system functioning. Research has focused on three main chronic stressors: conflict in interpersonal relationships, death of a spouse and care giving.

■ *Conflict in interpersonal relationships* – Couples whose interactions are negative and hostile show less adaptive immunological responses after these interactions. For example, individuals who report relationship conflict lasting more than one month have been found to be particularly at risk of developing illness when exposed to an infectious agent (Cohen 2005).

Kiecolt-Glaser *et al.* (2005) tested the impact of interpersonal conflict on wound healing. She found that blister wounds on the arms of married couples healed more slowly after conflictive than after supportive discussions. Some interesting gender differences have emerged in this area, with women often showing greater immune-system suppression following marital conflict than men (Mayne *et al.* 1997).

Interpersonal conflict has been found to have a negative effect on immune-system functioning

How can we deal with the negative effects of stress on immune-system functioning? Research has suggested a role for physical exercise in countering the effects of stress, particularly among older people. Ageing is associated with a reduced efficiency of the immune system (immunosenescence), putting older adults at much greater risk of infection. Emery *et al.* (2005) randomly assigned 28 healthy older adults (mean age 61 years) to either an exercise activity group or a no-exercise control group (to act as a comparison).

A month after the introduction of the exercise regime (the independent variable), all participants received a small wound, which was measured at three-week intervals to calculate the rate of wound healing (the dependent variable).

Wound healing occurred at a significantly faster rate in the exercise group (mean 29.2 days) than the control group (mean 38.9 days). The exercise group also reported much lower levels of perceived stress, suggesting that exercise activity may have important consequences for both the perception of stress *and* immune-system functioning. Research such as this offers a clear message (particularly for some of us older authors ...) concerning the value of exercise, and adds scientific credibility to the common belief that exercise is good for you.

■ *Death of a spouse* – The death of a close relative, such as a husband or wife, child or parent, is also associated with immune-system dysfunction. For example, individuals who had recently experienced an unexpected bereavement showed lower natural killer cell and lymphocyte activity compared to matched non-bereaved controls. This difference was observed 40 days after the death and, in some participants, still persisted after six months (Gerra *et al.* 2003). We should exercise some caution when interpreting these findings, however, as it is not clear to what degree stress, as opposed to other consequences of bereavement, such as disturbed sleep and depression, plays a role in this change in immune-system functioning. Research has also uncovered gender differences although, unlike the findings about effects of marital conflict, it is men who appear to be at greater risk of mortality following the death of their spouse (Kiecolt-Glaser and Newton 2001).

■ *Care giving* – Another form of chronic stressor associated with immune-system dysfunction is care giving, in particular caring for a spouse with dementia. Such caregivers are frequently socially isolated, experience overwhelming demands on their resources, both physical and psychological, and show higher levels of depression and anxiety. Compared to matched controls, spousal caregivers tend to show poorer immune function, including lower levels of natural killer cell activity and poorer resistance to viral infection (Kiecolt-Glaser *et al.* 2000).

Suppression of the immune system need not necessarily lead to illness and disease if immune function remains within the normal range. Even if it is not, you still have to be exposed to an infectious agent for illness to develop. Cohen *et al.* (1993) demonstrated this in a classic study. Participants filled in questionnaires on negative life events, how stressed they felt, and the degree of negative emotions (depression and hostility) they felt. These scores were combined into a 'stress index'. The participants were then exposed to low doses of the common cold virus. Some 82 per cent of the 394 participants became infected with the cold virus, and infection was highly correlated with their stress index score, i.e. the higher their score, the more likely they were to become infected. Although this was a correlational study, it strongly suggests that high levels of stress reduce immune function and make a person more vulnerable to viral infection.

Age and gender differences in the effects of stress on the immune system

A telephone survey (National Consumer League 2003) of over 1000 adult Americans found that:

■ women were significantly more likely to report problems and being stressed than men (84 per cent vs 76 per cent)

■ people under the age of 65 were more likely to report being stressed than older people (82 per cent vs 70 per cent).

However, these statistics do not tell us how these groups cope with stress, or *how* stress impacts on their immune-system functioning.

Kiecolt-Glaser *et al.* (2003) suggests there are significant differences between women and men in the way their immune system reacts to marital conflict, with women showing more adverse hormonal and immunological changes. Segerstrom and Miller (2004) claim that age may make people more vulnerable to stress-related decreases in immune function because age makes it harder for the body to regulate itself.

CHECK YOUR UNDERSTANDING

Check your understanding of stress as a bodily response by answering the following questions. Try to do this from memory. You can check your answers by looking back through Topic 1.

1 What is a stressor?

2 What is a stress response?

3 Who did the earliest systematic studies of the stress response?

4 Name the three stages in the General Adaptation Syndrome.

5 Describe the 'transactional' model of stress.

6 Name the two parts of the adrenal glands.

7 Outline the two main pathways of the body's stress response.

8 What does the body's immune system do?

9 What is immunosuppression?

10 How did Kiecolt-Glaser and colleagues measure activity of the immune system?

11 What general conclusions can be drawn from the work of Kiecolt-Glaser and colleagues?

12 How did Cohen and colleagues measure the stress levels of participants and how did they test immune function?

Topic 2: Stress in everyday life

As we saw at the beginning of this chapter, the common definition of stress is rooted in our perception of demands made on us. For example:

- *demands we make on ourselves* – e.g. am I happy enough, rich enough, do I look okay, will I meet this deadline?

- *demands other people make on us* – e.g. get this job done, make me happier, earn more money, be my friend

- *demands made by the environment we live in* – e.g. getting stuck in traffic jams, breaking down on the motorway, having our mobile phone stolen

- *demands made by friends and relations* – e.g. when they have accidents, become ill and when they die.

Whether we regard all or only some of these situations as stressful depends on our coping abilities.

Life changes and daily hassles

Stressors can be classified into two broad categories: discrete (i.e. one-off) or continuous (Wheaton 1996). Most of the research on discrete stressors has focused on the study of major life events, such as divorce or job loss, that require a significant degree of adjustment on the part of the individual. Continuous

Psychology in context

The positive side of traumatic life changes

We might imagine that negative life changes can result in only negative consequences for the individual, but research suggests this is not the case. While several surveys have reported the *negative* psychological impact on the general public of the terrorist attacks in the USA on 11 September 2001, evidence is beginning to emerge about *positive* changes in people's lives.

Survivors emerging from the smoke as the World Trade Center towers collapse

A survey of adults in Ottawa, Canada (Davies and Macdonald 2004) found that two years after the event, many reported positive changes in their lives (e.g. being closer to family and refocusing priorities) that they attributed to the attacks. The greater the initial distress, the greater the extent of positive changes reported. The same trend has been found in studies of rape victims (Frazier *et al.* 2004), with many survivors reporting some positive life changes after the assault, including increased social support and gaining perceived control over the recovery process. These findings are consistent with the claim that the perception of growth may grow directly out of one's personal experience of traumatic life events.

Consider any life changes that you, or someone you know, have experienced that seemed entirely negative at the time but which, later on, you realized helped you or the other person to grow and mature.

If you enjoy reading novels, you might like to read *Falling Man*, which examines the way a few people cope after being involved, directly and indirectly, in the attacks on the Twin Towers in New York in 2001. The novel was written by Don DeLillo and was published by Picador in 2007.

Table 5.1
The Social Readjustment Rating Scale (SRRS)

	Life event	LCU
1	Death of spouse	100
2	Divorce	73
3	Marital separation	65
4	Jail term	63
5	Death of close family member	63
6	Personal injury or illness	53
7	Marriage	50
8	Fired at work	47
9	Marital reconciliation	45
10	Retirement	45
11	Change in health of family member	44
12	Pregnancy	40
13	Sex difficulties	39
14	Gain new family member	39
15	Business readjustment	39
16	Change in financial status	38
17	Death of close friend	37
18	Change to different line of work	36
19	Change in number of arguments with spouse	35
20	Mortgage over US $10 000	31
21	Foreclosure of mortgage or loan	30
22	Change in responsibilities at work	29
23	Son or daughter leaving home	29
24	Trouble with in-laws	29
25	Outstanding personal achievement	28
26	Wife begins or stops work	26
27	Begin or end school	26
28	Change in living conditions	25
29	Revision of personal habits	24
30	Trouble with boss	23
31	Change in work hours or conditions	20
32	Change in residence	20
33	Change in schools	20
34	Change in recreation	19
35	Change in church activities	19
36	Change in social activities	18
37	Mortgage or loan less than US $10 000	17
38	Change in sleeping habits	16
39	Change in number of family get-togethers	15
40	Change in eating habits	15
41	Vacation	13
42	Christmas	12
43	Minor violation of the law	11

stressors, such as the ongoing problems of life and living, also permeate our daily reality. We begin this section by examining the impact of discrete major stressors, i.e. **life changes**, and then move on to examine the impact of continuous minor stressors, i.e. **daily hassles**.

Life changes

The Social Readjustment Rating Scale (SRRS)

A major way of measuring the relationship between life changes and wellbeing is the Social Readjustment Rating Scale (SRRS). This scale, developed by Thomas Holmes and Richard Rahe in 1967, is also known as the Holmes–Rahe Life Events Rating Scale. Together with some later variations, the SRRS has been the most widely used of all methods for assessing life stress.

Inevitably, things happen in life to which we have to make psychological adjustments. The more we have to adjust, the more stressful the event is. Holmes and Rahe made a list of major life events, based on their experience as clinicians. They then asked hundreds of men and women, of various ages and backgrounds, to rate the events in terms of the amount of readjustment they would require, i.e. their psychological impact. The death of a spouse came out top, and was given an arbitrary value (called a 'life change unit' or LCU) of 100. Other events were given ratings relative to this ranking, so that losing your job, for instance, came out as LCU 47, a house move as LCU 20, and holidays as LCU 13 (see Table 5.1).

Once the scale was constructed, it was simply a matter of asking participants to check off any of the 43 life events they had experienced over a given period, usually two years, but sometimes less. The researcher then totalled their score and used it as an index of that person's life stress. Using studies that were both *retrospective* (asking people with possible stress-related illnesses to look back at the previous two years) and *prospective* (assessing life stress and then observing participants over the following months), Holmes and Rahe proposed that a score of 150 or more increased the chances of stress-related health breakdown by 30 per cent, while a score of over 300 increased the odds by 50 per cent.

Figure 5.4 How life changes are linked to stress

Bereavement

All types of bereavement tend to be perceived by the survivor as stressful, but sudden or violent deaths are particularly distressing.

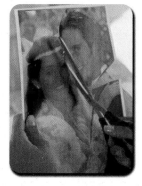

Divorce

Divorce can create high levels of stress for divorcing couples, making them more susceptible to depression (Hines 1997). Research also suggests that divorce negatively affects the immune system.

Research into sources of stress

A study of life changes as a source of stress (Rahe *et al.* 1970)

Aim	To find out if scores on the Holmes and Rahe Social Readjustment Rating Scale (SRRS) correlated with the subsequent onset of illness.
Procedure	■ 2500 male American sailors were given the SRRS to assess how many life events they had experienced in the previous six months. ■ The total score on the SRRS – the Life Change Score – was recorded for each participant. ■ Then, over the following six-month tour of duty, detailed records were kept of each sailor's health status. ■ The recorded Life Change Scores were correlated with the sailors' illness scores.
Findings	■ There was a positive correlation of +0.118 between Life Change Scores and illness scores. ■ Although the positive correlation was small (a perfect positive correlation would be 1.00 – see p. 20 and pp. 64–5), it did indicate that there was a meaningful relationship between LCUs and health (this is often referred to as a statistically significant correlation). As LCU scores increased, so did the frequency of illness.
Conclusion	■ The researchers concluded that as LCUs were positively correlated with illness scores, experiencing life events increases the chances of stress-related health breakdown. ■ Since the correlation was not perfect, life events cannot be the only factor contributing to illness.
Evaluation	■ A correlation does not imply causality or the direction of any effect; depression or anxiety may not be caused by life events, since depressed or anxious people may bring about life events such as separation or divorce. ■ The sample was restricted to male US Navy personnel; therefore, it was both ethnocentric (Americans only) and androcentric (males only). This reduces the validity of the study, and makes it difficult to generalize to other populations.
FURTHER ANALYSIS	The study does not take into account individual differences in reactions to stress, but on the positive side, these findings support other research that suggests that life-event scores do have a low but significant association with stress-related health breakdown.

Other research into life changes as a source of stress

Stone *et al.* (1987) had married couples complete daily checklists of events over a three-month period. The number of undesirable events that they experienced increased three to four days prior to the onset of illness, and desirable events decreased during the same period. Because a sequence of undesirable events preceded the onset of illness, this suggests that they might have been responsible for the stress-related illness. This is supported by the fact that the incidence of desirable events (which might buffer the individual from illness) *decreased* during the same period.

Michael and Ben-Zur (2007) studied 130 participants (mean age 49.4 years), approximately half of whom were male and half female. Half of these individuals had been recently divorced and half recently widowed. The findings showed that widowed individuals scored higher on life satisfaction before than after the loss, while divorced individuals showed the opposite pattern in relation to their separation from their partners. In part, this difference might be explained because those divorced were dating or living with a new partner, a trend that was not as obvious in widowed participants.

RESEARCH METHODS

Activity — **Measuring the impact of life events**

A correlation measures the relationship between two variables. In Rahe *et al.*'s (1970) research, there was a significant positive correlation of +0.118 between Life Change Units and illness scores.

1 What does this tell us about the relationship between life changes and illness?

2 What can this study *not* tell us about the relationship between life changes and illness?

3 How could we establish whether there is a causal relationship between life changes and illness?

Answers are given on p. 277 ▶

Activity Stressful life events

In 1967, Holmes and Rahe published a scale called the Social Readjustment Rating Scale (SRRS), reproduced in Table 5.1 on p. 158. This scale consists of a list of 43 major life events that were perceived as being potentially stressful because they forced people to make substantial psychological readjustments. Each life event in the list is allocated a point value to reflect the relative amount of change it requires. This is known as the 'life change unit' (LCU).

1 Look at the three photographs below. Why do you think that Holmes and Rahe included each of these events in their scale?

2 Why do you think that each event was allocated the rating it was?

Outstanding personal achievement is ranked 25 in the SRRS with a LCU of 28.

Vacation is rated 41 with a LCU of 13.

Marriage is ranked 7 in the SRRS with a LCU of 50.

Evaluation of the life changes approach

Many studies have been carried out on the link between life events and health breakdown using the SRRS. Although significant correlations are often found, they tend, like the study undertaken by Rahe *et al.* (1970) outlined on p. 159, to be relatively small (the highest at about 0.30), suggesting a relationship between stress and health, but not a strong one. However, it also became clear that there were problems with the scale:

- *Individual differences* – The scale's values for different events are arbitrary and will certainly vary from person to person. Some people really dislike holidays or Christmas, and would have them near the top of their list of stressors rather than at the bottom. Others might find marital separation a relief from a highly dysfunctional relationship. The stress of taking out a large mortgage depends on your income. Each of us could devise a personal rating scale, since the stressfulness of an event depends upon our perception of it.

- *Causality* – The relationship between SRRS score and health is correlational and so tells us nothing about causality. Depression or chronic physical illness may *lead to* life problems rather than being caused by them.

- *Positive life events* – Some life events are positive. People getting married probably see it as a positive change, while 'change in financial state' can clearly be positive or negative. The SRRS does not distinguish positive from negative because the model assumes that any life change is stressful, without evidence to support such an assumption.

- *Self-report* – Self-report of life events can be surprisingly unreliable. Raphael *et al.* (1991) asked participants to fill out a life-events scale for the previous year, and then repeated the exercise every month for another year. As time passed, the agreement on life events between the later reports and the first declined significantly.

- *Dated and androcentric* – Although Holmes and Rahe's approach using the SRRS scale generated a huge amount of research in the 30 years after its publication, it is now rather dated (e.g. 'mortgage over $10 000') and androcentric (e.g. 'wife begins or stops work'). More recent studies have used developments of this scale that focus more on contemporary issues that affect both males *and* females.

One general problem with any life-event approach is that it concentrates on events that are by their very nature unusual. In any given study, 10 to 30 per cent of participants may experience none of the items on the scale, while still not being free of stress. This is because incidents we would not count as major events – the everyday hassles of life – can be a source of considerable stress. These are everyday occurrences such as worrying about friendships, losing the car keys, concerns over appearance, keeping up with college courses and minor health problems. For most people, these have more daily impact than items included in scales such as the SRRS.

Daily hassles

'Any idiot can handle a crisis – it's this day-to-day living that wears you out.'
Anton Chekhov

Daily hassles are relatively minor events that arise in the course of a normal day. They include, for example, everyday concerns about work, such as disagreements with a colleague, or problems with your daily commute to college such as the bus being late. Some of these might be fairly routine (e.g. the bus is often late), while others might be more unexpected (e.g. a malfunctioning computer). The hassle and its associated emotional effects usually disappear after a short time.

Research suggests that the adverse effects of these daily hassles can be offset by the corresponding experience of daily *uplifts* – positive everyday experiences, such as receiving praise for a job well done, or receiving an unexpected tax rebate. In one study (Gervais 2005), nurses were asked to keep diaries for a month, recording daily hassles and uplifts connected with their job. They were also asked to rate their own performance over the same period. Results showed that nurses felt the uplifts usually counteracted the negative effects of their daily hassles, and also improved their performance and lowered stress levels.

Research on daily hassles

To assess these very real sources of stress, Lazarus and colleagues devised the Hassles Scale (Kanner *et al.* 1981). The original form had 117 items, although versions can be constructed for subgroups, such as students (e.g. unfriendly classmates, boring teachers). Since they thought that positive events in life could reduce the impact of daily hassles, the group also introduced an Uplifts Scale, with 135 items that cheer people up; items include getting on well with your partner and feeling healthy. See Table 5.2 for some examples taken from the Hassles and Uplifts Scales. Research findings on daily hassles include the following:

- Scores on the Hassles Scale correlate with levels of depression, anxiety and health problems (Kanner *et al.* 1981).

- DeLongis *et al.* (1982) compared Hassles scores with Life Events, and found that although both correlated significantly with health status, the association for Hassles scores was greater. No statistical relationship was found between Uplift scores and health outcomes.

- In an Australian study, Ruffin (1993) found that daily hassles produced greater psychological and physical dysfunction than major negative life events.

- Recent research (Bouteyre *et al.* 2007) has established a significant relationship between daily hassles and mental health of students during the initial transition period to university. A total of 233 first-year Psychology students at a French university answered a questionnaire based on the Beck Depression Inventory and the Hassles Scale. The results showed that 41 per cent of the students suffered from depressive symptoms, and that the daily hassles encountered during the first year at university could be considered a significant risk factor for depression.

The negative impact of daily hassles is now broadly accepted.

Why are daily hassles so stressful?

Two explanations have been proposed:

- Minor daily stressors affect wellbeing by accumulating over a series of days to create persistent irritations, frustrations and overloads that result in more serious stress reactions, such as anxiety and depression (Lazarus 1999). Many researchers suggest that the frequency and type of daily hassles experienced by individuals provide a better explanation for physical and psychological health than (relatively) rare major life events.

- An alternative explanation is that daily hassles arise from pre-existing chronic stressors and so amplify the effects of that existing stressor. Take, for

Table 5.2 Examples of hassles and uplifts

Examples of hassles
- Concerns about weight
- Health of a family member
- Rising prices of certain goods
- Home maintenance
- Too many things to do
- Misplacing or losing things
- Physical appearance

Examples of uplifts
- Relating well to spouse/partner/lover
- Relating well to friends
- Completing a task
- Feeling healthy
- Getting enough sleep
- Eating out
- Visiting, phoning or writing to someone

RESEARCH METHODS

Activity   Your hassles and uplifts

Keep a diary over the next week or so. At the end of each day, make a note of all the *hassles* that you have experienced (keeping the diary may be one of them!) and record the total number.

Beside your list of hassles for each day, make a note of all the *uplifts* you experienced on the same day and the total number.

Also, at the end of each day, give yourself a rating between 1 and 10 to indicate how you have felt that day: a rating of 1 indicates a very low sense of psychological wellbeing, while 10 indicates very high psychological wellbeing.

Finally, note down any health problems that you have experienced that day (e.g. headaches).

At the end of the week, prepare a bar chart to show the total number of hassles and uplifts for Day 1, Day 2 through to Day 7.

1 Does there appear to be any relationship between the number of hassles and uplifts on a particular day and the rating for general psychological wellbeing of that day?

2 Did you seem to experience more health problems after you had experienced a higher number of hassles?

3 How might you explain the possible relationship between the number of hassles, uplifts, general sense of psychological wellbeing and health problems?

example, a husband who is trying to cope with the loss of his wife and who experiences a relatively minor problem with the washing machine, or with a child who has wet the bed. He may experience higher than expected levels of distress given the relatively trivial nature of the situation because he was coping with chronic stress before the hassle arose. The existence of chronic stressors may deplete a person's resources for coping with daily hassles or prevent them from promoting a more positive appraisal of the situation.

Evaluation of research into daily hassles

- *Causality* – What does research tell us? Most of the data on daily hassles is correlational, which means we cannot draw *causal* conclusions about the relationship between daily hassles and stress-related problems. However, these correlations do indicate that the daily stress in our lives can *potentially* have adverse effects on our health and feelings of wellbeing.

- *Cultural differences* – Social support is an important protective factor against stress, and there are clear cultural variations in how it is used. Researchers have looked at the way different ethnic groups use social support as a protection against stressors, including daily hassles. Kim and McKenry (1998) looked at social support networks in a range of cultural groups living in America. They found that African-Americans, Asian-Americans and Hispanics all used the social support offered by significant others (e.g. parents and friends) more than White Americans did.

However, this is not always the case. Research by Sim (2000) found that Korean early adolescents reported having more daily hassles that contributed to maladjustment than they had social support from significant others. There appears, therefore, to be cross-cultural research supporting the claim that daily hassles contribute to health and social problems.

Workplace stress

Through its effects on psychological and physical health, stress can affect performance at work, whatever your job. All jobs involve a certain amount of stress, but there is a growing interest in work conditions that increase stress. Companies have an interest in maintaining productivity and performance, both of which are affected by stress-related illness. The study of **workplace stress** is an area of occupational psychology and is one of the fastest-growing fields of psychology.

Sources of stress in the workplace

Sources of stress in the workplace depend on the type of work or enterprise you are looking at. An assembly-line worker in a car factory has different problems from a middle-rank manager in a City bank. There are, however, some sources of stress which apply to most workers; for example:

- *Physical environment* – Space, temperature, lighting and arrangement of an office (open plan or separate rooms) can all affect the individual. Physical stressors make work more difficult, and more energy has to be expended to overcome them. The increased arousal can also lead to frustration, and many studies have shown that increased temperature (e.g. Halpern 1995) and exposure to intense noise (e.g. Evans *et al.* 1998) can lead to stress and aggression.

■ *Work overload* – We seem to be moving towards a culture in which long hours at work are seen as a mark of esteem, to the cost of both the individual and social structures, such as the family. Overload is frequently reported as one of the most stressful aspects of the workplace (Dewe 1992), and a key element in this is the impact long hours have on family life (the home–work interface).

■ *Lack of control* – In many organizations, other people often determine workload and work patterns. Both animal studies (e.g. the work on learned helplessness by Seligman 1975) and work with humans (e.g. Marmot *et al.*'s 1991 study, described below) show that a perceived lack of control increases the stress response and contributes to depression and illness.

■ *Role ambiguity* – This occurs when the requirements for a particular work role are unclear or poorly defined, and is a major factor contributing to work-related stress. This sometimes results either from having no clear guidelines separating one role from another, or ones that are contradictory. Role ambiguity will also contribute to other sources of workplace stress, such as relations with co-workers and lack of control.

Before reading on, look at the activity 'Categorizing workplace stressors' on the left and start planning how you might carry it out.

Sources of stress are highly significant to the individual concerned, but they also affect the organization. Stress can lead to physical and psychological consequences, which, in turn, affect productivity through decreased motivation at work and time off with health problems.

In the USA, and increasingly in companies in the UK, occupational psychologists are brought in to identify sources of stress in the workplace and to advise on methods of reducing them. By assessing the organizational structure and interviewing employees at all levels of the hierarchy, occupational psychologists try to pinpoint key problems and to identify solutions. These can involve changes in methods of communication or the physical arrangement of workplaces, or the introduction of different work schedules or management structures.

The key study on the next page, 'The workplace as a source of stress', describes one study of work stressors and the possible link with work-related illness.

Research on workplace stress

Many other studies have been carried out on stress in the workplace. For example, Marmot *et al.* (1991) carried out a three-year longitudinal study of over 3000 Whitehall civil servants, measuring job control and stress-related illness. They found that people with low job control (type and amount of work decided by others) were four times more likely to die of a heart attack than those with high job control (i.e. more independence in deciding the type and amount of work). Job control and illness were negatively correlated: as job control decreased, the chances of stress-related illness increased. This finding was supported by a review of research that concluded that a combination of high job demands and low control is associated with an increased chance of heart disease (Van der Doef and Maes 1998).

Evaluation of research on workplace stressors

■ *Extraneous variables* – Despite the apparent link between lack of job control and stress-related illness found in many studies, it is possible that important variables, such as personality, were not controlled for. It could be that people

A woman's place?

You may have wondered why your working mum always appears far more 'frazzled' at home than your working dad. Research may have provided the answer. As we saw on p. 151, adrenaline and noradrenaline levels are increased in stressful situations. At work, these stressors include work overload, too much responsibility and role conflicts, as well as having to endure monotonous and repetitive jobs. However, Lundberg and Frankenhaeuser (1999) found that for many female managers trying to juggle work *and* home responsibilities, the lack of 'unwinding time' after a hard day at work meant that stress levels remained high throughout the day (see Figure 5.5). This was not the case for their male colleagues, who could use the evening as a chance to wind down from the pressures of the day. This study demonstrates how psychological research can explain everyday observations, in this case why your mum often seems more frazzled than your dad!

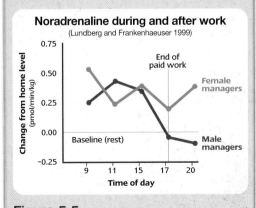

Figure 5.5
Noradrenaline during and after work

The workplace as a source of stress

A study by Johansson et al. (1978) into work stressors and stress-related illness.

RESEARCH METHODS

Aim	To investigate whether work stressors, such as repetitiveness, machine-regulated pace of work and high levels of responsibility, increase stress-related physiological arousal and stress-related illness.
Procedures	■ The researchers identified a high-risk group of 14 'finishers' in a Swedish sawmill. Their job was to finish off the wood at the last stage of processing timber. The work was machine paced, isolated, very repetitive yet highly skilled, and the finishers' productivity determined the wage rates for the entire factory. ■ The 14 'finishers' were compared with a low-risk group of 10 cleaners (the control group), whose work was more varied, largely self-paced, and allowed more socializing with other workers. ■ Levels of stress-related hormones (adrenaline and noradrenaline) in the urine were measured on work days and on rest days. ■ Records were kept of stress-related illness and absenteeism.
Findings	■ The high-risk group of 14 'finishers' secreted more stress hormones (adrenaline and noradrenaline) on work days than on rest days, and higher levels than the control group. ■ The high-risk group of 'finishers' also showed significantly higher levels of stress-related illness, such as headaches and higher levels of absenteeism, than the low-risk group of cleaners.
Conclusions	■ A combination of work stressors – especially repetitiveness, machine pacing of work and high levels of responsibility – lead to chronic (long-term) physiological arousal. This in turn leads to stress-related illness and absenteeism. ■ If employers want to reduce illness and absenteeism in their workforce, they need to find ways of reducing these work stressors, e.g. by introducing variety into employees' work and by allowing them to experience some sense of control over the pace of their work.
Evaluations	■ Some important variables, such as individual differences, are not controlled in this study; it may be that certain people who are vulnerable to stress (e.g. those exhibiting Type A behaviour – see opposite page) are attracted to high-risk, demanding jobs, such as 'finishing' in a sawmill. ■ In addition, the study does not identify which of the various work stressors may be the most stressful. The high-risk group was exposed to low levels of control through repetitive machine-paced work, physical isolation and high levels of responsibility. To separate out the effects of these different factors, a more controlled experimental study would have to be carried out but this would be at the expense of ecological validity.

RESEARCH METHODS   HOW SCIENCE WORKS

Eye on the exam

Drawing conclusions from graphs

As part of your *How Science Works* (AO3) assessment, you may be asked to 'draw a conclusion' from a graph. It pays to be attentive to detail, drawing a full conclusion that demonstrates that you really do understand what the graph shows. This involves studying the labels on both axes, any overall trends in the graph, and (if necessary) drawing a comparison between groups. From Figure 5.5 on the previous page, we can see that levels of noradrenaline are broadly the same for male and female managers throughout the working day, although peaking at different times. However, the graph also shows that for females, the high levels of noradrenaline continue for longer; this suggests that females, more than males, experience more non-work stressors that maintain their stress levels beyond the working day.

For more exam advice, visit
www.collinseducation.com/psychologyweb

with Type A personality are attracted to stressful jobs and this is what causes their health problems rather than any lack of job control. The role of Type A behaviour is discussed in the next section.

■ *Job control* – Furthermore, having high levels of job control can be stressful for some people. Schaubroeck *et al.* (2001) found that employees who perceived they had control over their job responsibilities but didn't have confidence in their ability to handle the demands of the role or who blamed themselves for negative outcomes were more likely to experience stress. This research shows that increasing job control can be harmful for individuals who lack the capacity to handle it or when this control increases their self-blame when things go wrong.

■ *Individual differences* – Research has shown that as other cultures (e.g. in Eastern Europe) take on the working practices of the West, a similar relationship between lack of control and stress-related illness is becoming evident. However, not all workers with low-control and high-demand jobs become ill, and the study of these individual differences is an important area of stress research.

Personality factors and stress: Type A behaviour

In the early 1960s, Friedman and Rosenman (1974) studied the behaviour of patients suffering from coronary heart disease (CHD), and proposed that a particular behaviour pattern was associated with increased vulnerability to this stress-related illness. This pattern is known as the **Type A behaviour** pattern and is characterized by constant time pressure (always being in a hurry), doing several tasks at once, being intensely competitive in work and social situations, and being easily frustrated by the efforts of others. The frequency with which this pattern is observed has led to it often being referred to as the Type A personality. (See the key studies left and below, and Table 5.3. The key study below is also relevant to the debate about the relationship between stress and physical illness.)

Recent research on Type A behaviour

Williams *et al.* (2003) reported on a 15-year study that focused on younger individuals who exhibited Type A personality. They found that certain aspects of Type A behaviour were unhealthier than others, with hostility and impatience putting individuals at increased risk of developing high blood pressure – a major precursor to heart attacks, strokes and other symptoms of cardiovascular disease.

A study of over 300 German managers (Kirkaldy *et al.* 2002) compared managers with Type A behaviour who also had an external locus of control (likely to believe

Table 5.3 Type A behaviour pattern

Time pressure
- working against the clock
- doing several things at once
- irritation and impatience with others
- unhappy doing nothing

Competitive
- always plays to win at games and at work
- achievement measured as material productivity

Anger
- self-critical
- hostile to the outside world
- anger often directed inwards

Key study: Type A behaviour and cardiovascular disorders
The Western Collaborative Group Study by Friedman and Rosenman (1974)

RESEARCH METHODS

Aim	To investigate links between the Type A behaviour pattern and cardiovascular (heart) disease.
Procedures	■ Using structured interviews (see Chapter 1, p. 29), 3200 Californian men, aged between 39 and 59, were categorized as either Type A, Type X (balanced between Type A and Type B) or Type B (the opposite of Type A, i.e. more relaxed and not showing the Type A characteristics of time pressure, competitiveness and anger). ■ This large sample was followed up for eight and a half years to assess their lifestyle and health outcomes.
Findings	■ By the end of the study, 257 men in the sample had developed coronary heart disease (CHD), of which 70 per cent were from the Type A group – twice the rate of heart disease found in the Type B group. ■ This difference in the incidence of CHD between the two groups was independent of lifestyle factors such as smoking and obesity that are known to increase the chances of heart disease.
Conclusions	■ The Type A behaviour pattern increases vulnerability to heart disease. ■ Behaviour modification programmes to reduce Type A behaviour should result in a reduced risk of heart disease.
Evaluations	■ Although some aspects of lifestyle were controlled for, there may have been other variables that could have affected vulnerability to heart disease, such as elements of hardiness (see p. 167). ■ This was not an experimental study, so cause and effect cannot be assumed; other studies have failed to show a relationship between Type A behaviour and heart disease.
FURTHER ANALYSIS	Whilst it is true that many studies have failed to demonstrate a relationship between Type A behaviour and heart disease, there are also new studies that do. For example, a meta-analysis of 35 studies (Myrtek 2001) found a significant association between Type A behaviour and heart disease, but only in studies that included angina (a narrowing of the coronary arteries) as an outcome, rather than some other aspect of coronary heart disease.

in bad luck and fate) with managers who had Type B behaviour and an internal locus of control (likely to believe that they were in charge of their own destiny). They found that the former group had greater perceived levels of stress, lower job satisfaction and poorer physical and mental health than the latter group.

This research appears to show that the negative health consequences of Type A behaviour, combined with an external locus of control, may outweigh the superficial attractiveness of Type A (hard working, competitive, self-critical) in a work setting.

Explaining the relationship between Type A behaviour and heart disease

Several mechanisms have been proposed to explain the link between Type A behaviour (or components of it, such as hostility) and an increased risk of coronary heart disease. Compared to Type Bs, Type A individuals respond more quickly and more strongly to stressful situations, both in their behaviour and in their physiological responses (e.g. increased heart rate and blood pressure). As a result, they experience more wear and tear on their cardiovascular system, making them more susceptible to heart disease than those with Type B behaviour.

Evaluation of Type A behaviour

- *Lack of consistent research support* – Since the original work by Friedman and Rosenman (1974), many studies have looked at the relationship between Type A behaviour and CHD. Some of these have been retrospective (looking at the previous behaviour of patients with CHD) and some prospective (measuring Type A behaviour using questionnaires and then following participants' health outcomes over months or years). Significant correlations have been found, but these are never very high, and many negative findings have been reported. Even the value of the Type A concept has been questioned (Evans 1990).

- *The role of hostility* – To try to make some sense of this, the Type A behaviour pattern has been more closely analyzed, and it turns out that a critical personality variable is hostility. When high levels of hostility are combined with other high levels of Type A behaviour, correlations with CHD are significantly increased (Matthews and Haynes 1986). Particularly vulnerable are individuals who repress high levels of hostility rather than express it (although that may be better for the rest of us, of course!).

- *Type A and hardiness* – Despite the fact that Type A behaviour seems to be a risk for stress-related illness, many Type A individuals survive quite happily with their pressured and competitive lives. In the last section of this chapter, which looks at stress-management techniques, we will see that one of the key factors in managing stress is a strong sense of commitment, control and challenge. These are key elements of the '**hardy personality**', which Kobasa proposes is resistant to the damaging effects of stress (see next page). There is no reason why Type A people should not also show high levels of commitment and control – in fact, they would be expected to. They are high achievers and so are likely to be very committed, and they like to do everything themselves, as they do not believe anyone else can do it as well, i.e. they have a strong sense of control.

- *Protective factors* – So, along with factors which make them vulnerable, such as haste, time pressure, doing too many things at once and hostility, the Type A person may also score highly on protective factors, such as control and commitment. There are also other less specific elements that have been shown to protect against stress, such as physical exercise and social support. These may also help the Type A person to avoid the negative effects of stress.

Personality factors and stress: the 'hardy personality'

According to Kobasa (Kobasa and Maddi 1977), the concept of 'hardiness' (or the 'hardy personality') is central to understanding why some people are vulnerable to stress and some resistant. Hardiness includes a range of personality factors that, if present, defend against the negative effects of stress. These factors are:

- *Control* – This is the belief that you can influence what happens in your life, rather than attributing control to outside influences. It is similar to locus of control, and attributional style, which is the tendency to attribute causes either to yourself (*dispositional* attribution) or to external factors over which you have no control (*situational* attribution).

- *Commitment* – This is a sense of purpose and involvement in the world around you, including people as well as jobs and careers. The world is seen as something to engage with, rather than to stand apart from. Committed people tend to resist giving up in times of stress.

- *Challenge* – Life changes are seen as challenges to be overcome, or as opportunities, rather than as threats and stressors. Those who possess a challenge orientation do not seek comfort and security as their main goals, but rather they look for change and growth.

Kobasa has presented evidence that people who have high scores on scales measuring hardiness are significantly less likely to suffer stress-related physical and psychological disorders than those with low hardiness scores. In theory, their positive approach means that life events are not seen as stressful, but as challenges and opportunities that can be overcome. This leads to less activation of the stress response and its negative consequences.

Kobasa's studies of personality and stress have identified other factors involved in coping with stress and have implications for stress management. Using previous work suggesting that physical exercise and social support also protected against stress-related illness, Kobasa *et al.* (1985) rated participants on the presence or absence of the three factors:

- hardiness
- social support
- regular exercise.

In this prospective study, they then followed the participants and assessed the severity of any subsequent psychological (depression and anxiety) or physical illnesses.

Results showed clearly that participants with no protective factors had higher scores on severity of illness scales than any other group. In addition, the presence of one, two or all three protective factors was associated with steadily decreasing illness scores. This implied that the factors acted additively in improving resistance to stress. Of the three, hardiness seemed to have the greatest impact.

Regular physical exercise is one of the factors that help protect against stress-related illness, according to Kobasa et al. (1985)

Evaluation of hardiness and the hardy personality

- *Participants* – Much of Kobasa's work has been carried out with male, white-collar workers, and so the findings may not be generalizable to other groups. For example, stressors and coping responses are known to differ between men and women.

- *Components of personality* – control, commitment and challenge have never been very clearly defined, so control, for instance, may be an important part of commitment and challenge rather than being separate from them. This would mean that Kobasa is only looking at the role of control in protection against stress rather than a full 'personality type'.

Emotion-focused and problem-focused coping

Folkman and Lazarus (1980) define *coping* responses as those 'cognitions (thoughts) and behaviours that a person used to reduce stress and to moderate its emotional impact'. In other words, coping is an attempt to manage stress effectively. Folkman and Lazarus measured a person's *style* of coping using the Ways of Coping Questionnaire (WCQ). This consists of 50 items that score individuals on eight different scales. These include *seeking social support* (e.g. talking to someone about a problem), *escape-avoidance* (e.g. hoping for a miracle) and *positive reappraisal* (e.g. changing one's perception of a problem so that it is less stressful).

Research using the WCQ has indicated that people use two major types of coping strategies to deal with stressful events:

- *Problem-focused coping* – strategies that attempt to do something active to alleviate or eliminate the stressful situation. These include taking control (e.g. finding out as much as possible about a disease), evaluating the pros and cons of different options, and suppressing competing activities (e.g. avoiding the temptation to surf the Internet for hours rather than revising).

- *Emotion-focused coping* – strategies that attempt to regulate the emotional distress associated with stressful or potentially stressful events. Emotion-focused coping includes denial (e.g. going on as if nothing had happened), focusing on and venting of emotions, and seeking social support (e.g. women maintain a network of close friends whom they can turn to in times of need). Emotion-focused coping is viewed as being more passive, that is, an internal process that merely involves changing thoughts or feelings about a stressful event as opposed to taking direct behavioural action to remedy it.

When is each coping strategy used?

The coping strategy used depends partly on personal style (e.g. some people are better problem solvers than others) and partly on the type of stressful event.

Several studies have shown that people typically use problem-focused coping to deal with events that are potentially controllable (e.g. work-based problems), whereas stressors perceived as less controllable (e.g. terrorist attacks or certain physical health problems) might prompt more emotion-focused coping (Ben-Zur and Zeidner 1995). In general, therefore, problem-focused coping is the most effective coping strategy *provided* the individual has a realistic chance of changing those aspects of the situation that are causing them stress.

Emotion-focused and problem-focused coping in action

To understand how these different strategies might operate, consider the example of a student facing three difficult examinations in a single week. She knows she must get good grades to get to university, so this situation is a potential source of stress. To cope, she could organize her revision timetable systematically and work through all the material she needs to learn for the exams (problem-focused coping). Alternatively, she may decide that she needs to relax and watch a bit of television (emotion-focused coping) before proceeding with her revision plan (problem-focused coping). She might decide to go out shopping with her friends to prevent her having to think about or study for her exams (emotion-focused coping).

Emotion-focused coping can be used successfully, however, as a short-term measure to help one step back from an overwhelming problem in order to reduce arousal levels prior to using a problem-solving approach. Emotion-focused strategies also help people deal with stressful situations where there are few options to change the situation itself. The predominant view among stress researchers, however, is that emotion-focused coping strategies are less effective than problem-focused strategies.

Research on emotion- and problem-focused coping

- *Health outcomes* – Research has tended to suggest that these different coping strategies are related to different health outcomes, emotion-focused coping being associated with a significantly higher incidence of depression. A study of nursing students (Penley *et al.* 2002) found that problem-focused coping was positively correlated with overall good health outcomes, whereas distancing, avoidance and wishful thinking (emotion-focused) were *negatively* correlated with overall good health outcomes.

  Nolen-Hoeksema (1994) has suggested that the ruminative type of emotion-focused strategy that women tend to engage in (i.e. thinking and worrying about a problem) is more likely to maintain depressive symptoms than the more active, distractive type of emotion-focused techniques that men tend to use (e.g. exercising, drinking).

- *Control and coping* – In a study by Park *et al.* (2004), undergraduates described their most stressful event, its controllability, how they coped and their daily mood. Results showed that problem-focused coping was positively related to positive mood when dealing with perceived highly controllable stressors.

  This relationship, however, is not always straightforward. **Fang *et al.* (2006) studied women who were at increased risk of developing ovarian cancer because they had a close relative with the disease. They found that women who felt more in control and who actively engaged in problem-focused coping strategies, actually suffered more distress over time than a group of women who did not use problem-focused coping. Why might this be? Possibly because feeling in control is only beneficial if it matches reality. The researchers suggest that there is currently little that a woman at risk of hereditary ovarian cancer can do to protect herself against developing the disease. The women, therefore, who perceived high control and reported high levels of problem-focused coping may have become increasingly distressed if their efforts to reduce their cancer risk did not lead to actual changes.**

- *Threat and coping* – Rukholm and Viverais (1993) examined the relationship between stress and coping, and concluded that if a person feels greatly threatened when exposed to a stressor, they need to deal with this anxiety through emotion-focused coping first. Only then can they make use of problem-focused coping.

Evaluation of the different coping styles

Problems of measurement

The Ways of Coping Questionnaire is organized around eight subscales, scores on which indicate the degree to which a person tends towards emotion-focused or problem-focused coping. However, some aspects of behaviour on this questionnaire (such as mobilizing social support) could be seen as either a problem-focused or an emotion-focused strategy. It may, for example, be used

Eye on the exam

Effective evaluation

In order to evaluate material *effectively* for the AO2 component of questions, it is important to ask yourself the question: what does this material tell me about whatever it is I'm evaluating – does it show it in a good light or a bad light?

For example, Baker and Berenbaum's (2007) research shows us when emotion-focused coping can be particularly effective in certain circumstances. This is obviously a strength of this form of coping, but we need to make that point explicit. Thus, you could write: '*The effectiveness of emotion-focused coping is demonstrated in a study by ...*', or '*The claim that emotion-focused coping can be effective is supported by ...*'

Similarly, the discovery that males and females differ in their preferred style of coping (e.g. Brody and Hall 1993) tells us that '*there are individual differences in the use of different coping styles, which is illustrated by the finding that ...*'

You might also (through your own research) discover *applications* of a particular avenue of research. For example, Reinecke and Didie (2005) found that teaching problem-focused coping was an effective form of treatment for clinically depressed adolescents. The fact that there is an application linked to a particular research area, and that the application has clearly positive outcomes, demonstrates a strength of that research and is a powerful affirmation of its value.

For more exam advice, visit **www.collinseducation.com/psychologyweb**

Activity — Problem-focused and emotion-focused approaches to coping with stress

You have forgotten your best friend's birthday. Which form of coping would you be using in each of these reactions?

1 'Well she forgot to wish me good luck for my driving test.'

2 'I must make a note in my diary of birthdays I want to remember so that this doesn't happen again.'

to help solve a problem or to obtain information (problem-focused) *or* to help calm the individual or distract them from the stressor (emotion-focused). The original eight-factor model developed by Folkman and Lazarus has been criticized by many researchers for being too general and not reflecting the reality of coping with specific types of stressor. Because of the general nature of this questionnaire, some researchers (e.g. Dunkel-Schetter *et al.* 1992) have adapted the categories to better fit specific stressors (e.g. for cancer patients).

Is emotion-focused coping always ineffective?

Although most studies appear to indicate that emotion-focused coping is ineffective as a way of dealing with stress, there are reasons to doubt that this is always the case:

- While some emotion-focused strategies encourage *avoidance* of the stressful situation (e.g. escape, denial), others encourage *approach* (recognizing one's feelings about the problem). For example, Stanton *et al.* (2000) found that men who used emotional-approach coping were better able to deal with the stress of infertility than those who did not. *Emotional-approach coping* involves actively identifying and expressing emotions, becoming aware of exactly how an event makes us feel, and using that information to identify the best course of action.

- Problem-focused coping can even be counterproductive if a person decides on a particular strategy *without* first recognizing their own emotions as a first step in helping to solve the problem.

- The important role of emotion-focused coping has been supported by the recent research of Baker and Berenbaum (2007). They found that individuals who were first encouraged to express their emotions were subsequently more effective in solving the problem posed by a stressful event. Men, in particular, benefited from using emotional coping – a strategy they usually do not use efficiently owing to social roles, lack of comfort and lack of practice.

Do males and females use different strategies?

A stereotypical view exists that when confronted with a stressful event, males are more likely to use problem-solving coping while females are more likely to use emotion-focused coping (Brody and Hall 1993). A number of studies have supported this presumed gender difference. For example, Stone and Neale (1984) found that men engaged in direct action when dealing with stressful events, whereas women were more likely to use relaxation, catharsis and distraction.

Likewise, Rosario *et al.* (1988) found that women consistently made more use of social support than did men when dealing with stressful situations. If this is the case, why do males and females cope differently with stress? Rosario and colleagues describe two theories that might account for such gender differences:

- *Socialization theory* argues that women have been socialized in a way that equips them with less effective coping strategies. According to this theory, women are taught to express their emotions openly, but to act in a more passive manner. Men, on the other hand, are taught to approach stressful situations in a more active, problem-focused way. According to socialization theory, therefore, gender differences in coping would be found across different situations, regardless of role.

- In contrast, *role constraint theory* argues that gender differences in coping responses are a product of the roles that males and females tend to occupy.

According to role constraint theory, if males and females occupy the same social role, their coping responses will be the same. Consistent with role constraint theory, Rosario and colleagues found that males and females in the same social roles did not differ in their reported use of problem-focused or emotion-focused coping strategies.

Similarly, in a study of college students, Ptacek *et al.* (1992) found no gender differences in the use of problem-focused coping, presumably because the students also shared the same social role. It is possible, therefore, that men and women have begun to adopt similar coping strategies, due at least in part to the fact that they are taking on more similar roles.

Methods of stress management

The public regards stress as one of the most prevalent 'diseases' of the last 20 years. It is also seen as fundamental to the way we live; as the pace of life increases, so, inevitably, does the stress of keeping up. In parallel with the increase in research into the negative effects of stress, such as psychological and physical disorders, an industry has grown up devoted to methods of **stress management**. These are by now many and varied, but methods of managing stress can be divided into two major categories:

- **physiological approaches** – the use of drugs and biofeedback to target directly the stress-response systems themselves

- **psychological approaches** – for example, cognitive and behavioural training to help people control specific stressors in their lives, and the use of techniques of relaxation and increasing hardiness to reduce the bodily arousal associated with stress.

Physiological methods of stress management: Drugs

The most commonly used drugs to combat stress are the **benzodiazepine** (BZ) anti-anxiety agents and **beta-blockers**.

Benzodiazepines (BZs)

BZs, such as librium (chlordiazepoxide) and valium (diazepam), are the most prescribed drugs for psychological disorders and can be very effective against states of stress and anxiety. They appear to act by reducing central (brain) arousal. BZs enhance the actions of a natural brain chemical, gamma-aminobutyric acid, or GABA. GABA tells the neurons that it contacts to slow down or stop firing. Since about 40 per cent of the neurons in the brain respond to GABA, this means it has a general quietening influence on the brain.

The way in which it does this is by reacting with special sites (GABA-receptors) on the outside of the receiving neuron (see Figure 5.6). This opens a channel that allows negatively charged chloride ions to pass to the inside of the neuron. These chloride ions make the neuron less responsive to other neurotransmitters that would normally excite it. BZs bind to special sites situated on the GABA-receptor, boosting the actions of GABA, so allowing more chloride ions to enter the neuron, and making it even more resistant to excitation.

The action of GABA is thus supported by BZs, which exert an extra inhibitory influence on neurons. As a result of this extra influence, the brain's output of excitatory neurotransmitters is reduced and the person feels calmer.

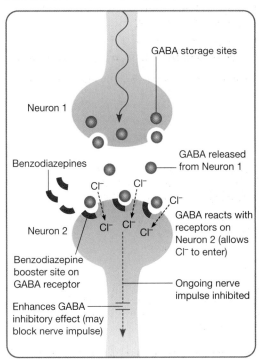

Figure 5.6 How benzodiazepines enhance the inhibitory role of GABA at the synapse

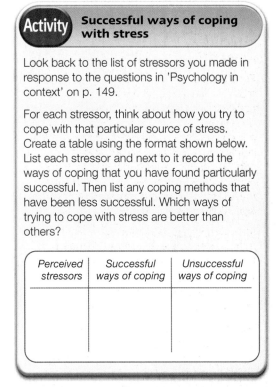

Activity Successful ways of coping with stress

Look back to the list of stressors you made in response to the questions in 'Psychology in context' on p. 149.

For each stressor, think about how you try to cope with that particular source of stress. Create a table using the format shown below. List each stressor and next to it record the ways of coping that you have found particularly successful. Then list any coping methods that have been less successful. Which ways of trying to cope with stress are better than others?

Perceived stressors	Successful ways of coping	Unsuccessful ways of coping

Beta-blockers

Beta-blockers, such as inderal, do not enter the brain, but directly reduce activity in pathways of the sympathetic nervous system around the body. As sympathetic arousal is a key feature of stressful states, beta-blockers can be very effective against symptoms such as raised heart rate and blood pressure. (They have also been used when bodily arousal can reduce performance in groups such as musicians and snooker players.)

Beta-blockers work by reducing the activity of adrenaline and noradrenaline, which are key agents in sympathetic arousal. Adrenaline and noradrenaline are produced as part of the sympathomedullary response to stress (see p. 150) and circulate in the bloodstream, stimulating beta-adrenergic receptors in various parts of the body, including the heart, brain, and blood vessels. For example, stimulation of beta-adrenergic receptors on heart cells causes an increase in the force and rate of the heartbeat. The beta-blocker drug binds to beta-adrenergic receptors and blocks the receptor from being stimulated. By blocking sympathetic arousal, beta-blockers slow the heartbeat, lessen the force with which the heart contracts and reduces blood vessel contraction. This results in a fall in blood pressure and therefore produces less stress on the heart.

Advantages of drugs as a method of stress management

Drugs have been shown to be a vital part of the armoury against the harmful effects of stress:

- *Speed and effectiveness* – Drugs can work quickly, rapidly reducing dangerous symptoms, such as raised blood pressure (beta-blockers), or reducing disabling levels of stress-related anxiety (BZs). Hedblad *et al.* (2001) found that regular, low doses of a beta-blocker drug significantly slowed the rate of progression of atherosclerosis (clogging of the arteries due in part to stress).

- *Research support* – A meta-analysis of studies focusing on the treatment of social anxiety (Hidalgo *et al.* 2001) found that BZs were more effective than other drugs, such as antidepressants. However, their effectiveness is not consistent across all forms of stress-related anxiety. For example, in a study of trauma survivors, Gelpin *et al.* (1996) found that although BZs may have beneficial short-term effects in alleviating distress following trauma, they do not prevent the onset of post-traumatic stress disorder (PTSD).

- *Availability* – Drugs can be prescribed immediately. In addition, the range of treatments available is increasing rapidly, with newer agents such as angiotensin-converting enzyme inhibitors (ACE inhibitors, e.g. Captopril) providing a variety of ways of tackling the symptoms of stress.

Weaknesses of drugs as a method of stress management

However, there are important weaknesses associated with the use of drugs:

- *Dependency* – Long-term use, especially of BZs, can lead to psychological and physical **dependency**. A proportion of people trying to come off BZs will experience a physical withdrawal syndrome, with symptoms such as increased anxiety, tremors and headaches. BZs should only be prescribed for short periods of a week or so, to help cope with short-term stress. Dependency is far less of a problem with beta-blockers, as they do not have a significant effect on central brain mechanisms.

Do the benefits of drugs outweigh the drawbacks when it comes to managing stress?

- *Tolerance* – **Tolerance** to the effects of BZs develops with regular use, i.e. the original dose of the drug has progressively less effect and so a higher dose is required to obtain the original effect.

- *Side effects* – All drugs have **side effects**. BZs can cause drowsiness and affect memory. BZs cause a specific deficit in *episodic* memory (memory for recent events), rather than other aspects of memory such as ability to remember a telephone number in short-term memory or recall of long-term memories. Most people who take beta-blockers experience no side effects, or only minor ones such as fatigue or cold extremities (e.g. hands and feet). With people suffering from asthma or other breathing difficulties, however, because beta-blockers can narrow the airways, this can make breathing symptoms worse

- *Only target symptoms* – Drugs treat symptoms, not causes. Many stressors are essentially psychological, so drugs, while helping in the short term, may prevent the real cause of stress being addressed. They are best used to manage acute (short-lived) stressors, such as the initial shock of a bereavement, or examinations (although see side effects, above). They are most effective when psychological coping techniques are employed at the same time.

- *NICE report (2006)* – The National Institute for Clinical Excellence recommended that beta-blockers should not be used to treat high blood pressure, except in a few specific cases. This was in part a response to the fact that other drugs, such as ACE inhibitors and diuretics, have been shown to be more effective in reducing the risk of stroke when compared to beta-blockers. There is also increasing evidence that the most frequently used beta-blockers carry a higher risk of provoking Type 2 diabetes than the new drugs.

Physiological methods of stress management: Biofeedback

The **biofeedback** technique involves recording the activity of the physiological systems of the body's stress response, such as heart rate, blood pressure or tension in the neck muscles that can lead to stress-induced headaches. Recording is usually made via electrodes on the skin that lead to a monitor held by the patient.

People are encouraged to try various strategies to reduce the physiological readings. These strategies can be muscle relaxation or meditation, or even altering their posture. The aim is to find a strategy to reduce, for instance, blood pressure consistently, and then to transfer the strategy to the world outside the laboratory and to practise it regularly.

Evaluation of biofeedback as a method of stress management

- *Effectiveness* – Biofeedback can be very successful for some individuals, especially children (Attanasio *et al.* 1985) who enjoy the technological aspects in controlling, for instance, migraine headaches.

- *Role of relaxation* – Biofeedback is often found to be no more effective than muscle **relaxation** procedures without biofeedback (Masters *et al.* 1987). This suggests that feedback on symptoms such as blood pressure is not a vital part of the procedure, but that training in relaxation techniques is.

Figure 5.7
Biofeedback: outline of the procedure

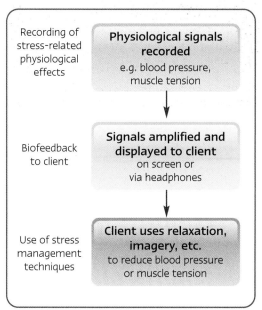

Recording of stress-related physiological effects

Physiological signals recorded
e.g. blood pressure, muscle tension

Biofeedback to client

Signals amplified and displayed to client
on screen or via headphones

Use of stress management techniques

Client uses relaxation, imagery, etc.
to reduce blood pressure or muscle tension

Roughly 50 to 60 per cent of the adult population are exposed to traumatic events, but less than 1 in 10 of these develop maladjusted stress responses such as post-traumatic stress disorder. Following the terrorist attacks in New York on 11 September 2001, only 7.5 per cent of Manhattan residents who were directly exposed developed clinical problems that could be attributed to this event. In London, following the bombings on 7 July 2005, less than 1 per cent of people caught up in the events sought professional help (Meichenbaum 2007).

What makes some people more able to deal with traumatic stress and others more vulnerable to its effects? Meichenbaum suggests that a key aspect of how people deal with significant stressors is the nature of the 'stories' they tell themselves and others about what is stressful in their lives. These stories influence how people think about themselves, how they feel and how they behave. There is now research evidence to indicate that individuals who experience marked distress following stressful events are more likely to use the following type of 'stories':

- seeing themselves as victims, shattering their beliefs about the world being a safe place and people being trustworthy
- engaging in self-blame and blaming others
- asking questions for which there are no satisfactory answers, making closure more difficult
- remaining avoidant and brooding and feeling guilty and unloved
- pining for the way things used to be
- keeping their experiences secret and delaying seeking help.

In contrast, individuals who cope well with traumatic events are more likely to:

- view themselves as 'survivors' than 'victims'
- find benefits for themselves or others as a result of having experienced stressful events
- transform their stressful experiences into something that can help others or themselves.

Therefore, how we replay our memories of stressful events can affect how we deal with future stressful events.

- *Expense* – Biofeedback is expensive in terms of equipment and time. If relaxation is the important feature, then the cost of the equipment could be avoided and training time would be much reduced.

Psychological methods of stress management: Cognitive Behavioural Therapy (CBT)

At the beginning of this chapter, we outlined the transactional model of stress. The trigger in stressful situations, according to this model, is the perceived gap between the demands being made on you and the coping responses you have available. So, a straightforward approach to stress management would be either to reduce the perceived demands or to improve your coping abilities or, preferably, both. **Cognitive behavioural** approaches aim to do this by encouraging the client to perceive and evaluate stressful situations accurately (often we overestimate the demands being made on us), and to improve coping skills and techniques by training and practice.

Stress-inoculation training

Meichenbaum's (Meichenbaum and Cameron 1983) **stress inoculation** training is a cognitive behavioural method designed specifically to prepare individuals for future stressors and to promote resilience. Following an initial phase of learning about the nature of stress, coping and resilience, a phase of skills training is provided. People are taught a range of coping strategies they might use to deal with stress. This is followed by exposure to a series of graduated challenges so that they can practise their newfound coping skills. By learning effective coping strategies, individuals are effectively 'inoculating' themselves against the harmful effects of future stressful situations, thus making themselves more resilient in the process.

The stress inoculation approach has three phases:

- *Conceptualization* – This is the main cognitive element. The client is encouraged to relive stressful situations and to analyze various features. What was actually stressful about it? How did they attempt to cope? Why wasn't it successful? If many situations are stressful, do they have elements in common, such as the presence of strangers or the knowledge that performance is being assessed, as in examinations and tests? These discussions can be individual or take place in groups, where the sharing of experience can help achieve a greater understanding of the nature of stress and the client's reactions to it. Clients reach a more realistic understanding of the demands being made on them.

- *Skills training and practice* – Once the key elements of the stressful situations have been identified, clients can be taught specific and non-specific strategies for coping with them. Relaxation techniques help them to cope with the initial arousing effects of stress. Training in particular skills then helps reduce the specific demands. For instance, if examinations are the problem, knowing the syllabus in detail and developing simple strategies for learning, revision and time allocation can reduce stress. Relaxation techniques can be used in the examination room to keep arousal under control. Mock examinations can be taken to practise stress management. Many people also find social interactions stressful. Surprisingly, perhaps, social skills such as body posture, eye contact and conversational give-and-take can be taught relatively easily and practised in the therapeutic setting. Again, general relaxation techniques help to limit stress-induced arousal.

Real-life application – The final stage is for the client to go out into the real world and to put the training to the test. Contact with the therapist is maintained, and follow-up sessions and further training are provided if necessary. The reinforcement of successful coping with examinations or social interactions then becomes self-sustaining.

Evaluation of stress inoculation training

- *Targeting symptoms and causes* – Meichenbaum's programme is directed at both ends of the stress problem, i.e. sources of stress and coping strategies. By reviewing the coping methods they have used in the past, clients can gain a clearer understanding of their strengths and weaknesses. By acquiring new skills and techniques, they reduce the gap between demands and coping resources, and clients gain more confidence in their ability to handle previously stressful situations.

- *Effectiveness* – The combination of cognitive therapy (i.e. thinking about situations in the past and using cognitive strategies as part of a general relaxation technique) and behavioural therapy (i.e. training in new skills) makes stress inoculation training a powerful method of stress management. However, few controlled studies of its effectiveness have been carried out, although Meichenbaum has reported some encouraging results (Meichenbaum and Turk 1982).

- *Practicality* – It takes time, application and money. Clients have to go through a rigorous programme over a long period, analyzing their responses to stress and learning new techniques. This requires high levels of motivation and commitment, so it is not a quick and easy fix.

- *Difficulties* – There is evidence that the way we cope with life's stressors can reflect basic aspects of our personality, possibly innate or acquired during early experience. Any technique aimed at improving stress management may be acting against habits that are well established, even if they are not very effective. Changing cognitions and behaviour will always be difficult.

Psychological methods of stress management: Progressive muscle relaxation

Although we all think we know how to relax, effective relaxation has, in practice, to be learned. Rather than simply thinking about nice things, progressive muscle relaxation is, strange as it may sound, an active approach to reducing bodily arousal. A standard procedure would be to train clients consciously to clench and unclench muscles, to get them used to the sensations of tension and relaxation. Whole-body relaxation would begin with the muscles of the toes, tensing and then relaxing them, and then working up through the legs, body, arms, shoulders and head (facial muscles).

Eventually, the client understands the sensations well enough to use progressive muscle relaxation in everyday life as a method to reduce bodily arousal. During relaxation, stress-response mechanisms are inactive, heart rate and blood pressure fall, and the parasympathetic subdivision of the autonomic nervous system is activated (see p. 150).

The activity on the right encourages you to experience the effects of progressive muscle relation for yourself.

Another way of managing stress

Activity **Dealing with stress**

How well prepared are you to deal with stress? Think of a recent stressful event that you experienced and analyze it using the steps below.

1 What did you feel and think during and after the event? How did you react and how did others respond to you? What, if anything could you have done differently?

2 What coping skills do you already have that help you deal with events such as this? What new coping skills do you think you need to add to your repertoire?

3 After stressful events such as this, what lingers on in your mind? How does this affect your view of yourself, the future and the world around you?

4 What lessons can you learn from watching resilient individuals deal with stress? How can you use this to help inoculate yourself against future stressors?

Activity ▪ Practising a relaxation technique

It is easier to focus on your studies when you are feeling relaxed. If you find this or any other chapter difficult to take in, it may be because you're feeling stressed and so find it difficult to concentrate. If you are feeling stressed, take a few minutes out to practise a relaxation technique.

The progressive muscle relaxation technique is most effective if you lie on the floor. Tense each of the areas in turn, starting with your toes and ending with your facial muscles. For each area, tense your muscles as hard as you can and count to five. Then relax the muscles, counting to five before moving on. By the end of the process, a lot of the tension in your body will have disappeared and you should feel a lot more relaxed as your heart rate and blood pressure reduce. Try it for yourself and use this technique whenever you are feeling stressed.

Relaxation techniques are an important part of stress management. Try for yourself by having a go at the activity above.

Evaluation of progressive muscle relaxation as a method of stress management

- *Effectiveness* – If practised regularly, relaxation techniques are effective in reducing stress, but are not practical in all situations due to space and time constraints – see the next point.

- *Practicality* – These techniques take time and space. If you are stuck in a traffic jam or in the middle of an examination, full progressive relaxation is inconvenient, if not impossible. However, the training also involves cognitive strategies to help relaxation, such as imagining yourself in pleasant, non-arousing surroundings, taking deep breaths, and consciously telling yourself to relax. Relaxation of some muscle groups is usually possible. Taking two minutes to run through a learned procedure like this can pay dividends in most stressful situations.

- *Targeting symptoms* – Relaxation techniques address bodily or physiological arousal by reducing activation of stress-response systems. This is undoubtedly beneficial, but long-lasting, severe stressors need more than non-specific relaxation; their source has to be identified and targeted, usually via cognitive and behavioural strategies. Relaxation can still remain as an important component of stress management, but long-term adjustment requires more focused intervention as well.

Psychological methods of stress management: Hardiness training

Kobasa's belief that hardiness (see p. 167) is an important element in stress management led her to propose ways in which it could be *increased*. As with stress inoculation training, the procedure has three aspects, the first two of which are quite similar to the first stage of stress inoculation training:

- *Focusing* – Clients are trained and encouraged to spot signs of stress, such as muscle tension, increases in heart rate and anxiety. This allows them to recognize stressful situations and therefore to identify sources of stress.

- *Reliving stressful encounters* – Clients analyze recent stressful situations in terms of how they were actually resolved, ways in which they could have turned out better, and ways in which they could have turned out worse. This gives them insight into their current coping strategies and how they may be more effective than they imagine.

- *Self-improvement* – Central to hardiness is the belief that you can cope with life's challenges. Often, however, we are faced with stressors that cannot be easily managed. It is important, then, to recognize and to take on challenges that we *can* cope with. In this way we confirm that we still have control over some events in our lives. It is this sense of personal control and effectiveness that is fundamental to stress management. So an essential part of hardiness training is to begin with challenges the client can cope with before moving on to more complex problems.

Evaluation of hardiness training

- *Theoretical issues* – The concept of hardiness itself has been criticized. The relative importance of the three factors – control, commitment, challenge – is unclear, although there is evidence for the role of control and commitment in reducing responses to stressors. As we shall see, the importance of control in stress management cannot be exaggerated, and the concept of hardiness overlaps substantially with issues of personal control and may not be very different from it.

- *Generalizability* – Kobasa's studies usually involve White, middle-class businessmen, so the results cannot reliably be generalized to women or to different classes and cultures.

- *Effectiveness and practicality* – There are few systematic studies of the effectiveness of hardiness training. As with stress inoculation training, it is lengthy and requires commitment and motivation, and would never be a rapid solution to stress-management problems. It also has the problem of addressing basic aspects of personality and learned habits of coping. These are notoriously difficult to modify.

CHECK YOUR UNDERSTANDING

Check your understanding of stress in everyday life by answering the following questions. Try to do this from memory. You can check your answers by looking back through Topic 2.

1. What is the name of the rating scale devised by Holmes and Rahe in 1967 to investigate life stress? How many life events were on this scale and which was given the highest score of 100?

2. Outline two criticisms of the Holmes and Rahe's scale and its use.

3. What term is used to describe incidents that we would not call major life events, but which nevertheless can be a source of stress?

4. Outline the procedures and findings of one study of stress in the workplace.

5. How did Johansson *et al.* (1978) measure levels of stress in their study of Swedish sawmill workers?

6. Describe two or more sources of stress in the workplace.

7. Describe the main characteristics of the Type A behaviour pattern.

8. Which characteristic of the Type A pattern seems to be especially important in increasing vulnerability to stress?

9. Why might some people with Type A behaviour be less vulnerable to stress-related illness than others who also have Type A behaviour?

10. Distinguish between emotion-focused and problem-focused coping.

11. Give two advantages and two disadvantages of each type of coping.

12. Describe the effects of two types of drug used to manage stress.

13. Outline one strength and one weakness of using drugs to manage stress.

14. Name and outline the three phases of stress inoculation training.

15. Outline one strength and one weakness of the stress inoculation approach.

16. Name and outline one other psychological method of stress management.

Eye on the exam

The skill of précis

There are many different types of question that could be asked on this topic, but one of the more demanding is the 'essay' question that requires both AO1 and AO2 content. The example below is typical of such a question.

Discuss one psychological method of managing stress. *(12 marks)*

However, you may instead see a very similar question, but with one important difference – the number of marks available.

Discuss one psychological method of managing stress. *(8 marks)*

Let's look at each question. Each uses the same words, but changes the number of marks available (i.e. either 8 or 12). The question is preceded by the word 'discuss' (it could also have been 'consider' or 'describe and evaluate' or even 'outline and evaluate'). However, in these 'extended essay' questions, you will need to provide equal amounts of AO1 (description) and AO2 (commentary). For the 8-mark version, you don't have to write as much to get maximum marks: work on the rough guide that 1 mark = about 20 words, therefore 8 marks = about 160 words and 12 marks = 240 words.

Consider the psychological methods of managing stress that we have covered in this chapter. Of these, Meichenbaum's stress inoculation theory was given the most coverage (because it is the only one that might be *specified* in an exam question). There is, of course, far too much material for you to include in an 8-mark answer. You must be *selective* in putting together your response to either of the above questions. Your task is to represent the gist of your chosen method in the appropriate number of words for the question.

It is an important skill to practise, writing descriptions and evaluations of different lengths to fit the possible questions. If you have 160 words in total, then you should have about 80 words of AO1 and 80 words of AO2. As marks are given for both breadth and depth, a suitable compromise would be to make four AO1 points (each about 20 words) and four AO2 points (again each about 20 words). If this was the 12-mark version, then you have the luxury of having an extra 80 words (40 for AO1 and 40 for AO2). You may choose to introduce two more AO1 points and two more AO2 points, or simply expand the ones you already have. Either way, you have moulded your response to fit the exact requirements of the question and the number of marks allocated to its answer.

For more exam advice, visit
www.collinseducation.com/psychologyweb

Chapter 5: Summary

Stress as a bodily response

Stress

A lack of fit between the perceived demands of a situation and a person's perceived ability to cope

Stress in everyday life

The body's response to stress

Pituitary–adrenal system

1 Higher brain centres activate hypothalamus
2 Hypothalamus releases CRF
3 Pituitary releases ACTH
4 Adrenal cortex releases corticosteroids into bloodstream
5 Corticosteroids cause 'fight-or-flight' changes

Evaluations

- 'Fight or flight' – a male stress response
- 'Tend and befriend' – a female response

Sympathomedullary pathway

1 Activation of SNS causes bodily arousal
2 SNS also activates adrenal medulla
3 Releases adrenaline and noradrenaline
4 Both support sympathetic activation

Evaluations

- Stress response adaptation to stressors faced by ancestors
- Fight-or-flight response prepared body for energy expenditure

Life changes and daily hassles

Life changes

- Discrete stressors
- Measured by SRRS
- Higher SRRS, more illness (Rahe *et al.* 1970)
- Link between undesirable life changes and illness

Evaluations

- Individual differences – impact varies
- Correlational rather than causal
- Doesn't distinguish between negative and positive events

Daily hassles

- Relatively minor events
- Higher hassles score, lower mental health
- May accumulate for more serious stress reactions
- May arise from pre-existing chronic stressors

Evaluations

- Correlational rather than causal
- Cultural differences important in buffering effects

Personality factors

- Type A personality (Friedman and Rosenman 1974)
- Hardiness (Kobasa and Maddi 1977)

Evaluations

Type A

- Lack of consistent research support
- Role of hostility

Hardiness

- Non-representative participants
- Components of personality not well defined

Workplace stressors

- Physical environment
- Work overload
- Lack of control

Evaluations

- Extraneous variables not controlled
- Job control – stressful for some people
- Individual differences – e.g. cultural differences

Stress and the immune system

- Immune system – seek outs and destroys antigens
- Stress may affect immune system directly
- May also have an indirect effect

Research on short-term stressors

- Natural killer cell activity
- Wound healing
- Additional stressors (e.g. daily hassles)

Research on chronic stress

- Conflict in interpersonal relationships
- Death of a spouse
- Care giving

Evaluations

- Women report more stress-related problems than men
- Younger people report more stress than older people
- Older people show more adverse changes in response to stress

Emotion-focused and problem-focused coping

Problem-focused coping

- Active to eliminate stressful situation
- Used to deal with potentially controllable events
- Associated with overall good health outcomes
- More by males

Emotion-focused coping

- Regulates emotional distress of stressful situations
- Short-term measure to reduce arousal levels
- Used first to deal with high anxiety levels
- More by females

Methods of stress management

Physiological methods

Drugs

- BZs – enhance GABA
- Beta-blockers – reduce arousal

+ve: fast action and effective

–ve: dependency, side effects, only targets symptoms

Biofeedback

- Strategies to reduce physiological measures
- Effectiveness – no more effective than muscle relaxation alone

Psychological methods

Stress inoculation

- Promotes confidence in ability to deal with stress
- Conceptualization; skills training and practice; real-life application

+ve: greater confidence to handle stressful situations

–ve: requires high levels of motivation and commitment

Hardiness training

- Increases hardiness and resilience
- Focusing; reliving stressful encounters; self-improvement
- Problems – theoretical issues and practicality

EXPLAINING THE SPECIFICATION

Specification content	The specification explained
Social influence	In this part of the specification you are required to know about how the presence and actions of other people might influence individuals to change their beliefs or behaviour. In particular, you need to know about the psychological processes that result in conformity and obedience – two responses to social influence. To do this, you need to be able to:
Types of conformity, including internalization and compliance Explain what is meant by conformity	■ Explain what is meant by conformity. ■ Describe (and recognize examples of) the two types of conformity that are specified, namely internalization and compliance. ■ Explain the difference between internalization and compliance.
Explanations of why people conform, including informational social influence and normative social influence	■ Describe two reasons why people conform: informational and normative social influence. ■ Explain how these different types of social influence may result in different types of conformity. ■ Outline and evaluate research into conformity (e.g line-length study by Asch and Zimbardo's study of conformity to social roles).
Obedience, including Milgram's work and explanations of why people obey	■ Explain what is meant by obedience and how it differs from conformity. ■ Outline and evaluate research on obedience. In particular, you need to be able to outline Milgram's research procedures, findings and conclusions and to evaluate these in terms of their validity and the ethical issues they raised. ■ The specification requires that you know about **at least two** explanations of why people obey, but no particular explanation is specified.
Social influence in everyday life	In this part of the specification you are required to know about reasons for independent behaviour and how research into social influence might explain or be significant in social change. To do this, you need to be able to:
Explanations of independent behaviour, including how people resist pressures to conform and pressures to obey authority	■ Explain at least two ways in which people can resist pressures to conform. ■ Explain at least two reasons why people can resist pressures to obey.
The influence of individual differences on independent behaviour, including locus of control	■ Describe and evaluate at least two ways in which individual differences (important personal factors that differentiate people) may affect independent behaviour. ■ You must include locus of control as one of the individual differences you study.
Implications for social change of research into social influence	■ Discuss how findings from social influence research might have implications (explanations or significance) for changes in society. ■ You will need to be able to describe and evaluate at least two such implications (e.g. how research on minority influence helps explain how minorities might bring about social change; the development of more stringent ethical guidelines for psychological research following Milgram's study).

Introduction

Social influence is an inevitable part of social life. Think how many times over the past few weeks people have tried to get you to think or behave as they want you to. These attempts might have taken the form, for example, of advertisements trying to persuade you to buy something or a parent's request that you tidy your room or do your homework. In addition to these examples of *active* social influence, there are many cases where social influence occurs without our being aware of it. A common example of this less obvious type of social influence is when we conform to **social norms** (rules of behaviour that prescribe what is acceptable in a given situation), such as what is appropriate clothing for different occasions.

In the first topic of the chapter, we shall look at conformity and obedience, two responses to social influence and among the most challenging and controversial topics in social psychology. Not only are the findings of studies in these areas at times unsettling, but the methods used by some researchers (e.g. Stanley Milgram) have come in for much criticism. Consequently, we shall consider some of the ethical issues that have arisen in social influence research when evaluating work in this area.

In the second topic of the chapter we turn our attention to independent behaviour and the reasons why people are sometimes able to resist pressures to conform or obey. We shall look at individual differences in people's susceptibility to social influence – what is it about some individuals that makes them more or less likely to conform or obey? Finally, we shall consider the implications of research findings about social influence, including minority influence, for social change.

Topic 1: Social influence

Social influence can be defined as the process by which an individual's attitudes, beliefs or behaviours are modified by the presence or actions of others. Some forms of social influence, such as when a teacher insists that you hand in work on time, are obvious (though not always successful). Other types of social influence are more subtle, sometimes unintended and, on occasions, even unnoticed by those who are influenced. Have a look at 'Psychology in context' on the right and try to answer the questions at the bottom.

Types of conformity

Conformity is the process of yielding to majority influence (i.e. a response to social influence) and is defined by David Myers (1999) as 'a change in behaviour or belief as a result of real or imagined group pressure'. Zimbardo *et al.* (1995) defined it as a 'tendency for people to adopt the behaviour, attitudes and values of other members of a reference group'. You may find it easier to identify with Myers' definition because it focuses upon the kind of experience most of us have had at one time or another: the feeling that others are putting pressure on us to change our minds or behaviour. However, the Zimbardo definition proposes that we tend to go along with those people with whom we compare ourselves when we are evaluating our status (i.e. our reference groups). If you accept that the process of conformity can occur without your being aware of it, then you may prefer the wording of the Zimbardo definition. Try the activity, 'Types of groups', now before reading on.

Psychology in context

Conforming behaviour

In the pictures above, you see some examples of conforming behaviour.

1 What are/were the advantages of conforming for the people in the pictures?

2 In what situations do you think that conformity is desirable?

3 What are the dangers of being over conformist?

Activity **Types of groups (based on Stainton Rogers 2003)**

- *Incidental group* – Members have little involvement or commitment, e.g. short-term practical or discussion group where members are assigned by a teacher.
- *Membership groups* – Members are committed to the norms of the group, e.g. sports club or hobby group, by virtue of being members.
- *Identity-reference group* – Members identify with the values, goals and motives of the group and obtain their social identity from their group membership.

1 List the incidental, membership and identity-reference groups to which you belong at present.
2 Which of the three groups above is likely to exert the most conformity pressures on its members?

Distinctions between the groups proposed by Stainton Rogers are not always clear-cut. However, members of an identity-reference group are more likely to experience pressures to conform to the group norms and be less individualistic than members of the other two groups.

Although most people think of themselves as autonomous (independent) individuals, they nevertheless tend to go along with (conform to) the social norms that their groups and societies have evolved. The social norms that indicate how we ought to behave may be explicit (e.g. 'Stand on the right' on London underground escalators), or they may be implicit (e.g. the unspoken but well understood norm in the UK of not standing too close to strangers). Such implicit norms are, nevertheless, powerful sources of social influence. Norms about 'personal space', for example, exist in all cultures but we may only become fully aware of the implicit norms about personal space in our own culture when someone makes us feel uncomfortable by trespassing on what we think of as our 'personal bubble'.

As long ago as 1958, Kelman identified three types of conformity, that is, three responses to social influence: compliance, identification and internalization.

Compliance

Compliance is publicly conforming to the behaviour or views of others in a group but privately maintaining one's own views. For example, if you are with a group of friends who support a particular football team, you might not reveal that you support a different one, even if asked directly!

Identification

Identification is adopting the views or behaviour of a group both publicly and privately because you value membership of that group. However, the new attitudes and behaviours are often temporary and not maintained on leaving the group. For example, when young people move away from home to go to college, they may begin to question the lifestyles they had previously taken for granted. New students often enthusiastically adopt the dress and behaviour codes of their new student groups. However, on graduating and moving into employment, they often change the way they dress and behave again.

Internalization

Internalization is a conversion or true change of private views to match those of the group. What distinguishes this type of conformity from identification is that the new attitudes and behaviours have become part of your value system; they are not dependent on the presence of the group. For example, a person searching for some greater meaning to life may be influenced to convert to a religious faith if the members of that faith seem able to provide the answers being searched for. A true conversion will survive even if the person loses contact with those who influenced them originally.

Why do people conform?

According to Deutsch and Gerard's dual process model (1955), there are two types of social influence that lead people to conform: normative and informational social influence (see Figure 6.1).

Figure 6.1
Different routes to compliance and internalization

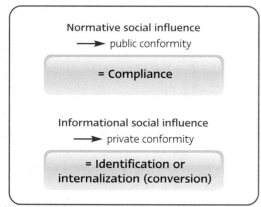

Normative social influence
→ public conformity

= Compliance

Informational social influence
→ private conformity

= Identification or internalization (conversion)

Normative social influence

Normative social influence is based on our desire to be liked. We conform because we think that others will approve of and accept us. The conformity that results from this desire to be liked is sometimes called compliance, that is, publicly going along with the majority but privately holding to one's own views (see previous page). If you have ever agonized over what to wear to a party because you wanted to fit in, and eventually phoned a friend to find out what they were going to wear, then you have experienced the power of normative social influence.

When are people most likely to conform to normative social influence? According to Latane's (1981) **social impact theory**, we respond most to normative influence when the group is very important to us and when we spend a lot of time with it. The effect of group size is less clear-cut. A group of four people may exert more normative influence than a group of two or three. If, however, the group consists of, say, 40 people then an increase in its size to 42 or 43 makes no difference to the influence it already exerts. (See Asch's study on conformity, p. 185, where he demonstrated that it does not take a large group to produce optimum normative social influence.)

Informational social influence

Informational social influence is based on our desire to be right. We look to others whom we believe to be correct, to give us information about how to behave, particularly in novel or ambiguous situations. Sherif's (1936) study of the emergence of group norms demonstrated that people will use each other as a source of information when a situation is unclear (see the panel on the right).

Informational social influence may be particularly strong when we move from one group to another and experience *situational ambiguity* (as Sherif's study). For example, young people moving from school to university might redefine themselves as students (no longer pupils) and look to other students to learn what are acceptable ways of behaving (the norms) in this new situation. You can probably think of occasions when you have looked to the behaviour of others to provide information about how to behave correctly. Informational social influence can sometimes lead to a genuine and long-lasting change of belief or attitude, called internalization (see previous page).

Although *situational ambiguity* is the most important factor in leading people to use others as a source of information, there are other factors that can produce conformity owing to informational social influence. These include emergencies and the presence of experts.

- In an *emergency*, we may be panicky and not have time to think calmly about the best course of action. In such a situation we may look to others for information about how best to respond. Other people, of course, may also be unsure and afraid and so not necessarily behave in the most rational manner.

- A third factor is the presence of someone with known *expertise or knowledge*. For example, we may be less likely to rush for the fire escape when we hear the fire alarm if our experienced teacher mutters 'not another fire practice!'.

Deutsch and Gerard's explanation of conformity is sometimes criticized for implying that the two types of social influence are separate and independent. Instead, Insko *et al.* (1983) claimed that normative influence and informational influence often complement each other, working together to affect levels of conformity.

The emergence of group norms
A study by Sherif (1935)

Sherif (1935) investigated the emergence of group norms using the autokinetic effect. This is an optical illusion experienced when a person is placed in a totally dark room in which a stationary point of light appears to move because the person's perceptual system has no frame of reference for it. In fact, the light remains stationary.

- Sherif asked *individual* participants to judge how far the light appeared to move on a number of trials. Each individual's estimates were relatively stable but between participants there was considerable variation, that is, the strength of the effect was seen differently by different people.

- When the same participants then worked in groups of three people, announcing their estimates aloud, their judgements converged until a group norm emerged.

- When Sherif altered his procedure so that participants made their first judgements in the group situation, he found that group norms emerged even more quickly than in the previous procedure.

- The participants who had worked in a group first, were then asked individually to estimate the movement of the light. They continued to give the answer that the group had arrived at earlier.

The study showed that when faced with an ambiguous situation, the participants looked to others in the group for guidance, that is, they experienced informational social influence. Furthermore, once a group norm had been established, participants continued to use it when they were asked to make individual judgements later.

Activity **Betty's friends**

Imagine that Betty and her three friends meet on the way to college. All Betty's friends decide to bunk off for the day and invite her along. Betty, however, wants to go to college.

In what ways might Betty's friends try to persuade her to go with them?

Suggest two ways that Betty might resist the pressure from her friends to skip college.

Activity — Identifying weaknesses of Asch's study of conformity

Read the key study on 'Majority influence' on the next page, up to and including the 'Conclusions'. Do not read the Evaluations. Note down any criticisms that you can identify in relation to:

1 the sample of participants he studied

2 the time and place of the study.

Compare your thoughts with the evaluations at the end of the study. When reading any research study, it is important to get into the habit of trying to identify any weaknesses. This will help you to develop your evaluation skills.

The set-up in Asch's studies, in which a minority of one (answering sixth out of seven) faces pressure to conform to an otherwise unanimous majority

Table 6.1
Factors affecting conformity levels

Factors increasing conformity levels

- Unanimous majority
- Difficult task
- Being deserted by a partner who had previously given correct answers

Factors decreasing conformity levels

- Non-unanimous majority
- Majority of only two people
- Writing responses rather than calling them aloud (i.e. private rather than public responding)

Asch's research into conformity

Many psychologists have attempted to answer the question 'Why do people conform' by conducting research studies in order to tease out the different factors that cause people to yield to majority social influence. The first of many researchers was Solomon Asch who carried out his highly influential work at Harvard University in the United States.

Asch (1951) thought that the convergence of judgements found in the Sherif study could be attributed to the ambiguity of the situation. He wondered what would happen if participants were exposed to normative social influence in a group situation where there could be no doubt about the correct answer to a question. How many participants would conform to the group, deny the evidence of their own eyes and give the wrong answer when it was their turn? Initially, Asch predicted that few would conform.

Try the activity on the left next and read the key study 'Majority influence' on the opposite page to find out what actually happened.

In addition to the specific criticisms made of Asch's study, he is also sometimes criticized for implying that conforming behaviour is 'bad' and that resisting (not yielding to) majority influence is somehow always good. Clearly, there are dangers involved if people are too conformist. Nevertheless, without widespread conformity, society could not function effectively. Conformity to prosocial norms, such as helping others in distress, is obviously highly desirable.

Extensions to Asch's research

In order to find out exactly which features of a situation made it more likely that someone would conform, Asch varied some of the situational factors in his original study. He introduced the following changes and observed the effects:

- *A non-unanimous majority* – Asch found that levels of conformity dropped dramatically (to only 5 per cent) when just one other participant dissented from the majority and supported the naive participant. A majority of three with no dissenters was more effective in producing conformity than a majority of eight with one dissenter.

- *The size of the majority* – When the majority consisted of only two people, conformity responses in naive participants dropped to 12.8 per cent of their total judgements. Optimum conformity effects (32 per cent of responses) were found with a majority of three. Increasing the size of the majority beyond three did not increase the levels of conformity found. Some psychologists have suggested that people may suspect collusion if the majority rises beyond three or four. When only one accomplice (confederate) was used, no conformity effects were found.

- *Losing a partner* – The naive participant started with a 'partner' who responded correctly to begin with but who 'deserted' to the majority in the middle of the procedure. This resulted in conformity levels of 28.5 per cent on critical judgements.

- *Gaining a partner* – When a participant who had started the procedure as a minority of one received a 'partner' part way through, this reduced conformity responses to 8.7 per cent.

- *The nature of the task* – The levels of conformity increased (see also Crutchfield's results on p. 186) as tasks were made more difficult.

Majority influence
A study of conformity by Asch (1951)

Aim

To see if participants would yield (conform) to majority social influence and give incorrect answers in a situation where the correct answers were always obvious.

Figure 6.2
A sample of the stimulus material used in Asch's experiments on conformity

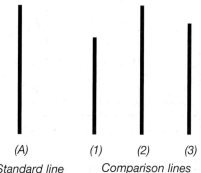

(A)   *(1)*   *(2)*   *(3)*
Standard line   *Comparison lines*

Procedure

- Seven male student participants looked at two cards: The 'test' card showed one vertical line; the other card showed three vertical lines of different lengths.
- The participants' task was to call out, in turn, which of the three lines was the same length as the test line. The correct answer was always obvious (see Figure 6.2 on the right).
- All participants, except one, were accomplices of the experimenter. The genuine participant called out his answer last but one.
- Accomplices gave unanimous wrong answers on 12 of the 18 trials. These 12 trials were called the 'critical' trials.
- In total, Asch used 50 male college students as naive, genuine participants in this first study.

Findings

- Participants conformed to the unanimous incorrect answer on 32 per cent of the critical trials. This might not strike you as a very high figure but remember that the correct answer was always obvious.
- 74 per cent of participants conformed at least once.
- 26 per cent of participants never conformed. Some of these 'independent' participants were confident in their judgements. More often, however, they experienced tension and doubt but managed to resist the pressure exerted by the unanimous majority.
- During post-experimental interviews, some conforming participants claimed to have actually seen the line identified by the majority as the correct answer. Others yielded because they could not bear to be in a minority of one and risk being ridiculed or excluded by the group. Most participants who had conformed, however, experienced a distortion of judgement: they thought that their perception of the lines must be inaccurate and for that reason they yielded to the majority view.

Conclusion

- Even in unambiguous situations, there may be strong group pressure to conform, especially if the group is a unanimous majority.
- However, after interviewing his participants, Asch concluded that people go along with the views of others for different reasons:
  - Some people experience *normative social influence* and feel compelled to accept the mistaken majority's norms or standards of behaviour to avoid being rejected.
  - Others experience *informational pressures* and doubt their own judgements – 'surely they can't all be wrong!'

Evaluation

- All the participants were male college students and so it was a very limited sample. For this reason it might not be valid to generalize the findings to a wider population.
- The time and place when the research was carried out might have affected the findings. In the 1950s, the USA was very conservative, involved in an anticommunist witch hunt against anyone who was thought to hold left-wing views (this became known as McCarthyism, named after the senator who spearheaded the witch hunt) and its educational institutions were more hierarchical than they are today.

FURTHER ANALYSIS

HOW SCIENCE WORKS

The importance of debriefing participants after an investigation is now widely recognized (see p. 57), especially if deception has been used. This is done to give participants information about the investigation and to reassure them if they feel foolish or upset. In this study we see yet another reason why thorough debriefing is important. Only by speaking to participants after the procedure was over was Asch able to uncover the feelings and different psychological experiences that the participants had undergone – to find out *why* the participants had behaved as they did. By using post-experimental interviews he found out that there were different reasons why the participants conformed: some experienced normative social influence, others experienced informational influence. Therefore, his careful debriefing procedure resulted in valuable findings.

Figure 6.3
Crutchfield's conformity-testing procedure: people sit in adjacent booths and answer questions shown on the wall in front of them after being told of other people's apparent responses

Which is bigger?

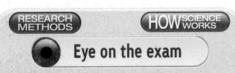

RESEARCH METHODS   HOW SCIENCE WORKS

Eye on the exam

Research studies into conformity are sometimes criticized for being unethical. Discuss one ethical issue which you think is raised by research in this area. *(4 marks)*

Take care that you discuss (outline and evaluate) only **one** ethical issue. Research studies into conformity often involve deceiving participants. Therefore, you could discuss (outline and evaluate):

- the ethical issue raised by use of deception and therefore the prevention of fully informed consent.

If you prefer, you could discuss:

- the risk of psychological harm to participants who may be embarrassed or stressed by the procedures used to investigate conformity (e.g. the procedure used by Asch 1951).

In addition you could discuss:

- the measures, such as thorough debriefing, that may be taken to overcome any harmful effects
- whether the benefits of the research findings outweigh the costs to the participants.

For more exam advice, visit
www.collinseducation.com/psychologyweb

- *Mode of response* – When Asch asked his participants to write their answers rather than call them out loud, conformity levels dropped sharply. This illustrates the difference between public compliance (overtly adhering to social norms) and private acceptance (actually thinking as others do).

Further research on conformity

Although many criticisms have been made of Asch's findings (see the key study on the previous page), one of the strengths of his work is the amount of subsequent research it generated.

When participants cannot see each other

Crutchfield (1955) thought that the face-to-face arrangement of participants in the Asch procedure might be responsible for the levels of conformity found. Therefore, he arranged his participants in booths out of sight of each other, but all able to see the stimulus cards (see Figure 6.3). This enabled him to collect data more economically by running several naive participants at the same time. Participants sat individually in booths with a row of switches and lights in front of them. They had to press the switch that corresponded to their judgement when their turn came to answer. They were told that the lights on the display panel showed the responses of the other participants. In fact, the experimenter controlled these lights and each participant saw an identical display. Despite the absence of an actual face-to-face group, Crutchfield found the following:

- Conformity levels were 30 per cent when using Asch's line comparison tasks.
- When the task was made more difficult, conformity increased.

Research on individual differences

Crutchfield was also interested in individual differences and how these might affect conformity. He found that participants (business and military men on a three-day assessment course) with high scores in intelligence and leadership ability displayed less conformity. However, there is insufficient evidence from subsequent studies to support any idea of a 'conforming personality'. (See pp. 206–9 for more information on individual differences as an influence on independent behaviour.) Crutchfield's studies can also be criticized for their artificial setting. The findings do, however, support those of Asch, suggesting that conformity pressures operate on people besides students.

Furman and Duke (1988) looked at how lack of confidence might make people more likely to conform. They asked students to listen to two versions of each of 10 musical excerpts. On their degree programme the students were majoring either in music or in another subject. Each student, on their own, selected a preferred version for each of the ten pairs. They were then individually tested in the presence of three confederates who unanimously stated a verbal preference from each pair of excerpts. Their findings were as follows:

- Music majors were not influenced to change their already stated preferences.
- However, the publicly stated preferences of *non-music majors* were significantly affected by the preferences of the confederates.

Research on historical and cultural contexts

Some observers have suggested that Asch's findings tell us more about the historical and cultural climate of the United States in 1951 than they do about fundamental psychological tendencies. Some later studies of conformity have failed to confirm Asch's findings.

- Perrin and Spencer (1980) replicated Asch's procedure, using British students. They found only one conforming response in 396 trials. They concluded that cultural changes over 30 years had led to a reduction in the tendency of students to conform. Another factor that might have influenced the results is the type of students used. They were drawn from engineering, chemistry and mathematics courses, and it is possible that the knowledge and skills acquired in their courses had equipped them to resist conformity pressures during a task of this sort. Another study by Perrin and Spencer (1981) using youths on probation as participants and using probation officers as the confederates demonstrated levels of conformity similar to those found by Asch in 1952. The researchers concluded that where the perceived costs for people of not yielding were high, conformity effects would still be demonstrated.

- Nicholson *et al.* (1985) compared conformity levels in British and in American students using the Asch procedure (paradigm). They found no significant differences between the two groups, suggesting some similarity in British and US student cultures, at least at that point in history. The students in 1985 were found to be significantly less conforming than their 1952 US counterparts but more conforming than the British students in 1981. Nicholson and colleagues have suggested that the experience of the Falklands War in 1982 (when Britain went to war with Argentina over the occupancy of the Falkland Islands) might have contributed to group cohesiveness and, in turn, to a higher degree of conformity. (The war took place in 1982, between the collection of Perrin and Spencer's data and the collection of their own data.)

- A more recent study that investigated whether conformity in an experimental setting could still be replicated outside American culture was carried out in Portugal by Neto (1995). The procedure of Asch's classic study was re-enacted using female psychology students as participants. On the critical trials, 59 per cent conformed at least once and 28 per cent yielded between three to twelve times. Neto concluded that conformity to a unanimous peer-group remains highly observable.

- Finally, Smith and Bond (1998) reviewed 31 studies of conformity conducted in different cultures using Asch's procedures. They concluded that people in collectivistic cultures show higher levels of conformity compared with those who live in individualistic cultures. In collectivistic cultures, people emphasize loyalty to the group and being concerned about the needs and interests of others. Group decision-making is preferred to individual decisions. In individualistic cultures, people are more concerned with their own and their family's self-interest and individual initiatives are valued.

Why might people be more likely to conform during times of war?

Zimbardo *et al.*'s (1973) investigation of conformity to social roles: the Stanford Prison Experiment

Philip Zimbardo and colleagues conducted one of the best-known and most controversial studies in psychology. They looked at how people conform to the expectations they have about social roles. He used a simulated prison set-up to see to what extent normal, well-balanced people would conform to new social roles. For example, Zimbardo wondered if participants who were assigned the role of guards would act in a way that conformed to their stereotyped view of how prison guards should behave. (In a simulation, participants are asked to act (role-play) as though the simulation is real. Psychologists use simulations in order to study behaviours to which they would not normally have access) (see key study, 'Conformity to social roles', on the next page).

Conformity to social roles

Stanford prison simulation experiment by Zimbardo *et al.* (1973)

Aim	To investigate how readily people would conform to new roles by observing how quickly people would adopt the roles of guard or prisoner in a role-playing exercise that simulated prison life. Zimbardo was interested to find out if the brutality reported among guards in American prisons was due to the sadistic personalities of the guards – called a dispositional explanation – or had more to do with the prison environment – a situational explanation.
Procedure	■ Well-adjusted, healthy male volunteers were paid $15 a day to take part in a two-week simulation study of prison life. ■ Volunteers were randomly allocated to the roles of prisoners or guards. ■ Local police helped by 'arresting' 9 prisoners at their homes, without warning. They were taken, blindfolded, to the 'prison' (actually the basement of Stanford University), stripped and sprayed with disinfectant, given smocks to wear and their prison number to memorize. From then on they were referred to by number only. ■ There were three guards on each shift who wore khaki uniforms, dark glasses and carried wooden batons. ■ No physical aggression was permitted.
Findings	■ The guards harassed and humiliated the prisoners and conformed to their perceived roles with such zeal that the study had to be discontinued after six days although it had been planned to last two weeks. ■ Prisoners rebelled against the guards after only two days. Guards quelled the rebellion using fire extinguishers. ■ Some prisoners became depressed and anxious; one prisoner had to be released after only one day! Two more prisoners had to be released on the fourth day. By day 6, prisoners were submissive to the guards.
Conclusion	■ The conforming behaviour of the participants can best be explained in terms of situational factors – the result of normative social influence – rather than dispositional (personality) factors. The situation of the 'prison environment' was an important factor in creating the guards' brutal behaviour (none of the participants who acted as guards had shown sadistic tendencies before the study). ■ People will readily conform to the social roles they are expected to play especially if the roles are as strongly stereotyped as those of prison guards. ■ The roles that people play shape their attitudes and behaviour. If it took only six days to alter the behaviour of the participants in this study, then the roles we play in real life will have even more far-reaching effects.
Evaluation	■ The study has received many ethical criticisms, including those about lack of fully informed consent by participants and the humiliation and distress experienced by those who acted as prisoners. Participants did not know, for example, that they would be arrested at home. Zimbardo thought, however, that withholding this type of procedural detail was justifiable given the nature of the study. Those acting as guards had to face up to the unpalatable fact that they had been willing to mistreat their prisoners and they as well as the 'prisoners' might have suffered psychological harm. However, Zimbardo's follow-up interviews with participants found no lasting negative effects. ■ According to Zimbardo, these results demonstrate how easily people can come to behave in uncharacteristic ways when placed in new situations and given new roles. Another possible explanation is that some of the volunteers might have tried to be 'good subjects' and behaved in the ways they thought the researcher wanted (called demand characteristics). ■ Zimbardo was wrong to act as both prison-superintendent and chief researcher as this produced a conflict of roles whereby he lost sight of the harm being done to the participants.
FURTHER ANALYSIS HOW SCIENCE WORKS	Haslam and Reicher (2005) have questioned Zimbardo's explanation that it was conformity to their social roles that was responsible for the guards' behaviour because not all the guards behaved brutally. Banyard (2007) also charges Zimbardo with being more responsible for the guards' tyrannical behaviour than he admits, owing to his role as prison superintendent. Banyard claims that 'it is not the roles that created the abusive behaviour in the guards but the manipulation of the Machiavellian superintendent' (p. 494). For example, at the beginning of the simulation, Zimbardo told the guards that they were to create a sense of powerlessness in the prisoners and advised on ways that this could be achieved. According to Haslam and Reicher (2008), 'the study of leadership must be a central component of any analysis of tyranny' (p. 19).

Ethics in Zimbardo's prison simulation study

- *Harm to participants* – Savin (1973) criticized Zimbardo's prison simulation study for the way it humiliated its participants (see key study on the previous page for more detail). After six days, the simulation, originally planned to last two weeks, was ended because of the unexpectedly extreme emotional and behavioural effects. Did the knowledge gained justify the means by which it was acquired? Savin thinks not; Zimbardo thinks it did. He reports that follow-ups over many years revealed no lasting negative effects; that student participants were healthy and able to bounce back from their 'prison' experience; that they had learned the important lesson that even the most intelligent and well-intentioned among us can be overwhelmed by social influences.

- *Need for independent surveillance* – In recent years, Zimbardo has acknowledged that he should not have acted as 'prison superintendent' as well as principal researcher, because he became trapped by the day-to-day business of his superintendent role, rather as the 'guards' and 'prisoners' became trapped in their roles. However, he argues that instead of banning research of this type, what is needed is better research – that is, where experiments are ethically sensitive, there should be an independent monitor and more vigilant surveillance by the institution concerned. In this way, he claims, participants could be protected while valuable information was acquired.

- *Deceiving participants* – Some critics of Zimbardo (and Milgram, see pp. 192–8) have suggested that deceiving participants is really not necessary in research and is particularly unethical when it might leave them feeling foolish or humiliated. They have proposed that other more ethically acceptable methods could be used, e.g. asking people to imagine how they or others would behave in certain situations. Zimbardo is scathing about the use of 'as if' procedures to replace simulations or experiments which he considers essential tools in the scientific study of behaviour. In an interview with Mark McDermott (1993), Zimbardo said:

'One of the subtle dangers arising out of the increase in concern for the ethics of experiments, is it gives social psychologists an easy out. To do behavioural experiments is very difficult. It's time consuming, it's labour intensive and you can replace it with an 'as if' paper-and-pencil, 30-minute self-report. The question arises, 'is that the same thing?' If, in fact, you could discover the same things about human nature from asking people to imagine how they would behave in a situation instead of observing how they do, it clearly doesn't make sense to do the behavioural simulation. There are situations you cannot imagine what it would be like until you are in them … Typically, even if you describe the situation, people will underestimate its power. There is no way until you are in it, that you begin to feel and become entrapped in the power of the situation.'

Owing to the ethical concerns raised by Zimbardo and colleagues' study, there have been no exact replications of this investigation, though the power of social roles has been explored in other simulation studies, such as the one by Orlando (1973) outlined on the next page. Without replicating a study it is impossible to question the reliability of its findings or the validity of its conclusions. However, in May 2002, the BBC, in collaboration with Haslam and Reicher, televised four hour-long documentaries that examined the ways in which relationships developed within and between groups within a mock prison scenario. Read the text on the next page and then try the activity on the right.

Eye on the exam

Zimbardo and conformity

'Discuss research findings in conformity.'
(12 marks)

Imagine you are answering this question in the exam and you want to include results from Zimbardo's prison simulation study as part of your answer. There are a couple of things that you need to make clear to ensure that you select relevant material:

- *What* it was the participants were conforming to – According to Zimbardo the participants conformed to the roles to which they had been assigned, that is, guard or prisoner.

- *Why* they conformed – They conformed owing to normative social influence, that is, situational pressure. Zimbardo claimed, for example, that the guards' aggression was a consequence of wearing uniforms which were associated with inherent power. In other words, he explained the findings in terms of situational, not dispositional, factors.

- Avoid being sidetracked into giving detailed descriptions of the more sensational aspects of the study. You need to *concentrate on the conformity aspects* if you are to keep focused on the requirements of the questions

For more exam advice, visit
www.collinseducation.com/psychologyweb

RESEARCH METHODS

Activity

Differences between Stanford Prison Experiment and the BBC 'prison study'

Read the key study on the opposite page and the description of the BBC's 'Prison study', described on the next page. Then answer the following questions:

1 Identify the differences between Zimbardo and colleagues' procedures, findings and conclusions and those of Haslam and Reicher.

2 To what extent do you think that the differences in the procedures explain the differences in the findings and conclusions?

Interpreting abuses of power at Abu Ghraib prison: Bad apples or bad barrels?

In 2007, Zimbardo published *The Lucifer Effect: How good people turn evil*, written in an effort to 'better understand the how and why of the physical abuses perpetrated on prisoners by American military police at the Abu Ghraib Prison in Iraq' (p. 18). Like many other people, Zimbardo was shocked and distressed when he saw the pictures (taken by the American guards themselves) of smiling men and women abusing their prisoners. However, he claims he was not surprised, because 30 years earlier he had witnessed similar scenes (e.g. of shackled prisoners with bags over their heads) in the psychology department of Stanford University. According to Zimbardo 'the college students role playing guards and prisoners in a mock prison experiment … were mirrored in the real guards and real prison in the Iraq of 2003' (p.20).

A US soldier watches coverage of the abuse of Iraqi prisoners in Abu Ghraib prison

Zimbardo does not accept that a 'few bad apples' were responsible for the torturing of prisoners at Abu Ghraib. Rather he claims that it is the 'barrel' (conditions and institutions) in which the apples operate that leads good people to carry out evil acts – the Lucifer effect. He had observed how decent, well-balanced young students could quickly become tyrannical when they role-played guards and were given wide-ranging powers over prisoners. Why, he argues, should we be surprised when real guards, apparently with the approval of some higher-ranking officers, humiliate and torture prisoners?

The Schlesinger Report (2004) acknowledged the parallels between the abuses at Abu Ghraib and those that occurred during the Stanford prison study.

> *'Findings from the field of social psychology suggest that the conditions of war and the dynamics of detainee operations carry inherent risks for human mistreatment … the landmark Stanford study provides a cautionary tale for all military detention operations.'* (from Zimbardo 2007, pp.401–2)

Another simulation study, by Orlando (1973)

A mock psychiatric ward study, lasting three days, was carried out by Orlando (1973) at a hospital in Illinois. Twenty-nine volunteer members of staff were held in a ward of their own, performing the role of 'patient'. Twenty-two regular staff carried out their usual roles. The procedure was videotaped.

- Within a short time, the behaviour of the mock patients became indistinguishable from that of the real patients.
- Some suffered withdrawal, depression or bouts of weeping and others tried to escape.
- Most of the 'patients' reported feelings of tension, anxiety, frustration, despair and a loss of identity.
- The positive outcome of this study was the insight gained by the staff-turned-patients into how real patients could feel in a situation where members of staff were disrespectful to them and where mistreatment could result. This led to a more cooperative way of working with patients and a conscious effort among all personnel to improve relationships between staff and patients.

The BBC 'Prison Study'

Haslam and Reicher used a set-up that was similar to that used by Zimbardo in his prison simulation study, e.g. participants were randomly allocated to role of prisoner or guard. However, the researchers did not act as prison superintendents and clinical psychologists and an ethics committee oversaw how the investigation was run. The set-up did not attempt to mimic a real prison, but guards were more powerful and had more resources (e.g. better food) than the prisoners. Both guards and prisoners were systematically observed and unobtrusively filmed for 10 days. One aim of the study was to see if the guards would abuse their power and if the prisoners would succumb or rebel against oppression. Several interesting findings emerged:

- The guards were uncomfortable about exercising their power and became divided and powerless. They never developed any sense of group identity.
- On the other hand, the prisoners, unhappy about the inequalities they experienced, supported each other, shared a social identity and challenged the guards' authority.
- A commune of both ex-guards and ex-prisoners was established but broke down when those who did not support the commune wanted to reinstate a more tyrannical version of the guard/prisoner system. At this point the study was ended.

Haslam and Reicher (2005) concluded that a shared social identity can create social power and lead to positive outcomes. Individuals, they argue, are not slaves to their social roles, but rather they contribute to the norms and values of the groups to which they belong. Turner (2006) has praised Haslam and Reicher's study for challenging the negative view of groups (and the power of social roles within them) to which Zimbardo and others have long subscribed. You may wish to consider to what extent the presence of television cameras and the knowledge that behaviour would be broadcast might have had on the behaviour of the participants.

Obedience to authority

My Lai Massacre
Interview with one of the American soldiers involved

During the Vietnam War, American soldiers rounded up hundreds of women, children and old men from My Lai village – and were ordered them to kill them. Mike Wallace from CBS News interviewed one of the soldiers, reported in *The New York Times*, 25 November 1969:

Q How many people did you round up?

A Well, there was about 40, 50 people that we gathered in the center of the village...

Q What kind of people – men, women, children?

A Men, women, children.

Q Babies?

A Babies. And we huddled them up. We made them squat down and Lieutenant Calley came over and said, "You know what to do with them don't you?" And I said yes. So I took it for granted that he just wanted us to watch them. And he left, and came back about 10 or 15 minutes later and said, "How come you ain't killed them yet?" And I told him that I didn't think you wanted us to kill them, that you just wanted us to guard them. He said, "No, I want them dead." So – ...

Q And you killed how many? At that time?

A Well I fired on them automatic, so you can't – You just spray the area on them and so you can't know how many you killed 'cause they were going fast. So I might have killed 10 or 15 of them.

Q Men, women, and children?

A Men, women, and children.

Q And babies?

A And babies ...

Q Why did you do it?

A Why did I do it? Because I felt like I was ordered to do it, and it seemed like that, at the time I felt like I was doing the right thing, because, like I said, I lost buddies...

Q What did these civilians – particularly the women and children, the old men – what did they do? What did they say to you?

A They weren't much saying to them. They [were] just being pushed and they were doing what they was told to do.

Q They weren't begging, or saying, "no ... no," or ...?

A Right. They were begging and saying "no, no". And the mothers was hugging their children, and ... but they kept right on firing. Well, we kept right on firing. They was waving their arms and begging ...

A guard supervises inmates of a Nazi concentration camp during World War II

Government troops violently quell protests by Buddhist monks in Burma, September 2007

Obedience is the result of social influence where somebody acts in response to a direct order from an authority figure (Cardwell 2000). It is assumed that without such an order the person would not have acted in this way. Obedience may sometimes be destructive, as when people comply with the orders of a malevolent authority.

'Obedience as a determinant of behaviour is of particular relevance to our time. It has been reliably established that from 1939 to 1945, millions of innocent persons were slaughtered on command; gas chambers were built, death camps were guarded, daily quotas of corpses were produced with the same efficiency as the manufacture of appliances. These inhumane policies may have originated in the mind of a single person, but they could only have been carried out on a massive scale if a very large number of persons obeyed orders.' (Milgram 1963, p.371)

Activity Obedience

Some questions for you to think about or debate:

- Why do you think that people obey orders from others?
- Why do you think people obeyed orders in the situations depicted above?
- Think of a situation when you obeyed an order and, as a consequence, you did something that you felt to be wrong. Why did you choose to obey? Why did you choose not to stick up for what you felt to be right?

Both obedience and conformity are outcomes of social influence. In the case of obedience, social influence takes the form of orders from an authority figure. In the case of conformity, the social norms of the majority exert influence on an individual to go along with the behaviour and attitudes of the group.

Identify two differences between conformity and obedience in terms of the psychological processes involved.

Answers are given on p. 277 ▶

RESEARCH METHODS

Activity   Other people's estimates of Milgram's findings

Milgram described this experimental procedure to three different groups of people: psychiatrists, college students and middle-class adults. He asked them to guess how people would respond.

1 Before reading on to find out what they said, how do *you* think that people would be likely to respond? The maximum number of shocks that could be delivered to the 'learner' was 30, starting at 15 volts – how many shocks do *you* think the participants would be prepared to deliver?

2 Describe the study to at least 10 other people (class members, friends or family members). Ask them how many shocks they think someone would be prepared to deliver in this kind of situation. Note down each of their answers.

3 Now calculate the average (mean) score by adding up all the scores (including your own score) and dividing by the total number of scores, or combine your answers with those collected by other members of your class so you have many more scores and then calculate the average. What is your answer?

On average, the people Milgram spoke to estimated an average of 9 out of the possible 30 shocks (i.e. 135 volts) and predicted that the participants would rebel against the instructions once that level was reached. Only a tiny handful predicted that participants would administer the maximum shock of 450 volts, which was labelled 'Danger, severe shock'.

Now read on to find out how many shocks the participants actually delivered in Milgram's study.

Similarly appalling events have occurred since then (e.g. the My Lai massacre during the Vietnam War, the slaughter of Kurds in Iraq, ethnic cleansing in Kosovo and the slaughter of nearly a million Tutsis and moderate Hutus in Rwanda in 1994). The list goes on. What induces people to obey their leaders' orders to torture and kill innocent human beings? Milgram was one of the first psychologists who tried to answer this question. He placed the issue of obedience in a social-psychological context, proposing that it is a *normative process*, a basic feature of human interaction.

Now try the activity on the left.

Milgram's studies of obedience

Stanley Milgram carried out a series of studies to try to shed some light on this aspect of human behaviour. In all, he studied over 1000 participants who were representative of the general population. He discovered that, under certain situational influences, most of us would obey orders that went against our conscience.

His original study took place in a laboratory at Yale University in the USA (see the key study, 'Obedience' on the next page). The experimenter, who wore a grey laboratory coat to reinforce his status and authority, introduced two participants to each other and they each drew lots, apparently to determine who would be the 'teacher' and who would be the 'learner'. The learner-accomplice was a mild-mannered 47-year-old man who mentioned that he had had a heart complaint in the past, but that he was willing to participate in the study nonetheless. As the learner-accomplice began making mistakes, the level of shock administered by the 'teacher' increased, and he was heard to protest until, at 180 volts he shouted that he could bear the pain no longer. At 300 volts he screamed and complained that his heart was troubling him. At 315 volts he refused to continue and from then on he made no responses to the teacher's requests that he answer. In reality, of course, the accomplice never received any shocks. His responses and pleadings were prerecorded.

You will not be surprised to learn that this procedure was very stressful for the 'teacher' participants. Most protested and wanted to stop. Many showed signs of extreme anxiety, biting their lips and trembling. However, whenever the teacher hesitated, the experimenter gave standardized prompts to encourage him to continue:

- Prod 1: 'Please continue' or 'Please go on'.
- Prod 2: 'The experiment requires that you continue'.
- Prod 3: 'It is absolutely essential that you continue'.
- Prod 4: 'You have no other choice, you must go on'.

Now try the activity on the left, 'Other people's estimates of Milgram's findings', before reading on.

Milgram's main results

Although most participants dissented verbally, they obeyed behaviourally and 65 per cent of participants went to the end of the shock generator, believing they had administered 450 volts to the 'learner'. Milgram was as surprised by these results as anyone since the people he had spoken to about the procedure before carrying out his study thought only a tiny handful would proceed to 450 volts. They were wrong. What was it about the situation that caused the participants to obey?

Obedience
Original study by Milgram (1963)

RESEARCH METHODS

Aim

To find out whether ordinary Americans would obey an unjust order from a person in authority to inflict pain on another person. Milgram wanted to discover what factors in a situation led people to obey.

Procedure

- 40 male volunteers, each paid $4.50, were deceived into thinking they were giving electric shocks.
- The participants were told that the study concerned the role of punishment in learning. The genuine participant always had the teacher's role and a confederate played the part of the learner whose task was to memorize pairs of words. When tested the 'learner' would indicate his choice using a system of lights. The teacher's role was to administer a shock every time the learner made a mistake. The teacher sat in front of the shock generator that had 30 levers, each of which indicated the level of shock to be given. The participant watched the accomplice being strapped into a chair in an adjoining room with electrodes attached to his arms (see photo right).

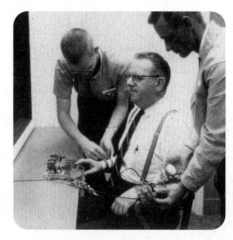

- To begin with, the accomplice answered correctly and then began to make mistakes. Every time he made an error he was to be given an electric shock administered by the participant. Shocks started at 15 volts and rose in 15-volt increments to 450 volts. If the teacher hesitated in administering the shocks the researcher encouraged him to continue.
- *No shocks were actually administered.*
- The experiment continued either until the teacher refused to continue or until 450 volts were reached and given four times. The participant was then debriefed and taken to meet the learner–accomplice (as shown in the photo on p. 196).

Findings

- All participants went to at least 300 volts on the shock generator.
- 65 per cent of participants went to the end of the shock generator. That is, they believed they had administered the full 450 volts!
- Most participants found the procedure very stressful and wanted to stop, with some showing signs of extreme anxiety. Although they dissented verbally, they continued, however, to obey the researcher who prodded them to continue giving the shocks.

Conclusion

- Under certain circumstances, most people will obey orders that go against their conscience.
- When people occupy a subordinate position in a dominance hierarchy, they become liable to lose feelings of empathy, compassion and morality and are inclined towards blind obedience.
- Atrocities such as those carried out in World War II may be largely explained in terms of pressures to obey a powerful authority. In other words, crimes, such as the torture or murder of innocent people, are caused by *situational* factors not the underlying characteristics (dispositions) of those who carry out the evil acts.

Evaluation

- The study has received many criticisms, most relating to the potential harm that might have been done to participants.
- Did participants really believe that they were giving electric shocks? Orne and Holland (1968) claimed that the study lacked **experimental (internal) validity** and that the Ps were only 'going along with the act' when they 'shocked' the learner, that they were not really distressed, just pretending in order to please the experimenter. Orne and Holland also claimed that the situation within Milgram's laboratory bore little resemblance to real-life situations where obedience is required and so it lacked **ecological validity**. (See pp. 194–5 for a fuller discussion of the experimental and ecological validity of this study.)

FURTHER ANALYSIS

Milgram claimed that he had no way of knowing beforehand that his study would cause distress. His follow-up procedures with his participants also showed that many said they were glad that they had taken part because they felt they had learned something important about themselves. (Turn to pp. 195–8 for a more detailed discussion of the ethical issues raised by Milgram's study.)

RESEARCH METHODS

Activity Experimental design: Variations to Milgram's procedures

When Milgram varied the procedures in his obedience studies, he showed how situational variables could alter obedience levels (as shown in Table 6.2). For each situational variation (called an experimental condition) he used a different group of participants.

1 What do you call the experimental design that uses different participants in each condition of the experiment (see Chapter 2, p. 41, if you are unsure)?

2 Why was it necessary for Milgram to use this particular design?

Answers are given on p. 277 ▶

Variations on Milgram's basic procedure

Milgram systematically varied a number of the features of his procedure in order to discover what elements of the situation made it more or less likely that participants would obey. It is clear from these results that obedience levels in a laboratory setting can be manipulated by controlling situational variables (see Table 6.2 below).

Table 6.2 Variations on Milgram's basic procedure

Variation	What happened	Obedience rate (those going to 450 volts)
Original experiment		65%
Venue moved to seedy offices in nearby town (Bridgeport)	Obedience fell when participants relocated to less prestigious surroundings.	47.5%
Learner agreed to participate on the condition that 'you let me out when I say so'	Obedience fell when the participant knew that the learner had agreed to only a limited contract.	40%
Teacher and learner in the same room	Obedience fell when participants were forced to see, as well as hear, the pain and distress caused by their actions.	40%
Teacher had to force learner's hand on to plate to receive shock	Obedience fell even further when participants were required to use physical force personally to administer the shocks (see photo on the left).	30%
Teacher given support from two other 'teachers' (confederates) who refuse to obey	Obedience fell when participants conformed to modelled disobedience by confederates.	10%
Experimenter left the room and instructed the teacher by telephone from another room	Obedience fell when the experimenter supervised participants less closely.	20.5%
Teacher paired with an assistant (confederate) who threw the switches	Obedience levels soared when someone else 'did the dirty work' of throwing the switches.	92.5%

Evaluating the validity of Milgram's studies

Most criticisms of Milgram's studies have dealt with ethical issues but before we consider those we shall look at the criticisms made by Orne and Holland (1968). Their criticisms concern lack of experimental (internal) validity and lack of ecological validity:

■ **Experimental (internal) validity** is a measure of whether experimental procedures actually work and the effects observed are genuine (i.e. caused by the experimental manipulation). Orne and Holland claimed that the participants in Milgram's studies were 'going along with the act' when they 'shocked' the learner. They argued that participants did not believe they were really giving electric shocks and that they were not really distressed, just pretending in order to please the experimenter and to continue to play their role in the study.

Milgram disputed both these claims. He cited evidence from films made of some of his investigations that clearly showed participants undergoing extreme stress. He also referred to evidence from post-experimental interviews and questionnaires to support his belief that the majority of participants believed they were administering real shocks. Furthermore, Orne and Holland do not explain why some participants refused to continue giving shocks if they were merely role-playing in the first place or why altering the location of the study (to rundown Bridgeport) reduced the levels of obedience.

- **Ecological validity** (mundane realism) is the degree to which the findings from a study can be generalized beyond the context of the investigation. Milgram's procedures have been replicated in other countries with higher levels of obedience found in Germany and lower levels found in Australia (Kilham and Mann 1974, see p. 200). In a Jordanian study, children aged between 6 and 16 exhibited high levels of obedience, with 73 per cent believing that they were administering the full 450 volts (Shanab and Yahya 1977). Therefore, there is plenty of evidence to support Milgram's contention that high levels of obedience can readily be obtained in laboratories other than his own.

  However, Orne and Holland have challenged the generalizability of Milgram's findings, claiming that the situation within Milgram's laboratory bore little resemblance to real-life situations where obedience is required. Given this criticism, the results of a study by Hofling et al. (1966) are interesting (see p. 198). This study appeared to provide support for the ecological validity of Milgram's findings by showing that blind obedience to an authority figure could occur just as readily in real life. However, Rank and Jacobson's later study (see pp. 198–9) called into question the ecological validity of the Hofling study!

Now try the activity on the right.

Evaluating the ethics of Milgram's studies: The case for the prosecution

Milgram's procedures have attracted much criticism. His work, however, has also received considerable support and has been stoutly defended by Milgram himself. If you have not already done so, look again at the ethical guidelines relating to informed consent, deception, debriefing and protection of participants (see Chapter 2, pp. 55–7):

- *Lack of respect for participants* – Baumrind (1964) believed that Milgram showed insufficient respect for his participants, that there were inadequate steps taken to protect them and that his procedures had the potential for causing long-term harm. The studies, it has been claimed, involved lack of informed consent, deception and possible psychological harm to his participants.

- *Lack of informed consent* – Voluntary informed consent and lack of deception are important principles to be adhered to if psychological research is to be ethical. Without doubt, Milgram's participants did not know the true purpose of his experiment and therefore they could not give informed consent. For the

Activity The case for and against Milgram's research

Re-read the description of Milgram's research on obedience and re-familiarize yourself with the ethical guidelines relating to informed consent, deception, protection of participants and debriefing (see Chapter 2, pp. 55–7).

Think carefully about these issues and then:

1 Make a list of the reasons why you think that this research should not have been carried out.

2 Make another list of all the reasons why you think it was important that Milgram carried out his studies.

When you have done this, compare your ideas with the points made in the text that follows below.

After the experiment, the participant is debriefed and taken to meet the learner–accomplice

experiment to work, deception was essential. The point at issue, however, is whether or not the deception can be justified in this case. Some researchers have advocated the use of role-playing to avoid the need for deception (see pp. 189 and 190).

- *Psychological harm to participants* – The criticism most often levelled against Milgram's experiments concerns the psychological harm that might have been done to participants. This harm, it is claimed, could result from several aspects of the procedure, including the stress of carrying out the instructor's orders to continue giving the shocks to the learner. For example, Milgram (1963) recorded that his participants often trembled, stuttered and sweated. Furthermore, there were the possible long-term psychological effects of learning that they had been willing to give potentially lethal shocks to fellow human beings, and feeling stupid and 'used' when they learned the true nature of the experiment and how they had been *deceived*. Allied to this is the likelihood that they would not trust psychologists or people in authority in the future.

- *Conversion to evil* – John Darley (1992), in his thought-provoking paper, 'Social organization for the production of evil', argues that the possibility of being evil is latent in all of us and it can be made active by a conversion process. He invites us to consider the possibility that Milgram may have begun the process of converting innocent participants into evil people. To support this theory, he points to Lifton's (1986) interviews with physicians who conducted horrific medical experiments in the Nazi death camps. He reported that the Nazi doctors were initially banal (ordinary) individuals. What they did, however, was not ordinary, and in performing their evil acts, they began a process that morally altered them. Could the same be true of those people who gave 450-volt shocks to the learners in Milgram's experiments?

- *Misapplying findings* – David Mandel (1998) has argued convincingly that the misapplication of Milgram's findings has led to an oversimplified explanation of the atrocities committed during the Holocaust (the genocide of European Jews). According to Mandel, to attribute the horrors of the Holocaust entirely to the sort of situational factors that caused obedience in Milgram's laboratory is oversimplified and misleading. It ignores other important factors that motivated the perpetrators of atrocities, including the chances for professional advancement and the opportunities for lucrative personal gains by plundering Jews and their corpses. Analysis of the behaviour of those who killed and tortured Jews has revealed some facts that do not accord with Milgram's laboratory findings:

  - Perpetrators did not always require close supervision by their superiors.
  - They were not inhibited by seeing the pain (and even the death) of those they victimized.
  - They were often willing to continue killing even when offered the opportunity to quit.

Evaluating the ethics of Milgram's studies: The case for the defence

Milgram has responded to his critics. The major plank of his defence is that participants themselves do not agree with the criticisms.

- *Benefits of participation* – Milgram responded to Baumrind's accusation that he had not respected his participants sufficiently, by drawing attention to the questionnaire distributed to participants. Eighty-four per cent replied that they were glad they had been involved. Seventy-four per cent said they had learned something of personal importance. Only 1.3 per cent reported negative feelings. Furthermore, one year after the study, a university psychiatrist interviewed 40 participants and reported no evidence of emotional harm that could be attributed to participation in the study.

- *Careful debriefing* – After each experimental session, a careful debriefing session was held when the reasons for the deception were explained and the true purpose of the study was revealed. Milgram claimed that the debriefing process was instrumental in helping to reassure and protect the participants (see the photo on the opposite page). Obedient participants were reassured that their behaviour was the norm in that investigation (i.e. there was not anything wrong with them). Disobedient participants were reassured that their behaviour was actually socially desirable, because they had stood up against a malevolent authority figure trying to coerce them into doing something they felt was wrong.

- *Healthy scepticism* – As regards the criticism that people might be distrustful of psychologists or others in authority in the future, Milgram (1964) replied that. he thought it would be 'of the highest value if participation in the experiment could inculcate a scepticism of *this* [inhumane] kind of authority' (p. 852).

- *Unpalatable findings* – Supporters of Milgram have rallied to his defence, agreeing with him that had the results of his studies been different, with participants declining to continue at the first sign of learner discomfort, no one would have protested. But, of course, we cannot be sure what the results of research will be. Milgram had not intended to cause discomfort to his participants. Indeed, the survey carried out beforehand predicted that few people would give shocks after the learner began to protest. Therefore, few participants should have experienced any discomfort. Even when participants did show distress, however, Milgram did not believe it sufficient to justify stopping the experiment. After Milgram's research was published, the American Psychological Association investigated it and found it ethically acceptable. He was, in fact, awarded a prize for his outstanding contribution to social psychological research.

- *Costs–benefits dilemma* – Elliot Aronson (1999) has suggested that psychologists face a particularly difficult dilemma when their wider responsibility to society conflicts with their more specific responsibilities to each individual research participant. This conflict is greatest when the issues under investigation are issues of social importance. Do the potential benefits of the research outweigh the costs to the individual participants? Unfortunately this 'costs–benefits' dilemma is not easy to resolve, as it is difficult to predict either costs or benefits before a study begins. Also, participants and investigators may have very different views as to what is an acceptable cost or a worthwhile benefit.

- *Follow-up care* – Darley's proposition that those who took part in Milgram's experiments may have entered on the slippery slope towards evil was made after Milgram's death (1984) and so Milgram did not have an opportunity to respond. He did, however, as already mentioned, arrange for a psychiatrist to interview a sample of his participants to see if any psychological damage could be detected. None was reported.

- *Caution when generalizing* – David Mandel's criticism relates to those who would misuse the findings from Milgram's study as an 'excuse' for atrocities.

Eye on the exam

'Discuss whether or not research into conformity and obedience was justified if it breached ethical guidelines.' *(12 marks)*

One way to approach this question is to:

1 Briefly identify some examples of where research into conformity and obedience has breached ethical guidelines and outline some of the criticisms made. You could outline some of accusations made (e.g. by Savin 1973 and Baumrind 1964) about use of deception, lack of fully informed consent and failure to protect participants. (Note that *debriefing* is not an ethical issue but rather an attempt to deal with possible ethical issues that might have arisen in the research.) Remember that you will earn only A01 marks (for knowledge and understanding) for these outlines. Hence, do not spend too much time giving unnecessary detail as only 6 A01 marks are available.

2 Use the counter arguments of Milgram, Zimbardo and their allies as a means of evaluating or commenting on the criticisms you have outlined and so earn A02 marks. For example, you could refer to the extensive debriefing that both Milgram and Zimbardo used, the social importance that is claimed for these studies and the 'costs–benefits' dilemma. Remember that you must use these points to construct an argument, not just describe them. For instance, if you use the argument that Milgram's findings help us understand the reasons for the Holocaust (and so are socially important) then you could also refer to the position taken by Mandel that Milgram's research gives an oversimplified explanation of atrocities committed during the Holocaust and might even be misused as an excuse or alibi for these crimes.

3 Finally, don't think that you have to come down firmly on one side of the debate – you may if you feel strongly and have formulated a sound argument but it is not obligatory.

For more exam advice, visit **www.collinseducation.com/psychologyweb**

Milgram himself acknowledged that his study did not provide an adequate explanation of the Nazis' behaviour toward Jews during the Holocaust. As he wrote in a letter to a young student,

'It is quite a jump from an experiment of this sort to general conclusions about the Nazi epoch, and I, myself, feel that I have sometimes gone too far in generalizing. Be cautious in generalizing' (in Blass 2004, p. 279).

Milgram recognized that the zeal with which many Nazis tortured and murdered their victims pointed to a deep-seated hatred of Jews. However, he argued that the processes of 'entering into the agentic state' (relinquishing responsibility) and accepting the authority's definition of the situation (Jews seen as vermin that could pollute German people) enabled those who did the killing to proceed without a guilty conscience.

- *Ethical guidelines* – A very positive outcome of Milgram's experiments has been the increased awareness among psychologists since then concerning how they should treat their participants. This, in turn, has led psychologists to draft codes and guidelines to be used for research (see Chapter 2, pp. 55–7). Remember that the sort of ethical guidelines used by research psychologists today were not formulated when Milgram carried out his research.

Hofling *et al.* (1966) – obedient nurses

The situation used was a hospital. They arranged for a nurse who was working alone on a late shift (the participant) to receive a phone call from an unknown doctor, who asked her to administer 20 milligrams of a drug called Astroten (a drug that was not known to these nurses) to a patient so that it would have taken effect before he arrived. If the nurse obeyed, she would be breaking several hospital rules:

- giving twice the maximum dose allowable for this drug
- administering a drug that was not on the ward stock list for that day
- taking a telephone instruction from an unfamiliar person
- acting without a signed order from a doctor.

Despite all this, 21 out of 22 of the participants started to give the medication (which was in fact a harmless placebo) until another nurse, who had been stationed nearby but out of sight, stopped them.

When interviewed afterwards, all the nurses said that they had been asked to do this type of thing before and that doctors became annoyed if they refused. These results are important as they highlight that pressures to obey are greater than most people imagine. When Hofling and colleagues asked nurses (not those in the study) what they thought the rate of obedience would be in this situation, they were all convinced that nurses would refuse to obey!

This study showed that high levels of obedience can be obtained in real-life settings and so appeared to provide support for the ecological validity of Milgram's findings. However, not all studies conducted in real-life settings do so. Before reading on, try the activity on the left.

Rank and Jacobson (1977) – not so obedient nurses

Rank and Jacobson were uneasy about two aspects of Hofling's study – that the nurses had no knowledge of the drug involved and that they had no opportunity to seek advice from anyone of equal or higher status. In most hospital situations, they argued, nurses would either have knowledge about a drug or would have

---

RESEARCH METHODS

Activity | **Criticism of Hofling and colleagues' study**

Did you notice any weakness in the way that Hofling and colleagues designed and carried out their study? Clue: think about the way that nurses might normally operate when asked to prescribe a drug that they did not know about from a doctor who was not known to them.

1. How might you change the design of the study to enable nurses to respond as they would normally? How do you think the results might differ?

2. What do you think are the practical implications (e.g. for nurse training and practice) of Hofling and colleagues' findings?

time to seek advice. Therefore, they replicated the procedure, but this time the doctor required the nurse to use the common drug Valium at three times the recommended level. The doctor who telephoned gave the name of a real doctor on the staff and nurses were able to speak to other nurses before they proceeded. Results showed that only two out of 18 nurses proceeded to prepare the medication as requested. Rank and Jacobson concluded that 'nurses aware of the toxic effects of a drug and allowed to interact naturally ... will not administer a medication overdose merely because a physician orders it' (p. 191).

Bickman (1974) – the power of uniforms!

Before reading any further, try the activity 'The power of uniforms' on the right.

In this interesting field study, Bickman found that visible symbols of authority, such as uniforms, increased levels of obedience. Three male experimenters dressed either in uniform (as a milkman or a guard) or as a civilian (in a coat and tie) made requests of passersby in a street in New York. For example, they asked them to pick up a bag for them or provide money for a parking meter. People were most likely to obey the experimenter who was dressed as a guard and least likely to obey the experimenter dressed as a civilian. A strength of this study is its real-life setting. However, the opportunity sample of participants (i.e. those people who just happened to be available) may have affected the findings. The results, nevertheless, supported those of Milgram who found higher levels of obedience at the visibly prestigious Yale University than at the run-down office in Bridgeport.

Now try the activity 'Bickman's field study' on the right.

Obedience in an interview setting

High levels of obedience have also been found in business settings. For example, Meeus and Raaijmakers (1986) carried out a study in the Netherlands. They asked 24 naïve participants to act as interviewers for job applicants. The applicants were actually accomplices of the researchers who had been trained to start the interview confidently but to appear increasingly upset as the interview progressed. The participant-interviewers were asked to stress the applicants by making 15 'stress remarks'. These derogatory remarks increased in severity as the interview went on. If required, interviewers were prodded to continue even when the job applicant complained about being interrupted or was clearly distressed. Twenty-two of the 24 participants ignored the interviewees' pleas and administered all 15 stress remarks. This study paralleled the structure of Milgram's laboratory study, using progressively more severe 'punishments' (stress remarks) and prods if the participants hesitated to obey. The findings illustrate the willingness of people in a face-to-face, real-life setting to obey the orders of an unjust authority figure even when they observed the pain and distress they were causing.

Explanations as to why people obey

Why do people obey? A number of explanations have been offered that look at the psychological processes involved in obedience (see Table 6.3 on p. 200).

Legitimate authority

One suggestion is that we feel obligated to those in power because we respect their credentials and assume they know what they are doing. Legitimate social

Activity The power of uniforms

In the photographs below, the same man is dressed in three different ways. If he asked you to do something, like wait inside a shop and stay there until told to, in which situation would you be most likely, and least likely, to obey? Explain your answer.

RESEARCH METHODS

Activity Bickman's field study

1. Identify the independent variable in the study.
2. Identify the dependent variable in the study.
3. How might the opportunity sample have affected the findings? How could you try to reduce such effects?

Answers are given on p. 277 ▶

Table 6.3 Why people obey

> ### Summary of reasons why people obey
>
> - Request by a legitimate authority
> - Gradual commitment by small increments
> - Feel a contractual obligation by initially agreeing to help
> - Accept semantic reframing that conceals what situation really involves
> - Experience agentic shift and see others as responsible
> - Buffered from consequences of own actions
> - Hold authoritarian attitudes

By simply agreeing to listen to a telemarketing person, are you being sucked into agreeing to the next request?

power is held by authority figures whose role is defined by society. This usually gives the person in authority the right to exert control over the behaviour of others, and others usually accept it (e.g. see the study by Hofling and colleagues described on p. 198). Although respect for authority permits orderly social interaction, there is the danger that it may be so deeply ingrained in us that we obey, even when we believe we are being asked to do something unethical or immoral. Clearly, the authority conveyed by a legitimate researcher at a prestigious university impressed the participants in Milgram's original experiment. When the location of the study was moved to a run-down office building, the level of obedience dropped (see Table 6.2 on p. 194). Bickman's study also showed that people are more inclined to obey those who display visible symbols of authority such as uniforms.

Respect for authority varies from country to country. For example, in Kilham and Mann's (1974) study in Australia, where there is a greater tradition of questioning authority than was the case in early 1960s United States, only 40 per cent of male and 16 per cent of female participants went to 450 volts on the shock generator, an overall obedience rate of 28 per cent – the lowest rate reported using Milgram's standard procedure. On the other hand, Mantell (1971) found 85 per cent obedience levels in Germany.

Gradual commitment

An important feature of Milgram's procedure was the gradual way in which participants became sucked into giving greater and greater levels of shock. They found it difficult to decide when to disengage from the procedure because each voltage increment was fairly small. Psychologists call this gradual commitment the *foot-in-the-door effect*. Once people comply with a trivial, seemingly harmless, request they find it more difficult to refuse to carry out more serious, escalating requests. This is explained by the desire to appear consistent.

Contractual obligation

Milgram also pointed out that participants felt that they had 'contracted' to help with the study. By coming along to the laboratory and publicly agreeing to accept the procedures, they saw themselves as helpful people, willing to aid scientific research. If they then were to refuse to continue, they might have to re-evaluate this flattering self-perception.

Altering the meaning of the situation

The unpleasant reality of what the participants were asked to do in Milgram's study was altered by framing the task in desirable language, for example, 'helping the experimenter', rather than 'giving painful electric shocks to a mild-mannered man'. We see this semantic reframing (altering the meaning by changing the wording) in advertising, for example, describing a tasteless breakfast cereal as healthy because it is low in sugar.

The agentic shift

Milgram's agency theory states that people operate on two levels:

- as *autonomous* individuals, behaving voluntarily and aware of the consequences of their actions

- on the *agentic level*, seeing themselves as the agents of others and not responsible for their actions.

The consequence of moving from the autonomous to the agentic level (known as the *agentic shift*) is that individuals attribute responsibility for their actions to the person in authority. At this agentic level, Milgram argued, people mindlessly accept the orders of the person seen as responsible in the situation. Milgram believed that this explained the behaviour of the participants in his study; they denied personal responsibility, merely 'doing what they were told'. They were also given the opportunity to abdicate responsibility for any negative outcomes when the experimenter said that he would take responsibility for anything that happened to the 'learner'. You probably know that when those responsible for atrocities during the Second World War were asked why they did what they did, their answer was simply: 'I was only obeying orders' (Arendt 1963). Similar defences have been offered by ex-torturers at the South African Truth and Reconciliation Commission.

What causes people to undergo the agentic shift? Milgram suggested that it is part of the socialization process: we train children from a very early age to be obedient to authority at home, in school and in society. Many rules and regulations exist to reinforce obedience, so that eventually we tend to accept unquestioningly what we are told to do because most requests are perceived to be both reasonable and appropriate. Additionally, there are factors that operate to keep one in the agentic state and to make the 'exit costs' high. These are known as *binding factors*. They include:

- fear of appearing rude or arrogant by disrupting a well-defined social situation such as a laboratory experiment – this would involve a breach of etiquette and require courage

- fear of increasing one's anxiety levels (likely to be high already among Milgram's participants) by challenging the authority figure.

Buffers

The term *buffer* is used here to describe any aspect of a situation that protects people from having to confront the consequences of their actions. Remember that the participants in Milgram's studies did not enjoy what they were doing. Why then did they continue? Milgram suggested that buffers acted as a mechanism to help people reduce the strain of obeying an immoral or unethical command. In turn, these buffers served to facilitate obedience. In the original Milgram study, the 'teacher' and 'learner' were in different rooms; the teacher was buffered (protected) from having to see his victim. In some real-life situations where obedience is required, the person merely has to press a button – the resulting destruction may not even be observed. In other cases, those carrying out orders are not told full details of their mission. This was the case with the aircrew that dropped the atomic bomb on Hiroshima.

Personality factors

Unlike the preceding situational factors, some dispositional (personality) factors have been proposed to explain Milgram's findings.

- *Authoritarian personality*: An authoritarian person has rigid beliefs, is intolerant of uncertainty or change, hostile to minorities but submissive to those in authority. Milgram (1974) found that participants who were highly authoritarian tended to give stronger shocks than those who were less authoritarian.

- *Psychopathic personality*: Miale and Selzer (1975) claimed that the obedience of Milgram's participants was a socially acceptable expression of their

Adolf Eichmann as a young officer in the Austrian army and during his trial for war crimes (1961/2). Is this the face of a monster? Would you have 'followed orders' in the same way as so many Nazi officers did?

In his final statement to the court, Eichmann claimed: 'My guilt is my obedience, my subjugation by duty, war obligations, procedures, and service oath.'

The correct answers can be found in the chapter.

Activity — Statements about obedience – True or False?

Below are ten statements about psychological research into obedience. Decide whether each statement is true or false. For those statements that you think are 'False', make a note of what the correct statement should be.

1 Milgram found lower levels of obedience when he moved his study to a run-down office block.

2 75 per cent of the participants in Milgram's original study gave shocks to the 'learner' up to the maximum 450 volts.

3 Another name for the gradual commitment felt by Milgram's participants is the foot-in-the-face effect.

4 Hofling's study of obedience amongst nurses supported Milgram's findings.

5 According to Milgram, participants who obeyed were probably psychopaths.

6 Orne and Holland challenged whether Milgram's findings could be generalized.

7 Zimbardo found that people who are given power over others exercise it responsibly.

8 Research suggests that obedience levels in a laboratory setting are unaffected by controlling situational variables.

9 Orne and Holland challenged the ecological validity of Milgram's findings.

10 Research findings suggest that respect for authority can vary from country to country.

The correct answers can be found in the chapter.

psychopathic (violent and psychologically disordered) impulses. Milgram refuted this account completely. He reminded us that when participants were able to select their own voltage levels they gave lower levels of shock. Hannah Arendt agreed with Milgram. She covered the trial of the Nazi war criminal Adolf Eichmann for crimes against humanity. She wrote:

'*It would have been comforting indeed to believe that Eichmann was a monster ... The trouble with Eichmann was precisely that so many were like him and the many were neither perverted nor sadistic ... [but] terribly and terrifyingly normal.*' (1963, p.276)

Remember that the main conclusion of Milgram's findings is that situational factors are important in derailing normally decent people from the moral straight and narrow.

CHECK YOUR UNDERSTANDING

Check your understanding of social influence by answering these questions. Try to do this from memory first. You can check your answers by looking back through Topic 1.

1 What do you understand by the terms: 'conformity' and 'obedience'?

2 Outline what is meant by: informational social influence and normative social influence.

3 Explain the difference between compliance and internalization.

4 Give the main findings and the main conclusions of Asch's study of conformity.

5 How did the results found by Perrin and Spencer in Britain in 1980 differ from those found by Asch in 1951? What explanation did Perrin and Spencer offer for this?

6 Where did Zimbardo's prison simulation study take place?

7 How long did the prison simulation study last? How long was it originally intended to last?

8 In what ways did the participants in Zimbardo's prison simulation study demonstrate conformity?

9 Give one criticism that has been made concerning the ethics of Zimbardo's study.

10 In what way did Zimbardo criticize his own role in the simulation study?

11 What was the specific aim of Milgram's study on obedience?

12 Briefly outline the procedures and main findings of Milgram's study.

13 In what way did Hofling's study of obedience in nurses support the ecological validity of Milgram's study?

14 Outline two criticisms that have been made concerning the ethics of Milgram's procedures. How did Milgram answer these criticisms?

15 Describe two psychological processes that help explain why people obey authority.

Topic 2: Social influence in everyday life

Explanations of independent behaviour

There are occasions when people appear not to conform – to behave independently. However, some apparently independent behaviour may really only be *anticonformity* – a consistent opposition to the norms of the group, such as deliberately choosing to dress or wear one's hair in a way that is different from others. It may seem paradoxical, but anticonformity is, in fact, a type of conformity as it is determined by the norms of the group; if the group favours long hair, anticonformists will wear theirs cut short; if the group decides that short hair is cool, anticonformists will wear theirs long.

On the other hand, a person who displays true *independence* is unresponsive to the norms of the group. **Independent behaviour** refers to behaviour that is not altered despite pressures to conform or obey. An example of this type of behaviour might be the case of a student who ignores the dress norms of her fellow students and who dresses only to please herself. Note that sometimes this student might dress like her friends if their dress sense happens to coincide with hers. She is not reacting against their code; she is just unaffected by it and is, therefore, truly independent. Similarly, independent people may go along with requests or instructions from those in authority as long as the requests coincide with their own values and beliefs.

Researchers in this area have looked at why some people act independently despite social influence pressures. In this next section we shall consider:

■ factors that contribute to resisting pressures to conform

■ factors that contribute to resisting pressures to obey authority.

Resisting pressures to conform

You will recall that in Asch's study, where participants were asked to judge the length of lines, most participants (74 per cent) conformed to majority social influence – but only part of the time. On many trials, these participants stuck to their own judgement, resisting the pressures from a unanimous majority. How did they manage to do this? Two key factors are thought to be important: desire for individuation and desire to maintain control.

■ *Desire for individuation* – We may wish to be like others some of the time but not wish to be exactly the same all the time! This desire to maintain a sense of our own individuality sometimes outweighs pressures to conform. In Western cultures, it seems that people feel uncomfortable if they appear exactly like everyone else. Snyder and Fromkin (1980) led one group of American students to believe that their most important attitudes were different from those of 10 000 other students. Another group was told that their most important attitudes were nearly identical to those of 10 000 others. Later, when those students who had been stripped of their identity participated in a conformity study, they resisted pressures to conform. Snyder argued that this was an attempt by them to assert their individuality.

■ *Desire to maintain control* – Most of us wish to hold on to the idea that we can control events in our lives, an idea that does not sit comfortably with yielding to social influence. If we experience obvious group pressure we may feel that our personal freedom and control have been threatened. People, however, differ in the extent to which they desire to maintain control.

Psychology in context

Going, going green ...

National and local governments spend considerable time and effort trying to persuade us to be 'greener'. You have probably seen newspaper articles and television programmes that encourage us to compost our garden waste, recycle more, use energy efficient light bulbs and insulate our houses better. These are all social influence attempts.

In the first part of this chapter we discussed the power of social influence to produce conformity and obedience.

1 With reference to the processes and techniques that you have learned about in this chapter, how might a local council set about trying to influence people in its area to adopt greener habits? Think, for example, about what you have learned from Milgram's study concerning the roles of gradual commitment (the foot-in-the-door approach), modelled behaviour and legitimate authority.

2 How might the power of normative and informational social influence be utilized?

Resisting pressures to conform

People resist pressures to conform when they:

● wish to maintain a sense of individuality

● wish to maintain control

● have previously expressed an opinion in public

● have time to think and find support.

The paragraphs on the left and on the next page look in more detail at these factors.

Russell Brand: anticonformity or true independence?

Burger (1992) has demonstrated that people with a high need for personal control are more likely to resist conformity pressures than those who have a lower need. One way in which this has been investigated was by looking at how people reacted to unasked-for help when working in pairs on a set of puzzles (Daubman 1993). The reactions of two groups were examined: those who had a high score when tested on a *Desirability of Control Scale* and those who had a low score. All participants were given the same feedback, that they were average in solving the puzzles, and that their partner had done better. Some participants were then given hints on how to do better. As predicted, those who scored low on the *Desirability of Control Scale* tended to welcome these hints. On the other hand, those with a high score felt worse after help was offered, over half of them expressing irritation at this unwelcome incursion into their personal control. These results support Burger's contention that other people's offers of advice or attempts at influence are seen as threats to the personal freedom of people who have a high need for personal control.

Other factors also shown to play a part in resistance to conformity pressures include the following:

- *Prior commitment* – Once people publicly commit themselves to an opinion, they are less likely to change their position than if their first opinion had been held privately. For example, football referees who have awarded penalties or shown a red card do not change their minds because members of the penalized team voice their objections. (However, you may have wondered if referees' decisions prior to being made public are sometimes influenced by social pressure!) A variation on Asch's procedure demonstrated the power of prior commitment. The naive participant publicly gave his judgement before any of the accomplices who then unanimously gave a different answer. When offered the chance to reconsider, participants almost never did (Deutsch and Gerard 1955). The fear of appearing indecisive encouraged people to stick to their original decision.

- *Time to think and find social support* – Zimbardo advises us to be mindful of situational demands, engage critical thinking and avoid going on automatic pilot. According to Aronson (1999) one of the best ways to stop ourselves being swept along by inappropriate social norms is to take time to think about what we are doing and to become aware of what type of normative social influence is operating – a necessary first step towards resistance. However, on its own, mere awareness is not sufficient to prevent conformity. Fear of rejection or ridicule may prevent us from *actively* resisting conformity. In such a situation, finding an ally – or several allies – will build confidence and aid resistance as we no longer face a unanimous majority. In Asch's study, conformity levels dropped to 8.7 per cent when the participant received social support from an ally.

Therefore, we can see that resisting pressures to conform relates to the circumstances of the situation (e.g. being able to find an ally) and to characteristics of the individual (e.g. desire for individuation or confidence levels). The influence of individual differences on independent behaviour is discussed below (see pp. 206–9).

Resisting pressures to obey authority

Just as people may resist pressures to conform to the norms of a majority, so also people sometimes resist pressures to obey. A significant minority of participants in Milgram's obedience study, for example, refused to complete the procedure, despite prodding by the experimenter. A number of key factors have been identified that contribute to this ability to resist pressures to obey a malevolent authority. The panel on the right summarizes these factors.

- *Feeling responsible and empathetic* – In Milgram's study, some participants disobeyed the experimenter and refused to continue giving shocks when they thought the learner was in distress. One such participant, in a follow-up study, when asked why, said that she had experienced too much pain in her own life, having grown up in Nazi Germany, and did not wish to inflict pain on someone else. According to Milgram, the triggering of painful memories had 'awakened' her from her agentic state. She felt responsible for any harm produced. The arrangement whereby the learner was in a separate room was an insufficient buffer for this particular participant who could imagine all too clearly the pain he must be suffering. Comments from other disobedient participants revealed that although they were uneasy about disobeying the experimenter, they were even more uneasy about the pain being suffered by the 'learner':

'I won't. The man … I can't, sir. It's against my wishes now. I don't like this myself this much … I can't, I'm sorry. I picture myself in his place. I wouldn't take it myself.'

Another participant was even more explicit:

'I can't do it to him. It's hurting him. I can't. How can I do it to him? If he doesn't want it how can I do it? Hey, would you punish your children like this? I wouldn't do it to my own. I have a choice. I can walk out of here. I can't hurt this man. He's a human being like me. I wouldn't want it done to myself' (reported in Blass 2000).

- *Disobedient models* – Exposing people to the actions of disobedient models, i.e. seeing others refuse to obey instructions from an authority figure, encourages disobedience. For example, when confederate participants refused to continue giving shocks, only 10 per cent of participants in Milgram's experiment continued (see Table 6.2 on p. 194).

- *Questioning motives and status of authority* – Questioning the motives, legitimacy and expertise of authority figures has been proposed as a way to prevent automatic obedience. Remember that when Milgram's study was transferred to a run-down office block, the levels of obedience dropped (see Table 6.2). The lack of prestigious surroundings made it easier for participants to question the legitimacy of the experimenter. See also Gamson and colleagues' study next.

- *Time for discussion* – In a study conducted by Gamson *et al.* (1982) to investigate under what circumstances people will refuse to go along with an unjust authority, participants were involved in making a video and signing statements that could be used in court proceedings. Participants, who worked in groups, gradually became suspicious about the true purpose of the study and refused to obey the requests of the experimenter. They realized that they were being manipulated into producing tapes that an oil company could exploit in court. However, in this study, participants had plenty of time to share information and to discuss their suspicions. They eventually began to question the legitimacy and the motives of the authority figures. One explanation given for their disobedience was the psychological process called reactance (see next page). Participants reported feeling very anxious and stressed in this study. Therefore, the research raises ethical concerns about protecting participants from psychological harm. After running 33 groups, the researchers felt obliged to abandon their plans to run the 80 groups they had originally intended.

Resisting pressures to obey

People resist obedience to a malevolent authority:

- when they feel responsible for their own actions
- when they observe others being disobedient (conformity effects)
- by questioning the motives of those giving the orders
- when they have time to think about what they are being asked to do
- when orders are so heavy handed and restrictive that people react against their freedom being threatened.

The paragraphs on the left look in more detail at these types of situation.

■ *Reactance* – The process of reactance may occur when we want to protect our sense of freedom. Gamson and colleagues found in their study that once someone had voiced their concern about what they were being asked to do, others quickly joined in and this was the start of rebellion against the unjust authority. Blatant attempts to restrict people's freedom can sometimes produce a *boomerang effect,* causing people to do the opposite of what is being asked. It has been suggested that reactance might contribute to underage drinking and the increase in cigarette smoking among young people, although peer pressure and conformity effects probably play a part as well.

Influence of individual differences on independent behaviour

Individual differences are important personal factors (such as personality, gender or culture) that differentiate people. Individual differences between people may affect how they respond to situations where social influence is applied.

Most early researchers into social influence were convinced that situational factors were sufficient to explain why people yielded or remained resistant to social pressure. Milgram, for example, has been called a 'standard-bearer for the situationist perspective' (Blass 2004, p. 290). However, in most cases where situational factors had significant effects on obedience, some participants still showed resistance to pressures to obey. In other words, given an identical situation, some people obeyed and others did not. Therefore, something in addition to situational variables was influencing behaviour. Blass (1991) has reviewed individual differences in people's responses to obedience pressures in a number of studies, many of which used Milgram's procedure (paradigm). The following results shed some light on the influence of individual differences on independent behaviour.

Moral reasoning

Kohlberg (1969), a colleague of Milgram's, who studied the processes of cognitive development, found that those who used more advanced stages of moral reasoning were more able to resist the exhortations of the experimenter and consequently showed higher levels of disobedience (independent behaviour). However, other research has shown that there is not an exact correspondence between moral reasoning and moral actions. 'One can reason in terms of principles and not live up to those principles' (Kohlberg 1973). The power of the situation may overwhelm moral reasoning.

Locus of control

The concept of **locus of control** (Rotter 1966) refers to individual differences in people's beliefs and expectations about what controls events in their lives. There are two extremes, as shown in Figure 6.4:

■ Those with an *internal locus* believe that what happens to them is largely a consequence of their own behaviour. A strong internal locus of control is associated with the belief that one can control much of one's life and succeed in difficult or stressful situations.

■ Those with an *external locus* tend to believe that what happens to them is controlled by external factors and agents. They have a sense that 'things happen to them' and are largely uncontrollable. Luck and fate are seen as

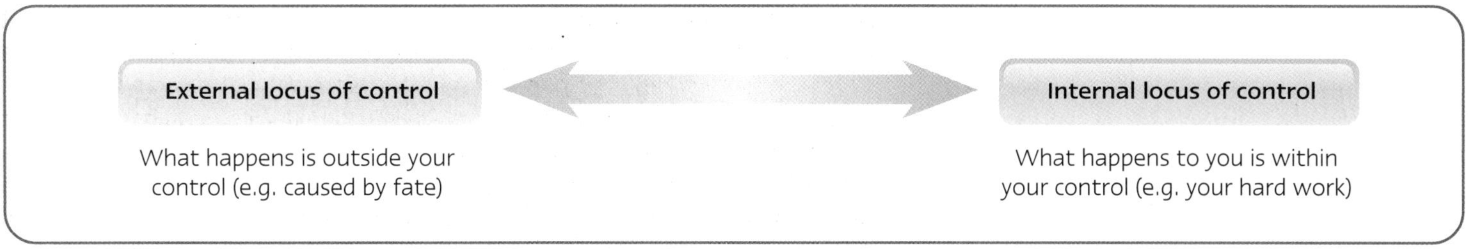

External locus of control		Internal locus of control
What happens is outside your control (e.g. caused by fate)		What happens to you is within your control (e.g. your hard work)

Figure 6.4 Locus of control

important factors. People with an external locus tend to face stressful situations with a more passive and fatalistic attitude.

Research on locus of control and independent behaviour

There are a few studies that have looked at the relationship between locus of control and independent versus obedient behaviour.

Holland (1967) investigated this relationship when he ran a number of variations on Milgram's procedure. He found no relationship between scores on Rotter's Internal-External Locus of Control Scale and levels of obedience. However, Blass (1991) has reanalyzed the data from Holland's investigation using the more sophisticated statistical techniques now available. He found that those with an internal locus of control were more resistant to pressures to obey and especially so if they felt they were being coerced and manipulated by the experimenter.

Participants in a study in Austria (Schurz 1985), using a procedure modelled on Milgram's obedience study, were instructed to apply increasingly painful 'ultrasound' stimulation to a 'learner' by pressing a switch. The 56 participants were told that, at its highest level on a 20-step continuum, the ultrasound could cause skin damage. Schurz's findings were as follows:

- Eighty per cent of participants pressed all 20 switches on the switchbox.

- Locus of control measures were *not* predictive of obedience.

- However, the 20 per cent of participants who were independent (disobedient) tended to take more responsibility for their actions than those who obeyed.

In his review of locus of control effects on obedience, Blass (1991) concludes that research findings in this area are unclear, with some studies finding no relationship between locus of control and obedience. The evidence that does exist tentatively suggests that 'internals' have a greater resistance to pressures to obey than 'externals'.

Confidence

Another individual difference between people that helps explain differences in resistance to conformity pressures is the level of confidence that people bring to a situation. One factor thought to have influenced the results of Perrin and Spencer's (1980) study (see p. 187) was the nature of the students who participated. They were drawn from engineering, mathematics and science courses where the skills gained probably enabled them to be more confident in rejecting the erroneous 'judgements' of the accomplices.

In his original study, however, Asch (1951) (see p. 185) discovered that some participants who lacked confidence nevertheless resisted pressures to conform. He closely observed the behaviour of the 'independent' participants – the 26 per cent who never conformed. He distinguished three main categories of independent behaviour:

Table 6.4

Rotter devised a set of statements to measure the extent of a person's internal or external locus of control (LOC). Some sample items from the LOC scale are given below.

Which of each pair of statements do you believe to be true? (There are no right or wrong answers.)

1 (a) Bad luck is what leads to many of the disappointments in life.

   (b) Disappointments are usually the result of mistakes you make.

2 (a) To become a leader you must be in the right place at the right time.

   (b) Those who are capable of leadership but don't lead, have failed to capitalize on the opportunities afforded to them.

3 (a) If something is meant to happen, it will; there is little you can do to change it.

   (b) You decide what will happen to you. You don't believe in fate.

If you wish to find out about your own place on the LOC scale, visit **www.mindtools.com** where you can complete the scale and have your score calculated and interpreted.

- independence based on participants' *confidence* that their perceptions were correct

- independence accompanied by *withdrawal*, where participants felt the need to isolate themselves from the others by avoiding eye contact in order to deliver independent judgements

- independence accompanied by *tension and doubt*, where the participants' behaviour revealed the discomfort they were experiencing.

Therefore, we see that the reasons for resisting conformity pressure are no more homogeneous than those for conforming behaviour. Not everyone who demonstrates independent behaviour is confident that they are right or comfortable with their position.

Gender differences

Milgram reported no differences between men and women's levels of obedience to authority. Most of Milgram's participants were male but he did run one study using 40 women and found 65 per cent were fully obedient (i.e. went to 450 volts on the generator). Although Milgram found no difference in obedience rates between male and female participants, the self-reported tension of obedient women was higher than that reported by obedient men.

Blass (1991) reviewed nine methodological replications of Milgram's procedure using both male and female participants. He found the following:

- Eight out of the nine studies reported no gender differences.

- The consistency of this finding is notable as the studies were conducted in different countries, with both male and female researchers.

- Only Kilham and Mann (1974) in Australia found that the obedience rate in men (40 per cent) was significantly higher than in women (16 per cent).

It seems fair to conclude, therefore, that there are no reliable gender differences in levels of independent behaviour when it comes to resisting pressures to obey.

Much of the early research investigating gender differences looked at differences in levels of conformity (rather than obedience) and, typically, females appeared to be less independent (i.e. more conforming) than males. However, such findings can usually be explained in terms of the conformity tasks used, that is, tasks with which females were unfamiliar (Eagly 1978).

Sistrunk and McDavid (1971) carried out a study to investigate the effects of different conformity tasks on males' and females' levels of conformity. Male and female participants were exposed to group pressure when identifying various stimuli. There were three conditions in the experiment, such that participants saw one of the following:

- stereotypically masculine items (e.g. types of wrench)

- stereotypically feminine items (e.g. types of needlework)

- neutral items (e.g. popular rock stars).

Results were as expected: females conformed more on masculine items, males more on feminine items and both groups equally on neutral items (see Figure 6.5). The findings suggest that gender differences in conformity are more illusory than real.

Figure 6.5 Conformity as a function of participant and sex-stereotypicality of task
Source: Hogg and Vaughan (1998) based on data from Sistrunk and McDavid (1971)

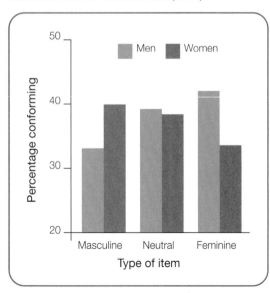

Eagly (1987) has proposed another reason why females might appear less independent than males in group-pressure situations where an audience can directly observe whether or not they conform. She suggests that the answer lies in the different social roles that men and women have traditionally been taught in Western society – women to be supportive and agreeable, men to be independent when put under pressure. Therefore, in public situations, both men and women conform to gender-consistent behaviours. However, in situations where decisions are made privately (e.g. deciding whether or not a speech has changed our earlier opinions) gender differences in succumbing to (or resisting) social pressure disappear.

There appears, therefore, to be no significant difference in the susceptibility of males and females to conform to majority influence.

Culture: time and place

- *Culture* – Smith and Bond's (1998) review of 31 conformity studies concluded that people from individualistic cultures were more likely to show independent behaviour (see p. 187).

- *Time* – Two correlational analyses by Blass (2000) of obedience outcomes (using Milgram's paradigm) and year of publication (from 1963 to 1985) found no relationship between when a study was conducted and how much obedience occurred.

To sum up: Other researchers have found that high self-esteem, high status, low need for social approval, and security in the group are all associated with high levels of independent behaviour. Crutchfield (1955), for example (see p. 186), found that participants with high scores in intelligence and leadership ability displayed greater independence when faced with pressures from a unanimous majority. However, the fact that people who are independent in one situation may conform in another, suggests that situational factors may be more important than personality in determining whether people conform or act independently.

Implications for social change of research into social influence

In this section we shall look at the meanings or significance of research into social influence for changes in society.

Implications from research on conformity and obedience

- *Resisting unwanted influences* – Psychological research on obedience has exposed the intellectual illusion that often hinders critical discussion about why people behave inhumanely: the belief that only evil people do evil acts. Research by Zimbardo and Milgram demonstrated that ordinary, decent people placed in powerful positions, without adequate structural constraints or put under pressure to obey an authority figure may commit evil acts. To reduce the likelihood of such behaviour, there is a need for all of us to be aware of the circumstances that lead, for example, to blind obedience or a failure to empathise with the plight of others. As recent events (e.g. in Iraq) have shown, we have a long way to go. Zimbardo (2007) recommends that each one of us should try to adopt a ten-step programme to resist unwanted influences (see Table 6.4 on the next page).

Eye on the exam

'Outline two explanations of how people sometimes resist pressures to conform'
(3 marks + 3 marks)

When faced with a question like this which requires *two* explanations, each with its own mark allocation, provide *two separate* accounts. The two explanations do not have to be exactly the same length but each must earn its own 3 marks. In other words, you cannot compensate for one weak explanation by providing a better, more detailed second one.

Material from the chapter that you might use to answer this question includes: desire for deindividuation or control, being confident or having made a prior commitment that differs from the majority opinion, finding someone who thinks the same as you do (see pp. 203–4).

For more exam advice, visit
www.collinseducation.com/psychologyweb

Table 6.4 Ten steps to resist unwanted influences (Zimbardo 2007)

1 *Admit mistakes* – Apologise; don't waste time trying to justify errors; move on.

2 *Be mindful* – Pay attention to the words and actions of those who try to influence us; encourage children to be critical thinkers.

3 *Be responsible* – Take responsibility for our actions and decisions.

4 *Assert your individuality* – Be clear about our identity and credentials; avoid the anonymity and secrecy that conceals wrongdoing.

5 *Respect just authority but rebel against unjust authority* – try to distinguish between those who have authority based on expertise and wisdom and those who lack substance.

6 *Balance desire for group acceptance with value of own individuality* – We are social animals but we need to determine when to follow group norms and when to reject them.

7 *Be frame-vigilant* – The way issues are described (framed) may be highly influential. For example, people prefer the odds described as a 60 per cent chance of winning to those described as a 40 per cent chance of losing! Being asked to 'go the extra mile to defend one's country', sounds less sinister than being asked to torture suspects to gain information.

8 *Develop a balanced time perspective* – Beware of 'going with the flow' if others are behaving badly. Remember past commitments and future consequences.

9 *Do not sacrifice freedoms for the illusion of security* – The sacrifices are real; the security may be a distant illusion (advice that has particular resonance at this time of the so-called 'war on terror' when our freedoms are being curtailed).

10 *Oppose unjust systems* – Although a daunting undertaking, individuals (such as whistleblowers who bring social injustices to public attention) along with others of the same mind can make a difference.

- *Educating nurses* – The findings from Hofling *et al.*'s (1966) obedience study of nurses' behaviour (see p. 198) raised awareness about the potential for senior staff to influence junior personnel to the point where they might break important hospital rules. The education of doctors and nurses now includes courses in psychology. One would expect that this, alongside the even more rigorous 'sign-off' procedures for administering drugs, should have changed practice for the better. However, mere awareness is no guarantee of behaviour change, as we see from research on the 'Enlightenment effect'.

- *'Enlightenment effect'* – In 1973, Gergen proposed that 'sophistication as to psychological principles liberates one from their behavioural implications'. The implication of this statement is that people will be less susceptible to blind obedience and unthinking conformity if they are knowledgeable about the processes involved in social influence. If we look at research findings, however, we see that this does not appear to be the case. As mentioned earlier, Blass (2000) found no correlation (relationship) between when studies of obedience (using Milgram's paradigm) were conducted and the levels of obedience found. Attempts to investigate the 'enlightenment effect' experimentally (as reported by Blass 2000) confirm that having information about obedience research will not necessarily change a person's behaviour once they are in an authority-dominated situation. One of Milgram's former participants, however, wrote in 1982 that he found it *'easier ... to recognise and avoid situations in which authority and obedience play significant roles ... than ... to defy authority within such situations'* (adapted from Blass 2000, p. 53)

- *The 'foot-in-the-door' technique* – This technique, used in Milgram's obedience studies, demonstrated that if you succeed in getting people to comply with a small request (e.g. administer a mere 15 volts) they may feel committed to go along with more important requests subsequently. This technique is commonly used by sales people or those looking for charitable donations. A few years ago, for instance, I was approached by a well-known cancer charity asking me to make a small, regular monthly donation. I agreed to this and since then have twice been induced to increase my donation. It might seem odd to you that the success of this type of foot-in-the-door technique actually relies on informational social influence. In this case, the information gained is about oneself. In my case, I see myself as someone who helps research efforts to find a cure for cancer. Once this image has been established, I am more likely to agree to increase my help, until of course the money runs out! Local authorities that wish to implement 'greener' policies to encourage less waste and more recycling might bear in mind the benefits of the incremental or foot-in-the-door technique.

- *Increasing empathy* – The experience of being placed in a mock psychiatric ward for only three days was sufficient for staff at the Elgin State Hospital in Illinois to change their attitudes towards their patients and to implement training programmes to enhance staff–patient relationships (Orlando 1973). The implications of this research are far reaching. Carers in positions of power need to empathise with those for whom they care if they are to treat them with respect. It is only through regular education, training and adequate staffing levels that vulnerable people will be given the care and respect they are due.

- *Implications for psychology codes and ethical guidelines* – Ethics is concerned with the rules or principles used to distinguish between right and wrong. Societies such as the British Psychological Society and the American

Psychological Association have devised ethical guidelines and codes of conduct in an effort to prevent unethical practices in psychological research. A major impetus for the development of these guidelines came from the ethical issues raised by research into social influence. Ethical guidelines of the sort we have today did not exist when Asch, Milgram and Zimbardo were carrying out their research. See Chapter 2, pp. 54–8, for a discussion of ethical guidelines in psychology today.

Implications from research on minority influence

Earlier in the chapter we saw how powerful a majority can be in influencing the behaviour of a minority of one (see pp. 184–5). Research has shown, however, that minorities also can be influential provided they adopt the appropriate style of behaviour. If people simply went along with the majority all the time and minority viewpoints never prevailed, there would be no change, no innovation. There are, of course, many instances where small minorities – or even lone dissenters – have influenced majority opinion. Nemeth (1986) believes that even when minorities are wrong, their views can stimulate productive thinking. Small minority groups may be dismissed initially by the majority as eccentrics or extremists. However, under certain circumstances and over a period of time, these small groups or even individuals can eventually become very influential. See the panel, right, on 'Differences between majority and minority influence'.

Behavioural styles of influential minorities

Following many investigations, Moscovici (1985) identified the behavioural styles which minorities must possess if they are to exert social influence on majorities:

- *Consistency* – They must be consistent in their opposition to the majority. Consistency, according to Moscovici, comprises 'resolution, certainty, clarity of definition, and coherence'. Consistency is generally recognized as the single most important factor for a minority to be influential.

- *Not dogmatic* – They must not appear dogmatic by rigidly reiterating the same arguments. They need to demonstrate a degree of flexibility.

Others psychologists (e.g. Hogg and Vaughan 1998) have also claimed that minorities are more likely to be influential if they are seen to:

- be acting from principle (not out of self-interest)
- have made sacrifices in order to maintain their position
- be similar to the majority in terms of class, age and gender
- advocate views that are consistent with current social trends (e.g. as our society becomes more concerned with environmental issues, so the views of certain minority groups, once derided, attract a wider audience and become more persuasive).

Why do people yield to minority influence?

The following explanations have been proposed for minority influence:

- *Consistency* – Consistency is generally recognized as the single most important factor for a minority to be influential. There are two types of consistency:

  - intra-individual, where a person maintains a consistent position over time
  - inter-individual, where there is agreement among members of the minority group.

Differences between majority and minority influence

Different processes

According to Moscovici (1980) majorities and minorities achieve influence through different processes:

- Majority influence involves public compliance (rather than private acceptance) where the person is more concerned with how they appear in front of others than with the issue itself. The majority, therefore, exerts normative social influence (as seen in Asch's experiments) to exact compliance from the minority.

- By contrast, minorities use informational social influence to persuade those in the majority to change their views. Minorities are aiming for conversion rather than compliance. They hope that by focusing on the issue, the majority will come to examine the arguments proposed by the minority. In turn, this may start the process of conversion whereby, at least in private, attitudes genuinely begin to shift

Instant versus delayed effects

Majority social influence may produce instant effects where people conform rather than appear foolish or risk rejection. However, there is no such risk in the case of minority influence. After all, who cares what a small minority thinks and, furthermore, minorities are often ridiculed for their unpopular positions. In fact, many people holding mainstream views would wish to avoid being associated with oddball minorities. Nevertheless, by using informational social influence, a consistent minority may plant the seed of doubt in the mind of someone holding a majority viewpoint. Over time, that doubt may lead to a change of view, albeit delayed, especially if others from the majority are seen to be wavering or converting to the minority position.

If members of a minority fail to demonstrate either of these forms of consistency, the majority is unlikely to pay them much attention.

■ *The snowball effect* – The term snowball effect (Van Avermaet 1996) is used to describe what sometimes happens in minority influence. Once a few members of the majority start to move towards the minority position, then the influence of the minority begins to gather momentum as more people gradually pay attention to the potential correctness of the minority view.

■ *Group membership* – According to Hogg and Vaughan (1998) we are most likely to be influenced by those we perceive to be like us (called our in-group). For example, the attitudes of straight males towards gay men are more likely to become more liberal if other straight males (the in-group) express such attitudes. However, even with an in-group, minority influence works slowly. The dissociation model provides one reason for this.

■ *The dissociation model* – Mugny and Perez (1991) and Perez *et al.* (1995) propose that minority groups influence majority group members through a process called social cryptoamnesia, meaning that minority ideas are assimilated into the majority viewpoint without those in the majority remembering where the ideas came from. In other words, the content and the source become dissociated. According to this model, minority ideas are so strongly associated with their source that to adopt the message risks assuming the negative identity of the source. If, on the other hand, the ideas can be dissociated from their source, the majority can resist overt identification with an out-group while still drawing inspiration from their ideas.

This may account for why the conversion effect, generated by minority groups, is often delayed. The process of assimilating ideas is slow because initially they have been resisted vigorously, purely because of their source. Over time, the ideas become detached from their source and begin to reappear in the individual's mind as their own. The dissociation model does not lend itself to experimental testing, but it does provide an appealing explanation as to how dominant ideas or trends within a culture (zeitgeists) can be launched by minority groups despite the strong resistance they encounter from majority positions.

Minority influence
A study by Moscovici *et al.* (1969)

Moscovici and colleagues wanted to see whether a consistent minority could influence a majority to give an incorrect answer in a perception task. In the experiment, six participants at a time estimated the colour of 36 slides, all of which were blue but of differing brightness. Two of the six participants were accomplices of the experimenter.

There were two conditions:

■ *Consistent* – the two accomplices called the slides green on all trials.

■ *Inconsistent* – the two accomplices called the slides green 24 times, and blue 12 times.

Findings showed the following:

■ Participants in the *consistent* condition called the slides green in 8.4 per cent of the trials and 32 per cent of these participants called a slide green at least once.

■ Participants in the *inconsistent* condition called the slides green on only 1.3 per cent of the trials.

RESEARCH METHODS

Activity Minority influence

Read about Moscovici and colleagues' research into minority influence in the panel on the right.

1 What conclusion do you draw from Moscovici and colleagues' findings?

2 Identify one potential confounding variable that the researchers would need to have controlled.

3 Why might this study be criticized for lacking validity?

Answers are given on p. 277 ▶

Benefits of minority dissent for creative thinking

Charlan Nemeth, a Professor of Psychology at the University of California, has studied the positive role that minorities play in creativity. Among her students are business executives. When she was asked how successfully the insights from minority influence research extend beyond the laboratory, she replied:

'Flexibility and innovation are indispensable elements in a global economy. In this context, dissent [by minorities] should be protected and valued. Many times, executives would rather learn how to get power and keep it, how to get their employees to do their bidding and "like it"… However, if they want an organization that anticipates changes in products or the market place, if they want one that is flexible and able to innovate, they must harness the power of dissenting views for the stimulation of thought that this provides … Perhaps the best application of all is the value of dissent for democracies. As John Stuart Mill noted, diversity, variety and choice, the allowance of refutation and the airing of different views are great strengths of democracies. They serve as a safeguard against tyranny but, importantly, they serve the detection of truth and the vitality of our beliefs.' (Cardwell et al. 2003, p. 167)

According to Nemeth, therefore, minority influence lies in its ability to stimulate thought so that, over time, people may be converted, for good or ill, to new ways of thinking and behaving.

Activity The behaviour of minorities

1 According to Moscovici et al. (1994), the message of the early Christian minority was not very distinctive or compelling. How then did Christianity develop to become such an influential religion?

2 Considering what you know about minority influence, to what extent do you think that the behavioural style of the early advocates of Christianity might have played a significant part in the growth of this religion?

Moscovici's suggestions are given on p. 277 ▶

CHECK YOUR UNDERSTANDING

Check your understanding of social influence in everyday life by answering these questions. Try to do this from memory first. You can check your answers by looking back through Topic 2.

1 What do you understand by the term 'independent behaviour'?

2 How many participants in Asch's line-length study of conformity acted independently throughout the procedure (see Topic 1)?

3 Outline three explanations that have been proposed for people resisting pressures to conform.

4 Outline three explanations that have been proposed for people resisting pressures to obey authority.

5 In what way have levels of moral reasoning been linked to the likelihood that a person will obey?

6 Explain the terms: 'internal locus of control' and 'external locus of control'.

7 According to Blass, under what circumstances were participants with an internal locus of control most likely to resist obedience pressures?

8 What gender differences (if any) did Milgram find in his research on obedience?

9 Outline the procedures and findings of the study by Sistrunk and McDavid (1971) that investigated gender differences in conformity.

10 What conclusion did Sistrunk and McDavid draw from their research?

11 What cultural differences have been found in people's responses to pressures to conform?

12 In what way did research into social influence (e.g. by Milgram and Zimbardo) affect how psychologists have addressed ethical issues when they have carried out research subsequently? (See also Chapter 2, p. 63, to help you answer the question.)

13 How should minorities behave if they are to be influential and bring about social change?

14 What is meant by the foot-in-the-door technique as a means of changing behaviour and whose research on social influence demonstrated its effectiveness?

15 What implications does Zimbardo's research on conformity to social roles have for the training of those in positions of power?

Chapter 6: Summary

Conformity

Result of social influence – people adopt behaviours and attitudes of reference group

Types of conformity

- Compliance
- Identification
- Internalization

> Difference between internalization and compliance

Why people conform

- Normative social influence
- Informational social influence

Research into conformity

- Asch (1951): face to face = 32% conforming responses
- Crutchfield (1955): separate booths = 30% conformity
- Furman and Duke (1988): confident music majors = less conformity
- Perrin and Spencer (1980): UK students = no conformity
- Nicholson *et al.* (1985): found increased conformity since Perrin and Spencer
- Neto (1995): Portugal = 59% conformed at least once
- Smith and Bond (1998): compared individualistic and collectivist cultures
- Zimbardo (1973): prison simulation. Ethical criticisms
- Haslam and Reicher (2005): BBC prison study

Social influence

Social influence

How an individual's attitudes, beliefs or behaviours are modified by presence or actions of others

Social influence in everday life

Explanations of independent behaviour

Resisting pressures to conform

- Individuation
- Control
- Prior commitment
- Time to think
- Find social support

Resisting pressures to obey

- Feeling responsible
- Disobedient models
- Question motives
- Time to think
- Reactance

Obedience

Result of social influence – act according to orders from authority figure

Why people obey

- Legitimate authority
- Gradual commitment
- Contractual obligation
- Alter meaning of situation
- Agentic shift
- Buffers
- Personality factors

Research into obedience

Milgram (1963):

- 65% participants 'administered' 450 volts
- Situational variations led to changes in obedience rates
- Experimental and ecological validity issues
- Ethical issues:
  - respect for participants
  - deception
  - damage to psychologists' reputation
  - misapplication of findings to explain Holocaust
- Milgram's response to criticisms

Later research

- Hofling *et al.* (1966) – obedient nurses
- Rank and Jacobson (1977) – not so obedient nurses
- Bickman (1974) – power of uniforms
- Kilham and Mann (1974) – Australian study
- Meeus and Raaijmakers (1986) – interviewer obedience

Research on social influence: Implications for social change

- Resisting unwanted influences
- Nurse/doctor education
- Questionable 'enlightenment effect'
- Use of foot-in-the-door technique to effect change
- Increasing empathy among carers
- Development of psychology ethical guidelines
- Influence of minorities for innovation and social change

Individual differences: Influences on independent behaviour

- High level of moral reasoning – not always enough
- Internal locus of control
- Confidence
- No gender differences
- Individualistic culture
- No correlation between obedience rates and date of study

Psychopathology (Abnormality)

EXPLAINING THE SPECIFICATION

Specification content	The specification explained
Defining and explaining psychological abnormality	**In this part of the specification you are required to discuss attempts that have been made to define and explain abnormality. To do this, you need to be able to:**
Definitions of abnormality, including deviation from social norms, failure to function adequately, and deviation from ideal mental health, and limitations associated with these definitions of psychological abnormality	■ Describe the three attempts to define abnormality that are listed on the left: – behaviour that deviates from social norms (i.e. deviates from what is socially acceptable) – behaviour that leaves an individual unable to function adequately, e.g. leading to personal distress or distress caused to others – a deviation from the ideal characteristics that people should possess if are to live with optimal (ideal) mental health. ■ Describe and evaluate the limitations of the attempts that have been made to identify the defining components of abnormality (psychopathology).
Key features of the biological approach to psychopathology	■ Describe and evaluate the main features of the biological explanation (approach), which claims that abnormal physiological processes, such as brain damage, genes or faulty biochemistry, are the cause of psychopathology (psychological abnormality).
Key features of psychological approaches to psychopathology including psychodynamic, behavioural and cognitive approaches	■ Describe and evaluate the main features of three psychological explanations (approaches) for psychopathology: – the psychodynamic approach: unconscious psychological processes cause abnormal behaviour – the behavioural approach: abnormal behaviours are learned – the cognitive approach: problems with thinking processes are important factors in psychopathology.
Treating abnormality	**In this part of the specification, you are asked to discuss the different ways in which psychopathology is treated. To do this, you need to be able to:**
Biological therapies, including drugs and ECT	■ Describe and evaluate at least two therapies (treatments) that are based on the biological approach. ■ You are required by the specification to know about: – drug treatment – electro-convulsive therapy (ECT).
Psychological therapies, including psychoanalysis, systematic desensitization and Cognitive Behavioural Therapy.	■ Describe and evaluate at least three psychological therapies. ■ You are required by the specification to know about: – psychoanalysis (based on the psychodynamic approach) – systematic desensitization (based on the behavioural approach) – Cognitive Behavioural Therapy (based on the cognitive approach).

Introduction

Abnormal psychology or 'psychopathology' is the field of psychological study that deals with mental, emotional and behavioural problems. It involves research into the classification, causation, diagnosis, prevention and treatment of psychological disorders. The range of disorders classified under this term is huge, but some well-known examples are phobias, clinical depression, eating disorders and schizophrenia.

It is difficult to define precisely what is meant by the term 'abnormality' as there is no single characteristic that applies to all instances of abnormal behaviour. Therefore, people have to make judgements about whether or not a particular behaviour is abnormal. As judgements are often influenced by social and cultural factors, people from different backgrounds may disagree about what is abnormal. However, there is general agreement about certain key components of abnormal behaviour and, in Topic 1, we shall look at some of the ways these have been used in attempts to define abnormality. Whilst most of these definitions have some practical value, we shall also consider their limitations in terms of operational or ethical difficulties. We need also to be aware that judgements about labelling human behaviour as 'normal' or 'abnormal' cannot be made in absolute terms but only within the context of a given culture (called cultural relativism).

In Topic 1, we shall also look at a number of explanations, using different approaches, for abnormal behaviour (psychopathology). Each approach leads to quite different ideas about how to treat mental disorders or psychological problems. We shall consider the biological approach and a number of psychological approaches to abnormality and, in Topic 2, we shall consider the implications for therapy of each of the approaches to abnormality discussed in Topic 1.

Topic 1: Defining and explaining psychological abnormality

Start this topic by reading 'Psychology in context: What's abnormal?' on the right and answering the questions.

Definitions of abnormality

The term 'abnormal' means deviating from the average (norm). Therefore, if we were to adopt a literal approach to defining **abnormality**, we would conclude that *any* rare behaviour or ability was abnormal. This, however, is not a useful way to define abnormality as it takes no account of whether or not the 'abnormal' behaviour or ability is desirable. Consider the example of intelligence. The average IQ score (the best-known measure of intelligence) is 100. One criterion for mental retardation, a psychological disorder, is an IQ score of 70 or under. However, it is equally rare to have an IQ score of over 130, but, of course, exceptionally high intelligence is not classified as a psychological disorder. Certain behaviours also are statistically rare, but would not be classified as psychologically abnormal because they are seen as desirable (e.g. high levels of heroism or exceptional artistic ability).

Defining abnormality is no easy matter, but this does not mean that the phenomenon of abnormality does not exist. In every society, people identify

Psychology in context

What's abnormal?

Look at these photos.

1 Is this way of dressing (or not dressing) normal?

2 Would you consider those who behave or dress in these ways to be abnormal or even psychologically disordered?

Read the descriptions below.

A 'Sian always puts things off until the last minute. She is always late with assignments and now she is in danger of being thrown off the course.'

B 'Ashok has gone to pieces since splitting up with his girlfriend two months ago. He sleeps all the time now and never wants to do anything. He often misses classes and today he told me that he couldn't see the point of going on.'

C 'Pete's really nervous. He hates standing up in class to read out anything – he gets all shaky. Now he's started to turn down all invitations to go out. People will stop asking him soon.'

D 'Kate has this weird habit – she says it's really important to chew an even number of times when eating. No one talks to her at mealtimes any more because she's so busy counting that she doesn't pay any attention.'

3 Which of the behaviours described do you consider normal and which abnormal?

4 *How* do you decide what is normal and what is abnormal?

behaviours that they consider abnormal. We shall consider three ways of defining abnormality plus the limitations associated with each.

- deviation from social norms
- failure to function adequately
- deviation from ideal mental health.

Deviation from social norms

Social norms are the explicit and implicit rules that a society has about what are acceptable behaviours, values and beliefs. Every society sets up rules for behaviour based on a set of moral standards. Some of these rules are explicit and to violate them may mean breaking the law, such as stealing, arson and driving on the wrong side of the road. Behaviours that violate legal norms are called criminal.

Other rules are implicit (unspoken), but are agreed as a matter of convention within a particular society. Such rules include not standing too close to someone in a face-to-face conversation (although what is considered 'too close' may vary from culture to culture), dressing according to a particular code or sitting silently during a play at the theatre. Rules (codes) of conduct, whether implicit or explicit (such as requests to turn off mobile phones in the cinema) become established as social norms. People who violate such norms are often regarded as deviant or abnormal. For example, showing inappropriate affect (emotion), e.g. laughing when told that someone has died or crying when watching a comedy show, may be seen as a symptom of schizophrenia (a serious psychotic disorder where the person loses touch with reality). Similarly, people with phobias often demonstrate bizarre behaviour when trying to escape their feared object.

Spiders are a common object of phobias

At a practical, everyday level, deviation from social norms can be a useful way to identify mental problems. We learn what to expect from individuals, and if their behaviour drastically deviates from this, we become concerned on their behalf. This may be vital in securing appropriate help. For example, people with clinical depression are often unable to motivate themselves to seek assistance and therefore depend on others to summon help. However, there are several limitations associated with this approach to defining abnormality.

Limitations of the deviation from social norms definition

- *Eccentric or abnormal* – Deviation from social norms does not always indicate psychological abnormality. We often decide that behaviours that deviate from the norm are merely 'eccentric' rather than abnormal in a pathological sense. Running naked across a rugby pitch, for example, or taking part in a marathon dressed as a giant rabbit may be regarded as strange, or idiosyncratic, but we would not necessarily assume that the person is mentally disturbed. However, if someone walks down the street talking out loud to an invisible person, or insists that Martians have taken over their brain, then we would be more likely to suspect a mental disorder. Thus, only particular kinds of 'abnormal' behaviour tend to be regarded as pathological.

On the other hand, behaviour usually regarded as eccentric may be judged as indicating mental illness if the degree of eccentricity is great enough. For example, someone who is known for blunt speaking to the point of rudeness might be considered eccentric or even deviant but not psychologically disturbed. However, rudeness that crosses the line into uncontrolled, foul-mouthed abusiveness may lead us to suspect some kind of psychological disorder. Now try the activity on the left.

Activity **Eccentric or abnormal?**

Look again at the three photographs on the previous page.

What do these photos tell us about the limitations of using deviation from social norms as a means of identifying psychological abnormality?

Abnormal or criminal – The behaviour of people who violate legal norms is usually regarded as criminal and the behaviour is rarely attributed to an underlying psychological disorder. Would you consider committing fraud, for example, a symptom of a psychological disorder? There are, however, types of behaviour, such as rape and mass murder, where it is difficult to accept that anyone normal could have carried them out. In such cases, there is a tendency to regard the perpetrators of the crimes as abnormal and their extreme antisocial behaviour as inherent in their personality. Otherwise, if they, as people, were regarded as 'normal' and merely their behaviour as 'abnormal' then the implication is that anyone could be a potential rapist or mass murderer – too unsettling a notion for most people to contemplate. On the other hand, studies in social psychology have shown that, in certain circumstances, so-called 'normal' people can behave in shocking and antisocial ways (see, for example, the studies carried out by Milgram and Zimbardo in Chapter 6). Now read the activity on the right.

The role of context – Much of our behaviour is context-specific, and out of context, it may seem bizarre. For example, what would you think if you were walking through the park and someone sitting on a bench suddenly jumped up and started singing and dancing? You would probably think that this person was rather odd. However, if you then saw a film crew you would contextualize the scene, assume the person was an actor and perhaps stay around to watch. Similarly, leaping up and down and yelling encouragement is socially acceptable at a football or tennis match but would be bizarrely abnormal in the context of a classical music concert or when shopping in a supermarket.

Change with the times – Beliefs about 'abnormality' and the social norms of morally acceptable behaviour change over time, so what is regarded as deviant by one generation may be perfectly acceptable to the next. Two examples serve to illustrate this:

- Until the early years of the 20th century, unmarried women in the UK who became pregnant were sometimes sent to mental institutions. In many cases the babies were taken away for adoption. Some of these women were in their early teens when they became pregnant and remained in mental institutions for the rest of their lives.

- In recent centuries, homosexuality has been regarded as a deviation from social norms. In the UK, homosexual acts were criminal offences, even among consenting adults, until 1967. In the USA, until 1973, the American Psychiatric Association classified homosexuality as a mental disorder.

Risk of abuse – If we adhere strictly to the view that social deviance equates to psychological abnormality there is a risk that those who deviate are labelled 'mad' and treated accordingly. For example, political dissidents in the old USSR used to be seen as abnormal because they did not toe the party line; they were diagnosed as insane and often detained in mental asylums. Thus the definition was used as a means of social control. In Japan, a diagnosis of insanity has been used as a threat to ensure a strong work ethic. According to Cohen (1988), because of Japan's drive for industrial success, 'loony-bins' are required for those who are unwilling to conform to the demands of industry. Therefore, in order to instil the appropriate terror, the 'bins' must be sufficiently unattractive. Conditions in Japanese mental hospitals are similar to the old Victorian asylums in the UK, being overcrowded, dirty and often brutal places.

Activity **Chessboard killer**

Alexander Pichushkin, a Russian supermarket worker, was jailed for life in October 2007 after being found guilty of carrying out 48 murders that he marked off on a chessboard. He actually confessed to 62 murders but evidence for only 48 was found. Pichushkin bragged of his passion for killing but said he felt no emotion when he killed his victims.

What do you think – abnormal (pathological) or just criminal? Why do you think so?

An example of cultural change: in December 2005, Sir Elton John and David Furnish became one of the first same-sex couples to register their civil partnership following a change in the law

The World Bog Snorkelling Championships, Llanwrtyd Wells, Wales

La Tomatina in Buñol, Spain

■ *Cultural issues* – In Western societies, there is a common assumption that the behaviour of the White population is the norm and that any deviation from this by another ethnic group indicates psychological abnormality. However, social norms vary: what is abnormal in one culture may be acceptable in another. For example, talking to an invisible person is considered normal in certain African and Indian cultures following bereavement, where people believe it is possible to remain in contact briefly with a lost loved one. What might people from different cultures make of the eccentric traditions of bog snorkelling (e.g. in mid-Wales), cheese-rolling races in Gloucestershire or La Tomatina in Buñol, Spain where, on the fourth Wednesday of August, people gather to throw over-ripe tomatoes at each other? See the pictures on the left.

Failure to function adequately

People with psychological disorders often experience considerable suffering and distress and a general inability to cope with their everyday activities, such as being unable to go to work or take part in social activities. So common is this failure to function among those with mental disorders that doctors are required to take it into account when diagnosing an individual with psychological problems. There are diagnostic manuals available to doctors when they are trying to identify particular mental disorders. One of the most widely used is the *Diagnostic and Statistical Manual of Mental Disorders* (1994), which requires doctors to assess people on various psychological and physical measures. One of these measures is called the 'Global Assessment of Functioning Scale' (GAF), shown in Table 7.1. This is an important part of the overall assessment, although a poor score on its own would not be seen as an indication of a psychological disorder.

Table 7.1 Global Assessment of Functioning Scale (GAF)

Consider psychological, social and occupational functioning on a hypothetical continuum of mental health–illness. Do not include impairment in functioning due to physical (or environmental) limitations.

Code (*Note: Intermediate codes can be used when appropriate e.g. 45, 68, 72.*)

100 Superior functioning in a wide range of activities. Life's problems never seem to get out of hand. Is sought out by others because of his or her many positive qualities. No symptoms.

90 Absent or minimal symptoms (e.g. mild anxiety before an exam), good functioning in all areas, interested and involved in a wide range of activities, socially effective, generally satisfied with life, no more than everyday problems or concerns (e.g. an occasional argument with family members).

80 If symptoms are present, they are transient and expectable reactions to psychosocial stressors (e.g. difficulty concentrating after family argument); no more than slight impairment in social, occupational, or school functioning (e.g. temporarily falling behind in school work).

70 Some mild symptoms (e.g. depressed mood and mild insomnia) OR some difficulty in social, occupational, or school functioning (e.g. occasional truancy, or theft within the household), but generally functioning pretty well, has some meaningful interpersonal relationships.

60 Moderate symptoms (e.g. flat effect and circumstantial speech, occasional panic attacks) OR moderate difficulty in social, occupational, or school functioning (e.g. few friends, conflicts with peers or co-workers).

50 Serious symptoms (e.g. suicidal ideation, severe obsessional rituals, frequent shoplifting) OR any serious impairment in social, occupational or school functioning (e.g. no friends, unable to keep a job).

40 Some impairment in reality testing or communication (e.g. speech is at all times illogical, obscure or irrelevant) OR major impairment in several areas, such as work or school, family relations, judgement, thinking or mood (e.g. depressed man avoids friends, neglects family and cannot work).

30 Behaviour is considerably influenced by delusions or hallucinations OR serious impairment in communication or judgement (e.g. sometimes incoherent, acts grossly inappropriately, suicidal preoccupation) OR inability to function in almost all areas (e.g. stays in bed all day, no job, home).

20 Some danger of hurting self or others (e.g. suicide attempts without clear expectation of death, frequently violent, manic excitement) OR occasionally fails to maintain minimal personal hygiene (e.g. smears faeces) OR gross impairment in communication (e.g. largely incoherent or mute).

10 Persistent danger of severely hurting self or others (e.g. recurrent violence) OR persistent inability to maintain minimal personal hygiene OR serious suicidal act with clear expectation of death.

0 Inadequate information.

The 'failure to function adequately' view of abnormality carries certain implications. If someone's behaviour appears strange or 'abnormal' to others, then provided they are not harming themselves or others, and provided their behaviour is not dysfunctional, such as preventing them from carrying on their daily lives, then no intervention is required. This view of abnormality, however, means that someone whose problem falls outside the criteria for a serious mental disorder should still be given appropriate professional help if they experience a dysfunction in their daily living. Unfortunately, NHS provision (in the UK) is not always available for people with less severe psychological problems and there are generally long waiting lists for treatment.

Limitations of the failure to function adequately definition

Using the criterion of failure to function adequately as a definition of abnormality may be the most humane way of addressing psychological problems and mental disorders, as it is left to the person (or others close to them) to decide whether they need or wish to seek help. However, there are some problems with this approach:

- *Not the whole picture* – This is not a true definition of 'abnormality'. Rather it is a way of determining the extent of a person's problems and the likelihood that they might need professional help. Comer (2005) points out that psychological abnormality is not necessarily indicated by dysfunction alone. For example, some people protest against social injustice by depriving themselves of necessities, such as food. It is when abnormal behaviour interferes with daily functioning, such that people lose the ability to work or the motivation to care for themselves properly, that the behaviour is viewed as abnormal.

- *Exceptions to the rule* – A student experiencing anxiety and distress about a forthcoming exam may behave uncharacteristically, even inadequately, but this would not necessarily be regarded as abnormal behaviour. Conversely, sociopaths (people with antisocial personalities) might exhibit violent or aggressive behaviour, but be unlikely to experience personal suffering, distress, or any general dysfunction, because of their amoral attitudes. Now try the activity 'Functioning adequately?' on the right.

- *Direction of causality: cultural issues* – It may be that the inability to cope with the demands of daily living is the cause rather than the outcome of mental disorder. This might explain why statistics show a higher incidence of psychological problems among people from minority ethnic groups, owing to the exploitation, deprivation and harassment they often experience. Cochrane and Sashidharan (1995) point out that racism and prejudice have a significant impact upon psychological wellbeing.

  If you are interested in other cultural issues relating to abnormality you should look at the panel 'Culture and subculture' on the next page.

Deviation from ideal mental health

Begin this section by attempting the activity 'Psychological health' on the right.

The notion of 'ideal mental health' was first put forward by Marie Jahoda in 1958. It turns the traditional approach to abnormality on its head, by looking at positives, rather than negatives – the notion of mental *health* rather than mental *illness*. Jahoda identified six major criteria for optimal living, which, she believed, promoted psychological health and wellbeing. Anyone lacking these qualities, she claimed, would be vulnerable to mental disorder.

Activity Functioning adequately?

As mentioned on the left, students preparing for stressful examinations may not function as well as they do normally. Look at Table 7.1 'The GAF Scale' on the opposite page.

Which of the symptoms mentioned on the scale have you experienced or observed in others when preparing for an important test or exam?

Activity Psychological health

So far, we have focused on negative aspects of life and deviations from what might be considered 'normal'. Before reading on, make a list of the qualities that you feel indicate a psychologically healthy person.

When you have done this, compare your list with the six criteria that Jahoda (1958) identified, discussed on pp. 222–3.

Culture and subculture

A major problem with all definitions of abnormality is the fact that they are culturally specific because abnormality means different things in different cultural contexts.

Groups of people within a wider culture who have their own particular set of norms and beliefs are said to have a distinctive subculture. Using a broad interpretation of the term subculture, it is interesting to look at social class and gender issues.

Social class

- *Stressful lives* – Research has indicated that the higher prevalence of severe mental disorders in socially disadvantaged groups is largely due to their exposure to more stressful life experiences, compared with those in more advantaged social groups. For example, the Midtown Manhattan Study (Srole *et al.* 1961) found the lowest levels of psychiatric impairment in the upper classes, slightly more in the middle classes and the highest levels in the lower classes. These findings were supported in a British study (Cochrane and Stopes-Roe 1980), which also found that lower social status was associated with higher risk of psychological problems. Try the activity on the left.

- *Social drift* – The 'social drift' hypothesis offers another explanation for the higher incidence of serious mental disorder in lower socio-economic groups: the early onset of a major mental disorder, such as schizophrenia, might reduce the chances of establishing a career so that the person subsequently 'drifts' down the socio-economic scale. This suggests that social class is largely a consequence of, rather than a contributory factor in, mental disorder. The higher incidence of schizophrenia in poor areas could reflect the number of people who move to those areas after the onset of their illness, because it is all they can afford, rather than that they had lived there all their lives (Cochrane 1983).

Gender

A number of psychologists have proposed reasons why certain psychological problems appear to be more prevalent in men or women.

- *Depressed women* – Howell (1981) points out that women's experience in British culture predisposes them to depression and therefore clinicians are diagnosing a situation rather than a person. Cochrane (1995) explains that depression can be related to the long-term effects of child abuse and also to gender-role socialization, which produces increased female vulnerability.

- *Alienated men* – Unemployed men have a high rate of psychiatric breakdown. Johnstone (1989) explains that by labelling the problem as a mental disorder, not only does the person have the stigma of a psychiatric label, but the problem is seen only in individual terms, rather than in the wider political and social context. Furthermore, Bennett (1995) believes that the socialization of men in industrialized societies has created masculine stereotypes that alienate men from seeking help for psychological problems.

RESEARCH METHODS

Activity — Correlational research

Consider the findings from the Midtown Manhattan Study (Srole *et al.* 1961), discussed in the panel on the right. This looked at the relationship between social class and psychological problems.

1 What type of correlation was found – positive or negative?

2 Has the study demonstrated that there is a causal link between social class and psychological problems? Give a reason for your answer.

Answers are given on p. 278 ▶

Jahoda's six criteria are:

1 *Positive attitudes towards the self* – This means having a positive self-concept and a sense of identity. Jahoda suggested that a mentally healthy attitude towards the self included self-respect, self-confidence, self-reliance and self-acceptance. Those with a positive attitude towards self have learned to live with themselves, accepting both their limitations and their possibilities. What is important here is to view oneself realistically and objectively. Unfortunately, many people develop a negative self-concept or low self-esteem because of the way they have been treated by others and perhaps made to feel small

and unimportant. Jahoda claimed that to be mentally healthy, people must know who they are and like what they see.

2 *Self-actualization of one's potential* – This idea was first proposed by Abraham Maslow (1968), who suggested that we all have potential (for example, intellectual, artistic, athletic) and that we constantly strive to fulfil this potential. Mental health problems occur when we are prevented from fulfilling our true potential.

3 *Resistance to stress* – Jahoda called this the ability to tolerate anxiety without disintegration. The mentally healthy person will have developed good coping strategies for dealing with stressful situations. Indeed, it does seem that people who are more vulnerable to stress and anxiety are more likely to develop psychological problems. A great deal of research has been undertaken to identify effective coping strategies to reduce stress (see Topic 2 in Chapter 5, starting on p. 171).

4 *Personal autonomy* – Autonomous people are reliant on their own inner resources and can remain relatively stable even in the face of hard knocks, frustrations and deprivations. This is because autonomous people are not dependent upon others. They are self-contained and depend upon their own resources. Jahoda describes personal autonomy as an ability to make our own decisions on the basis of what is right for ourselves, rather than to satisfy others.

5 *Accurate perception of reality* – This means seeing oneself and the world in realistic terms, rather than through either 'rose-tinted glasses' or in an overly pessimistic manner. Indeed, if someone continually distorts reality, then they are not really living in the real world and their views and behaviours are bound to appear abnormal to others. Those who only ever see the best in people may endear themselves to others, but they are also left vulnerable to those who may take advantage. Conversely, someone who is overly morbid and pessimistic is a likely candidate to develop a depressive disorder and would not endear themselves to others very easily.

6 *Adapting to and mastering the environment* – This means being competent in all areas of life: at work, in personal relationships and in leisure activities. It also involves being flexible rather than rigid, being able to adapt and adjust to change. Someone who is fixed in old ways of thinking and behaving may appear abnormal to younger people and to those who have been able to adjust to a changing environment.

Limitations of the deviation from ideal mental health definition

This is a refreshing approach in that it focuses on positive, rather than negative, aspects of life, but meeting all six criteria appears quite demanding. Most people are likely to fall short of 'ideal mental health'. Specific limitations include the following:

- *The difficulty of self-actualizing* – Unfortunately, in reality, very few people achieve their full potential in life. This may be because of their particular environment or owing to some failing within themselves. It would seem, then, that if self-actualization is a criterion for ideal mental health, most of us would be regarded as mentally unhealthy.

- *Possible benefits of stress* – As far as resistance to stress is concerned, some people actually work more efficiently in moderately stressful situations. For example, many actors say that they give their best performances when they experience a certain amount of anxiety.

Activity What causes mental illness?

Consider the woman in the picture who is suffering from depression. Her symptoms include sadness, having a pessimistic view of the future, being lethargic and uninterested in other people. She also finds it difficult to sleep and her interpersonal relationships are suffering.

What might be causing her depression? Make a note of all the possible causes you can think of and then read on to see whether or not your ideas are covered within the four explanations discussed on the following pages.

'The Interior of Bedlam', from A Rake's Progress by William Hogarth, 1763

■ *Cultural issues* – Jahoda's ideas are based on Western ideals of self-fulfilment and individuality. Seeking to fulfil one's own potential, for example, may be seen as a prime goal in life within some cultures but not in others. In some cultures, elders in the family plan the young person's future for them. This planning might include such things as career paths and arranged marriages, which are relatively common in Asian cultures. It may, therefore, be regarded as 'abnormal' to pursue your own individual goals if they are in conflict with those of your culture. The pursuit of self-actualization or personal happiness is, perhaps, a privilege for those living in an affluent, industrialized society where people are freed from the need to pursue the basic necessities for survival.

Similarly, with regard to personal autonomy, there is an overwhelming sense of duty to others in many cultures; it would not be regarded as 'normal' to put your own wishes before those of others.

Perceptions of reality differ over time (remember, people once thought the world was flat) and also differ between cultures. For example, seeing or hearing someone who has died would be considered normal in some cultures, but regarded as psychotic hallucinations in other cultures.

In the following sections, we shall examine four approaches used to explain psychopathology. Adopting a particular approach (conceptual model) is very important because it will influence the type of research that is conducted and also the methods of treatment used. Three of the approaches we shall look at are psychological: psychodynamic, behavioural and cognitive, each of which offers a different explanation for the origins of mental disorders. First, however, we shall look at the biological approach. Before reading on, try the activity, 'What causes mental illness?' on the left.

Biological approach to psychopathology

The **biological approach** (sometimes called the biomedical or medical model) sees mental disorders as caused by abnormal physiological processes such as genetic and biochemical factors. Psychological abnormality, according to this model, is an illness or disease. The biological approach has dominated the field of mental health for the past 200 years. In the Middle Ages, abnormality was seen as a sign of 'possession' by evil spirits and treatments involved trying to drive out these demons. From the 16th to 19th centuries, although little was known about the causes of insanity, asylums for the insane were built, initially as places of sanctuary. Later, however, the overflowing asylums became tourist sites where people could come and see the bizarre antics of the lunatics housed there.

The biological approach, first espoused by the ancient Greeks, began to re-emerge in the 19th century when it became apparent that some behaviours labelled as 'mad' were the result of strokes or infections. This led in time to the current biological (medical) approach that deviant behaviour arises out of biological abnormalities and so can be treated by biological interventions (see Topic 2).

Key features of the biological approach

Mental disorders equated with physical diseases

Mental disorders are thought to be related to the physical structure and functioning of the brain, that is, to have an organic (physical) basis.

Disorders where a clear organic cause has not been identified have been traditionally referred to as functional disorders. However, people who adopt the biological approach believe that research will eventually show that all mental disorders have an underlying physical cause.

Psychiatrists – advocates of the medical model – are medically qualified practitioners specializing in mental disorders. They approach psychological abnormality in the same way that they would investigate physical illness:

- Classify (label) the disorder as a recognised **syndrome** by identifying symptoms (as reported by the patient) and signs (observed by the doctor).

- Identify the underlying cause (see following paragraphs).

- Prescribe an appropriate treatment/therapy (see pp. 237–9 for biological therapies).

Physical causes of mental disorders

Four physical causes for mental disorders have been proposed and investigated:

- *Brain damage* – Abnormal behaviour may occur if the structure of the brain is damaged in some way. Once disease or brain damage has caused mental deterioration, there is, unfortunately, little that can be done to stop it. An example of this is Alzheimer's disease, a type of dementia caused by the malformation and loss of cells in a number of areas of the nervous system. Excessive use of alcohol and other drugs can damage the brain also and may result in hallucinations or other symptoms of mental disorder, such as Korsakoff's syndrome – a profound impairment of memory, most commonly caused by alcohol abuse.

- *Infection* – We are familiar with the idea of bacteria or viruses causing physical illness such as flu or meningitis. It seems, though, that infection can also give rise to mental illness. Indeed flu has been linked to schizophrenia. Recent research findings suggest that 14 per cent of schizophrenia cases may be linked to exposure to the flu virus in the womb during the first trimester (Brown *et al.* 2004). Syphilis, a sexually transmitted disease caused by a micro-organism, was identified in the 19th century as causing brain damage, resulting in symptoms of a mental illness known as general paresis – see the 'How science works' panel on the right.

- *Biochemistry* – During the 20th century, the medical profession has increasingly learned more about the role played by biochemistry in mental disorders.

  Neurotransmitters (chemicals that transmit nerve impulses from one nerve cell to the next) are thought to be out of balance in the nervous systems of individuals with certain psychological disorders. For example, schizophrenia has been associated with an excess of activity in the neurotransmitter dopamine (known as the dopamine hypothesis). Depression has been associated with decreased availability of serotonin. The use of PET scans to provide images of the brain and to measure the action of neurotransmitters has supported this association (Mann *et al.* 1996).

  Hormones (chemical messengers released by the pituitary adrenal system – see Chapter 5, p. 150) have also been implicated in the origins of some mental disorders. For example, people with depression are often found to have higher than normal levels of the hormone cortisol. The reasons why these chemical changes take place is not yet clear, but they may be due to infections, life stress or a genetic defect.

HOW SCIENCE WORKS

How science worked to uncover the origins of general paresis

In the 19th century, a cluster of symptoms (a syndrome) was identified that came to be known as 'general paresis' – one of the most widespread psychological disorders at that time. The symptoms included mental deterioration, paralysis and eventually death. The precise identification of the syndrome enabled it to be distinguished from other similar mental disorders. This, in turn, led to the suspicion that it was caused by syphilis (a sexually transmitted disease) because some sufferers were reported to have had syphilis earlier in life. Syphilis causes genital sores to develop but these disappear after a few weeks so that it appears that the sufferer has fully recovered. It was suspected, however, that the syphilitic bacterium remained in the body, where it attacked the nervous system.

However, such speculation was not sufficient to permit a firm conclusion about what caused general paresis. It was difficult to collect evidence, since people suffering from general paresis ('paretics') were unable or unwilling to admit that they had contracted syphilis and, most important, syphilis predated the onset of general paresis by anything up to 20 years. Therefore, a situation existed where some paretics were known to have had syphilis but others claimed never to have contracted the disease. There was no cure for syphilis at this time but it was known that people who once had the disease developed immunity and never developed symptoms again even when they were re-exposed to the syphilitic germ. This knowledge led to the idea for a risky experiment to answer the question once and for all: did syphilis cause general paresis?

Krafft-Ebing carried out his experiment in 1897. He injected nine paretic patients who denied they had ever had syphilis with the syphilitic bacterium. None of them developed syphilitic sores. At last, the conclusive link between syphilis and general paresis had been established. The link that had long been suspected was conclusively demonstrated by means of this scientific investigation. This finding is often used to support the biological approach to psychological abnormality, as it demonstrated that physical infection can lead to mental disorder.

Postscript: In 1906, a blood test was developed that detected syphilis. Over 90 per cent of paretics tested positively. With the advent of penicillin (in the 1940s) this disease is now rarely seen.

Activity The origins of general paresis: Krafft-Ebing's hypothesis

The discovery of what caused the psychological disorder, general paresis, is one of the best-known early scientific investigations of mental disorders. Read the panel on the previous page about Krafft-Ebing's investigation and then answer the following questions:

1 What was Krafft-Ebing's hypothesis before he injected the nine patients? See Chapter 2, p. 38, if you are unsure about hypotheses.

2 Did Krafft-Ebing accept or reject his hypothesis?

3 This study is ethically unacceptable by today's standards. Identify two principles from the BPS Code of Ethics and Conduct (see pp. 55–7) that this study violates.

Answers are given on p. 278 ▶

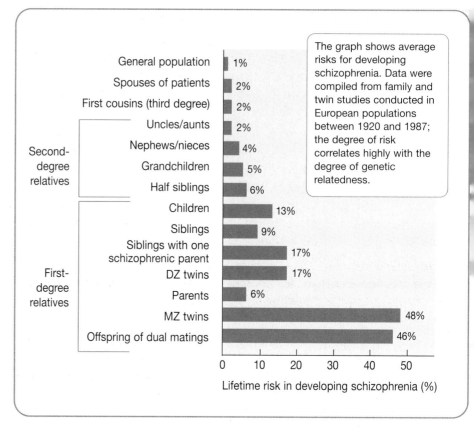

The graph shows average risks for developing schizophrenia. Data were compiled from family and twin studies conducted in European populations between 1920 and 1987; the degree of risk correlates highly with the degree of genetic relatedness.

Figure 7.1 Genetic risk of developing schizophrenia. Source: Zimbardo *et al.* (1995)

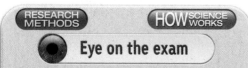 **Eye on the exam**

Biological factors in psychopathology

Some research into depression in twins has found 46 per cent concordance in identical (MZ) twins and 20 per cent in fraternal (DZ) twins for the condition. Concordance rates refer to the likelihood that if one twin has the disorder then the other twin does also.

1 Explain why these figures might suggest that there is a genetic basis to depression. *(2 marks)*

2 What factor(s) (other than a genetic basis) might explain the figures? *(2 marks)*

Answers are given on p. 278 ▶

For more exam advice, visit **www.collinseducation.com/psychologyweb**

■ *Genes* – Important new genetic research has highlighted the possibility that some people may be genetically at risk of developing a mental disorder, but so far the only strong evidence relates to conditions such as schizophrenia and bipolar depression (a disorder characterized by alternating periods of depression and mania). It has been demonstrated, for example, that a first-degree relative (e.g. son or daughter) of someone suffering from schizophrenia has approximately a 10 per cent chance of developing schizophrenia. This is far in excess of the 1 per cent risk to the normal population. Figure 7.1 above, 'Genetic risk of developing schizophrenia', shows that the degree of risk increases with the degree of relatedness.

In order to investigate genetic links, researchers carry out family, twin and adoption studies. Some of these studies can be difficult to interpret because the similarity of family members might simply reflect their shared environment rather than their shared biology. See the panel on the opposite page for more information about how family, twin and adoption studies are carried out and what the findings of these studies tell us about the role of genetics in schizophrenia.

Some physical disorders, such as muscular dystrophy, appear to arise from defects in single genes. It seems unlikely that this is the case for mental disorders such as schizophrenia. In disorders such as this, it is more likely that there are defects in several genes. The Human Genome Project, which is concerned with determining the sequence of all human DNA, will provide the means to establish genetic linkage in psychiatric disorders.

Advances in genetic research raise ethical and practical concerns about the consequences of trying to engineer a better society by genetic means.

valuation of the biological/medical model

No blame – A diagnosis of mental 'illness' implies that the person is not responsible for their abnormal behaviour and as such is not to blame. The concept of 'no blame' is generally thought to be humane and likely to elicit a sympathetic response from others as the person suffering from the mental disorder is in need of help not punishment.

Stigma – However, Szasz (1972), pointed out that, even more than physical illness, mental illness is something that people fear – largely because it is something they do not understand. In general, people do not know how to respond to someone diagnosed as mentally ill. There may also be fears that the person's behaviour might be unpredictable and potentially dangerous. Therefore, sympathy is more likely to give way to avoidance, which in turn leads to the person feeling shunned.

Relinquishing responsibility – Another criticism of the medical model is that people are encouraged to become passive patients, handing over responsibility for their 'wellness' to professionals, and so, not feeling responsible for their own recovery.

Research – A huge amount of research has been carried out within the framework of the medical model and this has greatly increased our understanding of the possible biological factors underpinning psychological disorders. For example, McGuffin *et al.* (1996) found 46 per cent concordance in MZ twins compared to 20 per cent in DZ twins for depression in a total of 109 twin pairs. This suggests a genetic component in depression. However, much of the evidence is inconclusive and findings can be difficult to interpret. For example, in family and twin studies, it is difficult to disentangle the effects of genes from the effects of environment. It can also be difficult to establish cause and effect. For example, raised levels of dopamine activity may be a consequence rather than a cause of schizophrenia

Reductionist – The biological explanation of abnormality is criticized for being reductionist. This means attempting to explain phenomena by breaking them down to the most fundamental level, i.e. it explains abnormal behaviour in terms of the activity of brain cells. It seems, however, much more likely that psychological disorders are caused by the interaction of many factors, including learned patterns of behaviour, ways of thinking and emotional experiences as well as biological factors.

Biological therapies are described and evaluated on pp. 237–9.

In the next sections, we shall look at the key features of three psychological approaches to psychopathology, that is, approaches that focus on psychological rather than biological factors that might cause mental disorders.

Psychodynamic approach to psychopathology

Freud (1856-1939) and others developed the psychodynamic approach (model) in the latter part of the nineteenth century through their clinical work with mentally disordered patients. They challenged the biomedical view that mental disorders had physical origins. The **psychodynamic approach** views abnormal behaviour as caused by unconscious, underlying psychological forces.

Investigating the role of genetics

Family studies

First-degree relatives share on average 50 per cent of their genes, while second-degree relatives (e.g. nephews/nieces) share approximately 25 per cent. To investigate the role of inheritance in a disorder, studies are carried out that compare the rates for the disorder in those who are related to already diagnosed cases, with those who are related to controls (i.e. people who do not have the disorder).

Twin studies

This offers another way of establishing genetic links, by comparing the differences in concordance rates (i.e. the likelihood of both twins being affected with the disorder) for identical (MZ) twins and fraternal (DZ) twins. Both share the same environment but only MZ twins have identical genes.

You can see from Figure 7.1 that there is a higher concordance rate for schizophrenia among MZ twins (48 per cent) than among DZ twins (17 per cent). What this means is that if one of an MZ twin pair has schizophrenia, then there is a 48 per cent chance that the other twin will also have the disorder.

Adoption studies

To separate out the effects of environmental and genetic factors, adopted children who later developed mental disorders are studied and compared with their biological and adoptive parents. For example, Wender *et al.* (1986) found there was an eight times greater risk of developing depression for biological relatives of people with depression rather than for adoptive relatives. Now try the activity below.

Activity Concordance rate in MZ twins

Family, twin and adoption studies have provided reliable evidence that the degree of risk of developing schizophrenia increases with the degree of genetic relatedness. However, the concordance rate in MZ twin studies falls far short of 100 per cent. What does this tell you about the role of genetic inheritance for developing schizophrenia?

Answers are given on p. 278 ▶

Structures of the personality

- *Id* – the unconscious, insatiable set of instincts with which people are born. The id is pleasure-orientated and completely selfish.
- *Ego* – the conscious, rational part of the personality (driven by the reality principle) that arbitrates between the demands of the id and the demands of the superego.
- *Superego* – the last part of the personality to develop – is concerned with right and wrong, that is, it is morality driven. The superego develops through the process of socialization when people learn the moral standards and expectations of their culture.

Key features of the psychodynamic approach

Psychopathology is psychological in origin

Freud believed that all behaviour – normal and abnormal – derived from unconscious forces and that psychopathology arose from the dynamic working of the personality (psyche), rather than from physical causes. In other words, psychopathology is psychological in origin. According to Freud, the psyche consists of three interrelated structures (see the panel on the left), and the id and the superego are bound to be in conflict. Therefore, the ego has a vital role to play if a healthy personality is to develop. Let's look at three possible scenarios:

- *Strong ego* – The well-adjusted person develops a strong ego that is able to cope with the demands of both the id and the superego by allowing each expression at appropriate times. If, however, the ego is weakened, then either the id or the superego, whichever is stronger, may dominate the personality.

- *Unchecked id impulses* – If id impulses emerge unchecked, they are expressed in destructiveness and immorality, which may result in conduct disorders in childhood and psychopathic (dangerously abnormal) behaviour in adulthood.

- *Too powerful superego* – When the superego is too powerful, it rigidly restricts the id to such an extent that the person will be deprived of even socially acceptable pleasures. According to Freud this would create neurosis, which could be expressed in the symptoms of anxiety disorders, such as phobias and obsessions.

Unconscious conflicts cause psychopathology

Psychological disturbances in adulthood are assumed to be the result of unconscious, unresolved psychological conflicts and experiences that date back to childhood.

- *Unresolved conflicts* – The ego may be unable to balance the competing demands of the id and the superego. Freud maintained that these internal conflicts occur at an unconscious level, so that we are unaware of their influence. Although conflict between the superego and the id can occur at any time in our life, it is most marked in early childhood because the ego is not yet fully developed. Freud also believed that children go through stages of psychosexual development: oral, anal, phallic, latency and genital. If conflicts arising within these stages are not satisfactorily resolved (called a fixation), then psychological or behavioural problems may arise later on, the type of problem being determined by the stage at which the unresolved conflict happened. For example, children who fail to identify with their parents during the phallic stage will find it impossible to develop a conscience and will be at risk of developing antisocial personality disorder (a lack of consideration for the rights and feelings of others and an absence of guilt or remorse).

- *Early experiences* – The immature ego is not developed fully enough to deal with external events such as maternal absences, parental shortcomings or competition with siblings. Traumatic or confusing events in childhood, therefore, are pushed into the unconscious – a process which Freud called **repression** – because they are too painful for the ego to bear, or because the child hasn't developed sufficient knowledge of the world to make sense of the event (A. Freud 1936). Distressing feelings around traumatic events do not disappear, however, simply because they are repressed. They find expression in dreams and irrational behaviour and may eventually erupt and express themselves in psychological disorders such as depression.

Each stage represents the focus for pleasure (libido) from different parts of the body.

1	**Oral stage** (0–18 months)	Pleasure gained, for example, from eating and sucking. Weaning is the most important developmental achievement.
2	**Anal stage** (18–36 months)	Pleasure gained from expelling or retaining faeces. Bowel and bladder control are important achievements.
3	**Phallic stage** (3–6 years)	At this most vital stage, the child becomes aware of its gender and the focus is on the genitals. At this stage, the Oedipus complex occurs for boys and the Electra complex for girls, when an unconscious rivalry develops between the child and its same-sex parent for the affection of its opposite-sex parent. At this time, boys experience castration anxiety and girls experience penis envy. According to Freud, this complex is resolved when the boy, repressing his desire for his mother, identifies strongly with his father and when the girl sublimates her penis envy into a desire to have a baby. Successful (normal) development through this stage requires the development of a firm gender identity. One of Freud's most famous case studies concerns a young boy who is in this stage of development (see case study 'Little Hans' below).
4	**Latency stage** (6 years to puberty)	The focus is on social rather than psychosexual development. This is sometimes seen as the calm before the storm of adolescence.
5	**Genital stage** (puberty to maturity)	If the conflicts experienced during the earlier stages have been satisfactorily resolved, the greatest pleasure comes from mature heterosexual relationships.

Table 7.2 Freud's stages of psychosexual development

For more background information about Freud's stages of psychosexual development, see Table 7.2 above. Then read the case study of 'Little Hans' below and try the activity on the right.

Little Hans
A case study of a phobia (Freud 1909)

Little Hans was a 5-year-old boy whose father wrote to Freud for help because his son had developed a phobia – a fear of horses. Freud's analysis of Little Hans was based on the information reported in the letters written by the boy's father. When he was 3 years old, Hans had shown 'a peculiarly lively interest in the part of his body which he used to describe as his widdler'. He invited his mother to touch his penis, was told that would be 'piggish' and was warned that his penis would be cut off if he continued touching it. According to Freud, Hans showed strong sexual urges, directed towards his mother and these were repressed for fear of castration by his father. About six months later, Hans was frightened when he saw a horse-drawn van tip over and thereafter he indicated he was afraid to go out in case he was bitten by a horse. Freud believed that the initial source of the boy's fear was his father but the fear was transposed to a horse (a symbol for his father). The muzzles and blinkers on the horses were seen to represent the father's moustache and spectacles. The boy's fear of horses represented his fear of castration at the hands of his father because Hans and his father were rivals for his mother's love. Freud advised Hans' father to continue being loving towards his son, to talk through his fears with him until the phobia disappeared and Hans identified with his father.

Activity Little Hans' fear of horses

Read the case study 'Little Hans'.

According to Freud, Hans' fear of horses represented his repressed fear of his father. Can you suggest another explanation? Keep a note of your ideas so that you can compare them with the behavioural explanation given later in the chapter.

Ego defence mechanisms

In order to balance the demands of the id and superego and to protect itself, the ego employs 'defence mechanisms' (see Table 7.3 on the next page).

These mechanisms distort or deny reality and are essential ways of protecting the ego from distress and allowing the person to cope with life. They have a

Mechanism	How it works	Example:
Repression	Prevents unacceptable desires, motivations or emotions from becoming conscious. Repression does not mean that you consciously cover up guilty secrets; it means that you make them unconscious so that you are not even aware of them. The repressed drives do not disappear; they remain in the unconscious where they influence behaviour in ways that we are unaware of, and may cause emotional difficulties.	A person who is normally placid acts in a violent way towards someone else and subsequently has no recollection of this.
Projection	When people's own unacceptable faults or wishes are attributed to someone else. In the extreme, this defence mechanism can become paranoia.	Accusing someone else of being angry, or secretive, or thoughtless, when it is actually you who are feeling angry or being secretive, or thoughtless.
Denial	People sometimes refuse to believe events or to admit they are experiencing certain emotions that provoke anxiety.	An alcoholic may deny that they are dependent on alcohol.
Regression	Sometimes people respond to anxiety by behaving in childish ways, such as adults who resort to stamping or kicking, which they may have found effective as children. People may also regress to an earlier type of behaviour when they suffer a traumatic experience.	A 9-year-old child whose parents are getting divorced may revert to thumb-sucking or bed-wetting.
Displacement	Diverting emotions on to someone else because the emotions cannot be expressed to the person concerned, or because accepting faults in ourselves will cause anxiety.	A child who feels angry towards their parents may resort to bullying a younger or weaker child at school. A student who fails an exam may blame the teacher.
Sublimation	Diverting emotions onto something else (rather than someone else). This is the socially acceptable form of displacement and a defence mechanism that is encouraged in our society.	Playing a vigorous sport as an expression of aggressive drives.

Table 7.3 Defence mechanisms

Activity   Using defence mechanisms

1 In what way can hard physical activity be a form of sublimation?

2 Spend a few minutes noting as many examples as you can think of when:
   – you might have used defence mechanisms
   – you have been aware of others using defence mechanisms.

3 Try to provide additional examples for any of the defence mechanisms from Table 7.3 that you have not already included in your examples.

powerful, yet unconscious, influence upon our behaviour, and everyone uses them. Freud said that they are perfectly natural and normal and offer a way of satisfying the demands of the id without upsetting the superego. Whilst useful for protecting the ego, however, they do not offer a long-term solution, and if defence mechanisms are adopted too frequently, or get out of proportion, they themselves can create psychological problems of their own.

According to Freud, the behaviour of all people is to some extent 'abnormal', in that none of us is free from the dynamic conflicts caused by our unconscious drives and repressed memories. Therefore it is perfectly 'normal' to experience anxiety. Abnormality is, therefore, both inevitable and beyond our conscious control. Now try the activity 'Using defence mechanisms' on the left.

Evaluation of the psychodynamic model

■ *Influential* – Freudian theory has been enormously influential and was the first model to establish talking therapy as an acceptable form of treatment in mainstream mental health practice (see p. 240). Freud's ideas about the unconscious have had a profound impact on the way we think about what motivates behaviour. The use of psychodynamic insights, for example to analyze and even create films and literature, is well known; for instance, in the film *Psycho*, Norman Bates is portrayed as having 'Oedipal problems'.

■ *Untestable* – However, the psychodynamic model has proved difficult to test scientifically. Kline (1988), nevertheless, claims that a theory is not invalidated merely because it cannot be tested scientifically; it just means that no one has yet found a way to do it. Zeldow (1995) points out that 'psychoanalytic theories have inspired more empirical research in the social and behavioural sciences than any other group of theories'.

Retrospective data – Although early traumatic experiences may not necessarily emerge in adulthood as psychological problems, research indicates that many people with psychological problems do recollect having experienced emotional trauma in childhood. However, it is important to understand that retrospective data collected during interviews (i.e. information from clients gathered years after the event) may be unreliable. Try the activity on the right.

Determinism – The psychodynamic model claims that abnormal behaviour results from unconscious psychic conflict related to innate, biological drives. The model also claims that early relationships with parents are important to psychological development. For these reasons, it has been claimed that the theory is deterministic, that is, individuals are portrayed as having very little conscious involvement in their own personality development.

Current experiences – Freud's psychoanalytic approach (the earliest version of the psychodynamic approach) has been criticized for underestimating the importance of current difficulties that clients might be facing. Even if repressed childhood experiences contribute to adult disorders, it is still important to take account of factors (such as loss of job or relationship break-up) that might be contributing to the person's psychological problems. Later psychodynamic approaches take adult experiences into account.

Ethical implications – The implicit assumption of the psychoanalytic approach is that people are not to blame for their own abnormal behaviour, but may be partially responsible for the development of abnormal behaviour in their offspring. This may prove a heavy burden for parents who feel they have 'done their best' and, according to the model, may also be grappling with their own inner emotional conflicts.

See pp. 240–1 for a description and evaluation of psychoanalysis, a psychodynamic therapy.

Behavioural approach to psychopathology

This approach focuses on the 'behaviour' of an individual in order to explain psychological problems. Advocates of the **behavioural approach** claim that abnormal behaviour is learned through experience in the same way as most other behaviour. Behaviourists see no need for concepts such as the mind or unconscious motivations. Even if a person has a biological predisposition towards pathological behaviour, behaviourists claim that the behaviour is maintained by environmental reinforcement. The behavioural approach explains the emergence of specific, maladaptive, or dysfunctional behaviours such as phobias, anxiety and depression, through the processes of classical conditioning, operant conditioning and social learning, described below.

Key features of the behavioural approach

Classical conditioning

The theory of **classical conditioning** (Pavlov 1927) explains how behaviour is learned through 'stimulus–response' associations. An event in the environment

 Eye on the exam

Definitions and explanations

In an exam you may be asked to:

Outline two attempts to define abnormality.
(3 marks + 3 marks)

There is a trap that students sometimes fall into with this type of question. They confuse definitions and explanations of abnormality. This question concerns definitions and if you write about explanations you will earn no marks. The same applies, of course, if you write about definitions when you have been asked for explanations (or approaches). Remember also that this type of question does not require any evaluation.

Are you clear about the difference between a '*definition of*' and an '*approach to*' abnormality?

- A definition of abnormality is an attempt to *describe* what is meant by abnormality, e.g. abnormal behaviour is behaviour that prevents an individual functioning adequately. In other words, a *definition* of abnormality answers the question 'What is abnormality?'

- An approach to abnormality (psychopathology) is a *type of explanation* of abnormality, e.g. abnormality is caused by physical factors such as faulty biochemistry or brain damage. In other words, an *approach* to abnormality answers the question 'Why does abnormality happen?'

For more exam advice, visit
www.collinseducation.com/psychologyweb

(stimulus) results in a physiological reaction (response) in the individual. The event and the reaction are then forged into an association. Phobias (irrational fears of objects or situations) are thought to develop in this way. For example, a person may climb to the top of a high building and, when looking down (environmental stimulus), experience nausea and dizziness (physiological response). This association may then develop into a fear of heights so strong that it becomes a phobia and the person will then be so afraid of heights that they will avoid all situations that involve heights. Think back to Freud's case study of Little Hans (see p. 229). The behavioural approach would explain his fear of horses in terms of classical conditioning: Hans was frightened when he saw a noisy accident involving a horse and thereafter associated horses with being afraid.

In classical conditioning, it is not the object, nor the situation, which is the cause of the fear but the conditioned response to the object or situation. For example, it is the response of feeling sick and dizzy when looking down from a high building that causes the fear of heights, not the height itself. What is important is that the person must have first experienced a fearful reaction to the situation or event, which is so extreme that they will avoid it (or anything similar) in the future. This may not be a problem if the person can avoid being in high places, but becomes dysfunctional if the person works in a tall office block for example, or has a job that involves airline travel. In such cases, the person either has to seek alternative employment or seek help from a therapist to overcome the phobia. In a classic study, Watson and Rayner (1920) demonstrated how phobias are learned by conditioning a young boy to fear a white rat (see the panel below).

After reading about the 'Little Albert' study, try the activity below left.

According to classical conditioning, fear of heights is caused not by the height itself, but by the response of feeling sick and dizzy when looking down from a high building

Activity: Ethical issues in the 'Little Albert' study

The 'Little Albert' experiment raises ethical issues. Remind yourself of the BPS code of conduct (see Chapter 2, pp. 55–7) and explain why an investigation like this would not receive approval from an ethics committee today.

Little Albert
An experiment in conditioning (Watson and Raynor 1920)

Watson and Rayner (1920) attempted to show how a phobia could be conditioned. They conducted an experiment using an 11-month-old child – known as Little Albert (with his parents' consent). A couple of months earlier his response to various stimuli (including a white rat, a rabbit and cotton wool) had been tested, but the only thing he showed fear of was the loud noise caused when a hammer struck an iron bar just behind his head (unconditioned response).

Albert was now introduced to a tame white rat (neutral stimulus) and he showed no fear. From time to time during the experiment, when Albert reached out to touch the rat the experimenters hit the metal bar with the hammer, making a loud noise (unconditioned stimulus). The noise startled and upset Albert and soon he became afraid to touch the white rat (conditioned response). In this classic study, Watson and Rayner showed that an association had been formed between touching the white rat and fear of the noise (see Figure 7.2). This conditioned fear of the rat then became generalized to other stimuli that resembled the white rat, like other fluffy animals and objects such as a cotton wool beard. A month after the conditioning procedure, Albert still showed fear when he was presented with the white rat. His parents withdrew him from the experiment before Watson and Rayner had the opportunity to try and extinguish Albert's fear response to the white rat and replace it with his original response. See p. 242 for how this might have been attempted.

Now look at the activity on 'Little Hans' on the opposite page.

Operant conditioning

In his theory of **operant conditioning**, Skinner (1974) explained how our behaviour is influenced by the consequences of our actions. We learn at an early age, for example, which of our actions are rewarded and which are

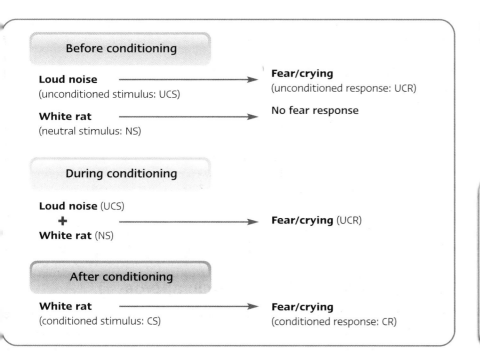

Before conditioning

Loud noise (unconditioned stimulus: UCS) → Fear/crying (unconditioned response: UCR)

White rat (neutral stimulus: NS) → No fear response

During conditioning

Loud noise (UCS)
+
White rat (NS) → Fear/crying (UCR)

After conditioning

White rat (conditioned stimulus: CS) → Fear/crying (conditioned response: CR)

Activity — Little Hans' fear of horses: a behavioural explanation

Do you recall the case study of Little Hans, who developed a fear of horses? In the activity on p. 229, you were asked to think of an alternative explanation to that offered by the psychodynamic approach for Hans' fear. Use Figure 7.2 on the left as a template to explain Hans' fear in terms of classical conditioning.

punished. Psychological disorders, such as antisocial personality disorder (see p. 228) have been explained in operant conditioning terms. If childhood aggression is rewarded, then the behaviour is likely to be repeated. Sometimes, behaviours that may appear maladaptive to others might be useful or adaptive for the individual. For example, anxiety or depression might receive reward in the form of attention and concern from others. The more attention received the more likely the behaviour will be repeated.

Social learning

According to social learning theory (Bandura 1973), many behaviours are learned through imitation, that is, by observing others who serve as models for behaviour. Observational learning is particularly powerful if those who model the behaviour are seen to be rewarded. For example, a child may learn antisocial behaviour by observing that others are rewarded for similar behaviour (e.g. bullying). Some specific phobias, such as fear of harmless spiders, may best be explained by social learning – by observing other people showing fear when they see a spider.

A study of monkeys by Mineka *et al.* (1984) showed how a phobia could be developed through observation alone. Young monkeys raised by parents who already had a fear of snakes did not automatically acquire this fear themselves, and so Mineka concluded that the fear was not genetically inherited. However, those monkeys who had the opportunity to observe their parents showing fearful reactions to real and toy snakes did acquire an intense and persistent fear.

Evaluation of the behavioural approach

Focus on behaviour – The behavioural approach overcomes the ethical issue raised by the medical model of labelling and thereby stigmatizing someone as 'abnormal'. Instead, the behavioural model concentrates on behaviour and whether it is 'adaptive' or 'maladaptive'. The assumption is that maladaptive learned behaviour can be replaced with new adaptive learned behaviour (see pp. 241–4 for therapies using the behavioural approach).

Does comforting serve to reinforce children's anxious behaviour?

Activity — Learning maladaptive behaviours

1 For each of the following behaviours, select one or more of the behavioural explanations outlined in this section to explain how the behaviour might have been learned:
 (a) an irrational fear (phobia) of dogs
 (b) a school phobia
 (c) bullying behaviour
 (d) an eating disorder.
2 To what extent do you think that the behavioural approach provides adequate explanations for these behaviours?

- *Focus on functioning* – Provided the behaviour presents no problems to the individual, or to other people, there is no reason to regard the behaviour as a mental disorder. It is the behavioural model that led to the definition of abnormality previously outlined as 'a failure to function adequately' (see p. 220).

- *Underlying causes* – Those who support the psychodynamic model, however, claim that the behavioural model focuses only on symptoms and ignores the causes of abnormal behaviour. They claim that symptoms are merely the tip of the iceberg – the outward expression of deeper underlying emotional problems. Whenever symptoms are treated without any attempt to ascertain the deeper underlying problems, then, according to the psychodynamic approach, the problem will only manifest itself in another way, through different symptoms. This is known as symptom substitution. Behaviourists reject this criticism, however, and claim that we need not look beyond behavioural symptoms because the symptoms are the disorder. Thus, there is nothing to be gained by searching for internal causes, either psychological or physical. Behaviourists point to the success of behavioural therapies in treating disorders such as phobias (Emmelkamp 1994). Others note that the effects of such treatments are not always long lasting (see p. 244).

- *Reductionism* – The behavioural approach is accused of being reductionist and simplistic because it seeks to explain complex behaviours in very narrow terms, that is, through the processes of conditioning and observation but ignoring the roles of biology, emotion or thinking (cognition). The importance of cognitive factors in explaining some cases of psychopathology is explored in the next section.

See pp. 241–4 for a description and evaluation of behavioural therapies.

Cognitive approach to psychopathology

The **cognitive approach** stresses the role of cognitive problems (such as irrational thinking) in abnormal functioning. This approach to understanding abnormality was founded by Albert Ellis (1962) and Aaron Beck (1963), who thought that the weakness of the behavioural model was that it did not take mental processes into account. The rationale behind the cognitive model is that the thinking (cognition) processes that occur between a stimulus and a response are responsible for the feeling that forms part of the response.

Key features of the cognitive approach

Irrational thinking (Ellis 1962)

The cognitive approach assumes that emotional problems can be attributed directly to distortions in our thinking processes (cognitions). These distortions take the form of negative thoughts, irrational beliefs and illogical errors, such as polarized thinking (e.g. believing you are totally worthless if you are not loved by everyone you know) and overgeneralization (drawing negative conclusions on the basis of a single event). These maladaptive thoughts, it is claimed, usually take place automatically and without full awareness.

Ellis maintained that everyone's thoughts are rational at times and irrational at other times. Psychological problems occur only if people engage in faulty thinking to the extent that it becomes maladaptive for them and others around them (see Figure 7.3 and Table 7.4 on the next page).

Activity **The cognitive triad**

Read the following case study of a depressed woman (adapted from Beck *et al.* 1979) and try to identify the features of the cognitive triad:

1 the negative thoughts that she expresses about herself

2 the negative thoughts that she expresses about her experiences

3 the negative thoughts that she expresses about the future.

Stella, a 36-year-old depressed woman, had withdrawn from the tennis games she had previously enjoyed. Instead, her daily behaviour pattern consisted of 'sleeping and trying to do the housework I've neglected'. Stella firmly believed she was unable to engage in activities as 'strenuous' as tennis and that she had become so poor at tennis that no one would ever want to play with her. Her husband arranged for a private tennis lesson in an attempt to help his wife overcome her depression. She reluctantly attended the lesson and appeared to be 'a different person' in the eyes of her husband. She showed agility and hit the ball well. Despite her good performance during the lesson, Stella concluded that her skills had 'deteriorated' beyond the point at which lessons would do any good. She misinterpreted her husband's positive response to her lesson as an indication of how bad her game had become because in her view, 'he thinks I'm so hopeless that the only time I can hit the ball is when I'm taking a lesson'.

She also stated that she didn't enjoy the tennis session because she didn't deserve any recreation time.

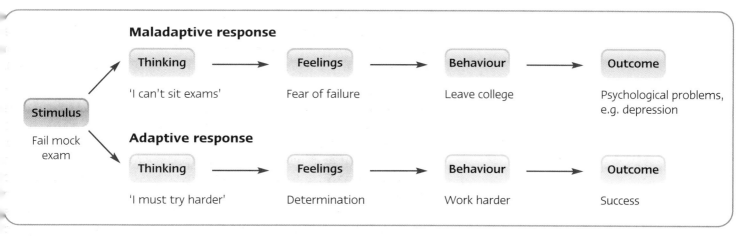

Figure 7.3 The rationale behind cognitive theory

According to Ellis, when we *think* rationally, we *behave* rationally and, as a consequence, we are happy, competent and effective. When we think irrationally, however, the result can be psychological disturbance, because people become accustomed to their disturbed thoughts. Ellis observed that irrational thinking is often revealed in the language that people use, in particular the use of words such as 'should', 'ought' and 'must'.

Examples of irrational thinking that could lead to psychological problems include:

- 'I *ought* to be good for my parents'
- 'David *should* be nice to me'
- 'I *must* do well in all my A levels'.

Ellis also claimed that some people tend to exaggerate or 'catastrophize' events. For example: 'I must be an awful person because Mary ignored me when I spoke to her this morning'. Such people fail to consider rational alternatives, e.g. that Mary was engrossed in thinking about something, or feeling ill, or she may be a moody type of person.

Table 7.4 Some irrational ways of thinking (Ellis 1962 and Beck 1967)

- **Polarized thinking** – seeing everything in black or white
- **Overgeneralization** – sweeping generalization from a single event
- **Tyranny of 'should', 'ought' and 'must'** – 'I must be loved by everyone'
- **Catastrophizing** – making a mountain out of a molehill

The cognitive triad and errors in logic (Beck 1967)

Beck, who also believed that negative thoughts underlie mental disorder, was particularly interested in finding out why people become depressed. He identified two mechanisms that he thought were responsible for depression:

- *Errors in logic* – He found that depressed people tend to draw illogical conclusions when they evaluate themselves. For example, you conclude that you are stupid because you once get a mediocre grade for an assignment even though you normally gain straight 'A's. This faulty logic is called overgeneralization – drawing a sweeping conclusion on the basis of a single event. Such negative thoughts lead to negative feelings, which, in turn, can result in depression.

- *Cognitive triad* – Beck identified three forms of negative thinking that he called the 'cognitive triad' and that he thought were typical of those suffering from depression (see Figure 7.4).

As these three components interact, they interfere with normal cognitive processing, leading to impairments in perception, memory and problem-solving and the person becoming obsessed with negative thoughts. Constant exposure to these faulty cognitions can lead to depression.

Now try the activity 'The cognitive triad' on the opposite page.

Figure 7.4 The cognitive triad that leads to depression (Beck 1967)

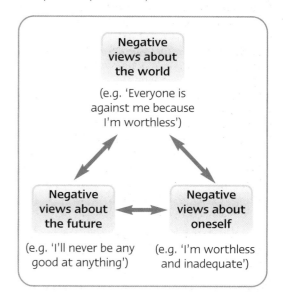

Evaluation of the cognitive model

■ *Research support* – Research has shown that many people suffering from mental disorders do exhibit thought patterns associated with maladaptive functioning. For example, Gustafson (1992) found that maladaptive thinking processes were displayed by many people with psychological disorders such as anxiety, depression and sexual disorders.

■ *Irrational thinking* – Cause or effect? A criticism of the model is that it does not attempt to examine the origins of irrational thinking, nor does the treatment address these origins. Beck (1991) himself has pointed out that, although cognitive processes are involved in many psychological disorders, they may well be a consequence rather than a cause of the problem.

■ *Individual is responsible* – The cognitive model has also been criticized because it suggests that everyone should be self-sufficient. Indeed, Ellis had little sympathy with those suffering from depression, regarding it as an 'indulgence' of self-defeating thoughts. A belief in self-sufficiency lays the blame for psychological problems firmly within the individual, rather than with the social environment. Consequently, attention may be drawn away from the need to improve social conditions that have a significant effect on the quality of life.

See pp. 244–6 for a description and evaluation of Cognitive Behavioural Therapy.

CHECK YOUR UNDERSTANDING

Check your understanding of defining and explaining psychological abnormality by answering the following questions. Try to do this from memory. You can check your answers by looking back through Topic 1.

1. What is meant by the term 'social' norm? Give one example of a social norm from your own culture.

2. Explain how the use of the social norm definition of abnormality could be used as a form of social control.

3. Why is context important when using the deviation from social norms definition of abnormality?

4. In the context of defining abnormality, what is meant by a failure to function adequately?

5. Outline two limitations of using the failure to function adequately definition of abnormality.

6. Name the six criteria that Jahoda identified for optimal living.

7. Outline two limitations of using the deviation from ideal mental health as a definition of abnormality.

8. Outline two key features of the biological approach to psychopathology.

9. What are the four possible causes of psychopathology according to the biological approach?

10. Give one strength and one weakness of the biological approach to psychopathology.

11. Name the three parts of the psyche according to Freud.

12. According to the psychodynamic approach, what are the two main causes of psychopathology?

13. Explain what is meant by the term 'defence mechanisms'.

14. Outline two evaluations of the psychodynamic approach to psychopathology.

15. According to the behavioural approach to psychopathology, what three processes explain how abnormal behaviours are acquired?

16. Give one strength and one weakness of the behavioural approach to psychopathology.

17. Outline the key features of the cognitive approach to psychopathology.

18. In the cognitive approach, what is meant by overgeneralization and polarized thinking? Give an example of each.

19. To which psychological disorder did Beck apply his 'cognitive triad'?

20. Give one strength and one weakness of the cognitive approach to psychopathology.

Topic 2: Treating abnormality

In Topic 2 we turn our attention to the therapies used to treat psychological abnormality. Before reading on, try answering the questions posed in Psychology in context.

Biological therapies

Those who advocate the biological approach to abnormality assume that deviant behaviour and mental disorders are caused by biological abnormalities and so are best treated by biological (physical/somatic) interventions.

Aim of biological therapies

Biological treatments are interventions that aim to redress biological abnormalities such as biochemical imbalances. The treatments fall into three main categories:

- drug treatment
- electro-convulsive therapy (ECT)
- psychosurgery.

Drug treatment

Drug therapy (chemotherapy) is the main treatment for mental disorders and is based on the assumption that chemical imbalance is at the root of the problem. Drugs for mental disorders include the following:

- *Anti-anxiety drugs*, e.g. minor tranquillizers called benzodiazepines (BZs) such as Valium – These have a calming effect by inhibiting the nervous system and causing muscles to relax. BZs work by enhancing the action of the chemical messenger (neurotransmitter), GABA, which acts to calm brain activity (see Chapter 5, p.171 for more information on GABA)

- *Anti-depressant drugs*, e.g. MAOIs (monoamine-oxidase inhibitors), TCAs (tricyclics) and SSRIs (selective serotonin re-uptake inhibitors) – These improve mood by increasing the availability of neurotransmitters such as serotonin. For example, MAOIs block the action of an enzyme that breaks down serotonin, so increasing its availability in the nervous system.

- *Anti-psychotic drugs*, e.g. major tranquillizers such as the phenothiazines – These sedate and alleviate symptoms (e.g. hallucinations and delusions) of the person suffering from psychotic disorders such as schizophrenia. They seem to work by blocking the D2 receptor for dopamine.

Evaluation of drug treatment

- *Efficacy* – Drug treatment has been found to be effective in relieving the symptoms of mental disorders in many (but not all) people. For example, before the introduction of phenothiazines, schizophrenia was seen as untreatable and patients were interned in institutions. Despite the claims made for some modern drug treatments, however, there are critics and the use of drugs remains controversial. Fisher and Greenberg (1989) believe they have limited beneficial effects. Others (e.g. Kirsch and Sapirstein 1998) assert that beneficial effects are caused in large part by the placebo effect. They argue

Psychology in context

Approaches and treatments

In Topic 1, you read about four approaches to psychopathology: biological, psychodynamic, behavioural and cognitive.

1 Make a list of all the films you and some of your fellow students have seen that deal with mental illness. For example: *One Flew over the Cuckoo's Nest*, *A Beautiful Mind* and *Girl Interrupted*.

2 What approach (e.g. biological, psychodynamic) did each film adopt for representing, explaining or treating the mental illnesses it depicted?

3 Were the mental illnesses in the films depicted sympathetically/non-sympathetically, humorously/seriously, accurately or exaggeratedly?

4 Now read the five cases below and decide which approach is being used to determine the treatment described.

A Rebecca has a spider phobia and is no longer able to stay in the house alone with her young daughter whilst her partner goes to work every day. She is being treated by systematic desensitization, which is teaching her to relax and confront her fear of spiders in a relaxed setting, so that she learns to associate a feeling of calm with the presence of a spider.

B Lynda has been diagnosed as suffering from schizophrenia. She regularly takes the drug chlorpromazine that helps to keep her severe symptoms in check and enables her to live with her family and keep her job.

C Rational-emotive therapy is being used to treat Karl's bouts of depression. In his twice-weekly session with the therapist, Karl is being helped to recognise the irrational assumptions that he has about his life and change these into more positive views of himself and his situation.

D Bill suffers from severe depression that has not improved with the drugs that he was prescribed. He has recently been admitted to hospital for electroconvulsive therapy (ECT) which involves passing an electric current through the brain.

E Tom is experiencing anxiety. His psychoanalyst encourages him to free associate on dreams and early childhood memories by letting his mind wander and saying aloud whatever comes into his mind. This may bring uncomfortable desires or repressed thoughts into conscious awareness. The psychoanalyst interprets his words, dreams and behaviour and helps him make sense of his experience and come to terms with it and work through repressed thoughts.

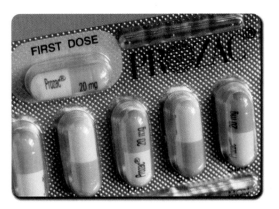

Drug therapy is the main treatment for mental disorders

that therapy produces beneficial effects often because of the attention given and because the patient develops an expectation of success when treatment is offered. In other words, the patient's condition improves owing to their belief that they are receiving appropriate treatment (in this case, a beneficial drug). Of course, the placebo effect can play a part in the response to any type of therapy, not just drug treatment.

- *Side effects* – Drugs may also have side effects that may be considered worse than the original symptoms of the disorder. Some patients suffering from schizophrenia refuse to take phenothiazines because of the unpleasant side effects, the worst of which include symptoms associated with Parkinson's disease, such as stiffness and tremors. Nevertheless, there is an expectation that patients will comply with medication, despite the fact that, as the British National Formulary (an index of pharmaceutical drugs and preparations) indicates, most medication carries side effects and often long-term dependency upon the drugs.

- *Treating the symptoms* – Psychologists have criticized psychiatry for focusing on symptoms and assuming that relieving symptoms with drugs cures the problem. Unfortunately, in many cases when drug treatment is ceased, the symptoms recur, suggesting that drugs are not addressing the true cause of the problem or helping patients learn to cope with experiences in their lives that may have contributed to the disorder in the first place (Hewstone *et al.* 2005)

- *Ethical issues in use of drugs* – There has traditionally been a good deal of criticism levelled at the use of drugs for psychological problems, particularly in mental institutions where patients had no choice. Were they being administered to alleviate suffering in the patient, or to sedate patients so that they were more compliant with institutional regimes? More recently, there has been greater emphasis on voluntary agreement and the right to refuse treatment – see Mental Health Act (2007).

Electro-convulsive therapy (ECT)

The procedure

The patient lies on a bed, in loose clothes, and receives an anaesthetic and muscle relaxant before treatment. ECT involves passing a current (70-130 volts) through the brain for approximately half a second. This is done by fixing electrodes to the patient's temples. In the past, electrodes were put on each side of the forehead. Nowadays it is more common to use unilateral ECT by fixing one electrode to the non-dominant hemisphere (the right side for most people) as this reduces side effects such as memory loss. The current induces convulsions (a seizure similar to an epileptic fit) that last for approximately one minute. Once the patient comes round from the anaesthetic they recall nothing about the procedure.

A patient receives electro-convulsive therapy

Use of ECT

Originally ECT was used by Cerletti and Bini (1938) in an attempt to help a patient suffering from schizophrenia. However, it is now used mainly to treat people with severe depression. Treatments are given typically two or three times a week for three or four weeks. ECT was particularly popular in the 1940s, fell out of favour during the 1950s but is still widely used today. Over 11,000 patients in England and Wales were given ECT in 1999 (Johnstone 2003). Two thirds of these patients were women.

Evaluation of ECT

- *Efficacy* – ECT is a quick form of treatment compared with drugs or psychological therapies. It can be an effective short-term treatment for depression with 60-70 per cent of patients showing improvement (Sackheim 1988). However, approximately 60 per cent of patients will become depressed again within a year (Sackheim *et al.* 1993)

- *When to use* – ECT should only be administered if anti-depressant drugs have no effect and if there is a risk that the person will commit suicide. Some psychiatrists argue that the prevention of suicide is sufficient justification for its use.

- *Mode of action* – It is not clear exactly how ECT works, but it may increase the availability of certain neurotransmitters in the brain and the secretions of hormones that may improve a depressed mood.

- *Side effects* – When ECT was first introduced there were serious side effects including bone fractures and memory loss. Side effects have been reduced (e.g. after the change from bilateral to unilateral ECT) but opinions are divided regarding the severity of cognitive and emotional impairments following treatment.

- *Ethical issues* – ECT has a history of abuse, being used as a means of punishing or controlling people in mental hospitals.

The Mental Health Act (2007), however, states that ECT is prohibited if the patient is capable of making a decision and refuses treatment – known as 'capacitous refusal' of treatment – unless it is immediately necessary to save life or immediately necessary to prevent a serious deterioration in the person's condition. Parents are prohibited from overriding the 'capacitous refusal' of treatment by 16 or 17 year olds.

In the film One Flew Over the Cuckoo's Nest, *the main character, McMurphy (played by Jack Nicholson), causes persistent problems for the staff – attempts are made to control him using drugs, ECT and finally psychosurgery*

Psychosurgery

Psychosurgery is brain surgery to treat psychological disorders. It is the most invasive form of biological therapy because it involves removal of brain tissue and the effects are irreversible. The first modern psychosurgery technique was the pre-frontal lobotomy, developed in the 1930s as a cure for schizophrenia. This method involved destroying the fibres that connect the higher thought centres of the frontal cortex from the lower centres of the brain. Despite early optimism about the procedure, no reliable evidence was found that the lobotomy provided an effective form of treatment.

Nowadays, psychosurgery techniques involve less damage to neural tissue.

Psychosurgery is rarely used, and is only offered as a last resort for treating otherwise intractable conditions.

Evaluation of psychosurgery

- *Controversial treatment* – In the 1950s, psychosurgery was performed on thousands of people in the absence of other effective treatments and in an attempt to reduce the numbers of people crammed into mental institutions.

- *A last resort* – Although psychosurgery is rarely performed today and is seen as a treatment of last resort, some procedures, carried out to alleviate the symptoms of severe anxiety or obsessive-compulsive disorders, have been beneficial (Beck and Cowley 1990).

Psychological therapies

The term 'psychological therapy' – usually called psychotherapy – covers any treatment that addresses psychological rather than biological factors associated with mental disorder. Each psychological approach to (model of) abnormality has its own therapies, based on its own particular perspective. There are many different types of psychotherapy, including:

- psychoanalysis – based on the psychodynamic approach
- systematic desensitization – based on the behavioural approach
- aversion therapy – based on the behavioural approach
- token economy – based on the behavioural approach
- Cognitive Behavioural Therapy – based on the cognitive approach.

Psychoanalysis (psychodynamic approach)

Freud was instrumental in changing ways of thinking about people who are mentally ill. He developed a method of treatment for psychological distress known as 'psychoanalysis', which is often called the 'talking cure'. From this many other psychodynamic therapies have evolved.

Aim of psychoanalysis

Psychoanalysis seeks to:

- bring repressed impulses and traumatic memories into conscious awareness
- facilitate **insight** into the conflicts and anxieties that are the underlying causes of abnormal behaviour
- cure neurotic symptoms, such as phobias or anxiety.

The belief is that if someone can understand what happened in the past and what is going on at an unconscious level within their psyche, they can better deal, at a conscious level, with situations that are happening in their life now.

Methods of psychoanalysis

- *Dream analysis* – According to psychodynamic theory, the unconscious is revealed in dreams; therefore, one of the techniques of psychoanalysis is the analysis of dreams. Freud believed that repressed memories and impulses appeared in dreams in disguised (symbolic) form.
- *Free association* – In free association, clients are encouraged to let their thoughts wander and say whatever comes into their heads without editing or censorship. The idea is that such uncensored thoughts will reveal underlying conflicts and uncomfortable or unfulfilled wishes. The analyst is then able to piece together patterns of association and offer an interpretation of the client's words and behaviour. In this way, the analyst helps make the thoughts that had been repressed available to the client's conscious mind. Successful free association leads to catharsis – the process whereby the expression of a pent up emotion removes its pathological effect as repressed memories and urges are brought to conscious awareness.
- *Transference* – An important part of psychoanalysis is when the client projects (transfers) on to the analyst the characteristics that are unconsciously associated with parents or other important people. When this happens

repressed feelings towards, say, a parent, are directed towards the analyst who is 'standing in' for the parent. Repeated experiences of this sort help reveal to the client their repressed feelings and, gradually, neurotic symptoms disappear. It is important that the analyst remains neutral throughout this process and does not get drawn into countertransference – showing their unconscious feelings towards the client!

Evaluation of psychoanalysis

■ *Expense* – Psychoanalysis tends to be time-consuming and expensive (compared to many behavioural treatments), taking place over a number of years. By and large, it is only available to those who can afford to pay for it. However, some shorter psychodynamic therapies, focusing more on the client's current concerns, have been developed. These provide quicker improvements and so are more affordable.

■ *Types of disorders* – Psychoanalysis is generally considered more appropriate for treating neurotic disorders such as anxiety, but it is less suitable for patients with psychotic disorders such as schizophrenia. Fonagy (2000), in a review of several studies looking at people before and after psychoanalysis, found that the treatment consistently helped those who had mild neurotic disorders (e.g. mild anxiety). Results were less consistent for more serious disorders.

■ *Does it work?* – Figures published by Eysenck (1952) suggested that psychodynamic therapies (including psychoanalysis) were a waste of time and money. However, when Bergin (1971) re-analysed Eysenck's data using different outcome criteria (for what counted as success or failure) the results showed that 83 per cent of those receiving psychoanalysis improved compared with only 30 per cent of those in control groups (on a waiting list). Corsini and Wedding (1995) claim that the success of psychotherapy ranges from 30 to 60 per cent depending on the outcome criteria involved.

■ *Difficulty in evaluating effectiveness* – it may not be possible to evaluate psychoanalysis scientifically because concepts such as insight, transference and repression are vague and difficult to measure. The concept of insight, in particular, poses difficulties. If a client's behaviour improves, then insight is deemed to have taken place. If the client's behaviour does not improve, then it is assumed that insight did not happen (rather than that insight occurred but was ineffective in producing improvement) – a circular argument.

■ *Ethical issues* – Masson (1988) has criticized the therapeutic relationship in psychoanalysis as one where all the power lies with the analyst. In any therapeutic situation there is a risk that the therapist might abuse their power. However, in psychoanalysis the disparity in power between client and analyst is particularly pronounced. The analyst possesses all the expertise while clients are expected to accept a view of themselves as prescribed by the analyst.

■ *Behaviourists' criticism* – Those who adopt a behavioural approach to psychopathology think the abnormal behaviour *is* the disorder and so it is better to concentrate on changing the problem behaviour rather than spend time delving into distant childhood conflicts. In the next section we shall look at some therapies based on the behavioural approach.

Why is it important that the analyst should remain neutral throughout the therapeutic process?

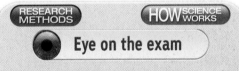

Eye on the exam

The psychodynamic approach to psychopathology

One assumption of the psychodynamic approach to psychopathology is that abnormality is caused by unconscious psychological forces.

Explain **one** psychoanalytic technique that has been used to investigate the role of unconscious forces in abnormality.

(4 marks)

You could, for example, focus on one aspect of psychoanalysis, such as free association, and explain:

● the assumption concerning the link between unconscious forces and abnormality

● the process of free association, including (for example) the nature and purpose of catharsis.

For more exam advice, visit
www.collinseducation.com/psychologyweb

Systematic desensitization (behavioural approach)

If maladaptive or dysfunctional behaviours have been learned through classical and operant conditioning (see pp. 231–3), it should be possible to change them through the same processes. Behavioural therapy, therefore, takes a practical, problem-solving approach. Therapies based on classical conditioning include systematic desensitization and aversion therapy.

Aim of systematic desensitization

Systematic desensitization uses reverse (counter) conditioning and aims to replace a maladaptive response (e.g. fear) to a situation or object (e.g. an animal) by eliciting another healthier response (i.e. relaxation) to the situation or object that is incompatible with the undesirable response (see Figure 7.5).

Figure 7.5 Diagram showing reverse (counter) conditioning whereby an original response (R1) to a given stimulus (S) is eliminated by producing a new response (R2) to the same situation

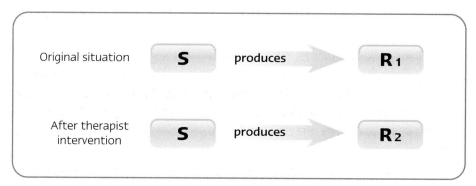

Original situation — **S** produces **R₁**

After therapist intervention — **S** produces **R₂**

Procedures in systematic desensitization

One of the earliest reported uses of systematic desensitization was carried out by Mary Cover Jones (1924). She worked with a little boy who had a fear of rabbits. She fed the boy in the presence of a rabbit but started by keeping the animal several feet distant from the child. On successive occasions the rabbit was moved closer. Eventually the fear (R1) associated with the rabbit (S) was eliminated by the stronger positive feelings associated with eating (R2). This is the type of procedure that Watson and Rayner might have tried with Little Albert had he not been removed from their care by his parents before this could be attempted (see p. 232)

- *Relaxation* – Typically, systematic desensitization starts with teaching an individual how to relax using muscle relaxation techniques.

- *Hierarchy of anxiety-provoking situations* – The individual then imagines a graded series (i.e. a hierarchy) of anxiety-provoking situations, starting with those that arouse least anxiety and gradually progressing to those that arouse most anxiety.

- *Reciprocal inhibition* – the concept of reciprocal inhibition states that two incompatible emotional states cannot exist at the same time. Therefore, anxiety and relaxation cannot exist together. During the procedure, relaxation techniques are practised and, to begin with, relaxation is associated with the least anxiety-provoking situation. When completely relaxed, the client moves on to imagine the next level in the hierarchy of situations and so *systematically* the hierarchy is worked through. Relaxation tends to inhibit any anxiety that might be felt. If anxiety returns at any point then the client calls a halt, usually by raising a hand, rests and starts again when fully relaxed. Over a number of sessions, a client will manage to tolerate increasingly difficult situations in the hierarchy.

- *Complete treatment* – Treatment ends when the client is *desensitized* – able to work through the entire hierarchy without anxiety.

- *In vivo and in vitro* – This procedure can be carried out either through imagined situations (*in vitro*) or in real-life (*in vivo*) as was the case with Jones' (1924) study of the little boy who had a fear of rabbits (see opposite page). Therapists often advise clients to place themselves in progressively more anxiety-provoking real-life situations between therapy sessions in order to help them move from merely imagined to actual situations.

Evaluation of systematic desensitization

- *Research support* – Evidence exists to show that the ability to tolerate imagined stressful situations is followed by a reduction in anxiety in real-life situations (e.g. Emmelkamp 1994).

- *Alternatives to imagination* – The procedure depends upon the individual's ability to imagine vividly the feared situations or objects. Not everyone is able to do this. Some therapists use photographs of the feared object or situation or go straight to an *in vivo* procedure. Evidence suggests that *in vivo* procedures are more effective and longer-lasting than techniques using imagery (Emmelkamp 1994).

- *Quicker alternatives* – 'Flooding' is an alternative to systematic desensitization; a client is exposed to a feared object (e.g. spider) or situation (e.g. heights) without any gradation of exposure or attempt to reduce prior anxiety. Escape from the feared object or situation is prevented. Thus the therapist forces the person to continue to confront what causes the anxiety until the anxiety decreases. Such procedures are too traumatic for some people and the technique must be used with caution.

  In 'implosion therapy', the same principle of non-graded exposure to the feared situation is employed but using the *in vitro* technique. High levels of anxiety cannot be sustained indefinitely, and eventually anxiety disappears (implodes) because the client has suffered no harm. Both 'flooding' and 'implosion therapy' provide outcomes that are often as successful, but much quicker, than those achieved using systematic desensitization.

- *Symptom substitution* – Systematic desensitization is commonly used to treat phobias. Psychoanalysts argue, however, that a phobia is a symptom of an underlying condition and that when one phobia is removed by using a behavioural technique such as systematic desensitization, another will emerge to take its place. There is, however, little evidence to support this criticism of systematic desensitization.

Aversion therapy (behavioural approach)

Aversion therapy is another behavioural treatment based upon classical conditioning. It aims to rid an individual of an undesirable habit (e.g. excessive drinking) by pairing the habit with unpleasant (*aversive*) consequences.

Procedure in aversion therapy

Aversion therapy is used to deal with addictions such as smoking or alcoholism. For example, someone who wishes to stop drinking excessively may be given an alcoholic drink which is laced with an emetic (a nausea-inducing substance). After a few pairings of alcohol and feeling nauseous, the person will wish to avoid the smell or taste of alcohol.

Aversion therapy is one approach used to combat alcohol addiction

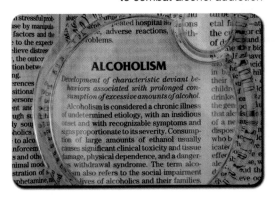

Alex (played by Malcolm McDowell), the sociopath protagonist in the film A Clockwork Orange, *is subjected to aversion therapy to 'cure' him of his violent tendencies. His eyes are clamped open, forcing him to watch an extremely violent film. Before watching the film, he has been given an emetic so that he learns to associate violence with feelings of nausea.*

HOW SCIENCE WORKS

Shaping behaviour through positive reinforcement

Isaacs *et al.* (1960) reported the case of a 40-year-old man with schizophrenia. For 19 years he had not spoken. By accident, someone noticed that he loved chewing gum. It was decided to use the gum as a reinforcement to get him to speak.

Initially, the gum was held up and if the man looked at it he was given the gum. This led to the patient paying attention to the therapist and looking at the gum as soon as it was taken from the therapist's pocket. The next step required that the patient move his lips when he saw the gum if he was to receive it. Next, he was given the gum only if he made a sound when he saw it. Once this behaviour was established, the therapist then asked him to say the word 'gum'. After 19 weeks, the patient said the word and six weeks later he spontaneously said 'Gum please'. Soon after this, the man began talking to the therapist. This approach is called behaviour shaping.

Adapted from Gross and McIlveen (1996)

Evaluation of aversion therapy

- *Research evidence* – Some studies have shown support for the claim that nausea paired with alcohol can result in conditioned aversions (e.g. Baker and Brandon 1988). However, there are doubts about the aversion being maintained after the negative pairings have been discontinued for any length of time.

- *Combined therapies* – Therapists who use aversive procedures tend also to use other more positive techniques to teach new behaviours to replace those that have been eliminated. Therefore, even if the effects of aversion therapy are short-lived, they may offer a 'window of opportunity' when other more appropriate behaviours can be learned.

- *Ethical issues* – Even when clients agree to a particular therapy, they cannot always anticipate what will happen during the course of the therapy and many psychologists are unhappy about inflicting pain or discomfort on people even when they asked for it. Critics of this and other behavioural therapies (e.g. flooding or implosion therapy) claim they are dehumanizing and unethical.

Behaviour modification (behavioural approach)

Behaviour modification is a procedure based on operant conditioning (see pp. 232–3). It aims to *modify* (change) behaviour that is antisocial or maladaptive by reinforcing appropriate behaviour and ignoring inappropriate behaviour. Behaviour modification has been used in institutions such as prisons, schools or mental hospitals. See panel 'Shaping behaviour through positive reinforcement'.

Token economy is a behaviour modification procedure where tokens are given when desirable behaviour is performed. The tokens can later be exchanged for goods or privileges. This procedure has been used to encourage self-care and social skills, for example, in people with learning disabilities.

Evaluation of behaviour modification

- *Research evidence* – Many studies have shown the effectiveness of token economy in changing behaviour. Isaacs *et al.*'s (1960) study of a man with schizophrenia is a case in point (see the panel on the left).

- *Institutional bias* – Critics of behaviour modification programmes such as token economy claim that whenever goals (appropriate behaviour) are imposed by others there is a risk that what is considered desirable is influenced by the needs of the institution rather than the well being of the individual.

- *Token learning* – Baddeley (1990) has warned that people whose behaviour has been shaped by reinforcement might not behave in the same way if the reinforcement is withdrawn. In other words, they become dependent on the token economy regime and find it difficult to think for themselves outside the institutional setting.

Cognitive Behavioural Therapy (cognitive approach)

The rationale behind Cognitive Behavioural Therapy (CBT) is that thoughts (cognitions) interact with and influence emotions and behaviour. If thoughts are persistently negative and irrational, they can lead to maladaptive behaviour. See pp. 234–6 for a description of the cognitive approach to psychopathology.

The aim of Cognitive Behavioural Therapy

CBT is aimed at encouraging people to examine the beliefs and expectations underlying their unhappiness and to replace irrational, negative thoughts with a more positive, adaptive pattern of thinking. Therapists and clients work together to set new goals for the clients in order that more realistic and rational beliefs are incorporated into their ways of thinking.

Procedures in Cognitive Behavioural Therapy

A therapy session involves both *cognitive* and *behavioural* elements, with homework between sessions.

- *Cognitive element* – the therapist encourages the client to become aware of beliefs that contribute to anxiety or depression or are associated with general dysfunction in daily life. This involves direct questioning, such as, 'Tell me what you think about …' Diagrams (such as the ABC model in Figure 7.6) can be used to help the client understand better where their faulty cognitions are leading them.

- *Behavioural element* – The client and therapist decide together how the client's beliefs can be reality-tested through experimentation, either as role play or as homework assignments. The aim is that clients will themselves come to recognize the consequences of their faulty cognitions. The client and therapist then set new goals for the client in order that more realistic and rational beliefs are incorporated into ways of thinking. These are usually in graded stages of difficulty so that clients can build on their own success.

Examples of Cognitive Behavioural Therapy

- *REBT* – Ellis (1962) developed Rational-Emotive Behaviour Therapy (REBT), using the ABC model (see Figure 7.6), based on his theoretical model of how psychological problems emerge. He claimed that REBT helps people to 'cure' themselves in an elegant way because they become less disturbed and less anxious and they maintain this over a long period, or even permanently. The ultimate aim is that REBT should be incorporated into a person's way of life, in order to overcome procrastination and eradicate self-defeating thoughts.

- *Beck's cognitive therapy* (Beck *et al.* 1985) – This is used mainly for people with depression and is aimed at training clients to monitor situations where they make negative assumptions. It encourages them to challenge these distorted thoughts and to take part in activities (such as logical question and answer sessions in which the client's irrational beliefs are challenged) that will help them to see that such assumptions are unfounded. Beck devised the 'Beck Depression Inventory' – an assessment scale for depression (Beck *et al.* 1961). From this other scales have been devised including the 'Suicide Intent Scale'. These scales are used by clinical psychologists to monitor depression in clients. Subsequently, Beck has applied his techniques to phobias, anxieties and personality disorders.

- *Meichenbaum's stress inoculation model* – Meichenbaum's (1972) stress inoculation therapy (SIT) has been widely used in stress management training and is discussed in Chapter 5 on p. 174.

- *CBT and treating schizophrenia* – In the main, cognitive-behavioural therapies are considered appropriate only for those who have developed good problem-solving skills and who are capable of gaining reasonable insight into their problems. However, both Beck and Meichenbaum see a role for CBT with schizophrenic patients. Hole *et al.* (1979) encouraged patients to reality-test

Figure 7.6
An example of the ABC model in action
Source: adapted from Ellis (1991)

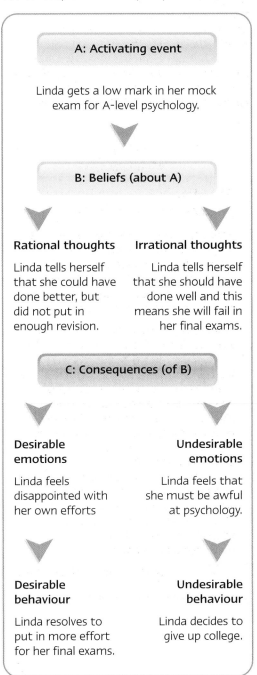

their delusions and found that half of the patients could reduce the pervasive (saturating) nature of their delusions. Cognitive-behavioural techniques for schizophrenia continue to be developed but they do not offer a cure, rather a way of 'normalizing' symptoms.

Evaluation of Cognitive Behavioural Therapies

- *Diverse applications* – Cognitive Behavioural Therapies are becoming more popular and diverse in their applications. They are increasingly becoming the most widely used therapy by clinical psychologists in the National Health Service, partly because they are short-term and economic. Cognitive behavioural therapies are used in stress management, as well as in treating educational, marital and family problems.

- *Appeal of CBT* – CBT appeals to clients who find insight therapies (e.g. psychoanalysis) too threatening. CBT could be criticized for not addressing underlying causes, but it does attempt to empower clients by educating them into self-help strategies. However, despite this, clients sometimes do become dependent on their therapist.

- *Use of CBT in treating depression* – Research shows that CBT is at least as effective as drugs in treating depression (Hollon *et al.* 1992). See key study by Fava *et al.* (1998) 'Combining drugs and CBT to treat depression' and then try the activity on the left.

- *Ethics* – CBT is a collaborative therapy that aims for a relatively equal relationship between the client and the therapist: the client and therapist together agree what the problem is and what the goals of therapy should be. This collaborative aspect of CBT exempts the therapy from the criticism sometimes levelled against psychoanalysis that the therapist holds all the power and expertise to 'make the client better'.

RESEARCH METHODS

Activity — **Combining drugs and CBT to treat depression**

1 What research method was used by Fava *et al.* in their study?

2 Identify the independent and dependent variables.

3 Why was it important to allocate patients randomly to the treatment conditions?

Answers are given on p. 278 ▶

Combining drugs and CBT to treat depression
A study by Fava *et al.* (1998)

RESEARCH METHODS

Aim	To see if using drug therapy followed by CBT reduced relapse rates for patients with depression compared with using drugs only.
Procedure	Forty patients, who had experienced at least three episodes of depression, were randomly assigned to one of two treatment conditions: ■ drugs followed by CBT ■ drugs and standard clinical management (including reviewing progress and giving advice if necessary).
Findings	During a two-year follow up: ■ 25% of patients who had drug therapy followed by CBT had relapses ■ 80% of patients who had only drug therapy and standard clinical management had relapses.
Conclusion	For some patients, CBT offers a successful alternative to long-term drug treatment for preventing relapse.
Evaluation	■ Previous studies have shown that drug therapy and CBT can be equally effective in treating depression (e.g. Hollon *et al.* 1992). However, using CBT and drug therapy at the same time (concurrently) produces no better results than administering either alone. This study, however, shows the advantage of administering the treatments sequentially (i.e. one after the other rather than at the same time) to help patients suffering from chronic depression. ■ A drawback of this study (along with other studies in this area) is the small sample size, which makes it difficult to generalize findings with confidence.

CHECK YOUR UNDERSTANDING

Check your understanding of treating abnormality by answering the following questions. Try to do this from memory. You can check your answers by looking back through Topic 2.

1 What is the aim of biological therapies?

2 Name three types of drugs used to treat mental disorders.

3 Outline one strength and one weakness of drug treatment for mental disorders.

4 What do the initials ECT stand for?

5 Outline the procedure used in ECT.

6 Give one advantage and one disadvantage of ECT.

7 What are the aims of psychoanalysis?

8 Briefly outline three techniques employed by psychoanalysts.

9 For what type of disorder is psychoanalysis thought to be appropriate?

10 Give two criticisms of psychoanalysis.

11 Outline the procedure used in systematic desensitization. On what type of conditioning is it based?

12 What is meant by *in vivo* and *in vitro* in systematic desensitization procedures?

13 Name two alternatives to systematic desensitization for treating phobias more quickly.

14 What is meant by aversion therapy? For what conditions might it be used?

15 Name one treatment based on operant conditioning. Give an example of when it could be used.

16 What do the initials CBT stand for?

17 Outline the main procedures used in CBT.

18 For what condition is Beck's cognitive therapy mainly used?

19 Give two reasons why CBT has become so widely used to treat mental disorders.

20 In what way has CBT helped individuals with schizophrenia?

Eye on the exam

We have just finished a detailed look at four different approaches to abnormality. You will now have a good understanding of where each of these models stands on the causes and treatments of abnormal behaviour. However, it is always wise to keep a careful eye on the exam and the kind of questions that could be asked. Note, this is not meant to be an exhaustive list:

1 Outline the key features of the biological (psychodynamic, behavioural, cognitive...) approach to psychopathology. *(6 marks)*

2 Outline one or more biological (psychodynamic, behavioural, cognitive...) therapy for treating abnormality. *(6 marks)*

3 Give two evaluations of the biological (psychodynamic, behavioural, cognitive...) approach to psychopathology.
(3 + 3 marks)

4 Discuss the biological (psychodynamic, behavioural, cognitive...) approach to psychopathology. *(12 marks)*

What does this tell us? Although you may know a great deal about a particular approach, in an exam you will only ever get the chance to offer a précis of that approach. A well-prepared student thinks ahead and can fit what they know to what is required in the exam. Look again at the questions detailed above and think what is actually required in response to each:

1 requires a précis of one of these four approaches concerning the causes of abnormality (you will, of course, need to be able to do this for all four models)

2 requires a précis of one of these four therapies concerning the treatment of abnormality

3 requires a short description of two evaluative points of one of these four approaches – remember evaluations can be positive as well as negative

4 requires a précis of one of these four approaches concerning the causes of abnormality together with an evaluation of that approach.

Performing well in an examination is only partly to do with having a good understanding of the material. It is also important to have good editorial skills, knowing what to leave out as much as what to put in. In the exam, you will write you answers on the exam paper. Space will be limited, so take care to choose your words carefully.

Practising these skills will pay off when you have to do it for real.

For more exam advice, visit
www.collinseducation.com/psychologyweb

Chapter 7: Summary

Psycho-pathology (Abnormality)

Biological approach to psycho-pathology

Biological approach

Mental disorders = physical disease

Causes

- Brain damage
- Infection
- Biochemistry
- Genes – family, twin, adoption studies

Evaluations

- Should be no blame, but mental disorders stigmatized
- Encourages passivity
- Research support
- Reductionist

Therapies

- **Drugs** – for anxiety, depression and schizophrenia)
- **ECT** – for severe depression
- **Psychosurgery** – for severe anxiety and obsessive-compulsive disorder

Evaluations

- Drugs:
  - sometimes effective but side effects
  - might treat only symptoms
  - ethical issues
- ECT
  - quick and sometimes effective
  - used to prevent suicide
  - mode of action unclear
  - ethical issues
- Psychosurgery
  - used as last resort
  - controversial

Definitions of abnormality

Definitions

Deviation from social norms

= Behaviour that violates explicit and implicit rules of what is acceptable in a society

Limitations

- Norms not fixed – change over time
- Abnormal, eccentric or criminal?
- Role of context including culture
- Risk of abuse

Failure to function adequately

= Inability to pursue normal activities

Limitations

- Not the whole picture
- Exceptions
- Direction of causality

Deviation from ideal mental health

= Deviation from characteristics required to meet Jahoda's six criteria for optimal living

Limitations

- Most people fail on some criteria
- Stress may be beneficial
- Culture bound by Western ideals of self-fulfilment and individuality

Psychological approaches to psycho-pathology

Psychodynamic

Abnormal behaviour caused by unconscious forces:

- Unresolved conflicts in psyche (id, ego and superego out of balance)
- Early traumatic experiences during stages of psychosexual development: oral, anal, phallic, latency, genital

> Little Hans case study

Defence mechanisms to protect the ego (e.g. repression)

Evaluations

- Influential
- Difficult to test scientifically
- Deterministic
- Problems with retrospective data
- Underestimates current difficulties
- Ethical issues

Therapy

Psychoanalysis – for anxiety disorders

- Dream analysis
- Free association
- Transference

Evaluations

- Expensive and time-consuming
- Limited usefulness
- Difficult to evaluate effectiveness
- Ethical issues – power disparity
- Criticized by behaviourists

Behavioural

Abnormal behaviours are learned by:

- Classical conditioning (CC)

> Little Albert case study

- Operant conditioning (OC)
- Social learning (observation)

Evaluations

- Focus on behaviour does not stigmatize individual
- Focus on functioning
- Ignores underlying causes
- Reductionist

Therapies

Systematic desensitization (based on CC) – for phobias

Aversion therapy (CC) – for addictions

Behaviour modification (OC) – for maladaptive behaviours

Evaluations

- Research support for systematic desensitization but implosion and flooding are quicker
- Some research support but ethical concerns over aversion therapy
- Research support for token economy but risk of institutional bias and token learning

Cognitive

Emotional problems caused by irrational thinking, e.g. overgeneralization, polarized thinking, catastrophizing

Beck's cognitive triad: negative thoughts about:

- self
- experiences
- future

Evaluations

- Research support
- Irrational thinking – cause or effect?
- Holds individual responsible

Therapy

Cognitive Behavioural Therapy

Two elements: cognitive and behavioural

Types of CBT:

- REBT – for anxiety/depression
- Beck's therapy – for depression, phobias and anxiety
- Stress inoculation therapy (SIT)

Evaluations

- Diverse applications
- Economic and quick
- Empowers clients
- Effective in treating depression
- Ethics – collaborative therapy

CHAPTER 8

Preparing for the AS examination

Introduction

It is our aim in this final chapter to give you the fullest possible understanding of how the AS examination 'works', including how questions are set and marked, so that you can prepare for the exam with this in mind. If you use this chapter in conjunction with the chapters that provide the psychological knowledge, topic by topic, you should be well prepared to achieve your best possible grade.

We will start by looking at the nature of the AS examination in Topic 1. Here we focus on the different types of questions that are set in the exam and the different skills they are designed to test (these are labelled AO1, AO2 and AO3). Topic 2 goes on to describe what examiners will be looking for when they mark your answers.

In Topic 3, we see how this works in practice by looking at some sample questions, together with examiner advice as to how you might approach these questions if you came across them in an exam. By focusing on what to do and what not to do, you will see how to achieve good marks in the answers you write.

Finally, Topic 4 contains 11 top tips for doing well in your psychology AS exam.

Topic 1: The nature of the AS examination

Assessment objectives

AS-level questions set for AQA Psychology Specification A assess three types of skill. These skills, which are known as 'assessment objectives', are:

- AO1: Knowledge and understanding of science and of *How Science Works*

- AO2: Application of knowledge and understanding of science and of *How Science Works*

- AO3: *How Science Works* – Psychology.

You will notice that *How Science Works* is referred to in each assessment objective. This phrase is used to describe the way that students are helped to understand how scientists investigate phenomena scientifically in their attempt to explain the world about us. To do this, you will need to develop and demonstrate your understanding of the following:

- the underpinning concepts, principles and theories that form the subject content

- the procedures associated with the valid testing of ideas and, in particular, the collection, interpretation and validation of evidence

- the role of the scientific community in validating evidence and also in resolving conflicting evidence.

There are two AS exams – Unit 1 (PSYA1) and Unit 2 (PSYA2) – and all the questions in each exam are compulsory, so there is no choice.

You will have $1\frac{1}{2}$ hours to answer each paper, and the total marks for each paper will be 72.

Assessment Objective 1 (AO1)

AO1 involves the *demonstration* of knowledge and understanding of science and of *How Science Works* through clear and effective communication. You should be able to:

- recognize, recall and show understanding of scientific knowledge
- select, organize and communicate relevant information in a variety of forms.

It is important to realize that knowledge and understanding are not the same thing. For example, I know that I have to press my foot down on the accelerator pedal to make my car go faster, but I must confess that I don't understand how this 'works', i.e. what actually happens as a result of 'putting my foot down'. Similarly, I may 'know' what the main features of Bowlby's theory of attachment are (see p. 120), but this knowledge may be quite superficial, with no real understanding underpinning it.

The best way to develop your understanding (which builds on your knowledge) is always to try to make notes and explain important ideas in your own words. If you can do this accurately and fairly easily, then you have almost certainly achieved a good understanding of a topic. If, however, you rely on rote learning, you will find it more difficult to shape your answer to the question asked. So, don't be tempted to rely on learning things off by heart in a list-like fashion. If you depend on memory, it may well let you down, especially if you are feeling anxious, but once achieved, true understanding will never let you down.

Assessment Objective 2 (AO2)

AO2 involves the *application* of knowledge and understanding of science and of *How Science Works*. To achieve this, you should be able to:

- analyze and evaluate scientific knowledge and processes
- apply scientific knowledge and processes to unfamiliar situations, including those related to issues
- assess the validity, reliability and credibility of scientific information.

Analysis, evaluation and application are the key skills here. Think of analysis as taking something apart, stripping it down to its basic elements and then carrying out a detailed examination of these. For example, we might look at whether a theory has research support, whether it fits the facts, and so on.

Evaluation involves making an informed judgement about the value or worth of something, or considering how it might be used, for example, to influence decision-making in society and possibly the formulation of social policy. For example, it is one thing to know the factual elements of Bowlby's theory of attachment, but quite another to make an informed judgement about the quality or worth of his theory. Making a judgement of worth about a theory entails a consideration of, for example, its application (an indication of its value) and whether it is subject to gender, age or cultural differences (an indication of its possible limitations as an explanation).

You may have noticed that the phrase used above was 'informed judgement'. This means that the judgement should be based on solid information and evidence and so can be substantiated. For example, the statement that 'Milgram's work was ethically unacceptable' is a form of evaluation, but has no substance. It requires a clear outline of the specific reasons *why* his research was ethically unacceptable.

The AQA specification also includes the criteria of validity, reliability and credibility under its AO2 heading. Validity and reliability were discussed in Chapter 2 (see p. 50) and are concerned with how much we can trust measurements taken in a study to be a true reflection of a particular behaviour (its validity) and a consistent reflection of that behaviour over time (its reliability). If either of these is lacking, then the credibility of a particular research study is reduced.

Assessment Objective 3 (AO3)

AO3 focuses entirely on *How Science Works* in psychology. To demonstrate your skills in this area, you should be able to:

- describe ethical, safe and skilful practical techniques and processes, selecting appropriate qualitative and quantitative methods
- know how to make, record and communicate reliable and valid observations and measurements with appropriate precision and accuracy, through using primary and secondary sources
- analyze, interpret, explain and evaluate the results and impact of investigative activities in a variety of ways.

AO3 tests the research methods part of the specification within the broader framework of *How Science Works*. It is your chance to demonstrate that you understand the research methods that psychologists use and can apply your understanding to the areas of psychology that are covered in Chapters 3 to 7 of this book. The exam questions assess your ability to think carefully about a piece of stimulus material. For example, you may need to consider *why* the researchers used a pilot study, or *how* the design of a research study could be improved, or *interpret* the information presented in a graph. Activities marked with a 'Research Methods' or '*How Science Works*' icon will provide plenty of practice in tackling AO3-type questions.

A word of advice

Remember, the AS exam is clearly structured around three distinct assessment objectives (AO1, AO2 and AO3), and examiners marking your work will allocate marks according to your success (or otherwise) in each of these. Note, however, that the same material can sometimes be used as description (AO1) and at other times as evaluation (AO2). For example, if you were asked to outline and evaluate the learning theory explanation of attachment, you would probably include the study of rhesus monkeys by Harlow and Harlow (1962). What transforms this study into evaluation is what you do with it. Merely describing this study shows knowledge and understanding (AO1), but stating that 'This study shows the limitations of the learning theory explanation because ...' turns it into AO2. It is very important to be clear about this distinction because time is short in the exam and you need to have thought of the different ways you can use material before you enter the exam hall.

Throughout this book, we have used an icon to highlight those activities which are specifically designed to develop your understanding of research methods and *How Science Works* (AO3). Don't be tempted to skip over these activities; they are crucial to your learning and preparation for the AS examination.

The structure of the examination

UNIT 1

The Unit 1 exam is divided into two sections and each of these sections is worth a total of 36 marks (72 marks in total). The two sections are outlined below.

Section A: Cognitive Psychology and Research Methods

This section includes all of the three assessment objectives (AO1, AO2 and AO3) in equal measures, each worth 12 marks. The subject matter is memory, but this can be assessed in the following manner:

- knowledge of models, research, etc., related to memory (AO1)

- evaluation of models, research, etc., related to memory (AO2)

- application of models, research, etc., to hypothetical situations (also AO2)

- research methods questions related to real or hypothetical studies of memory (AO3).

Section B: Developmental Psychology and Research Methods

This section also includes all three of the assessment objectives (AO1, AO2 and AO3) in equal measures, with each worth 12 marks. The subject matter is attachment, but this can be assessed in the following manner:

- knowledge of models, research, etc., related to attachment (AO1)

- evaluation of models, research, etc., related to attachment (AO2)

- application of models, research, etc., to hypothetical situations (also AO2)

- research methods questions related to real or hypothetical studies of attachment (AO3).

UNIT 2

The unit 2 exam is divided into three sections and each of these sections is worth 24 marks (a total of 72 marks). The three sections are outlined below.

Section A: Biological Psychology

- focuses on the topic of stress

Section B: Social Psychology

- focuses on the topic of social influence

Section C: Individual Differences

- focuses on the topic of psychopathology (abnormality)

As with Unit 1, each section assesses the skills of description (AO1), evaluation (AO2) and How Science Works (AO3), but this time they are not assessed in equal measures. AO1 and AO2 are each worth 10 marks, with 4 marks available for AO3.

Although the section headings for the Unit 2 exam do not explicitly refer to research methods, as they do in Unit 1, each of the three sections of the Unit 2 exam also include a 4-mark research methods element. For example, in Section B, an AO3 question might ask you to interpret a graph from a hypothetical study of conformity, or to comment on the ethical issues that emerged in Milgram's study of obedience.

Types of questions

The following are examples of the types of questions that are used to assess AO1, AO2 and AO3 (for a wider variety of question types see **www.collinseducation.com** and **www.aqa.org.uk**). In a $1\frac{1}{2}$-hour exam, you will be aiming for 72 marks in 90 minutes.

AO1 questions

These questions assess your *knowledge and understanding* of the material outlined in the specification. Examples of these questions are given below.

Table completion

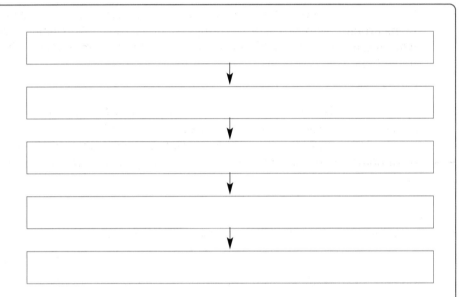

Place the phrases below in order to complete the diagram showing the pituitary–adrenal response to stress.

- Adrenal cortex releases corticosteroids into the bloodstream
- Corticosteroids produce changes in the body
- Higher brain centres perceive a situation as stressful
- Hypothalamus releases corticotrophin releasing factor
- Pituitary releases adrenocorticotrophic hormone

Describe/outline

Questions that ask you to describe something require a relatively detailed account of a particular theory, model or research study. Outline questions require a *précis*, which is a summary of the key elements and points relating to a particular model, study, feature, etc.

For example:

- Describe the learning theory of attachment.
- Describe the biological approach to psychopathology.
- Outline two explanations of attachment.
- Outline two reasons why people yield to majority influence.

In the examination, the terms 'describe' and 'outline' may well be used interchangeably, so the best guide as to the appropriate amount of detail in an answer is to look at the marks allocated to the question.

AO2 questions

AO2 questions involve *analysis*, *evaluation* and *application* of the material outlined in the specification. Examples of these questions are given below.

Analysis

AO2 questions test your ability to *evaluate* material and to apply this knowledge to new situations. The ability to *analyze* material is what makes your answers effective in this context.

For example:

> The passage below contains a statement about conformity. Identify whether this is an example of internalization or compliance and explain why this is the case. *(3 marks)*
>
> 'I started hanging round with the other lads from the estate. They were so cool I loved being around them. Some of the things we did, though, like nicking cars and smashing windows, made me feel a bit uneasy, but I had to do them because otherwise they'd make fun of me.'

In the first part of this question you are asked a simple AO1 question – is it internalization or compliance (it is compliance), which is worth just 1 mark. The second part asks you to analyze the passage, looking for clues as to why it is an example of compliance; this is the AO2 part of the question, which is worth 2 marks.

Evaluation

Other AO2 questions tend to be more traditional. For example:

- Explain **one** limitation of the use of drugs as a means of treating stress.
- Give **two** weaknesses of Milgram's study of obedience to authority.

In evaluative questions (as with all AO2 questions), it is important to go beyond merely identifying the critical point. Try to do three things:

1 Outline the critical point (e.g. 'Drugs have side effects').

2 Justify it (e.g. 'These were demonstrated in a study by…').

3 Answer the question 'so what?' (e.g. 'This means their effectiveness is diminished because people may stop taking them because of the unpleasant side effects').

Differences

Sometimes AO2 questions will test your ability to determine differences between two things. For example:

- Explain how the behavioural approach differs from the biological approach to psychopathology.

Another example is given at the top of the next page.

- Complete the following table by selecting six phrases and placing them in the appropriate column to indicate the key differences between problem-focused and emotion-focused coping.

Deals with stressor
Deals with distress
Deals with stress
Passive response
Active response
May involve denial
May involve taking control

Problem-focused	Emotion-focused

Application

AO2 questions will also test your ability to *apply* your knowledge. For example:

> Your younger brother is hanging around with other kids from the estate. You are worried about him getting into trouble, particularly when he tells you what they have been up to. From your knowledge of social psychology, suggest two ways that your brother might resist the pressure to conform, and explain why each of the two ways you suggest should help him adopt more independent behaviour.

In this type of question, marks are given not only for identifying appropriate ways of resisting pressures to conform, but also for appropriate elaboration – i.e. saying *why* these would work in this context. It is important to remember when answering such questions that you must always remember the context of the scenario, and make this clear in your answer.

AO1 + AO2 questions

Some questions are worth either 8 or 12 marks and they have equal measures of AO1 and AO2. In a 12-mark question, 6 marks are given for the AO1 content, and 6 for the AO2 content. It is important to remember this mark division when planning your response, so that half of your answer is AO1 and the other half is AO2. The examples that follow assume a 6+6 mark division between AO1 and AO2 (in 8-mark questions this would be 4+4 marks). Some questions make it very clear how you might divide your answer into description (AO1) and evaluation (AO2). For example:

- Outline and evaluate …
- Give a brief account of and evaluate …

Sometimes, however, it is up to you to decide how you will divide your answer into AO1 and AO2. For example:

- Discuss research into …
- Consider the view that …

It is always worth spending a couple of minutes looking carefully at exactly what the question is asking so that you are clear what is required, and then plan your answer carefully to reflect this, with the appropriate balance of description (AO1) and evaluation (AO2).

AO3 questions

These questions assess your ability to use your knowledge of research methods in the context of the material in a specific unit. In Unit 1, the AO3 questions are worth the same number of marks as the AO1 and AO2 parts of the question (see p. 253). In Unit 2, they are worth fewer marks, i.e. 4 marks per section. There are two main types of AO3 question, as described below.

1 Research methods questions that relate to studies included in the specification

Below is an example of a research methods question that relates to a specific study.

> Milgram's study of obedience was an example of an experiment in social psychology.
>
> 1 Identify **one** independent and **one** dependent variable used in Milgram's study. *(2 marks)*
>
> 2 Explain **one** advantage of using an experiment in this study. *(2 marks)*
>
> 3 Describe **one** ethical objection that has been raised concerning Milgram's obedience experiment. *(2 marks)*

2 Research methods questions that relate to hypothetical studies

An example of a research methods question of this type is shown in question 7 on p. 262.

Remember, for more practice on the different types of question that might be in the exams, go to **www.collinseducation.com/psychologyweb**.

Topic 2: How your work will be marked

A key factor of success is having a good understanding of what the examiners are looking for and how they will mark your work. An uninformed student will write, *hoping* that this is what the examiner is looking for, while an informed student will write, *knowing* that it is what the examiner is looking for.

Before they mark any exam papers, all examiners attend a one-day standardization meeting, during which they work through a large number of exam answers. They work alongside all the other examiners and are led by the Principal Examiners who set the question papers. This rigorous process ensures that:

- All examiners mark to the same standard, so it makes no difference which examiner marks your work. There is no such thing as a hard or soft marker!

- All the examiners mark to the same set of criteria and guidelines. This is important because these criteria are made public by the examining board, so you can know in advance what the examiners are looking for.

Before we look at the marking criteria, three other important general points need to be emphasized:

- Examiners mark according to a standard that it is reasonable to expect a notional 17 year old to display when working under exam conditions. They appreciate that you will be anxious and tense. They will also bear in mind that you have limited time at your disposal, are answering questions that you have only just encountered, and are not allowed to consult your books, notes, etc.

- In psychology, there is rarely a single, right answer (other than occasionally for research methods questions). Therefore, there is no single, correct answer to learn by heart when preparing for the exam and, perhaps most importantly, there is no single answer that the examiner is looking for.

- Examiners do not mark with pass or fail in mind. They do not even mark with grades in mind. Grades are decided by an Awarding Committee of examiners and teachers after the marking has been completed. Examiners award marks solely according to the marking criteria, which we will now explore.

Marking allocations

The summary tables below give an indication of where the marks come from in the extended questions, where 6 marks are available for AO1 and 6 for AO2. Smaller mark allocations will be distilled from these larger tables, so it is worth pointing out the different criteria for AO1 and AO2 marks here.

AO1 marking allocation

AO1 marks are awarded on the basis of four criteria:

- *Accuracy and detail* – Is the material accurate and how detailed is the description?

- *Knowledge and understanding* – Does the material reflect a good grasp of the topic?

- *Selection of material* – Is the presented material entirely appropriate for the question asked, or rather marginal?

- *Presentation of material* – Is the structure of the answer clear and coherent?

Table 8.1 Indicative summary of marks for AO1 (Knowledge and understanding of science and of *How Science Works*)

Marks	Accuracy and detail	Knowledge and understanding	Selection of material	Presentation of information
6	Accurate and reasonably detailed	Sound	Appropriate	Clear and coherent
5–4	Generally accurate, less detailed	Relevant	Some evidence	Appropriate
3–2	Basic	Some relevant	Little evidence	Appropriate
1	Very brief/flawed	Very little	Largely or wholly inappropriate	

AO2 marking allocation

AO2 marks are awarded on the basis of three criteria:

- *Use of material* – Are evaluative points used effectively? (e.g. Has the answer gone further than just identifying a critical point and shown *why* it is critical?)

■ *Range of issues/evidence* – Has a suitable balance between breadth and depth been demonstrated?

■ *Expression of ideas* – Have appropriate psychological terminology, correct grammar and spelling, etc., been used? (This is the 'Quality of written communication' element of your assessment.)

Table 8.2 Indicative summary of marks for AO2 (Application of knowledge and understanding of science and of *How Science Works*)

Marks	Use of material	Range of issues and/or evidence	Expression of ideas, specialist terms, spelling, etc.
6	Effective	Broad range in reasonable depth, or narrower range in greater depth	Clear and good range, few errors
5–4	Not always effective	Broad range in limited depth, or narrower range in greater depth	Reasonable, some errors
3–2	Basic	Superficial coverage of restricted range	Lacks clarity, some specialist terms, errors
1	Rudimentary	Just discernible	Poor, few specialist terms

AO3 marking allocation

You will remember that *How Science Works* (AO3) is referred to in each assessment objective and this is reflected in the AO1 and AO2 marking allocation tables (see Tables 8.1 and 8.2). Questions that examine AO3 skills are spread throughout the two AS exams – Unit 1 (PSYA1) and Unit 2 (PSYA2). Examples of the type of question that assess *How Science Works* (AO3) are given below:

> 1 Explain **one** disadvantage of ...   *(2 marks)*

To gain these 2 marks, you would need to state a disadvantage (1 mark) and then elaborate on that disadvantage in an appropriate context for the second mark (1 mark).

> 2 Identify **one** ethical issue in this investigation and explain how the researcher could have dealt with it.   *(3 marks)*

To gain these three marks, you would need to identify an ethical issue (1 mark) and then explain how the researcher could have dealt with the ethical issue within the specific context of the investigation that you have identified in order to gain further marks (2 marks).

> 3 Explain why studies of eyewitness testimony have been criticized as lacking validity.   *(5 marks)*

For questions such as this, a proportion of the marks available (e.g. 2 marks) are given for *identification* of validity problems for studies of eyewitness testimony (e.g. use of laboratory experiments, lack of realism). To gain the full 5 marks, however, there must be an *explanation* of why these threaten validity (e.g. in laboratory experiments, participants know it is not a real crime, so do not take it as seriously).

Topic 3: Sample exam questions with commentary

In this section, we will be reviewing a range of sample exam questions from Units 1 and 2, together with some examiner advice should you meet these or similar questions in *your* examination.

UNIT 1

Section A: Cognitive Psychology and Research Methods

Question 1: Examiner advice

As with all questions it is important to read this carefully. There is a requirement for *two* differences (that's 2 marks for each), and the question requires differences between STM and LTM rather than just two characteristics of each. For each difference there would be 1 mark for identifying the difference (STM is short-duration/LTM long duration) and a second mark for elaborating on this difference (a few seconds/more or less permanent). It is a good idea to link the two by the word 'whereas' to ensure you focus explicitly on differences between the two.

Question 2: Examiner advice

As with the previous question, there are two distinct requirements, so 2 marks each. Again, if there are 2 marks for each technique, the general rule, is 1 mark for correctly identifying a technique and second for elaborating on it within the context of the question (in this case examination revision). Consider the following answers on one of the two techniques required – which do you think would get 2 marks?

- Answer 1 – One technique that could be used is mnemonics such as ROYGBIV (Richard of York gave battle in vain) to remember the colours of the rainbow. This is Red, Orange, Yellow, Green, Blue etc., in the order they occur in the rainbow. This technique could be very useful for exam revision.

- Answer 2 – One technique could be the method of loci, associating each piece of information to be learned (e.g. parts of a psychological theory) with a specific physical location and then taking a mental 'walk' from location to location. In an exam, the student could simply revisit each location in turn and recall the different parts of the theory.

> **Question 1**
>
> Give **two** differences between short-term and long-term memory.
>
> *(4 marks)*

> **Question 2**
>
> A student at your school who is not studying psychology approaches you. She is worried about not being able to remember sufficient information in her forthcoming exams. Suggest **two** techniques that might help improve her memory, and explain how these would be helpful for examination revision.   *(4 marks)*

Question 3

In order to assess the effectiveness of the cognitive interview, two police forces were selected to take part in a field experiment to compare the use of cognitive and traditional interviewing of witnesses to non-violent crimes. The study took place over a six-month period, and Figure 1 shows the percentage of crimes that each force was able to solve over that time period.

(a) What is meant by a 'field experiment'?   *(2 marks)*

(b) Suggest a suitable directional hypothesis for this experiment.   *(2 marks)*

(c) What does Figure 1 tell us about the crime solution rates for the two types of interview?   *(4 marks)*

(d) Identify **two** possible weaknesses in the design of this study and suggest how these might be overcome.   *(4 marks)*

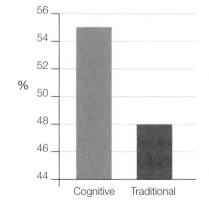

Figure 1 Crimes solved over 12-month period

Type of interviewing method used

Question 3: Examiner advice

(a) This straightforward question simply asks you to recall a definition of a field experiment, e.g. 'A field experiment is where there is an independent variable (e.g. the type of interviewing method used) but this is manipulated in a natural setting rather than in a laboratory'. If you find it difficult to recall textbook-style definitions, answer in your own words, and perhaps use an example to elaborate. Remember that the stimulus material can be a useful source of information for your example.

(b) In Chapter 2 (pp. 38–9), we emphasized the importance of phrasing hypotheses correctly. The hypothesis should state the predicted difference and operationalize all variables, i.e. 'Using a cognitive interview with witnesses of non-violent crimes leads to a higher crime-solution rate than using more traditional interviewing methods'.

(c) Here, you need a little more than the statement that 'the cognitive interview was better than the traditional interview', but there is no need for precise percentages. Ask yourself, 'better at what?' (i.e. percentage of crimes solved) and 'how much better?' (i.e. approximately 15 per cent more crimes solved). Don't fall into the trap of saying 'more than twice as many', because this isn't what the graph shows (pay attention to the scale used in the graph).

(d) As before, careful division of time will be necessary – two design weaknesses (1 mark each) and a suggestion how each might be overcome (1 mark for each). One weakness might be that the type of crimes being dealt with across the two police forces might be different and therefore harder to solve. This could be dealt with by matching two police forces based on the type of crimes dealt with over a previous 12-month period. A second weakness might be that the police doing the interviewing are different and may be more or less skilled at interviewing generally. This can be solved by using a repeated measures design, and using the same police for both types of interview.

Question 4: Examiner advice

This question contains both an AO1 ('Give a brief account of…') and an AO2 ('…and evaluate') component, so requires equal amounts of each. A question of this nature requires you to outline concisely the key elements of the multi-store model (see p. 89). This model is described at length in Chapter 3, but in the exam you will only be able to provide a brief account. It is important, therefore, to practise doing this by identifying the most important characteristics of this model.

For the AO2 component of the answer, you should aim for a balance of breadth (i.e. how many evaluative comments you make) and depth (i.e. how much you elaborate each). Higher marks are awarded for answers which address both breadth and depth. Thus, it is better to give two elaborated evaluative points than it is to give four or five more superficial ones.

> **Question 4**
>
> Give a brief account of, and evaluate, the multi-store model of memory.
>
> *(8 marks)*

Section B: Developmental Psychology and Research Methods

Question 5: Examiner advice

This type of question invites common-sense answers (e.g. 'that they are happy'), but they would get no marks. What is important in this question is the phrase 'based on your study of attachment behaviour', and so is testing your knowledge of research on secure attachment behaviour (see p. 124). An examiner would be looking for something like 'The mother is able to comfort the infant when distressed', and 'The infant feels able to explore strange environments when the mother is present'.

> **Question 5**
>
> Based on your study of attachment behaviour, identify **two** behaviours that a mother might look for to suggest that her infant is securely attached.
> *(2 marks)*

Question 6

Explain how the evolutionary explanation (Bowlby's theory) differs from the behavioural explanation of attachment.   *(4 marks)*

Question 6: Examiner advice

A common fault with many answers to this type of question is that they merely detail facts about each theory without considering how they actually differ. This is a typical AQA-style question, as you have not been taught how these explanations differ, it's something you have to work out for yourself. If you just list characteristics of each explanation without making the differences explicit, then the most you can hope for is 2 marks. It is your choice how many differences you cover – you are not asked for more than one, so one difference (such as innate programming versus learning or the possibilities for reversibility in each explanation) would suffice. If you don't have enough to say using just one difference, then add a second (or even a third).

Question 7

A researcher sets out to compare the effect of day nurseries on children's aggression. After first carrying out a pilot study, she visits four day nurseries in Lancashire and four in Surrey regularly over a period of six months. During her visits, she and her colleagues interview staff and mothers, and observe children at play. Based on the results of her interviews and observations, she collects data on the amount of time children spend in day care per week and the aggression rating given to each child (with 1 being not at all aggressive and 10 extremely aggressive).

(a) Suggest **one** conclusion that might be drawn from the data presented in the scattergram in Figure 2.   *(2 marks)*

(b) Give **one** strength and **one** limitation of using correlational data in this study.   *(4 marks)*

(c) The researcher also collected some qualitative data from her interviews with staff and mothers. Explain **one** advantage of using **qualitative** data in this study.   *(2 marks)*

(d) Suggest **two** reasons why the researcher would have used a pilot study.   *(2 marks)*

Figure 2 Hours of day care per week and aggression rating

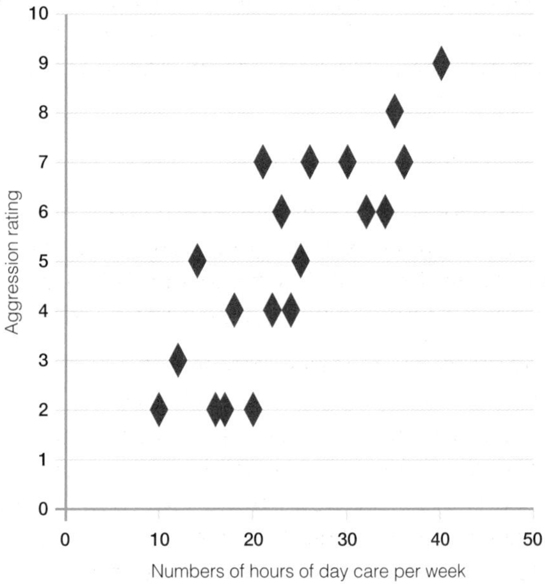

Question 7: Examiner advice

(a) It is important to distinguish between a 'finding' and a 'conclusion' here. A finding refers to the behaviour of the people that actually took place in the study. So among the children studied, there was a strong positive correlation between the number of hours' day care per week and the aggression rating of the children concerned. A conclusion from this would make a more general statement about what this finding tells us about the relationship between day care and aggression, which might be that the more hours of day care children have per week, the more aggressive behaviour they display. Mind the obvious trap here – this is a correlation, so you cannot make any statements about causality. Do not, therefore, conclude that day care makes children more aggressive.

(b) Note that this question asks for both a strength and a limitation (not two strengths or two limitations, although it is easy to miss that). It is vital to elaborate your answer in terms of the context of the study rather than just giving a answer on correlational data generally. So, for example, you might suggest that correlational data provides a measure of how strong the relationship is between day care and aggression (strength) so researchers can predict how aggressive a child might be with different amounts of day care (elaboration). Although there is a strong positive correlation between hours of day care and aggression, this does not mean that one caused the other (limitation), but that a third variable might have influenced both (e.g. parental stress) (elaboration).

(c) Remember that you must do more than just identify an advantage, but demonstrate why it would be an advantage in this particular study. Using qualitative data might 'allow the researcher to gather more in-depth data, e.g. she may discover information about the children's background that might explain why they act so aggressively'.

(d) The mark allocation here is a clue to the length of answer that is required. Just 1 mark is available for each reason, so one reason might be the need to check procedures, e.g. that she is asking the right questions, and a second might be to check that all researchers are assessing and recording data in the same way. In the exam, another important clue will be the space that is made available to write your answer.

Question 8: Examiner advice

As with question 4 earlier, this question requires equal amounts of AO1 and AO2. It is, however, slightly less straightforward to unpack, as there is no obvious split between the AO1 and AO2 components. This is only the case on first reading, as closer examination of this question should reveal what these are.

First, you are asked to present research into the effects of day care on children's development (see pp. 137–42) with peer relations and aggression being suggested as examples. You are then asked 'to what extent …', which does tend to throw students. However, what this means in practice is that having described your research, you can now consider whether this really does tell us anything worthwhile about the link between day care and social development. For example, you might evaluate the research in terms of its reliability, validity, applications (see pp. 144–5), research support, individual differences and so on. There is no need to come to a conclusion (which many people see as being required by the 'to what extent' instruction).

> **Question 8**
>
> To what extent has day care been shown to have effects on children's social development (e.g. relations with peers or aggression)?
> *(12 marks)*

UNIT 2

Section A: Biological Psychology

Question 1: Examiner advice

Students frequently get stressed when studying the underlying physiology of the stress response, but there is no need. Questions such as this are fairly low key, in that they merely ask for a précis of just one type of stress response (such as the pituitary–adrenal pathway, see p. 150). The easiest way to deal with a question such as this is to think of four main stages (e.g. higher brain centres detect stressor, hypothalamus releases CRF, pituitary releases ACTH, adrenal cortex releases corticosteroids into bloodstream). These can then be expanded into a four-mark answer. Remember that your answer is limited to the space available in the answer book, and that diagrams might be used if you find that helpful.

> **Question 1**
>
> Outline **one** way in which the body responds to stress. *(4 marks)*

Question 2

Anna is becoming increasingly stressed at work, particularly as she is constantly driven to meet deadlines and produce high-quality work. She finds it hard to cope and has started getting regular headaches. From your knowledge of workplace stressors, suggest **one** reason why Anna is experiencing such high levels of stress. From your knowledge of stress management, outline **one** way in which she might reduce these high levels of stress. *(4 marks)*

Question 3

In a study that compared the effectiveness of two different physiological methods of stress management, psychologists gave one group a drug known to reduce stress, and another group a placebo (i.e. a drug with no therapeutic value). They measured stress levels before and after the drug trials to see which had produced the greater change.

(a) Identify the independent and dependent variables in this study.
(2 marks)

(b) Identify **one** ethical issue in this study and explain how researchers should deal with it. *(2 marks)*

Question 4

Your younger brother is hanging around with other kids from the estate. You are worried about him getting into trouble, particularly when he tells you what they have been up to. From your knowledge of social psychology, suggest **two** ways that your brother might resist the pressure to conform, and explain why **each of the two** ways you suggest should help him adopt more independent behaviour. *(4 marks)*

Question 2: Examiner advice

There are two distinct parts of this question – why Anna is experiencing such high levels of stress and how she might reduce these. The question also states 'from your knowledge of workplace stressors', so would require something more than 'she has to work hard' or 'she should take it easy and have a day off'. Anna appears to be stressed because of pressure of work, but what has research told us about that? For example, Johansson *et al.* (see p. 164) found this to be one of the most stressful aspects of any job. Linking an assertion to a piece of supporting evidence is a useful way of elaborating a point and demonstrating your familiarity with the underlying psychology.

She could reduce her levels of stress in a number of ways, but your suggestions should be limited to actual techniques you have studied (e.g. stress inoculation training, see p. 174). It is important that your outline of stress inoculation takes into account the specific stressors faced by Anna, e.g. she would learn techniques for dealing with demanding employers, and learn how to recognize and deal effectively with the symptoms of stress related to her job.

Question 3: Examiner advice

(a) For 1 mark you do need not to be that thorough, but you still need to be accurate. So the IV is not just 'the drug' but 'the stress-reducing drug'. The DV is not just 'the stress levels' but 'the change in stress levels after treatment'. It is always wise to think carefully even about one-mark answers to ensure your answer matches the precise requirements of the question set.

(b) Simply saying something like 'They should get the participants' consent before they give them the drug' would not be enough to get 2 marks. The main ethical issue is perhaps informed consent (rather than just 'consent') and to 'get it' would involve 'informing participants of any potential risks of participation, and then asking them if they are willing to take part'.

Section B: Social Psychology

Question 4: Examiner advice

The key phrase is 'from your knowledge of social psychology', so you should resist the chance to offer advice from your own experience! If you revisit pp. 203–4, you can see that there are a number of suggestions how our fictional younger brother could resist the pressure to conform. These include finding social support (i.e. finding another person who does not want to engage in deviant behaviour) and prior commitment (i.e. people who commit to a particular point of view are less likely to change their mind later on). Note that this is just the first component of the question – you must also suggest why each of these might help him adopt more independent behaviour. For example, with the latter way, when he finds himself in a situation where he is under pressure to conform, he will have a reason for not doing the same as everyone else.

Question 5: Examiner advice

(a) Remember that 'conclusions' differ from 'findings'. The fact that male locus of control mean scores are 9.8 and female mean scores are 8.4 is not a conclusion but a *finding*. To make this into a conclusion means translating this into a more general statement about *all* males and females, i.e. males are more external in their locus of control compared to females, who are more internal. A second *finding* is that the standard deviation for female locus of control scores is higher than the standard deviation for male locus of control scores – but what general conclusion might you draw from this?

(b) There are 2 marks for this question, with the first being for a definition of the term 'investigator effects' (i.e. when some characteristic of the investigator or their behaviour affects the participants) and the second for a reason why they might be operating in this particular context. It is very important to bear the importance of context in mind here – merely saying that, for example, 'they might have smiled at one group more than another' is not in context, and so would not be worth the extra mark. However, saying 'the fact that the researcher is female may have affected the male and female participants differently, influencing their responses to the questionnaire' shows engagement with the study, and so would get the extra mark.

Question 6: Examiner advice

There is a temptation to unload everything you know about Milgram's obedience research and ignore the real purpose of the question, which is about the *validity* of such research. There are two main issues of validity in obedience research. The first of these is experimental validity, a measure of whether the procedures used in the study actually worked. The second issue concerns ecological validity, i.e. whether the findings can be generalized beyond the context of the investigation. The most effective way of answering this question is to outline the main arguments for a particular view (e.g. Orne and Holland claimed that participants saw through the deception; Milgram claimed the same processes were operating in his study as in real-life events such as the Holocaust). The AO2 component could then be a critical response to these claims, such as Milgram's argument that participants did believe the shocks were real, and Mandel's claim that Milgram's study did not explain the behaviour of Holocaust perpetrators (see p. 196).

Section C: Individual Differences

Question 7: Examiner advice

As explained on p. 251, *real* understanding means being able to demonstrate an in-depth knowledge of a particular concept that goes beyond just learning the examples given. From the coverage of definitions of abnormality on pp. 217–24, you would need to understand each sufficiently to work out why each of the examples given in the question would fit its 'parent' definition. Remember, sometimes there will be an extra choice on the table to avoid a merely random distribution of examples across the three definitions given.

Question 5

In an analysis of independent behaviour, a female researcher collects locus of control scores from male and female students to investigate whether there are any gender differences. The means, medians and standard deviations of these scores are presented in the table below (low scores are associated with internal locus of control, high scores with external locus of control).

	Mean	Median	Standard deviation
Males	9.8	9	1.6
Females	8.4	9	2.4

(a) Give **two** conclusions that might be drawn from the above table. *(2 marks)*

(b) This study might be criticized for its investigator effects. What is meant by the term 'investigator effects' and why might they be evident here? *(2 marks)*

Question 6

To what extent have studies of obedience been shown to lack validity? *(8 marks)*

Question 7

In the table below, place each behaviour with its appropriate definition of abnormality. *(3 marks)*

A Being unable to eat in front of others

B Making decisions merely to satisfy others

C Shouting at passers-by

Deviation from social norms	
Failure to function adequately	
Deviation from ideal mental health	

Question 8

(a) Explain the key features of the cognitive approach to psychopathology. *(6 marks)*

(b) Give **two** criticisms of the cognitive approach to abnormality. *(4 marks)*

Question 9

Becky is frightened of moths and butterflies and seeks help to overcome this fear. It is decided that systematic desensitization would be most appropriate.

(a) Which approach to psychopathology would be most likely to advocate the use of systematic desensitization? *(1 mark)*

(b) Explain how systematic desensitization might be used to cure Becky's fear of moths and butterflies. *(4 marks)*

Question 8: Examiner advice

(a) What, you might ask, do we mean by the 'key features' of an approach? For 6 marks, we might, as a very rough guide, expect about five to six separate points, each of about 15 words or so. The cognitive approach to psychopathology is covered on pp. 234–6, but an answer might include the following:

- The cognitive approach explains psychopathology in terms of distortions of thinking.
- These distortions include negative thoughts and irrational beliefs, such as the belief that everyone should like us.
- Beck claimed that depressed people drew illogical conclusions about themselves, particularly when things go badly. These negative thoughts lead to negative feelings and these can then lead to depression.
- The cognitive triad comprises negative thoughts about oneself, our experiences and about the future.
- This interferes with normal cognitive functioning, as the person becomes obsessed with negative thoughts.

This overview of the cognitive approach is sufficiently broad (five distinct points are made) and detailed to justify full marks. Giving examples, although they aid understanding, might be a bit of a luxury in an answer such as this, so description of the approach should take precedence.

(b) A simple and effective rule for criticisms is to (1) identify the criticism, (2) justify it, and (3) state what you can conclude from this criticism. With just 2 marks available for each criticism, you could identify and justify, or, alternatively, identify and state a conclusion. So, for example, the cognitive approach has been criticized because the cause of person's problems is seen as a problem of their own thought processes rather than the world in which they live (identification). As a result, this draws attention away from aspects of the environment (e.g. life events or family problems) that might be responsible for the disorder (conclusion). Similarly, the claim that distorted thinking is a feature of psychopathology is supported by research evidence (identification). For example, Gustafson (1992) found that cognitive distortions were evident in the thinking of people with a variety of disorders, including depression and sexual disorders (justification).

Question 9: Examiner advice

(a) You have studied a number of approaches to psychopathology, so hopefully you would recognize that systematic desensitization (see pp. 241–3) is an example of a behavioural approach. There is no need for anything other than just a simple statement of 'the behavioural approach'.

(b) You would find this type of question easier by simply listing the different stages of systematic desensitization rather than writing in terms of continuous prose. Two points are particularly relevant here. First, you should remember that your answer should be in context, so frequent mention of Becky and her fear of moths and butterflies is necessary to stay focused. Second, you are not asked to evaluate this technique, so don't waste your time doing so.

- Becky would first be taught to relax.
- She and the therapist construct a fear hierarchy, beginning with a cartoon and moving up to the most feared scenario, a butterfly in her hair.
- She works through the stages whilst practising relaxation. When relaxed at one stage, she is moved to the next step.
- Because fear and relaxation are incompatible, eventually she will have overcome her fear of moths and butterflies.

Topic 4: Doing well in the exam – 11 tips for success

Exam tip 1: Look for clues within the exam questions

It is important to remember that there are crucial clues within an exam question that will help you to answer it.

- The *language of the question* will give you a clear indication as to which skills – description or evaluation – the question is assessing. Look back to the section in this chapter on the different types of question (see pp. 254–6).

- The *structure of the question* will give you a clue as to how to organize your answer. Make sure that where a question is divided into parts, you read all parts before you attempt to answer, so that you are certain to answer each part of the question appropriately.

- The *mark allocation* will guide you as to how much content to include in your answer and also the depth of answer required.

- The *space provided* for you to write your answer will also give you a very clear indication as to what is considered an appropriate length for your answer.

So, if you are given 4 marks and 10 lines, don't answer in a single sentence, and if you are given 2 marks and just a few lines, don't try to cram in hundreds of words. Remember, always look carefully at the number of marks on offer and the specific demands of the question, and ensure that you tailor your answer to both of these and answer within the specific context of the question rather than giving a general answer.

Exam tip 2: Organization and planning

One of the best examples of efficient preparation concerns organization and planning. Good students break their work up into manageable chunks and set themselves goals to achieve. These goals may correspond to what your tutor will know as 'learning outcomes'. Examples would be:

- 'By the end of my revision today I will be able to write an accurate and detailed description and evaluation of Bowlby's maternal deprivation hypothesis.'

- 'By the end of my revision today I will be able to explain physiological approaches to stress management.'

It helps to make a chart so that you know exactly what you need to demonstrate in the exam. We have included revision summaries at the end of each topic so you can do this. For Developmental Psychology, Topic 1, your revision summary can be broken down and set out in a chart in the format shown in Table 8.3 on the next page.

Table 8.3 Possible format for a revision summary

	Tick if you could make only a basic attempt	Tick if you could make a reasonable attempt	Tick if you have complete mastery of this
Definition of attachment			
Definition of secure attachment			
Definition of insecure attachment			

By breaking your topics into small and more tangible skills, you can keep a careful eye on your own progress. The three columns roughly equate to the division of marks, so a *basic* performance might get you 1 out of 3 marks or 2 out of 6 marks. A *reasonable* performance might get 2 out of 3, or 3/4 out of 6 marks, and a *good* performance would get 3 out of 3, or 5/6 out of 6. It may help motivate you to know that it is possible to get a Grade A on just two-thirds of the marks available, so don't get too dispirited if you don't get too many ticks in the third column. You must, however, aim for at least a tick in the second column for every item.

Setting yourself tangible targets will motivate you and will help you keep a check on how you are progressing, what you have achieved and what still remains for you to do. Two final points:

- Don't set yourself huge, impossible goals, e.g. 'Tonight I will learn everything about abnormality'.

- Remember to revisit what you have already learned. If skills and knowledge are not regularly re-addressed and reviewed, they can decay. This review often only takes a matter of a few minutes. Do this regularly for maximum impact.

Exam tip 3: Gain access to materials

The AQA examining board (at Stag Hill House, Guildford, Surrey GU2 5XJ) makes available a wide range of support material for the AS examination: specimen examination papers, marking schemes, suggestions for reading, and much, much more. Most of this is written for tutors but if you believe (as I think you should) that you should make sure that as much of your future is in your own hands as possible, then reading these will put you in the driving seat. The Chief Examiner writes a highly detailed report at the end of each exam series and by reading this you will be aware of the shortcomings of fellow students in the previous exam and so be able to avoid these yourself. Most important of all, get yourself a copy of the relevant specification for this exam. Know the specification and there will be no unpleasant surprises in the exam. You can download this free from **www.aqa.org.uk** (follow the links to Qualifications).

Exam tip 4: Use a wide variety of sources

Of course the writers of this book want to include everything possible that you will need in order to do well, but it is always good practice to cast your net wide. There are a number of magazines and periodicals written for psychologists and psychology students, and you should aim to make good, intelligent use of the Internet. As well as a lot of unmitigated junk, the Internet also contains a wealth of superb and bang-up-to-date material which cannot fail to impress your examiner, as well as increasing your interest and involvement with the topic. You may, of course, find some of the material held on these sites to be quite advanced (a good deal will be written for undergraduates and professionals) but there *will* be plenty to interest and help you.

Exam tip 5: Get plenty of exam practice

There is no substitute for practising the skills on which you will finally be assessed, in the actual situation in which they will be assessed. If you practise answering questions from mock papers under exam conditions – no books, with time limits, answering questions you have not seen before – every week during your revision, building up to the exam, the exam will hold no terrors for you.

As the exam approaches you should spend at least two hours a week doing 'mock exams' on your own. Your teacher will be able to supply you with typical exam questions and you should aim to work on these under exam conditions, two questions in one hour, with no books and so on. When you have finished, you should check your answers through – with your books this time – and see how accurate and detailed your answers are. If you read the sample answers and examiner comments, you and your friends can assess each others' answers and talk about the merits and shortcomings of each one. It may be a bit embarrassing to start with, but it soon gives you mastery over the assessment side of the specification.

Exam tip 6: Know what will come up in the exam

We have already discussed the skills and content areas you will need to know about, but we can be even more specific. The detail of the specification shows exactly what you need to know. Put simply, if it's not in the specification, it can't be in a question.

If you have a copy of the specification, you can get inside the head of the Principal Examiner who sets the questions for each examination. He or she does not try to trip you up, but merely samples different areas of the specification for each examination. Remember that you cannot ignore *any* part of the specification because each subsection (e.g. stress as a bodily response, stress and illness, stress management) is sampled in every examination. However, because questions are set to the wording of the specification, you have a pretty good idea what a question in a particular area will look like. Try the activity on the right.

Activity Predicting exam questions

Use the information in Topic 1 in this unit to work out what questions could be asked for the following subsection of the specification, and compare your list with that of a friend.

Defining abnormality

Definitions of abnormality, including deviation from social norms, failure to function adequately and deviation from ideal mental health, and limitations associated with these definitions of psychological abnormality.

Exam tip 7: Answer the question

This may sound obvious – even patronizing – but many candidates simply don't answer the questions set. Some candidates seem to think that the actual wording of a question doesn't really matter too much, as long as they write an answer 'in the general area'. Others seem to prepare too rigidly and go into the exam hall simply intent on reproducing 'prewritten' answers. For whatever reasons, the answers do not 'fit' the questions. You must go into the exam hall prepared to be flexible and deal with the specific demands of the paper in front of you.

To use two analogies, *don't* think of yourself as an actor in a play whose task it is to repeat the lines they have learned, word perfect. *Instead*, think of yourself as a doctor who has to deal with whatever comes your way in a particular surgery session.

Make sure you read the questions carefully, and don't start writing your answers until you have really thought about what you are being asked to do and planned your responses. Remember, it isn't just what you put into your answers; it's also to do with what you leave out. Almost certainly you will know a lot more

Outline and evaluate the use of biological therapies for the treatment of abnormality. *(12 marks)*

psychology than you can write down in the exam. The trick is to make sure that you offer the examiner those parts of your psychological knowledge that are most relevant to the questions in front of you. Don't fall into the trap of writing what you want to; write what the examiner wants.

Exam tip 8: Plan your answers carefully

Some questions have both descriptive (AO1) *and* evaluative (AO2) components, so it is important to spend time planning how you will tackle these questions so that you address each (equally weighted) component.

The two-paragraph technique

This is probably the most straightforward way of responding to these questions. Remember that these questions (usually worth either 8 or 12 marks) are one-half AO1 and one-half AO2. By presenting all your AO1 material in the first paragraph and your AO2 in the second paragraph, you can be confident that you have the right balance, making it more likely that you achieve more of the marks available for these two skills. Take the example question on the left.

- Paragraph 1: An outline of the use of drugs and ECT.

- Paragraph 2: An evaluation of the use of drugs and ECT.

In order to construct an entirely AO2 paragraph, you have many alternative forms of critical commentary. You may, for example, look at research support (or challenge), gender or cultural differences (which limit the universality of a particular theory or finding), useful applications, ethical issues and so on.

Another advantage of using this approach is that you can impose some clear time and space divisions on your work. In a 12-mark question, if you allow about 100 words per paragraph (in our example above, this would mean 50 words on drugs and 50 on ECT and the same for AO2), this can seem far less intimidating than having to write a mini-essay (of 200 words) just on biological therapies. Remember that the amount of physical space allocated for each question is determined by the answer book, but how you divide that space is in your hands.

Working backwards from your conclusion

If you want to get somewhere, it is often a good idea to use a map to find the place you are going to, and then work backwards in an attempt to plan your route. Take a look at the question above – what do you think of biological therapies? Are they good, bad, or are there good points and bad points? Think about this for a while, and then decide what arguments you will put together to justify that conclusion. There are three stages to this approach:

- What is my conclusion?

- What evidence would lead to that conclusion? This might be research evidence that supports your point of view or challenges the views of others. It might be the views of critics or supporters of this point of view.

- What arguments (or evidence) might I encounter along the way, and how would I discount them?

Finally, and perhaps most importantly, when thinking about the AO2 component of an answer, is the *effective* use of material. This is often what causes students the most problems. Students frequently *describe* relevant studies rather than use them as part of a critical argument (e.g. that a study supports or perhaps *challenges* a theory). The examiner may be aware that there is a link between the study and the point the candidate was trying to make, but the student does not actually make that link explicit! In other words, the student has the material, but does not use it effectively to answer the question.

Exam tip 9: Good time management

It is important to your exam success that you allocate your time carefully so that you spend an equal amount of time on each section of the exam paper, as these earn equal marks. This includes reading the questions, planning your answers and then checking them at the end.

Good time management is, therefore, essential, because without it you will find yourself spending too long on questions that do not have the marks available to justify the extra time, and then (inevitably) too little time will be left for the questions that do. You should aim to move on at the appropriate time points throughout your exam to ensure that you answer all the required parts, and don't run out of time because you have spent too much time on earlier questions. You can always revisit a question if you have time left at the end of the exam.

Exam tip 10: Dealing with research methods

On the AS psychology examination, the assessment of research methods is of key importance. As you read through this book, pay attention to the specific details of a study. Some studies are experiments, some observations; some rely on questionnaires and others on correlational data. You may well be asked to comment on why a particular method was best for a particular study or what might be the strengths or weaknesses of that particular approach. One thing is certain, however: you will need to discuss this within the context of that particular study. So, if you were asked what were the advantages of using a natural experiment as the most appropriate approach to a study looking at the effects of stress on the immune system, you would not just list the *general* advantages of natural experiments, but tailor your answer to that particular context.

Questions do tend to be very specific, so look carefully for *how many* of something you are being asked for (e.g. 'one' 'two' or perhaps 'one strength and one weakness'). Given that so many marks are available for research methods (particularly on Unit 1), this is a skill you need to practice – so why not generate your own questions, and swap them with your friends. You will eventually be heartily sick of doing research methods questions, but you will have developed a very valuable skill.

Exam tip 11: Remember what you have learned

For this final tip, we could suggest stress management techniques, memory improvement strategies, a healthy diet, clever use of revision groups, and so on, but one of the most important parts of this course is that you should be able to apply what you have learned to real life. We always tell psychology students that they have an important advantage over other students because they are studying themselves. In this course, you have learned how your memory works, as well as how to improve it. In biological psychology, you have learned about sources of stress (such as exams), about emotion-focused and problem-focused coping, and about effective forms of stress management. In social psychology, you will have learned techniques for avoiding the pressure to conform to your non-studious friends, and in individual differences you will have discovered that failure is merely a state of mind. So, for exam tip number 11, you should take heed of your own advice by applying your psychological knowledge and insights when studying and also when preparing for, and sitting, an exam.

Answers to activities

Chapter 1: Psychology, psychologists and research methods

Identifying independent and dependent variables, p. 15

1   IV – the acoustic similarity of the words
    DV – serial memory recall scores

2   IV – level of difficulty of the anagrams (i.e. easy and difficult)
    DV – memory retention (i.e. memory scores)

3   IV – location of the memory test/instructions to imagine a particular environment
    DV – the number of words correctly recalled.

The Stroop effect, p. 16

1   The IV is whether the stimulus sheets consisted of coloured words or coloured ink blocks.

2   The DV is the time taken to name the ink colours.

3   There were two conditions: experimental and control.

4   The data were quantitative.

5   The findings suggest that when colour names are written in a conflicting ink colour, it takes longer to name the ink colour than when the ink colour is presented as a block.

Bowlby's '44 thieves' study, p. 21

1   Bowlby's study of 44 juvenile thieves is a correlational study (a study using a correlational analysis) carried out in a child guidance clinic.

2   Bowlby was testing the maternal deprivation hypothesis. He was interested in whether a disrupted early childhood, including separation from their mothers, was associated with later behavioural disorders, including 'affectionless psychopathy'.

3   The findings did support the hypothesis: they suggested a link between early separation/maternal deprivation and later behavioural maladjustment, including – in its most severe form – affectionless psychopathy.

4   Correlational data.

5   No: correlational data highlight an association (relationship) between variables, but do not allow us to claim a causal relationship.

6   It would not be possible to design a true experiment to establish whether the relationship between early separation/maternal deprivation and subsequent social and emotional maladjustment is causal. Having identified a possible link between early deprivation and subsequent social and emotional maladjustment, it would not be ethical to allocate young children randomly to either a group that experienced early separation group or a control group that did not. At best, a natural experiment could be designed, but the loss of control of the independent variable (early deprivation) would mean that a causal relationship could not be unequivocally demonstrated.

Rosenhan's study, p. 23

1   Rosenhan's observational research involves undisclosed participant observation.

2   The findings of Rosenhan's study suggest that the ongoing diagnosis of mental illness, once a patient had been admitted to hospital and labelled as 'schizophrenic', was not based on observed symptoms of schizophrenia, but rather on staff expectations that people in a psychiatric hospital are mentally ill. The lack of symptoms therefore went unnoticed.

3   Given the role they played, we can assume that the eight participants (the 'pseudopatients') gave their fully informed consent to take part in Rosenhan's study. However, the hospital staff were not aware they were participating in an observational study and that things they said and noted in the records of the 'pseudopatients' were being recorded as data in the study. As a hospital is not a public place, where those being observed would expect to be observed by strangers, the staff involved might claim that Rosenhan had not respected their privacy and psychological wellbeing.

    Using today's ethical guidelines, the staff would need to be debriefed and the nature of the deception disclosed at the earliest possible opportunity. The staff would have the right to request that their data were excluded from the study and destroyed. Professional support and advice would need to be offered to any staff who, following debriefing, became distressed by their involvement in the study. All the research data should remain confidential and the anonymity of all those involved should be protected in any report of the research.

4   If Rosenhan's study were to be replicated, it might produce similar results if diagnostic practices have not changed much since the 1970s. In that case, the expectations of staff would again prevail. However, if the results of Rosenhan's study have been widely discussed as part of the education of health professionals working in psychiatric hospitals, then the effects of labelling and expectations should no longer be as powerful and the results of a replicated study might be different. The lack of schizophrenic symptoms in the pseudopatients while in hospital might be noted and their *true* status recognized.

Chapter 2: Investigation design, data analysis and presentation

Writing hypotheses, p. 39

See the table below.

Study	Alternative hypothesis	D or ND	Null hypothesis
Loftus (1979) – a study of the role of anxiety in eyewitness testimony	People who experience anxiety when witnessing an event will differ in their accuracy when recalling that event compared with people who do not experience anxiety.	ND	There is no effect of anxiety when witnessing an event on the accuracy of eyewitnesses' recall of that event.
Godden and Baddeley (1975) – an experiment to investigate the effect of retrieval context on learning	Divers who learn and recall words in the same context will have better recall of the words than divers who learn words in one context and recall them in a different context.	D	Divers who learn and recall words in the same context will *not* have better recall of the words than divers who learn words in one context and recall them in a different context.
Kiecolt-Glaser et al. (2000) – a study of chronic stress	People who provide long-term care for their spouses will show poor immune function compared with similar people who do not act as caregivers for their spouses.	D	There will be no difference in immune function between those who provide long-term care for their spouses and those who do not.
Johansson et al. (1978) – a study of stress in a Swedish sawmill	Work stressors increase stress-related physiological arousal and the incidence of stress-related illness.	D	There is no effect of work stressors on stress-related physiological arousal and the incidence of stress-related illness.
Moscovici et al. (1969) – a study of minority influence	There will be a difference in the influencing effect on visual judgements of a consistent minority compared with an inconsistent minority.	ND	There will *not* be a difference in the influencing effect on visual judgements of a consistent minority compared with an inconsistent minority.

Identifying the design used in research studies, p. 44

▪ The study of the duration of very long-term memory by Bahrick et al. (1975) is an independent groups design: some participants were asked to *recognize* the names of the people in the photos from a list of potential names, while other participants were asked to name the people in the photos without being given a list of potential names (the *recall* group). A potential weakness associated with this independent groups design is that there may be individual differences in the memory ability of the two groups that could affect the memory scores. However, since a large number of participants were tested (N=392), individual differences in memory ability should be eliminated by random allocation of participants to the two groups.

An alternative would be a matched pairs design, whereby the researcher would match participants in each group for their memory ability at the start of the study. This would retain the benefits of an independent groups design (i.e. no order effect), but would eliminate the potential confounding variable of memory ability.

▪ The study of the effects of stress on the immune system by Kiecolt-Glaser et al. (1984) is a natural experiment, using a repeated measures design (blood samples were taken at two points from all participants). Although some students may have experienced other stressors besides their exams during the investigation, the confounding impact of any such additional stressors would be minimized due to the use of a repeated measures design.

An independent groups design could have been used, but with only 75 participants, fewer data would be available for analysis, and the effect of any additional stressors would have a greater confounding effect on the findings. With only a relatively small pool of 75 medical students, it would not be possible to match the students effectively for a matched pairs design.

▪ Glanzer and Cunitz's 1966 study of the multi-store model of memory employs an independent groups design. A potential weakness of this design is the individual differences between the groups that could affect the recall scores. A repeated measures design could be used and would overcome this weakness, in which case counterbalancing could be employed to avoid order effects.

▪ This natural experimental study of stress in a Swedish sawmill by Johansson et al. (1978) is also an independent groups design. Possible weaknesses include the very small number of 24 self-selected participants (an opportunity sample) for an independent groups design – 14 'finishers' and 10 cleaners. With such small numbers, important individual differences between the two groups are possible (see the Evaluation section of the key study on p. 164) which could affect the results of the study. However, no alternative design could have been used.

Observing and recording interactions, p. 45

This type of activity could be used to study the interpersonal relationships within small groups, such as committees (e.g. in education or industry) that make recommendations or take decisions. Observing and recording interactions in such groups provides insight into who is most influential and who is least influential in decision-making.

Your views on the BPS *Code of Ethics and Conduct*, p. 54

The key ethical issues that need to be considered in any psychological study involving human participants include:

- informed consent
- confidentiality and anonymity
- the right to withdraw from a study part way through
- use of deception
- the protection of participants (including privacy and psychological wellbeing, the risk of harm, protection from stress, the use of inducements, availability of professional advice/support)
- debriefing.

1 If all psychologists were to follow the detailed guidance in the British Psychological Society (BPS) *Code of Ethics and Conduct* then the interests of all those who participate in psychological research in the UK should be fully protected.

2 Researchers who are members of the BPS and who seriously violate the *Code of Ethics and Conduct* would be expelled from the BPS, which could have serious consequences for their future employment. However, at present, a psychologist undertaking research is not required to be a member of the BPS. If a psychologist is not a member of the BPS, then there are no sanctions that can be applied against them if they do not follow the ethical guidance issued by the BPS.

Protection is also provided by ethics committees, which vet research proposals and can ensure that ethical guidance is followed. An ethics committee will not give its formal permission for a study to proceed if it decides that the research does not demonstrate the required ethical standards. Furthermore, if a researcher does not follow the procedures that were agreed by the ethics committee, this is formally reported to the organization that sponsored the research. The final sanction is that the organization concerned would not be permitted to sponsor any further research.

3 The studies carried out by Milgram and Zimbardo still remain highly controversial today. Some would argue vehemently that the research was unethical and should never have been carried out. Others might argue that the implementation of safeguards around the use of deception, careful debriefing, emphasizing participants' right to withdraw at any time during the study, and the provision of professional advice and support following debriefing, are sufficient for the study to proceed. Their view would be further strengthened by the argument that there is no other means of obtaining such important scientific insights into obedience to authority, so the outcome (important new knowledge) justifies the means, as long as ethical guidance is meticulously followed.

Ethical issues, p. 58

Ethical issues you could have chosen to discuss include the following:

- In a laboratory experiment: using deception; risks of psychological harm; lack of informed consent.
- In a naturalistic observation: lack of informed consent; invasion of privacy; difficulty of debriefing.
- In a study using questionnaires: importance of confidentiality if anonymity is not possible; protection from harm; importance of consent and right to withdraw data; debriefing and support.
- In interview research: similar issues as for questionnaires, plus risk of humiliation (psychological harm).
- In case study research: same issues as arise in observations and interviews, as well as the risk of excessive intrusion.

Presenting data, p. 63

Figure 2.12
Graph produced by salesperson

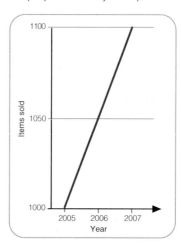

Figure 2.13
Graph produced by management

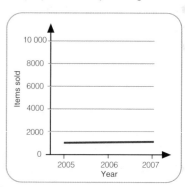

Measures of central tendency: advantages and weaknesses, p. 69

Definition	Advantages	Weaknesses
Median The middle value of a set of numbers that have been placed in numerical order	• Unaffected by outlying values • Useful when data sets are skewed • Can be used with ordinal data	• Should not be used with small data sets • Easily affected by any change of central values in a data set
Mean The arithmetic average	• Makes use of all available data (unlike the median or mode) and therefore the most powerful measure of central tendency • Most appropriate measure for interval or ratio data	• Decimal points in calculated means may lack meaning if all the original data are whole numbers • Often inappropriate for use with ordinal data • Unsuitable for data sets that have extreme outlying values (median is preferable in these circumstances)
Mode The value in any set of scores that occurs most frequently	• The mode is a figure that always occurs in a sequence (unlike the mean or the median) • Easy to identify • Can be calculated from any type of data, including nominal data	• Very small changes in a data set can radically alter the mode • There may not be a single mode – the bimodal value may still be useful, but the more modes in a data set, the less useful the measure • Reveals nothing about other values in the distribution

Chapter 3: Memory

Difference between findings and conclusions in research studies, p. 83

These were the conclusions from Peterson and Peterson's (1959) study:

1 STM is very short (only 20 seconds approximately) if we are unable to repeat what we are trying to remember.

2 Maintenance rehearsal is necessary to prevent information vanishing rapidly from STM.

3 Information in STM is lost through decay (i.e. it fades away) if maintenance rehearsal is prevented.

Conrad's study of acoustic confusion, p. 84

1 A well-designed experiment allows a researcher to draw conclusions about the cause-and-effect relationship between the independent variable and the dependent variable. Conrad concluded that the nature of the stimuli (i.e. whether or not the letters sounded similar) affected the accuracy of participants' recall. Because people confused letters that sounded alike, he concluded that they used acoustic encoding in STM.

2 Independent variable – type of consonants.
Dependent variable – number of recall errors made by the participants.

3 An appropriate hypothesis: Participants will make more errors when trying to recall acoustically similar consonants than when recalling acoustically dissimilar consonants.

4 This study was a laboratory experiment that used artificial stimuli, not necessarily reflecting what we try to remember in everyday life. The study could, therefore, be criticized for lacking ecological validity.

Natural experiments, p. 87

1 The IV was the different number of years that the participants had lived since graduating from high school and being asked to recognize faces of classmates.

2 Because this IV was naturally occurring and not controlled by the researchers, we cannot be entirely confident that it is solely responsible for any differences in recognition rates between the groups (the DV).

Differences between STM and LTM, p. 88

	Capacity	Duration	Encoding
STM	Very limited: 7 ± 2 chunks of information or what can be articulated in 2 seconds	Very short – a matter of seconds	Mainly acoustic (by sounds)
LTM	Unlimited	Potentially up to a lifetime	Mainly semantic (by meaning)

Evidence in support of the multi-store model, p. 91

1 Recalling the words immediately or after a 30-second delay.

2 The number of words correctly recalled.

3 Unlike the immediate recall group, the delayed recall group showed no recency effect.

The interactive flow of information between STM and LTM, p. 91

1 Enthusiasms or special expertise may be used to increase the capacity of STM. Experts (such as football enthusiasts in this case) can draw on their knowledge (e.g. about the results of past matches) held in LTM to help retrieve information from STM, thus showing a flow of information from LTM to STM.

2 Chess experts are better than non-chess players at recalling (from STM) the positions of chess pieces on a board, given the pieces are placed in positions that the rules of chess permit. They can draw on their knowledge (held in LTM) about possible patterns of chess pieces.

Christianson and Hubinette (1993), p. 98

1 A natural experiment.

2 By collecting evidence from real-life events, researchers achieve a level of realism that is lacking in most laboratory studies.

3 This might approximate more to what happens in real life than the procedures used in laboratory experiments. Witnesses are not always questioned immediately after the incident in which they were involved, and giving testimony in court may happen years after the event itself.

A skull in the office!, p. 99

1 The bizarre nature of the skull in an office context probably meant it was attended to longer than other items and so was better recalled.

2 This finding challenges early schema theory but provides evidence to support an extension of schema theory, called the 'schema copy plus tag hypothesis' (Smith and Graesser 1981). The hypothesis states that what is memorized from an event is the underlying schema we already possess for that event plus any bizarre (atypical) details.

Based on a study by Bransford and Johnson, p. 100

The appropriate schema for the passage is 'washing clothes'.

Bransford and Johnson found the following:

■ Participants who lacked the clothes-washing schema before they started reading, on average rated the passage at 2.29 for comprehensibility and recalled fewer than three out of the possible 18 points in the passage.

■ Participants who had been given the appropriate schema before reading the passage rated it 4.5 for comprehensibility and recalled twice as many points.

Chapter 4: Early social development

Harlow and Harlow's research study, p. 119

1 The independent variable (IV) in this study is the type of 'mother surrogate' (i.e. either 'lactating' or contact comfort).

2 The dependent variable (DV) is the amount of time monkeys spend on each surrogate 'mother'.

3 An experiment gave the researchers the additional advantages of: (a) control over extraneous variables, such as light and noise, which might affect behaviour; and (b) the opportunity for precise measurement of behaviour that might be impossible in a non-experimental situation.

4 The term 'unethical' is used when an experiment does not follow the ethical guidelines for that particular type of research. Ethical guidelines for animal research include advice on the stress of captivity, and whether any deprivation is justified. This research might be considered unethical on both these grounds because the monkeys clearly suffered as a result.

Research into types of attachment, p. 122

1 This is a bar chart. (How do we know this? The data are nominal, the height of the bars is proportional to the magnitude of relationship success scores, and a continuous variable is not implied.)

2 We may conclude that people who were securely attached fared better than insecurely attached people in both friendships and romantic relationships. We may also conclude that insecure–avoidant types fare better than insecure–resistant types as regards friendships, but worse as regards romantic relationships.

3 One weakness relates to the way the participants were obtained – through an advertisement in a newspaper. This means there is a sampling bias (e.g. only readers of that newspaper, people likely to volunteer). A second weakness relates to the way 'relationship success' was measured, e.g. number of friends. Measuring the 'success' of our relationships *quantitatively* does not really give us any indication of whether participants are capable of forming deep and enduring relationships, as predicted by attachment theory.

Validity, p. 125

1 A lack of validity would be a problem because the Strange Situation may not actually be measuring attachment but something else completely different, such as temperament or the relationship with that particular adult. A lack of ecological validity may indicate that the findings have no relevance outside that particular (artificial) situation.

2 A lack of reliability would be a problem because it would mean that the Strange Situation was not a consistent measure of attachment, and would therefore be likely to produce different results on different occasions.

3 The ecological validity of the Strange Situation could be assessed by using it in a variety of different settings (e.g. with different population groups). If different children responded in the same way in the various stages of the Strange Situation, this would indicate high ecological validity.

4 The reliability of the Strange Situation could be assessed by repeating it with the same mother–infant pairs on more than one occasion. If the same results are found, this would indicate high reliability.

Criticizing Takahashi's study, p. 127

1 Research with children, especially infants, needs to be especially careful in terms of potential psychological harm to the participants.

Takahashi showed sensitivity by stopping those observations when the infants became too distressed. However, the study itself was not stopped, even though it became obvious that extreme distress was likely.

2 Takahashi's study was carried out on a limited sample of only middle-class, home-reared infants (as was the original study by Ainsworth and Bell). It may therefore not be reasonable to generalize these findings to all Japanese people, although the results do demonstrate that there are important cultural or subcultural differences in attachment.

The High/Scope Perry Pre-school Project (Schweinhart *et al.* 1993), p. 139

1 It was important to assign children randomly to groups because otherwise the selection of children for the programme and no-programme groups might have been both non-representative and biased. For example, those in the programme group might have come from less deprived areas or had families that encouraged home learning more.

2 The purpose of the control (no-programme) group in this study is to provide a point of comparison of a similar group who had not received the independent variable (i.e. the child-planned learning activities and weekly home visits to families).

3 Weekly visits to families were necessary to reinforce and extend the learning activities of the daily High/Scope Perry Pre-school Programme. As home background is an important factor in a child's development, parents would have to be trained how to motivate their children to learn, and then monitored on a regular basis to ensure they maintained their commitment to the programme.

4 Children who had not received the High/Scope Perry Pre-school Programme at age 3 to 4 were far more likely to be receiving welfare as adults compared to those who had taken part in the programme, and were over four times as likely to have five or more arrests as adults.

Using control groups, p. 143

1 The independent variable was the training that was received by one group of caregivers but not by the other.

2 It would have been important to make sure that the control group was as closely comparable as possible to the group receiving the IV. For example, this would have meant ensuring that the control and experimental groups included caregivers of the same age and with a similar amount of experience with children.

3 This study is likely to have been an independent groups design because the caregivers in the experimental group (with the IV) and in the control group (without the IV) were different people.

4 An advantage of an independent groups design is that there are no order effects, which would occur if each participant took part in each condition. For example, if caregivers were tested without training and then with training, the positive effects of training may actually be a consequence of the extra 'practice' with the child as a result of the earlier 'non-training' condition. A weakness of this design is that there is the possibility of individual differences between the two groups. Efforts can be made to make the experimental and control groups as similar as possible, but with relatively small numbers in each group (as would probably be the case in this study), the influence of differences in caregiver aptitude, empathy with the child, etc., could influence the results.

Chapter 5: Stress

Stress and the immune system, p. 154

1 There are some clear advantages to this arrangement. For example, participants in Kiecolt-Glaser's study were less conscious about taking part in a study compared to participants in a laboratory experiment, and so would be less likely to alter their behaviour to fit the experimenter's expectations.

2 There is a lack of control in the study, which greatly increases the likelihood of confounding variables affecting the results. For example, we cannot be sure that other aspects of the students' lives were not contributing to the drop in immune system function (for example, lack of sleep during the examination period or seasonal fluctuations in the functioning of their immune systems). Although natural experiments such as this provide valuable insights into human behaviour without the problems of artificiality associated with laboratory experiments, this inevitably comes at a cost. The task for researchers is often to weigh up the benefits of a method against its costs.

3 Because other variables might have contributed to the change in immune system functioning around the time of the exams, the researchers should be cautious in concluding that stress caused deterioration in the efficiency of the immune system.

4 Students may be a special group and generalizations should be made with caution.

Measuring the impact of life events, p. 159

1 It tells us that as one variable increases (in this case the score on the SRRS), so does the other (illness scores), but that this is fairly low (i.e. doesn't apply in all cases). The relationship is significant, meaning that it is unlikely to have occurred by chance, and so we can be fairly confident that these two variables really are related in some way.

2 Even if there was a very strong relationship between life changes and illness, we cannot assume that one causes the other. Knowing that the number of life changes experienced and the amount of illness over a given period were correlated does not mean that the illness was a consequence of the life changes. It is also possible that both were influenced by a third variable (e.g. temperament or age). Even if we have reason to believe that there may be a causal relationship between the two variables, it remains a possibility that the causal direction is the other way around. For example, illness might cause someone to be less able to do their job (particularly true in the pressurized life of the US Navy), or be less attractive as a partner.

3 The only way to do this is by carrying out an experiment. You might like to ponder the ethical implications of carrying out such a study!

Chapter 6: Social influence

Differences between obedience and conformity, p. 192

- Public compliance and private change – Obedience often involves no more than public compliance, with private attitudes left unchanged. Conformity, however, may involve a more long-lasting and even more fundamental shift of attitudes and beliefs if the conformity takes the form of identifying with the group or internalizing the views of the majority.

- Conscious versus unconscious effects – Figures who command obedience often display signs of their authority (e.g. uniforms) and individuals are usually well aware when they have obeyed such a figure. Indeed, many people have pleaded 'I just did what I was told' as an excuse for carrying out reprehensible acts. In the case of conformity, however, individuals are often unaware that they have been subjected to conformity pressures and may refute the idea that others have influenced them to modify their views or behaviour.

Experimental design: Variations to Milgram's procedures, p. 194

1 Milgram used an independent groups design, but note that a matched pairs design also uses different (but matched) participants in each condition of the experiment.

2 Order effects would have made a repeated measures design impractical. The way participants had acted in one condition would have interfered with how they acted in another. A matched pairs design was not practical as it would have required a large number of prospective participants from whom to select the matched pairs.

Bickman's field study, p. 199

1 IV – the way the researchers were dressed

2 DV – how often people obeyed the experimenter's requests

3 It is possible that the samples of people available just happened to be different during the different conditions of the study. If this happened, it might mean that the different rates of obedience observed (the dependent variable) were caused by differences in the participants, not differences in the way the experimenters were dressed (the independent variable). Apart from the way the experimenters were dressed, you would need to keep variables as constant as possible across conditions. For example, you would want the locations, time and day of the week to be the same.

Minority influence, p. 212

1 Those in a minority must behave consistently if they are to influence a majority to change its mind.

2 It would be important to check before the study began that all participants had good eyesight. All participants in this study had good eyesight.

3 The artificiality of the laboratory setting is unlike real-life situations where minorities such as pressure groups exert their influence on the prevailing majority opinion. Therefore, the study might be accused of lacking ecological validity.

The behaviour of minorities, p. 213

Moscovici and colleagues claim that it was not *what* the early Christian advocates said, but *how* they said it that was important. In other words, their behavioural style – their conviction (acting from principles), certainty, consistency and courage (e.g. willingness to be martyrs) – won converts.

Chapter 7: Psychopathology (Abnormality)

Correlational research, p. 222

1 Negative correlation. The higher the social class, the lower the rate of psychological disorder.

2 No. This was a correlational study which demonstrated a relationship (not causal link) between two variables: social class and psychological problems. If a causal link does exist, we cannot be sure about the direction of causality. It could be that the stress of poverty causes psychological problems, or that psychological problems determine in which social class people end up. See the 'social drift' hypothesis in the panel 'Culture and subculture' on p. 222.

The origins of general paresis: Krafft-Ebing's hypothesis, p. 226

1 Patients would be immune to syphilis and not develop syphilitic sores (showing that they had contracted the disease in the past).

2 He accepted it.

3 ■ Participants were already suffering from a mental disorder and so were unable to give fully informed consent.

■ The participants were potentially at risk – If the hypothesis had not been supported by the findings, then paretic patients would also have had to deal with the symptoms of syphilis.

Eye on the exam: Biological factors in psychopathology, p. 226

1 If there was no genetic basis to depression, you would expect concordance levels to be the same for both types of twins. However, concordance in MZ twins is more than twice the level it is in DZ twins. This means that, compared to fraternal twins, there is a greater likelihood that if one identical twin has depression, then the other twin will also, suggesting that genes play a part in one's susceptibility to depression.

2 MZ twins may share more similar experiences than DZ twins. Both MZ and DZ twins may share similar environments, but it is possible that MZ twins have even more similar environments than DZ twins. This might come about because MZ twins are treated more alike because they look so similar. Consequently, environmental factors that might cause depression in one MZ twin are likely to be experienced by the other twin also.

Concordance rate in MZ twins, p. 227

If genes were entirely responsible for schizophrenia, then concordance rates in MZ twins would be 100 per cent. Therefore, factors other than genetic inheritance play a part in the development of schizophrenia.

Retrospective data collected during clinical interviews, p. 231

Reasons why the data collected might be unreliable:

■ People do not have perfect memories of past events, particularly if they happened a long time ago. See Chapter 3.

■ Furthermore, if someone is suffering from anxiety or depression this might affect how they interpret past events and make them more likely to recall negative events than individuals who are not anxious or depressed.

■ There is also the possibility of the social desirability bias (a demand characteristic – see Chapter 1, p. 16) affecting what a client reports – wanting to 'look good' and recall incidents that are thought to be relevant.

Combining drugs and CBT to treat depression, p. 246

1 The experimental method

2 IV = the treatment regime experienced – either drugs only or drugs followed by CBT

DV = the rate of relapse among the patients

3 In order to demonstrate that the IV (type of treatment) caused the DV, it was important to ensure that characteristics of the patients did not differ systematically between each condition. For example, it would have been undesirable to have had all the most severe cases in one condition. Of course, random allocation does not guarantee that this will never happen, but it makes it very unlikely.

Glossary

Abnormality: see **Psychological abnormality** or **Psychopathology**.

Adult Attachment Interview: a set of 20 questions that ask the individual about their experiences with parents and other attachment figures. It assesses the individual's strategies for protecting themselves from the perceived dangers of intimate relationships.

Aim: the intended purpose of an investigation, i.e. what it is actually trying to discover.

Alternative hypothesis (may be referred to as the **experimental hypothesis** in an experiment): predicts that something other than chance alone has produced the results obtained; in a well-designed experiment, this should be the effects of the independent variable.

Anxiety: a state of apprehension, worry or fear.

Attachment: a strong emotional and reciprocal bond between two people, especially between an infant and its caregiver(s). Attachments serve to maintain proximity between infant and caregiver because each experiences distress when separated.

Aversion therapy: a behavioural treatment that aims to rid the individual of an undesirable habit (e.g. smoking) by pairing the habit with unpleasant (aversive) consequences.

Bar chart: a series of vertical bars of equal width used to illustrate the frequencies of a non-continuous variable displayed on the x-axis. It is superficially similar to a histogram.

Behaviour categories (or **behavioural categories**): categorizing behaviour is a process carried out in observational research where the investigator(s) classify examples of the behaviour to be observed. For example, behaviours in a discussion group might include categories of 'giving advice', 'asking for advice', 'seeming friendly' and 'seeming unfriendly'.

Behavioural approach to psychopathology: a view that abnormal behaviours are maladaptive, learned responses which can be replaced by more adaptive responses.

Benzodiazepines (BZs): anti-anxiety drugs often used for the short-term relief of severe anxiety.

Beta-blockers: used in the treatment of high blood pressure (hypertension), these reduce activity in the sympathetic nervous system.

Biological (somatic) therapies: an approach to the treatment of mental disorders that relies on the use of physical or chemical methods. Biological therapies include drug treatment, electroconvulsive therapy and psychosurgery.

Biological approach to (or **biomedical model of**) **psychopathology**: a view of abnormality that sees mental disorders as being caused by abnormal physiological processes such as genetic and biochemical factors. According to this model, abnormality is seen as an illness or disease.

Capacity: the amount of information that can be stored in memory at any particular time.

Case study: case study research typically involves the in-depth study over time of a single individual or small group and is usually undertaken within a real-life context.

Catharsis: in psychoanalysis, catharsis is the process whereby the expression of an emotion removes its pathological effect – the release of pent-up emotion that happens when a client recalls and relives a repressed earlier emotional catastrophe and re-experiences the tension and unhappiness.

Central executive: the most important component of Baddeley's working memory model, it controls attention.

Chemotherapy: treatment by using drugs.

Classical conditioning: a form of learning where a neutral stimulus is paired with a stimulus that already produces a response, such that over time, the neutral stimulus also produces that response.

Cognitive approach to psychopathology: a view that stresses the role of cognitive problems (such as illogical or irrational thought processes) in abnormal functioning

Cognitive behavioural therapy (CBT): a technique that involves helping clients to identify their negative, irrational thoughts and to replace these with more positive, rational ways of thinking.

Cognitive development: the changes that take place throughout one's life with respect to mental abilities, including memory, perception, language and intelligence.

Cognitive Interview/Cognitive Interview Schedule (CI): a method for questioning witnesses that requires them to recreate the context, recall all details, recall events in different orders, and use different perspectives to aid memory recall.

Compliance publicly conforming to the behaviour or views of others in a group while privately maintaining one's own views.

Conditioning: a learning process in which an organism's behaviour becomes dependent on a learned association with an existing stimulus (classical conditioning) or on the consequences of that behaviour (operant conditioning).

Conformity: a result of social influence where people adopt the behaviours, attitudes and values of the majority members of a reference group.

Confounding variable: an uncontrolled variable that produces an unwanted effect on the dependent variable and so distorts the findings by obscuring any effect of the independent variable.

Content analysis: a systematic research technique for analyzing transcripts of interviews and other documents; it involves formally categorizing and counting how often things in the text (such as words or ideas) occur.

Correlation: a term that refers to the extent to which values on (usually two) different variables co-vary.

Correlation coefficient: a descriptive statistic with a numerical value on a scale between –1 and +1. It demonstrates the strength and direction of any relationship that exists between two sets of data. The sign of the coefficient tells us if the relationship is positive or negative. The numerical part describes the magnitude of the relationship.

Correlational analysis: a technique used to test a hypothesis using an association that is measured between two variables that are thought likely to co-vary (e.g. height and weight).

Counterbalancing: a technique used in a repeated measures design to overcome the impact of order effects, practice, boredom and fatigue on performance in an experiment. It involves ensuring that each condition is equally likely to occur in a particular order within the study. If there are only two conditions, then each is equally likely to be carried out first or second by participants.

Counterconditioning: a therapeutic technique for treating phobias. A phobic patient is helped to relax while imagining the feared situation (going from the least feared to the most feared situation). The relaxation response is incompatible with the fear previously associated with the situation. This leads to the fear being extinguished.

Critical period: a period of time during development when the brain is open to a particular type of experience, resulting in the development of a particular characteristic. Outside this 'window of opportunity', such development is no longer possible.

Cross-cultural variation: variations between people of different cultures. A culture is a set of beliefs and customs, e.g. about child-rearing practices, that bind a group of people together.

Cultural relativism: the idea that judgements about definitions of human behaviour (e.g. abnormal behaviour) cannot be made in absolute terms, but only within the context of a given culture.

Daily hassles: relatively minor events arising out of day-to-day living, such as the everyday concerns of work, caring for others and commuting.

Day care: a form of care for infants and children, offered by someone other than close family, taking place outside the home. Day care differs from institutional care, which refers to long-term, 24-hour care.

Decay: the process whereby memory trace fades away with time, so that the memory is no longer available.

Deception: withholding information or misleading research participants. Deception may be trivial when only a few details of a hypothesis are withheld. On the other hand, deception is of more ethical concern when it involves deliberately providing false information that may influence a participant's willingness to take part.

Demand characteristics: occur when participants try to make sense of a research situation that they find themselves in and act accordingly.

Dependent variable (DV): in an experiment, the variable that is assumed to be directly affected by changes in the independent variable (IV). In a well-designed experiment, any changes in the DV are presumed to have been caused by the IV.

Deprivation: to have something taken away, such as food or warmth, i.e. a loss. In the context of attachment, deprivation refers to the loss of emotional care which results in the breaking of emotional bonds.

Deviation from ideal mental health: A deviation from the ideal characteristics that people *should* possess if they are to live optimally (e.g. being autonomous and having a positive attitude to self) first proposed by Jahoda (1958).

Deviation from social norms: behaviour that violates implicit and explicit rules and moral standards of a given society (e.g. paedophilia and sexual exhibitionism violate moral standards concerning sexual behaviour in British society).

Directional hypothesis: an alternative hypothesis that predicts the direction in which any differences (or any correlation in an investigation using correlational analysis) in the results of an investigation are expected to occur. (See also **Non-directional hypothesis**.)

Displacement: the process whereby items currently in STM are pushed out to make room for incoming new ones.

Duration: the length of time that information can be kept in memory.

Ecological validity: the degree to which the findings from a study can be generalized beyond the context of the investigation. Problems with ecological validity tend to emerge only when

other researchers try to rerun the study in different situations.

Electro-convulsive therapy (ECT): a form of treatment sometimes used for people with severe depression. It involves passing a high current through the brain for approximately half a second to induce convulsions. Patients are anaesthetized before treatment and recall nothing once the anaesthetic has worn off.

Encoding specificity principle (ESP): states that information is remembered best when the conditions during recall are similar to the original conditions during encoding.

Encoding: changing sensory input into a form or code to be processed by the memory system.

Episodic buffer: a more recent addition to Baddeley's working memory model, it integrates information from different sources including LTM for use in working memory.

Ethical guidelines: are the prescriptive guidance given by professional associations (such as the British Psychological Society) on how psychologists should practise (e.g. as clinical psychologists) or carry out their research. Guidelines attempt to deal with the key issues that face psychologists in their work with humans and animals, and are regularly updated by the organizations that issue them.

Ethical issue: an ethical issue will arise in research where there is a conflict between the rights and dignity of participants and the goals and outcomes of research. For example, there may be conflict between the rights of participants to give fully informed consent and the importance of studying behaviour in as natural a setting as possible.

Ethics: in psychology, ethics are fundamental principles, which respect the rights and feelings of those taking part in research.

Experiment: an investigative technique involving changes to one variable (the independent variable) in order to see its effect on another variable (the dependent variable), and to establish cause-and-effect relationships.

Experimental (internal) validity: a measure of whether the experimental procedures actually worked and the effects observed were genuine (i.e. caused by the experimental manipulation). The conclusions of a study are justified when there is a high level of experimental validity.

Experimental method: a term used to describe the method used by researchers when carrying out an experiment to establish cause-and-effect relationships.

External validity: is concerned with the extent to which results can be generalized to other settings beyond that of the study concerned. A distinction can be drawn here between **population validity** (the extent to which results

from research can be generalized to other groups of people) and **ecological validity** (the extent to which research findings can be generalized to situations outside the research setting).

Extraneous variables: anything other than the independent variable that could affect the dependent variable.

Eyewitness testimony (EWT): an area of memory research that investigates the accuracy of memory following an accident, crime or other significant event, and the types of errors that are commonly made in such situations.

Failure to function adequately: an assessment of an individual whose disability prevents them from pursuing normal activities and goals (e.g. alcoholic addiction preventing normal performance at work or interfering with social activities).

Field experiment: an experiment carried out in a real-world setting (such as a classroom) rather than the more artificial setting of the laboratory.

Focus group: a collective interview carried out with a small group of people (usually no more than eight) who meet to discuss the issue(s) that the researcher wants to find out their views on.

Forgetting: the loss of the ability to recall or recognize something previously learned.

Frequency polygon: a form of graphical representation used to present data on interval or ratio levels of measurement. It consists of a line linking points that represent the frequencies of the variable placed on the x-axis.

Frequency table: this type of table displays frequency data, i.e. the number of cases occurring in specific categories of interest.

Grouped frequency table: this type of table is similar to a frequency table, except that the categories of interest are clustered together to reduce the number of categories displayed. It is used when the data set includes too many categories to be included in a standard frequency table.

Hardy personality: Hardiness includes a range of personality characteristics that provide defences against the negative effects of stress. These factors are: belief that you have control over what happens in your life, commitment (a sense of involvement in the world); challenge (seeing life changes as opportunities rather than threats).

Histogram: a form of graphical representation used to present data on interval or ratio levels of measurement. It consists of a series of vertical bars of equal width, which represent the frequencies of the variable placed on the x-axis.

Hypothesis: a testable statement. A **research hypothesis** is a general prediction made at the beginning of an investigation about what a researcher expects to happen.

Iconic memory: visual sensory memory.

Identification: adopting the views or behaviour of a group both publicly and privately because you value membership of that group. However, the new attitudes and behaviours are often temporary and not maintained on leaving the group.

Immediate digit span: the number of digits one can recall in correct order immediately after hearing them.

Immune system: system that protects the body against infection; a network of cells and chemicals that seek out and destroy invading particles.

Implications of research for social change: the meanings or significance of research for changes in society.

Independent behaviour: in the context of social influence research, independent behaviour refers to behaviour that is not altered despite pressures to conform or obey.

Independent groups design: an experimental design that involves using different participants in each condition of the experiment.

Independent variable (IV): the variable manipulated by the experimenter that is presumed to have a direct effect on the dependent variable.

Individual differences: in psychology, this refers to important differences between people that may affect the way the respond to or experience the world. Psychologists study, for example, differences in gender, intelligence, personality and mental health.

Individuation: desire to differentiate oneself from others by emphasizing one's uniqueness.

Informed consent: an ethical requirement that participants should have sufficient information about a research study to enable them to make an informed judgement about whether or not to take part.

Innate: present at birth rather than being acquired through experience or learning.

Insecure attachment: a less optimal form of attachment, at least in Western culture. Insecurely attached children show disturbed behaviour during separation and reunion.

Insight: in psychoanalysis, this refers to an understanding of unconscious reasons for one's maladaptive behaviour.

Interference: the process whereby memory traces are disrupted or obscured by other information.

Internal validity: is concerned with the extent to which we can be sure that research findings are due to the mechanisms suggested (such as manipulation of the independent variable in an experiment) and not to the action of some

other unwanted (**extraneous**) variable, such as individual differences or the effects of practice.

Internal working model: an inner representation of the parent–child bond that subsequently becomes an important part of an individual's personality. It serves as a set of expectations about the availability of attachment figures and the likelihood of receiving support from them. This model becomes the basis for all future close relationships during childhood, adolescence and adult life.

Internalization: a conversion or true change of private views to match those of the group, whose attitudes and behaviours have become part of one's value system.

Interquartile range: the distance between the first and third quartile in a distribution; it is the spread of the middle 50 per cent of a set of scores after they have been ranked in order from the lowest to the highest. It is a measure of the dispersion in a set of data.

Interview: a self-report technique involving a face-to-face encounter where one person (the interviewer) asks another person (the respondent) a series of questions. These questions may be structured, semi-structured or unstructured.

Introspection: a form of observation that was used by early psychologists (such as Wundt and colleagues) to record and analyze the elements of their own conscious mental processes under controlled conditions.

Investigator effects: result from the effects of a researcher's behaviour and characteristics on an investigation. They include expectation effects and the effects the presence of a researcher can have on the behaviour of participants, resulting in their behaving in ways different from those that would normally be displayed.

Laboratory experiment: an experiment carried out in a laboratory, allowing the researcher to exert a high level of control over the independent variable, and to eliminate or control for confounding variables.

Leading question: question phrased in such a way that it biases a respondent's reply.

Life changes: major life events, such as marriage, divorce, moving house, having a baby, that are scored according to their psychological impact within the Social Readjustment Rating Scale (SRRS) and are used to investigate the relationship between life changes and stress-related health breakdown.

Locus of control: refers to individual differences in people's beliefs and expectations about what controls events in their lives. There are two extremes: (a) *internal locus* – the belief that what happens is largely under one's own control (associated with the belief that one can control much of one's life and succeed in

stressful or difficult situations); (b) an *external locus* – the belief that what happens to one is controlled by external factors and agents, such as luck and fate (associated with the tendency to face stressful situations with a more passive and fatalistic attitude).

Long-term memory (LTM): an unlimited capacity system for storing information for long periods.

Matched pairs design: an experimental design that involves matching each participant in one of the experimental conditions as closely as possible with another participant in the second condition on variables considered to be relevant to the experiment in question.

Mean: the arithmetic average of a set of scores, calculated by adding all the scores together and dividing by the number of scores.

Measure of central tendency: a descriptive statistic that provides a single value that is representative of a set of numbers by indicating the most typical (average) value. The **mode**, **median** and **mean** are measures of central tendency.

Measure of dispersion: descriptive statistics that enable us to examine the variability within sets of data; they help us to understand whether scores in a given set of data are similar to, or very different from, each other. The **range** and **standard deviation** are measures of dispersion.

Median: the middle value of a set of scores arranged in ascending or descending order.

Memory: the mental processes involved in registering, storing and retrieving information.

Minority influence: a form of social influence where a persuasive minority exerts pressure to change the attitudes, beliefs or behaviours of the majority. Minorities are most influential when they appear consistent and principled.

Misleading information: in the study of EWT, this usually takes the form of a question or statement following an eyewitness experience which wrongly implies that something happened when it did not.

Mnemonics: techniques for improving memory based on encoding information in special ways so that a strong memory trace is established along with effective retrieval cues.

Mode: the most frequently occurring value in a data sequence.

Model: a term that is used synonymously with theory. In psychopathology, it refers to an explanation of the causes of psychological disorders.

Multi-store model of memory: an explanation of memory as a flow of information through a series of stages in a fixed sequence. The best-known model of this type was proposed by Atkinson and Shiffrin.

Natural experiment: a type of quasi-experiment where the allocation of participants to the different experimental conditions is outside the control of the researcher, but instead reflects naturally occurring differences in the independent variable (e.g. two schools using different methods to teaching reading).

Negative correlation: a measurement of the extent to which high values on one variable are associated with low values on another. A negative correlation is indicated by a correlation coefficient between zero and –1.

Non-directional hypothesis: an alternative hypothesis which does not predict the direction in which any differences (or any correlation in an investigation using correlational analysis) in the results of an investigation are expected to occur.

Null hypothesis: predicts no differences between the results from the different conditions of an experiment (it predicts no correlation in an investigation using correlational analysis). Under the null hypothesis, any difference (or correlation) found is due to chance alone.

Obedience: an outcome of social influence where an individual acts according to orders, usually from an authority figure. It is assumed that without such an order the person would not have acted in this way.

Observation: a research technique where behaviour is observed either in its natural context or in a laboratory setting, usually without intrusion by the person who is doing the observing.

Operant conditioning: an explanation of learning that sees the consequences of behaviour as of vital importance to the future appearance of that behaviour. If a behaviour is followed by a desirable consequence, it becomes more frequent; if it is followed by an undesirable consequence, it becomes less frequent.

Operational definition: the specific observable and measurable criteria used to identify an abstract variable so that it can be studied systematically.

Operationalization: the process of achieving precise descriptions of particular key terms in research – for example, what researchers understand by key variables such as the independent variable and the dependent variable. Operationalizing these variables usually results in a narrowing-down of the research focus.

Opportunity sample: a type of sample where the researcher selects anyone who is available to take part from any given population (sometimes called a convenience sample).

Phonological loop: a component of Baddeley's working memory model, it stores a limited number of speech-based sounds for brief periods. It consists of a phonological store (inner ear) and the articulatory control process (inner voice).

Physiological methods of stress management: the use of drugs and biofeedback to target directly the stress-response systems themselves.

Pilot study: a small-scale prototype of a research investigation. It is carried out on a small number of participants in order to find out whether there are any problems with the design, the instructions for participants or the measuring instruments used.

Pituitary–adrenal system: In response to stressful situations, the hypothalamus stimulates the pituitary gland, which in turn acts on the adrenal gland to produce stress hormones that have a range of effects throughout the body.

Positive correlation: a measurement of the extent to which high values on one variable are associated with high values on another. A positive correlation is indicated by a correlation coefficient between zero and +1.

PQRST method: a five-stage strategy for remembering material from a textbook, based on organizing and elaborating material and practising retrieval: **p**reviewing, **q**uestioning, **r**eading, **s**elf-recitation and **t**esting.

Privation: a lack of the necessities of life. In the context of attachment, privation refers to a complete lack of emotional care, especially during the first few years of life, such that no attachments are formed.

Protection of participants from psychological harm: an ethical requirement that research participants should be protected from undue risk during an investigation. Risks that they should be protected from include humiliation, embarrassment and loss of dignity or self-esteem.

Psychoanalysis: a theory and a therapeutic method in which a person is given insights into the unconscious psychological conflicts that are seen as the cause of their symptoms.

Psychodynamic approach to psychopathology: a view that abnormal behaviour is caused by underlying psychological forces of which the individual is probably unaware.

Psychological abnormality: behaviours and psychological functioning that are considered different from the normal behaviour within a given society, e.g. harmful or distressing behaviour.

Psychological methods of stress management: this includes (a) general psychological approaches such as the use of techniques of relaxation and meditation to reduce bodily arousal associated with stress, and (b) specific psychological approaches such as cognitive and behavioural training to help people control specific stressors in their lives.

Psychopathology (abnormality): abnormal functioning (e.g. behaviours, cognitive processes) that could be described as deviant, distressful, dysfunctional or dangerous.

Psychosurgery: a treatment that involves cutting brain tissue in order to alleviate the symptoms of severe psychological disorder.

Qualitative data: information collected in the course of a research study that is in non-numerical, narrative form, such as the transcript of what was said during a series of interview.

Quantitative data: information collected in the course of a research study that is in a quantified (numerical) form (e.g. speed of response in milliseconds).

Quasi-experiment: a design of experiment where at least one of the key characteristics of a true experiment – manipulation, randomization or control – is lacking.

Questionnaire: a self-report technique that uses a structured set of questions, for asking a large sample of people about their views and behaviours, etc. Questionnaire surveys may be conducted in person, by telephone, by post, via the Internet, etc.

Random sample: a subset of a target population in which every person or item stands an equal chance of being selected for inclusion. This requires the researcher to be able to identify every person or item in the target population before selection of a sample takes place. The selection process therefore takes place in a completely unbiased way.

Randomization: a selection process through which each individual person or element in a given population has the same chance of being chosen for inclusion in a study (usually referred to as 'random sampling') or is allocated to a particular group or sample within a study (usually referred to as 'random allocation to conditions'). It is used to avoid bias.

Range: the difference between the highest and lowest scores in a given set of data, with one added if the scores are all whole numbers.

Reliability: a term that means dependability or consistency. If the findings are replicated consistently, then the outcome can be said to be reliable.

Repeated measures design: an experimental design that involves exposing every participant to each of the experimental conditions, so that participants are, in effect, used as their own controls.

Retrieval cue: a prompt or clue that helps us to recall stored information from LTM.

Retrieval failure: the process whereby items stored in LTM cannot be accessed because no suitable retrieval cues are available.

Sample: a subset of a target population that shares the characteristics of the population despite its smaller size.

Scattergram (or **scattergraph** or **scatterplot**): a graphical technique used to illustrate sets of data that are being correlated with each other. Data from one of the variables being correlated are presented on the x-axis, and data from the same individual for the second variable on the y-axis.

Schema: a knowledge package built up through experience that enables us to make sense of familiar situations and interpret new information.

Secure attachment: the optimal form of attachment, associated with healthy emotional and social development. Securely attached infants feel content to explore a strange environment using their caregiver as a safe base.

Self-report techniques: techniques that enable those participating in a study to provide information about specific things about themselves (e.g. what they think, believe or do), as opposed to the researcher actually observing these things directly.

Semi-structured interview: a type of interview based on a predetermined list of topics to be explored. The interviewer aims to have a fairly natural conversation with each participant about each topic and decides whether sufficient information has been provided.

Sensory memory: storage system in memory that holds information in unprocessed form for fractions of a second after the physical stimulus is no longer present.

Separation: to be physically set apart from something – in the context of attachment, to be physically apart from one's caregiver, especially one's mother figure.

Short-term memory (STM): a limited capacity system for storing information for short periods.

Social development: the changes that take place throughout one's life with respect to social behaviour, such as relationships with friends and family, popularity, ability to negotiate with peers, friendliness and aggressiveness.

Social impact theory: Latane's theory that conforming to social influence depends upon the strength (importance), immediacy (presence) and number of other people in the group.

Social influence: the process by which a person's attitudes, beliefs or behaviours are modified by the presence or actions of others. There are two types of social influence that lead people to conform: normative social influence (based on our desire to be liked) and informational social influence (based on our desire to be right).

Social norms: rules of behaviour that prescribe what is acceptable in a given situation.

Standard deviation: used to measure the variability (i.e. the typical deviation) of a given sample of scores from its mean. Standard deviation is the most powerful of the measures of dispersion available to the researcher.

Strange Situation: a research technique developed by psychologist Mary Ainsworth that is used in the assessment of attachment type. The goal of this procedure is to provide an infant with an environment that arouses both the motivation to explore and also the urge to seek security.

Stress management: methods of managing the negative effects of stress. These include: (a) the use of drugs and biofeedback; (b) the use of relaxation and meditation; (c) cognitive and behavioural training; and (d) the use of exercise and social support networks.

Stress: there are three ways of defining stress: (a) as a *response* or reaction to something in the environment; (b) as a *stimulus* or stressor, i.e. a feature of the environment that produces a stress-response; (c) as a *lack of fit* between the perceived demands of the environment and the perceived ability to cope with those demands; this *transactional model* of stress is the most popular among psychologists.

Stressor: is any stimulus in the environment that produces the stress-response, as described by Selye. For example, life events such as dealing with death and bereavement or the breakdown of a long-term relationship; events associated with the workplace such as workload, conflict between home and work, keeping up with changes or lack of career prospects.

Structured interview: a type of interview where the questions are pre-set and ordered, and participants have to choose their answer from a set of fixed options.

Survey: a research method that involves using a set of questions (either in a questionnaire or an interview) to ask a large sample of people about their views, beliefs, attitudes or behaviours.

Sympathomedullary pathway: refers to the pathway in the body involving the sympathetic part of the autonomic nervous system acting on the adrenal medulla, which in turn produces adrenaline and noradrenaline into the bloodstream.

Syndrome: a set of symptoms that occur together.

Systematic desensitization: a behaviour therapy used to treat phobias and anxieties. After being trained in relaxation techniques, the phobic person is gradually exposed to situations that are more and more anxiety-provoking, until the fear response is replaced by one of relaxation.

Target population: a group of people who share a given set of characteristics about which a researcher wishes to draw conclusions.

Test validity: psychologists use various techniques to assess the validity of a specific psychological test, including face validity, content validity, concurrent validity and predictive validity.

Token economy: a behavioural technique that reinforces appropriate behaviour by awarding tokens that can be exchanged for goods or privileges.

Transference: in psychoanalysis, when a client directs repressed feelings towards someone (e.g. a parent) onto the analyst.

Type A behaviour: A particular behaviour pattern associated with increased vulnerability to coronary heart disease (CHD). This Type A behaviour pattern is characterized by constant time pressure, competitiveness in work and social situations, and anger, i.e. being easily frustrated by the efforts of others.

Unstructured interview: a type of interview where participants are asked a series of open questions that enable them to respond in whatever way they think is appropriate. The answers to an unstructured interview have to be transcribed and usually generate a significant volume of qualitative data.

Validity: a concept that is concerned with the extent to which a research instrument measures what it sets out to measure. A distinction may be drawn between different types of validity, including internal validity, external validity and ecological validity.

Variable: any phenomenon that varies and can either be given a specific quantitative (numerical) value or can be categorized (e.g. male/female).

Visuo-spatial scratchpad: a component of Baddeley's working memory model that stores visual and spatial information.

Volunteer sample: a type of sample where individuals volunteer to take part in a study (e.g. by responding to an advert).

Working memory: a model of memory formulated by Baddeley and Hitch to replace the concept of short-term memory. It proposes a multi-component, flexible system concerned with active processing and storage of short-term information.

Workplace stressor: any stimulus in the workplace environment that produces the stress-response, such as work overload or role ambiguity.

References

Ainsworth, M.D.S. (1967) *Infancy in Uganda: Child Care and the Growth of Love*, Baltimore: John Hopkins University Press

Ainsworth, M.D.S. (1989) 'Attachment beyond infancy', *American Psychologist,* 44, pp.709–16

Ainsworth, M.D.S. and Bell, S.M. (1970) 'Attachment, exploration, and separation: illustrated by the behavior of one-year-olds in a Strange Situation', *Child Development*, 41, pp.49–65

Ainsworth, M.D.S., Bell, S.M. and Stayton, D.J. (1974) 'Infant/mother attachment and social development as a product of reciprocal responsiveness to signals', in M.P.M. Richards (ed.) *The Integration of the Child into a Social World*, Cambridge: Cambridge Univ. Press

Arendt, H. (1963) 'Eichmann in Jerusalem: a report on the banality of evil', New York: Viking Press, cited in A.G. Miller (1986) *The Obedience Experiments*, New York: Praeger Publishers

Aronson, E. (1999) *The Social Animal* (7th edn), New York: W.H. Freeman

Asch, S.E. (1951) 'Effects of group pressure upon the modification and distortion of judgements', in H. Guetzkow (ed.) *Groups, Leadership and Men*, Pittsburg: Carnegie Press

Atkinson, R.C. and Shiffrin, R.M. (1968) 'Human memory: a proposed system and its control processes', in K.W. Spence and J.T. Spence (eds) *The Psychology of Learning and Motivation*, Vol. 2, London: Academic Press

Attanasio, V., Andrasik, F., Burke, E.J., Blake, D.D., Kabela, E. and McCarran, M.S. (1985) 'Clinical issues in utilising biofeedback with children', *Clinical Biofeedback and Health*, 8, pp.134–41

Baddeley, A.D. (1966) 'Short-term memory for word sequences as a function of acoustic, semantic and formal similarity', *Quarterly Journal of Experimental Psychology*, 18, pp.362–5

Baddeley, A.D. (1986) *Working Memory*, Oxford: Clarendon Press

Baddeley, A.D. (1988) 'But what the hell is it for?', in M.M. Gruneberg, P.E. Morris and R.N. Sykes (eds) *Practical Aspects of Memory: Current Research and Issues*, Vol. 1, Chichester: John Wiley & Sons

Baddeley, A.D. (1990) *Human Memory*, Hove: Lawrence Erlbaum Associates

Baddeley, A.D. (1997) *Human Memory: Theory and Practice* (revised edition), Hove: Psychology Press

Baddeley, A.D. (2000) 'The episodic buffer: a new component of working memory?', *Trends in Cognitive Sciences*, 4(11), pp.417–23

Baddeley, A.D. and Hitch, G. (1974) 'Working memory', in G.H. Bower (ed.) *The Psychology of Learning and Motivation*, Vol. 8, London: Academic Press

Baddeley, A.D., Grant, S., Wight, E. and Thomson, N. (1973) 'Imagery and visual working', in P.M.A. Rabbitt and S. Dornic (eds) *Attention and Performance V*, London: Academic Press

Baddeley, A.D., Thomson, N. and Buchanan, M. (1975) 'Word length and the structure of short-term memory', *Journal of Verbal Learning and Verbal Behaviour*, 14, pp.575–89

Bahrick, H.P. and Hall, L.K. (1991) 'Lifetime maintenance of high school mathematics content', *Journal of Experimental Psychology: General*, 120, pp.20–33

Bahrick, H.P., Bahrick, P.O. and Wittlinger, R.P. (1975) 'Fifty years of memory for names and faces: a cross sectional approach', *Journal of Experimental Psychology: General*, 104, pp.54–75

Baker, J.P. and Berenbaum, H. (2007) 'Emotional approach and problem-focused coping: A comparison of potentially adaptive strategies', *Cognition and Emotion,* 21(1), pp.95–118

Baker, M.J., Gruber, J, and Milligan, K. (2005) 'Universal childcare, maternal labor supply and family well-being', *National Bureau of Economic Research Working Paper*, No. 11832, Cambridge, MA

Baker, T. and Brandon, T.H. (1988) 'Behavioural treatment strategies', in *A Report of the Surgeon General: The health consequences of smoking: Nicotine addiction*, Rockville, Md: U.S. Department of Health and Human Services

Bales, R.F. (1970) *Personality and Social Behaviour*, New York: Holt, Rinehart & Winston.

Bandura, A. (1973) *Aggression: A Social Learning Analysis*, London: Prentice Hall

Banister, P., Burman, E., Parker, I., Taylor M. and Tindall, C. (1994) *Qualitative Methods in Psychology: A Research Guide*, Buckingham: Open University Press

Banyard, P. (2007) 'Tyranny and the tyrant: from Stanford to Abu Ghraib', *Psychologist*, 20(8), pp.494–5

Bartlett, F.C. (1932) *Remembering*, Cambridge: Cambridge University Press

Baumrind, D. (1964) 'Some thoughts on ethics of research after reading Milgram's "Behavioural study of obedience"', *American Psychologist*, 19, pp.421–3

Beck, A.T. (1963) 'Thinking and depression', *Archives of General Psychiatry*, 9, pp.324–33

Beck, A.T. (1967) *Depression: Clinical, Experimental and Theoretical Aspects*, New York: Hoeber

Beck, A.T. (1991) 'Cognitive therapy: a 30-year retrospective', *American Psychologist*, 46, pp.382–9

Beck, A.T. and Cowley, G. (1990) 'Beyond lobotomies', *Newsweek*, 26 March, p.44

Beck, A.T., Emery, G. and Greenberg, R.I. (1985) *Anxiety Disorders and Phobias: A Cognitive Perspective,* New York: Basic Books

Beck, A.T., Rush, A.J., Shaw, B.F. and Emery, G. (1979) *Cognitive Therapy of Depression*, New York: Guildford Press

Beck, A.T., Ward, C.H., Mendelson, M., Mock, J. and Erlbaum, J. (1961) 'An inventory for measuring depression', *Archives of General Psychiatry*, 4, pp.561–71

Bee, H. (1999) *The Developing Child* (9th edn), Boston: Allyn & Bacon

Bekerian, D.A. and Bowers, J.M. (1983) 'Eye-witness testimony: were we misled?', *Journal of Experimental Psychology: Learning, Memory and Cognition*, 9, pp.139–45

Bekerian, D.A. and Dennett, J.L. (1993) 'The cognitive interview: reviving the issues', *Applied Cognitive Psychology*, 7, pp.275–97

Bellezza, F.S. (1996) 'Mnemonic methods to enhance storage and retrieval', in E.L. Bjork (eds) *Memory*, San Diego, California: Academic Press

Belsky, J. (1988) 'Infant daycare and socioemotional development: The United States', *Journal of Child Psychology and Psychiatry*, 29(4), pp.397–406

Belsky, J. (1998) 'Paternal influence and children's well-being: Limits of and new directions for understanding', In A. Booth and A.C. Crouter (eds) *Men in Families: When Do They Get Involved? What Difference Does It Make?,* Mahwah, NJ: Lawrence Erlbaum

Belsky, J. and Rovine, M.J. (1987) 'Temperament and attachment security in the Strange Situation: A rapprochement', *Child Development*, 58, pp.787–95

Belsky, J. and Rovine, M.J. (1988) 'Non-maternal care in the first year of life and the security of parent–infant attachment', *Child Development*, 59, pp.157–167

Belsky, J. and Steinberg, L.D. (1978) 'The effects of day care: A critical review', *Child Development*, 49, pp.929–49

Bennett, M. (1995) 'Why don't men come to counselling? Some speculative theories', *Counselling*, 6(4), pp.310–13

Ben-Zur, H. and Zeidner, M. (1995) 'Coping patterns and affective reactions under community crisis and daily routine conditions', *Anxiety, Stress and Coping*, 8, pp.185–201

Bergin, A.E. (1971) 'The evaluation of therapeutic outcomes', in A.E. Bergin and S.L. Garfield (eds) *Handbook of Psychotherapy and Behaviour Change: An Empirical Analysis,* New York: Wiley

Berkowitz, L. (1970) 'The contagion of violence: an S-R meditational analysis of observed aggression' in W.J. Arnold and M.M. Page (eds) *Nebraska Symposium on Motivation*, 18, Lincoln: Univ. of Nebraska Press

Bickman, L. (1974) 'The social power of a uniform', *Journal of Applied Social Psychology*, 4, pp.47–61

Blass, T. (1991) 'Understanding behaviour in the Milgram obedience experiment: The role of personality, situations and their interactions', *Journal of Personality and Social Psychology*, 60(3), pp.398–413

Blass, T. (ed.) (2000) *Obedience to Authority: Current Perspectives on the Milgram Paradigm*, Mahwah, NJ: Lawrence Erlbaum Associates

Blass, T. (2004) *The Man Who Shocked the World: The Life and Legacy of Stanley Milgram*, New York: Basic Books

Bouteyre, E., Maurel, M. and Bernaud, J.-L. (2007) 'Daily hassles and depressive symptoms among first year psychology students in France: the role of coping and social support', *Stress and Health*, 23, pp.93–9

Bower, G.H. and Clark, M. (1969) 'Narrative stories as mediators for serial learning', *Psychonomic Science*, 14, pp.181–2

Bower, G.H. and Winzenz, D. (1969) 'Group structure, coding and memory for digit series', *Journal of Experimental Psychology*, Monograph 80 (No. 2, Pt 2), pp.1–17

Bower, G.H., Clark, M.C., Lesgold, A. and Winzenz, D. (1969) 'Hierarchical retrieval schemes in recall of categorized word lists', *Journal of Verbal Learning and Verbal Behaviour*, 8, pp.323–43

Bowlby, J. (1944) 'Forty-four juvenile thieves: their characters and home lives', *International Journal of Psychoanalysis*, 25, pp.107–27

Bowlby, J. (1953; 2nd edn 1965) *Child Care and the Growth of Love,* Harmondsworth: Penguin

Bowlby, J. (1969) *Attachment and Loss*, Vol. 1, *Attachment,* London: Hogarth Press

Bowlby, J., Ainsworth, M., Boston, M. and Rosenbluth, D. (1956) 'The effects of mother–child separation: a follow-up study', *British Journal of Medical Psychology*, 29, pp.211–47

Brandimonte, M.A., Hitch, G.J. and Bishop, D.V.M. (1992) 'Influence of short-term memory codes on visual image processing: evidence from image transformation tasks', *Journal of Experimental Psychology: Learning, Memory and Cognition*, 18, pp.157–65

Bransford, J.D. and Johnson, M.K. (1972) 'Contextual prerequisites for understanding; some investigations of comprehension and recall', *Journal of Verbal Learning and Verbal Behaviour*, 11, pp.717–26

Brewer, W.F. and Treyens, J.C. (1981) 'Role of schemata in memory for places', *Cognitive Psychology*, 13, pp.207–30

British Psychological Society (2006) *Code of Ethics and Conduct*. Leicester: BPS

Brody, L.R. and Hall, J.A. (1993) 'Gender and emotion', in M. Lewis and J.M. Haviland (eds) *Handbook of Emotions*, New York: Guildford Press, pp.447–60

Brown, A.S., Begg, D., Gravenstein, S., Schafer, C., Wyatt, R.J., Bresnahan, M., Babulas, V.P. and Susser, E.S. (2004) 'Serologic evidence of prenatal influenza in the etiology of schizophrenia', *Archives of General Psychiatry*, 61, pp.774–80

Bryson, C., Kazimirski, A. and Southwood, H. (2006) 'Childcare and early years provision: A study of parents' use, views and experiences, *National Centre for Social Research*, Brief No. RB723

Burger, J.M. (1992) *Desire for Control: Personality, Social and Clinical Perspectives*, New York: Plenum.

Campbell, F.A., Pungello, E.P., Miller-Johnson, S., Burchinal, M. and Ramey, C.T. (2001) 'The development of cognitive and academic abilities: Growth curves from an early childhood experiment', *Developmental Psychology*, 37(2)

Cannon, W. (1914) 'The interrelations of emotions as suggested by recent physiological researches', *American Journal of Psychology*, 25, pp.256–63

Cardwell, M., Clarke, E. and Meldrum, C. (2003) *Psychology for AS-Level* (3rd edn), London: CollinsEducational

Cardwell, M.C. (2000) *The Complete A–Z of Psychology Handbook* (2nd edn), London: Hodder & Stoughton

Cassel, W.S., Roeberts, C.E.M. and Bjorklund, D.F. (1996) 'Developmental patterns of eyewitness responses to repeated and increasingly suggestive questions', *Journal of Experimental Child Psychology*, 61, pp.116–33

Ceci, S.J. and Bruck, M. (1993) 'Suggestibility of the child witness: a historical review and synthesis', *Psychological Bulletin*, 113, pp.403–39

Cerletti, U. and Bini, L. (1938) 'L'elettroshock', *Arch. Gen. Neuro. Psychiat. & Psychoanal.,* 19, pp.266–8

Christianson, S.A. and Hubinette, B. (1993) 'Hands up! A study of witnesses' emotional reactions and memories associated with bank robberies', *Applied Cognitive Psychology,* 7, pp.365–79

Clarke, A.D.B. and Clarke, A.M. (1979) 'Early experience: Its limited effect upon later development', in D. Shaffer and J. Dunn (eds) *The First Year of Life*, Chichester: John Wiley

Clarke-Stewart, K.A., Gruber, C.P. and Fitzgerald, L.M. (1994) *Children at Home and in Day Care*, Hillsdale, NJ: Erlbaum

Clutton-Brock, T.H. and Albon, S.D. (1979) 'The roaring of red deer and the evolution of honest advertisement', *Behaviour,* 69, pp.145–70

Cochrane, R. (1983) *The Social Creation of Mental Illness*, London: Longman

Cochrane, R. (1995) 'Women and depression', *Psychology Review*, 2(1), pp.20–4

Cochrane, R. and Sashidharan, S.P. (1995) 'Mental health and ethnic minorities: a review of the literature and implications for services', Paper presented to the Birmingham and Northern Birmingham Health Trust

Cochrane, R. and Stopes-Roe, M. (1980) 'Factors affecting the distribution of psychological symptoms in urban areas of England', *Acta Psychiatrica Scandinavica*, 61, pp.445–60

Cohen, D. (1988) *Forgotten Millions: The Treatment of the Mentally Ill – A Global Perspective*, London: Paladin

Cohen, G. (1993) 'Everyday memory', in G. Cohen, G. Kiss and M. LeVoi, *Memory: Current Issues* (2nd edn) Buckingham: Open University Press

Cohen, S. (2005) Keynote presentation at the Eight International Congress of Behavioral Medicine: 'The Pittsburgh Common Cold Studies: Psychosocial predictors of susceptibility to respiratory infectious illness', *International Journal of Behavioral Medicine*, 12(3), pp.123–31

Cohen, S., Tyrrell, D.A.J. and Smith, A.P. (1993) 'Negative life events, perceived stress, negative affect, and susceptibility to the common cold', *Journal of Personality and Social Psychology*, 64, pp.131–40

Comer, R.J. (2005) *Fundamentals of Abnormal Psychology* (4th edn), New York: Worth Publishers

Condor, S. (1991) 'Sexism in psychological research: A brief note', in *Feminism and Psychology*, 1, pp.430–4

Conrad, R. (1964) 'Acoustic confusions in immediate memory', *British Journal of Psychology,* 55, pp.75–84

Corsini, R.J. and Wedding, D. (1995) *Current Psychotherapies* (5th edn), Illinois: F.E. Peacock Publishers

Craik, F.I.M. and Watkins, M.J. (1973) 'The role of rehearsal in short-term memory', *Journal of Verbal Learning and Verbal Behaviour*, 12, pp.599–607

Crowder, R.G. (1993) 'Short-term memory: Where do we stand?', *Memory and Cognition*, 21, pp.142–5

Crutchfield, R.S. (1955) 'Conformity and character', *American Psychologist*, 10, pp.191–8

Cumberbatch, G. (1990) 'Television advertising and sex role stereotyping: a content analysis', Working Paper IV for the Broadcasting Standards Council, Communications Research Group, Birmingham: Aston University

Curtiss, S. (1977) *Genie: A Psycholinguistic Study of a Modern-day 'Wild Child'*, London: Academic Press

Darley, J.M. (1992) 'Social organization for the production of evil', *Psychological Inquiry,* 3(2), pp.199–218

Daubman, K.A. (1993) 'The self-threat of receiving help: A comparison of the threat-to-self-esteem model and the threat to interpersonal-power model', Unpublished manuscript, Gettysburg, PA: Gettysburg College

Davies, C. and Macdonald, S. (2004) 'Threat appraisals, distress and the development of positive life changes after September 11th in a Canadian sample', *Cognitive Behaviour Therapy*, 33(2), pp.68–78

DeLongis, A., Coyne, J.C., Dakof, G., Folkman, S. and Lazarus, R.S. (1982) 'Relationship of daily hassles, uplifts, and major life events to health status', *Health Psychology*, 1, pp.119–36

Deutsch, M. and Gerard, H.B. (1955) 'A study of normative and informational influence upon individual judgement', *Journal of Abnormal and Social Psychology*, 51, pp.629–36

Dewe, P.J. (1992) 'Applying the concept of appraisal to work stressors: some exploratory analysis', *Human Relations*, 45, pp.143–64

REFERENCES

DiLalla, L.F. (1998) 'Daycare, child, and family influences on preschoolers' social behaviors in a peer play setting', *Child Study Journal*, 28(3), pp.225–45.

Dollard, J. and Miller, N.E. (1950) *Personality and Psychotherapy: An Analysis in terms of Learning, Thinking and Culture*, New York: McGraw-Hill

Donovan, J.J. and Radosevich, D.J. (1999) 'A meta-analytic review of the distribution of practice effects: Now you see it, now you don't', *Journal of Applied Psychology*, 84, pp.795–805

Dunkel-Schetter, C., Feinstein, L.G., Taylor, S.E. and Falke, R.L. (1992) 'Patterns of coping with cancer', *Health Psychology*, 11, pp.79–87

Dyer, C. (1995) *Beginning Research in Psychology: A Practical Guide to Research Methods and Statistics*, Oxford: Blackwell

Eagly, A.H. (1978) 'Sex differences in influenceability', *Psychological Bulletin*, 85, pp.86–116

Eagly, A.H. (1987) *Sex Differences in Social Behaviour: A Social Role Analysis'*, Hillsdale, NJ: Erlbaum

Egeland, B. and Hiester, M. (1995) 'The long-term consequences of infant day-care and mother–infant attachment', *Child Development*, 66, pp.474–85

Eich, J.E. (1980) 'The cue-dependent nature of state-dependent retrieval', *Memory and Cognition*, 8, pp.157–73

Ellis, A. (1962) *Reason and Emotion in Psychotherapy*, New Jersey: Citadel

Ellis, A. (1991) 'The revised ABCs of rational-emotive therapy', *Journal of Rational-Emotive and Cognitive-Behaviour Therapy*, 9, pp.139–92

Emery, C.F., Kiecolt-Glaser, J.K., Glaser, R., Malarkey, W.B. and Frid, D.J. (2005) 'Exercise accelerates wound healing among healthy older adults: A preliminary investigation', *Journal of Gerontology: Medical Sciences*, 60A(11), pp.1432–6

Emmelkamp, P.M. (1994) 'Behaviour therapy with adults', in A.E. Bergen and S.L. Garfield (eds) *Handbook of Psychotherapy and Behaviour Change* (4th edn), New York: Wiley

Evans, G., Bullinger, M. and Hygger, S. (1998) 'The effects of chronic exposure to aircraft noise', *Psychological Science*, 9, pp.75–7

Evans, P.D. (1990) 'Type A behaviour and coronary heart disease: when will the jury return?', *British Journal of Psychology*, 81, pp.147–57

Eysenck, H.J. (1952) 'The effects of psychotherapy: an evaluation', *Journal of Consulting Psychology*, 16, pp.319–24

Eysenck, M.W. (2005) *Psychology for AS Level* (3rd edn), Hove: Psychology Press

Fang, C.Y., Daly, M.B., Miller, S.M., Zerr, T., Malick, J. and Engstrom, P. (2006) 'Coping with ovarian cancer risk: The moderating effects of perceived control on coping and adjustment', *British Journal of Health Psychology*, 11(4), pp.561–80

Fava, G.A., Rafanelli, C., Grandi, S., Conti, S. and Belluardo, P. (1998) 'Prevention of recurrent depression with cognitve behavioural therapy: Preliminary findings', *Archives of General Psychiatry*, 55, pp.816–20

Field, T. (1991) 'Quality infant day care and grade school behavior and performance', *Child Development*, 62, pp.863–70

Fisher, R.P., Geiselman, R.E. and Amador, M. (1989) 'Field test of the cognitive interview: enhancing the recollection of actual victims and witnesses of crime', *Journal of Applied Psychology*, 74, pp.722–7

Fisher, S. and Greenberg, R.P. (eds) (1989) *The Limits of Biological Treatments for Psychological Distress*, Hillsdale NJ: Lawrence Erlbaum and Associates

Flanagan, C. (1996) *Applying Psychology to Early Child Development*, London: Hodder & Stoughton

Folkman, S. and Lazarus, R. (1980) 'An analysis of coping in a middle-aged community sample', *Journal of Health and Social Behavior*, 21, pp.219–39

Fonagy, P. (2000) 'The outcome of psychoanalysis: the hope of a future', *The Psychologist*, 13(12), pp.620–3

Foster, R.A., Libkuman, T.M., Schooler, J.W. and Loftus, E.F. (1994) 'Consequentiality and eyewitness person identification', *Applied Cognitive Psychology*, 8, pp.107–21

Fox, N. (1977) 'Attachment of Kibbutz infants to mother and metapelet', *Child Development*, 48, pp.1228–39

Frazier, P., Steward, J. and Mortensen, H. (2004) 'Perceived control and adjustment to trauma: A comparison across events', *Journal of Social and Clinical Psychology*, 23, pp.303–24

Freud, A. (1936) *The Ego and the Mechanisms of Defence*, London: Chatto and Windus

Freud, S. (1909, reprinted 1990) 'Case study of Little Hans' in *Sigmund Freud 8, Case Histories I*, London: Penguin Books

Friedman, M. and Rosenman, R.H. (1974) *Type A Behavior and Your Heart*, New York: Knopf

Furman, C.E. and Duke, R.A. (1988) 'Effect of majority consensus on preferences for recorded orchestral and popular music', *Journal of Research in Music Education*, 36(4), pp.220–31

Gale, A. (1995) 'Ethical issues in psychological research', in A.M. Colman (ed.), *Psychological Research Methods and Statistics*, London: Longman Essential Psychology

Gallo, P.S., Smith, S. and Mumford, S. (1973) 'Effects of deceiving subjects upon experimental results', *Journal of Social Psychology*, 89, pp.99–107

Gamson, W.B., Fireman, B. and Rytina, S. (1982) *Encounters with Unjust Authority*, Homewood, IL: Dorsey Press

Gauld, A. and Stephenson, G.M. (1967) 'Some experiments relating to Bartlett's theory of remembering', *British Journal of Psychology*, 58, pp.39–50

Geiselman, R.E. (1988) 'Improving eyewitness testimony through mental reinstatement of context', in G.M. Davies and D.M. Thomson (eds) *Memory in Context: Context in Memory*, Chichester: Wiley

Geiselman, R.E. and Padilla, J. (1988) 'Cognitive interviewing with child witnesses', *Journal of Police Science and Administration*, 16, pp.236–42

Geiselman, R.E., Fisher, R., Mackinnon, D. and Holland, H.L. (1985) 'Enhancement of eyewitness testimony with the cognitive interview', *American Journal of Psychology*, 99, pp.385–401

Gelpin, E., Bonne O., Peri ,T., Brandes, D.,and Shalev, A.Y. (1996) 'Treatment of recent trauma survivors with benzodiazepines: a prospective study', *Journal of Clinical Psychiatry*, 57(9), pp,390–4

Gergen, K.J. (1973) 'Social psychology as history', *Journal of Personality and Social Psychology*, 26, pp.309–20

Gerra, G., Monti, D., Panerai, A.E., Sacerdote, P., Anderlini, R., Avanzini, P., Zaimovic, A., Brambilla, F. and Franceschi, C. (2003) 'Long-term immune-endocrine effects of bereavement: relationships with anxiety levels and mood', *Psychiatry Research*, 121(2), pp.145–58

Gervais, R. (2005) 'Daily hassles beaten back by uplifting experiences', Poster presented at British Psychological Society Annual Conference, University of Manchester

Glanzer, M. and Cunitz, A.R. (1966) 'Two storage mechanisms in free recall', *Journal of Verbal Learning and Verbal Behaviour*, 5, pp.351–60

Glaser, R. and Kiecolt-Glaser, J.K. (2005) 'Stress is bad for your immune system and your health', *Discovery Medicine*, 26, pp.165–9

Godden, D. and Baddeley, A. (1975) 'Context-dependent memory in two natural environments: on land and under water', *British Journal of Psychology*, 66, pp.325–31

Goodman, G.S. and Reed, R.S. (1986) 'Age differences in eyewitness testimony', *Law and Human Behaviour*, 10, pp.317–32

Goodwin, D.W., Powell, B., Bremer, D., Hoine, H. and Stern, J. (1969) 'Alcohol and recall: state dependent effects in man', *Science*, 163, p.1358

Gross, J. and Hayne, H. (1996) 'Eyewitness identification by 5- to 6-year-old children', *Law and Human Behaviour*, 20(3), pp.359–73

Gross, R. and McIlveen, R. (1996) *Abnormal Psychology*, London: Hodder & Stoughton

Gross, R.D. (2005) *Psychology: The Science of Mind and Behaviour* (5th edn), London: Hodder Arnold

Grossmann, K.E. and Grossmann, K. (1991) 'Attachment quality as an organizer of emotional and behavioural responses in a longitudinal perspective', in C.M. Parkes, J. Stevenson-Hinde and P. Marris (eds), *Attachment across the Life Cycle*, London: Tavistock/Routledge

Gustafson, R. (1992) 'The relationship between perceived parents' child-rearing practices, own later rationality, and own later depression', *Journal of Rational-Emotive and Cognitive Behaviour Therapy*, 10(4), pp.253–8

Halpern, D. (1995) *More Bricks and Mortar? Mental Health and the Built Environment*, London: Taylor & Francis

Harlow, H.F. and Harlow, M.K. (1962) 'Social deprivation in monkeys', *Scientific American*, 207(5), pp.136–146

Harvey, E. (1999) 'Short-term and long-term effects of early parental employment on children of the National Longitudinal Survey of Youth', *Developmental Psychology*, 35(2), pp.445–59

Haslam, S.A. and Reicher, S.D. (2005) 'The psychology of tyranny', *Scientific American Mind*, 16(3), pp.44–51

Haslam, S.A. and Reicher, S.D. (2008) 'Questioning the banality of evil', *The Psychologist*, 21(1), pp.16–19

Hazan, C. and Shaver, P.R. (1987) 'Romantic love conceptualised as an attachment process', *Journal of Personality and Social Psychology*, 52, pp.511–24

Hedblad, B., Wikstrand, J., Janzon, L., Wedel, H. and Berglund, G. (2001) 'Low dose metoprolol CR/XL and fluvastatin slow progression of carotid intima-media thickness: main results from the Beta-blocker Cholesterol-lowering Asymptomatic Plaque Study (BCAPS)', *Circulation*, 103, pp.1721–6

Hewstone, M., Fincham, F.D. and Foster, J. (eds) (2005) *Psychology*, Oxford: BPS Blackwell

Hildalgo, R.B., Barnett, S.D. and Davidson, R.T. (2001) 'Social anxiety disorder in review: two decades of progress', *The International Journal of Neuropsychopharmacology*, 4, pp.279–98

Hines, A.M. (1997) 'Divorce related transitions, adolescent development, and the role of the parent-child relationship: A review of the literature', *Journal of Marriage and the Family*, 59, pp.375–88

Hodges, J. and Tizard, B. (1989) 'Social and family relationships of ex-institutional adolescents', *Journal of Child Psychology and Psychiatry*, 30(1), pp.77–97

Hofling, C.K., Brotzman, E., Dalrymple, S., Graves, N. and Pierce, C.M. (1966) 'An experimental study in nurse-physician relationships', *Journal of Nervous and Mental Disease*, 143, pp.171–80

Hogg, M.A. and Vaughan, G.M. (1998) *Social Psychology: An Introduction*, Hemel Hempstead: Prentice Hall/Harvester Wheatsheaf

Hole, R.W., Rush, A.J. and Beck, A.T. (1979) 'The cognitive investigation of schizophrenic illusions', *Psychiatry*, 42, pp.312–19

Holland, C.D. (1967) 'Sources of variance in the experimental investigation of behavioral obedience', *Dissertation Abstracts International*, 29, 2802A (University Microfilms No. 69-2146)

Holliday, R.E. (2003) 'The effect of a prior cognitive interview on children's acceptance of misinformation', *Applied Cognitive Psychology*, 17, pp.443–57

Hollon, S.D., DeRubeis, R.J., Evans, M.D., Weimer, M.J., Garvey, M.J., Grove, W.M. and Tuason, V.B. (1992) 'Cognitive therapy and pharmacotherapy for depression: singly and in combination', *Archives of General Psychiatry*, 49, pp.774–809

Holmes, T.H. and Rahe, R.H. (1967) 'The social readjustment rating scale', *Journal of Psychosomatic Research*, 11, pp.213–18

Howell, E. (1981) 'The influence of gender on diagnosis and psychopathology', in E. Howell and M. Bayes (eds) *Women and Mental Health*, New York: Basic Books

Howes, C., Galinsky, E. and Kontos, S. (1998) 'Caregiver sensitivity and attachment', *Social Development*, 7(1), pp.25–36

Insko, C.A., Drenan, S., Soloman, M.R., Smith, R. and Wade, T.J. (1983) 'Conformity as a function of the consistency of positive self-evaluation and being liked and being right', *Journal of Experimental Social Psychology*, 19, pp.341–58

Isaacs, W., Thomas, J. and Goldiamond, I. (1960) 'Application of operant conditioning to reinstate verbal behaviour in psychotics', *Journal of Speech and Hearing Disorders*, 25, pp.8–12

Isabella, R.A., Belsky, J. and Von Eye, A. (1989) 'Origins of infant–mother attachment: an examination of interactional synchrony during the infant's first year', *Developmental Psychology*, 25, pp.12–21

Jahoda, M. (1958) *Current Concepts of Positive Mental Health*, New York: Basic Books Inc

James, W. (1890) *The Principles of Psychology*, New York: Henry Holt & Co

Johansson, G., Aronsson, G. and Linstrom, B.O. (1978) 'Social psychological and neuroendocrine stress reactions in highly mechanised work', *Ergonomics*, 21, pp.583–99

Johnstone, L. (1989) *Users and Abusers of Psychiatry: A Critical Look at Traditional Psychiatric Practice*, London: Routledge

Johnstone, L. (2003) 'A shocking treatment', *The Psychologist*, 16(5), pp.236–9

Jones, D.N., Pickett, J., Oates, M.R. and Barbor, P. (1987) *Understanding Child Abuse* (2nd edn), London: Macmillan

Jones, M.C. (1924) 'The elimination of children's fears', *Journal of Experimental Psychology*, 7, pp.382–90

Juffer, F. and Van Ijzendoorn, M.H. (2005) 'Behavioral problems and mental-health referrals of international adoptees: a meta-analysis', *Journal of the American Medical Association*, 20, pp.2501–15

Kagan, J. (1982) *Psychology Research on the Human Infant: An Evaluative Summary*, New York: W.T. Grant Foundation

Kang, D.H., Coe, C.L., McCarthy, D.O., Jarjour, N.N., Kelly, E.A., Rodriguez, R.R. and Busse, W.W. (1997) 'Cytokine profiles of stimulated blood lymphocytes in asthmatic and healthy adolescents across the school year', *Journal of Interferon Cytokine Research*, 17, pp.481–87

Kanner, A.D., Coyne, J.C., Schaefer, C. and Lazarus, R.S. (1981) 'Comparison of two modes of stress measurement: daily hassles and uplifts versus major life events', *Journal of Behavioural Measurement*, 4, pp.1–39

Kelman, H.C. (1958) 'Compliance, identification and internalisation: three processes of attitude change', *Journal of Conflict Resolution*, 2, pp.51–60

Kent, M.A. and Yuille, J.C. (1987) 'Suggestibility and the child witness', in S.J. Ceci, M.P. Toglia and D.F. Ross (eds) *Children's Eyewitness Memory*, New York: Springer-Verlag

Kiecolt-Glaser, J.K. and Glaser, R. (1991) 'Stress and immune function in humans', in R. Ader, D. Fetten and N. Cohen (eds), *Psychoneuroimmunology*, pp.849–67

Kiecolt-Glaser, J.K. and Newton, T.L. (2001) 'Marriage and health: His and hers', *Psychological Bulletin*, 127, pp.472–503

Kiecolt-Glaser, J.K., Bane, C., Glaser, R. and Malarkey, W.B. (2003) 'Love, marriage, and divorce: Newlywed's stress hormones foreshadow relationship changes', *Journal of Consulting and Clinical Psychology*, 71, pp.176–88

Kiecolt-Glaser, J.K., Dura, J.R., Speicher, C.E., Trask, O.J. and Glaser, R. (1991) 'Spousal caregivers of dementia victims: longitudinal changes in immunity and health', *Psychosomatic Medicine*, 53, pp.345–62

Kiecolt-Glaser, J.K., Fisher, L.D., Ogrocki, P., Stout, J.C., Speicher, C.E. and Glaser, R. (1987) 'Marital quality, marital disruption, and immune function', *Psychosomatic Medicine*, 49, pp.13–34

Kiecolt-Glaser, J.K., Garner, W., Speicher, C., Penn, G.M., Holliday, J. and Glaser, R. (1984) 'Psychosocial modifiers of immunocompetence in medical students', *Psychosomatic Medicine*, 46, pp.7–14

Kiecolt-Glaser, J.K., Glaser, R., Cacioppo, J.T. and Malarkey, W.B. (1998) 'Marital stress: immunologic, neuroendocrine, and autonomic correlates', *Annals of the New York Academy of Sciences*, 840, pp.656–63

Kiecolt-Glaser, J.K., Loving, T.J., Stowell, J.R., Malarkey, W.B., Lemeshow, S., Dickinson, S. L. and Glaser, R. (2005) 'Hostile marital interactions, proinflammatory cytokine production and wound healing', *Archives of General Psychiatry*, 62, pp.1377–84

Kiecolt-Glaser, J.K., Manucha, P.T., Malarkey, W.B., Mercado, A.M. and Glaser, R. (1995) 'Slowing of wound healing by psychological stress', *The Lancet*, 346, pp.1194–6

Kilham, W. and Mann, L. (1974) 'Level of destructive obedience as a function of transmitter and executant roles in the Milgram obedience paradigm', *Journal of Personality and Social Psychology*, 29, pp.696–702

Kim, H.K. and McKenry, P.C. (1998) 'Social networks and support: A comparison of African Americans, Asian Americans, Caucasians, and Hispanics', *Journal of Comparative Family Studies*, 29, pp.313–36

Kirkcaldy, B.D., Trimpop, R.M. and Williams, S. (2002) 'Occupational stress and health outcome among British and German managers', *Journal of Managerial Psychology*, 17(6), pp.491–505

Kirsch, I. and Sapirstein, G. (1998) 'Listening to Prozac but hearing placebo: A meta-analysis of antidepressant medication', *Prevention and Treatment*, 1, Article 0002a (posted 26 June 1998 at http://journals.apa.org/prevention/volume 1/toc-jun26-98.html)

Kline, P. (1988) *Psychology Exposed, or, The Emperor's New Clothes*, London: Routledge

Knight, R. and Knight, M. (1959) *A Modern Introduction to Psychology*, London: University Tutorial Press

Kobasa, S.C. and Maddi, S.R. (1977) 'Existential personality theory', in R. Corsini (ed.) *Current Personality Theories*, Itasca: Peacock

Kobasa, S.C., Maddi, S.R., Puccetti, M.C. and Zola, M.A. (1985) 'Effectiveness of hardiness, exercise and social support as resources against illness', *Journal of Psychosomatic Research*, 29, pp.525–33

Kohlberg, L. (1969) 'Stage and sequence: the cognitive-developmental approach to socialization', in D.A. Goslin (ed.), *Handbook of Socialization Theory and Research*, Chicago: Rand McNally

Kohlberg, L. (1973) 'Continuities in childhood and adult moral development revisited', in P.B. Baltes and K.E. Schaie, *Lifespan Development Psychology* (2nd edn), New York: Academic Press

Koluchová, J. (1976) 'A report on the further development of twins after severe and prolonged deprivation', in A.M. Clarke and A.D.B. Clarke (eds) *Early Experience Myth and Evidence*, London: Open Books

Koriat, A. and Goldsmith, M. (1996) 'Memory metaphors and the real life/laboratory controversy: correspondence versus storehouse conceptions of memory', *Behavioural and Brain Sciences*, 19, pp.167–228

Koriat, A., Goldsmith, M., Schneider, W. and Nakash-Dura, M. (2001) 'The credibility of children's testimony: can children control the accuracy of their memory reports?', *Journal of Experimental Child Psychology*, 79, pp.405–37

Lamb, M.E. (1977) 'The development of mother–infant and father–infant attachments in the second year of life', *Developmental Psychology*, 13, pp.637–48

Larner, M. *et al.* (1989) 'The peer relations of children reared in day care centers or home settings: a longitudinal analysis', *Paper presented at the Biennial Meeting of the Society for Research on Child Development*, 21st, Kansas City, MO

Latane, B. (1981) 'The psychology of social impact', *American Psychologist*, 36, pp.343–56

Lazarus, R.S. (1999) *Stress and emotion: A new synthesis*, New York: Springer

Leach, P., Barnes, J., Malmberg, L.E., Sylva, K., Stein, A. and the FCCC Team (in press 2007) 'The quality of different types of child care at 10 and 18 months: A comparison between types and factors related to quality', *Early Child Development and Care*

Leichtman, M.D. and Ceci, S.J. (1995) 'The effects of stereotypes and suggestions on preschoolers' reports', *Developmental Psychology*, 31, pp.568–78

Ley, P. (1988) *Communicating with Patients*, London: Chapman and Hall

Lifton, R.J. (1986) *The Nazi Doctors: Medical Killing and the Psychology of Genocide*, New York: Basic

List, J.A. (1986) 'Age and schematic differences in reliability of eyewitness testimony', *Developmental Psychology*, 22, pp.50–57

Loftus, E.F. (1975) 'Leading questions and the eyewitness report', *Cognitive Psychology*, 7, pp.560–72

Loftus, E.F. (1979) 'Reactions to blatantly contradictory information', *Memory and Cognition*, 7, pp.368–74

Loftus, E.F. and Burns, H.J. (1982) 'Mental shock can produce retrograde amnesia', *Memory and Cognition*, 10, pp.318–23

Loftus, E.F. and Ketcham, K. (1991) *Witness for the Defence*, New York: St Martin's Press

Loftus, E.F. and Loftus, G.R. (1980) 'On the permanence of stored information in the human brain', *American Psychologist*, 35, pp.409–20

Loftus, E.F. and Palmer, J.C. (1974) 'Reconstruction of automobile destruction: an example of the interaction between language and memory', *Journal of Verbal Learning and Verbal Behaviour*, 13, pp.585–9

Loftus, E.F., Miller, D.G. and Burns, H.J. (1978) 'Semantic integration of verbal information into a visual memory', *Journal of Experimental Psychology: Human Learning and Memory*, 4, pp.19–31

Lorenz, K.Z. (1937) 'The companion in the bird's world', *Auk*, 54, pp.245–73

Lorenz, K.Z. (1952) *King Solomon's Ring: New light on animal ways*, London: Methuen & Co

Lundberg, U. and Frankenhaeuser, M. (1999) 'Stress and workload of men and women in high ranking positions', *Journal of Occupational Health Psychology*, 4, pp.142–51

McCarthy, G. (1999) 'Attachment style and adult love relationships and friendships: A study of a group of women at risk of experiencing relationship difficulties', *British Journal of Medical Psychology*, 72, pp.305–21

Maccoby, E.E. (1980) *Social Development: Psychological Growth and the Parent–child Relationship*, San Diego: Harcourt Brace Jovanovich

McDermott, M. (1993) 'On cruelty, ethics and experimentation: profile of Philip G. Zimbardo', *The Psychologist*, 6(10), pp.456–9

McGeoch, J.A. and MacDonald, W.T. (1931) 'Meaningful relation and retroactive inhibition', *American Journal of Psychology*, 43, pp.579–88

McGuffin, P., Katz, R., Watkins, S. and Rutherford, J. (1996) 'A hospital-based twin register of the heritability of DSM-IV unipolar depression', *Archives of General Psychiatry*, 53, pp.129–36

Main, M. and Cassidy, J. (1988) 'Categories of response to reunion with the parent at age six: predicted from infant attachment classifications and stable over a one-month period', *Developmental Psychology*, 24, pp.415–26

Main, M. and Weston, D. (1981) 'Security of attachment to mother and father: Related to conflict behavior and readiness to establish new relationships', *Child Development*, 52, pp.932–40

Mandel, D.R. (1998) 'The obedience alibi: Milgram's account of the Holocaust reconsidered', *Analyse und Kritik: Zeitschrift für Sozialwissenschaften*, 20, pp.74–94

Mann, J.J., Malone, K.M., Diehl, D.J., Perel, J., Cooper, T.B. and Mintun, M.A. (1996) 'Demonstration in vivo of reduced serotonin responsivity in the brain of untreated depressed patients', *American Journal of Psychiatry*, 153, pp.174–82

Mantell, D.M. (1971) 'The potential for violence in Germany', *Journal of Social Issues*, 27, pp.101–12

Marmot, M.G., Smith, G.M., Stansfield, S., Patel, C., North, F., Head, J., White, I., Brunner, E. and Feeney, A. (1991) 'Health inequalities among British Civil Servants: the Whitehall II study', *The Lancet*, 337, pp.1387–93

Marshall, G.D. Jr, Agarwal, S.K., Lloyd, C., Cohen L., Henninger, E.M. and Morris, G.J. (1998) 'Cytokine dysregulation associated with exam stress in healthy medical students', *Brain, Behaviour and Immunity*, 12, pp.297–307

Maslow, A.H. (1968) *Towards a Psychology of Being* (2nd edn), Princeton, NJ: Van Nostrand Reinhold

Masson, J. (1988) *Against Therapy: Emotional Tyranny and the Myth of Psychological Healing*, New York: Athaneum

Masters, J.C., Burish, T.G., Hollon, S.D. and Rimm, D.C. (1987) *Behavior Therapy: Techniques and Empirical Findings* (3rd edn), San Diego: Harcourt Brace Jovanovich

Matthews, K. and Haynes, S. (1986) 'Type A behavior pattern and coronary disease risk', *American Journal of Epidemiology*, 123, pp.923–7

Maurer, D. and Maurer, C. (1989) *The World of the Newborn*, London: Viking

Mayne, T.J., O'Leary, A., McCrady, B, *et al.* (1997) 'The differential effects of acute marital distress on emotional, physiological and immune functions in martially distressed men and women', *Psychological Health*, 12, pp.277–88

Meeus, W.H.J. and Raaijmakers, Q.A.W. (1986) 'Administrative obedience: carrying out orders to use psychological-administrative violence', *European Journal of Social Psychology*, 16, pp.311–24

Meichenbaum, D.H. (1972) 'Cognitive modification of test anxious college students', *Journal of Consulting and Clinical Psychology*, 39(3), pp.370–80

Meichenbaum, D.H. (2007) 'Stress inoculation', *Psychology Review,* 13(2)

Meichenbaum, D.H. and Cameron, R. (1983) 'Stress inoculation training: toward a general paradigm for training coping skills', in D. Meichenbaum and M.E. Jarenko (eds) *Stress Reduction and Prevention*, New York: Plenum

Meichenbaum, D.H. and Turk, D. (1982) 'Stress, coping, and disease: a cognitive-behavioral perspective', in R.W.J. Neufield (ed.) *Psychological Stress and Psychopathology*, New York: McGraw-Hill

Melhuish, E.C. (1993) 'Behaviour measures: a measure of love? An overview of the assessment of attachment', *ACPP Review and Newsletter*, 15(6), pp.269–75

Melhuish, E.C. (2004) 'A literature review of the impact of early years provision upon young children, with emphasis given to children from disadvantaged backgrounds', *Report to the Comptroller and Auditor General,* London: National Audit Office

Miale, F.R. and Selzer, M. (1975) *The Nuremberg Mind: The Psychology of the Nazi Leaders*, New York: Quadrangle

Michael, K. and Ben-Zur, H. (2007) 'Stressful life events: coping and adjustment to separation or loss of spouse', *Illness, Crisis, and Loss*, 15(1), pp.53–67

Milgram, S. (1963) 'Behavioural study of obedience', *Journal of Abnormal and Social Psychology*, 67, pp.371–8

Milgram, S. (1964) 'Issues in the study of obedience: a reply to Baumrind', *American Psychologist*, 19, pp.848–52

Milgram, S. (1974) *Obedience to Authority,* London: Tavistock

Miller, G.A. (1956) 'The magical number seven, plus or minus two: some limits on our capacity for processing information', *Psychological Review*, 63, pp.81–97

Milner, B. (1966) 'Amnesia following operation on the temporal lobes', in C.W.M. Whitty and O.L. Zangwill (eds) *Amnesia*, London: Butterworth

Mineka, S., Davidson, M., Cook, M. and Keir, R. (1984) 'Observational conditioning of snake fear in rhesus monkeys', *Journal of Abnormal Psychology*, 93, pp.355–72

Mixon, D. (1972) 'Instead of deception', *Journal of the Theory of Social Behaviour*, 2, pp.139–77

Moore, J. (2006) 'Theatre of Attachment: Using drama to facilitate attachment in adoption', *Adoption and Fostering Journal,* 30(2), pp.64–73

Morris, P.E., Tweedy, M. and Gruneberg, M.M. (1985) 'Interest, knowledge and the memorizing of soccer scores', *British Journal of Psychology*, 76, pp.415–25

Moscovici, S. (1980) 'Towards a theory of conversion behaviour', in L. Berkowitz (ed.) *Advances in Experimental Social Psychology*, London: Academic Press

Moscovici, S. (1985) 'Social influence and conformity', in G. Lindzey and E. Aronson (eds) *Handbook of Social Psychology* (3rd edn), New York: Random House

Moscovici, S., Faina, A.M. and Maass, A. (1994) *Minority Influence,* Chicago: Nelson-Hall

Moscovici, S., Lage, E. and Naffrechoux, M. (1969) 'Influence of a consistent minority on the responses of a majority in a colour perception task', *Sociometry*, 32, pp.365–80.

Mugny, G. and Perez, J. (1991) *The Social Psychology of Minority Influence*, Cambridge: Cambridge University Press

Murdock, B.B. (1961) 'The retention of individual items', *Journal of Experimental Psychology,* 62, pp.618–25

Murstein, B.I. (1972) 'Physical attractiveness and marital choice', *Journal of Personality and Social Psychology*, 22, pp.8–12

Myers, D.G. (1999) *Social Psychology* (6th edn), Boston: McGraw-Hill College

Myrtek, M. (2001) 'Meta-analyses of prospective studies on coronary heart disease, type A personality, and hostility', *International Journal of Cardiology*, 79, pp.245–51

National Consumer League (2003) *Dealing with Stress,* National Consumer League, Washington DC., www.nclnet.org/stress/summary.htm

Naveh-Benjamin, M. and Ayres, T.J. (1986) 'Digit span, reading rate, and linguistic relativity', *Quarterly Journal of Experimental Psychology*, 38, pp.739–51

Neisser, U. (1978) 'Memory: what are the important questions?', in M.M. Gruneberg, P.E. Morris and R.N. Sykes (eds) *Practical Aspects of Memory*, London: Academic Press

Nemeth, C. (1986) 'The differential contributions of majority and minority influence', *Psychological Review*, 93, pp.23–32

Neto, F. (1995) 'Conformity and independence revisited', *Social Behaviour and Personality*, 23(3), pp.217–22

NICE report (2006) 'NICE implementation uptake report: drugs used in the management of hypertension in primary care in England', *National Institute for Health and Clinical Excellence Report*

NICHD Early Child Care Research Network (2003) 'The NICHD study of early child care: Contexts of development and developmental outcomes over the first seven years of life', in J. Brooks-Gunn and L.J. Berlin (eds), *Early Childhood Development in the 21st century*, New York: Teachers College Press

Nicholson, N., Cole, S.G. and Rocklin, T. (1985) 'Conformity in the Asch situation: a comparison between contemporary British and US university students', *British Journal of Social Psychology*, 24, pp.59–63

Nolen-Hoeksema, S. (1994) 'An interactive model for the emergence of gender differences in depression in adolescence', *Journal of Research in Adolescence*, 4, pp.519–34

Orlando, N.J. (1973) 'The mock ward: a study in simulation', in O. Milton and R.G. Wahlers (eds) *Behaviour Disorders: Perspectives and Trends* (3rd edn), Philadelphia: Lippincott

Orne, M.T. (1962) 'On the social psychology of the psychology experiment with particular reference to demand characteristics and their implications', *American Psychologist*, 16, pp.776–83

Orne, M.T. and Holland, C.C. (1968) 'On the ecological validity of laboratory deceptions', *International Journal of Psychiatry*, 6(4), pp.282–93

Park, C.L., Armeli, S. and Tennen, H. (2004) 'Appraisal-coping goodness of fit: A daily Internet study', *Personality and Social Psychology Bulletin*, 30, pp.558–69

Parke, R.D. (1981) *Fathers*, Cambridge, MA: Harvard University Press

Parker, K.C. and Forrest, D. (1993) 'Attachment disorder: An emerging concern for school counselors', *Elementary School Guidance and Counseling*, 27(3), pp.209–15

Pavlov, I.P. (1927) *Conditioned Reflexes*, Oxford: Oxford University Press

Penley, J.A. and Tomaka, J. (2002) 'Associations among the big five, emotional responses and coping with acute stress', *Personality and Individual Differences*, 32(7), pp.1215–28

Perez, J., Papastamou, S. and Mugny, G. (1995) 'Zeitgeist and minority influence – where is the causality? A comment on Clark (1990)', *European Journal of Social Psychology*, 25, pp. 703–10

Perrin, S. and Spencer, C. (1980) 'The Asch effect – a child of its time', *Bulletin of the British Psychological Society*, 33, pp.405–6

Perrin, S. and Spencer, C. (1981) 'Independence or conformity in the Asch experiment as a reflection of cultural and situational factors', *British Journal of Social Psychology*, 20, pp.205–9

Peterson, L.R. and Peterson, M. (1959) 'Short-term retention of individual verbal items', *Journal of Experimental Psychology*, 58, pp.193–8

Ptacek, J.T., Smith, R.E. and Zanas, J. (1992) 'Gender, appraisal, and coping: A longitudinal analysis', *Journal of Personality*, 60(4), pp.746–70

Quinton, D., Rutter, M. and Liddle, C. (1985) 'Institutional rearing, parenting difficulties, and marital support', *Annual Progress in Child Psychiatry and Child Development*, pp.173–206

Rahe, R.H., Mahan, J. and Arthur, R. (1970) 'Prediction of near-future health-change from subjects' preceding life changes', *Journal of Psychosomatic Research,* 14, pp.401–6

Rank, S.G. and Jacobson, C.K. (1977) 'Hospital nurses' compliance with medication overdose orders: a failure to replicate', *Journal of Health and Social Behaviour*, 18, pp.188–93

Raphael, K.G., Cloitre, M. and Dohrenwend, B.P. (1991) 'Problems of recall and misclassification with checklist methods of measuring stressful life events', *Health Psychology*, 10, pp.62–74

Rattner, A. (1988) 'Convicted but innocent: wrongful conviction and the criminal justice system', *Law and Human Behaviour*, 2, pp.283–93

Reicher, S.D. (1984) 'The St Paul's riot: an explanation of the limits of crowd action in terms of a social identity model', *European Journal of Social Psychology*, 14, pp.1–21

Reicher, S.D. and Potter, J. (1985) 'Psychological theory as intergroup perspective: a comparative analysis of "scientific" and "lay" accounts of crowd events', *Human Relations*, 38, pp.167–89

Reinecke, M.A. and Didie, E.R. (2005) 'Cognitive-Behavioral Therapy with suicidal patients', in R.I. Yufit and D. Lester (eds) *Assessment, Treatment and Prevention of Suicidal Behaviour*, New Jersey: John Wiley & Sons Inc.

Richardson, J.T.E. (1984) 'Developing the theory of working memory', *Memory and Cognition*, 12, pp.71–83

Robbins, T.W., Anderson, E.J., Barker, D.R., Bradley, A.C., Fearnyhough, C., Henson, R., Hudson, S.R. and Baddeley, A.D. (1996) 'Working memory in chess', *Memory and Cognition*, 24 (1), pp.83–93

Robertson, J. and Robertson, J. (1971) 'Young child in brief separation', *Psychoanalytic Study of the Child*, 26, pp.264–315

Robles, T.F., Shaffer, V.A., Malarkey, W.B. and Kiecolt-Glaser, J.K. (2006) 'Positive behaviors during marital conflict: Influences on stress hormones', *Journal of Social and Personal Relationships*, 23(2), pp.305–25

Rosario, M., Shinn, M., Morch, H. and Huckabee, C.B. (1988) 'Gender differences in coping and social supports: Testing socialization and role constraint theories', *Journal of Community Psychology*, 16, pp.55–69

Rosenhan, D.L. (1973) 'On being sane in insane places', *Science*, 179, pp.250–8

Rotter, J.B. (1966) 'Generalised expectancies for internal versus external control of reinforcement', *Psychological Monographs*, 80, pp.1–28

Ruffin, C.L. (1993) 'Stress and health: Little hasslers vs. major life events', *Australian Psychologist*, 28, pp.201–8

Rukholm, E.E. and Viverais, G.A. (1993) 'A multifactorial study of test anxiety and coping responses during a challenge examination', *Nurse Education Today*, 13, pp.91–9

Rutter, M. (1976) 'Parent–child separation: psychological effects on the child', in A.M. Clarke and A.D.B. Clarke (eds) *Early Experience: Myth and Evidence*, London: Open Books

Rutter, M. (1981) *Maternal Deprivation Reassessed* (2nd edn), Harmondsworth: Penguin

Rutter, M., Anderson-Wood, L., Beckett, C., Bredenkamp, D., Castle, J., Dunn, J., Ehrich, K., Groothues, C., Harborne, A., Hay, D., Jewett, J., Keaveney, L., Kreppner, J., Messer, J., O'Connor, T., Quinton, D. and White, A. (1998) 'Developmental catch-up and deficit, following adoption after severe global early privation', *Journal of Child Psychology and Psychiatry*, 39, pp.465–76

Rutter, M., Beckett, C., Castle, J., Colvert, E., Kreppner, J., Mehta, M., Stevens, S. and Sonuga-Barke, E. (2007) 'Effects of profound early institutional deprivation: an overview of findings from a UK longitudinal study of Romanian adoptees', *European Journal of Developmental Psychology*, 4(3), pp.332–50

Rymer, R. (1993) *Genie: Escape from a Silent Childhood*, London: Michael Joseph

Sackheim, H.A. (1988) 'The efficacy of electrconvulsive therapy', *Ann. NY Academic Science*, 462, pp.70–5

Sackheim, H.A., Nordlie, J.W. and Gur, R.C. (1993) 'Effects of stimulus intensity and electrode replacement on the efficacy of the effects of electroconvulsive therapy', *New England Journal of Medicine*, 328, pp.839–46

Sammons, P., Sylva, K., Melhuish, E., Siraj-Blatchford, I., Taggart, B. and Elliot, K. (2003) 'The Effective Provision of Pre-School Education (EPPE) Project: *Technical Paper 8b – Measuring the Impact of Pre-school on Children's Social/behavioural Development'*, London: Institute of Education, University of London

Sandelowski, M. (1996) 'One is the liveliest number: the case orientation of qualitative research', *Research in Nursing and Health*, 19, pp.525–9

Sapolsky, R.M. (1994) *Why Zebras Don't Get Ulcers*, New York: Freeman

Savin, H.B. (1973) 'Professors and psychological researchers: conflicting values in conflicting roles', *Cognition*, 2(1), pp.147–9

Saywitz, K.J. (1987) 'Children's testimony age-related patterns of memory errors', in S.J. Ceci, M.P. Toglia and D.F. Ross (eds) *Children's Eyewitness Memory*, New York: Springer-Verlag

Schaffer, H.R. (1998) *Making Decisions about Children*, Oxford: Blackwell

Schaffer, H.R. (2004) *Introducing Child Psychology*, Oxford: Blackwell Publishing

Schaffer, H.R. and Emerson, P.E. (1964) *The Development of Social Attachments in Infancy*, Monographs of the Society for Research in Child Development, 29(3), Serial No. 94

Schaubroeck, J., Jones, J.R. and Xie, J.L. (2001) 'Individual differences in utilizing control to cope with job demands: Effects on susceptibility to infectious disease', *Journal of Applied Psychology*, 86, pp.265–78

Schlesinger report (2004) in Zimbardo (2007) *The Lucifer Effect: How Good People Turn Evil*, London: Rider

Schurz, G. (1985) in Blass, T. (1991) 'Understanding behaviour in the Milgram obedience experiment: The role of personality, situations and their interactions', *Journal of Personality and Social psychology*, 60(3), pp.398–413

Schwartz, P. (1983) 'Length of daycare attendance and attachment behaviour in 18-month infants', *Child Development*, 54, pp.1073–8

Schweickert, R. and Boruff, B. (1986) 'Short-term memory capacity: magic number or magic spell?', *Journal of Experimental Psychology: Learning, Memory and Cognition*, 12, pp.419–45

Schweinhart, L.J., Barnes, H.V. and Weikart, D.P. (1993) 'Significant Benefits: The High/Scope Perry Preschool Study through Age 27', *Monographs of the High/Scope Educational Research Foundation*, 10, Ypsilanti, MI: High/Scope Press

Sebrechts, M.M., Marsh, R.L. and Seamon, J.G. (1989) 'Secondary memory and very rapid forgetting', *Memory and Cognition*, 17, pp.693–700

Segerstrom, S.C. and Miller, G.E. (2004) 'Psychological stress and the human imm une system: A meta-analytic study of 30 years of inquiry', *Psychological Bulletin*, 130(4), pp.601–30

Seligman, M.E.P. (1975) *Helplessness: On Depression, Development and Death*, London: W.H. Freeman

Selye, H. (1956) *The Stress of Life*, New York: McGraw-Hill

Shanab, M.E. and Yahya, K.A. (1977) 'A behavioural study of obedience in children', *Journal of Personality and Social Psychology*, 35, pp.530–6

Sherif, M. (1935) *The Psychology of Social Norms*, New York: Harper & Row

Sim, H.-O. (2000) 'Relationship of daily hassles and social support to depression and antisocial behavior among early adolescents', *Journal of Youth and Adolescence*, 29, pp.647–59

Singer, L.M., Brodzinsky, D.M., Ramsay, D., Steir, M. and Waters, E. (1985) 'Mother–infant attachment in adoptive families', *Child Development*, 56, pp.1543–51

Sistrunk, F. and McDavid, J.W. (1971) 'Sex variables in conforming behaviour', *Journal of Personality and Social Psychology*, 2, pp.200–7

Skeels, H. (1966) 'Adult status of children with contrasting early life experiences: A follow-up study', *Monographs of Society for Research of Child Development*, 31(3), whole issue

Skeels, H. and Dye, H.B. (1939) 'A study of the effects of differential stimulation on mentally retarded children', *Proceedings and Addresses of the American Association on Mental Deficiency*, 44, 114–36

Skinner, B.F. (1974) *About Behaviourism*, New York: Knopf

Smith, D.A. and Graesser, A.C. (1981) 'Memory for actions in scripted activities as a function of typicality, retention interval and retrieval task', *Memory and Cognition*, 9, pp.550–9

Smith, E., Nolen-Hoeksema, S. and Fredrickson, B. (2002) *Atkinson and Hilgard's Introduction to Psychology*, Fort Worth, TX: Harcourt Brace

Smith, P.B. and Bond, M.H. (1998) *Social Psychology across Cultures: Analysis and Perspectives*, Massachusetts: Allyn & Bacon

Smith, S.M. (1979) 'Remembering in and out of context', *Journal of Experimental Psychology: Human Learning and Memory*, 5, pp.460–71

Snedecor, G.W. (1956) *Statistical Methods*, Iowa State University Press

Snyder, C.R. and Fromkin, H.L. (1980) *Uniqueness: The Human Pursuit of Difference*, New York: Plenum

Spitz, R.A. and Wolf, K.M. (1946) 'Anaclitic depression', *Psychoanalytic Study of the Child*, 2, pp.313–42

Srole, L., Langner, T.S., Michael, S.T. and Opler, M.K. (1961) *Mental Health in the Metropolis*, New York: McGraw-Hill

Sroufe, L.A., Carlson, E.A., Levy, A.K., and Egeland, B. (1999) 'Implications of attachment theory for developmental psychopathology', *Development and Psychopathology*, 11, pp.1–13

Stainton Rogers, W. (2003) *Social Psychology: Experimental and Critical Approaches,* Buckingham: Open University Press

Stambor, Z. (2006) 'How reliable is eyewitness testimony?', *Monitor on Psychology*, www.apa.org/monitor/apr06/eyewitness.html

Stanton, A.L., Kirk, S.B., Cameron, C.L. and Danoff-Burg, S. (2000) 'Coping through emotional approach: Scale construction and validation', *Journal of Personality and Social Psychology, 78,* pp.1150–69

Stone, A.A. and Neale, J.M. (1984) 'New measure of daily coping: Development and preliminary results', *Journal of Personality and Social Psychology*, 46, pp.892–906

Stone, A.A., Reed, B.R. and Neale, J.M. (1987) 'Changes in daily event frequency precede episodes of physical symptoms', *Journal of Human Stress*,13(2), pp.70–4

Stroop, J.R. (1935) 'Studies of interference in serial verbal reactions', *Journal of Experimental Psychology*, 18, pp.643–62

Sylva, K., Melhuish, E., Sammons, P., Siraj-Blatchford, I. and Taggart, B. (2003) '*The Effective Provision of Pre-school Education: Final Report*', Nottingham: DfES Publications

Szasz, T. (1972) *The Manufacture of Madness*, London: Routledge and Kegan Paul

Takahashi, K. (1990) 'Are the key assumptions of the 'strange situation' universal?' *Human Development*, 33, pp.23–30

Taylor, S.E., Klein, L.C., Lewis, B.P., Grunewald, T.L., Gurung, R.A.R. and Updegraff, J.A. (2000) 'Biobehavioural responses in stress in females: tend-and-befriend, not fight-or-flight', *Psychological Review*, 107, p.3

Thomas, L.K. (1998) 'Multicultural aspects of attachment', http://www.bereavement.demon.co.uk/lbn/attachment/lennox.html. *See also* Thomas, L.K. (1995) 'Psychotherapy in the context of race and culture', in S. Fernando (ed.) *Mental Health in a Multi-ethnic Society*, London: Routledge

Thomson, D. (1988) 'Reliability and credibility of children as witnesses', in J. Vernon (ed.) *Children as Witnesses*, Proceedings of a conference held in May 1988, AIC Conference Proceedings, No. 8, Australian Institute of Criminology

Tizard, B. (1979) 'Language at home and at school', in C.B. Cazden and D. Harvey (eds), *Language in Early Childhood Education*, Washington, DC: National Association for the Education of Young Children

Triseliotis, J. (1984) 'Identity and security in adoption and long-term fostering', *Early Child Development and Care*, 15(2-3), pp.149–70

Tronick, E.Z., Morelli, G.A. and Ivey, P.K. (1992) 'The Efe forager infant and toddler's pattern of social relationships: Multiple and simultaneous', *Developmental Psychology*, 28, pp.568–77

Tulving, E. (1983) *Elements of Episodic Memory*, Oxford: OUP

Tulving, E. and Osler, S. (1968) 'Effectiveness of retrieval cues in memory for words', *Journal of Verbal Learning and Verbal Behaviour*, 5, pp.381–91

Tulving, E. and Thompson, D.M. (1973) 'Encoding specificity and retrieval processes in episodic memory', *Psychological Review*, 80, pp.352–73

Tunstill, J., Allnock, D., Akhurst, S., Garbers, C. and NESS Research Team. (2005) 'Sure Start Local Programmes: Implications of case study data from the national evaluation of Sure Start', *Children and Society*, 19, pp.158–71

Turner, J.C. (2006) 'Tyranny, freedom and social structure: Escaping our theoretical prisons', *British Journal of Social Psychology,* 45, pp.41–6

Tyler, S.W., Hertel, P.T., McCallum, M.C. and Ellis, H.C. (1979) 'Cognitive effort and memory', *Journal of Experimental Psychology: Human Learning and Memory*, 5(6), pp.607–17

Ucros, C.G. (1989) 'Mood-state dependent memory: a meta-analysis', *Cognition and Emotion*, 3, pp.139–67

Underwood, B.J. (1957) 'Interference and forgetting', *Psychological Review*, 64, pp.49–60

Van Avermaet, E. (1996) 'Social influence in small groups', in M. Hewstone, W. Stroebe, G.M. Stevenson (eds), *Introduction to Social Psychology*, Oxford: Blackwell

Van der Doef, M. and Maes, S. (1998) 'The job demand-control (-support) model and physical outcomes: a review of the strain and buffer hypotheses', *Psychology and Health,* 13, pp.909–36

Van IJzendoorn, M.H. and Kroonenberg, P.M. (1988) 'Cross-cultural patterns of attachment: A meta-analysis of the Strange Situation', *Child Development*, 59, pp.147–56

Van IJzendoorn, M.H., Sagi, A. and Lambermon, M.W.E. (1992) 'The multiple caretaker paradox: Data from Holland and Israel', in R.C. Pianta (ed.) *Beyond the Parent: The Role of Other Adults in Children's Lives*, San Francisco, CA: Jossey-Bass Publishers

Wartner, U.G., Grossman, K., Fremner-Bombik, I. and Guess, G.L. (1994) 'Attachment patterns in south Germany', *Child Development,* 65, pp.1014–27

Watson, J.B. and Rayner, R. (1920) 'Conditioned emotional reactions', *Journal of Experimental Psychology*, 3, pp.1–14

Wender, P.H., Kety, S.S., Rosenthal, D., Schulsinger, F., Ertmann, J. and Lunde, I. (1986) 'Psychiatric disorders in the biological and adoptive families of adopted individuals with affective disorders', *Archives of General Psychiatry*, 43, pp.923–9

Wheaton, B. (1996) 'The domains and boundaries of the stress concepts', in J.B. Kaplan (ed.), *Psychological stress: Perspectives on Structure, Theory, Life-course, and Methods*, San Diego, CA: Academic Press

Williams, R.B., Barefoot, J.C. and Schneiderman, N. (2003) 'Psychosocial risk factors for cardiovascular disease: More than one culprit at work', *Journal of American Medical Association,* 290(16), pp.2190–2

Willis, L., Thomas, P., Garry, P.J. and Goodwin, J.S. (1987) 'A prospective study of response to stressful life events in initially healthy elders', *Journal of Gerontology*, 42, pp.627–30

Yarmey, A.D. and Jones, H.P.T. (1983) 'Is the psychology of eyewitness identification a matter of commonsense?' in S.M.A. Lloyd-Bostock and S.R. Clifford (eds) *Evaluating Witness Evidence: Recent Psychological Research and New Perspectives*, Chichester: Wiley

Yuille, J.C. and Cutshall, J.L. (1986) 'A case study of eyewitness memory of a crime', *Journal of Applied Psychology*, 71, pp.291–301

Zeldow, P.B. (1995) 'Psychodynamic formulations of human behaviour', in D. Wedding (ed.) *Behaviour and Medicine* (2nd edn), St. Louis, MO: Mosby Year Book

Zimbardo, P.G. (2007) *The Lucifer Effect: How Good People Turn Evil*, London: Rider

Zimbardo, P.G., Banks, P.G., Haney, C. and Jaffe, D. (1973) 'Pirandellian prison: the mind is a formidable jailor', *New York Times Magazine*, 8 April, pp.38–60

Zimbardo, P.G., McDermot, M., Jansz, J. and Metaal, N. (1995) *Psychology: A European Text*, London: Harper Collins

Index